COMPLETE
ATLAS
OF THE
WORLD

Director of Publishing
David Gibbon

Director of Production
Gerald Hughes

Production
Ruth Arthur
Joanna Keywood
Pamela Simpkins

Editorial
Gill Waugh
Fleur Robertson
Pauline Graham

Designed and Produced by Engineering Surveys
Reproduction Ltd.

Cartographic Design and Production Manager
Keith Brook

Senior Cartographic Editor
Zoë Goodwin

Cartographic Editor
Lindsay Evans

Cartographers
Nicky Chapman
Mike Larby
Gill Dalton
David Handley-Clarke
Chris Major

Cartographic Consultant
Allan Marles

Cartographic Illustrator
Janos Marffy

Illustrator
Tom McArthur

The publishers wish to thank all those involved in the
production of this atlas, and in particular the photo
technicians at ESR Ltd, Richard Ross, John Gill,
Michael Hodson Designs, Apollo Colour Repro Ltd.,
E.S. Computing Ltd., Typogram Ltd., Link-Line Ltd.

COMPLETE
ATLAS
OF THE
WORLD

Bramley Books

FOREWORD

In 1636 a bound collection of maps was published by Gerard Mercator and John Hondt with a frontispiece illustrating the titan Atlas bearing the world on his shoulders. As a result, the word 'atlas' entered the vocabulary as a synonym for a book of maps. In the seventeenth century only the very rich could afford the luxury of an atlas. Cartographic masterpieces by Dutch map engravers offered their patrons the first view of a world the horizons of which were being swiftly broadened by maritime discovery.

Today, most households can afford an atlas even if they do not own one. Certainly, the need for and the attraction of the atlas have never been greater. Never have so many people been on the move around the world. Never have so many been concerned with the impact of world events. 'Atlas-eaters', Dylan Thomas called those who were hungry for world news. The atlas, through its co-ordinates of latitude and longitude, can answer the question 'Where?'. Or, perhaps, more precisely, the index to the atlas provides the answer – hence the importance of the extended index to the Atlas of the World.

In an atlas, the science of map-making is married to the art of map presentation. Techniques of production are increasingly refined; sources of information are increasingly precise. Satellite imagery, photogrammetry and computerisation have transformed map production. Most of the Atlas of the the World consists of topographical maps, with our own respective home areas receiving generous treatment. The thematic maps of the introductory section, necessarily selective in the topics that they treat, offer perspectives on the world distribution of a number of critically important phenomena.

An atlas is no substitute for a globe. The two are complementary, for not even the larger globes can include a fraction of the information that is packed into an atlas. The task of projecting the globe onto a flat surface has taxed the ingenuity of mathematicians since the Greeks first attempted to measure the circumference of the Earth. The variety of formidably-named projections employed in the Atlas of the World illustrates the extended range of options available to present-day cartographers.

Atlases have a romantic appeal as well as a utilitarian value. The novelist Alan Sillitoe, in a memorable essay on maps, recalls the flights of fancy set in motion by his 'first cheap layer-tinted atlas'. To turn the pages of the Atlas of the World – to contemplate the controlling features of land and sea, to reflect upon the boundaries that define the outlines and shape the destinies of countries and to respond to the magic of the infinity of place-names – is to experience a stimulus to the imagination as well as to the intellect.

William R. Mead
PROFESSOR EMERITUS OF GEOGRAPHY, UNIVERSITY COLLEGE LONDON.

CONTENTS

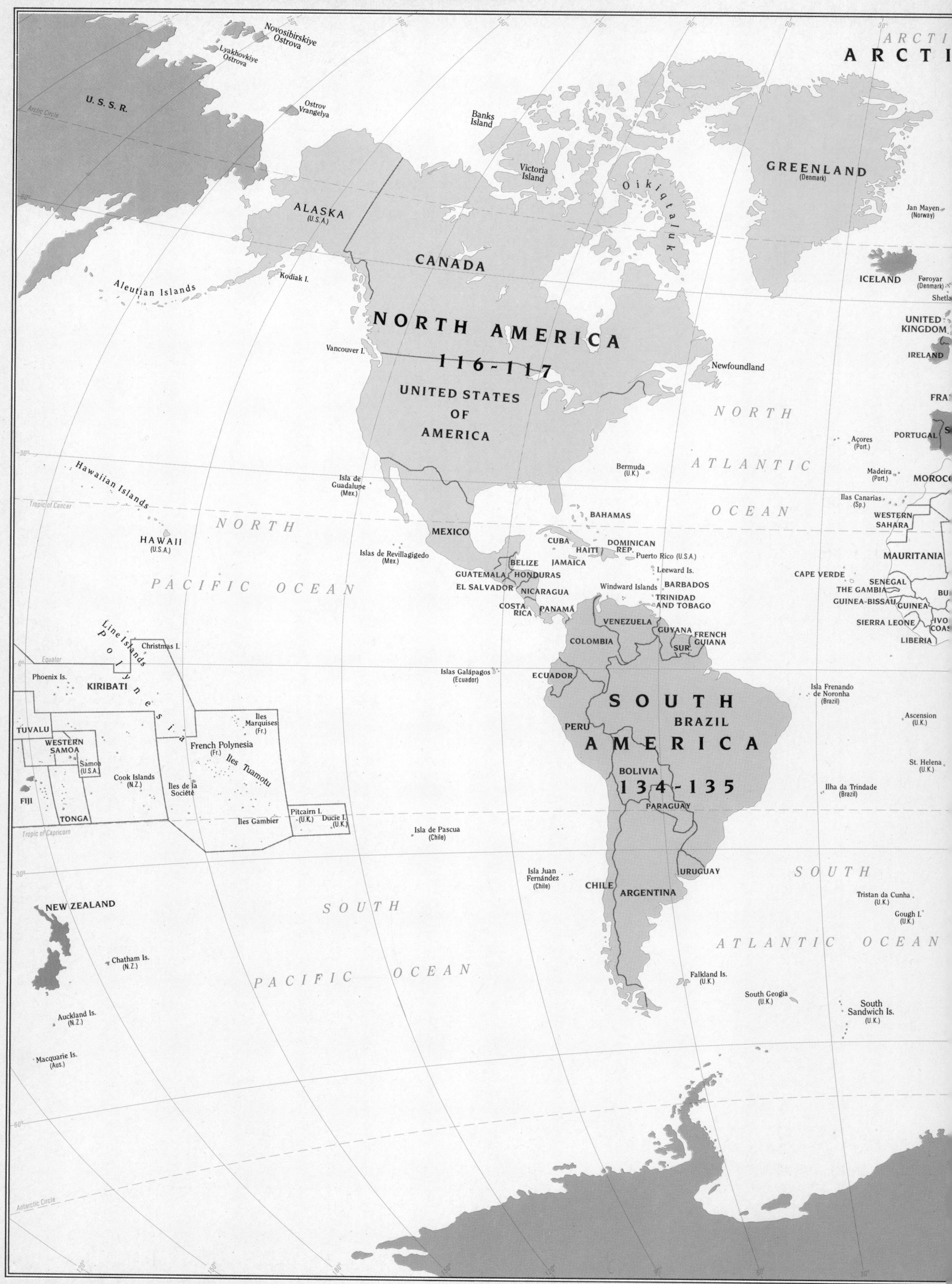

© COLOUR LIBRARY BOOKS

1:73,000,000 (Scale at the Equator)

West of Greenwich

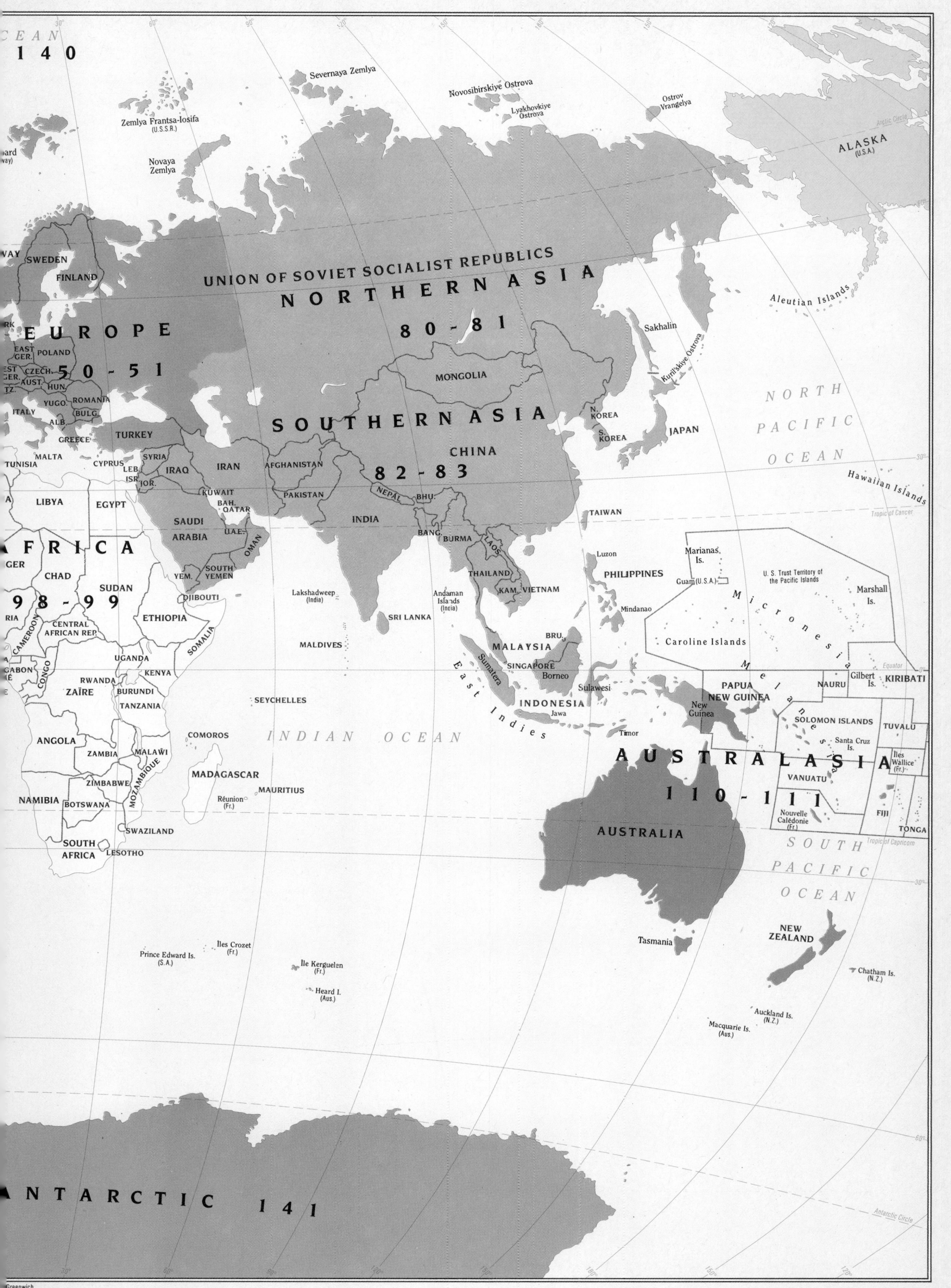

OCEAN

140

SWEDEN
FINLAND

Zemlya Frantsa-Iosifa
(U.S.S.R.)

Novaya
Zemlya

Severnaya Zemlya

Novosibirskiye Ostrova

Lyakhovskiye
Ostrova

Ostrov
Vrangelya

Arctic Circle

ALASKA
(U.S.A.)

UNION OF SOVIET SOCIALIST REPUBLICS

NORTHERN ASIA

80-81

Aleutian Islands

Sakhalin

EUROPE

50-51

EAST
GER. POLAND
CZECH.
AUST.
HUN.
YUGO.
ITALY
BULG.
ROMANIA
ALB.
GREECE
TURKEY
MALTA
CYPRUS
SYRIA
LEB.
TUNISIA
ISR.
JOR.
IRAQ
IRAN

MONGOLIA

SOUTHERN ASIA

CHINA
82-83

N. KOREA
S. KOREA

JAPAN

Kuril'skiye Ostrova

NORTH

PACIFIC

OCEAN

30°

LIBYA
EGYPT
KUWAIT
BAH.
QATAR
SAUDI
ARABIA
U.A.E.

AFGHANISTAN
PAKISTAN
NEPAL
BHU.

INDIA
BANG.
BURMA

TAIWAN

Hawaiian Islands

Tropic of Cancer

AFRICA

98-99

NGER
CHAD
SUDAN

YEM.
SOUTH
YEMEN
OMAN

DJIBOUTI

ETHIOPIA

SOMALIA

Lakshadweep
(India)

SRI LANKA

Andaman
Islands
(India)

LAOS
THAILAND
KAM.
VIETNAM

Luzon

PHILIPPINES

Mindanao

Marianas
Is.

Guam (U.S.A.)

U. S. Trust Territory of
the Pacific Islands

Marshall
Is.

Micronesia

CAMEROON
CENTRAL
AFRICAN REP.
UGANDA
KENYA
GABON
CONGO
RWANDA
ZAÏRE
BURUNDI
TANZANIA

MALDIVES

SEYCHELLES

MALAYSIA
SINGAPORE
Borneo

Caroline Islands

BRU.

Sumatera
East Indies

Sulawesi
INDONESIA
Jawa

Melanesia

NAURU
Gilbert
Is.
KIRIBATI

PAPUA
NEW GUINEA
New
Guinea

SOLOMON ISLANDS

Equator

TUVALU

ANGOLA
ZAMBIA
MALAWI
COMOROS

INDIAN OCEAN

Timor

Santa Cruz
Is.

Iles
Wallice
(Fr.)

NAMIBIA
ZIMBABWE
BOTSWANA
MOZAMBIQUE
MADAGASCAR
MAURITIUS
Réunion
(Fr.)

AUSTRALASIA

110-111

VANUATU

Nouvelle
Calédonie
(Fr.)

FIJI

SOUTH
AFRICA
SWAZILAND
LESOTHO

AUSTRALIA

SOUTH

PACIFIC

OCEAN

Tropic of Capricorn

TONGA

30°

Iles Crozet
(Fr.)

Prince Edward Is.
(S.A.)

Ile Kerguelen
(Fr.)

Heard I.
(Aus.)

Tasmania

NEW
ZEALAND

Chatham Is.
(N.Z.)

Auckland Is.
(N.Z.)

Macquarie Is.
(Aus.)

60°

ANTARCTIC 141

Antarctic Circle

Greenwich

Designed and produced by E.S.R.

THE SOLAR SYSTEM

Modern scientific and astronomical studies have increased our knowledge of the universe and the Earth's place within it immensely. Space exploration has solved many mysteries, but there is still much to be learnt.

The Earth is one of nine planets and numerous smaller bodies that orbit the Sun. The Sun is part of a much larger group of perhaps 100 billion stars that make up the Milky Way. This in turn is only one of the billions of galaxies in an incomprehensibly large universe.

Orbiting the Sun
Under the control of the Sun's gravitational force each planet maintains an elliptical orbit. Except for Mercury and Pluto, which are inclined 7° and 17° respectively, the orbits of the other planets lie within 3° of the plane of the Sun's equator.

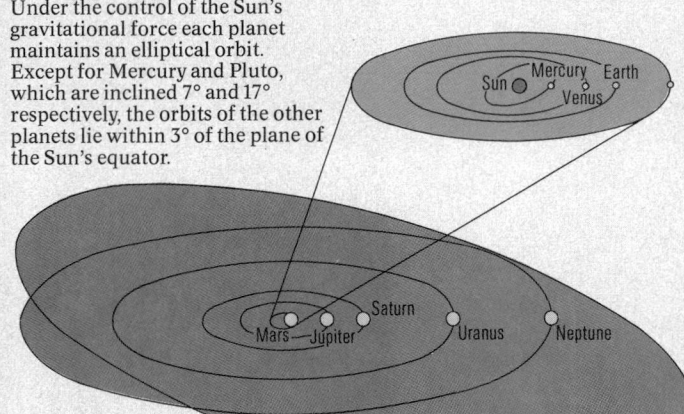

	Sun	Mercury	Venus	Earth	Mars	Jupiter	Saturn
Distance from the Sun (mean) millions of km	-	57·9	108·2	149·6	227·9	778·3	1427
Orbit (sidereal period) days	-	88	224·7	365·25	687	4332·5	10759·2
Rotation d=days hr=hours	24·6d	58·65d	243d	23·93hr	24·62hr	9·8hr	10·2hr
Orbital inclination	-	7°	3°23'	0°	1°52'	1°18'	2°29'
Equatorial diameter km	1392530	4878	12104	12756	6787	142800	120600
Mass (Earth=1)	333000	0·055	0·815	1 5.97×10^{24}kg	0·012	317·8	92·2
Density (water=1)	1·41	5·43	5·24	5·52	3·94	1·32	0·7
Number of satellites	-	0	0	1	2	16	17

The Sun is a huge, brilliant star at the centre of the Solar System. It is thought to be about five billion years old; halfway through its stable period of existence. The source of the Sun's immense energy is the continuous fusion of hydrogen into helium. Temperatures in the photosphere can reach 5500°C. Above the photosphere lies the chromosphere, the top layer of which contains numerous spicules that reach into the lower corona. The corona extends far beyond the Sun and produces a bright glow. Solar prominences often appear as great arches extending into the corona. The most conspicuous features on the surface of the Sun are dark blemishes called sunspots. These groups may be associated with violent solar flares.

Mercury is the smallest of the terrestrial planets and the closest to the Sun. The surface is distinctly lunar in appearance, extensively cratered, with smoother volcanic plains. Long lines of cliffs and scarps cut across the plains and craters alike. These probably resulted from crustal shortening as the planet cooled and shrank. Mercury has the greatest temperature extremes of any planet, rising to 480°C during daylight and falling to −180°C at night. This, as well as the virtual lack of atmosphere, indicates that no known form of life could survive there.

Venus is the planet most similar to Earth in both size and mass. However, it is altogether a more hostile world. A dense atmosphere (96 per cent carbon dioxide) obscures the surface under permanent cloud whilst maintaining a temperature of about 480°C. Radar mapping has revealed a landscape of highland 'continents', 'lowlands' and undulating plains. There are also shallow craters, large volcanoes and some rift valleys and trenches. Space probes have shown that the surface is strewn with smooth rocks.

Earth is the largest of the inner planets. The lower atmosphere consists mainly of nitrogen and oxygen. Ozone in the upper layers protects the Earth from the Sun's harmful radiation. The Earth is unique in having a surface largely covered with water (70 per cent), the remainder by continental land masses. Plate tectonics is the dominant process responsible for the structure of the surface, which is then subjected to erosional forces, creating a changing landscape.

Mars has a thin atmosphere which is mainly carbon dioxide (95 per cent). The mean surface temperature is about −40°C, ranging from −138°C at the winter pole to 27°C at the equator, causing strong atmospheric circulation. Dust storms can occur, enveloping the planet, and may take months to settle. Surface features include craters that are often filled with dust, lava plains and giant volcanoes such as Olympus Mons (25km high and 500km across its base), immense canyons, winding river-like valleys, the formation of which is subject to speculation, and polar ice caps which expand and contract with the seasons.

Asteroids are probably the remains of the debris from which the planets formed. They range in diameter from 1000km (the largest, Ceres), to less than 1km. The orbits of most asteroids lie between Mars and Jupiter.

Jupiter is the largest and most massive of the planets. It rotates faster than any other planet. This causes the equatorial region to bulge and the poles to flatten. The atmosphere is composed primarily of hydrogen and helium. The immense heat emanating from the planet's interior produces huge convection currents in the atmosphere. This drives strong wind systems that generate the alternate light- and dark-coloured bands of cloud that encircle the planet. A prominent feature is the Great Red Spot, which was first seen in the 17th century. It is thought to be a huge storm. Other storms have been observed, but none have survived for more than a few days. Jupiter's ring system appears to consist of particles temporarily entrapped by the planet's intense magnetic field. Its satellite system has at least 16 moons.

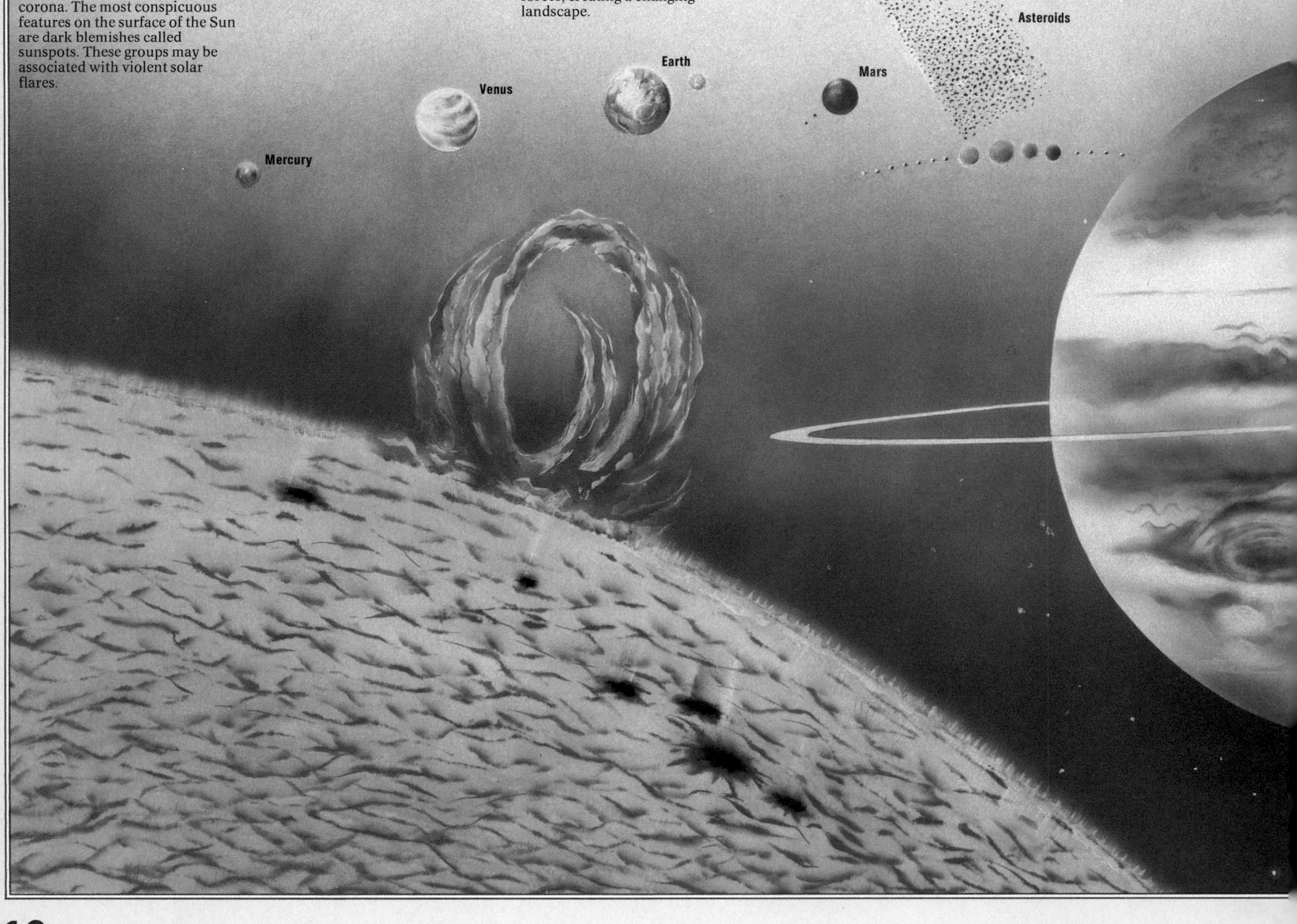

Uranus	Neptune	Pluto
1870	4497	5900
30684·8	60190·5	90465
16·3hr	18·2hr	6·38d
0°46′	1°46′	17°12′
51800	48600	3000
14·5	17·2	0·002
1·27	1·76	1·1?
5	2	1

Saturn, broadly similar in structure and composition to Jupiter, has a significantly lower mean density, and a greater degree of polar flattening. The atmosphere consists mainly of hydrogen, with some helium. It is thought that droplets of helium formed in Saturn's upper atmosphere sink towards the core, heating the interior as they descend. This may explain why the planet emits over twice as much heat as it receives. Saturn's belt-zone pattern is less conspicuous, and large cloud features are scarce. Strong zonal winds are symmetrical about the equator. The equatorial jet can blow at a speed of 1800km per hour. The most prominent feature of Saturn is its ring system, which is composed of small particles coated with water ice orbiting the planet in nearly circular paths. Seventeen satellites have so far been detected.

Uranus is thought to have a rocky, metallic core surrounded by a deep envelope of water, methane and ammonia 'ices', with a deep atmosphere composed mainly of hydrogen, helium and methane. Its axis is inclined by 98°, causing strong seasonal effects. The poles receive more solar radiation during each orbit than the equator. This, coupled with the lack of an internal heat source, suggests that atmospheric circulation is weak. Uranus has nine slightly elliptical rings of debris orbiting its equatorial region. It is also known to have five satellites.

Neptune was discovered due to the irregularities in the motion of Uranus's orbit which indicated the existence of another planet. Its composition is thought to be very similar to that of Uranus. However, as it emits twice as much heat as it receives, an internal heat source is thought to be responsible. Neptune has a 'bluish' appearance that has been attributed to the methane in the atmosphere. It has two satellites: Triton and Nereid.

Pluto lies on the fringe of the Solar System. Although a planet was believed to exist beyond the orbit of Neptune, Pluto was not found until 1930. Its satellite, Charon, was not discovered until 1978. The planet is thought to be made up of a mixture of frozen gases and rock. It has an eccentric orbit, which is presently inside the orbit of Neptune, where it will remain until the end of the century.

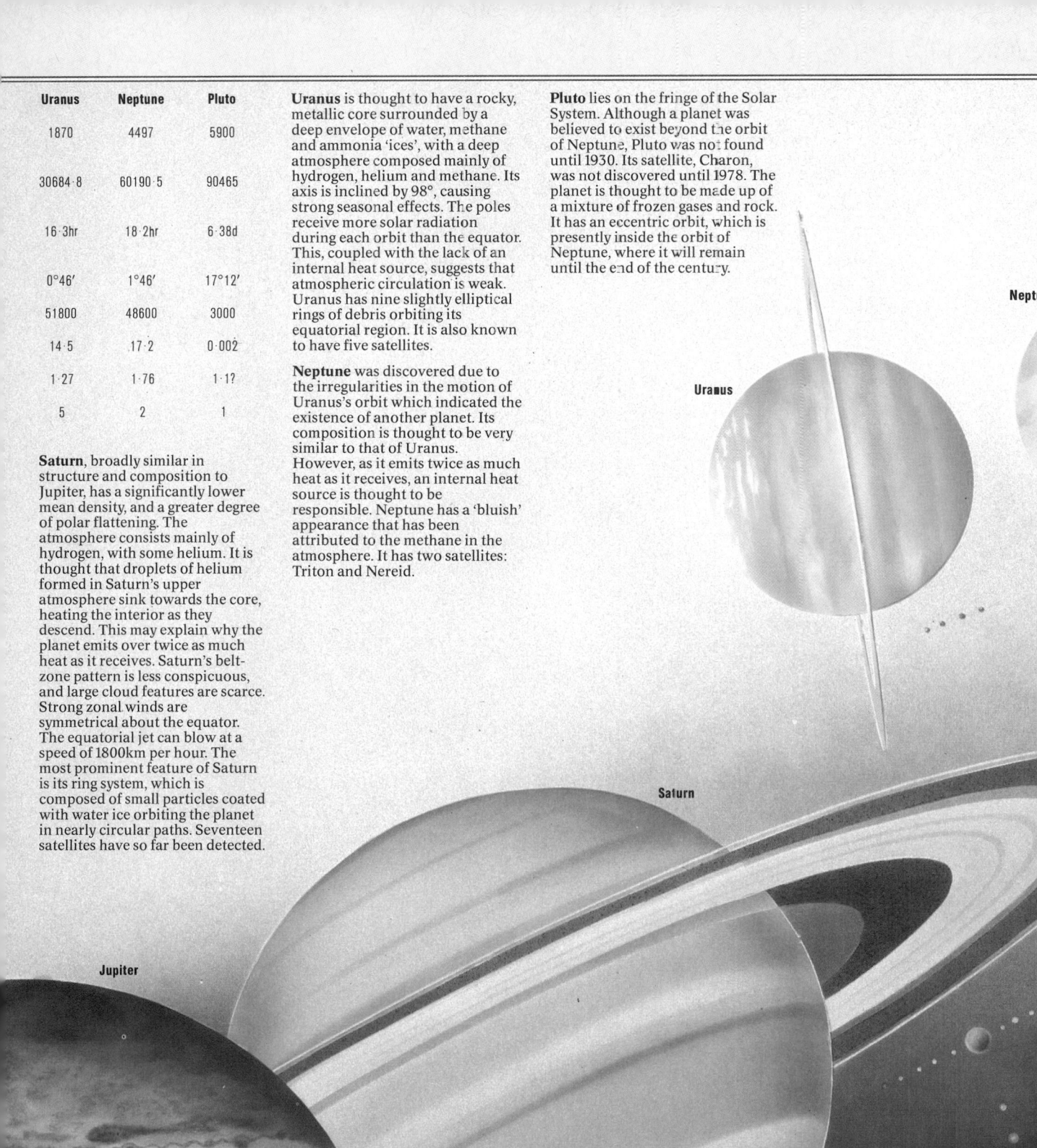

Pluto

Neptune

Uranus

Saturn

Jupiter

Designed and produced by E.S.R.

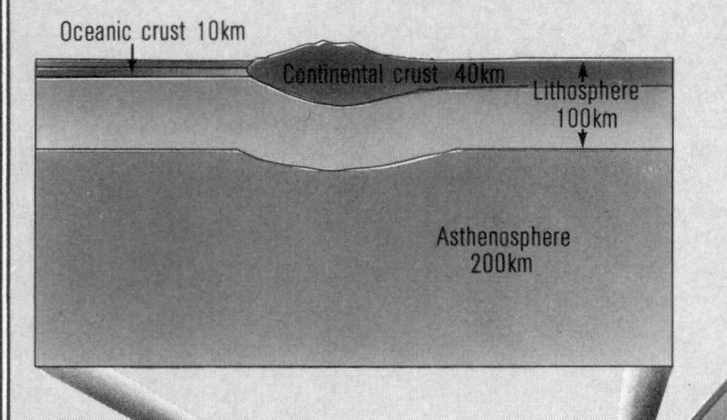

Oceanic crust 10km
Continental crust 40km
Lithosphere 100km
Asthenosphere 200km

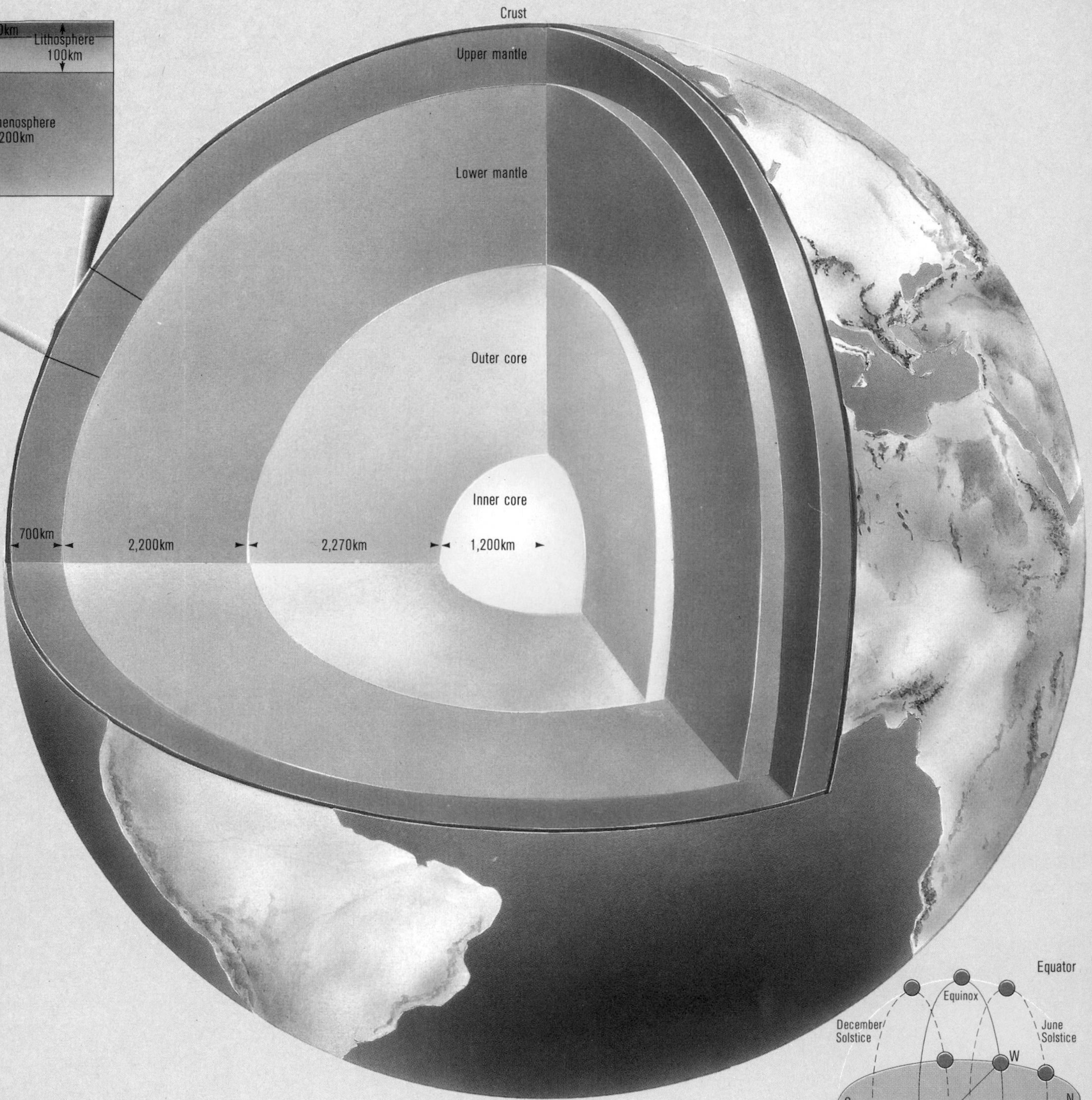

Crust
Upper mantle
Lower mantle
Outer core
Inner core

Internal structure of the Earth
There are four distinct layers to the Earth's interior: the crust, the mantle, the outer core and the inner core. The crust is the outermost layer. Its thickness varies greatly; beneath the oceans it is 5-11km thick, whereas continental crust averages about 40km, but in some places reaches depths of over 90km. The largest part of the mantle is the mesosphere, above which is the asthenosphere. The temperature in the asthenosphere is close to its melting point and it is thus partially fluid. Above the asthenosphere is the lithosphere. The sharp boundary between the crust and the mantle is known as the Mohorovičić discontinuity (Moho for short). The Gutenberg discontinuity marks the mantle-core boundary. The outer core is the only layer that is thought to be liquid. This is separated from the solid inner core.

700km   2,200km   2,270km   1,200km

Density	5·517g/cm³
Sideral period	365·26d
Sideral day (mean)	23h 56m·04s
Axial inclination	23·5°
Distance from Sun (mean)	149·6 million km
Equatorial diameter	12756 km
Equatorial circumference	400075 km
Surface gravity	981·183 cm/sec²
Orbital velocity	29·6 km/sec

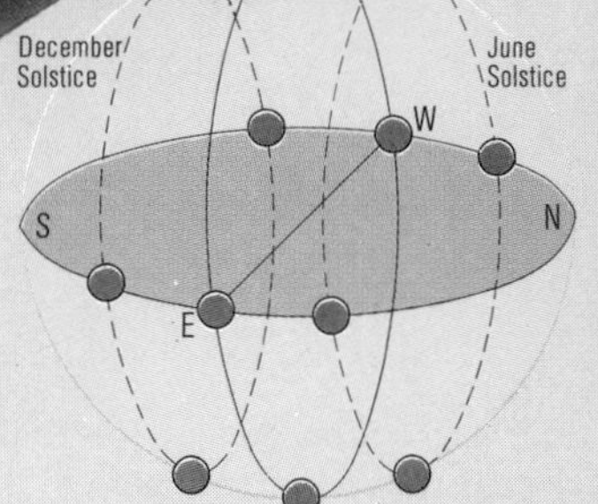

Since the Earth's formation from the solar nebula 4600 million years ago, immense changes have taken place. Not only has the planet evolved, but during the brief span of our existence our knowledge of the processes involved, and of the Earth's relationship with the Solar System, has increased. It was once believed that the Earth occupied a privileged position at the centre of the universe; a view that was not dispelled until the 17th century.

The Earth lies in the middle of the ecosphere, the region around the Sun where temperatures are neither too hot nor too cold for life to develop. The size, atmosphere and nature of the Earth's surface, which is made up largely of water, means that the Earth is the only known planet capable of supporting life.

Time
The world is divided into 24 time zones, each centred on meridians at 15° intervals. This is the longitudinal distance the Sun appears to travel every hour. The Greenwich meridian passes through the centre of the first zone. The International Date Line approximately follows the 180° meridian. For practical purposes, standard time is used so that times are fixed over extensive north-south zones that take into account international boundaries.

Seasons
Seasonal effects arise because of the tilt of the Earth's axis (23.5°), combined with its orbit around the Sun. This causes periodic variations in the amount of sunlight reaching the northern and southern hemispheres.
The north pole is tilted at its greatest angle towards the sun at summer solstice: thus the northern hemisphere experiences summer, and the southern hemisphere winter. This is reversed at winter solstice. In between, at the spring and autumn equinoxes, the tilt is neither towards nor away from the Sun. This also explains why the Sun will appear to take different paths across the sky when viewed from different parts of the Earth.

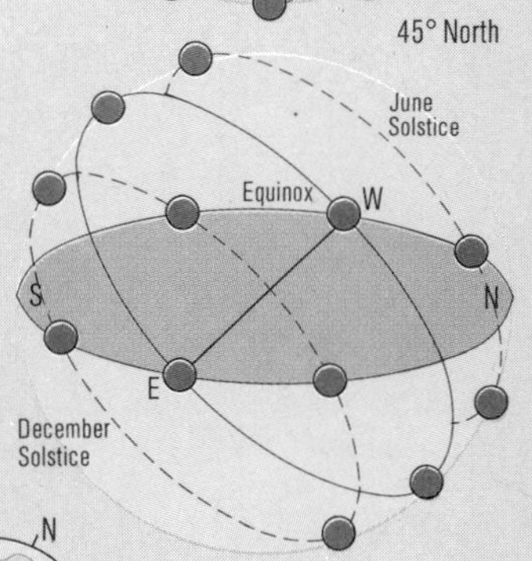

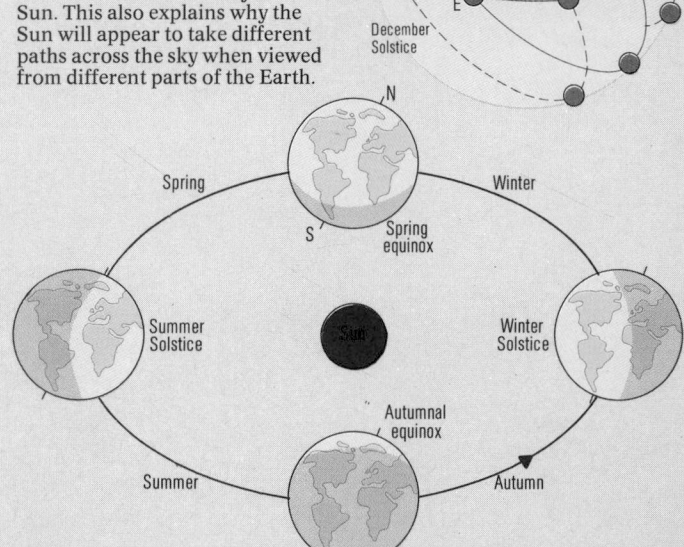

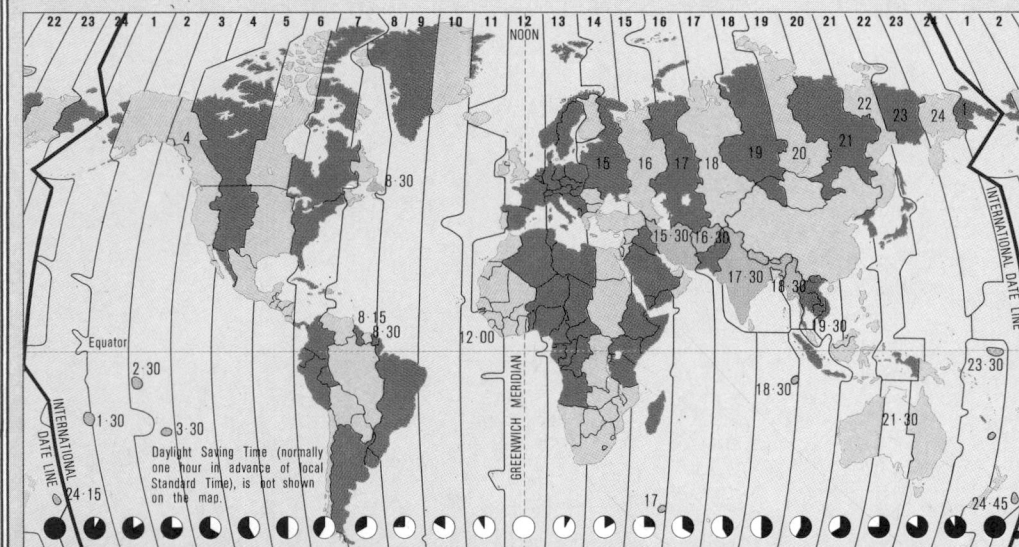

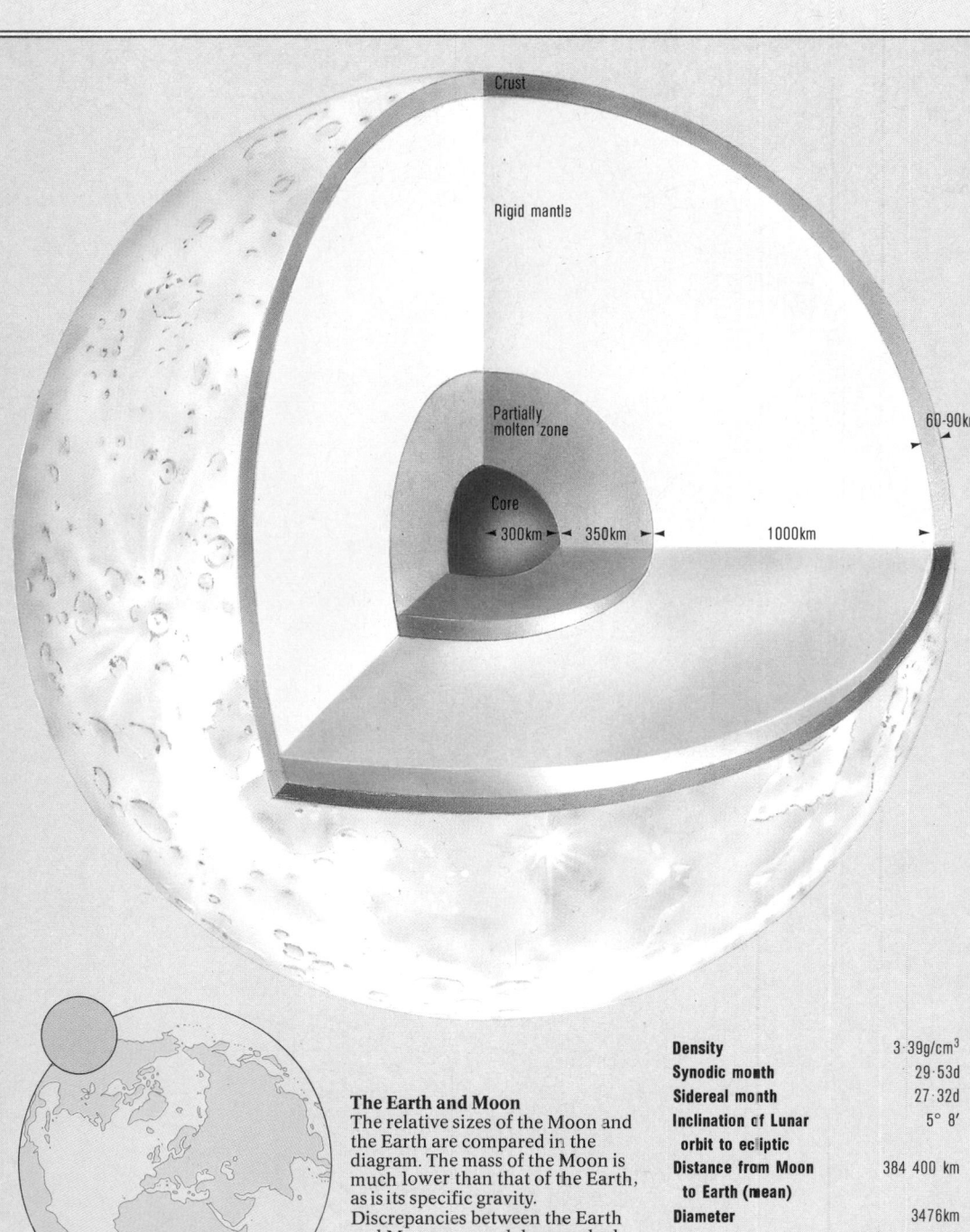

Crust

Rigid mantle

Partially molten zone

60-90km

Core

300km   350km   1000km

Moon

The Moon is our closest neighbour in space. Some features of the lunar landscape can be seen with the naked eye. It was not until the invention of the telescope, however, that serious observation could begin. Since then our knowledge of the Moon has increased; man has even walked on its surface. Yet some theories remain unresolved and exploration continues. Scientific analysis has established that the Earth and Moon are about the same age – 4500 to 5000 million years, yet they have undergone different evolutionary sequences. There is no atmosphere or weather on the Moon as its gravity is insufficient to hold any gases.

Moon

The lunar interior has been investigated by means of heat flow experiments and seismometers during Apollo missions. The core of the Moon appears to be relatively much smaller than that of the Earth, and it is probably extremely rich in iron. Surrounding the core is the lunar mantle overlaid by the crust, which is covered by a rocky 'topsoil' known as the regolith. The surface of the Moon has several distinctive features. The maria or 'seas' were probably created by vast lava flows. The craters which dominate the landscape are thought to originate from volcanic activity and the impact of vast meteorites. Other features are narrow trenches, rilles and mountain ranges reaching heights over 4500m.

Origin of the Moon

Various theories have been suggested as to how the Moon originated, and it is still a matter of conjecture. It might originally have been part of the Earth's mantle that became unstable and broke away. However, the Moon's composition is different from that of the Earth's mantle and neither appears to have sufficient angular momentum to enable the separation to have taken place. The Moon may have formed elsewhere and been subsequently 'captured' by the Earth, though this is thought to be a statistically unlikely event. Another possibility is that the Moon condensed from the solar nebula close to the Earth, but independently of it. The Moon could have formed from a cloud of material which once surrounded the Earth.

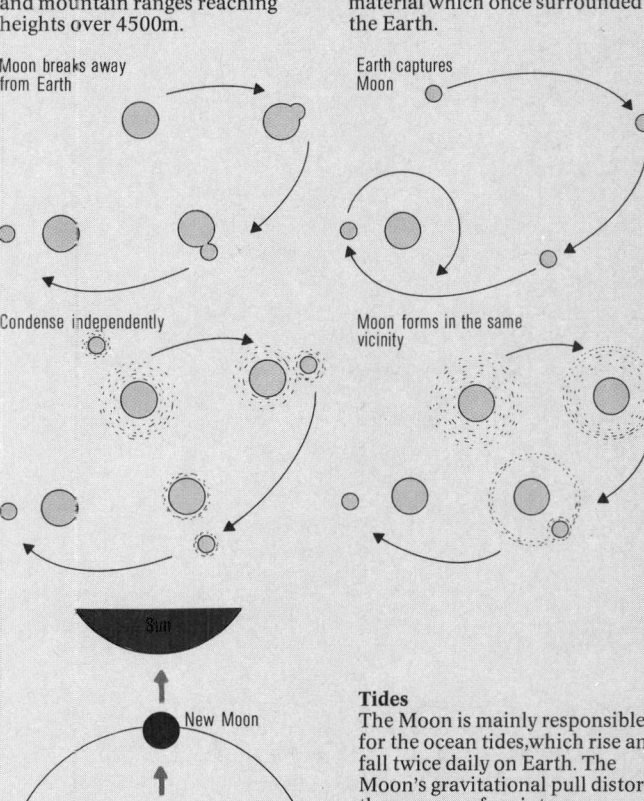

Moon breaks away from Earth

Earth captures Moon

Condense independently

Moon forms in the same vicinity

The Earth and Moon

The relative sizes of the Moon and the Earth are compared in the diagram. The mass of the Moon is much lower than that of the Earth, as is its specific gravity. Discrepancies between the Earth and Moon are much less marked than those between other planets and their satellites. The Earth-Moon system is regarded by some as a double planet.

Density	3·39g/cm³
Synodic month	29·53d
Sidereal month	27·32d
Inclination of Lunar orbit to ecliptic	5° 8'
Distance from Moon to Earth (mean)	384 400 km
Diameter	3476km
Temperature	−150°C to ±130°C
Surface gravity	162·2 cm/sec²
Orbital velocity	1·024 km/sec
Escape velocity	2·4 km/sec

Eclipses

When the Sun, Moon and Earth are in exact alignment, the Moon covers the whole disk of the Sun. A total eclipse is seen within the umbra (the area of deepest shadow) and a partial eclipse from the penumbra.
If the Moon is near apogee (farthest point from Earth) the Sun is not completely covered and a ring of sunlight remains around the dark lunar disk. This is known as an annular eclipse.
A lunar eclipse takes place when the Full Moon passes into the shadow cast by the Earth instead of passing above or below the shadow. If the Moon brushes the umbra it will be partially eclipsed; a total eclipse occurs when the Moon lies completely within the Earth's umbra.

Phases of the Moon

The Moon completes a cycle of phases every 29.5 days. The Moon shines by reflecting sunlight; at any moment one hemisphere is lit while the other is dark. When a New Moon lies directly in line with the sun, the hemisphere that faces the Earth is dark. The Moon then moves to the east of the Sun. More of the illuminated hemisphere becomes visible as the angle between the Sun and Moon increases, from a thin crescent to a fully illuminated disk when opposite the Sun, eventually returning to a New Moon.

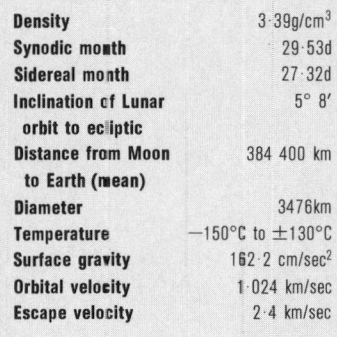

Sun

New Moon

Last quarter

Earth

First quarter

Full Moon

Tides

The Moon is mainly responsible for the ocean tides, which rise and fall twice daily on Earth. The Moon's gravitational pull distorts the ocean surface into an ellipsoidal shape. When the Sun and Moon are aligned (New and Full Moon), higher 'spring' tides occur. When they are pulling at right angles (first and last quarter), lesser 'neap' tides arise. Although the height of the rise in mid-ocean is approximately a metre, the effect in coastal waters is complicated by local factors, and a much greater tidal range can occur.

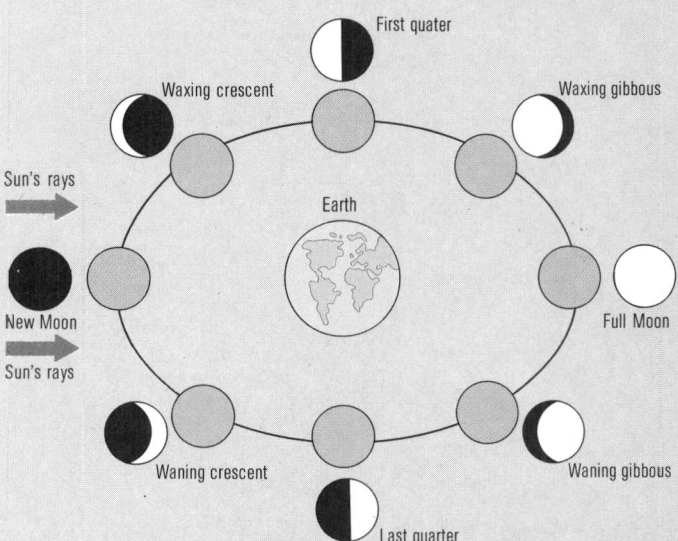

First quarter

Waxing crescent

Waxing gibbous

Sun's rays

Earth

New Moon

Full Moon

Sun's rays

Waning crescent

Waning gibbous

Last quarter

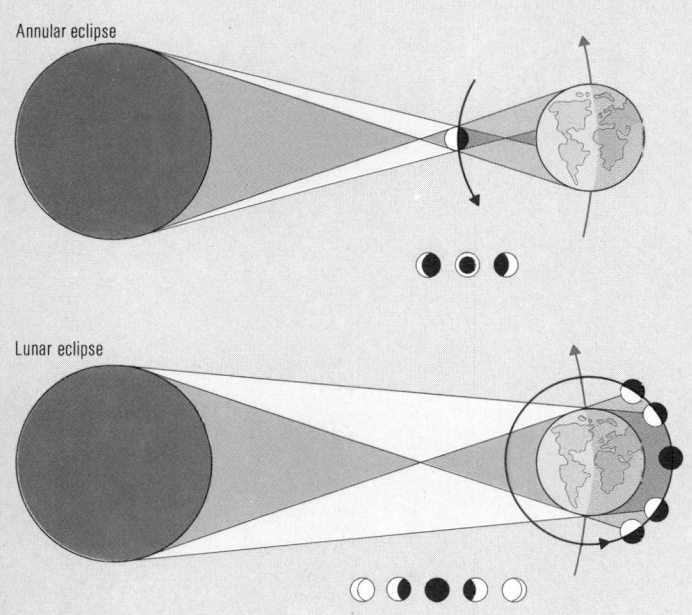

Solar eclipse

Annular eclipse

Lunar eclipse

MOVING CONTINENTS

The Earth's development is still a matter of much conjecture and debate. Until comparatively recently the view that the structure of the Earth has remained essentially fixed throughout geological time was common. The matching of many pairs of coastlines (strictly, continental shelves) led to the first detailed geological and structural comparisons. Palaeomagnetism has probably proved to be the most influential proof of continental drift, in conjunction with palaeontology, palaeoclimatology and other geological evidence.

Plate tectonics, the field of Earth studies which encompasses the theory of continental drift, offers an explanation for many of the Earth's varied structural and geophysical phenomena. According to theory, the lithosphere consists of rigid segments called plates. These can contain both oceanic and continental crust, which 'float' across the more mobile asthenosphere. Major interactions occur along the plate margins.

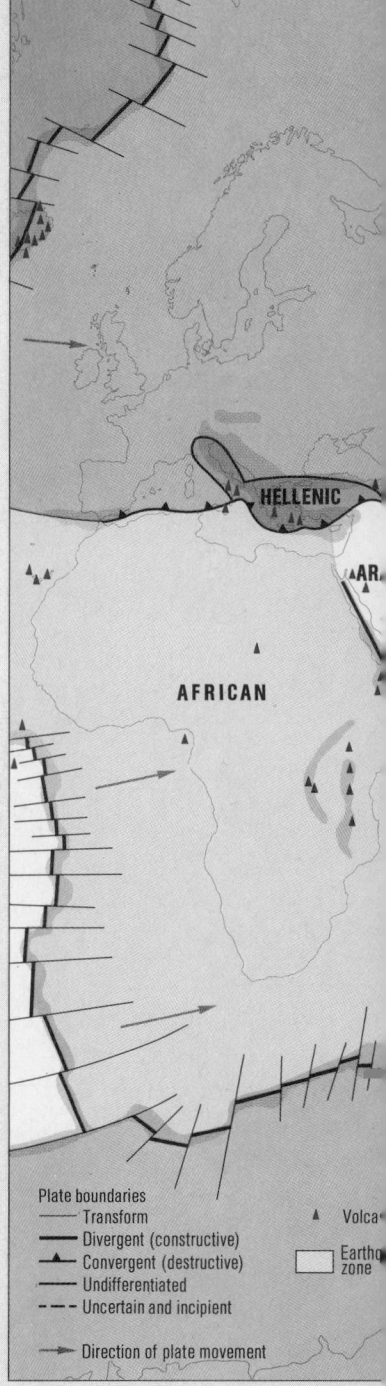

Cratons over 2000 million years old
Palaeozoic rock and mobile belt
Cretaceous and Tertiary coastal basin
Mesozoic and Cenozoic mobile belt
Maximum extent of ice movement

Glossopteris
Mesosaurus

Drifting continents
180 million years ago
The fragmentation of the supercontinent Pangaea began about 200 million years ago. Two major rifts initiated the breakup. The rift zone between North America and Africa generated a northern continental group, Laurasia. The rift that separated the southern landmass of Gondwanaland sent India in a northward direction and simultaneously split South America and Africa from Australia and Antarctica.

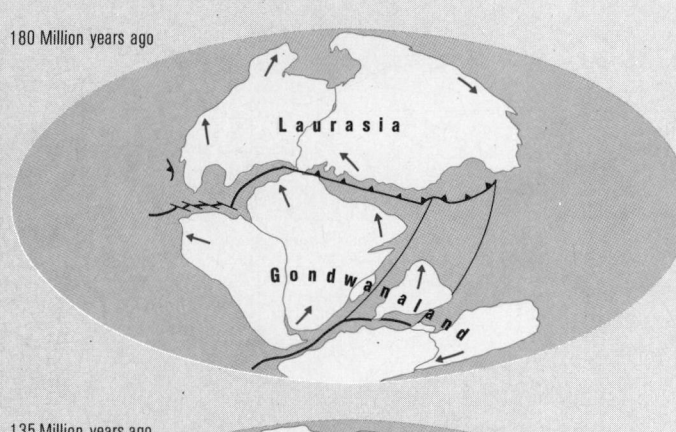

180 Million years ago

Laurasia

Gondwanaland

135 million years ago
Both Gondwanaland and Laurasia continued to drift northwards. Africa and South America began splitting apart to form the origins of the South Atlantic. India continued heading northwards to Asia. The southern part of the North Atlantic had widened considerably.

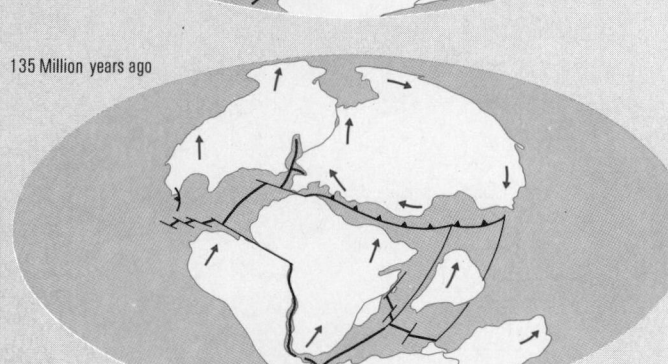

135 Million years ago

65 million years ago
South America had completely separated from Africa and the South Atlantic emerged as a full-fledged ocean. Madagascar had broken away from Africa. In the south, Australia was still connected to Antarctica.

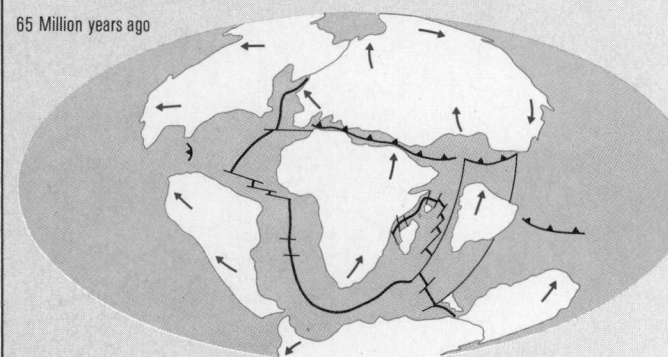

65 Million years ago

Proving continental drift
Evidence to support the theory of continental drift and the idea that today's continents were once joined comes from various geological and geophysical investigations. Rocks from 'matching coastlines' such as South America and Africa, are often similar in age, type and structure. Fossil remains of the reptile *Mesosaurus* have been found on both sides of the South Atlantic. Similarly the remains of the fossil fern *Glossopteris* also indicates that the continents were once joined. Comparisons of palaeomagnetism in rocks of various ages and the Earth's changing magnetic field seems to confirm continental movement.

Plate tectonics
The mobile behaviour of the material within the asthenosphere allows the motion of lithospheric plates, which form a rigid outer shell to the Earth. Each plate moves as a distinct unit. Most earthquakes, volcanoes and mountain building occur along the plate margins.

There are three types of plate boundary: Divergent (constructive) where plates move apart and upwelling of material from the mantle creates oceanic ridges; Convergent (destructive) where plates collide, causing the lithosphere of one plate to be consumed along a subduction zone; Transform margin, along which plates slide, neither creating nor destroying the lithosphere.

HELLENIC

AR

AFRICAN

Plate boundaries
Transform
Divergent (constructive)
Convergent (destructive)
Undifferentiated
Uncertain and incipient
Direction of plate movement
Volca
Earth
zone

Present
The northward movement of India has led to a collision with Asia, from which the Himalayas resulted. The separation of Greenland from Eurasia is also a recent event in geological time. South America has connected with North America, whilst Australia has drifted north away from Antarctica. Africa is moving away from the Arabian peninsula as the Red Sea rift widens.

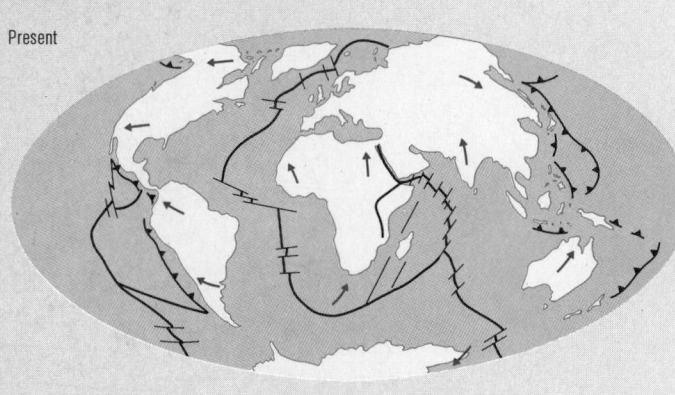

Present

50 million years ahead
By extrapolating plate movements into the future, important changes can be seen. A new sea emerges as East Africa parts company with the mainland. Australia and Papua New Guinea migrate north. The Baja peninsula slides past the North American plate along the San Andreas Fault. The continents will undoubtedly continue to change shape and position: exactly how must still be speculative.

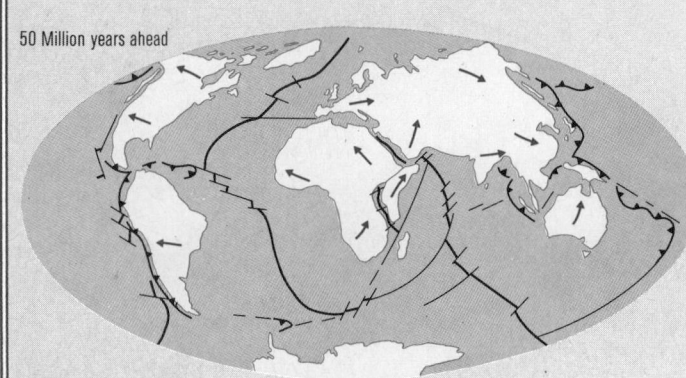

50 Million years ahead

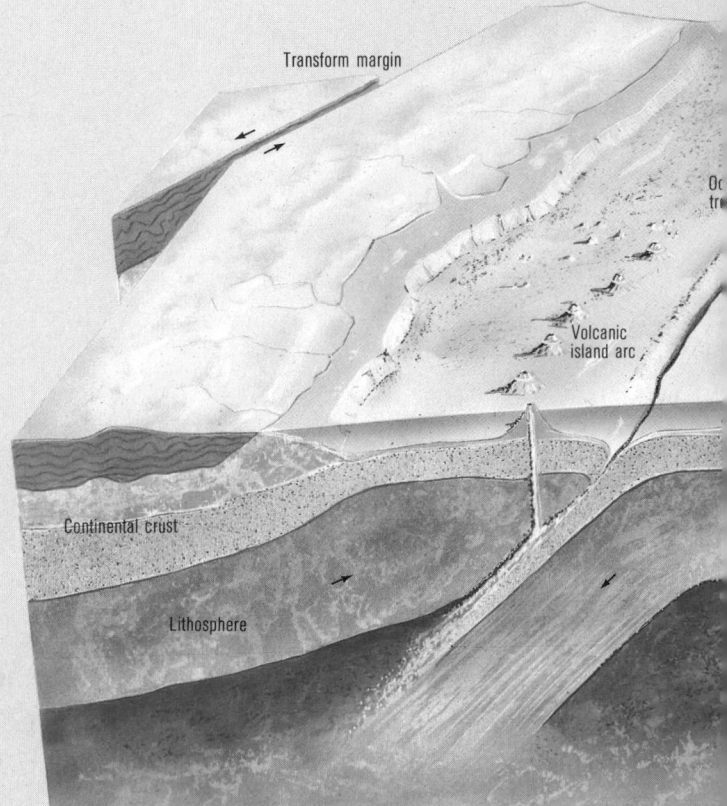

Transform margin
Oc
tr
Volcanic island arc
Continental crust
Lithosphere

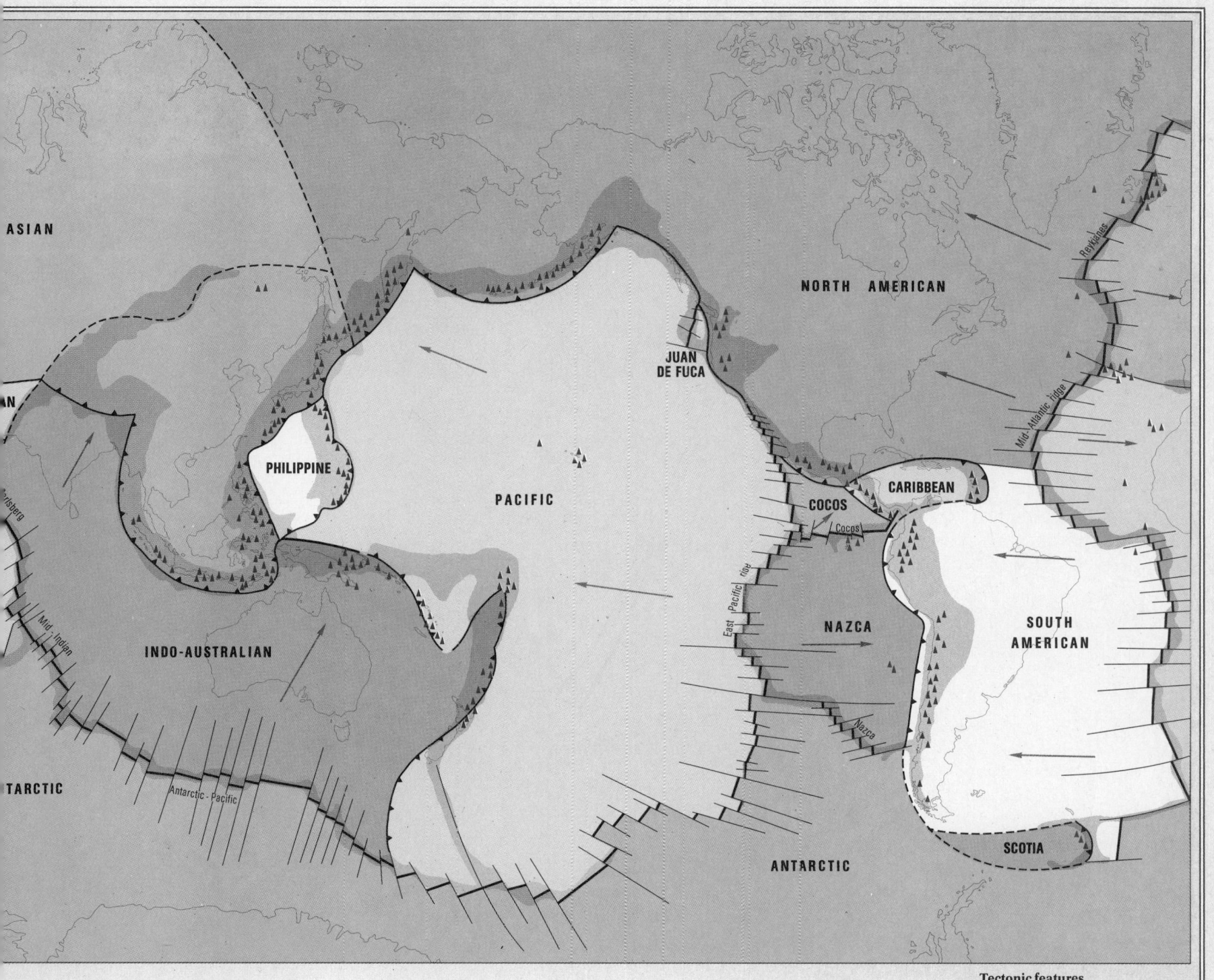

ASIAN

NORTH AMERICAN

JUAN
DE FUCA

PHILIPPINE

PACIFIC

CARIBBEAN

COCOS

Cocos

East Pacific ridge

Mid-Atlantic ridge

Reykjanes

NAZCA

SOUTH
AMERICAN

Mid-Indian

Carlsberg

INDO-AUSTRALIAN

Nazca

TARCTIC

Antarctic - Pacific

ANTARCTIC

SCOTIA

Oceanic
ridge

Ocean
trench

Volcanic
arc

Transform fault

Rift
valley

Fold
mountains

Oceanic crust

Subduction
zone

Asthenosphere

Tectonic features

At a divergent plate margin molten material rises to form new lithosphere. When the magma reaches the surface it cools, solidifies and continues to diverge. The ocean floors are thus in a state of continuous creation and spreading. The Red Sea is believed to be the site of a recently formed divergent boundary. Lateral spreading within a continent can generate large down-faulted valleys, or rifts, like the Great Rift Valley of East Africa.

Plate destruction occurs along subduction zones, often indicated by seismic activity. Continents will remain at the surface while the denser oceanic lithosphere is consumed in an ocean trench. The subducting lithosphere re-enters the Earth's interior, slowly melts and becomes reassimilated. Some magma may eventually migrate to the surface producing volcanic arcs, of which the Andes are an example. Island arcs, such as the Aleutian Islands, are often associated with descending oceanic plates.

If continental plates converge new mountain ranges will result. These are composed of deformed sedimentary rocks and fragments of volcanic arc compressed together. The most recently formed are the Himalayas, but the Alps and the Urals are also thought to have originated in this manner.

At transform margins tectonic effects are less dramatic as plates slide against one another. However, as in southern California increased seismic and volcanic activity occurs.

Designed and produced by E.S.R.

THE EARTH'S LANDSCAPE

The landscape around us is the result of a complex system of natural processes. Different rocks of igneous, sedimentary or metamorphic origin comprise the underlying structure. These can be brought to the surface of the Earth by various forces. When exposed to the elements of nature they are slowly weathered, leading to the disintegration and decomposition of the rock. The debris is then carried away and deposited elsewhere. In turn this may be acted upon by other agents. The Earth's surface reflects the processes at work at any given time. Although the forces which shape the landscape appear to act very slowly, in geological terms the alterations are very swift.

The number of people inhabiting the Earth has risen exponentially, and technology has expanded in conjunction with this growth. The human impact on the landscape has thus become increasingly significant. Construction, excavation, reclamation, hydrological work and farming create the most visible features of this changing environment.

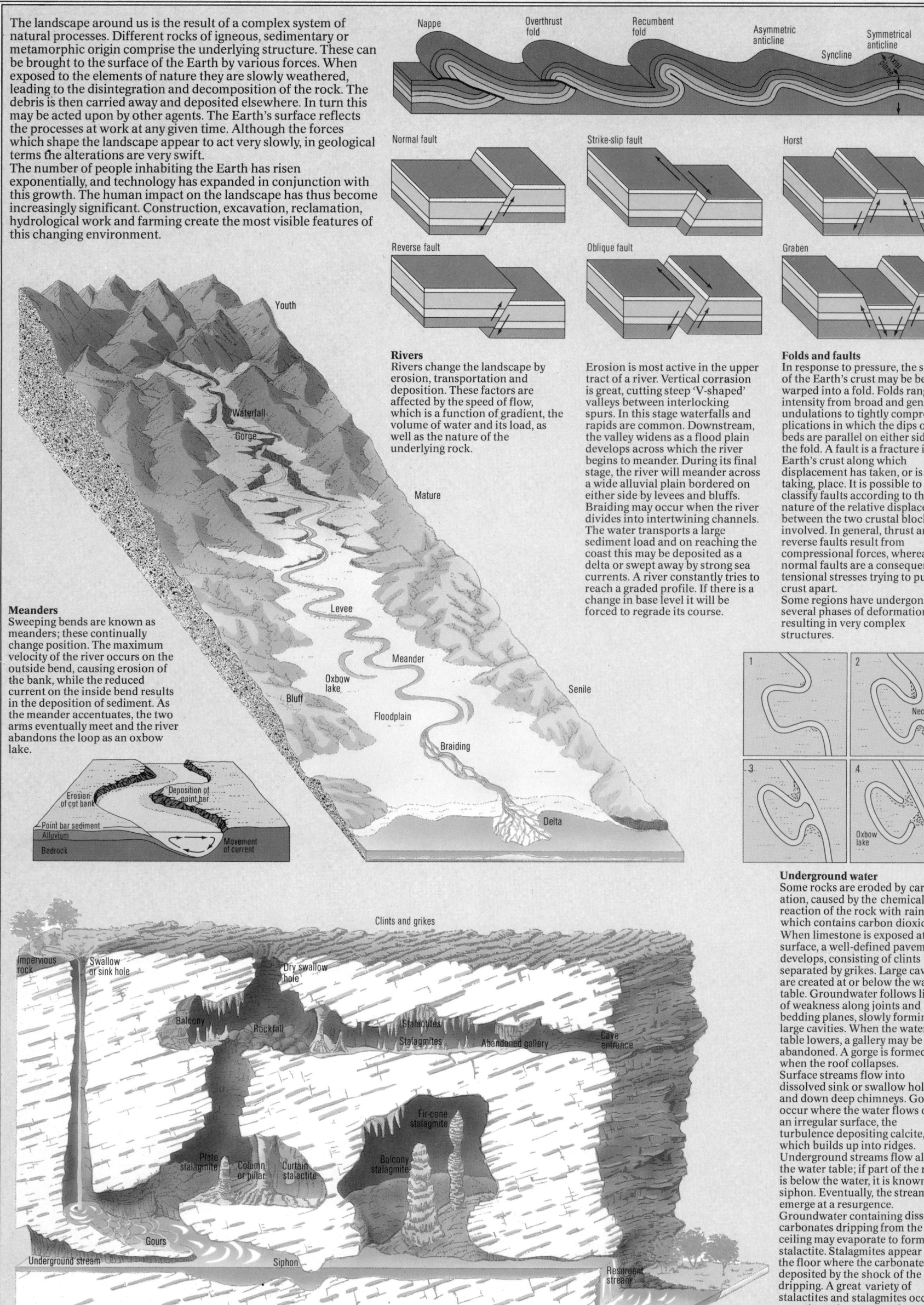

Meanders
Sweeping bends are known as meanders; these continually change position. The maximum velocity of the river occurs on the outside bend, causing erosion of the bank, while the reduced current on the inside bend results in the deposition of sediment. As the meander accentuates, the two arms eventually meet and the river abandons the loop as an oxbow lake.

Rivers
Rivers change the landscape by erosion, transportation and deposition. These factors are affected by the speed of flow, which is a function of gradient, the volume of water and its load, as well as the nature of the underlying rock.

Erosion is most active in the upper tract of a river. Vertical corrasion is great, cutting steep 'V-shaped' valleys between interlocking spurs. In this stage waterfalls and rapids are common. Downstream, the valley widens as a flood plain develops across which the river begins to meander. During its final stage, the river will meander across a wide alluvial plain bordered on either side by levees and bluffs. Braiding may occur when the river divides into intertwining channels. The water transports a large sediment load and on reaching the coast this may be deposited as a delta or swept away by strong sea currents. A river constantly tries to reach a graded profile. If there is a change in base level it will be forced to regrade its course.

Folds and faults
In response to pressure, the strata of the Earth's crust may be bent or warped into a fold. Folds range in intensity from broad and gentle undulations to tightly compressed plications in which the dips of the beds are parallel on either side of the fold. A fault is a fracture in the Earth's crust along which displacement has taken, or is taking, place. It is possible to classify faults according to the nature of the relative displacement between the two crustal blocks involved. In general, thrust and reverse faults result from compressional forces, whereas normal faults are a consequence of tensional stresses trying to pull the crust apart.

Some regions have undergone several phases of deformation resulting in very complex structures.

Underground water
Some rocks are eroded by carbonation, caused by the chemical reaction of the rock with rainwater, which contains carbon dioxide. When limestone is exposed at the surface, a well-defined pavement develops, consisting of clints separated by grikes. Large caverns are created at or below the water table. Groundwater follows lines of weakness along joints and bedding planes, slowly forming large cavities. When the water table lowers, a gallery may be left abandoned. A gorge is formed when the roof collapses. Surface streams flow into dissolved sink or swallow holes and down deep chimneys. Gours occur where the water flows over an irregular surface, the turbulence depositing calcite, which builds up into ridges. Underground streams flow along the water table; if part of the roof is below the water, it is known as a siphon. Eventually, the stream will emerge at a resurgence. Groundwater containing dissolved carbonates dripping from the ceiling may evaporate to form a stalactite. Stalagmites appear on the floor where the carbonate is deposited by the shock of the dripping. A great variety of stalactites and stalagmites occur; sometimes they meet to form a continuous pillar or column.

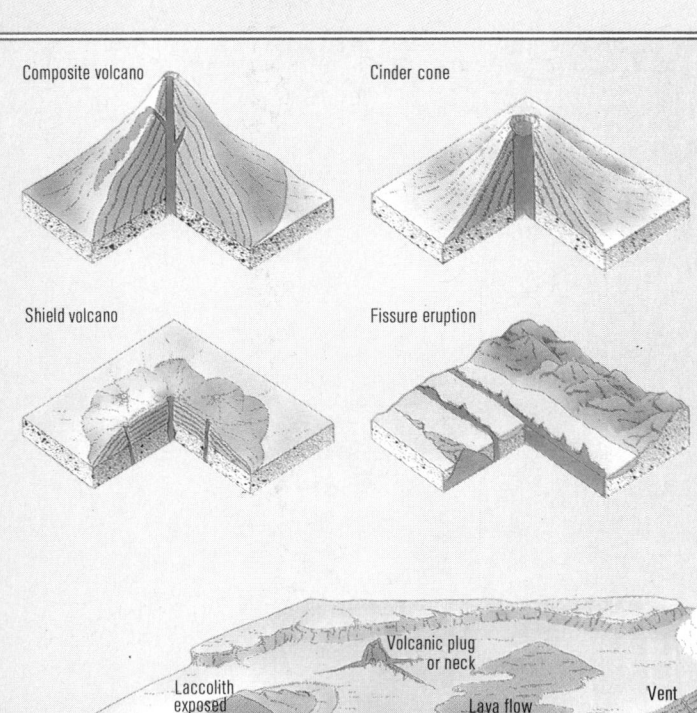

Composite volcano

Cinder cone

Shield volcano

Fissure eruption

Volcanoes and igneous activity

Volcanoes that eject ash form cinder cones comprising layers of cinder and dust from successive eruptions. More commonly, a volcano will produce alternate layers of lava and cinder. If the lava is plentiful, a shield volcano can occur, built up from many lava flows and covering a large area. Fissure eruptions release flows of very fluid lava that can extend over great distances. Magma does not always reach the surface and often cools at depth to form batholiths, laccoliths that arch the overlying strata upward, dykes that cut through strata, and sills injected between strata. Hot springs, gas vents and geysers may also occur. When igneous rocks are exposed, they form distinctive scenery as they are more resistant to erosion than the surrounding rocks.

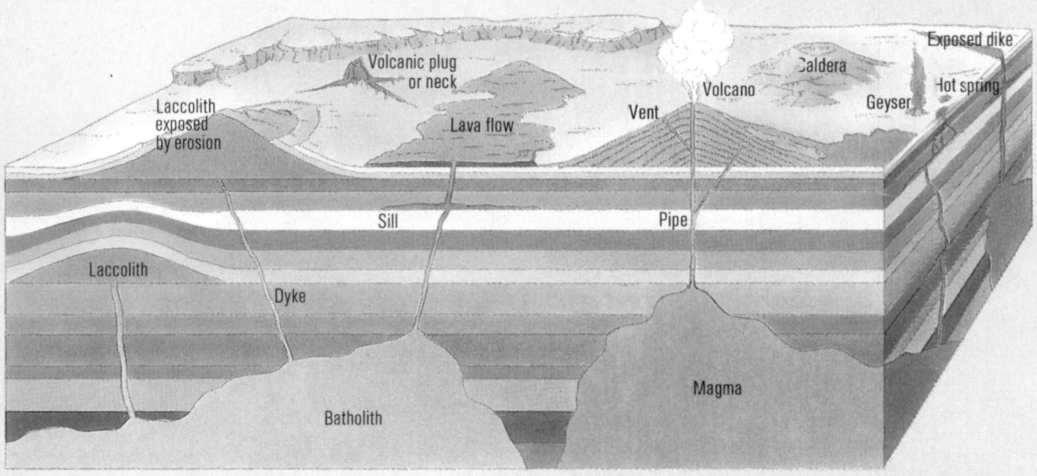

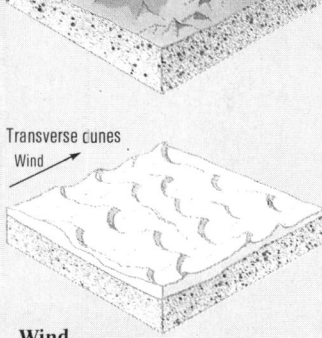

Irregular dunes

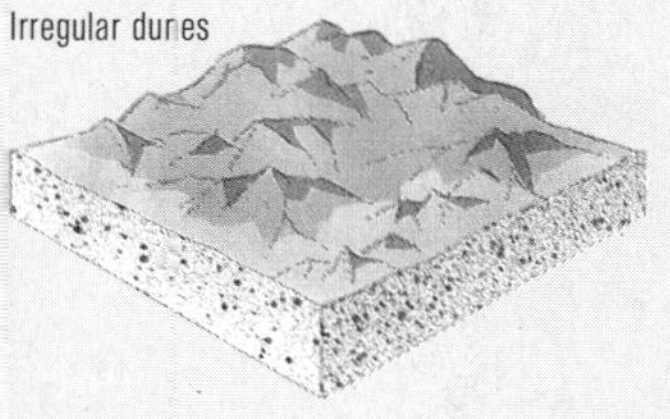

Seif dunes

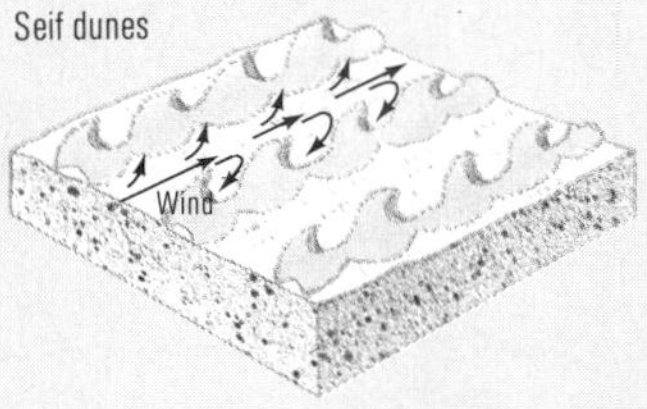

Wind

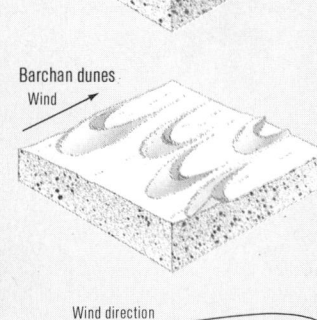

Transverse dunes

Wind

Barchan dunes

Wind

Volcanic plug or neck · Caldera · Exposed dike · Volcano · Geyser · Hot spring · Laccolith exposed by erosion · Lava flow · Vent · Sill · Pipe · Laccolith · Dyke · Magma · Batholith

Wind

Wind action is most effective in arid and semi-arid regions. Accumulations of sand as dunes can assume surprisingly consistent patterns. Crescent shaped Barchan dunes slowly migrate downwind. Transverse dunes form a series of long ridges that are separated by troughs, orientated at right angles to the prevailing wind. Seif or longitudinal dunes form parallel to the prevailing wind on bare rock surfaces. Where wind direction is variable, irregular star-shaped dunes may develop.
Exposed rock surfaces are eroded by abrasion, often causing strange shapes and effects. Fine particles seldom travel more than a metre above the surface. The wind's sandblasting effect is thus limited in vertical extent. Continued erosion at the base of a rock, however, may leave it precariously balanced.

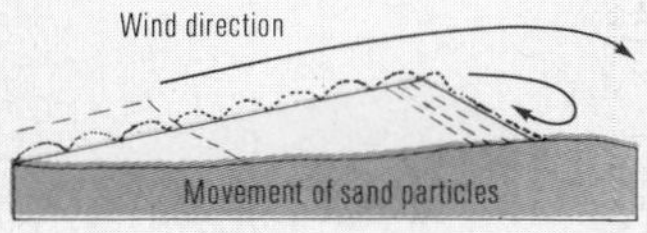

Wind direction

Movement of sand particles

Ice – a valley glacier

Glaciers cover nearly ten per cent of the Earth's land surface. However, in the recent geological past ice sheets extended over vast areas. Many present-day landscapes resulted from the action of these glaciers.
There are three main types of glaciers: valley glaciers, which originate above the snow line in mountain areas; piedmont glaciers, formed when valley glaciers join and spread out at the foot of mountains; and ice caps or sheets, which spread out laterally from their source area.
The immense abrasive power of debris caught in the ice erodes 'U' shaped valleys. Interlocking spurs are truncated and tributary valleys left hanging above the deepened main valley.
Sediments within the ice and moraine carried along the surface are deposited ungraded as till at the glacier snout. Meltwater carries deposits over the outwash plain where kettleholes and drumlins can be seen. Eskers are deposits from streams which were once under the ice.

Waves

Coastlines are continually changing: they may have resulted from land emergence or submergence and are shaped by erosional and depositional activities of waves, currents and tides.
Material transported by longshore drift may be deposited as a spit across a bay. This can develop into a baymouth bar which seals off the bay, completely enclosing a lagoon. A tombolo, a form of spit, links an island to the mainland. Caves caused by wave erosion on either side of a headland may unite to form a natural arch. When the arch collapses, sea stacks remain.

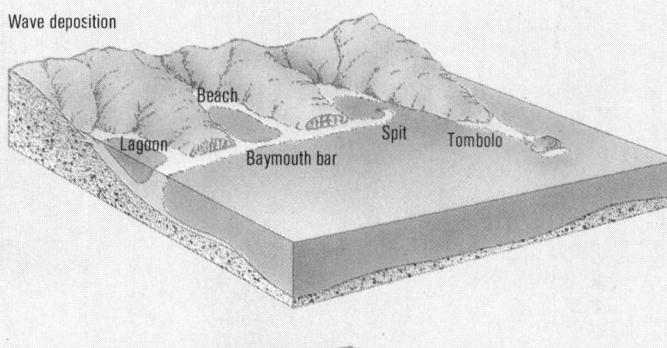

Wave deposition

Beach · Lagoon · Baymouth bar · Spit · Tombolo

Wave erosion

Headland · Cliff · Arch · Cave · Stack

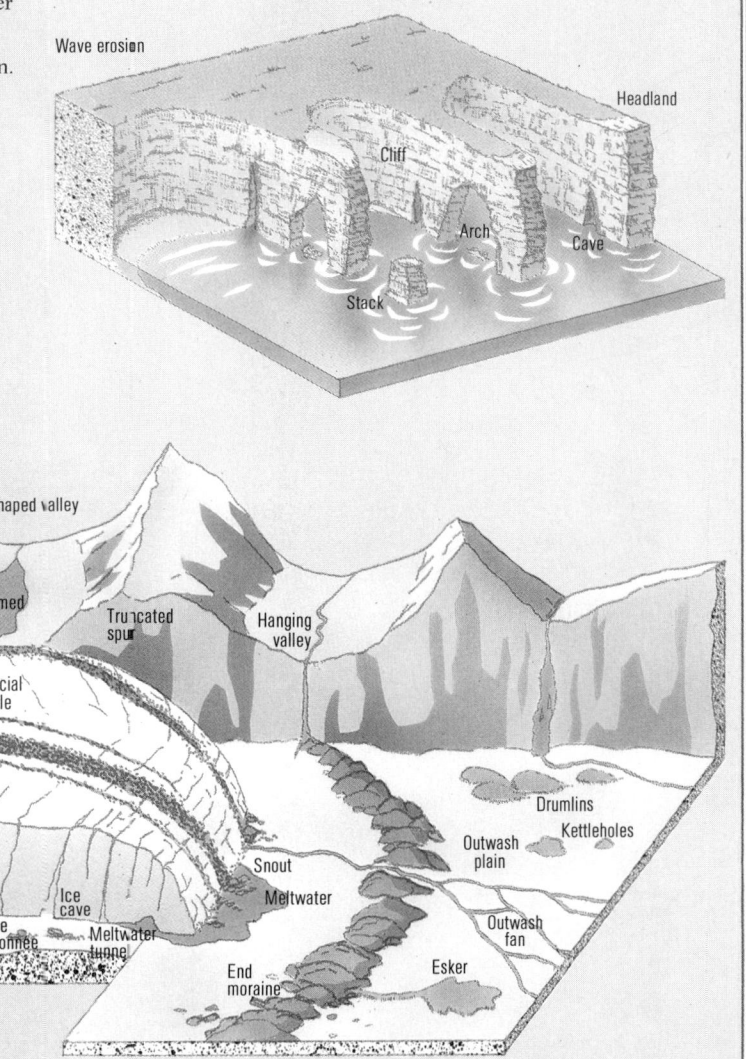

Pyramidal peak · Bergschrund · Firn (compacted snow) · Cirque · Marginal crevasses · Arête · Transverse crevasses · Sérac · Icefall · Lateral moraine · Medial moraine · Glacial table · 'U' shaped valley · Ice dammed lake · Truncated spur · Hanging valley · Englacial moraine · Subglacial moraine · Striations · Roche moutonnée · Ice cave · Snout · Meltwater · Meltwater dune · End moraine · Drumlins · Kettleholes · Outwash plain · Outwash fan · Esker

Designed and produced by E.S.R.

THE ATMOSPHERE

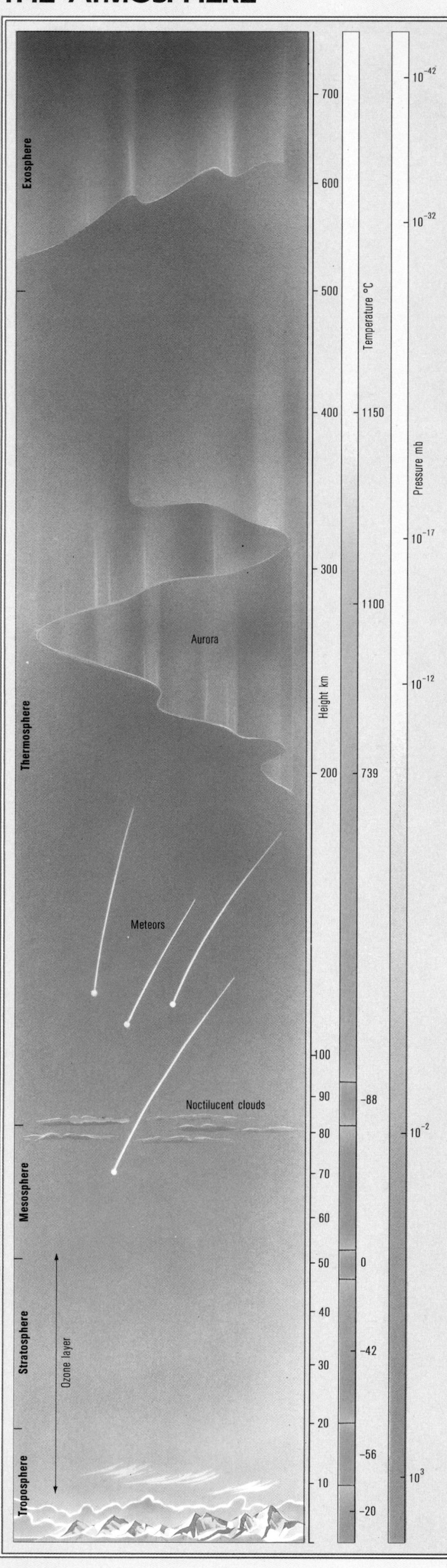

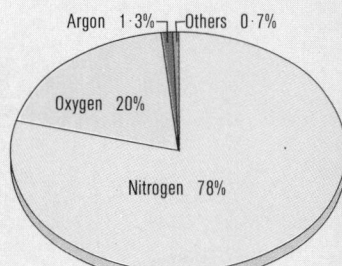

The atmosphere, which is unlike that of any other planet, encircles and protects the Earth. Changes in the composition of the atmosphere are closely associated with the evolution of the Earth. One of the most important transitions was the increase in oxygen when photosynthetic plants evolved.

The atmosphere is a mixture of gases, the largest proportion of which is nitrogen. The most important is oxygen, without which life could not be sustained; other gases are present in quite small quantities.

Near the Earth's surface, gravitational pull increases the density of the atmosphere. We do not feel this air pressure because of the equal air pressure inside our bodies. Variation in air pressure has a major influence on weather, as does the amount of water vapour in the atmosphere. These elements are in turn affected by a number of factors such as the evaporation of water from the oceans, wind movements and the topography of the Earth.

Structure of the atmosphere
The atmosphere can be divided into various layers, depending on its physical properties. Variations in temperature and pressure result from the distribution of solar heating and help to distinguish the different zones.

Exosphere
merges into the vacuum of space. It is extremely rarefied and is composed mainly of hydrogen and helium.

Atmospheric composition
The composition of the Earth's atmosphere has changed as the planet has evolved. At present the largest proportion is formed of nitrogen followed by oxygen. Argon and carbon dioxide can also be found, as well as other inert gases such as neon and helium. The atmosphere also contains variable amounts of water vapour, up to three per cent, and small quantities of sulphur dioxide.

Thermosphere
absorbs ultraviolet radiation. Temperatures rise steeply with height to several thousand degrees. This region is the source of the ionosphere, disturbances in this region appear as glowing lights of varying colours – aurorae. They occur primarily over the poles because the charged particles from the Sun are channelled there by the Earth's magnetic field. Short-wave and long-wave radio transmissions are also reflected at various layers within the ionosphere.

It would appear that human activities are altering the natural atmospheric conditions of the planet. To what extent this is happening is still a matter of great debate.

The ozone (a form of oxygen), in the upper atmosphere, screens the Earth from the Sun's ultraviolet rays and is deteriorating. The use of man-made refrigerant gases such as chlorofluorocarbons (CFCs) are a contributing factor. Conversely, other pollutants, such as methane, are by a complex set of chemical reactions increasing ozone levels nearer the ground, which may be adding to the 'greenhouse effect', a phrase which has been used to describe a general warming of the atmosphere.

Since the industrial revolution, carbon dioxide levels have increased by 30 per cent. This is a direct result of burning fossil fuel and destroying vast tracts of forest. The carbon dioxide traps outgoing radiation, which leads to an increase in temperatures. It has been predicted that an average rise of 3°C is possible, and as much as 8-10°C at the poles. Sea levels would rise as a result of melting ice and thermal expansion of the oceans. Many areas of low-lying land would then be flooded and island nations swamped. Accompanying these temperature rises would be changes in rainfall patterns which could affect agricultural productivity. In general it is also thought that tropical conditions would gradually extend northwards.

Mesosphere
extends to a height of about 80km and in it there is a marked fall in temperature to −120°C. Meteorites from space tend to burn out in this region as they meet increased air resistance.

Stratosphere
contains the ozone layer, which absorbs the Sun's harmful ultraviolet light. As a result, the temperature rises to about 10°C before decreasing again in the stratopause. Noctilucent clouds may form from compressed meteoric dust in this region.

Other forms of atmospheric pollution are also causing concern. Industrial emissions of sulphur oxide and nitrogen oxide dissolve in rain, which is often transported great distances before returning to Earth as sulphuric and nitric acids. Their deposition as 'acid rain' can have dire effects on ecosystems. Forests are affected, soils leached and water supplies contaminated. Exhaust-caused smogs and lead emitted from vehicles also have a detrimental effect on the atmosphere.

It is known that the atmosphere and climate of the planet have changed with time. Our knowledge, however, is far from complete in many areas. Whether changes in atmospheric conditions are natural or man-made is to some degree still a matter of speculation and controversy.

Troposphere
is the lowest layer of the atmosphere and contains all the climatic activities that affect us. It reaches about 8km above the poles and 15km above the equator. Pressure is at its greatest due to the weight of the layers above, and 80 per cent of the mass of the atmosphere is found here. Near ground level, visible and infrared radiation is absorbed. Temperature decreases with height until the tropopause is reached.

Greenhouse effect
The balance of the incoming and outgoing solar radiation is disturbed by the increased amount of carbon dioxide which traps infrared radiation. This causes a general warming of the atmosphere known as the greenhouse effect.

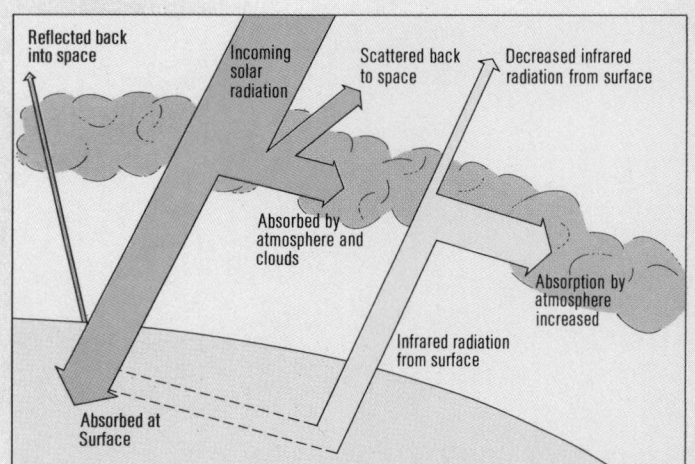

Clouds

Clouds can be classified on the basis of their appearance and height. The basic forms are cirrus, stratus and cumulus. Other clouds reflect one of these forms or are combinations or modifications of them.

Cirrus thin, delicate, fibrous ice-crystal clouds. Sometimes appear as hooked filaments called 'mares tails', often the first sign of an approaching depression.

Cirrocumulus thin, white ice-crystal clouds in the form of ripples, waves or globular masses all in a row. May produce a 'mackerel sky'.

Cirrostratus thin sheet of white ice-crystal clouds that may give the sky a milky look. Sometimes produce haloes around the Sun or Moon.

Altocumulus white to grey clouds often composed of separate globules. Frequently indicates unsettled weather.

Altostratus stratified veil of clouds that are generally thin and may produce very light precipitation.

Stratocumulus soft, grey clouds in globular patches or rolls. Rolls may join together to make a continuous cloud.

Stratus low uniform layer, forms dull, overcast skies. Associated with depressions, may often produce drizzle and rain.

Nimbostratus amorphous layer of dark grey clouds. One of the chief precipitation-producing clouds.

Cumulus dense, billowy clouds often characterised by flat bases. May occur as isolated clouds or closely packed.

Cumulonimbus towering cloud sometimes spreading out on top to form an 'anvil head'. Associated with heavy rainfall, thunder, lightning, hail and tornadoes.

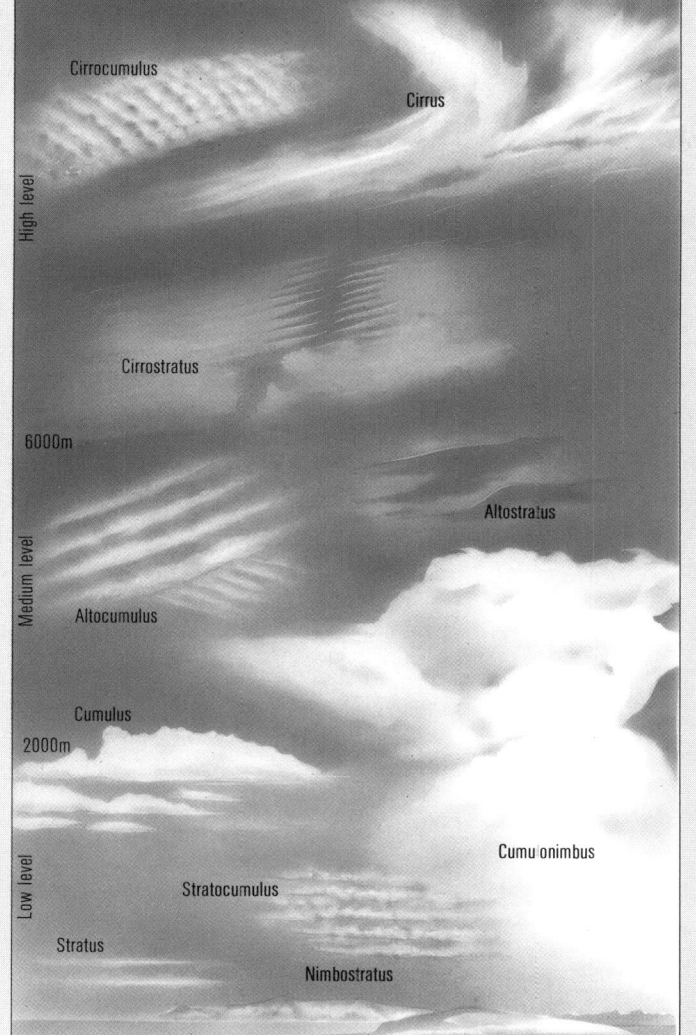

Clouds

Without clouds there would be no precipitation. Variations in the amount of precipitation from place to place as well as local differences from time to time have a significant impact not only on the nature of the physical landscape but also on people's life-styles.

Clouds consist of microscopic drops of water or ice crystals suspended in the atmosphere. Formation occurs when air that contains water vapour becomes saturated and reaches its dew point. This is usually the result of the air rising and thus cooling. The water vapour then condenses around dust particles.

Wind

The unequal heating of the Earth by solar radiation generates pressure differences. These inequalities cause the movement of air from areas of higher pressure to areas of lower pressure. A system of general circulation is thus generated by semipermanent cells of high and low pressure over the oceans. Wind direction is then subject to deflection by the Coriolis effect, to the right in the northern hemisphere, to the left in the southern hemisphere. This is complicated by seasonal pressure changes over land, which can give rise to seasonal reversals of wind known as monsoons.

Circulation of the air
The temperature differences between the poles and the equator provide the thermal energy to drive atmospheric circulation. Warm air at the equator rises and flows towards the poles at high levels. Cold polar air moves towards the equator at low levels to replace it. Once the effect of rotation is added, the Coriolis effect, this simple convection system breaks down into smaller cells.

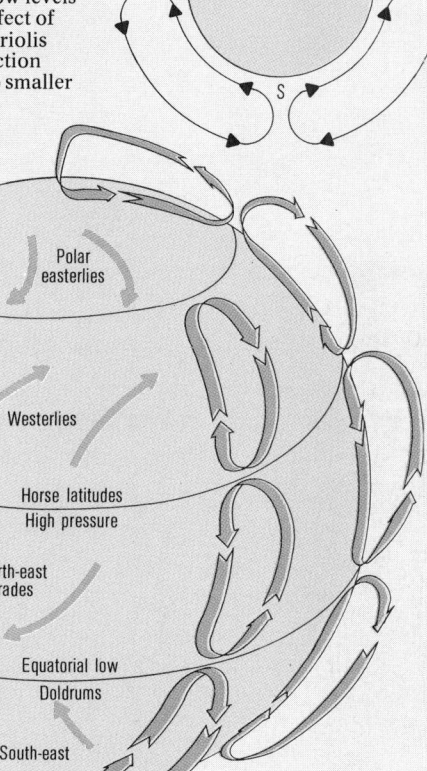

A Depression
Variable weather in the middle latitudes often results from the development of low pressure areas known as depressions, a common feature of which is the formation of warm and cold fronts. The warm, light air rises above the cool air along the warm front. Behind, the cold air forces its way under the warm air along the cold front. Gradually, the cold front catches up with the warm front and the warm air is pushed above the cold in an occlusion. In the northern hemisphere, the air circulates in an anticlockwise direction and in the southern, it circulates clockwise.

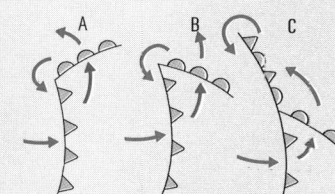

Climate

The climate of an area is its characteristic weather considered over a long period of time. Differences in latitude, prevailing air masses, either local or regional, the relative distribution of land and sea, as well as the topography, will all have an effect on the climatic conditions experienced. The most popular climatic classification is that devised by Wladimir Köppen. It is based on the seasonal variations of temperature and rainfall and their effect on vegetation growth. The range of climates can broadly be defined according to latitude. Hot, tropical climates are dominated by equatorial air masses throughout the year. Temperate climates of the mid-latitudes are very variable, subjected alternately to subpolar and subtropical air masses as well as seasonal shifts. Polar climates of high latitudes are strongly seasonal, influenced by subpolar and polar air masses. Geological evidence suggests that during other periods the planet experienced a more uniform climate. The present variable pattern may be due, in part, to the fact that the earth is still recovering from the last Ice Age, although opinion varies as to whether fluctuations in climate should be regarded as abnormal.

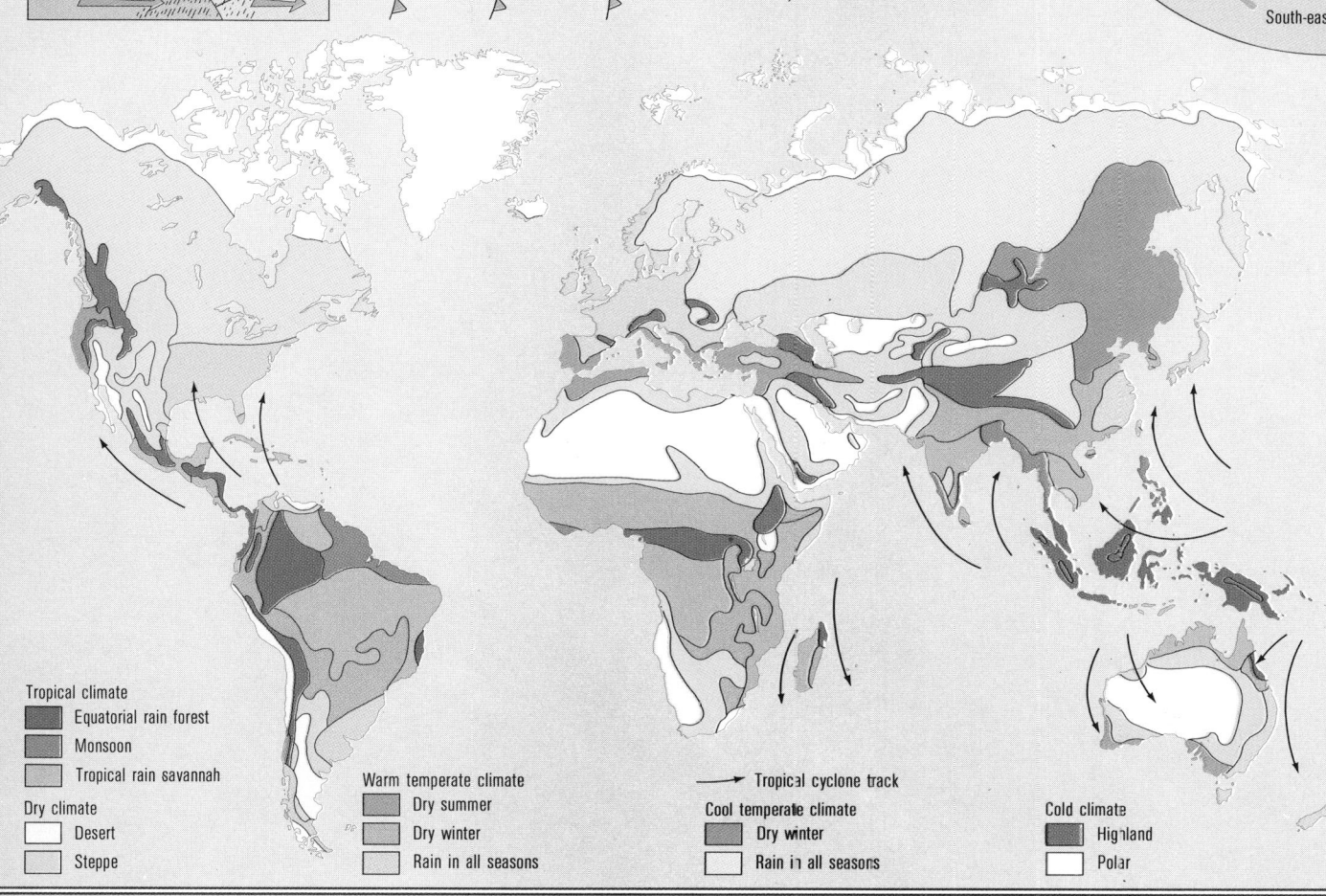

Tropical climate
- Equatorial rain forest
- Monsoon
- Tropical rain savannah

Dry climate
- Desert
- Steppe

Warm temperate climate
- Dry summer
- Dry winter
- Rain in all seasons

Cool temperate climate
- Dry winter
- Rain in all seasons

→ Tropical cyclone track

Cold climate
- Highland
- Polar

Designed and produced by E.S.R.

EVOLUTION OF LIFE

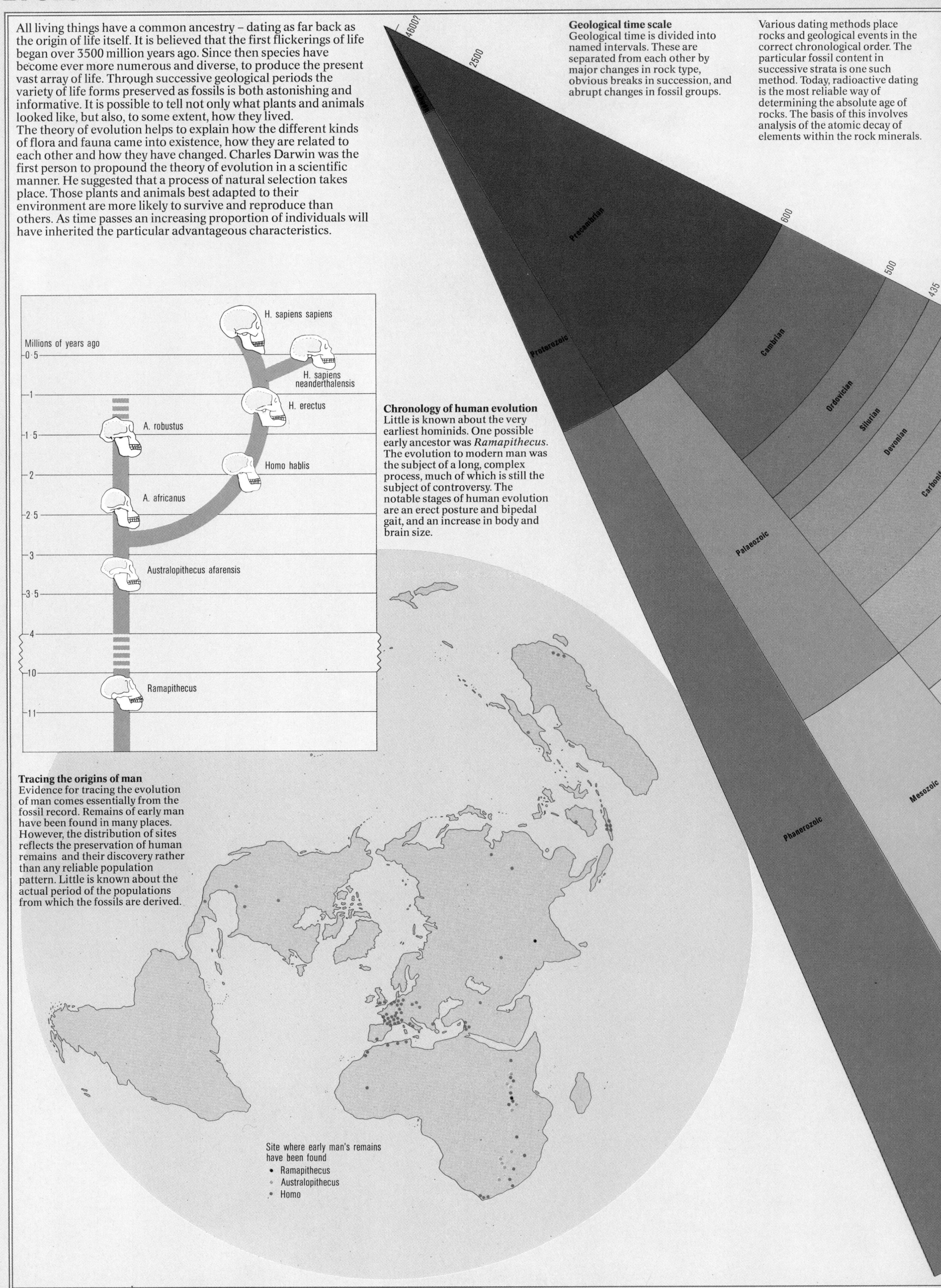

All living things have a common ancestry – dating as far back as the origin of life itself. It is believed that the first flickerings of life began over 3500 million years ago. Since then species have become ever more numerous and diverse, to produce the present vast array of life. Through successive geological periods the variety of life forms preserved as fossils is both astonishing and informative. It is possible to tell not only what plants and animals looked like, but also, to some extent, how they lived.

The theory of evolution helps to explain how the different kinds of flora and fauna came into existence, how they are related to each other and how they have changed. Charles Darwin was the first person to propound the theory of evolution in a scientific manner. He suggested that a process of natural selection takes place. Those plants and animals best adapted to their environment are more likely to survive and reproduce than others. As time passes an increasing proportion of individuals will have inherited the particular advantageous characteristics.

Geological time scale
Geological time is divided into named intervals. These are separated from each other by major changes in rock type, obvious breaks in succession, and abrupt changes in fossil groups.

Various dating methods place rocks and geological events in the correct chronological order. The particular fossil content in successive strata is one such method. Today, radioactive dating is the most reliable way of determining the absolute age of rocks. The basis of this involves analysis of the atomic decay of elements within the rock minerals.

Chronology of human evolution
Little is known about the very earliest hominids. One possible early ancestor was *Ramapithecus*. The evolution to modern man was the subject of a long, complex process, much of which is still the subject of controversy. The notable stages of human evolution are an erect posture and bipedal gait, and an increase in body and brain size.

Tracing the origins of man
Evidence for tracing the evolution of man comes essentially from the fossil record. Remains of early man have been found in many places. However, the distribution of sites reflects the preservation of human remains and their discovery rather than any reliable population pattern. Little is known about the actual period of the populations from which the fossils are derived.

Site where early man's remains have been found
- Ramapithecus
- Australopithecus
- Homo

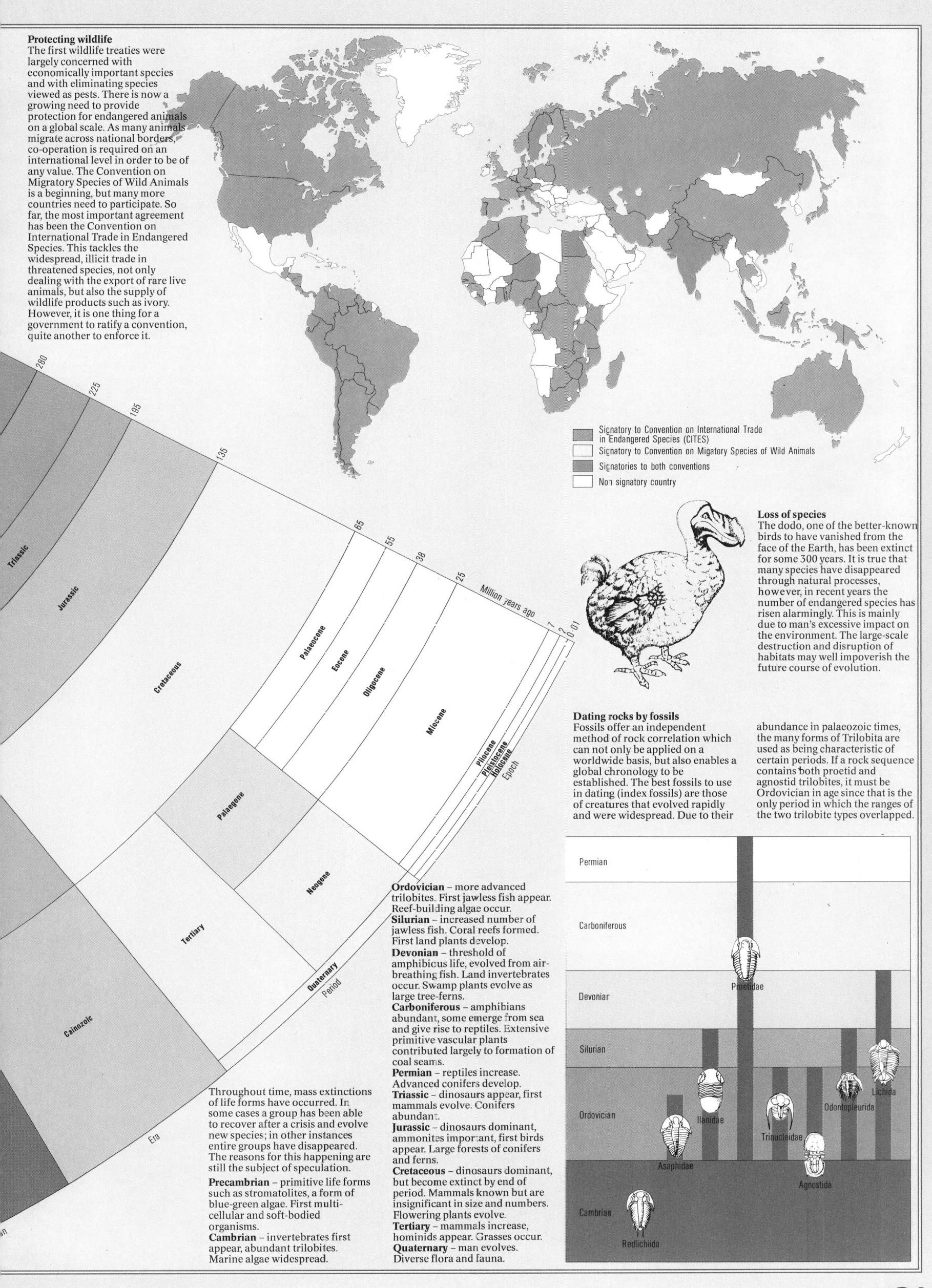

Protecting wildlife
The first wildlife treaties were largely concerned with economically important species and with eliminating species viewed as pests. There is now a growing need to provide protection for endangered animals on a global scale. As many animals migrate across national borders, co-operation is required on an international level in order to be of any value. The Convention on Migratory Species of Wild Animals is a beginning, but many more countries need to participate. So far, the most important agreement has been the Convention on International Trade in Endangered Species. This tackles the widespread, illicit trade in threatened species, not only dealing with the export of rare live animals, but also the supply of wildlife products such as ivory. However, it is one thing for a government to ratify a convention, quite another to enforce it.

Signatory to Convention on International Trade in Endangered Species (CITES)
Signatory to Convention on Migratory Species of Wild Animals
Signatories to both conventions
Non signatory country

Loss of species
The dodo, one of the better-known birds to have vanished from the face of the Earth, has been extinct for some 300 years. It is true that many species have disappeared through natural processes, however, in recent years the number of endangered species has risen alarmingly. This is mainly due to man's excessive impact on the environment. The large-scale destruction and disruption of habitats may well impoverish the future course of evolution.

Dating rocks by fossils
Fossils offer an independent method of rock correlation which can not only be applied on a worldwide basis, but also enables a global chronology to be established. The best fossils to use in dating (index fossils) are those of creatures that evolved rapidly and were widespread. Due to their abundance in palaeozoic times, the many forms of Trilobita are used as being characteristic of certain periods. If a rock sequence contains both proetid and agnostid trilobites, it must be Ordovician in age since that is the only period in which the ranges of the two trilobite types overlapped.

Throughout time, mass extinctions of life forms have occurred. In some cases a group has been able to recover after a crisis and evolve new species; in other instances entire groups have disappeared. The reasons for this happening are still the subject of speculation.

Precambrian – primitive life forms such as stromatolites, a form of blue-green algae. First multi-cellular and soft-bodied organisms.
Cambrian – invertebrates first appear, abundant trilobites. Marine algae widespread.

Ordovician – more advanced trilobites. First jawless fish appear. Reef-building algae occur.
Silurian – increased number of jawless fish. Coral reefs formed. First land plants develop.
Devonian – threshold of amphibious life, evolved from air-breathing fish. Land invertebrates occur. Swamp plants evolve as large tree-ferns.
Carboniferous – amphibians abundant, some emerge from sea and give rise to reptiles. Extensive primitive vascular plants contributed largely to formation of coal seams.
Permian – reptiles increase. Advanced conifers develop.
Triassic – dinosaurs appear, first mammals evolve. Conifers abundant.
Jurassic – dinosaurs dominant, ammonites important, first birds appear. Large forests of conifers and ferns.
Cretaceous – dinosaurs dominant, but become extinct by end of period. Mammals known but are insignificant in size and numbers. Flowering plants evolve.
Tertiary – mammals increase, hominids appear. Grasses occur.
Quaternary – man evolves. Diverse flora and fauna.

EXPLORATION AND DISCOVERY

The early explorers who travelled beyond their own shores were accomplished shipbuilders and seamen. The Vikings, Chinese and Arabs were among those who first reached distant lands. Some merchants and missionaries reached remote inland areas. Within a relatively short space of time the great voyages of discovery had charted the vast expanses of sea and largely determined the extent and shape of the continental landmasses. These geographical explorations were later expanded and consolidated by expeditions of a more scientific nature.

Antarctic explorers

— Bellingshausen 1819-21
—··— Weddell 1820-24
—— Biscoe 1831-32
– – – Wilkes 1839-40
—·— Ross 1840-43
—··— Shackleton 1907-9
– – – Scott 1910-12
—— Amundsen 1911-12
········ Hillary-Fuchs 1955-58

Great explorations
Much early exploration was prompted by the search for a new route to India and the Far East. Columbus believed that he had reached the East Indies by an Atlantic route, and not a 'new' world. Magellan did reach South-east Asia, and in doing so he was the first to circumnavigate the globe. Later exploration, such as the voyages of Captain Cook, was inspired as much by scientific curiosity as by the hope of commercial advantage. Livingstone's African journeys made him one of the greatest explorers ever known.

ARCTIC OCEAN

Barentsevo More

Nova Zemlya

ASIA

Caspian Sea

Black Sea

Karakorum

Constantinople (Istanbul)

Trabzon

Tabriz

Kashgar

Beijing

Acre

Tarabulus

El Qâhira (Cairo)

Mediterranean Sea

Ormuz

Chengdu

Yunnan (Kunming)

Fuzhou

Canton (Guangzhou)

Pagan

NORTH PACIFIC OCEAN

Bering Sea

Tropic of Cancer

Arctic Circle

Arabian Sea

Goa

Calicut

Bay of Bengal

Ceylon (Sri Lanka)

Malacca

Philippines

Gonder

AFRICA

(Congo) *Zaire*

L. Victoria

Dar es Salaam

Tanganyika

L. Nyasa

Zambezi

Sofala (Beira)

INDIAN OCEAN

Java

Equator

AUSTRALIA

Darwin

Brisbane

Port Jackson (Sydney)

Adelaide

Albany

Tasman Sea

Van Diemen's Land (Tasmania)

Torres Str.

Cape Town

Cape of Good Hope

Tropic of Capricorn

Cook Str.

New Zealand

Antarctic Circle

Greenwich

15th Century and earlier
– · – · – Rubruck 1252-55
– · · – Marco Polo 1271-95
· · · · · · Bartolomeu Diaz 1486-88
– – – – Columbus 1492-93
– – – Cabot 1497-98
———— Vasco da Gama 1497-99

16th Century
——— Piñeda 1519-20
——— Magellan 1519-22
——— Cortes 1519-25
–·–·– Verrazano 1524
· · · · Pizarro 1524-33
• • • • Almagro 1535
——— De Soto 1539
· · · · · Coronado 1540
– + – + Orellana 1541
——— Frobisher 1576
——— Drake 1577-80
——— Barentz 1594-97

17th Century
– ·· – Hudson 1610-11
——— Tasman 1642-44
– – – Marquette and Jolliet 1673

18th Century
——— Bering 1728-29, 1741
——— Cook 1768-71, 1772-75, 1776-80
– – – Bruce 1769-72
· · · · · Mackenzie 1793
– · – · Park 1795-97

19th Century
–◆–◆– Lewis and Clark 1804-8
• • • • Denham and Clapperton 1823-25
–◇–◇– Caillé 1827-28
–•–•– Sturt 1829
——— Eyre 1841
——— Leichhardt 1844
– – – McClure 1853
——— Livingstone 1853-56, 1856-63, 1866-73
–○–○– Stuart 1859-62
——— Speke 1859-63
•••••• Rohlfs 1861-69, 1873-80
——— Warburton 1873
· · · · · Cameron 1873-76
——— Stanley 1874-77
– – – Nordenskiöld 1878-79

23

Designed and produced by E.S.R.

Today's large number of nations is a relatively recent phenomenon. As colonialism declined, the number of independent nations grew. Some of the recently established national boundaries have created artificial divisions which often divide tribal lands and separate ethnic communities. Many newly emergent countries have been beset by instability, civil war and other turbulent events. The outcome of disputes within and between nations is now often dependent upon global opinion or intervention.

Nations are becoming more involved in each others affairs by virtue of trade, technology and aid. Also, problems such as terrorism, pollution, ecological issues and many more may be tackled more effectively through collaborative effort. An array of international and regional bodies, consultative agencies and other cohesive groupings reflect this growing interdependence of nations. There has been a rapid growth in recent years in the number of non-governmental organisations. They range from development groups like OXFAM to conservation groups such as Greenpeace and Friends of the Earth. These and other pressure groups seek to influence governments and international agencies. Some highly effective campaigns have increased world awareness of the disasters and problems faced in other parts of the globe as well as bringing to the fore many environmental issues.

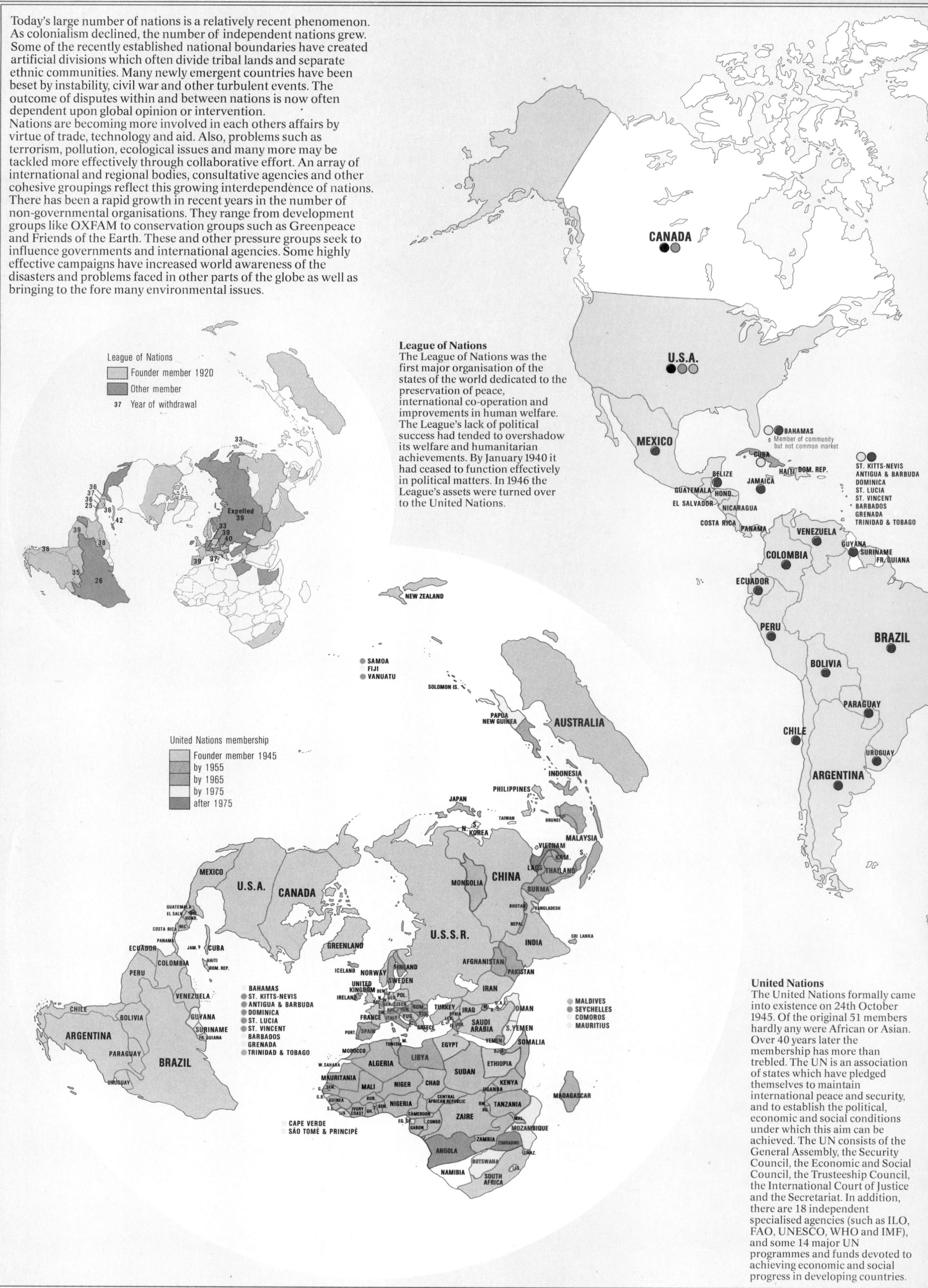

League of Nations

The League of Nations was the first major organisation of the states of the world dedicated to the preservation of peace, international co-operation and improvements in human welfare. The League's lack of political success had tended to overshadow its welfare and humanitarian achievements. By January 1940 it had ceased to function effectively in political matters. In 1946 the League's assets were turned over to the United Nations.

League of Nations
- Founder member 1920
- Other member
- 37 Year of withdrawal

United Nations membership
- Founder member 1945
- by 1955
- by 1965
- by 1975
- after 1975

United Nations

The United Nations formally came into existence on 24th October 1945. Of the original 51 members hardly any were African or Asian. Over 40 years later the membership has more than trebled. The UN is an association of states which have pledged themselves to maintain international peace and security, and to establish the political, economic and social conditions under which this aim can be achieved. The UN consists of the General Assembly, the Security Council, the Economic and Social Council, the Trusteeship Council, the International Court of Justice and the Secretariat. In addition, there are 18 independent specialised agencies (such as ILO, FAO, UNESCO, WHO and IMF), and some 14 major UN programmes and funds devoted to achieving economic and social progress in developing countries.

24

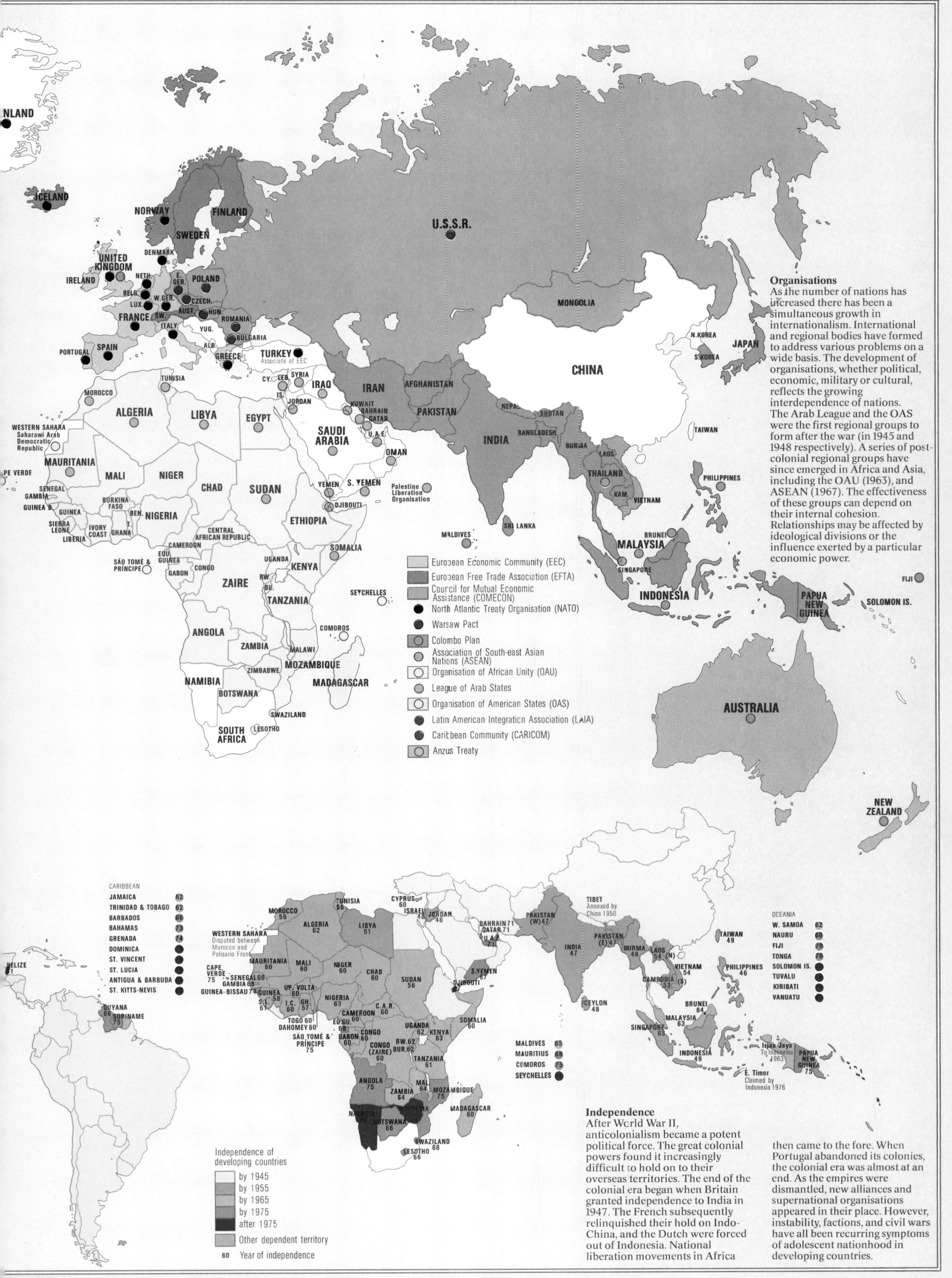

NLAND

ICELAND

NORWAY
SWEDEN
FINLAND

DENMARK
UNITED
KINGDOM
IRELAND
NETH.
BELG.
LUX.
FRANCE
SW.
ITALY
PORTUGAL SPAIN
E. GER.
W. GER.
AUST.
HUN.
POLAND
CZECH.
ROMANIA
YUG.
BULGARIA
ALB.
GREECE
TURKEY
Associate of EEC

U.S.S.R.

MONGOLIA

N.KOREA
JAPAN
S.KOREA
CHINA
TAIWAN

MOROCCO
ALGERIA
LIBYA
EGYPT
TUNISIA
CY.
LEB.
IS.
JORDAN
SYRIA
IRAQ
IRAN
AFGHANISTAN
PAKISTAN
KUWAIT
BAHRAIN
QATAR
U.A.E.
SAUDI
ARABIA
OMAN

WESTERN SAHARA
Saharawi Arab
Democratic
Republic
PE VERDE
MAURITANIA
MALI
NIGER
CHAD
SUDAN
SENEGAL
GAMBIA
GUINEA B.
GUINEA
SIERRA
LEONE
LIBERIA
IVORY
COAST
T.
GHANA
BURKINA
FASO
BEN.
NIGERIA
CAMEROON
EQU.
GUINEA
GABON
CONGO
CENTRAL
AFRICAN REPUBLIC
SÃO TOMÉ &
PRÍNCIPE
ZAIRE
RW.
BU.
UGANDA
KENYA
TANZANIA
ETHIOPIA
SOMALIA
DJIBOUTI
YEMEN
S. YEMEN
Palestine
Liberation
Organisation
SEYCHELLES
MALDIVES
SRI LANKA
INDIA
NEPAL
BHUTAN
BANGLADESH
BURMA
LAOS
THAILAND
KAM.
VIETNAM
PHILIPPINES
BRUNEI
MALAYSIA
SINGAPORE
INDONESIA
PAPUA
NEW
GUINEA
SOLOMON IS.
FIJI

ANGOLA
ZAMBIA
MALAWI
ZIMBABWE
MOZAMBIQUE
NAMIBIA
BOTSWANA
MADAGASCAR
COMOROS
SWAZILAND
SOUTH
AFRICA
LESOTHO

AUSTRALIA

NEW
ZEALAND

Organisations
As the number of nations has increased there has been a simultaneous growth in internationalism. International and regional bodies have formed to address various problems on a wide basis. The development of organisations, whether political, economic, military or cultural, reflects the growing interdependence of nations. The Arab League and the OAS were the first regional groups to form after the war (in 1945 and 1948 respectively). A series of post-colonial regional groups have since emerged in Africa and Asia, including the OAU (1963), and ASEAN (1967). The effectiveness of these groups can depend on their internal cohesion. Relationships may be affected by ideological divisions or the influence exerted by a particular economic power.

European Economic Community (EEC)
European Free Trade Association (EFTA)
Council for Mutual Economic Assistance (COMECON)
North Atlantic Treaty Organisation (NATO)
Warsaw Pact
Colombo Plan
Association of South-east Asian Nations (ASEAN)
Organisation of African Unity (OAU)
League of Arab States
Organisation of American States (OAS)
Latin American Integration Association (LAIA)
Caribbean Community (CARICOM)
Anzus Treaty

CARIBBEAN
JAMAICA 62
TRINIDAD & TOBAGO 62
BARBADOS 66
BAHAMAS 73
GRENADA 74
DOMINICA
ST. VINCENT
ST. LUCIA
ANTIGUA & BARBUDA
ST. KITTS-NEVIS

BELIZE
81

GUYANA
66
SURINAME
75

MOROCCO
56
TUNISIA
56
ALGERIA
62
WESTERN SAHARA
Disputed between
Morocco and
Polisario Front
LIBYA
51
CYPRUS
60
ISRAEL
48
JORDAN
46
BAHRAIN 71
QATAR 71
U.A.E.
S.YEMEN
67
PAKISTAN
(W) 47
TIBET
Annexed by
China 1950
PAKISTAN
(E) 47
INDIA
47
BURMA
48
LAOS
54 (N)
TAIWAN
49
W. SAMOA 62
NAURU 68
FIJI 70
TONGA 70
SOLOMON IS.
TUVALU
KIRIBATI
VANUATU

CAPE
VERDE
75
MAURITANIA
60
MALI
60
NIGER
60
CHAD
60
SUDAN
56
SENEGAL 60
GAMBIA 65
GUINEA-BISSAU 74
UP. VOLTA
60
GUINEA
58
S.L.
61
I.C.
60
GH.
57
TOGO 60
DAHOMEY 60
NIGERIA
60
CAMEROON
60
C.A.R.
60
EQ GU
68
SÃO TOMÉ &
PRÍNCIPE
75
GABON
60
CONGO
(ZAIRE)
60
UGANDA
62
KENYA
63
RW.62
BUR.62
TANZANIA
61
SOMALIA
60
DJIBOUTI
VIETNAM
54
CAMBODIA
53
PHILIPPINES
46
CEYLON
48
SINGAPORE
65
BRUNEI
84
MALAYSIA
63
INDONESIA
49
Irian Jaya
To Indonesia
1963
PAPUA
NEW
GUINEA
75
E. Timor
Claimed by
Indonesia 1976

MALDIVES 65
MAURITIUS 68
COMOROS 75
SEYCHELLES 76

ANGOLA
75
ZAMBIA
64
MAL
64
MOZAMBIQUE
75
NAMIBIA
BOTSWANA
66
MADAGASCAR
60
SWAZILAND
68
LESOTHO
66

Independence
After World War II, anticolonialism became a potent political force. The great colonial powers found it increasingly difficult to hold on to their overseas territories. The end of the colonial era began when Britain granted independence to India in 1947. The French subsequently relinquished their hold on Indo-China, and the Dutch were forced out of Indonesia. National liberation movements in Africa then came to the fore. When Portugal abandoned its colonies, the colonial era was almost at an end. As the empires were dismantled, new alliances and supranational organisations appeared in their place. However, instability, factions, and civil wars have all been recurring symptoms of adolescent nationhood in developing countries.

Independence of
developing countries
by 1945
by 1955
by 1965
by 1975
after 1975
Other dependent territory
60 Year of independence

25

Designed and produced by E.S.R.

POPULATION

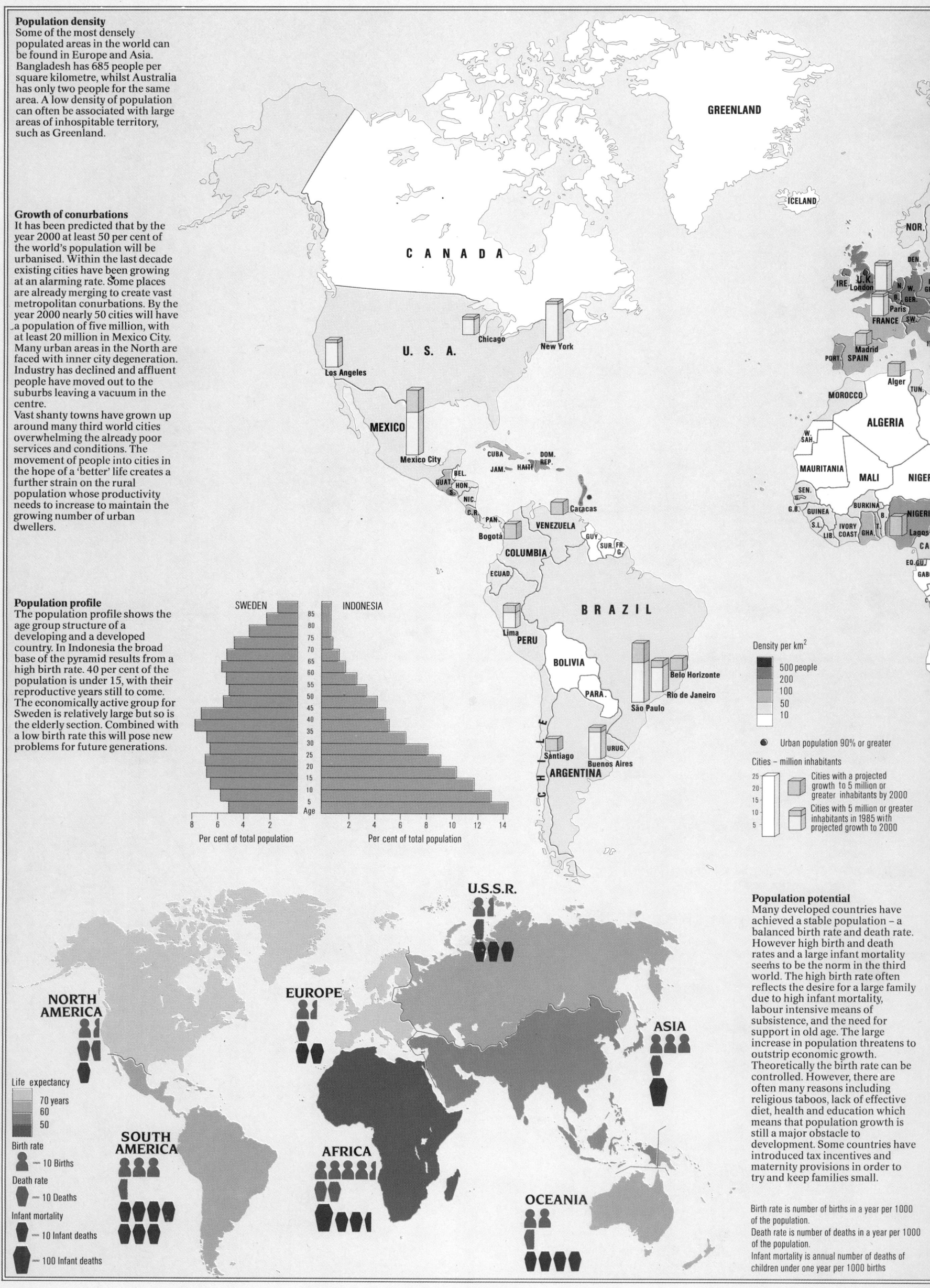

Population density

Some of the most densely populated areas in the world can be found in Europe and Asia. Bangladesh has 685 people per square kilometre, whilst Australia has only two people for the same area. A low density of population can often be associated with large areas of inhospitable territory, such as Greenland.

Growth of conurbations

It has been predicted that by the year 2000 at least 50 per cent of the world's population will be urbanised. Within the last decade existing cities have been growing at an alarming rate. Some places are already merging to create vast metropolitan conurbations. By the year 2000 nearly 50 cities will have a population of five million, with at least 20 million in Mexico City. Many urban areas in the North are faced with inner city degeneration. Industry has declined and affluent people have moved out to the suburbs leaving a vacuum in the centre.

Vast shanty towns have grown up around many third world cities overwhelming the already poor services and conditions. The movement of people into cities in the hope of a 'better' life creates a further strain on the rural population whose productivity needs to increase to maintain the growing number of urban dwellers.

Population profile

The population profile shows the age group structure of a developing and a developed country. In Indonesia the broad base of the pyramid results from a high birth rate. 40 per cent of the population is under 15, with their reproductive years still to come. The economically active group for Sweden is relatively large but so is the elderly section. Combined with a low birth rate this will pose new problems for future generations.

Population potential

Many developed countries have achieved a stable population – a balanced birth rate and death rate. However high birth and death rates and a large infant mortality seems to be the norm in the third world. The high birth rate often reflects the desire for a large family due to high infant mortality, labour intensive means of subsistence, and the need for support in old age. The large increase in population threatens to outstrip economic growth. Theoretically the birth rate can be controlled. However, there are often many reasons including religious taboos, lack of effective diet, health and education which means that population growth is still a major obstacle to development. Some countries have introduced tax incentives and maternity provisions in order to try and keep families small.

Birth rate is number of births in a year per 1000 of the population.

Death rate is number of deaths in a year per 1000 of the population.

Infant mortality is annual number of deaths of children under one year per 1000 births

Density per km²

500 people
200
100
50
10

● Urban population 90% or greater

Cities – million inhabitants

25
20
15
10
5

Cities with a projected growth to 5 million or greater inhabitants by 2000

Cities with 5 million or greater inhabitants in 1985 with projected growth to 2000

Life expectancy

70 years
60
50

Birth rate
— 10 Births

Death rate
— 10 Deaths

Infant mortality
— 10 Infant deaths
— 100 Infant deaths

26

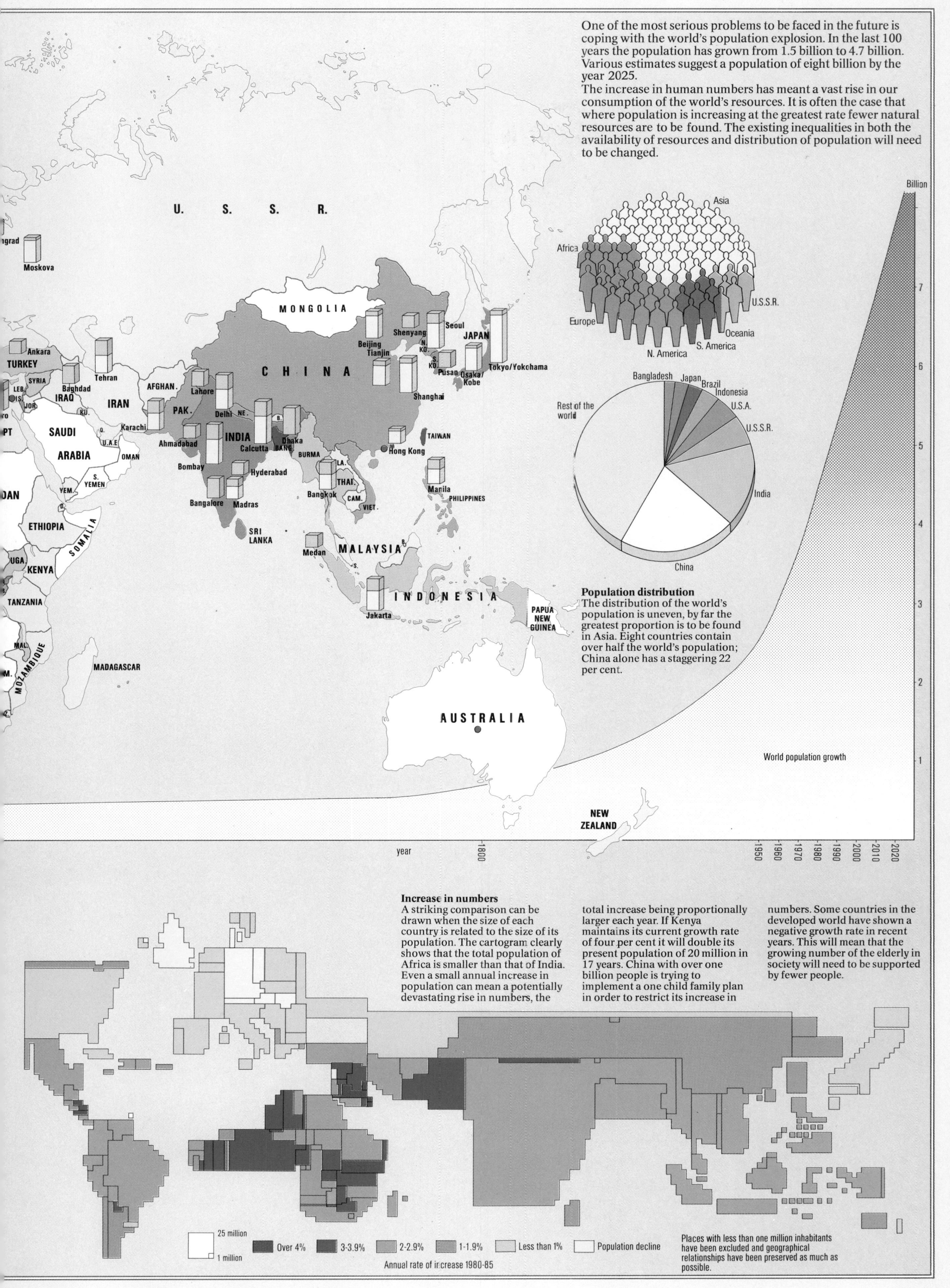

One of the most serious problems to be faced in the future is coping with the world's population explosion. In the last 100 years the population has grown from 1.5 billion to 4.7 billion. Various estimates suggest a population of eight billion by the year 2025.

The increase in human numbers has meant a vast rise in our consumption of the world's resources. It is often the case that where population is increasing at the greatest rate fewer natural resources are to be found. The existing inequalities in both the availability of resources and distribution of population will need to be changed.

Population distribution
The distribution of the world's population is uneven, by far the greatest proportion is to be found in Asia. Eight countries contain over half the world's population; China alone has a staggering 22 per cent.

World population growth

Increase in numbers
A striking comparison can be drawn when the size of each country is related to the size of its population. The cartogram clearly shows that the total population of Africa is smaller than that of India. Even a small annual increase in population can mean a potentially devastating rise in numbers, the total increase being proportionally larger each year. If Kenya maintains its current growth rate of four per cent it will double its present population of 20 million in 17 years. China with over one billion people is trying to implement a one child family plan in order to restrict its increase in numbers. Some countries in the developed world have shown a negative growth rate in recent years. This will mean that the growing number of the elderly in society will need to be supported by fewer people.

25 million
1 million

Over 4% | 3-3.9% | 2-2.9% | 1-1.9% | Less than 1% | Population decline

Annual rate of increase 1980-85

Places with less than one million inhabitants have been excluded and geographical relationships have been preserved as much as possible.

27

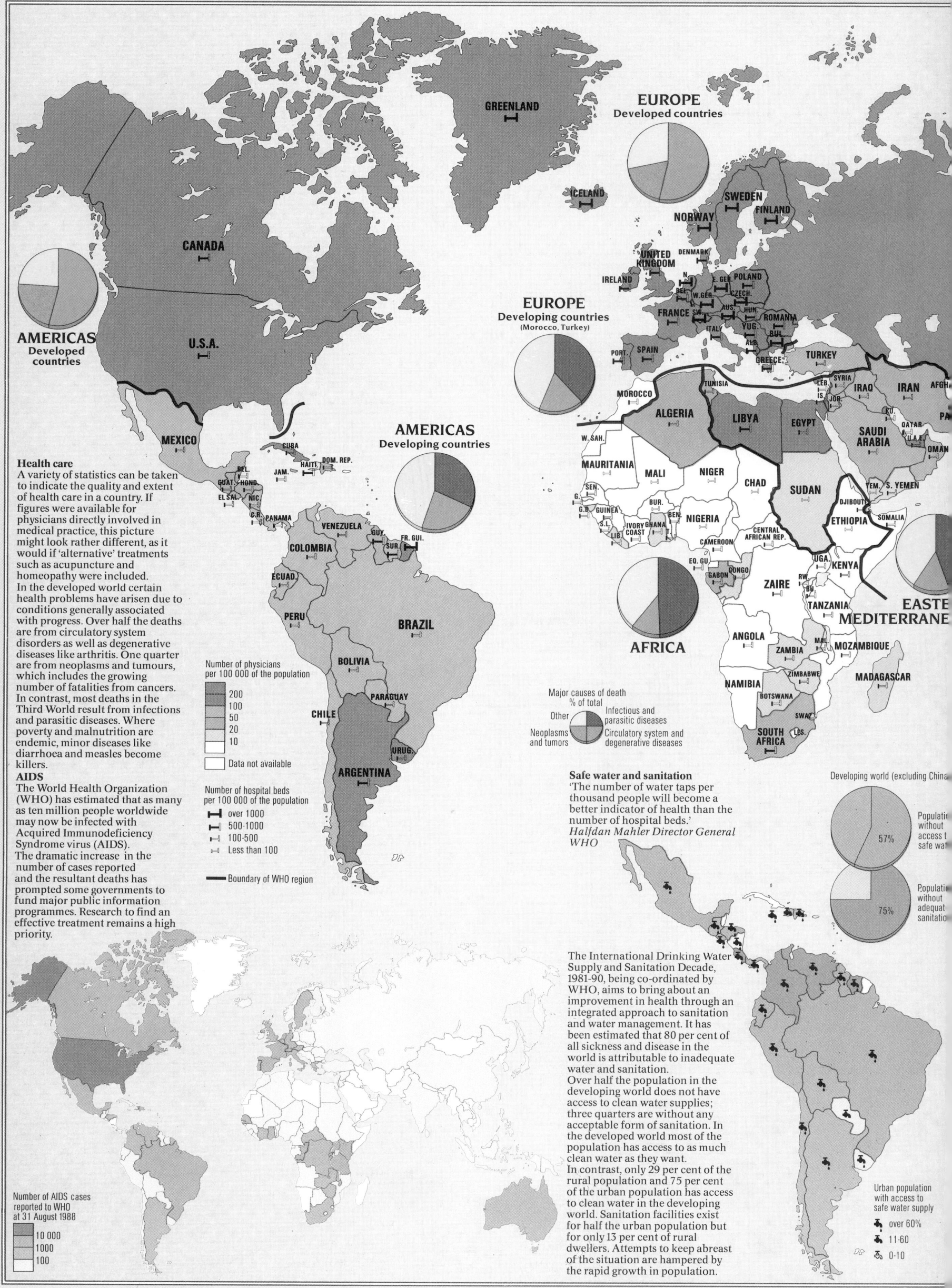

EUROPE
Developed countries

EUROPE
Developing countries
(Morocco, Turkey)

AMERICAS
Developed
countries

AMERICAS
Developing countries

AFRICA

**EASTE
MEDITERRANE**

Health care
A variety of statistics can be taken to indicate the quality and extent of health care in a country. If figures were available for physicians directly involved in medical practice, this picture might look rather different, as it would if 'alternative' treatments such as acupuncture and homeopathy were included.
In the developed world certain health problems have arisen due to conditions generally associated with progress. Over half the deaths are from circulatory system disorders as well as degenerative diseases like arthritis. One quarter are from neoplasms and tumours, which includes the growing number of fatalities from cancers. In contrast, most deaths in the Third World result from infections and parasitic diseases. Where poverty and malnutrition are endemic, minor diseases like diarrhoea and measles become killers.

AIDS
The World Health Organization (WHO) has estimated that as many as ten million people worldwide may now be infected with Acquired Immunodeficiency Syndrome virus (AIDS).
The dramatic increase in the number of cases reported and the resultant deaths has prompted some governments to fund major public information programmes. Research to find an effective treatment remains a high priority.

Number of physicians
per 100 000 of the population

- 200
- 100
- 50
- 20
- 10
- Data not available

Number of hospital beds
per 100 000 of the population
- over 1000
- 500-1000
- 100-500
- Less than 100

— Boundary of WHO region

Major causes of death
% of total

Other — Infectious and parasitic diseases

Neoplasms and tumors — Circulatory system and degenerative diseases

Safe water and sanitation
'The number of water taps per thousand people will become a better indicator of health than the number of hospital beds.'
Halfdan Mahler Director General WHO

Developing world (excluding China

Populati
without
access t
safe wa
57%

Populati
without
adequat
sanitati
75%

The International Drinking Water Supply and Sanitation Decade, 1981-90, being co-ordinated by WHO, aims to bring about an improvement in health through an integrated approach to sanitation and water management. It has been estimated that 80 per cent of all sickness and disease in the world is attributable to inadequate water and sanitation.
Over half the population in the developing world does not have access to clean water supplies; three quarters are without any acceptable form of sanitation. In the developed world most of the population has access to as much clean water as they want.
In contrast, only 29 per cent of the rural population and 75 per cent of the urban population has access to clean water in the developing world. Sanitation facilities exist for half the urban population but for only 13 per cent of rural dwellers. Attempts to keep abreast of the situation are hampered by the rapid growth in population.

Number of AIDS cases
reported to WHO
at 31 August 1988
- 10 000
- 1000
- 100

Urban population
with access to
safe water supply
- over 60%
- 11-60
- 0-10

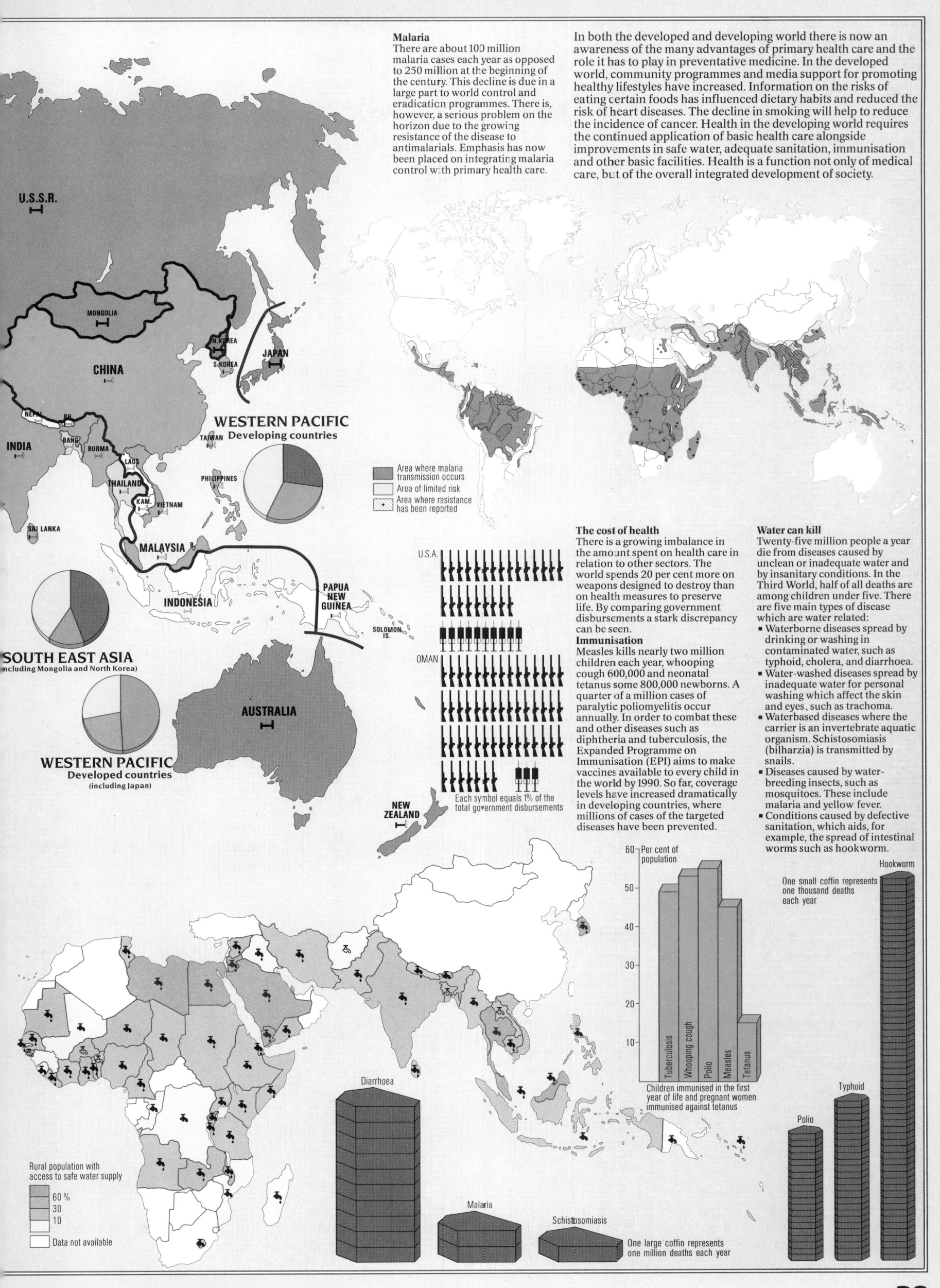

Malaria
There are about 100 million malaria cases each year as opposed to 250 million at the beginning of the century. This decline is due in a large part to world control and eradication programmes. There is, however, a serious problem on the horizon due to the growing resistance of the disease to antimalarials. Emphasis has now been placed on integrating malaria control with primary health care.

In both the developed and developing world there is now an awareness of the many advantages of primary health care and the role it has to play in preventative medicine. In the developed world, community programmes and media support for promoting healthy lifestyles have increased. Information on the risks of eating certain foods has influenced dietary habits and reduced the risk of heart diseases. The decline in smoking will help to reduce the incidence of cancer. Health in the developing world requires the continued application of basic health care alongside improvements in safe water, adequate sanitation, immunisation and other basic facilities. Health is a function not only of medical care, but of the overall integrated development of society.

U.S.S.R.

MONGOLIA

CHINA

N. KOREA

JAPAN

S. KOREA

NEPAL

BH.

INDIA

BANG.

BURMA

LAOS

THAILAND

TAIWAN

WESTERN PACIFIC
Developing countries

KAM.

VIETNAM

PHILIPPINES

SRI LANKA

MALAYSIA

Area where malaria transmission occurs
Area of limited risk
Area where resistance has been reported

SOUTH EAST ASIA
(including Mongolia and North Korea)

INDONESIA

PAPUA NEW GUINEA

SOLOMON IS.

AUSTRALIA

WESTERN PACIFIC
Developed countries
(including Japan)

U.S.A.

OMAN

Each symbol equals 1% of the total government disbursements

NEW ZEALAND

The cost of health
There is a growing imbalance in the amount spent on health care in relation to other sectors. The world spends 20 per cent more on weapons designed to destroy than on health measures to preserve life. By comparing government disbursements a stark discrepancy can be seen.

Immunisation
Measles kills nearly two million children each year, whooping cough 600,000 and neonatal tetanus some 800,000 newborns. A quarter of a million cases of paralytic poliomyelitis occur annually. In order to combat these and other diseases such as diphtheria and tuberculosis, the Expanded Programme on Immunisation (EPI) aims to make vaccines available to every child in the world by 1990. So far, coverage levels have increased dramatically in developing countries, where millions of cases of the targeted diseases have been prevented.

Water can kill
Twenty-five million people a year die from diseases caused by unclean or inadequate water and by insanitary conditions. In the Third World, half of all deaths are among children under five. There are five main types of disease which are water related:
- Waterborne diseases spread by drinking or washing in contaminated water, such as typhoid, cholera, and diarrhoea.
- Water-washed diseases spread by inadequate water for personal washing which affect the skin and eyes, such as trachoma.
- Waterbased diseases where the carrier is an invertebrate aquatic organism. Schistosomiasis (bilharzia) is transmitted by snails.
- Diseases caused by water-breeding insects, such as mosquitoes. These include malaria and yellow fever.
- Conditions caused by defective sanitation, which aids, for example, the spread of intestinal worms such as hookworm.

Per cent of population

Tuberculosis
Whooping cough
Polio
Measles
Tetanus

Children immunised in the first year of life and pregnant women immunised against tetanus

Hookworm

One small coffin represents one thousand deaths each year

Diarrhoea

Typhoid

Polio

Malaria

Schistosomiasis

One large coffin represents one million deaths each year

Rural population with access to safe water supply

60 %
30
10
Data not available

Designed and produced by E.S.R.

It has been argued that the kind of education provided by schools may be less important than 'traditional' wisdom derived from experience, especially in cultures other than those in the industrialised world. Education in the Third World has often been modelled on imported curricula which reflect the needs and conditions of a different society. Though newly independent nations introduce more suitable subjects, they may often lack the resources for relevant teaching materials.

Illiteracy

An illiterate person, one who is unable to read or write, is at a basic disadvantage in a world where literacy is an increasingly critical skill. Despite many literacy programmes, the total number of illiterates – over 800 million people, most of them in developing countries – continues to grow. These nations have only 12 per cent of the world's education budget. Most African countries spend less than ten per cent of GNP on education. There is a noticeable gap between the levels of male and female illiteracy, the latter being higher. This is often due to cultural differences and religious attitudes.

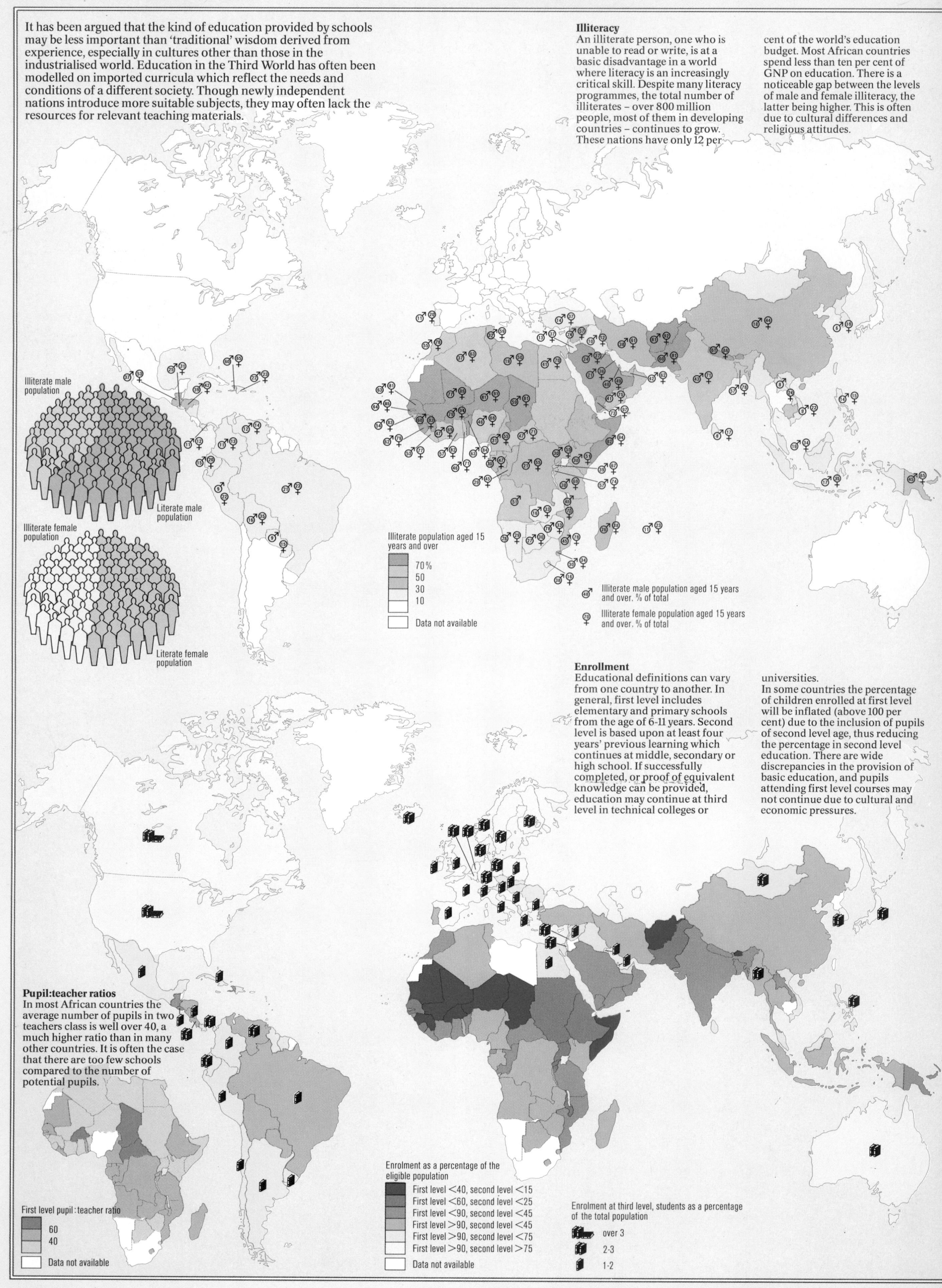

Illiterate male population

Literate male population

Illiterate female population

Literate female population

Illiterate population aged 15 years and over

70 %
50
30
10

Data not available

♂ Illiterate male population aged 15 years and over. % of total

♀ Illiterate female population aged 15 years and over. % of total

Enrollment

Educational definitions can vary from one country to another. In general, first level includes elementary and primary schools from the age of 6-11 years. Second level is based upon at least four years' previous learning which continues at middle, secondary or high school. If successfully completed, or proof of equivalent knowledge can be provided, education may continue at third level in technical colleges or universities.

In some countries the percentage of children enrolled at first level will be inflated (above 100 per cent) due to the inclusion of pupils of second level age, thus reducing the percentage in second level education. There are wide discrepancies in the provision of basic education, and pupils attending first level courses may not continue due to cultural and economic pressures.

Pupil:teacher ratios

In most African countries the average number of pupils in two teachers class is well over 40, a much higher ratio than in many other countries. It is often the case that there are too few schools compared to the number of potential pupils.

First level pupil : teacher ratio

60
40

Data not available

Enrolment as a percentage of the eligible population

First level <40, second level <15
First level <60, second level <25
First level <90, second level <45
First level >90, second level <45
First level >90, second level <75
First level >90, second level >75

Data not available

Enrolment at third level, students as a percentage of the total population

over 3
2-3
1-2

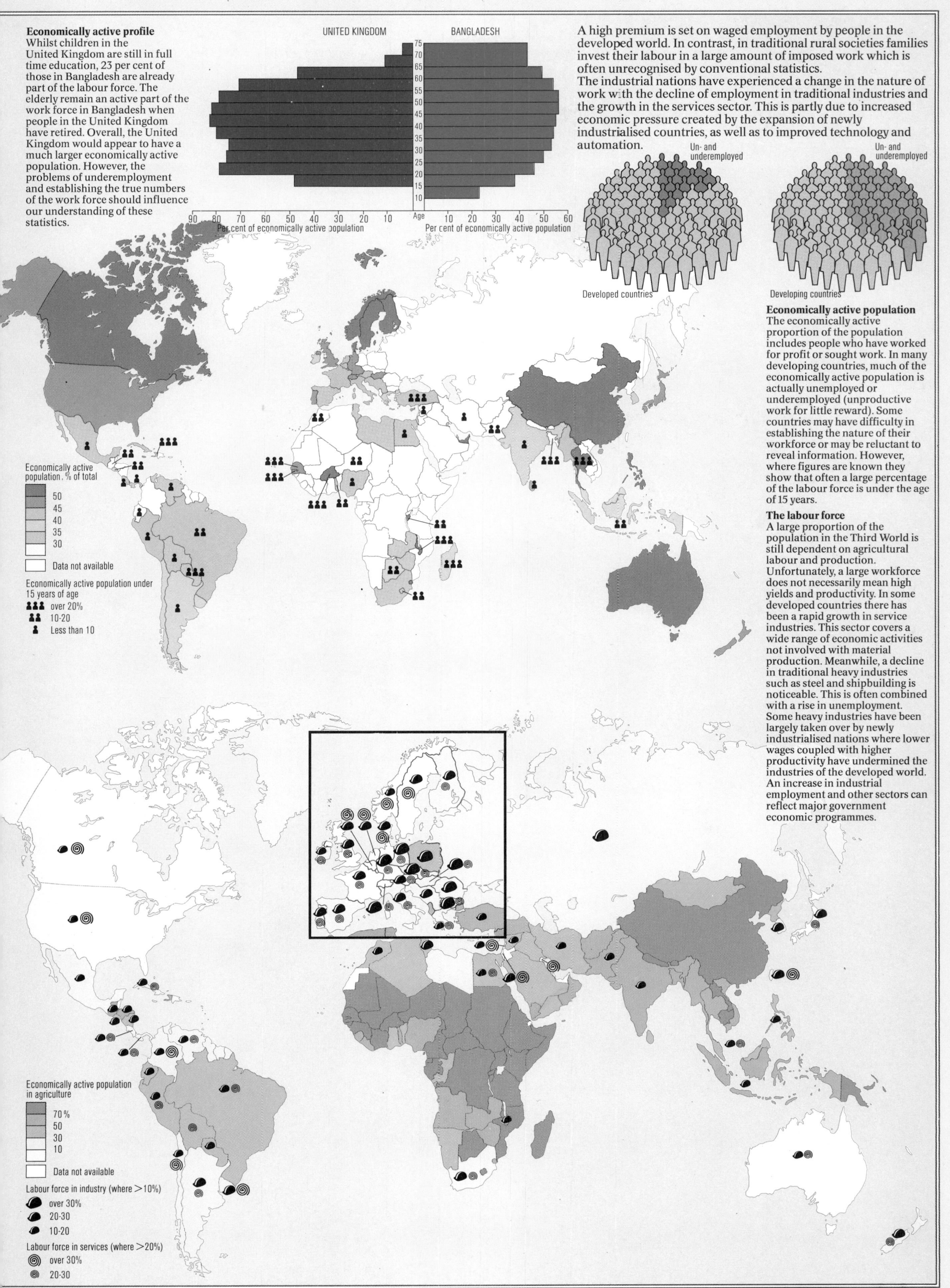

Economically active profile
Whilst children in the United Kingdom are still in full time education, 23 per cent of those in Bangladesh are already part of the labour force. The elderly remain an active part of the work force in Bangladesh when people in the United Kingdom have retired. Overall, the United Kingdom would appear to have a much larger economically active population. However, the problems of underemployment and establishing the true numbers of the work force should influence our understanding of these statistics.

UNITED KINGDOM

BANGLADESH

Age

Per cent of economically active population

Per cent of economically active population

A high premium is set on waged employment by people in the developed world. In contrast, in traditional rural societies families invest their labour in a large amount of imposed work which is often unrecognised by conventional statistics.
The industrial nations have experienced a change in the nature of work with the decline of employment in traditional industries and the growth in the services sector. This is partly due to increased economic pressure created by the expansion of newly industrialised countries, as well as to improved technology and automation.

Un- and underemployed

Un- and underemployed

Developed countries

Developing countries

Economically active population
The economically active proportion of the population includes people who have worked for profit or sought work. In many developing countries, much of the economically active population is actually unemployed or underemployed (unproductive work for little reward). Some countries may have difficulty in establishing the nature of their workforce or may be reluctant to reveal information. However, where figures are known they show that often a large percentage of the labour force is under the age of 15 years.

The labour force
A large proportion of the population in the Third World is still dependent on agricultural labour and production. Unfortunately, a large workforce does not necessarily mean high yields and productivity. In some developed countries there has been a rapid growth in service industries. This sector covers a wide range of economic activities not involved with material production. Meanwhile, a decline in traditional heavy industries such as steel and shipbuilding is noticeable. This is often combined with a rise in unemployment. Some heavy industries have been largely taken over by newly industrialised nations where lower wages coupled with higher productivity have undermined the industries of the developed world. An increase in industrial employment and other sectors can reflect major government economic programmes.

Economically active population, % of total
50
45
40
35
30
Data not available

Economically active population under 15 years of age
over 20%
10-20
Less than 10

Economically active population in agriculture
70%
50
30
10
Data not available

Labour force in industry (where >10%)
over 30%
20-30
10-20

Labour force in services (where >20%)
over 30%
20-30

Designed and produced by E.S.R.

LAND USE

Over the millenia the earth's landscape has changed significantly, due in no small part to man. The population explosion has put vegetation at risk as the need for agricultural land has increased. In order to meet the demand, forests have been cleared and degraded and marginal lands exhausted. Once fertile soils are rapidly becoming mineral-stressed. The requirement for forest products has risen, leading to even greater demolition of our woodlands. Man's expansion and construction has put all land uses under pressure.

The advancing desert
Over one quarter of land is now affected by rapidly encroaching deserts. 'Desertization' refers to instances in which the process is natural. Desertification usually occurs in arid and semi-arid areas and involves additional human factors. Expanding populations move onto marginal lands, where deforestation, over-cultivation and over-grazing occur, often accompanied by drought. This reduces the productivity of the land, which quickly degrades under stress.

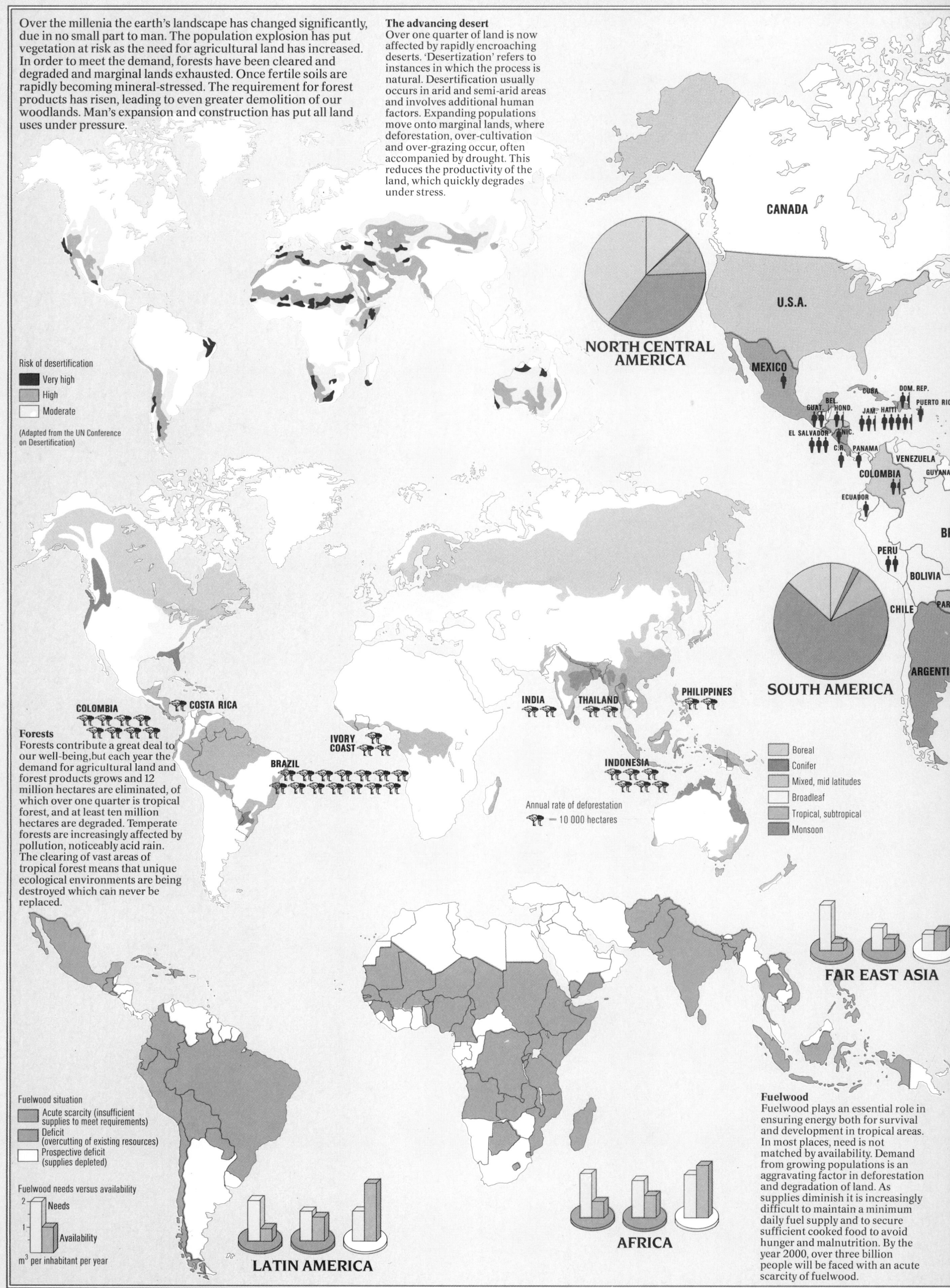

Risk of desertification
- Very high
- High
- Moderate

(Adapted from the UN Conference on Desertification)

CANADA

U.S.A.

NORTH CENTRAL AMERICA

MEXICO

CUBA · DOM. REP.
GUAT. · BEL · HOND. · JAM. · HAITI · PUERTO RICO
EL SALVADOR · NIC.
C.R. · PANAMA
VENEZUELA · GUYANA
COLOMBIA
ECUADOR
BR.
PERU
BOLIVIA
CHILE · PARA
ARGENTIN

SOUTH AMERICA

Forests
Forests contribute a great deal to our well-being, but each year the demand for agricultural land and forest products grows and 12 million hectares are eliminated, of which over one quarter is tropical forest, and at least ten million hectares are degraded. Temperate forests are increasingly affected by pollution, noticeably acid rain. The clearing of vast areas of tropical forest means that unique ecological environments are being destroyed which can never be replaced.

COLOMBIA   COSTA RICA
INDIA   THAILAND   PHILIPPINES
IVORY COAST
BRAZIL
INDONESIA

Annual rate of deforestation
= 10 000 hectares

- Boreal
- Conifer
- Mixed, mid latitudes
- Broadleaf
- Tropical, subtropical
- Monsoon

FAR EAST ASIA

Fuelwood situation
- Acute scarcity (insufficient supplies to meet requirements)
- Deficit (overcutting of existing resources)
- Prospective deficit (supplies depleted)

Fuelwood needs versus availability
2 — Needs
1 — Availability
m³ per inhabitant per year

LATIN AMERICA

AFRICA

Fuelwood
Fuelwood plays an essential role in ensuring energy both for survival and development in tropical areas. In most places, need is not matched by availability. Demand from growing populations is an aggravating factor in deforestation and degradation of land. As supplies diminish it is increasingly difficult to maintain a minimum daily fuel supply and to secure sufficient cooked food to avoid hunger and malnutrition. By the year 2000, over three billion people will be faced with an acute scarcity of fuelwood.

32

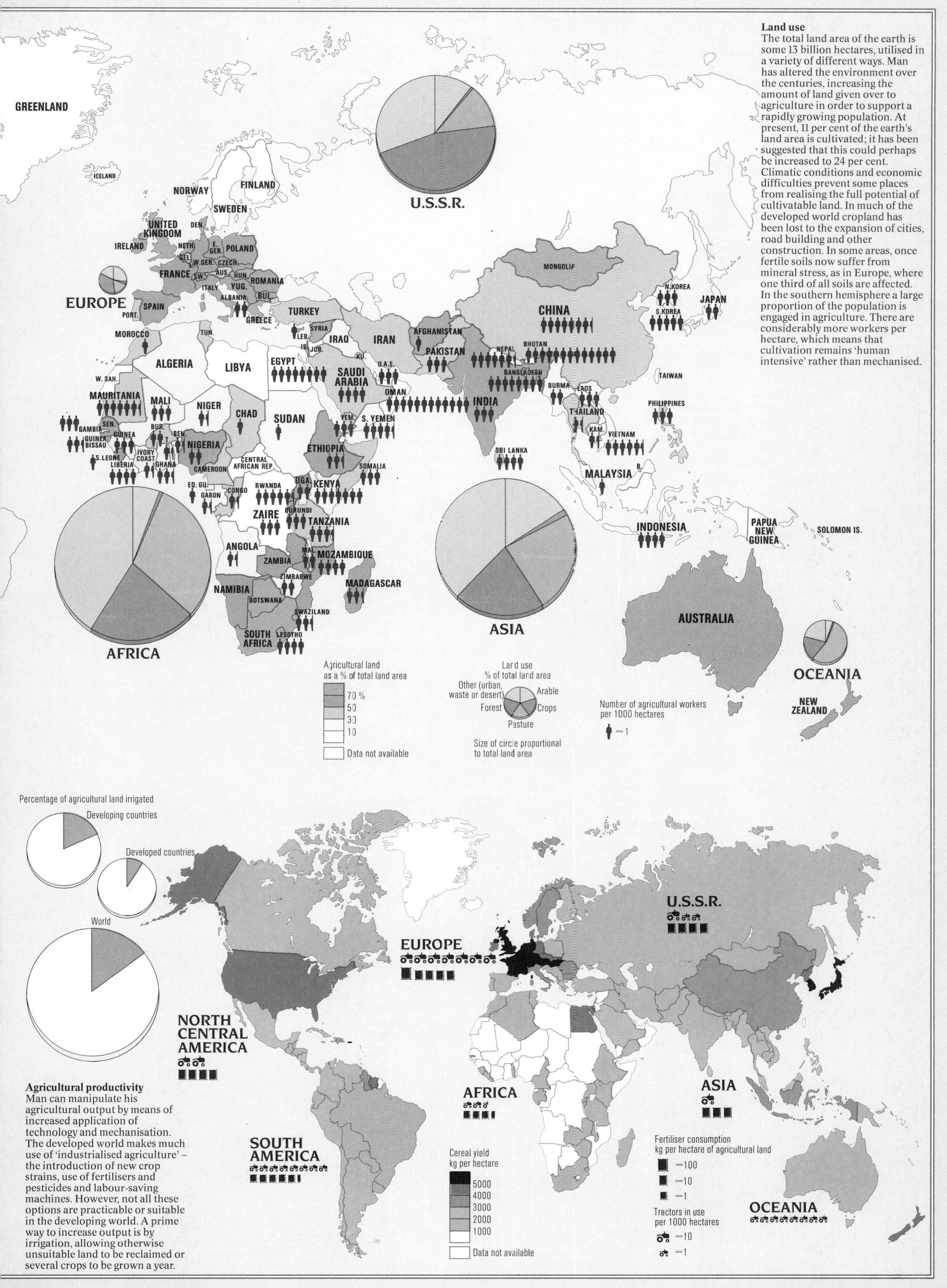

Land use
The total land area of the earth is some 13 billion hectares, utilised in a variety of different ways. Man has altered the environment over the centuries, increasing the amount of land given over to agriculture in order to support a rapidly growing population. At present, 11 per cent of the earth's land area is cultivated; it has been suggested that this could perhaps be increased to 24 per cent. Climatic conditions and economic difficulties prevent some places from realising the full potential of cultivatable land. In much of the developed world cropland has been lost to the expansion of cities, road building and other construction. In some areas, once fertile soils now suffer from mineral stress, as in Europe, where one third of all soils are affected. In the southern hemisphere a large proportion of the population is engaged in agriculture. There are considerably more workers per hectare, which means that cultivation remains 'human intensive' rather than mechanised.

Agricultural land
as a % of total land area

70 %
50
30
10

Data not available

Land use
% of total land area

Other (urban,
waste or desert)   Arable

Forest   Crops

Pasture

Size of circle proportional
to total land area

Number of agricultural workers
per 1000 hectares

= 1

Percentage of agricultural land irrigated
Developing countries

Developed countries

World

Agricultural productivity
Man can manipulate his agricultural output by means of increased application of technology and mechanisation. The developed world makes much use of 'industrialised agriculture' – the introduction of new crop strains, use of fertilisers and pesticides and labour-saving machines. However, not all these options are practicable or suitable in the developing world. A prime way to increase output is by irrigation, allowing otherwise unsuitable land to be reclaimed or several crops to be grown a year.

Cereal yield
kg per hectare

5000
4000
3000
2000
1000

Data not available

Fertiliser consumption
kg per hectare of agricultural land

= 100
= 10
= 1

Tractors in use
per 1000 hectares

= 10
= 1

Designed and produced by E.S.R.

FOOD

Enough food is produced globally to feed all of the population. Millions starve each year, millions suffer from malnutrition and are thus susceptible to disease and death. Somewhere the equation does not balance; resources are not necessarily matched to the areas of greatest demand.

Technological advances to increase output have created a new set of problems, including surpluses, mineral stressed soils, and vast erosion of topsoil. Emphasis on cash crops needs to be reversed in order for many countries to move towards self sufficiency. Combining this change with an increase in research to develop locally adapted strains and cultivation techniques relevant to local surroundings would help feed the hungry.

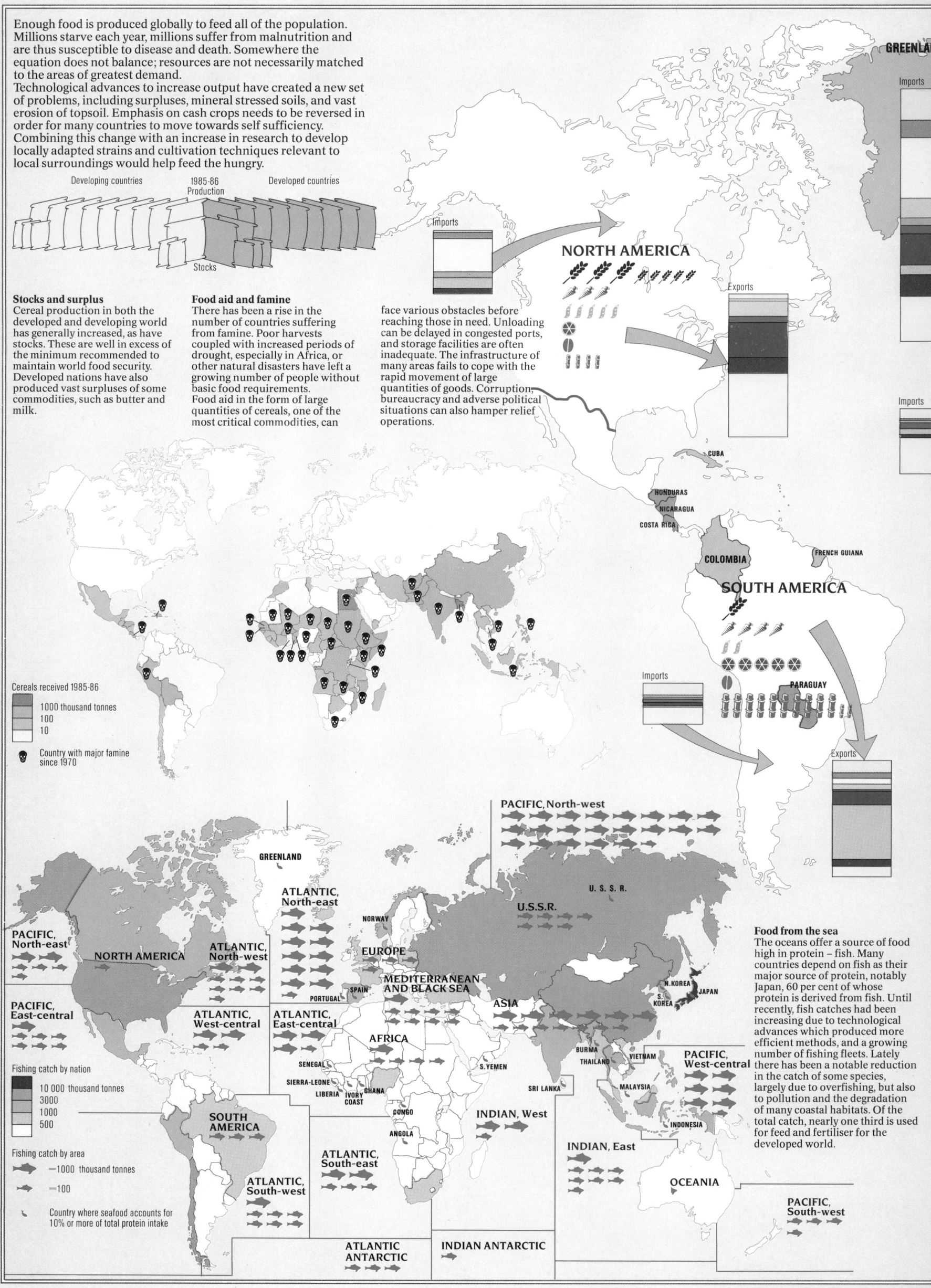

Stocks and surplus
Cereal production in both the developed and developing world has generally increased, as have stocks. These are well in excess of the minimum recommended to maintain world food security. Developed nations have also produced vast surpluses of some commodities, such as butter and milk.

Food aid and famine
There has been a rise in the number of countries suffering from famine. Poor harvests coupled with increased periods of drought, especially in Africa, or other natural disasters have left a growing number of people without basic food requirements.

Food aid in the form of large quantities of cereals, one of the most critical commodities, can face various obstacles before reaching those in need. Unloading can be delayed in congested ports, and storage facilities are often inadequate. The infrastructure of many areas fails to cope with the rapid movement of large quantities of goods. Corruption, bureaucracy and adverse political situations can also hamper relief operations.

Cereals received 1985-86
- 1000 thousand tonnes
- 100
- 10

☠ Country with major famine since 1970

Food from the sea
The oceans offer a source of food high in protein – fish. Many countries depend on fish as their major source of protein, notably Japan, 60 per cent of whose protein is derived from fish. Until recently, fish catches had been increasing due to technological advances which produced more efficient methods, and a growing number of fishing fleets. Lately there has been a notable reduction in the catch of some species, largely due to overfishing, but also to pollution and the degradation of many coastal habitats. Of the total catch, nearly one third is used for feed and fertiliser for the developed world.

Fishing catch by nation
- 10 000 thousand tonnes
- 3000
- 1000
- 500

Fishing catch by area
- —1000 thousand tonnes
- —100
- Country where seafood accounts for 10% or more of total protein intake

34

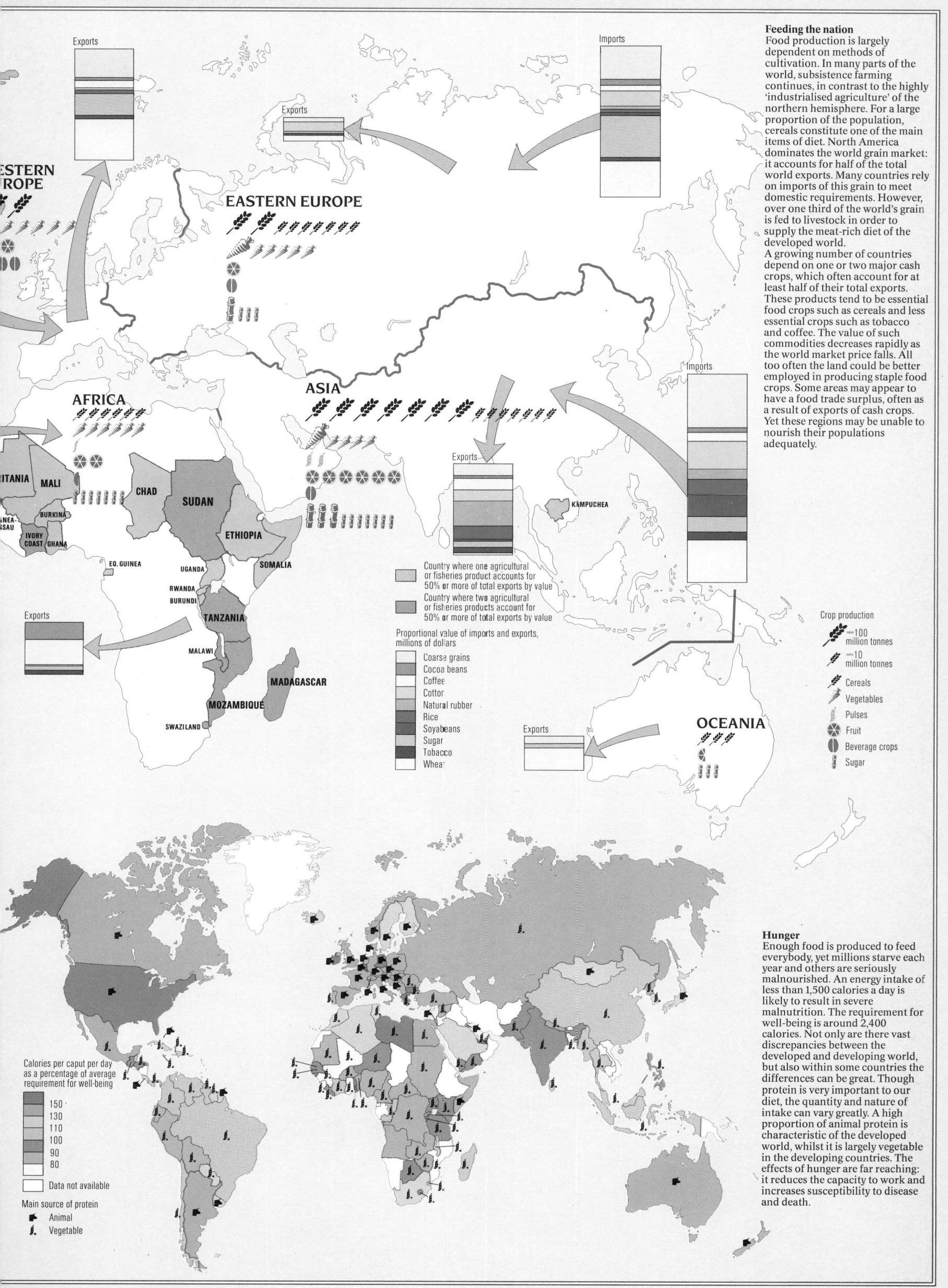

Exports

Imports

EASTERN
ROPE

EASTERN EUROPE

Exports

Imports

AFRICA

ASIA

KAMPUCHEA

ITANIA

MALI

CHAD

SUDAN

BURKINA

ETHIOPIA

NEA-
SSAU

IVORY
COAST GHANA

EQ. GUINEA

UGANDA

SOMALIA

RWANDA

BURUNDI

Exports

TANZANIA

Exports

MALAWI

MADAGASCAR

MOZAMBIQUE

OCEANIA

SWAZILAND

Exports

Country where one agricultural
or fisheries product accounts for
50% or more of total exports by value

Country where two agricultural
or fisheries products account for
50% or more of total exports by value

Proportional value of imports and exports,
millions of dollars

Coarse grains
Cocoa beans
Coffee
Cotton
Natural rubber
Rice
Soyabeans
Sugar
Tobacco
Wheat

Crop production

—100
million tonnes

—10
million tonnes

Cereals

Vegetables

Pulses

Fruit

Beverage crops

Sugar

Feeding the nation
Food production is largely
dependent on methods of
cultivation. In many parts of the
world, subsistence farming
continues, in contrast to the highly
'industrialised agriculture' of the
northern hemisphere. For a large
proportion of the population,
cereals constitute one of the main
items of diet. North America
dominates the world grain market:
it accounts for half of the total
world exports. Many countries rely
on imports of this grain to meet
domestic requirements. However,
over one third of the world's grain
is fed to livestock in order to
supply the meat-rich diet of the
developed world.
A growing number of countries
depend on one or two major cash
crops, which often account for at
least half of their total exports.
These products tend to be essential
food crops such as cereals and less
essential crops such as tobacco
and coffee. The value of such
commodities decreases rapidly as
the world market price falls. All
too often the land could be better
employed in producing staple food
crops. Some areas may appear to
have a food trade surplus, often as
a result of exports of cash crops.
Yet these regions may be unable to
nourish their populations
adequately.

Calories per caput per day
as a percentage of average
requirement for well-being

150
130
110
100
90
80

Data not available

Main source of protein

Animal

Vegetable

Hunger
Enough food is produced to feed
everybody, yet millions starve each
year and others are seriously
malnourished. An energy intake of
less than 1,500 calories a day is
likely to result in severe
malnutrition. The requirement for
well-being is around 2,400
calories. Not only are there vast
discrepancies between the
developed and developing world,
but also within some countries the
differences can be great. Though
protein is very important to our
diet, the quantity and nature of
intake can vary greatly. A high
proportion of animal protein is
characteristic of the developed
world, whilst it is largely vegetable
in the developing countries. The
effects of hunger are far reaching:
it reduces the capacity to work and
increases susceptibility to disease
and death.

35

ENERGY AND MINERALS

Energy from fossil fuels is limited by geology, and supplies are being exhausted. Even if new discoveries are made and extraction is viable there is still a limit to how long these will last. There is a growing awareness of the environmental damage caused by the increased use of coal. The many problems of nuclear power have made it a high risk option, and not the energy panacea envisaged by many. As a result, interest in renewable sources of energy has grown: wind, geothermal, power from the sea, hydro and solar are all possible alternatives for the production of energy.

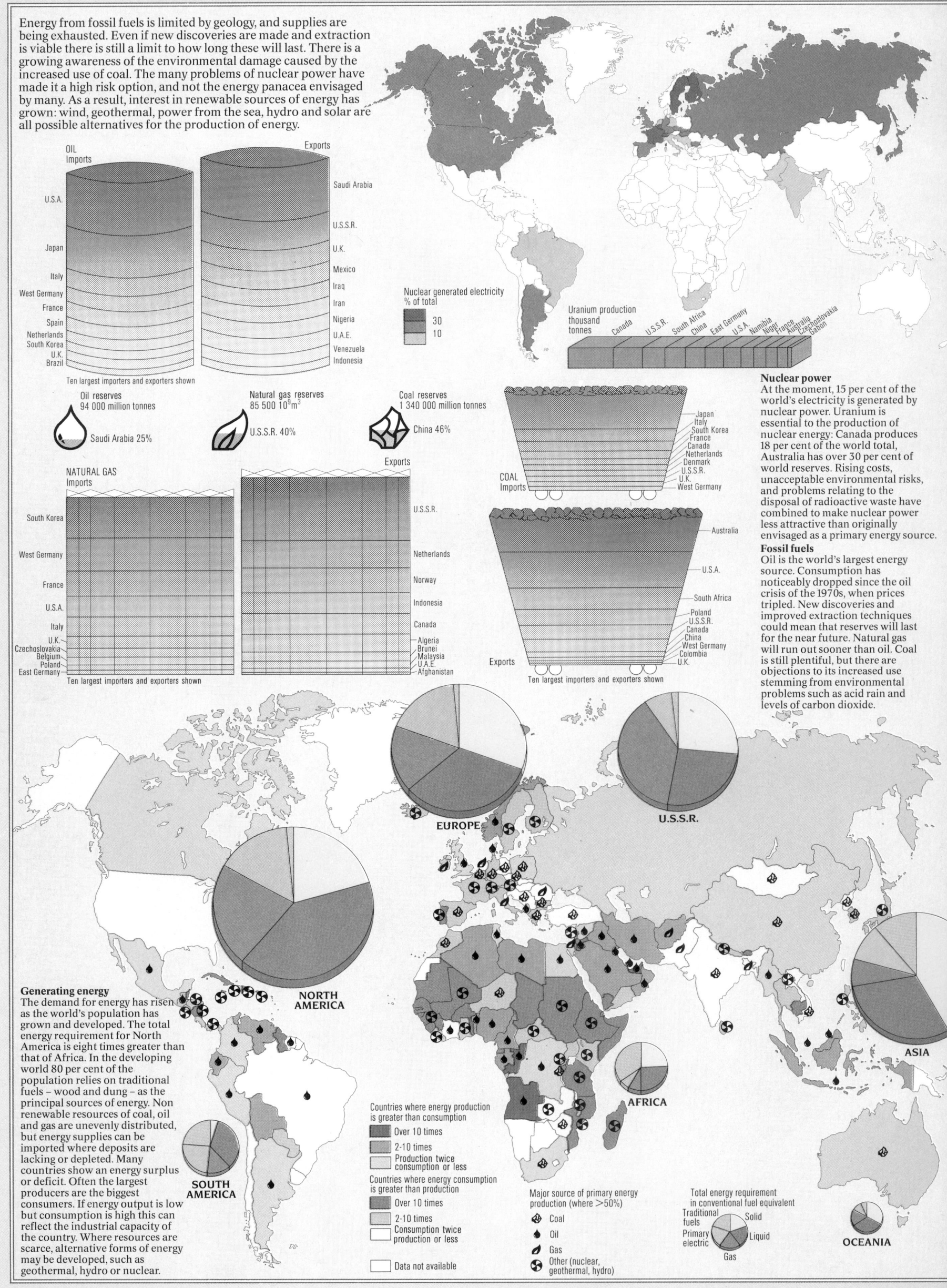

OIL
Imports

U.S.A.
Japan
Italy
West Germany
France
Spain
Netherlands
South Korea
U.K.
Brazil

Exports

Saudi Arabia
U.S.S.R.
U.K.
Mexico
Iraq
Iran
Nigeria
U.A.E.
Venezuela
Indonesia

Ten largest importers and exporters shown

Oil reserves
94 000 million tonnes
Saudi Arabia 25%

Natural gas reserves
85 500 10⁹m³
U.S.S.R. 40%

Coal reserves
1 340 000 million tonnes
China 46%

NATURAL GAS
Imports

South Korea
West Germany
France
U.S.A.
Italy
U.K.
Czechoslovakia
Belgium
Poland
East Germany

Exports

U.S.S.R.
Netherlands
Norway
Indonesia
Canada
Algeria
Brunei
Malaysia
U.A.E.
Afghanistan

Ten largest importers and exporters shown

Nuclear generated electricity
% of total
30
10

Uranium production
thousand tonnes

Canada, U.S.S.R., South Africa, China, East Germany, U.S.A., Namibia, Niger, France, Australia, Czechoslovakia, Gabon

COAL
Imports

Japan
Italy
South Korea
France
Canada
Netherlands
Denmark
U.S.S.R.
U.K.
West Germany

Exports

Australia
U.S.A.
South Africa
Poland
U.S.S.R.
Canada
China
West Germany
Colombia
U.K.

Ten largest importers and exporters shown

Nuclear power
At the moment, 15 per cent of the world's electricity is generated by nuclear power. Uranium is essential to the production of nuclear energy: Canada produces 18 per cent of the world total, Australia has over 30 per cent of world reserves. Rising costs, unacceptable environmental risks, and problems relating to the disposal of radioactive waste have combined to make nuclear power less attractive than originally envisaged as a primary energy source.

Fossil fuels
Oil is the world's largest energy source. Consumption has noticeably dropped since the oil crisis of the 1970s, when prices tripled. New discoveries and improved extraction techniques could mean that reserves will last for the near future. Natural gas will run out sooner than oil. Coal is still plentiful, but there are objections to its increased use stemming from environmental problems such as acid rain and levels of carbon dioxide.

EUROPE
U.S.S.R.
NORTH AMERICA
AFRICA
ASIA
SOUTH AMERICA
OCEANIA

Generating energy
The demand for energy has risen as the world's population has grown and developed. The total energy requirement for North America is eight times greater than that of Africa. In the developing world 80 per cent of the population relies on traditional fuels – wood and dung – as the principal sources of energy. Non renewable resources of coal, oil and gas are unevenly distributed, but energy supplies can be imported where deposits are lacking or depleted. Many countries show an energy surplus or deficit. Often the largest producers are the biggest consumers. If energy output is low but consumption is high this can reflect the industrial capacity of the country. Where resources are scarce, alternative forms of energy may be developed, such as geothermal, hydro or nuclear.

Countries where energy production is greater than consumption
Over 10 times
2-10 times
Production twice consumption or less

Countries where energy consumption is greater than production
Over 10 times
2-10 times
Consumption twice production or less

Data not available

Major source of primary energy production (where >50%)
Coal
Oil
Gas
Other (nuclear, geothermal, hydro)

Total energy requirement in conventional fuel equivalent
Traditional fuels
Primary electric
Gas
Solid
Liquid

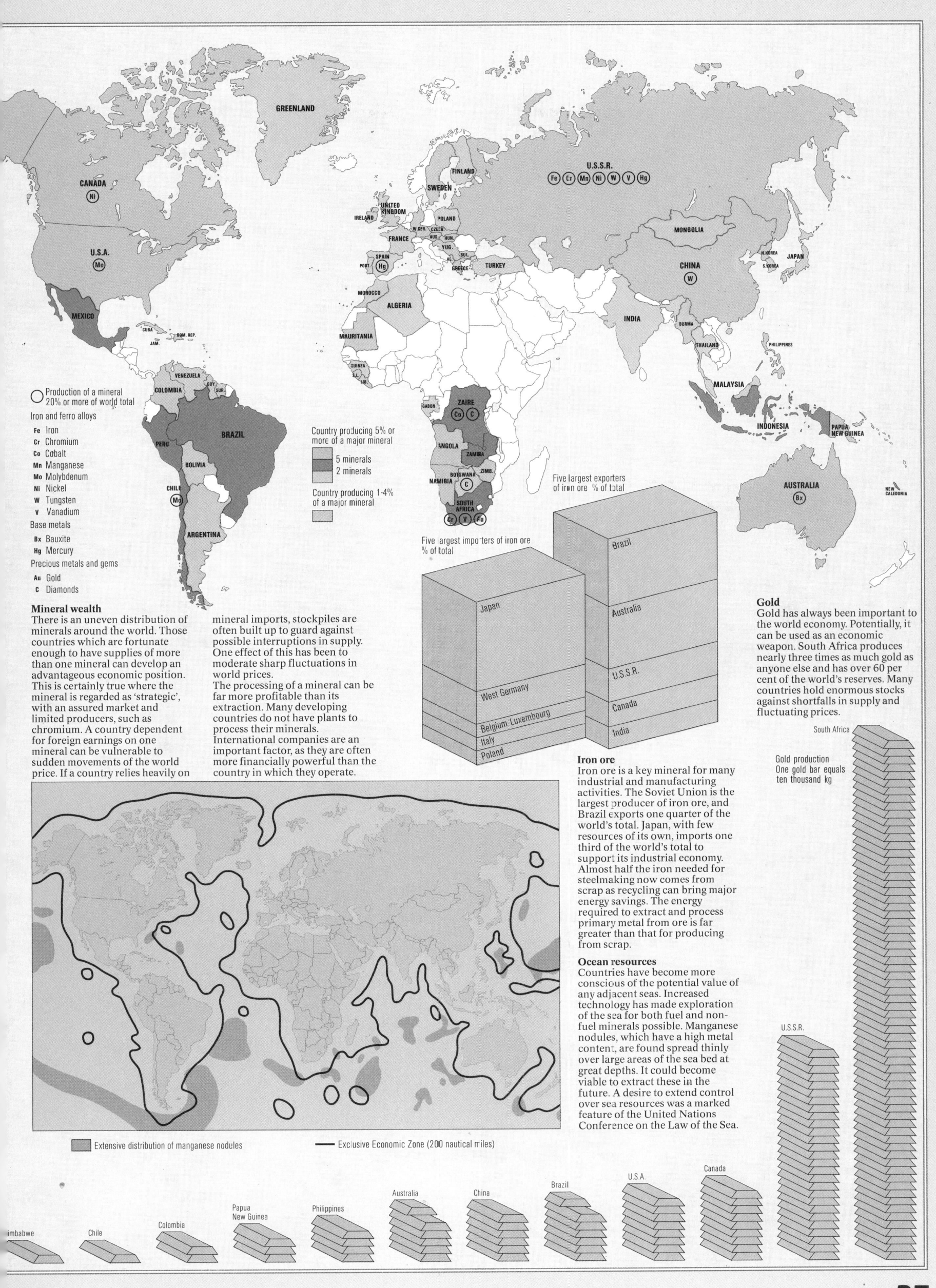

Mineral wealth

There is an uneven distribution of minerals around the world. Those countries which are fortunate enough to have supplies of more than one mineral can develop an advantageous economic position. This is certainly true where the mineral is regarded as 'strategic', with an assured market and limited producers, such as chromium. A country dependent for foreign earnings on one mineral can be vulnerable to sudden movements of the world price. If a country relies heavily on mineral imports, stockpiles are often built up to guard against possible interruptions in supply. One effect of this has been to moderate sharp fluctuations in world prices.

The processing of a mineral can be far more profitable than its extraction. Many developing countries do not have plants to process their minerals. International companies are an important factor, as they are often more financially powerful than the country in which they operate.

Legend

Production of a mineral 20% or more of world total

Iron and ferro alloys

Fe Iron
Cr Chromium
Co Cobalt
Mn Manganese
Mo Molybdenum
Ni Nickel
W   Tungsten
v   Vanadium

Base metals

Bx Bauxite
Hg Mercury

Precious metals and gems

Au Gold
C   Diamonds

Country producing 5% or more of a major mineral
- 5 minerals
- 2 minerals

Country producing 1-4% of a major mineral

Five largest exporters of iron ore % of total

Five largest importers of iron ore % of total

Iron ore

Iron ore is a key mineral for many industrial and manufacturing activities. The Soviet Union is the largest producer of iron ore, and Brazil exports one quarter of the world's total. Japan, with few resources of its own, imports one third of the world's total to support its industrial economy. Almost half the iron needed for steelmaking now comes from scrap as recycling can bring major energy savings. The energy required to extract and process primary metal from ore is far greater than that for producing from scrap.

Ocean resources

Countries have become more conscious of the potential value of any adjacent seas. Increased technology has made exploration of the sea for both fuel and non-fuel minerals possible. Manganese nodules, which have a high metal content, are found spread thinly over large areas of the sea bed at great depths. It could become viable to extract these in the future. A desire to extend control over sea resources was a marked feature of the United Nations Conference on the Law of the Sea.

Gold

Gold has always been important to the world economy. Potentially, it can be used as an economic weapon. South Africa produces nearly three times as much gold as anyone else and has over 60 per cent of the world's reserves. Many countries hold enormous stocks against shortfalls in supply and fluctuating prices.

Gold production
One gold bar equals ten thousand kg

Extensive distribution of manganese nodules

Exclusive Economic Zone (200 nautical miles)

Designed and produced by E.S.R.

TRADE

As trade has expanded, the production of goods has become increasingly specialised – components and raw materials from one country are shipped overseas for assembly or processing, then returned to their country of origin, or re-exported elsewhere. The dominance of established industrial countries is under threat from rapidly expanding industrial nations. Multinational corporations also play a large part in trade flows: they are mainly based in the developed world, which has a commanding influence on markets. Many developing countries, in order to achieve economic growth, face the dilemma between gearing production to satisfy overseas demands, while importing goods needed at home, or orientating production to domestic needs and increasing infrastructure at home. If trade is to prosper, the mutual interdependence of the developed and developing world both in demand and supply of goods needs to be recognised.

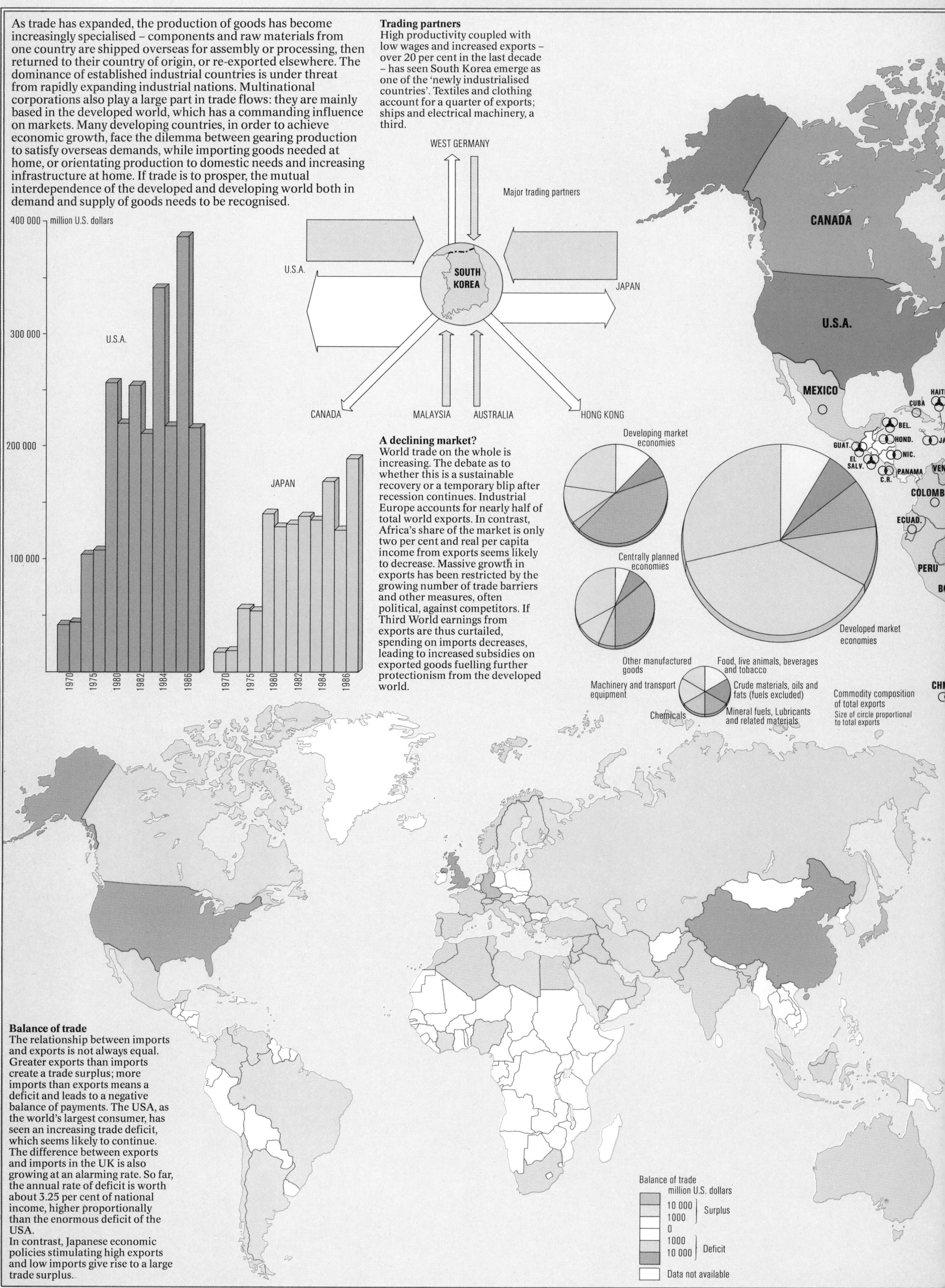

Trading partners
High productivity coupled with low wages and increased exports – over 20 per cent in the last decade – has seen South Korea emerge as one of the 'newly industrialised countries'. Textiles and clothing account for a quarter of exports; ships and electrical machinery, a third.

WEST GERMANY

Major trading partners

U.S.A.

SOUTH KOREA

JAPAN

CANADA   MALAYSIA   AUSTRALIA   HONG KONG

400 000 — million U.S. dollars

300 000

U.S.A.

200 000

JAPAN

100 000

1970 1975 1980 1982 1984 1986   1970 1975 1980 1982 1984 1986

A declining market?
World trade on the whole is increasing. The debate as to whether this is a sustainable recovery or a temporary blip after recession continues. Industrial Europe accounts for nearly half of total world exports. In contrast, Africa's share of the market is only two per cent and real per capita income from exports seems likely to decrease. Massive growth in exports has been restricted by the growing number of trade barriers and other measures, often political, against competitors. If Third World earnings from exports are thus curtailed, spending on imports decreases, leading to increased subsidies on exported goods fuelling further protectionism from the developed world.

Developing market economies

Centrally planned economies

Developed market economies

Other manufactured goods

Machinery and transport equipment

Chemicals

Food, live animals, beverages and tobacco

Crude materials, oils and fats (fuels excluded)

Mineral fuels, Lubricants and related materials

Commodity composition of total exports
Size of circle proportional to total exports

CANADA

U.S.A.

MEXICO

HAIT   CUBA   BEL.   HOND.   NIC.   JA
GUAT.   EL SALV.   PANAMA   VEN
C.R.   COLOMB

ECUAD.

PERU   B

CH

Balance of trade
The relationship between imports and exports is not always equal. Greater exports than imports create a trade surplus; more imports than exports means a deficit and leads to a negative balance of payments. The USA, as the world's largest consumer, has seen an increasing trade deficit, which seems likely to continue. The difference between exports and imports in the UK is also growing at an alarming rate. So far, the annual rate of deficit is worth about 3.25 per cent of national income, higher proportionally than the enormous deficit of the USA.
In contrast, Japanese economic policies stimulating high exports and low imports give rise to a large trade surplus.

Balance of trade
million U.S. dollars

10 000   Surplus
1000
0
1000   Deficit
10 000

Data not available

38

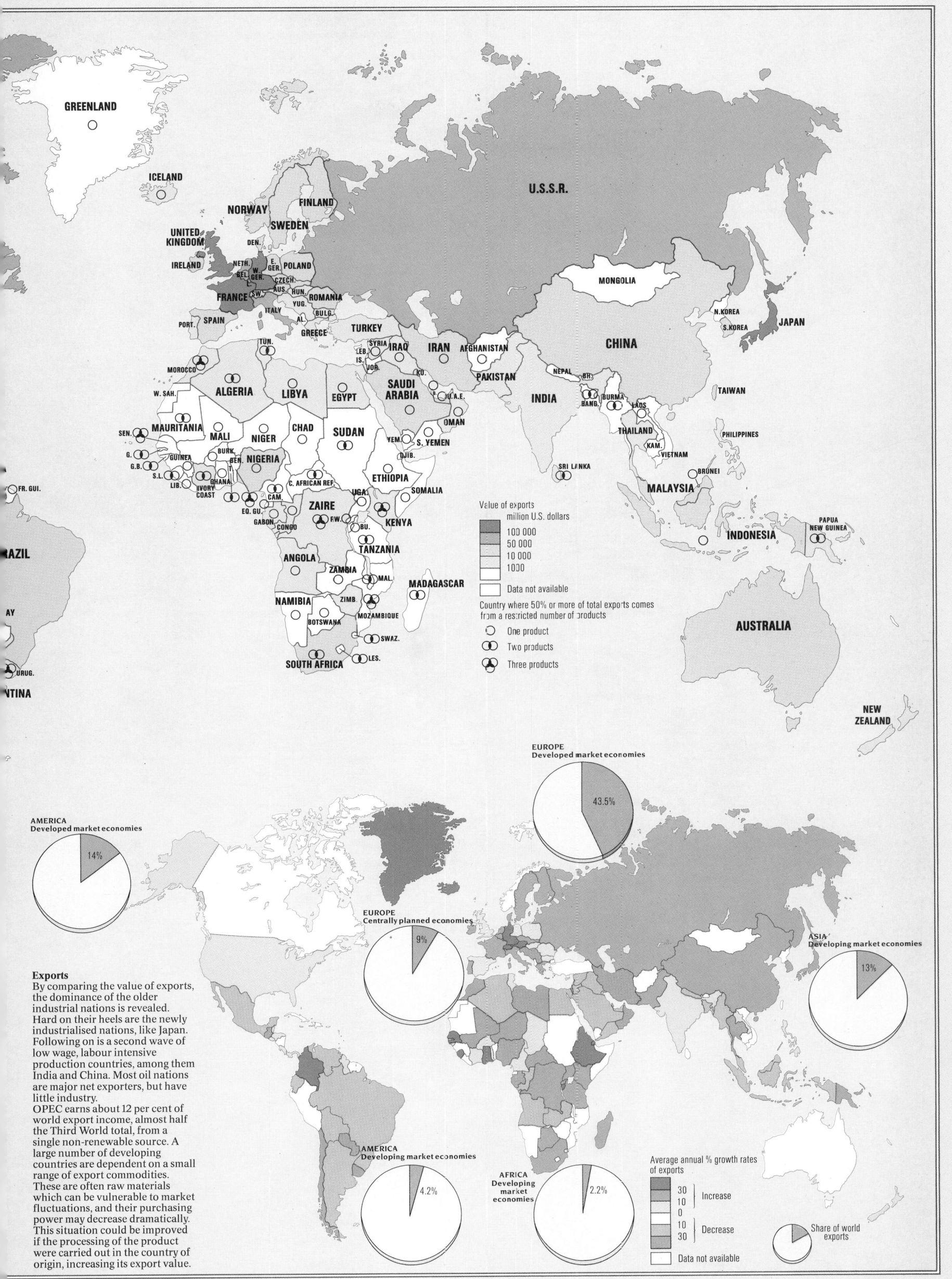

GREENLAND

ICELAND

NORWAY
SWEDEN
FINLAND

UNITED
KINGDOM
IRELAND
DEN.
NETH.
BEL.
W. GER.
E. GER.
POLAND
AUS.
CZECH.
HUN.
ROMANIA
YUG.
BULG.
FRANCE
SW.
ITALY
AL.
SPAIN
PORT.
GREECE
TURKEY

U.S.S.R.

MONGOLIA

N.KOREA
S.KOREA
JAPAN

TUN.
MOROCCO
W. SAH.
ALGERIA
LIBYA
EGYPT
SYRIA
LEB.
IS.
JOR.
IRAQ
KU.
IRAN
AFGHANISTAN
PAKISTAN
NEPAL
BH.
CHINA
TAIWAN

SEN.
MAURITANIA
MALI
NIGER
CHAD
SUDAN
SAUDI
ARABIA
U.A.E.
OMAN
YEM.
S. YEMEN
DJIB.
INDIA
BANG.
BURMA
LAOS
THAILAND
KAM.
VIETNAM
PHILIPPINES

G.
G.B.
GUINEA
S.L.
LIB.
BURK.
BEN.
NIGERIA
GHANA
IVORY
COAST
C. AFRICAN REF.
CAM.
EQ. GU.
GABON
CONGO
ZAIRE
UGA.
R.W.
BU.
KENYA
TANZANIA
ETHIOPIA
SOMALIA
SRI LANKA
MALAYSIA
BRUNEI
INDONESIA
PAPUA
NEW GUINEA

FR. GUI.

BRAZIL

ANGOLA
ZAMBIA
MAL.
MADAGASCAR
NAMIBIA
ZIMB.
BOTSWANA
MOZAMBIQUE
SWAZ.
SOUTH AFRICA
LES.

AUSTRALIA

AY

URUG.

NTINA

NEW
ZEALAND

Value of exports
million U.S. dollars
100 000
50 000
10 000
1000
Data not available

Country where 50% or more of total exports comes
from a restricted number of products
◖ One product
◖◖ Two products
◕◖ Three products

EUROPE
Developed market economies
43.5%

AMERICA
Developed market economies
14%

EUROPE
Centrally planned economies
9%

ASIA
Developing market economies
13%

Exports
By comparing the value of exports,
the dominance of the older
industrial nations is revealed.
Hard on their heels are the newly
industrialised nations, like Japan.
Following on is a second wave of
low wage, labour intensive
production countries, among them
India and China. Most oil nations
are major net exporters, but have
little industry.
OPEC earns about 12 per cent of
world export income, almost half
the Third World total, from a
single non-renewable source. A
large number of developing
countries are dependent on a small
range of export commodities.
These are often raw materials
which can be vulnerable to market
fluctuations, and their purchasing
power may decrease dramatically.
This situation could be improved
if the processing of the product
were carried out in the country of
origin, increasing its export value.

AMERICA
Developing market economies
4.2%

AFRICA
Developing
market
economies
2.2%

Average annual % growth rates
of exports
30
10
0
10
30
Increase

Decrease

Data not available

Share of world
exports

Designed and produced by E.S.R.

WEALTH AND DEBT

The chasm between the rich and poor nations of the world is widening. Existing methods of reducing the difference involve loans and aid from governments, UN organisations and aid agencies. In the future the international economic system needs to be redesigned to finance and invest in sustainable development of national resources and programmes to combat poverty.

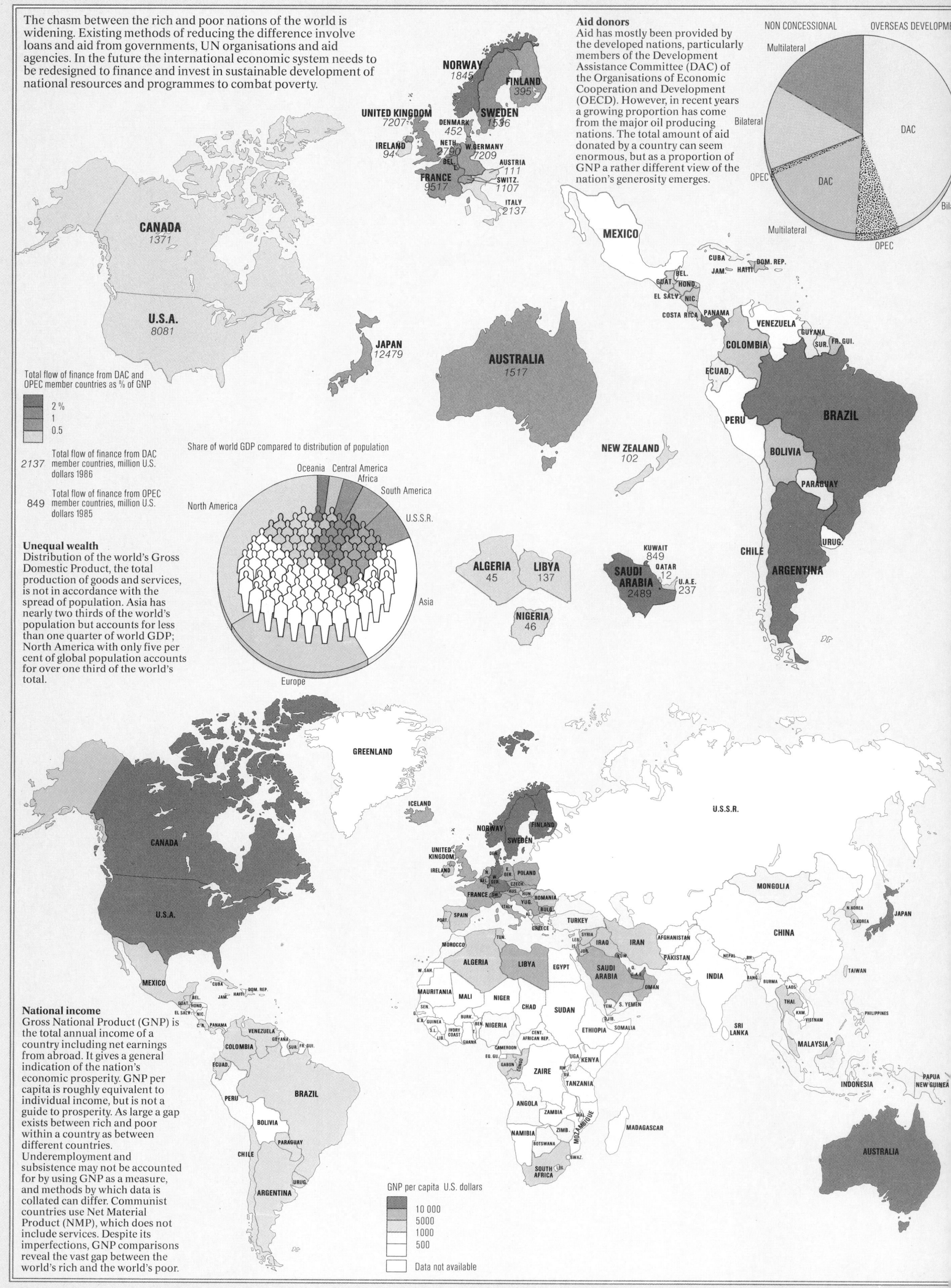

Aid donors
Aid has mostly been provided by the developed nations, particularly members of the Development Assistance Committee (DAC) of the Organisations of Economic Cooperation and Development (OECD). However, in recent years a growing proportion has come from the major oil producing nations. The total amount of aid donated by a country can seem enormous, but as a proportion of GNP a rather different view of the nation's generosity emerges.

NON CONCESSIONAL   OVERSEAS DEVELOPME

Multilateral
Bilateral
DAC
OPEC
DAC
Multilateral
OPEC
Bila

NORWAY 1845
FINLAND 395
SWEDEN 1536
UNITED KINGDOM 7207
DENMARK 452
IRELAND 94
NETH. 2780
BEL.
W.GERMANY 7209
AUSTRIA 111
FRANCE 9517
SWITZ. 1107
ITALY 2137

CANADA 1371

U.S.A. 8081

JAPAN 12479

AUSTRALIA 1517

NEW ZEALAND 102

MEXICO

CUBA
BEL.
GUAT. HOND.
EL SALV.
DOM. REP.
JAM. HAITI
NIC.
COSTA RICA PANAMA

VENEZUELA
COLOMBIA
GUYANA
SUR. FR. GUI.
ECUAD.
PERU
BRAZIL
BOLIVIA
PARAGUAY
CHILE
URUG.
ARGENTINA

ALGERIA 45
LIBYA 137
NIGERIA 46

KUWAIT 849
SAUDI ARABIA 2489
QATAR 12
U.A.E. 237

Total flow of finance from DAC and OPEC member countries as % of GNP
- 2 %
- 1
- 0.5

2137 Total flow of finance from DAC member countries, million U.S. dollars 1986

849 Total flow of finance from OPEC member countries, million U.S. dollars 1985

Unequal wealth
Distribution of the world's Gross Domestic Product, the total production of goods and services, is not in accordance with the spread of population. Asia has nearly two thirds of the world's population but accounts for less than one quarter of world GDP; North America with only five per cent of global population accounts for over one third of the world's total.

Share of world GDP compared to distribution of population

Oceania
Central America
Africa
South America
North America
U.S.S.R.
Asia
Europe

National income
Gross National Product (GNP) is the total annual income of a country including net earnings from abroad. It gives a general indication of the nation's economic prosperity. GNP per capita is roughly equivalent to individual income, but is not a guide to prosperity. As large a gap exists between rich and poor within a country as between different countries. Underemployment and subsistence may not be accounted for by using GNP as a measure, and methods by which data is collated can differ. Communist countries use Net Material Product (NMP), which does not include services. Despite its imperfections, GNP comparisons reveal the vast gap between the world's rich and the world's poor.

GREENLAND
ICELAND
CANADA
U.S.A.
MEXICO
NORWAY
SWEDEN
FINLAND
UNITED KINGDOM
IRELAND
DEN.
POLAND
E. GER.
CZECH.
FRANCE
SWITZ.
AUS. HUN.
ROMANIA
YUG.
BULG.
SPAIN
PORT.
ITALY
GREECE
TURKEY
U.S.S.R.
MONGOLIA
N. KOREA
S. KOREA
JAPAN
CHINA
AFGHANISTAN
SYRIA
LEB.
IRAQ
IRAN
MOROCCO
TUN.
ALGERIA
LIBYA
EGYPT
SAUDI ARABIA
OMAN
PAKISTAN
NEPAL
BH.
INDIA
BANG.
BURMA
TAIWAN
LAOS
THAI.
KAM.
VIETNAM
PHILIPPINES
W. SAH.
MAURITANIA
MALI
NIGER
CHAD
SUDAN
SEN.
G.B. GUINEA
S.L.
IVORY COAST
BEN.
NIGERIA
GHANA
CAMEROON
CENT. AFRICAN REP.
ETHIOPIA
SOMALIA
TEM. S. YEMEN
EQ. GU.
GABON
ZAIRE
UGA.
KENYA
RW.
TANZANIA
SRI LANKA
MALAYSIA
INDONESIA
PAPUA NEW GUINEA
ANGOLA
ZAMBIA
MALAWI
MOZAMBIQUE
MADAGASCAR
NAMIBIA
ZIMB.
BOTSWANA
SOUTH AFRICA
SWAZ.
LES.
CUBA
BEL.
GUAT. HOND.
EL SALV. NIC.
PANAMA
DOM. REP.
JAM. HAITI
VENEZUELA
GUYANA
COLOMBIA
SUR. FR. GUI.
ECUAD.
PERU
BRAZIL
BOLIVIA
PARAGUAY
CHILE
URUG.
ARGENTINA
AUSTRALIA

GNP per capita U.S. dollars
- 10 000
- 5000
- 1000
- 500
- Data not available

40

© COLOUR LIBRARY BOOKS

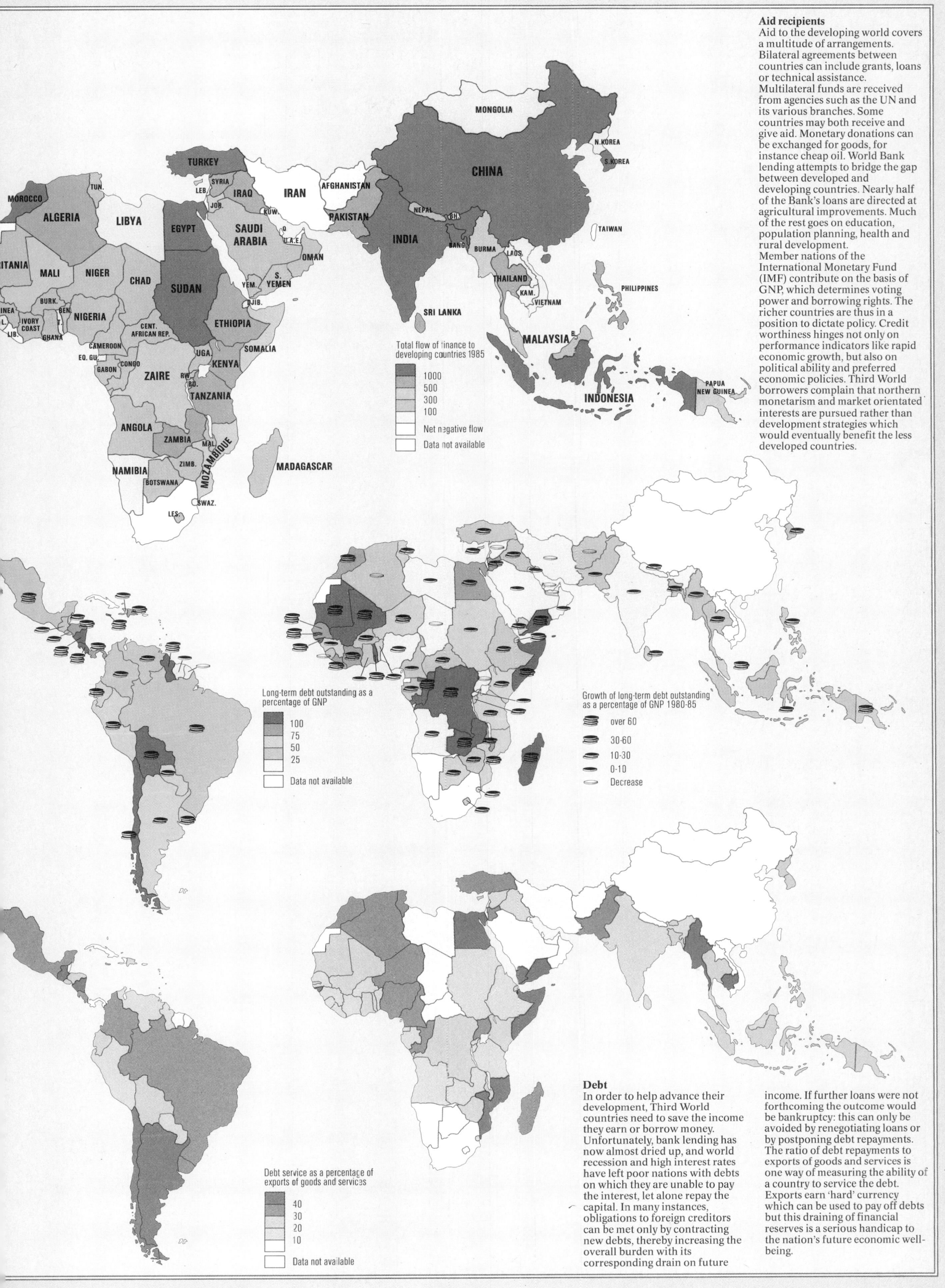

Aid recipients
Aid to the developing world covers a multitude of arrangements. Bilateral agreements between countries can include grants, loans or technical assistance. Multilateral funds are received from agencies such as the UN and its various branches. Some countries may both receive and give aid. Monetary donations can be exchanged for goods, for instance cheap oil. World Bank lending attempts to bridge the gap between developed and developing countries. Nearly half of the Bank's loans are directed at agricultural improvements. Much of the rest goes on education, population planning, health and rural development.
Member nations of the International Monetary Fund (IMF) contribute on the basis of GNP, which determines voting power and borrowing rights. The richer countries are thus in a position to dictate policy. Credit worthiness hinges not only on performance indicators like rapid economic growth, but also on political ability and preferred economic policies. Third World borrowers complain that northern monetarism and market orientated interests are pursued rather than development strategies which would eventually benefit the less developed countries.

Total flow of finance to developing countries 1985

1000
500
300
100
Net negative flow
Data not available

Long-term debt outstanding as a percentage of GNP

100
75
50
25
Data not available

Growth of long-term debt outstanding as a percentage of GNP 1980-85

over 60
30-60
10-30
0-10
Decrease

Debt service as a percentage of exports of goods and services

40
30
20
10
Data not available

Debt
In order to help advance their development, Third World countries need to save the income they earn or borrow money. Unfortunately, bank lending has now almost dried up, and world recession and high interest rates have left poor nations with debts on which they are unable to pay the interest, let alone repay the capital. In many instances, obligations to foreign creditors can be met only by contracting new debts, thereby increasing the overall burden with its corresponding drain on future income. If further loans were not forthcoming the outcome would be bankruptcy: this can only be avoided by renegotiating loans or by postponing debt repayments. The ratio of debt repayments to exports of goods and services is one way of measuring the ability of a country to service the debt. Exports earn 'hard' currency which can be used to pay off debts but this draining of financial reserves is a serious handicap to the nation's future economic well-being.

Designed and produced by E.S.R.

MAP LEGEND

SETTLEMENT

For scales larger than 1:2,000,000   Population

	BIRMINGHAM	>1,000,000
	GLASGOW	500,000–1,000,000
	CARDIFF	250,000–500,000
	LIMERICK	50,000–250,000
•	**Dover**	10,000–50,000
•	Lossiemouth	5,000–10,000
○	Church Stretton	<5,000

	CROYDON	London Borough

For scales between 1:2,000,000 and 1:12,000,000

	NEW YORK	>5,000,000
	RANGOON	2,500,000–5,000,000
■	**KUYBYSHEV**	1,000,000–2,500,000
•	**Hyderabad**	500,000–1,000,000
•	Adelaide	100,000–500,000
○	Baden-Baden	<100,000

For scales smaller than 1:12,000,000

■	**DAR ES SALAAM**	>1,000,000
•	**Maracaibo**	500,000–1,000,000
•	Tiranë	<500,000

Lisboa   National capital   **Winnipeg**   State, provincial capital

COMMUNICATIONS

────────	Motorway
========	Motorway under construction
────────	Principal road
────────	Principal road under construction
────────	Other main road
─ ─ ─ ─	Track, seasonal road
→─── ─←──	Road tunnel
────────	Principal railway
─ ─ ─ ─	Principal railway under construction
→─── ─←──	Railway tunnel
✈	International, main airport

BOUNDARIES

▬▬▬▬	International
▬ ▬ ▬	Undefined, disputed
────────	Internal, state, provincial
─ ─ ─ ─	Armistice, cease-fire line

The representation of a boundary in this atlas does not denote its international recognition and therefore the *defacto* situation has been depicted.

HYDROGRAPHIC FEATURES

～～～	River, stream
～～～	Intermittent watercourse
～～～	Waterfall, rapids
────	Dam, barrage
────	Irrigation, drainage channel
────	Canal
～～～	Lake, reservoir
～～～	Intermittent, seasonal lake
～～～	Salt pan, mud flat
•	Oasis
▦	Marsh, swamp
～～～	Reef

Depth of sea in metres

Scales larger than 1:12,000,000

0
200
3000

Scales smaller than 1:12,000,000

0
1000
5000

OTHER FEATURES

▲ 3798	Elevation above sea level (metres)
▼ −133	Depression, below sea level (metres)
≍	Pass
●──▲──■	Oil, gas pipeline with field

ENVIRONMENTAL TYPES

	Permanent ice and snow
	Mountain and moorland
	Tundra
	Coniferous forest
	Deciduous forest
	Tropical forest
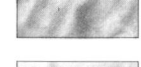	Prairie
	Temperate agriculture
	Mediterranean scrub
	Savannah
	Desert

This representation of the environment and its associated vegetation gives an overview of the landscape. It is not intended to be definitive.

CONVERSION SCALES

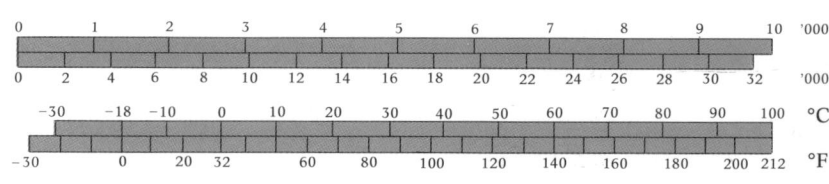

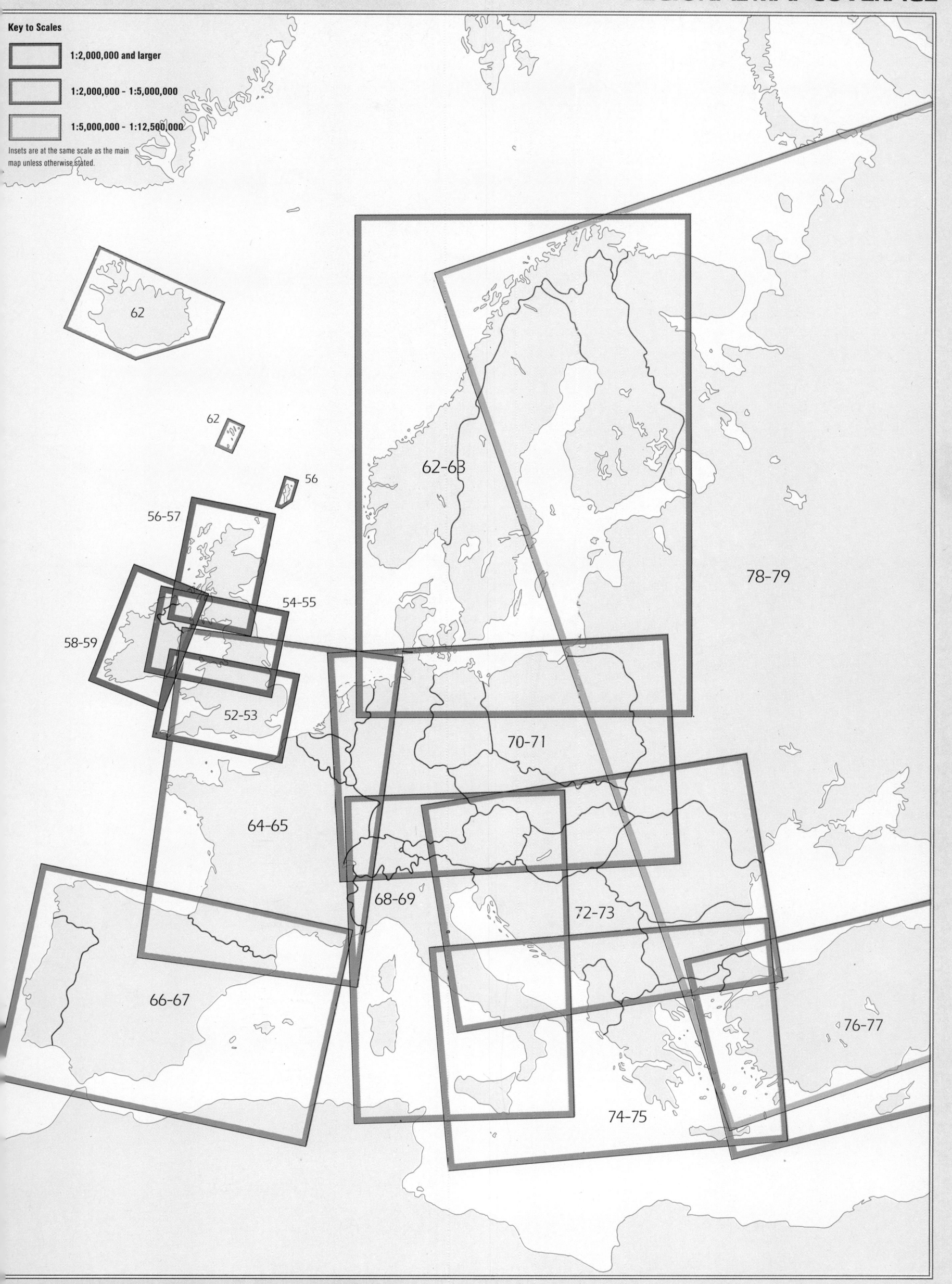

Key to Scales

1:2,000,000 and larger

1:2,000,000 - 1:5,000,000

1:5,000,000 - 1:12,500,000

Insets are at the same scale as the main map unless otherwise stated.

62

62

56

56-57

54-55

58-59

52-53

62-63

78-79

70-71

64-65

68-69

72-73

66-67

74-75

76-77

Designed and produced by E.S.R.

84-85

78-79

86-87

76-77

94-95

96-97

92-93

97

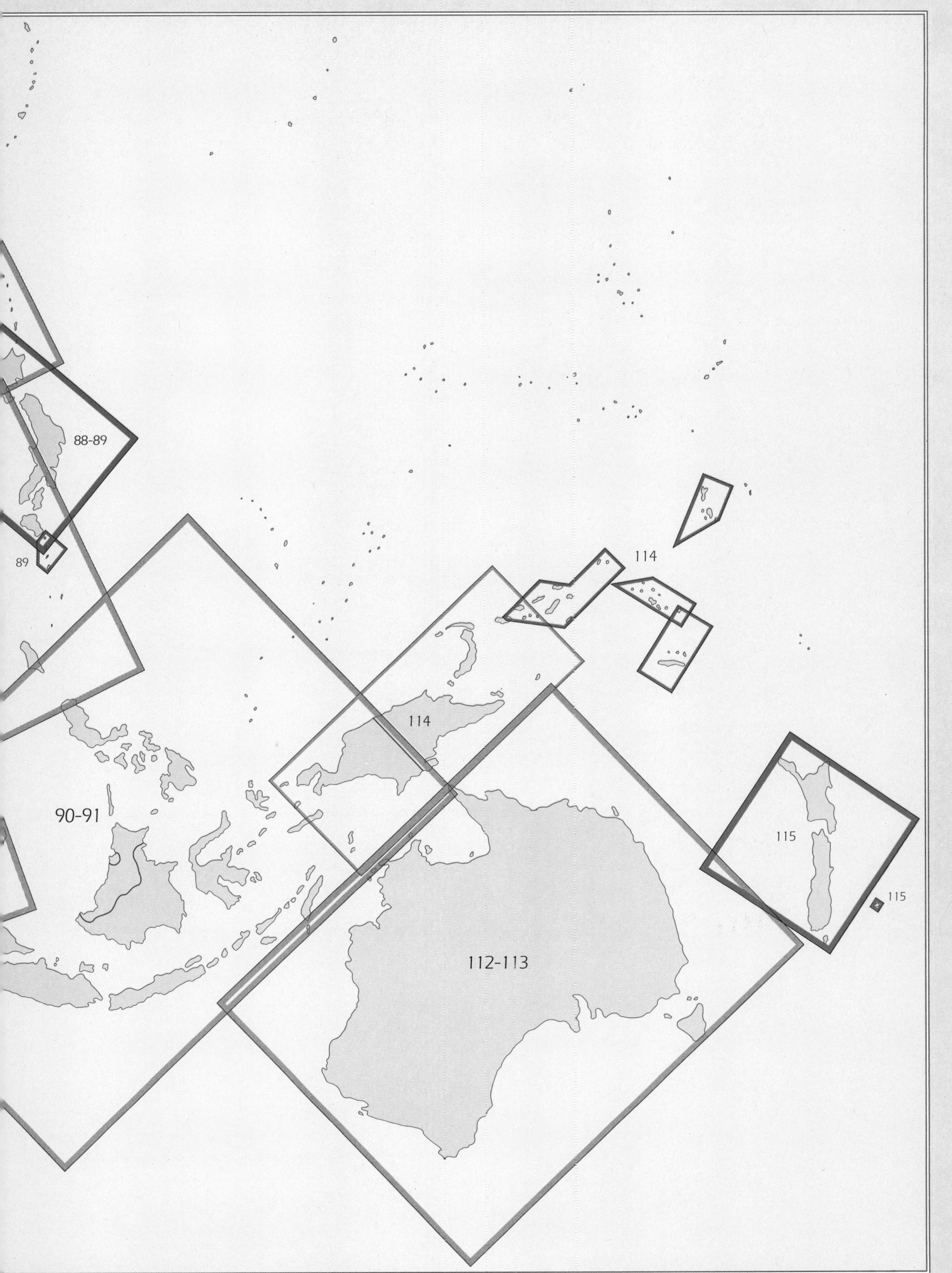

88-89

89

114

90-91

114

115

115

112-113

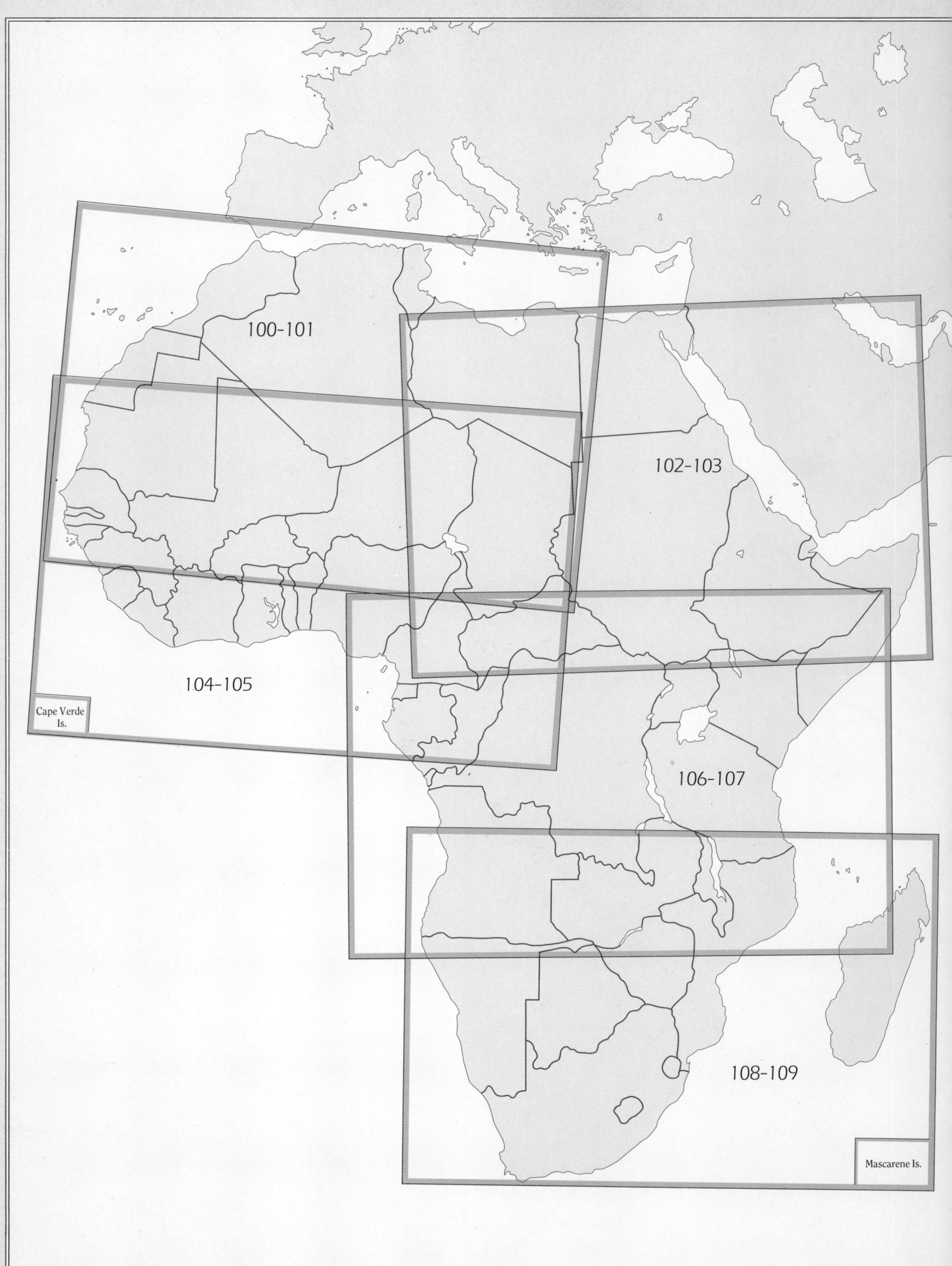

100-101

102-103

104-105

Cape Verde
Is.

106-107

108-109

Mascarene Is.

46

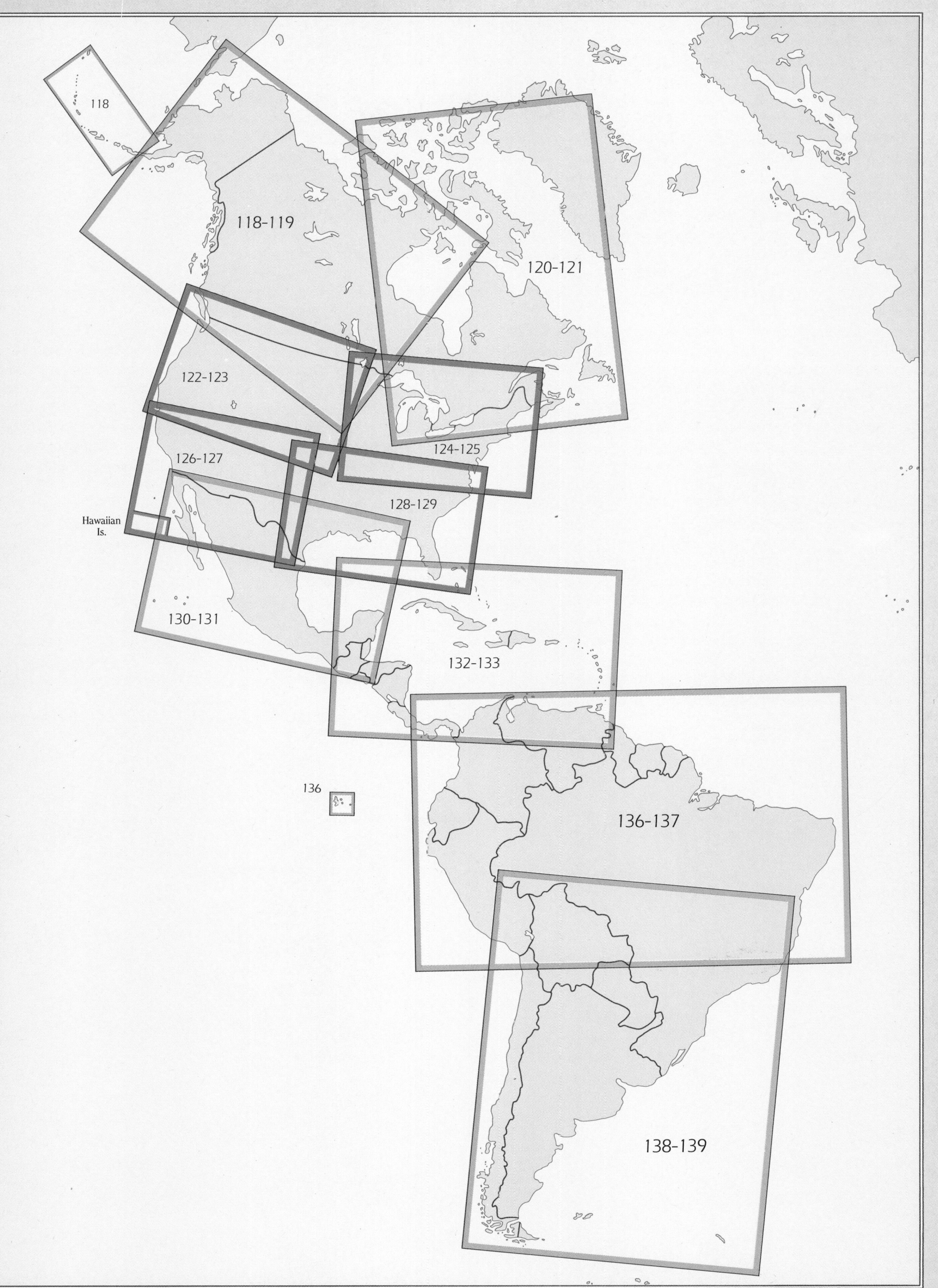

118

118-119

120-121

122-123

124-125

126-127

128-129

Hawaiian
Is.

130-131

132-133

136

136-137

138-139

East of Greenwich | 30° | H | 60° | J | 90° | K | 120° | L | 150° | M | East of Greenwich 180° West of Greenwich

ARCTIC OCEAN

Zemlya Frantsa-Iosifa
(U.S.S.R.)

Severnaya Zemlya

Novosibirskiye Ostrova

Karskoye More

More Laptevykh

Novaya Zemlya

Lyakhovskiye Ostrova

Vostochno Sibirskoye More

Ostrov Vrangelya

Barentsevo More

Nordkapp

Poluostrov Yamal

Cydanskiy Poluostrov

Gory Byrranga

Ozero Taymyr

Kolmskaya Nizmennost

Arctic Circle

SWEDEN

Lappland

Gulf of Bothnia

Beloye More

Plato Putorana

Verkhoyanskiy Khrebet

Khrebet Cherskogo

Khrebet Kolymskiy

Anadyrskiy Zaliv

Bering Strait

Helsingfors

FINLAND

Ozero Ladozhskoye

Poluostrov Yamal

S r e d n e

S i b i r s k o y e

Bering Sea

Stockholm

LENINGRAD

Uralskiy Khrebet

Ob

P l o s k o g o r y e

50°

Baltic Sea

MOSKVA

Pechora

Dvina

UNION OF SOVIET SOCIALIST REPUBLICS

Kuybyshevskoye Vodokhranilishche

Okhotskoye More

Kubenhavn

Berlin

Warszawa

POLAND

Dnieper

Prikaspiyskaya Nizmennost

Kirgiz Step'

Irtysh

Ozero Baykal

Sakhalin

Aleutian Islands

Praha

CZECH.

Wien

AUST.

Budapest

HUNG. **ROM.**

Beograd

Bucuresti

YUGO.

Caspian Sea

Aral'skoye More

Kyzylkum

Ozero Balkhash

MONGOLIA

Gobi

Sea of Japan

NORTH

Roma

Tirana

BULG.

Sofiya

Black Sea

6642 EL'BRUS

Karakumy

Ulaanbaatar

Anadyr

Kamchatka

Kuril'skiye Ostrova

Kuril Trench

PACIFIC

ALB.

GREECE

Athina

Ankara

Karakumy

Tien Shan

Tarim Pendi

-154

BEIJING

TIANJIN

N. KOREA

Pyongyang

JAPAN

TÖKYÖ

OCEAN

Valletta

MALTA

Tarābulus

TURKEY

SYRIA

TEHRAN

Kabul

Hindu Kush

Kunlun Shan

Taklimakan Shamo

Xizang Gaoyuan

S KOREA

SÖUL

Japan Trench

CYPRUS

Levkosia

Bayrūt

Dimashq

IRAQ

IRAN

Kūhhā ye Zagros

AFGHANISTAN

Islamabad

Huang He

SHANGHAI

LIBYA

Yerushalayim

-133

Amman

JOR.

Baghdād

PAKISTAN

DELHI

Kathmandu

Himalaya

CHINA

Chang Jiang

30°

EL QAHIRA

Al Kuwayt

KUW.

Thar Desert

New Delhi

EVEREST

BHU.

NEP.

EGYPT

Al Manamah

BAH.

Ad Dawhah

QAT.

KARACHI

INDIA

CALCUTTA

Dhaka

BANG.

Tropic of Cancer

Nile

Ar Riyād

Abu Zabi

U.A.E.

Masqat

BOMBAY

BURMA

Hanoi

HONG KONG

(U.K.)

Ta-pei

TAIWAN

SAUDI ARABIA

OMAN

Arabian Sea

Deccan

MADRAS

Bay of Bengal

Rangoon

LAOS

THAI-LAND

Viangchan

VIETNAM

MANILA

Luzon

Marianas Is.

CHAD

N'djamena

El Khartum

SUDAN

San'ā

SOUTH YEMEN

'Adan

Suqutrā

(S.Yem.)

Lakshadweep

(India)

Colombo

SRI LANKA

Andaman Islands

(India)

KRUNG THEP

KAM.

Phnom Penh

PHILIPPINES

Mindanao

Guam (U.S.A.)

Caroline Islands

U.S. Trust Territory of the Pacific Islands

Marshall Is.

Bangui

CENTRAL AFRICAN REP.

Adis Abeba

ETHIOPIA

DJIB.

SOMALIA

Muqdisho

Malé

MALDIVES

MALAYSIA

Kuala Lumpur

SINGAPORE

Bandar Seri Begawan

BRU.

Borneo

Sumatera

Maluku

Sulawesi

M i c r o n e s i a

NAURU

Tarawa

Gilbert Is.

Phoenix Is.

Equator

CAMEROON

Yaounde

Congo Basin

ZAÏRE

UGANDA

Kampala

KENYA

Nairobi

Victoria

SEYCHELLES

JAKARTA

Jawa

INDONESIA

Laut Arafura

New Guinea

PAPUA NEW GUINEA

Port Moresby

SOLOMON ISLANDS

Honiara

Santa Cruz Is.

TUVALU

Fanafuti

W. SAMOA

Apia

Ile Wallice

(Fr.)

Kinshasa

Luanda

ANGOLA

Kigali

RW.

Bujumbura

BUR.

Dodoma

TANZANIA

KILIMANJARO

5895

Victoria

COMOROS

Moroni

INDIAN OCEAN

Timor

Laut Timor

Coral Sea

VANUATU

Vila

Nouvelle Calédonie

(Fr.)

FIJI

Suva

TONGA

Nuku'alofa

5

ZAMBIA

Lusaka

MALAWI

Lilongwe

MOZAMBIQUE

Harare

ZIMBABWE

MADAGASCAR

Antananarivo

Rëunion

(Fr.)

MAURITIUS

Port Louis

Gt. Barrier Reef

Gt. Dividing Range

Tropic of Capricorn

Tonga Trench

NAMIBIA

Windhoek

BOTSWANA

Gaborone

Kalahari

Pretoria

Maputo

Mbabane

SWAZILAND

Maseru

LESOTHO

AUSTRALIA

L. Eyre

Gt. Victoria Desert

Darling

Murray

30°

Orange

SOUTH AFRICA

C. Leeuwin

Canberra

Tasman Sea

Kermadec Trench

Good Hope

Iles Crozet

(Fr.)

Prince Edward Is.

(S.A.)

Ile Kerguelen

(Fr.)

Heard I.

(Aus.)

NEW ZEALAND

Wellington

Tasmania

Chatham Is.

(N.Z.)

Auckland Is.

(N.Z.)

Macquarie Is.

(Aus.)

6

G | 30° | H | 60° | J | 90° | K | 120° | L | 150° | M | 180°

1:12,500,000

West of Greenwich · East of Greenwich

| 0 | 100 | 200 | 300 | 400 | 500 | 600 | 700 | 800 KILOMETRES |

| 0 | 100 | 200 | 300 | 400 | 500 STATUTE MILES |

© COLOUR LIBRARY BOOKS

Miller Oblated Stereographic Projection

Designed and produced by E.S.R.

Transverse Mercator Projection

1:1,175,000

© COLOUR LIBRARY BOOKS

| 0 | 10 | 20 | 30 | 40 | 50 | 60 | 70 | 80 KILOMETRES |

| 0 | 10 | 20 | 30 | 40 | 50 STATUTE MILES |

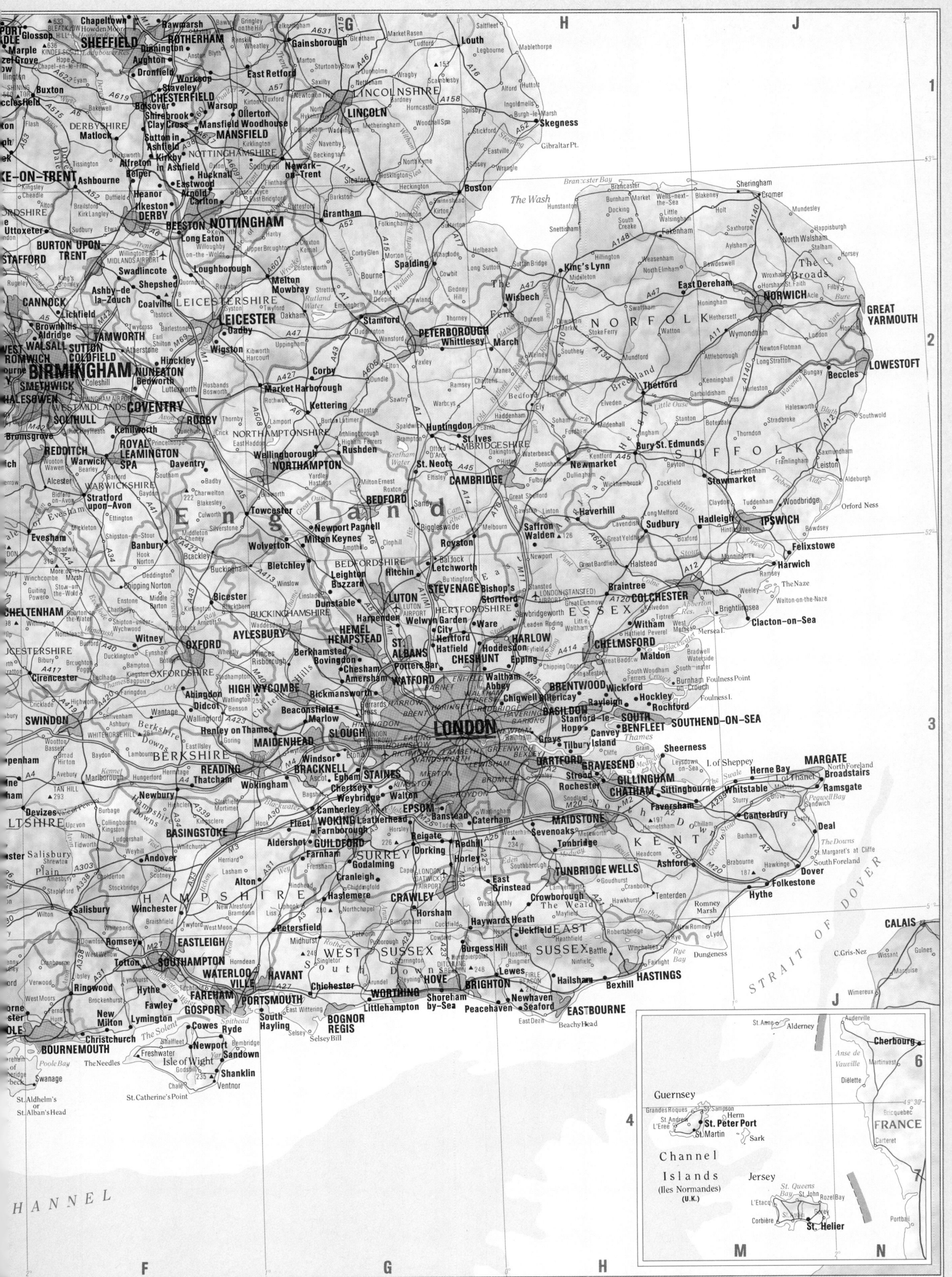

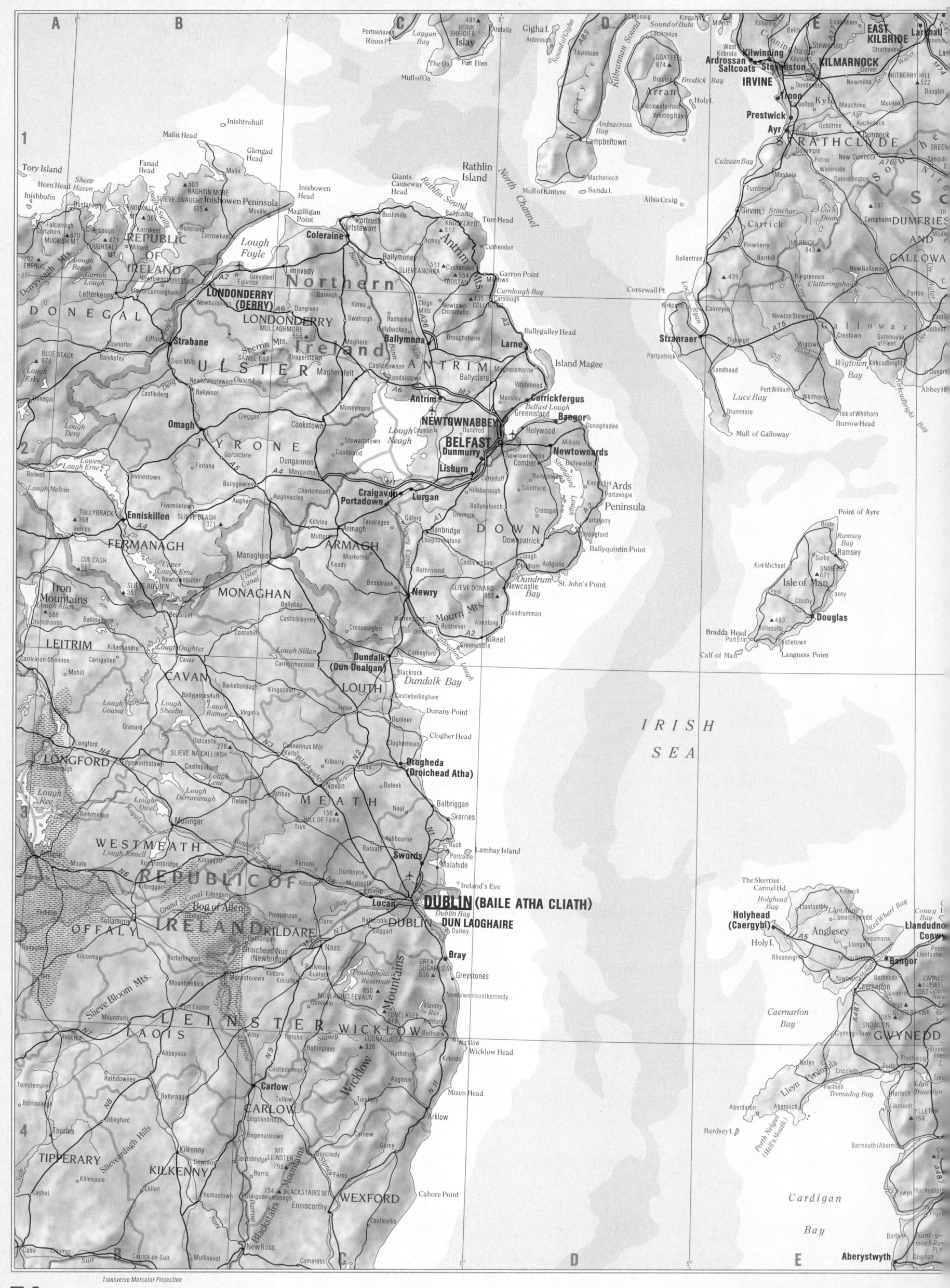

Transverse Mercator Projection

1:1,175,000

© COLOUR LIBRARY BOOKS

Designed and produced by E.S.R.

West of Greenwich   East of Greenwich

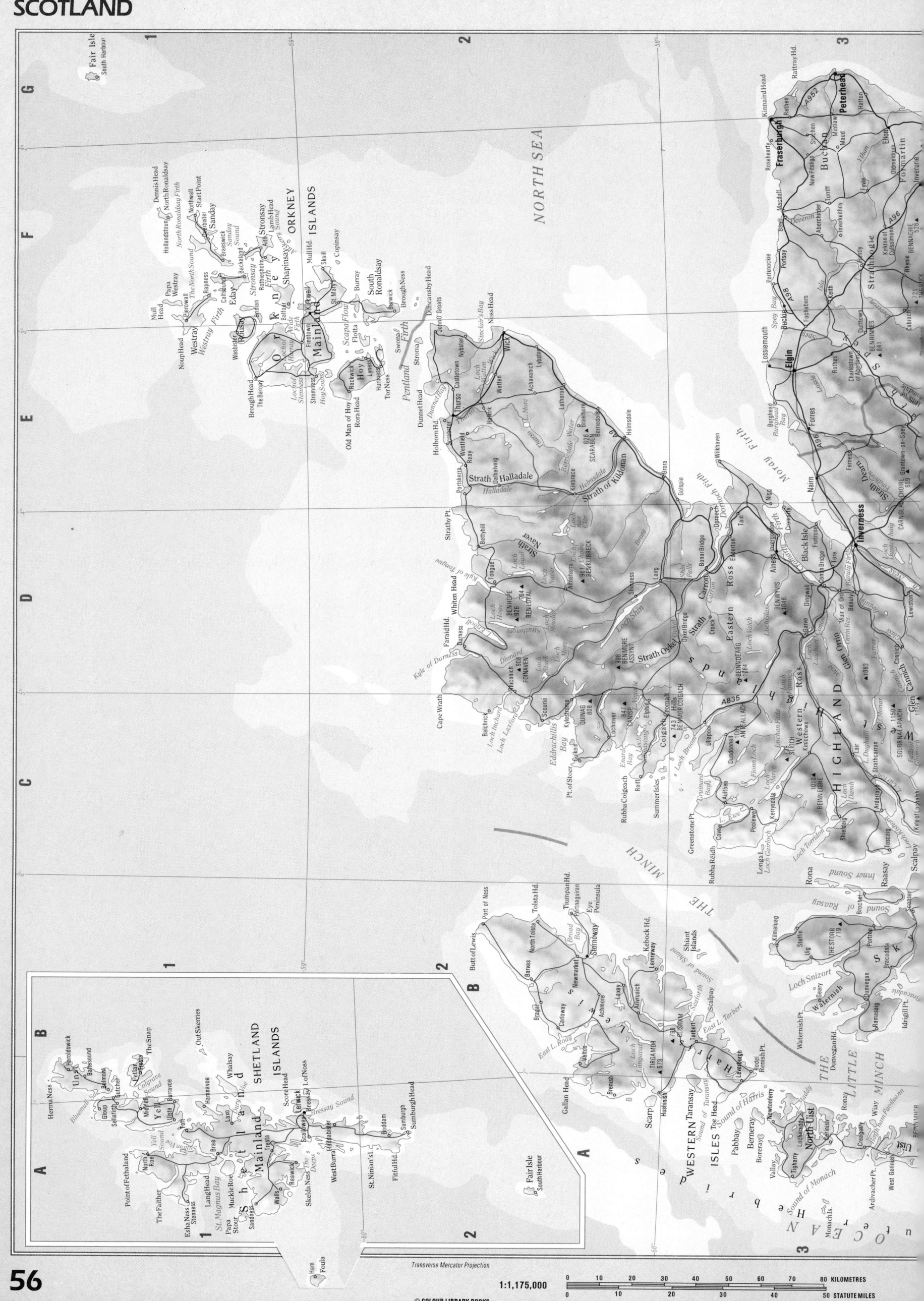

Fair Isle
South Harbour

ORKNEY ISLANDS

Dennis Head
North Ronaldsay
North Ronaldsay Firth
Northwall
Start Point
Hollandstoun
Sanday
Papa Westray
Westray
Braeswick
Sanday
Backaland
Rapness
Brinian
Eday
Mull Hd.
Stronsay
Auth
Lamb Head
Shapinsay
Copinsay

Mull Head
Noup Head
Westray
Pierowall
Westray Firth
Rousay
Egilsay
Wyre
Balfour
Shapinsay Sound
Mainland
St. Mary
Skaill
Burray
South Ronaldsay

Brough Head
The Barony
Loch of Stenness
Stromness
Scapa Flow
Flotta
Burwick
Brough Ness

Old Man of Hoy
Rora Head
Hoy
Rackwick
Lyness
Tor Ness
Swona
Pentland Firth
Stroma
Duncansby Head
John o' Groats

NORTH SEA

Dunnet Hd.
Holborn Hd.
Dunnet Bay
Thurso
Castletown
Nybster
Loch Wester
WICK
Sinclair's Bay
Noss Head
Westfield
Reay
Halkirk
Watten
Hestor
Portskerra
Dalhalvaig
Strath Halladale
Halladale
Thrumster
Bridge of Dunbeath
Latheron
Lybster

Strathy Pt.
Strathy
Bettyhill
Naver
Kinbrace
Helmsdale
Strath of Kildonan
Brora
Helmsdale

Whiten Head
Kyle of Tongue
Tongue
BEN LOYAL
Lairg
Golspie
Dunrobin

Faraid Hd.
Durness
BEN HOPE
Loch Hope
Loch Loyal
Loch Shin
Shin Falls
Bonar Bridge
Dornoch
Dornoch Firth
Tain

Cape Wrath
Kyle of Durness
FOINAVEN
Loch Stack
BEN MORE ASSYNT
Oykel Bridge
Strath Oykel
CARN CHUINNEAG
Edderton
Alness
Black Isle
INVERNESS

Balchrick
Scourie
Lochinver
Inchnadamph
Coigach
Strath
Eastern Ross
Invergordon
Nigg
Kessock Bridge

Pt. of Stoer
Loch Assynt
SUILVEN
Conon Bridge
Dingwall
Beauly
Kirkhill

Rubha Coigeach
Summer Isles
AN TEALLACH
Garve
Muir of Ord
Reiff
Loch Broom
Ullapool
Western Ross
Glen Orrin
Drumnadrochit

Greenstone Pt.
Loch Maree
Kinlochewe
Kyle of Lochalsh

Rubha Réidh
Loch Torridon
Shieldaig
Dornie

Longa I.
Loch Gairloch
Applecross
Lochcarron

THE MINCH

Scalpay
Raasay
Inner Sound
Rona
Sound of Raasay
Portree
THE STORR

Butt of Lewis
Port of Ness
Tolsta Hd.
Flodabay
Staffin
Uig

Barvas
North Tolsta
Broad Bay
Tiumpan Hd.
Kilmaluag
Loch Snizort
Dunvegan
Waternish Pt.

Newmarket
STORNOWAY
Eye Peninsula
Shant Islands
W. Waternish
Dunvegan Hd.

Bragar
Carloway
Lemreway
Kebock Hd.
Sound of Scalpay
Portnalong
Broadford

Braah
East L. Roag
Lazy
Achmore
Ardvourlie

WESTERN ISLES

Gallan Head
Brenish
Scarp
Taransay
Hushinish
Taransay
Toe Head
Sound of Harris
Harris
Tarbert
East L. Tarbert
Scalpay
Leverburgh
Rodel
Renish Pt.

NORTH SEA

Fraserburgh
Kinnaird Head
Rattray Hd.
Rosehearty
Rathen
Peterhead
Buchan
New Pitsligo
Maud
Mintlaw
Strichen
Ellon

Banff
Macduff
Turriff
Aberchirder
Inverurie
BENNACHIE
Rhynie

Lossiemouth
Spey Bay
Buckie
Portsoy
Cullen
Fochabers
Keith
Huntly
Dufftown

Elgin
Forres
Nairn
Charlestown of Aberlour
Grantown-on-Spey

Strath Spey
Kingussie

Loch Ness

WESTERN HIGHLAND

BEINN DEARG
Loch Monar
Cannich
Glen Cannich
Invermoriston

Loch Cluanie
Loch Quoich

OCEAN

North Uist
Bayhead
Lochmaddy
Sound of Monach
Monachs
Grimsay
Benbecula

Sound of Barra

Transverse Mercator Projection

1:1,175,000

0 10 20 30 40 50 60 70 80 KILOMETRES
0 10 20 30 40 50 STATUTE MILES

© COLOUR LIBRARY BOOKS

Designed and produced by E.S.R.

ATLANTIC OCEAN

North Channel

IRISH

NORTHERN IRELAND

U L S T E R

Counties and regions: ANTRIM, LONDONDERRY, TYRONE, DOWN, ARMAGH, FERMANAGH, MONAGHAN, CAVAN, DONEGAL, LEITRIM, SLIGO, MAYO, ROSCOMMON, LONGFORD, LOUTH

Scotland (Kintyre): Kintyre, Mull of Kintyre, Campbeltown, Machrihanish, Claonaig, Tarbert, Gigha, Ardminish, Jura, Feolin Ferry, Port Askaig, Islay, Bridgend, Bruichladdich, Sanaigmore, Portnahaven, Port Ellen, Mull of Oa

Towns and cities: BELFAST, Bangor, Newtownards, Carrickfergus, Larne, Whitehead, Holywood, Comber, Newtownabbey, Dunmurry, Lisburn, Antrim, Ballymena, Coleraine, Ballymoney, Portrush, Portstewart, Newry, Portadown, Lurgan, Craigavon, Armagh, Newcastle, Downpatrick, Dundalk (Dún Dealgan), Drogheda (Droichead Átha), LONDONDERRY (DERRY), Strabane, Omagh, Cookstown, Magherafelt, Limavady, Dungiven, Maghera, Enniskillen, Monaghan, Cavan, Longford, Sligo, Ballina, Castlebar, Westport

Physical features: Antrim Mountains, Sperrin Mts, Mourne Mountains, Slieve Donard, Sawel, Derryveagh Mountains, Blue Stack Mts (Croaghgorm Mts), Slieve League, Errigal, Muckish Mt, Nephin Beg Range, Croagh Patrick, Slieve Gamph (Ox Mts), Cuilcagh, Truskmore, Benbradagh

Loughs: Lough Neagh, Lough Foyle, Lough Swilly, Lough Erne, Lower Lough Erne, Upper Lough Erne, Strangford Lough, Belfast Lough, Carlingford Lough, Dundrum Bay, Lough Conn, Lough Mask, Lough Gill, Lough Allen, Lough Gara, Lough Oughter, Lough Melvin, Lough Derg, Lough Eske, Lough Beagh

Islands and headlands: Rathlin Island, Rathlin Sound, Giants Causeway, Inishowen Head, Malin Head, Inishtrahull, Fanad Head, Horn Head, Tory Island, Inishbofin, Aran Island, Achill Island, Clare Island, Rossan Point, Slieve League, Dawros Head, St. John's Point, Dunany Point, Clogher Head, Garron Point, Torr Head, Fair Head, Ballygalley Head, Magilligan Pt., Bloody Foreland, The Rosses, Crohy Head, Gweebarra Bay, Donegal Bay, Sligo Bay, Killala Bay, Broad Haven, Blacksod Bay, Clew Bay, The Mullet, Corraun Peninsula, Erris Head, Benwee Head, Downpatrick Head, Annagh Head, Mullaghmore

Lambert Conformal Conic Projection

1:1,000,000

0 10 20 30 40 50 60 70 80 KILOMETRES
0 10 20 30 40 50 STATUTE MILES

© COLOUR LIBRARY BOOKS

Designed and produced by E.S.R.

West of Greenwich

Mercator Projection

1:85,000,000 (Scale at the Equator)

© COLOUR LIBRARY BOOKS

BRITISH ISLES AND CENTRAL EUROPE

1:5,000,000

© COLOUR LIBRARY BOOKS

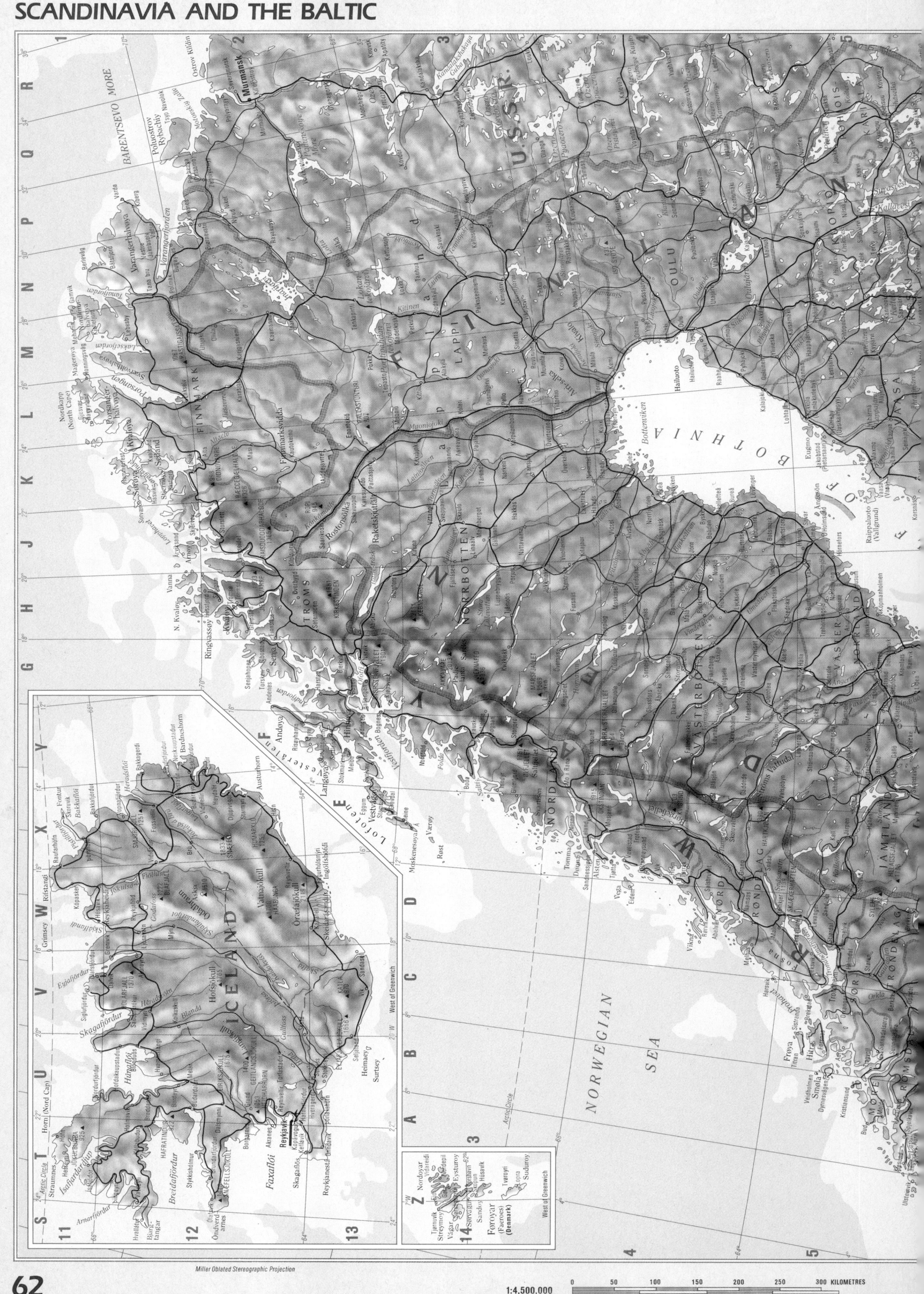

Miller Oblated Stereographic Projection

1:4,500,000

© COLOUR LIBRARY BOOKS

Conic Projection

1:3,000,000

| 0 | 25 | 50 | 75 | 100 | 125 | 150 | 175 | 200 KILOMETRES |

| 0 | 25 | 50 | 75 | 100 | 125 STATUTE MILES |

© COLOUR LIBRARY BOOKS

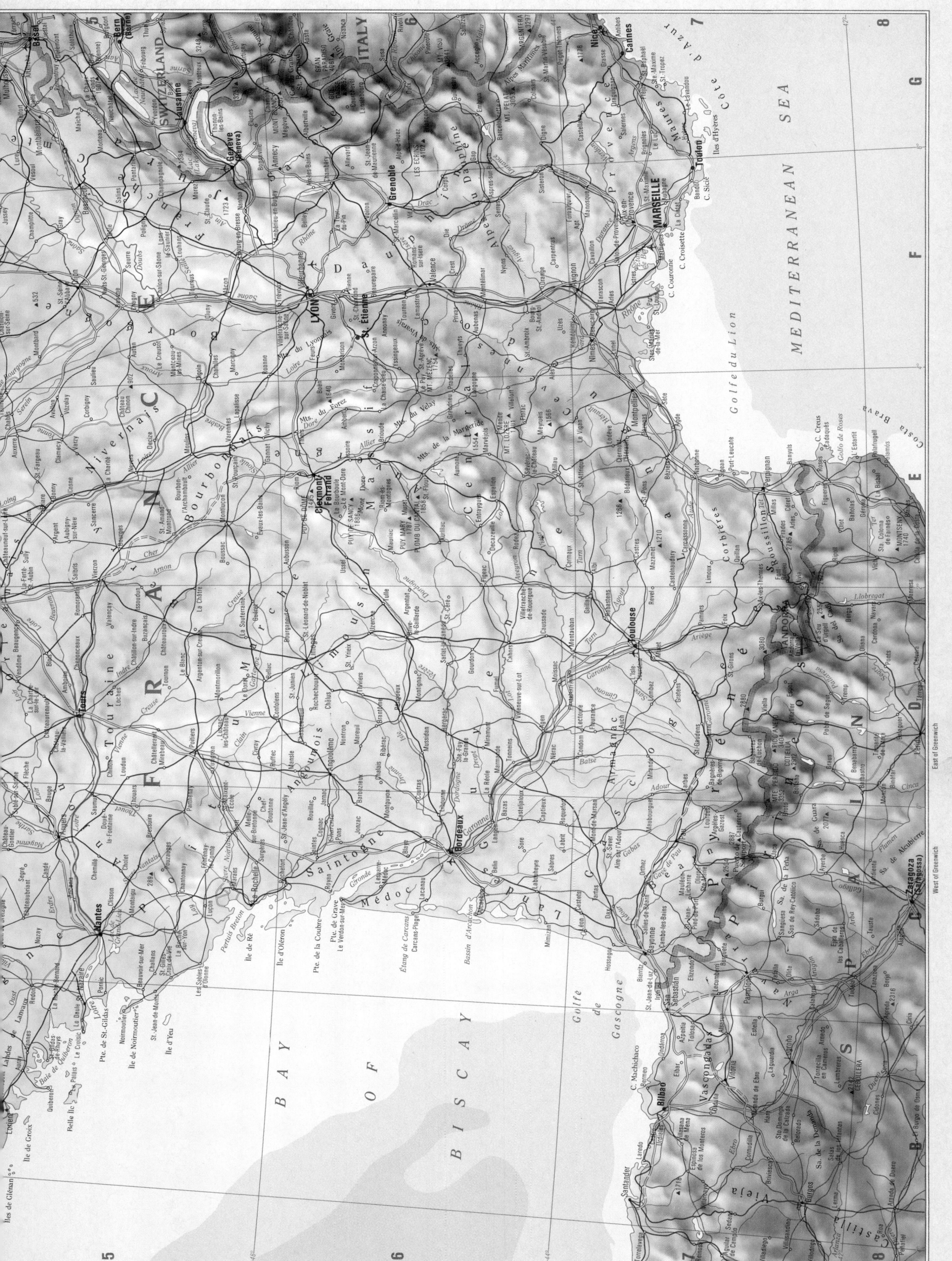

65

Conic Projection

1:3,000,000

© COLOUR LIBRARY BOOKS

| 0 | 25 | 50 | 75 | 100 | 125 | 150 | 175 | 200 KILOMETRES |

| 0 | 25 | 50 | 75 | 100 | 125 STATUTE MILES |

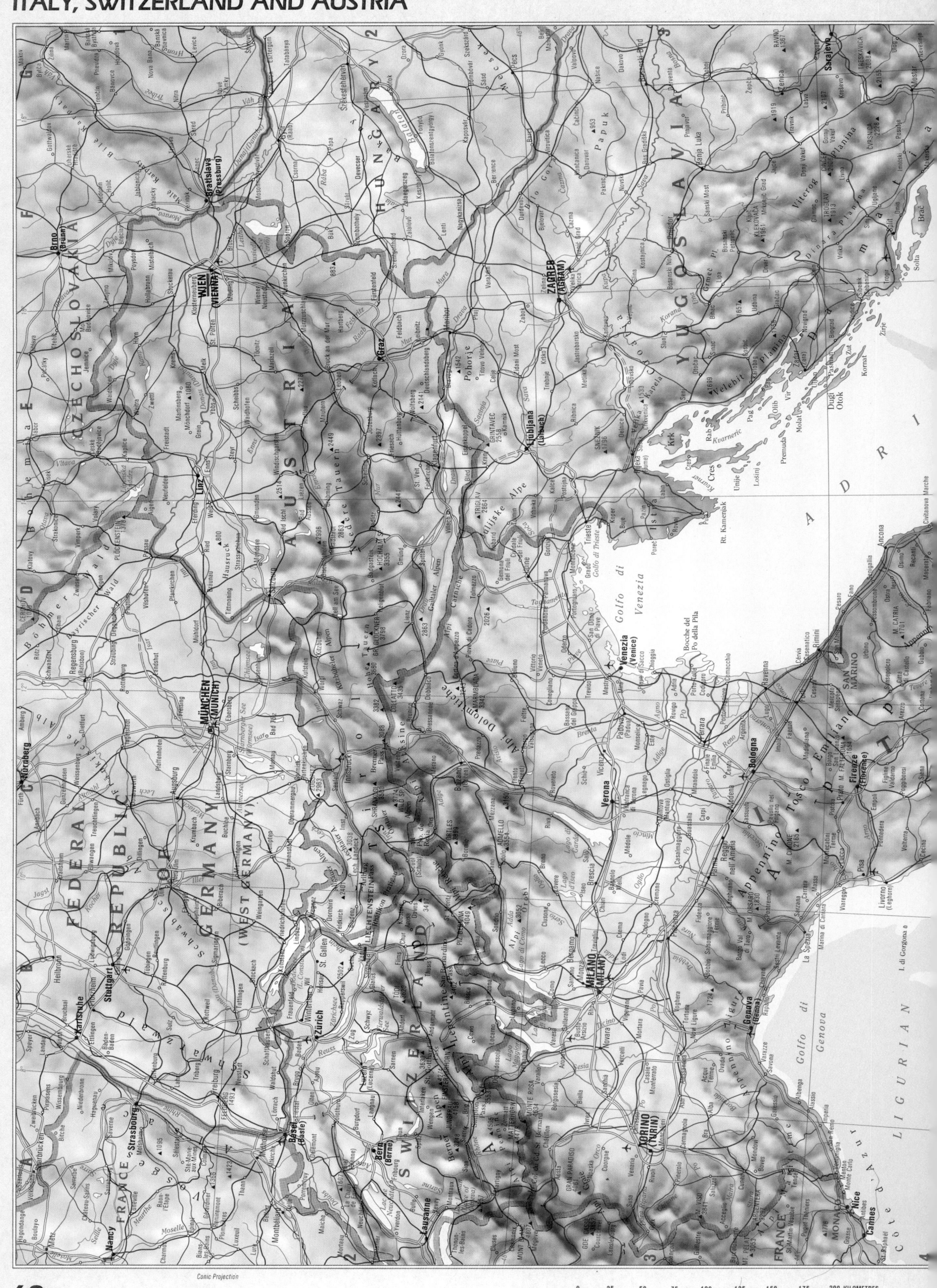

Conic Projection

1:3,000,000

© COLOUR LIBRARY BOOKS

Conic Projection

1:3,000,000

| 0 | 25 | 50 | 75 | 100 | 125 | 150 | 175 | 200 KILOMETRES |

| 0 | 25 | 50 | 75 | 100 | 125 STATUTE MILES |

© COLOUR LIBRARY BOOKS

Conic Projection

1:3,000,000

0   25   50   75   100   125   150   175   200 KILOMETRES

0   25   50   75   100   125 STATUTE MILES

© COLOUR LIBRARY BOOKS

73

Conic Projection

1:3,000,000

© COLOUR LIBRARY BOOKS

75

Lambert Conformal Conic Projection

1:3,500,000

© COLOUR LIBRARY BOOKS

Designed and produced by E.S.R.

East of Greenwich

Miller Oblated Stereographic Projection

1:8,000,000

| 0 | 100 | 200 | 300 | 400 | 500 | 600 KILOMETRES |
| 0 | 50 | 100 | 150 | 200 | 250 | 300 | 350 | 400 STATUTE M |

© COLOUR LIBRARY BOOKS

Conic Projection

1:17,000,000

| 0 | 100 | 200 | 300 | 400 | 500 | 600 | 700 | 800 KILOMETRES |

| 0 | 100 | 200 | 300 | 400 | 500 STATUTE MILES |

© COLOUR LIBRARY BOOKS

Designed and produced by E.S.R.

East of Greenwich

Lambert Azimuthal Equal Area Projection

1:25,000,000

| 0 | 200 | 400 | 600 | 800 | 1000 KILOMETRES |

| 0 | 100 | 200 | 300 | 400 | 500 | 600 STATUTE MILES |

© COLOUR LIBRARY BOOKS

Designed and produced by E.S.R.

East of Greenwich

Miller Oblated Stereographic Projection

1:11,500,000

© COLOUR LIBRARY BOOKS

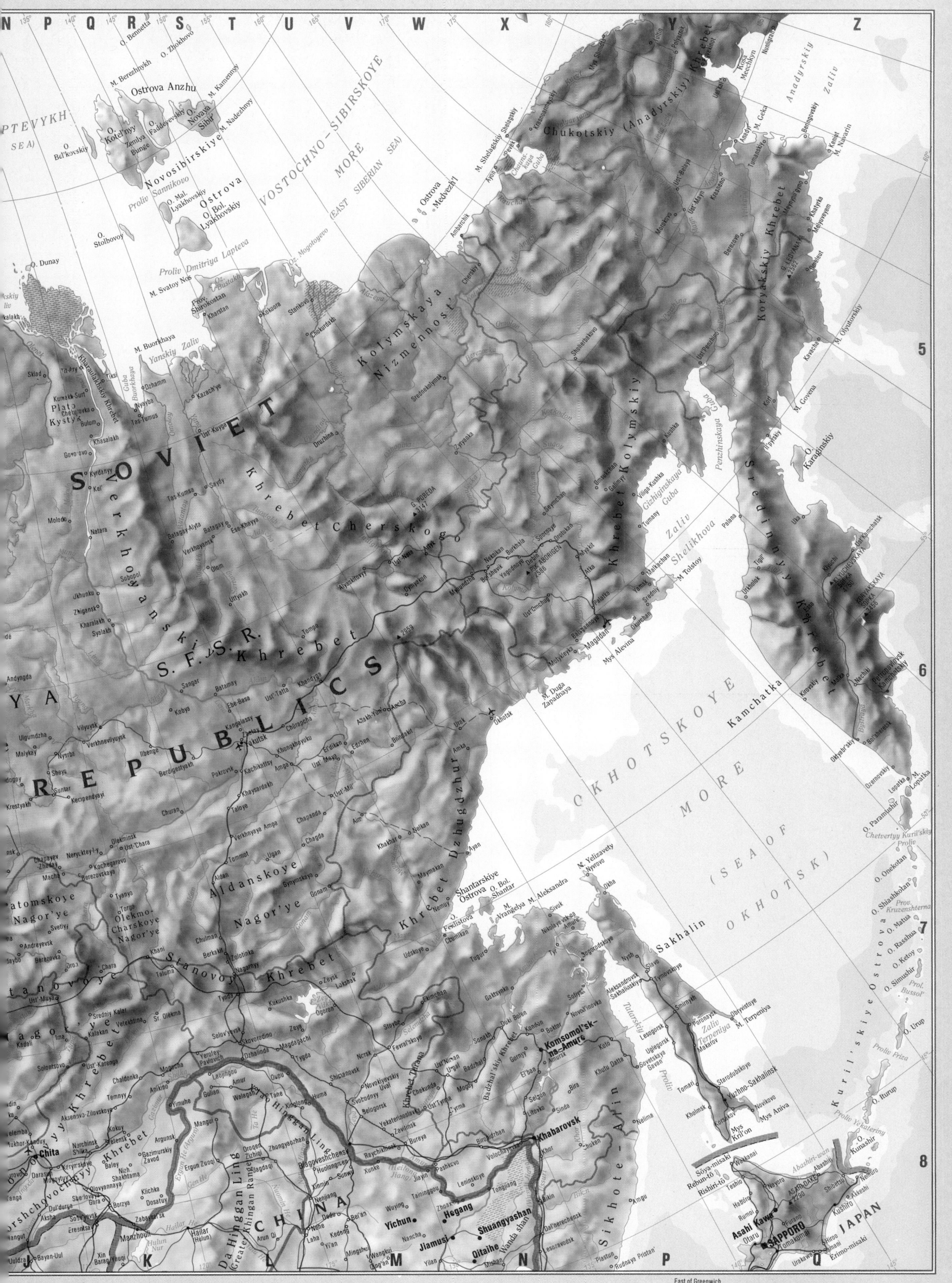

Miller Oblated Stereographic Projection

1:11,500,000

| 0 | 100 | 200 | 300 | 400 | 500 | 600 | 700 | 800 KILOMETRES |

| 0 | 50 | 100 | 150 | 200 | 250 | 300 | 350 | 400 | 450 | 500 STATUTE MILES |

© COLOUR LIBRARY BOOKS

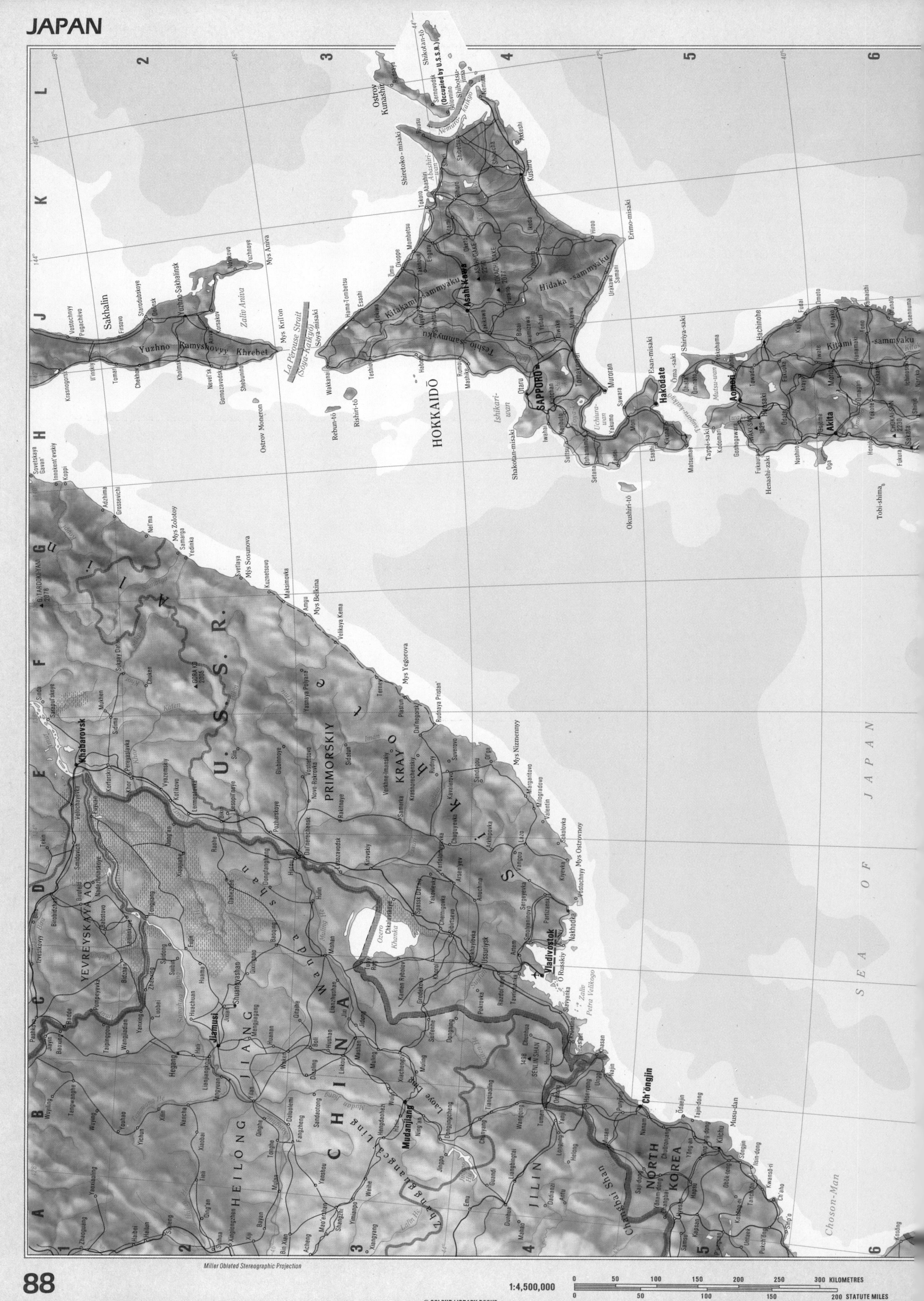

L

2

3

4

5

6

K

J

I

H

G

F

E

D

C

B

A

Ostrov
Kunashir

Shikotan-tō

Samovodsk
-jima
(Occupied by U.S.S.R.)
Shibotsu-
jima
Nemuro
Nemuro kaikyo

Shiretoko-misaki
Abashiri
Ōmu
Tokoro
Shari
Kushiro
Akkeshi

Monbetsu
Engaru
Kitami
Kushiro
Akan
TOKACHI-DAKE
2077
Hiroo
Erimo-misaki

Hama-Tombetsu
Esashi

Kitakami-sammyaku
ASAHI-DAKE
2290
Asahikawa
Furano
Hidaka-sammyaku
Urakawa
Samani

Teshio
Teshio-sammyaku
Bihoro
Biei
Iwamizawa
Yubari
Mukawa

Wakkanai
Rumoi
Mashike

Rebun-tō
Rishiri-tō

HOKKAIDŌ
Otaru
SAPPORO
Tomakomai
Muroran

Ishikari-
wan
Shakotan-misaki
Yakumo

Uchiura-
wan

Esan-misaki
Shiriya-saki
Oma-saki
Hakodate
Shimokita
Mutsu

Setana
Matsumae
Tappi-saki
Aomori
Towada
Hachinohe

Okushiri-tō
Kodomari
Goshogawara
1625
Akita
Towada
Noshiro
Oga

Tobi-shima

La Pérouse Strait
(Soya-kaikyo)
(Soya-misaki)

Mys Krilon
Zaliv Aniva

Sakhalin
Yuzhno-Sakhalinsk
Korsakov
Mys Aniva
Ozernovskoye
Firsovo
Dolinsk
Starodubskoye
Vostochnyy
Pugachevo
Mys Anlva

Yuzhno-Kamyshovyy Khrebet
Kholmsk
Nevel'sk
Gornozavodsk
Shebunino

Tomari
Chekhov
Il'inskiy
Krasnogorsk
Koppi

Ostrov Moneron

Mys Yegorova

Svetlaya

Adzhima

Nel'ma
Mys Zolotoy
Samarga
Yedinka

Grossevichi

Kuznetsovo
Maksimovka

Mys Sosunova

Angu
Velikaya Kema

Mys Belkina

B. TARDOKI-YANI
2078
Chukon

GORA KO
2006

Koppi

U.   S.   S.   R.

Khabarovsk

Svetlaya

Katen

Bikin

Sidatun
Vasya-Polyana
Plastun
Rudnaya Pristan'

PRIMORSKIY
Imman

KRAY

Dal'nerechensk

Kirovskiy

Verkhne-Imantsky
Krasnorechenskiy
Rudny
Olga
Mys Ostrovnoy
Margaritovo
Valentin

Nakhodka

Vladivostok

O Russkiy
Zaliv
Petra Velikogo

SEA   OF   JAPAN

SEA   OF   JAPAN

HEILONGJIANG

CHINA

Jiamusi

Mudanjiang

YEVREYSKAYA AO

JILIN

Changbai Shan
Chang Bai Ling

NORTH
KOREA

Ch'ŏngjin

Choson-Man

Miller Oblated Stereographic Projection

1:4,500,000

| 0 | 50 | 100 | 150 | 200 | 250 | 300 KILOMETRES |

| 0 | 50 | 100 | 150 | 200 STATUTE MILES |

© COLOUR LIBRARY BOOKS

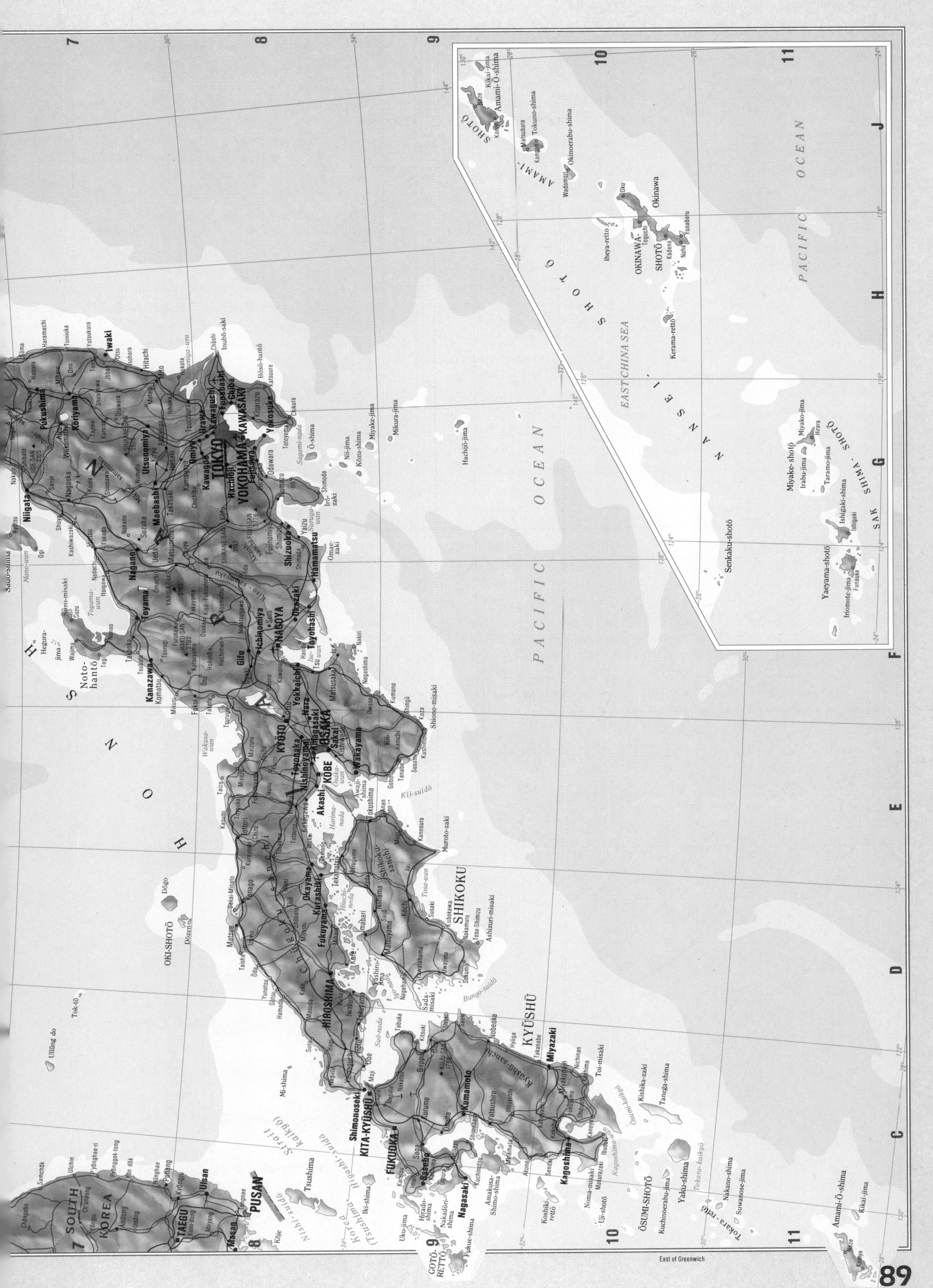

SOUTH-EAST ASIA

Mercator Projection

1:12,000,000

© COLOUR LIBRARY BOOKS

KAOHSIUNG Pingtung **TAIWAN** **G** **H** **J** **K** **L**

Bashi Haixia

Itbayat Batan
Basco Islands
Batan
Luzon
Strait
Balintang Channel

Babuyan
Calayan Babuyan Islands
Dalupiri Camiguin
Fuga
Mayraira Point Babuyan Chan.
Bangui Cape Engaño
Laoag San Vincente
Aparri

Vigan Tuguegarao
Bontoc Ilagan
Tagudin MT. PULOG Palanan Point

Luzon
San Fernando
Bolinao Baguio Casiguran
Lingayen Cabanatuan
San Carlos Baler Cape San Ildefonso

Iba Angeles San Fernando Polillo Islands
Olongapo Valenzuela Lamon Bay
MANILA **QUEZON CITY**
Cavite Pasig Calagua Islands
Muntinlupa San Pablo
Lubang Batangas Daet Catanduanes
Islands Lucena Naga Pandan
Cape Calavite Mamburao Boac Mulanay Virac
Mindoro Calapan Legaspi Sorsogon
MT. HALCON Romblon Burias Laoang Cape Espiritu Santo
SIBUYAN Sibuyan Masbate Oras
Calamian Busuanga *SEA* Jose Tablas Catarman **Samar**
Group Semirara Mandaon Calbayog Borongan
Culion Islands Pandan Roxas Catbalogan Guiuan
Crawford Point El Nido Cuyo San Jose *VISAYAN* Catbalogan
Islands de Buenavista *SEA* Tacloban
Dalanganem Taytay Islands Dao Cadiz Bogo **Leyte**
Islands **Panay** **Iloilo** **Bacolod** *Leyte Gulf*
Barton Dumaran Bayo Point Cebu Maasin Dinagat
Cagayan Islands **Cebu** Siargao
Puerto Princesa **Negros** Bohol Cauit Point
Aborlan Sipalay Tagbilaran *BOHOL* Tandag
Palawan Dumaguete Siquijor Camiguin Butuan *SEA*
Tubbataha Reefs Tagolo Point Surigao
Tubbataha Reefs Dipolog Oroquieta Iligan Bislig
SULU SEA Liloy MT. DAPIAN Malaybalay
Siocon Pagadian **Cagayan de Oro**
Cagayan Sulu **Mindanao**
Pangutaran Cotabato **Davao** Tagum
Group Datu Piang Mati
Zamboanga Basilan *Moro Gulf* Lebak
Jolo Basilan Cape San Agustin
Samales Kiamba General Santos
Tapul Group
Sandakan Group Jolo Tinaca Point
Bambing Tawitawi
Group *Sulu Archipelago*

Kepulauan Kepulauan Nanusa
Karkaralong Karakelong
Kepulauan
Salebabu **Talaud**
Kaburuang

PACIFIC

OCEAN

Ulithi Atoll

Yap Is.

Ngulu Atoll

Palau
Islands Babelthuap

C a r o l i n e   I s l a n d s
(U.S.A. Trust Territory of the Pacific Islands)

Sonsorol Is.

Pulo
Anna
Merir

Tobi Helen I.

LAUT

SULAWESI

Siau
Tahulandang
Biaro

Tg. Polisan

Minahassa Peninsula Manado Kema
Tg. Arus Tolitoli Tondano
Tg. Mangkalihat Issimu Boroko
Tomini Kotamubagu
G. OGOMAS Moutong Belang
2565 Marisa Gorontalo

Kepulauan
Togian
Donggala Parigi Ampana
Luwuk Sukon
Tg. Pemali
Poso Tataba Peleng
Tg. Lereh Sabulu Banggai
Budungbudung Paso Kepulauan
Sulawesi Wotu Banggai
(Celebes) Teluk Tolo
Mamuju Kolonodale
Mamuju Densongi
Majene

N

ujung Pandang
(Makassar) LIMPOBOTTANG

Kepulauan
Salabana

LAUT FLORES

G. TAMBORA
2821
umbawa

Sumba

G

G. GAMKUNORO
1635
Jailolo **Halmahera**
Ternate Maba
Soa-Siu Weda Patani
Maidi Cenga

Kasiruta *LAUT*
Labuha *HALMAHERA*
Bacan Guaedidalem

Tg. Libobo

Mangole Kepulauan
Taliabu **Obi**
Kepulauan Sula Sanana
Tg. Waka Lisabata
Tg. Palpetu Piru Waha
Fogi Namlea Wasisi Bergoi Hoti
Buru Amahai
Tifu Masohi **Seram**
Ambon **(Ceram)**
Kepulauan
Gorong
Kepulauan
Banda
Kepulauan
Watubela

Waigeo Natabu
Selat Dampier
Sorong Mega KWOKA
Salawati Klamono 3060
Seget Konda
Misoöl Mogoi
Inanwatan Arandai
Teluk Berau
Kokas
Faklak Weri
Ibonma
Karufa Kwatisore

New Guinea

Mubrani Manokwari Korido
Mega Ransiki Biak
Mogoi Wasian Yapen
Arandai Wasior Serui
Ransiki *Teluk Cendrawasih*
Waren Barapasai

IRIAN JAYA
Pegunungan Van Rees
Umari Wanapiri
Kokenau
Uta
Pirimapun

Kepulauan
Tayancu Tual Kai Besar
Dobo Banda Elat
Kai Kecil Tg. Wecuar
Rebb **Kepulauan**
Aru
Wokam Kobroor
Trangan

Nila
Teun
Wuliaru Kepulauan
Larat Tanimbar
Damar Babar Yamdena
Kepulauan Amdassa
Babar Selaru Saumlakki
Tg. Ngabordamlu

LAUT **BANDA**

Wetar Kisar Moa
Romang Ilwaki
Iliwaki Sagres
Kepulauan Barat Daya
Atauro *Selat Wetar* Baukau
Dili Loré
Maubara Ilomar
Timor
Hatohudo
Kefamenanu Tilomar
Kupang Roti *LAUT* **TIMOR**

LAUT SAWU

LAUT **ARAFURA**

Tg. Deyong Mappi
Tg. Dolak
Pulau Jos Sodarso
(Dolak)
Tg. Vals

Komoran

Merauke

Jayapura Genyem Vanimo
Sarmi Aitapé
Green River
PK. JAYA Kubkain
G. LEONARD DARWIN PAPUA
Peg. Jayawijaya PK. YAMIN NEW
Pegunungan Maoke 4595 GUINEA
PK. TRIKORA Nomad
PK. MANDALA
Lake Murray

Morehead

91

East of Greenwich

Designed and produced by E.S.R.

Miller Oblated Stereographic Projection

© COLOUR LIBRARY BOOKS

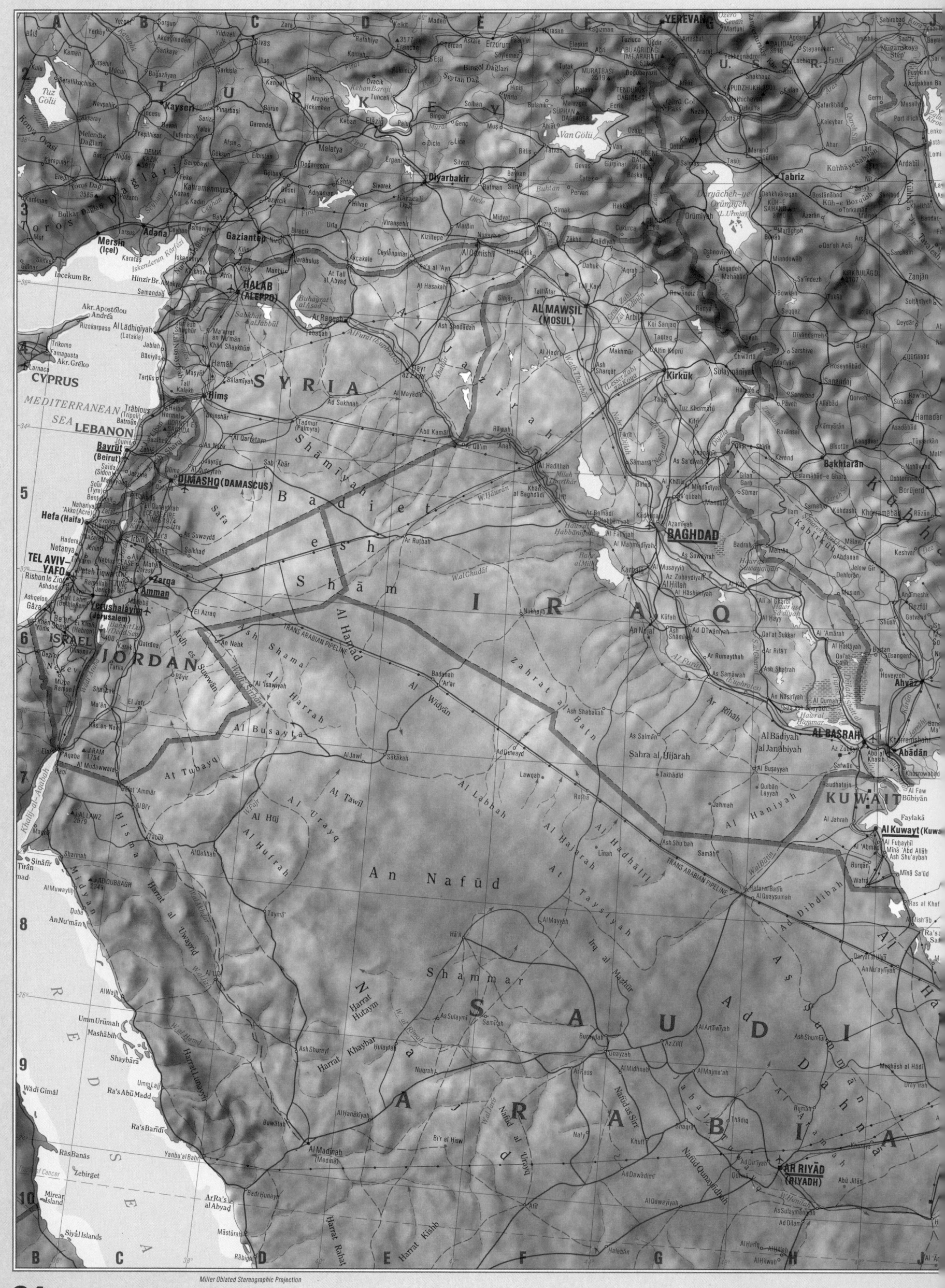

Miller Oblated Stereographic Projection

1:6,000,000

| 0 | 50 | 100 | 150 | 200 | 250 | 300 | 350 | 400 | 450 | 500 KIL. |

| 0 | 50 | 100 | 150 | 200 | 250 | 300 STATUTE |

© COLOUR LIBRARY BOOKS

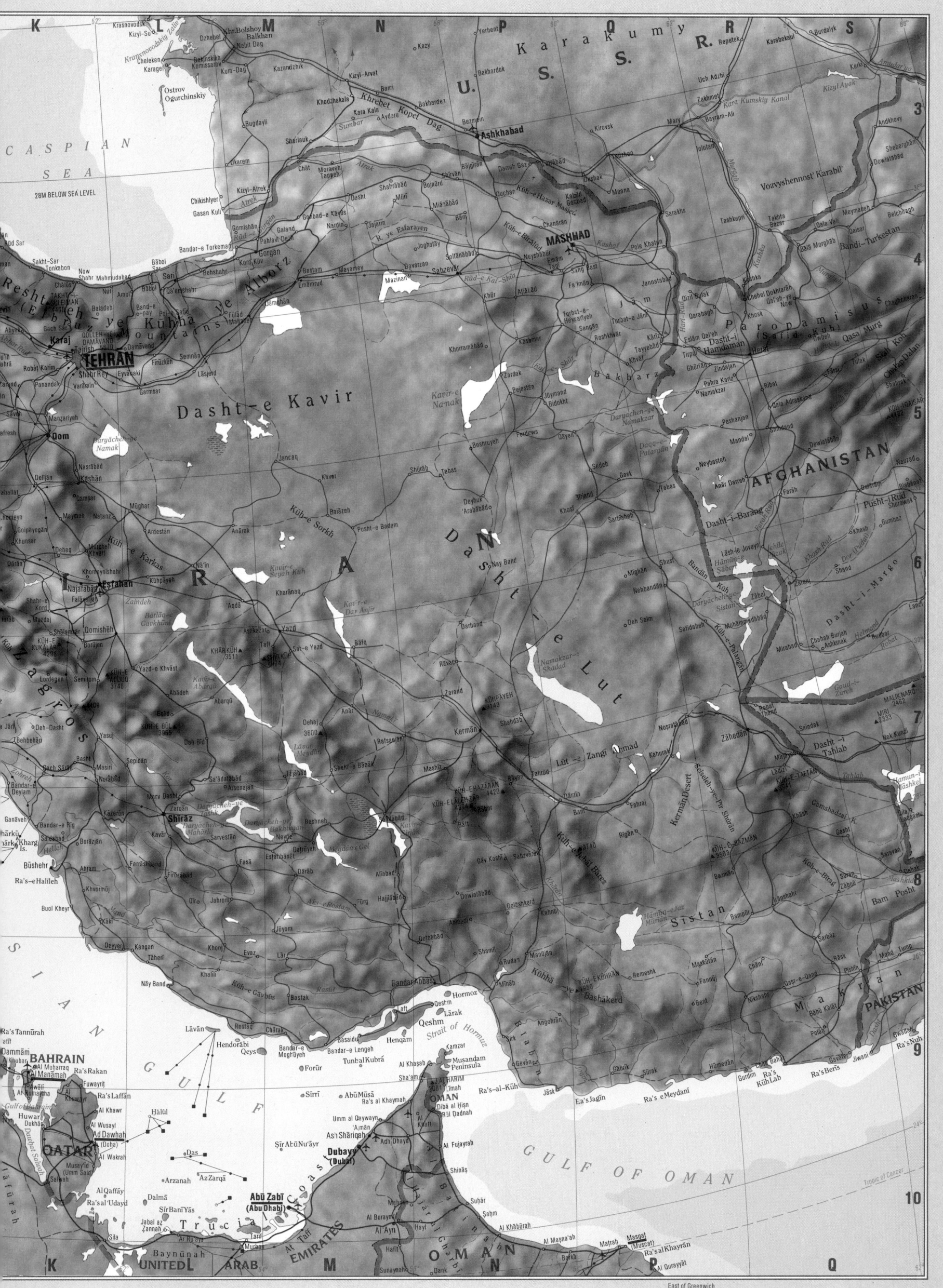

Designed and produced by E.S.R.

East of Greenwich

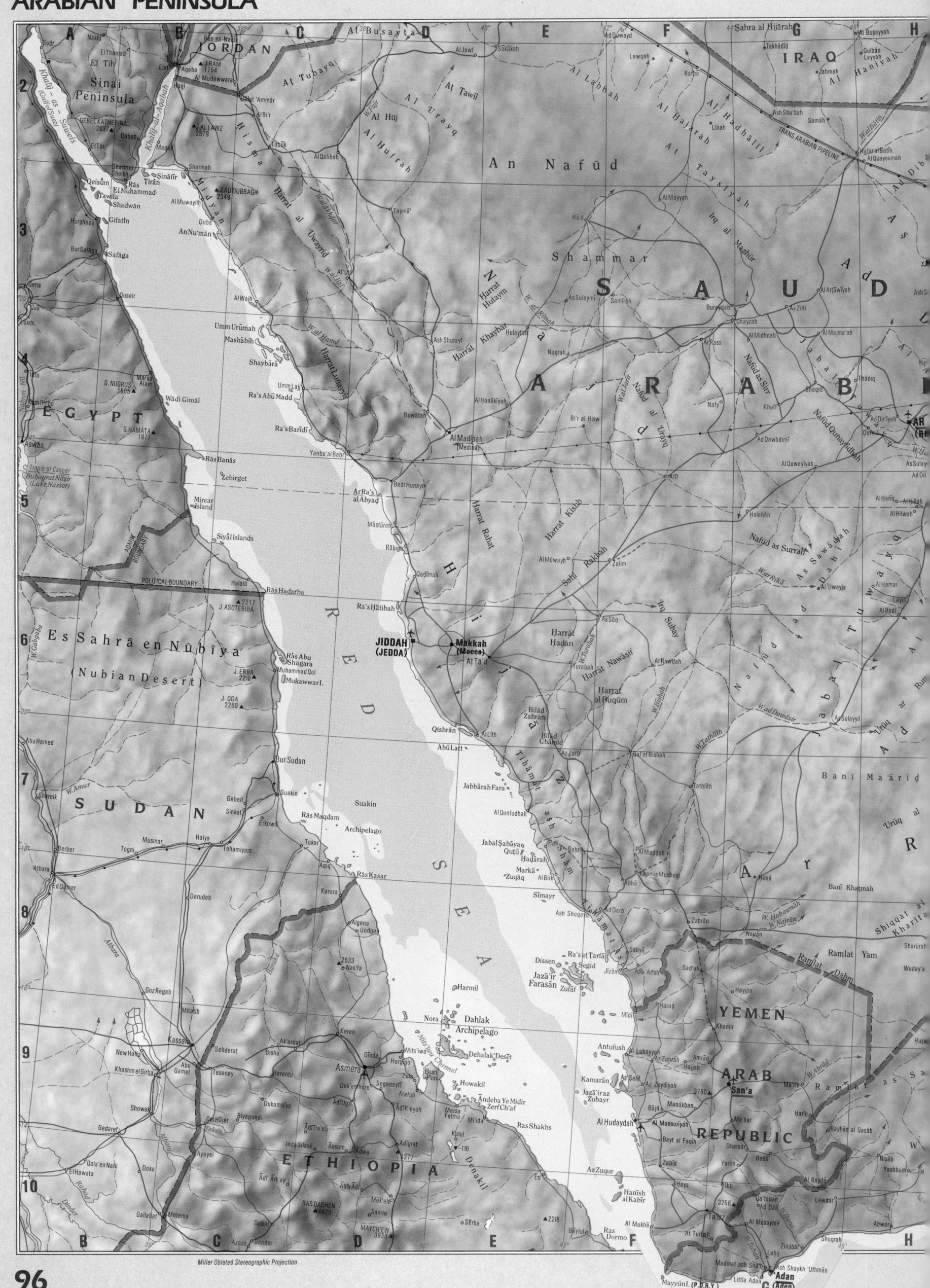

Miller Oblated Stereographic Projection

© COLOUR LIBRARY BOOKS

Miller Oblated Stereographic Projection

1:23,000,000

© COLOUR LIBRARY BOOKS

	0	250	500	750	1000	1250	1500	KILOMETRES
	0	100	200	300	400	500	600	700	800	900	1000 STATUTE MILES

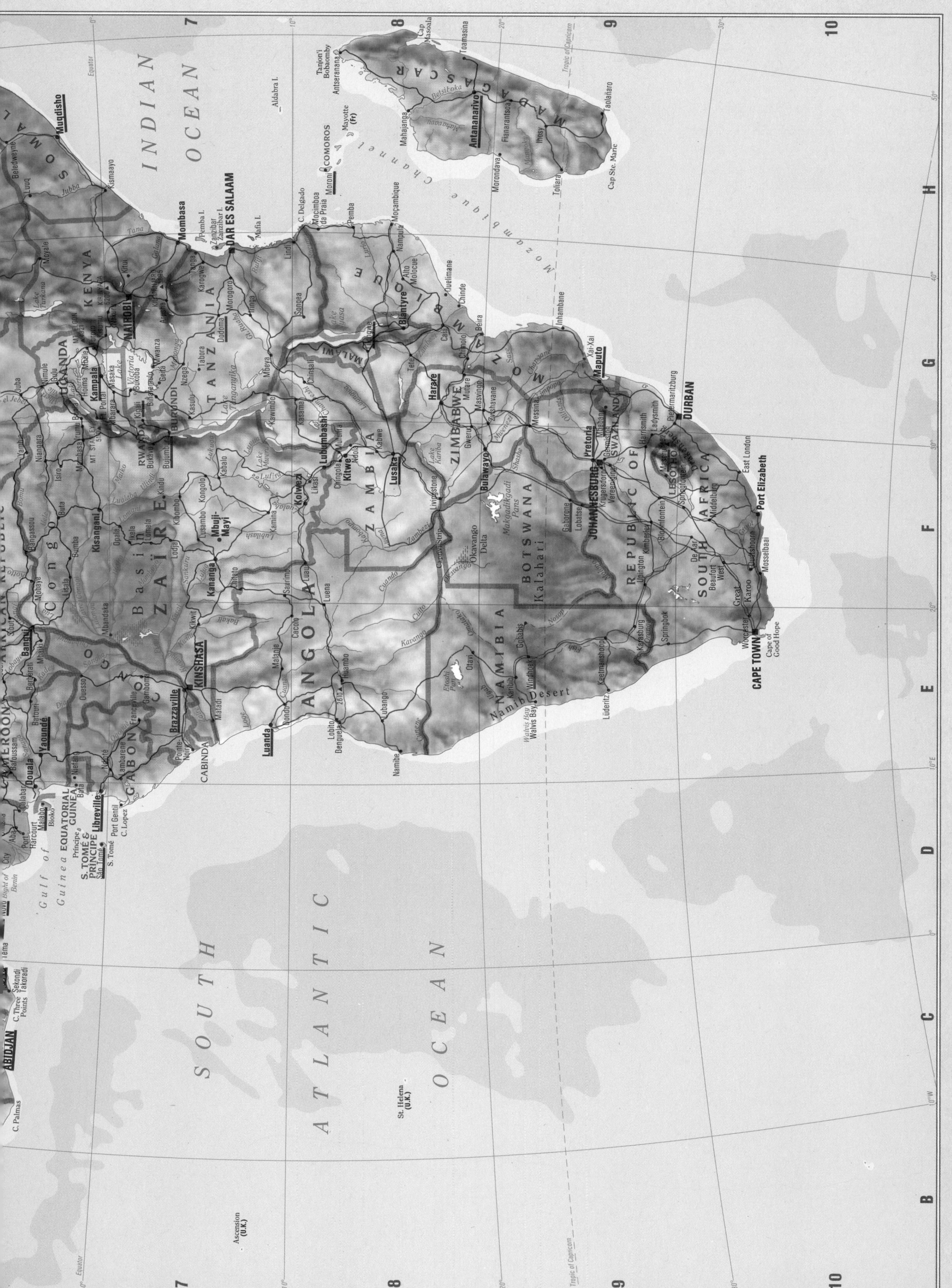

Designed and produced by E.S.R.

Miller Oblated Stereographic Projection   West of Greenwich

1:9,000,000

© COLOUR LIBRARY BOOKS

MEDITERRANEAN SEA

GREECE

Rodhos

Kastélli Khaniá Iráklion Sitía
Kríti
(Crete)

ITALY
Sicilia
(Sicily) Catania
Siracusa
Agrigento
Ragusa

MALTA
Valletta

Pantelleria
(Italy)

Linosa
(Italy)

Lampedusa
(Italy)

DJAZAÏR
(ALGIERS)

Cap Bougaroun
Dellys
Jijel Skikda 'Annaba
Bejaïa Guelma
Blida Tizi
Medea Ouzou
Constantine Souk Ahras
Sétif El Eulma
Bou Saâda Batna Aïn Beïda (Daou)
Khenchela Tébessa

Bizerte
Mateur
Béja Tunis
Kabeul
Sousse
Monastir
Mahdia

TUNISIA

Cap Bon
Kelibia

Tarābulus
(Tripoli)
Al Khums
Zliten
Misrātah

Banghāzī
(Benghazi)

Al Jabal al Akhdar
Shahhat (Cyrene)
Al Bayda Al Qubbah
Darnah (Derna)
Ras al Muraysah
Tubruq
As Sallūm Sidi Barram Matrūh

EGYPT

Es Sahra'el
Gharbīya
(Western Desert)

Gulf of Sirte

Sabkhat
Tāwurgha

Surt
(Sirte)

Ajdābiyā

Qaminis

Ed-Déffa

Munkhafed
el Qattāra
-133
(Qattāra
Depression)

Al Jaghbūb

Siwa

L I B Y A

Libyan

Desert

Grand Erg Oriental

El Golea

Ghadāmis

Al Hammādah
al Hamrā'

Waddān

Brāk

Al Fuqahā'
(Uled Saïdan)

Sabhā

Awbārī

Murzuq

Tāzirbū

Ramlat Rabyānah

Al Khufrah
(Al Jawf)

Idhān Murzuq

Ghāt

Tassili
N'Ajjer

Djanet
(Fort Charlet)

MT TAHAT
2918

Tamanrasset

Hoggar

Tassili
Oua-n
Ahagar

Meniet

In Ekker

S a h a r a

Toummo
(Bi'r al Wa'r)

PIC TOUSSIDE
3295

Bardaï

Zouar

Tibesti

Jef Jef
el Kebir

Ténéré du
Tafassásset

Djado

Bilma

Ounianga Kébir

Depression
du Mourdi

Grand Erg
de Bilma

Faya-Largeau

Fada

Ennedi

Aïr
(Azbine)

Agadez

N I G E R

Djourab

C H A D

Oum Chalouba

Biltine Guéréda

Abéché

Kutum JEBEL
GURGEÏ
2391

SUDAN

JEBEL
MARRA
3070

Tahoua

Dakoro

Zinder

Tanout

Nguigmi

Mao

N'Gouri

Moussoro

Ati

Adré Geneina

Goz Beïda

Zalingei

Birni n' Konni

Madaoua

Tessaoua

Gouré

Diffa
Maïné
Seroa

Lake Chad
(Lac Tchad)

Bol

Massakori

Bokoro

Mongo

Abou Deïa

Am Timan

Birao

NIGERIA

Kano

Katsina

Maïduguri

Ndjamena (Ft. Lamy)

CENTRAL AFRICAN
REPUBLIC

CAMEROON

East of Greenwich

101

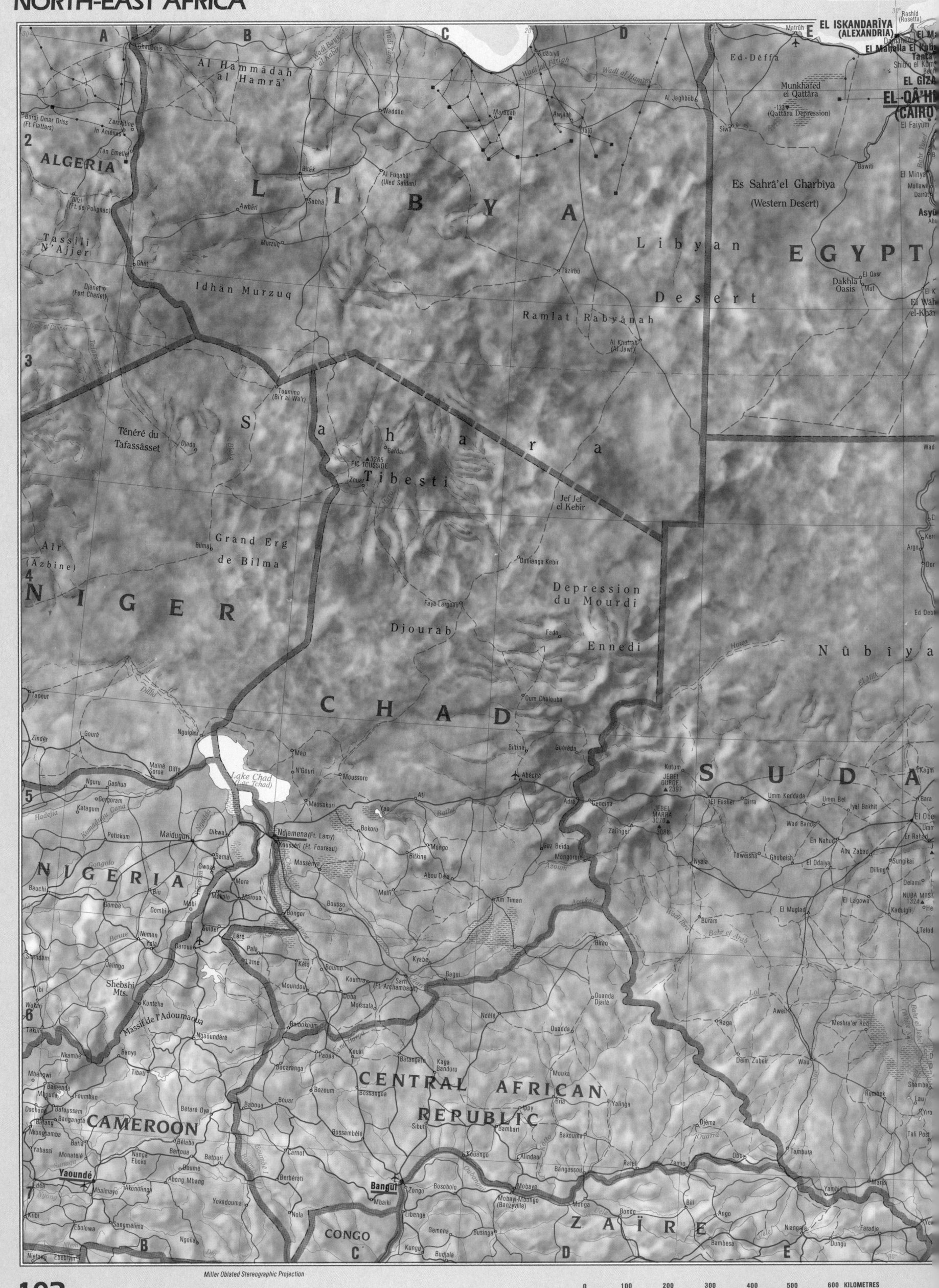

Miller Oblated Stereographic Projection

1:9,000,000

| 0 | 100 | 200 | 300 | 400 | 500 | 600 | KILOMETRES |

| 0 | 50 | 100 | 150 | 200 | 250 | 300 | 350 | 400 | STATUTE MILES |

© COLOUR LIBRARY BOOKS

WESTERN SAHARA

MAURITANIA

MALI

S a

Nouakchott

SENEGAL

Cape Vert
Dakar

THE GAMBIA

Banjul
(Bathurst)

GUINEA
BISSAU

Bissau

Arquipelago
dos Bijagos

GUINEA

Labé

Conakry

SIERRA
LEONE

Freetown

Sherbro Island

Nzérékoré

LIBERIA

Monrovia

Kankan

Bamako

BURKINA FASO

Ouagadougou

IVORY COAST

GHANA

Kumasi

ABIDJAN

Accra

Cape Three Points

A T L A N T I C

O C E A N

B

Santo
Antão

Porto Novo
Mindelo
São Vincente

São Nicolau

CAPE
VERDE

Fogo

Brava

São
Tiago

Praia

Sal

Boa Vista

Maio

C

Equator

Miller Oblated Stereographic Projection

West of Greenwich

1:9,000,000

0   100   200   300   400   500   600 KILOMETRES
0   50 100 150 200 250 300 350 400 STATUTE MILES

© COLOUR LIBRARY BOOKS

Designed and produced by E.S.R.

EQUATORIAL AFRICA

Miller Oblated Stereographic Projection

1:9,000,000

© COLOUR LIBRARY BOOKS

| 0 | 100 | 200 | 300 | 400 | 500 | 600 KILOMETRES |

| 0 | 50 | 100 | 150 | 200 | 250 | 300 | 350 | 400 STATUTE MILES |

Designed and produced by E.S.R.

East of Greenwich

SOUTHERN AFRICA

Miller Oblated Stereographic Projection

1:9,000,000

© COLOUR LIBRARY BOOKS

0 100 200 300 400 500 600 KILOMETRES

0 50 100 150 200 250 300 350 400 STATUTE MILES

TANZANIA

MALAWI

MOZAMBIQUE

COMOROS
Moroni
Grande
Comore
Moheli
Anjouan
Dzaoudzi
Mayotte
(France)

Juan de Nova
(France)

Bassas
da India
(France)

I. de l'Europa
(France)

I. do Bazaruto
I. Benguérua
Vilanculos
P. S. Sebastião

Tanjon'i Bobaomby
Antseranana
(Diégo-Suarez)
Nosy
Mitsio
Nosy Bé
Hell-Ville
Ambilobe
Vohimarina
(Vohémar)
Ambanja
Massif du
▲2876
Tsaratanana
Sambava
Bealanana
Analalava
Antsohihy
Andapa
Antalaha
Befandriana
Moreantsetra
Port-
Bergé
Sofia
C. Masoala
Mahajanga
Marovoay
Mananara
Soalala
Ambato-Boeny
Miarinrivo
Nosy Boraha
(Sainte-Marie)
Mahabe
Tsaratanana
Ambodifototra
Maevatanana
Stampiky
Fenoarivo Atsinanana
Maintirano
Morafenobe
A'tomainty
Ankazobe
Betsiboka
Toamasina
(Tamatave)
Antsalova
Bekopaka
Tsiroanomandidy
Anjozorobe
Mofomango
Andevoranto
Antananarivo
(Tananarive)
Murinarivo
Arivonimamo
Ambatolampy
Soavinandriana
Vatomandry
Anosibe
an'Ala
Belo-Tsiribihina
Betafo
Antsirabe
Morondava
Mahabo
Fandriana
Marolambo
Ambositra
Mananjara
Nosy-Varika
A'tofinandrahana
Tsitondroina
Fianarantsoa
Ifanadiana
Marja
Ankilliabo
Beroroha
Vohilaza
Ikongo
Manakara
Morombe
Mangoky
Ambalavao
Manakara
Vohipeno
Ankazoabo
Ihosy
Farafangana
Fitsitika
Vangaindrano
Tsiliara
(Tuléar)
Betroka
Soalara
Onilahy
Betioky
Mandrare
Midongy
Atsimo
Bekily
Mf.de l'Ivakoany
1956
Beampingaratra
Itampolo
Ampanihy
Amboyombe
Taolañaro
(Fort Dauphin)
C. Sainte Marie
Faux Cap

MADAGASCAR
Plateau du Bemaraha
Massif du Makay
Andringitra

INDIAN

OCEAN

MAURITIUS
Port Louis
Beau Bassin
Curepipe
Mahébourg
Réunion
(France)
St. Denis
St. Benoît
St. Pierre
Mascarene
Islands

Tropic of Capricorn

East of Greenwich

109

Designed and produced by E.S.R.

Bonne Projection

East of Greenwich

1:19,000,000

| 0 | 200 | 400 | 600 | 800 KILOMETRES |

| 0 | 100 | 200 | 300 | 400 | 500 STATUTE MILES |

© COLOUR LIBRARY BOOKS

N P Q R S T U V W

NAURU
Banaba

Gilbert Islands (Kiribati)
Nonouti
Beru
Nukunau
Kingsmill Group
Onotoa
Tamana
Arorae

Howland I.
Baker I. (U.S.A.)

KIRIBATI

Winslow Reef

Equator

ailau Tauu Is.
Nukumanu Is.

Kanton I.
McKean I. Birnie I. Enderbury I.
Rawaki
Nikumaroro Orona Manra

inville
Ontong Java Atoll

Nanumea
Niutao
Nanumanga

Carondelet Reef
Phoenix Islands (Kiribati)

2

SOLOMON
Choiseul
ISLANDS
New Georgia Santa Isabel
Vangunu
Russell Is. Malaita
Florida Is. Honiara Maramasike
Guadalcanal
San Cristóbal
Stewart Is.

Nui
Vaitupu
Nukufetau

5°

3

Reef
Indispensable Reefs
Rennell I.

Nupani Swallow Is.
Tinakula
Ndeni
Utupua
Vanikoro Is.
Cherry
Tikopia
Mitre
Santa Cruz Is.

Duff Is.

Funafuti
TUVALU
Nukulaelae

Niulakita

Tokelau (N.Z.)
Atafu
Nukunono
Fakaofo

3

Reef

Torres Is. Vot Tandé
Ureparapara
Vanua Lava **Banks**
Santa Maria **Islands**
Cap Nahoi Méré Lava
Espíritu Aoba Maéwo
Santo
Malo Pentecost I.
Malakula Ambrym
VANUATU Épi
Shepherd Is.

Rotuma
Eaglestone Reef

Iles Wallis (Fr.)
Uvea

WESTERN SAMOA
Swains I.

Pukapuka
Nassau

10°

4

Iles Chesterfield (Fr.)
Sable
Récifs d'Entrecasteaux
Iles Bélep

Éfaté
Vila
Erromango

Tanna

Futuna **Iles de Horn (Fr.)**
Alofi

Vanua Levu
Yasawa
Group
FIJI Taveuni **Lau**
Nadi Koro **Group**
Viti Levu Gau
Suva Lakeba
Kadavu

Niuafo'ou
Tafahi
'Niuatoputapu

Savaii **S a m o a n I s.** Manua
Upolu Apia Tau Rose I.
Tutuila

Suvorov I.

Cook Islands
(New Zealand)

MT. PANIÉ
1628
Ouvéa
Lifou
Bourail
Nouvelle Thio
Calédonie
(France) Maré
Nouméa
Ile des Pins
Is. Loyauté (Fr.)

Walpole
Matthew
Hunter

Ceva-i-Ra

Aneityum (Anatom)

Vatoa
Ono-i-Lau
Tuvana-i-Tholo Tuvana-i-Ra

Fonualei
Late Vava'u Group
Kao
Tofua Ha'apai Group
Nomuka
TONGA
Nuku'alofa Tongatapu
Tongatapu 'Eua
Group
Ata

Niue (N.Z.)

Palmerston I.

15°

5

Caye de
l'observatoire
Bellona
Reefs

Minerva Reefs

20°

6

Tropic of Capricorn

Middleton Reef
Elizabeth Reef

Norfolk I.
Philip I.² **(Aust.)**

Raoul

25°

7

Lord Howe I.
(Aust.)

Kermadec Is. (N.Z.)
Macauley I.
'Curtis I.
L'Esperance Rock

Three Kings Is.
C. Maria van Diemen North Cape
Kaitaia

8

S M A N
S E A
Dargaville Whangarei
Great Barrier I.
Auckland Manukau
Hamilton Thames
North Island Rotorua Tauranga
Whakatane East Cape
New Plymouth RUAPEHU Gisborne
2797 Mahia Peninsula
Hawera Napier
Wanganui Hastings
C. Farewell Palmerston
Motueka Picton North Masterton
Westport Blenheim **NEW**
South Island **Wellington** Cook Strait
Greymouth Kaikoura **ZEALAND**
Hokitika Rangiora
COOK Christchurch
4764 Lyttelton
Cascade Pt. Ashburton
L. Wakat Timaru
Southern Oamaru
L. Te Anau C. Saunders
Alexandra Dunedin
C. Providence Gore
Invercargill
Foveaux Strait
Stewart I.

8

35°

9

40°

Chatham Is. (N.Z.)
Pitt I.

Snares Is.

Bounty Is. (N.Z.)

10

Antipodes Is. (N.Z.)

Auckland Is. (N.Z.)

45°

Campbell I. (N.Z.)

11

quarie I.
(Aust.)

P Q R S T U V W X Y Z

West of Greenwich

Miller Oblated Stereographic Projection

1:10,500,000

© COLOUR LIBRARY BOOKS

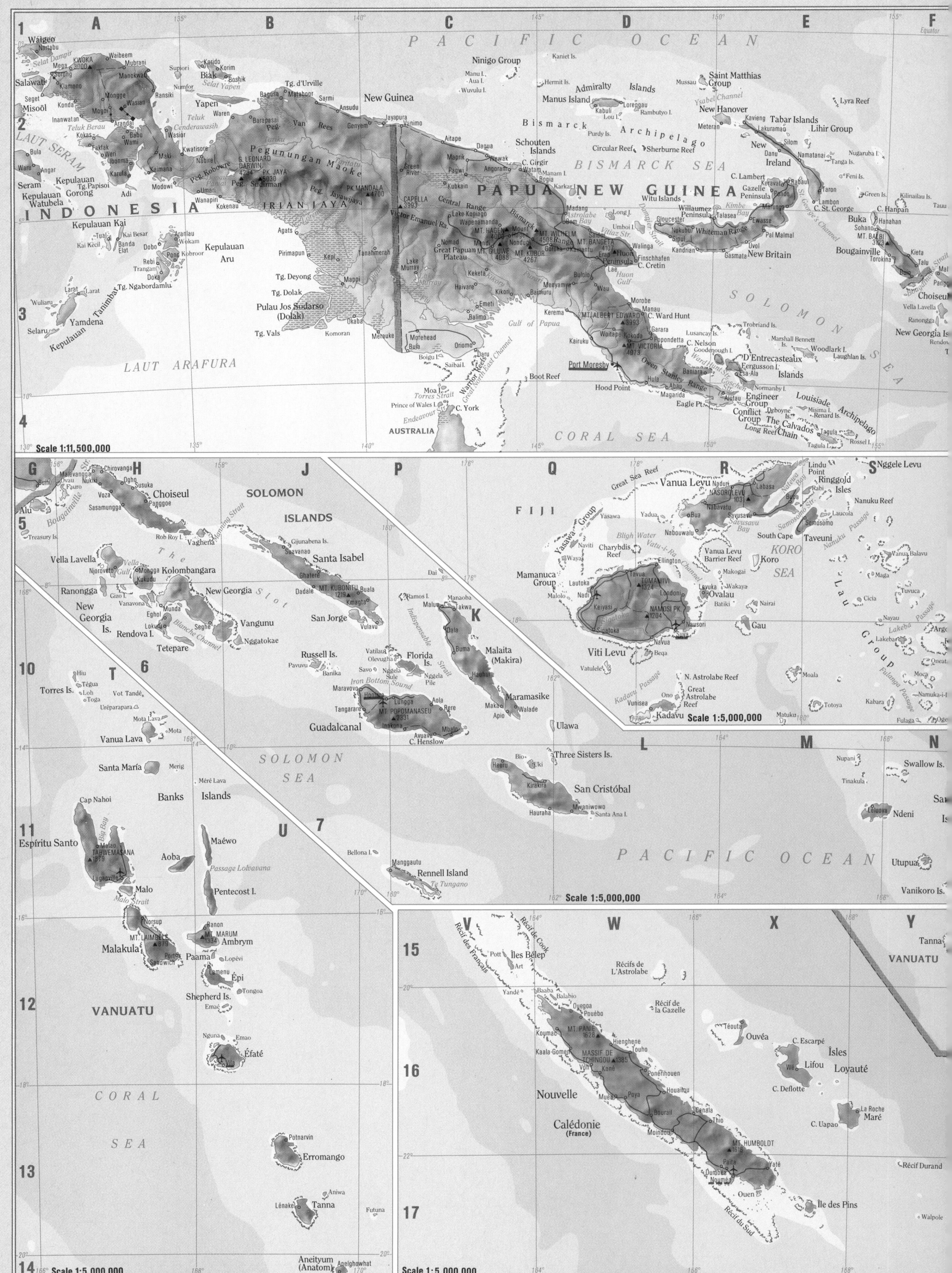

Miller Oblated Stereographic Projection

© COLOUR LIBRARY BOOKS

NEW

ZEALAND

North Island

South Island

TASMAN SEA

PACIFIC OCEAN

1:4,500,000

Lambert Azimuthal Equal Area Projection

1:20,000,000

© COLOUR LIBRARY BOOKS

| 0 100 200 300 400 500 600 700 800 900 1000 KILOMETRES |
| 0 100 200 300 400 500 600 STATUTE MILES |

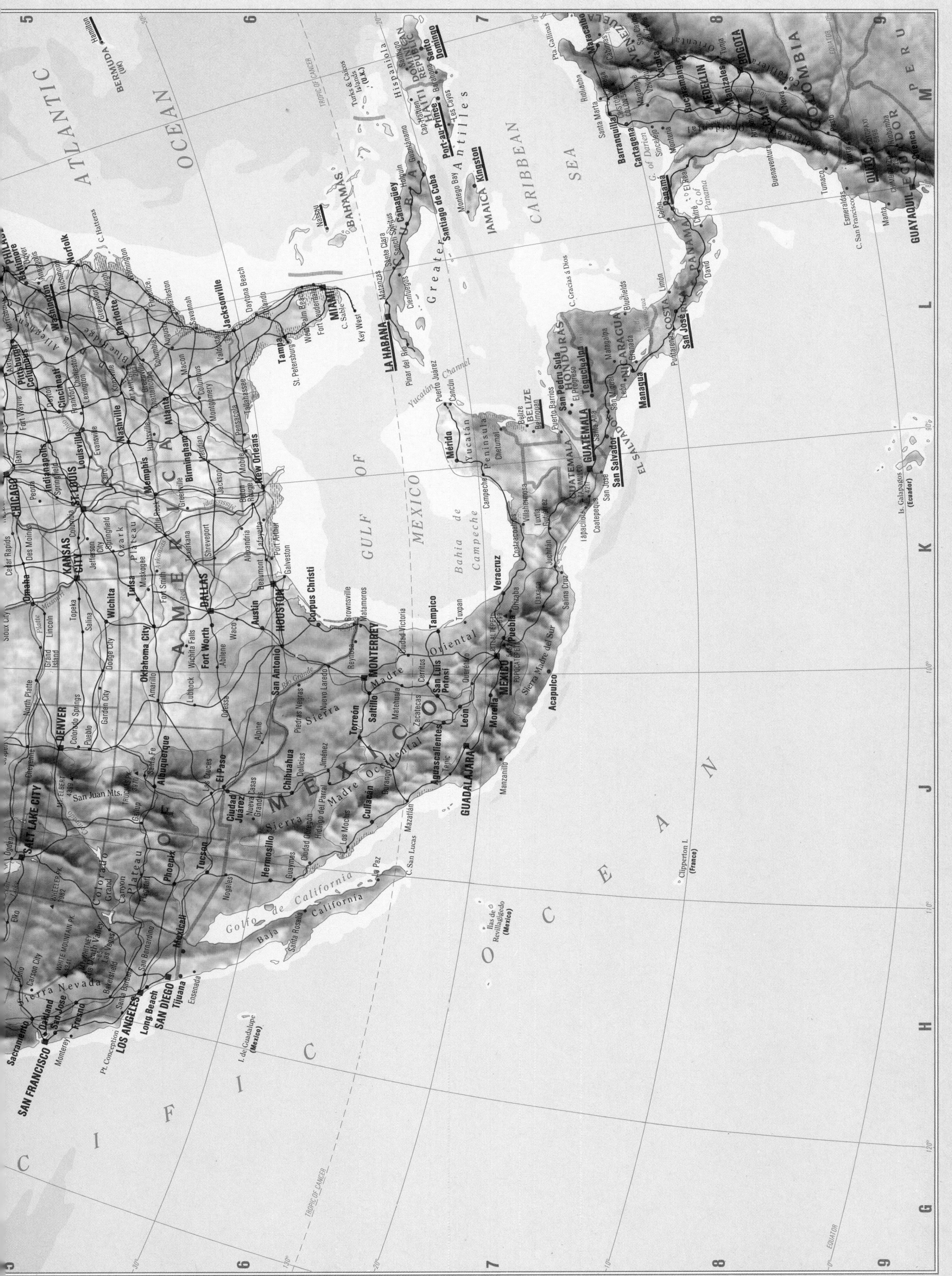

ATLANTIC OCEAN

BERMUDA (UK)

Hamilton

PHILA
Baltimore
Washington
Norfolk
C. Hatteras

Richmond
Raleigh
Greensboro
Charlotte
Wilmington
Columbia
Charleston
Augusta
Savannah
Jacksonville
Daytona Beach
Orlando
Tampa
St. Petersburg
MIAMI
Fort Lauderdale
West Palm Beach
C. Sable
Key West

BAHAMAS
Nassau

Turks & Caicos
Islands (U.K.)

Hispaniola
HAITI DOMINICAN
REPUBLIC
Cap Haïtien
Port-au-Prince
Santo
Domingo

Santiago
San Pedro
Barahona

Lesser Antilles

Pinar del Río
LA HABANA
Matanzas
Santa Clara
Cienfuegos
Sancti Spíritus
C U B A
Camaguey
Holguín
Santiago de Cuba
Guantánamo
Montego Bay
JAMAICA
Kingston

Greater Antilles

CARIBBEAN SEA

Pta. Gallinas
Santa Marta
Barranquilla
Cartagena
Maracaibo
VENEZUELA
Coro
Valencia CARACAS
Maracay

MEDELLÍN
BOGOTÁ
Manizales
Pereira
Ibagué
Cúcuta
Bucaramanga
COLOMBIA

Cordillera Oriental

PERU

QUITO
ECUADOR
GUAYAQUIL

Esmeraldas
Manta
C. San Francisco
Tumaco
Buenaventura
Cali
Neiva

Buga
Palmira

PANAMÁ
Colón
David
Chiré
G. of Darién
G. of Panama
El Real
Limón
Bluefields

COSTA RICA
San José
Puntarenas
NICARAGUA
Managua
Granada
León
Matagalpa
HONDURAS
Tegucigalpa
San Pedro Sula
El Progreso
La Ceiba
C. Gracias á Dios

Yucatán Channel

Puerto Juárez
Cancún
Chetumal
BELIZE
Belize
Belmopan
GUATEMALA
Puerto Barrios
Santa Ana
San Salvador
EL SALVADOR
San Miguel

Mérida
Yucatán Peninsula
Campeche
Ciudad del Carmen
Villahermosa
Coatzacoalcos
Minatitlán
Tuxtla Gutiérrez

Bahía de
Campeche

GULF OF
MEXICO

A M E R I C A

CHICAGO
Gary
Fort Wayne
Indianapolis
Columbus
Cincinnati
Louisville
Lexington
Frankfort
Springfield
St. Louis
KANSAS
CITY
Columbia
Jefferson
City
Cedar Rapids
Des Moines
Omaha
Lincoln
Topeka
Wichita
Tulsa
Springfield
Fort Smith
Muskogee
Oklahoma City
Little Rock
Memphis
Nashville
Birmingham
Atlanta
Montgomery
Columbus
Macon
Jackson
Shreveport
Monroe
Alexandria
Baton Rouge
New Orleans
Mobile
Pensacola
Tallahassee
Jackson
Greenville
Vicksburg
Natchez
Lafayette
Beaumont
Port Arthur
Galveston
HOUSTON
Corpus Christi
Brownsville
Matamoros
DALLAS
Fort Worth
Waco
Austin
San Antonio
Laredo
Nuevo Laredo
Reynosa
MONTERREY
Saltillo
Torreón
Ciudad Victoria
Tampico
Tuxpan
Veracruz
Xalapa
Puebla
MÉXICO
Toluca
Morelia
León
Guadalajara
Aguascalientes
Acapulco

Sierra Madre
Oriental

Sierra Madre del Sur

Oaxaca
Salina Cruz
Tehuantepec
Juchitán

M E X I C O

Sierra Madre Occidental

Chihuahua
Ciudad Juárez
El Paso
Nuevo Casas
Grandes
Hidalgo del Parral
Durango
Zacatecas
Culiacán
Los Mochis
Mazatlán
Tepic
Manzanillo

Hermosillo
Guaymas
Ciudad Obregón
Nogales
Tucson
Phoenix

DENVER
Colorado Springs
Pueblo
Garden City
Dodge City
Wichita Falls
Lubbock
Abilene
Amarillo
Odessa
Alpine
Santa Fe
Albuquerque
Las Cruces
Gallup

SALT LAKE CITY
Provo
Ogden

San Juan Mts.

Colorado
Plateau

Grand
Canyon

WHEELER PK.

SAN FRANCISCO
Sacramento
Oakland
San Jose
Monterey
Fresno
Bakersfield
Los Angeles
Long Beach
San Bernardino
San Diego
Tijuana
Ensenada
Mexicali

Sierra Nevada

I. de Guadalupe
(Mexico)

Golfo de California
Baja California
La Paz
C. San Lucas
Santa Rosalía

PACIFIC OCEAN

Clipperton I.
(France)

Islas de
Revillagigedo
(Mexico)

Is. Galápagos
(Ecuador)

GULF OF MEXICO

TROPIC OF CANCER

EQUATOR

West of Greenwich

117

ALASKA

A | B | C | D | E | F | G | H | J | K

Beaufort Sea

U.S.S.R.

Chukotskiy
Mechigmen
Zalив
Provedeniya
Uelen
C. Dezhneva
M. Chaplina
O. Arakamchechen
Chukchi Sea
Bering Strait
C. Krusenstern
Kotzebue Sound
Kobuk
Noatak

Icy C.
Wainwright
Pt. Franklin
Pt. Barrow
Pt. Barrow
Dease Inlet
Smith B.
C. Halkett
Harrison Bay
Colville
Teshekpuk Lake

De Long Mts.
Baird Mountains
Brooks
Endicott Range Mts.
2869

Prudhoe Bay
Martin Pt. Kaktovik
MT. MICHELSON 2699
Herschel I.
Mackenzie Bay
Richards I.
Tuktoyaktuk

C. Dalhousie
Baillie I.
C. Bathurst
Liverpool B.

BEAUFORT SEA

C. Kellett
Sachs
Amund
Franklin
Parry Pen.
Melv

Gambell
N. Cape
St. Lawrence I.
Savoonga
Northeast C.
Southeast C.
C. Rodney
Nome
Norton Sound
C. Darby
Norton B.
C. Denbigh
Stuart I.
St. Michael
Shaktoolik

Seward Peninsula
Koyuk
Buckland
Selawik L.
Shungnak

ALASKA
(U.S.A.)

MT. BOONERAK
Chandalar
Wiseman
Ray Mts.
Rampart
White Mts.
Fort Yukon
Circle

Davidson Mts.
Old Crow
Fort McPherson
Arctic Red River
Inuvik

INUVIK
Porcupine
Aklavik
1576

N
Franklin Mts.
Fort Good Hope
Norman Wells
Fort Norman

BERING SEA

Southeast C.
BERING SEA

C. Romanzof
Scammon Bay
Hooper Bay
Yukon Delta
Pastol
Mountain Village
Holy Cross
Kaiyuh Mts.
Galena
Koyukuk
Innoko

Fairbanks
Nenana
Delta Junction
Salcha
Eagle
Dawson

Ogilvie Mts.
Keno Hill
Mayo

Mackenzie

YUKON

Keele Pk.

Kuskokwim
Bethel
Kilbuck Mts.
2636
Dillingham
Togiak
C. Newenham
C. Constantine

Kuskokwim Mountains
Sleetmute
Aniak
Stony
Mulchatna

Alaska
MT. McKINLEY
6194
MT. FORAKER
Talkeetna
Talkeetna Mts.
Range
MT. HAYES
4216
MT. KIMBALL
2755
Tok
Northway Junction

MT. SANFORD
4950
McCarthy
MT. BONA
5005

Dawson Range
Carmacks
Ross River
MT. SIR JAMES McBRIEN
2758

Bristol Bay
Ugashik
Port Heiden
Meshik
Pilot Pt.
C. Constantine
Naknek
King Salmon
Iliamna Lake
MT. DENISON
2318
KATMAI VOL. 2047

Augustine I.
Kachemak B.
Kenai
Kenai Peninsula
Kenai Mts.
Seward
Anchorage
MT. MARCUS BAKER
4016
Palmer
Glennallen
Copper Center
Valdez
Cordova
MT. ST. ELIAS
5489
MT. LOGAN
6050

St. Elias Mountains
Kluane
Klukshu
Whitehorse
Carcross
Teslin

Pelly Mountains

Cassiar Mts.

Watson Lake

Aleutian Range
Chignik
Perryville
Seal C.
Sutwik I.
Chirikof I.
MT. GIOTTOF
1643
MT. DENISON
Afognak I.
Kodiak
Kodiak I.
Shelikof Str.
Barren Is.
Pt. Banks
Montague I.
Hinchinbrook
Kayak I.
Prince William Sound
Knight I.
MT. STELLER
3238
Bering Gl.
Icy B.
Malaspina Gl.
Yukutat B.
Yakutat
Dry B.
MT. FAIRWEATHER
4670

Chichagof I.
Cross Sd.
Juneau
DEVILS PAW
2616
White Pass
Skagway
Haines

Teslin

Cassiar Mts.

Coal River
Toad River
1095
MT. ROOSEVELT
2146
CHURCHILL
PK.
Sifton Pass
Dease Lake
Telegraph Creek
Stikine Mts.
Ware

GULF OF ALASKA

PACIFIC

OCEAN

Kruzof I.
Baranof I.
Sitka
Admiralty I.
Kupreanof I.
Kuiu I.
Wrangell
Petersburg

Alexander

Archipelago
C. Ommaney
Coronation I.
Prince of Wales I.
Revillagigedo I.
Ketchikan
Dall I.
C. Muzon

Coast

Mountains
2755
SEVEN SISTERS
Hazelton
Manson Cr.

BRIT

COLUM

Dixon Entrance
C. Knox
Rose Pt.
Prince Rupert
Terrace
Kitimat
Kemano
Stewart
Fort S

Graham I.
Skidegate
Banks I.
Pitt I.
Bella

Queen Charlotte Islands
Moresby I.
Aristazabal I.
Bella Bella

MONARCH
3533
MT. WADDINGTON
4042

Kunghit I.
C. St. James
Queen Charlotte Sound
Calvert I.
C. Scott
C. Cook
Bella Coola
VICTORIA PK.
2163

Vancouver Island
Port Hardy
Port Alice
Courtenay

Bipolar Oblique Conic Conformal Projection

1:9,000,000

© COLOUR LIBRARY BOOKS

| 0 | 100 | 200 | 300 | 400 | 500 | 600 KILOMETRES |
| 0 | 50 | 100 | 150 | 200 | 250 | 300 | 350 | 400 STATUTE MILES |

Inset (Aleutian Islands)

E | F | G | H

Aa | Ab | Ac | Ad | Ae | Af | Ag

St. Paul I.
Pribilof Is.
St. George I.

BERING SEA

Attu I.
Near Islands
Agattu I.
Buldir I.
Bowers Bank
Kiska I.
Segula I.
Little Sitkin I.
Rat Islands
Amchitka I.
Semisopochnoi I.

Aleutian Islands
Tanaga I.
Garefoi I.
Amatignak I.
Kanaga I.
Adak I.
KOROVIN VOL.
1553
Gt. Sitkin I.
Atka I.
Atka
Amlia I.
Seguam I.
Yunaska I.

Andreanof Islands

Islands of the Four Mts.

Umnak I.
MAKUSHIN VOL.
Dutch Harbor
Unalaska I.
Akutan I.
TULIK VOL.
2025
SHISHALDIN VOL.
2856
Unimak I.
False Pass
Sanak I.
Krenitzin Is.

Fox Islands

Alaska Peninsula
Meshik
Nelson Lagoon
Fort Randall
VENIAMINOF VOL.
2507
PAVLOF VOL.
2714
Perryville
Kupreanof Pt.
Shumagin Is.

Aleutian Trench

1:12,500,000

3 | 4 | 5 | 8 | 9 | 6

BERING
SEA

Aleutian Trench

Designed and produced by E.S.R.

West of Greenwich

Bipolar Oblique Conic Conformal Projection

1:9,000,000

| 0 | 100 | 200 | 300 | 400 | 500 | 600 KILOMETRES |

| 0 | 50 | 100 | 150 | 200 | 250 | 300 | 350 | 400 STATUTE MILES |

© COLOUR LIBRARY BOOKS

Designed and produced by E.S.R.

Bipolar Oblique Conic Conformal Projection

1:5,000,000

© COLOUR LIBRARY BOOKS

West of Greenwich

Bipolar Oblique Conic Conformal Projection

1:5,000,000

| 0 | 50 | 100 | 150 | 200 | 250 | 300 | 350 | 400 KILOMETRES |

| 0 | 50 | 100 | 150 | 200 | 250 STATUTE M |

© COLOUR LIBRARY BOOKS

Designed and produced by E.S.R.

1:5,000,000

© COLOUR LIBRARY BOOKS

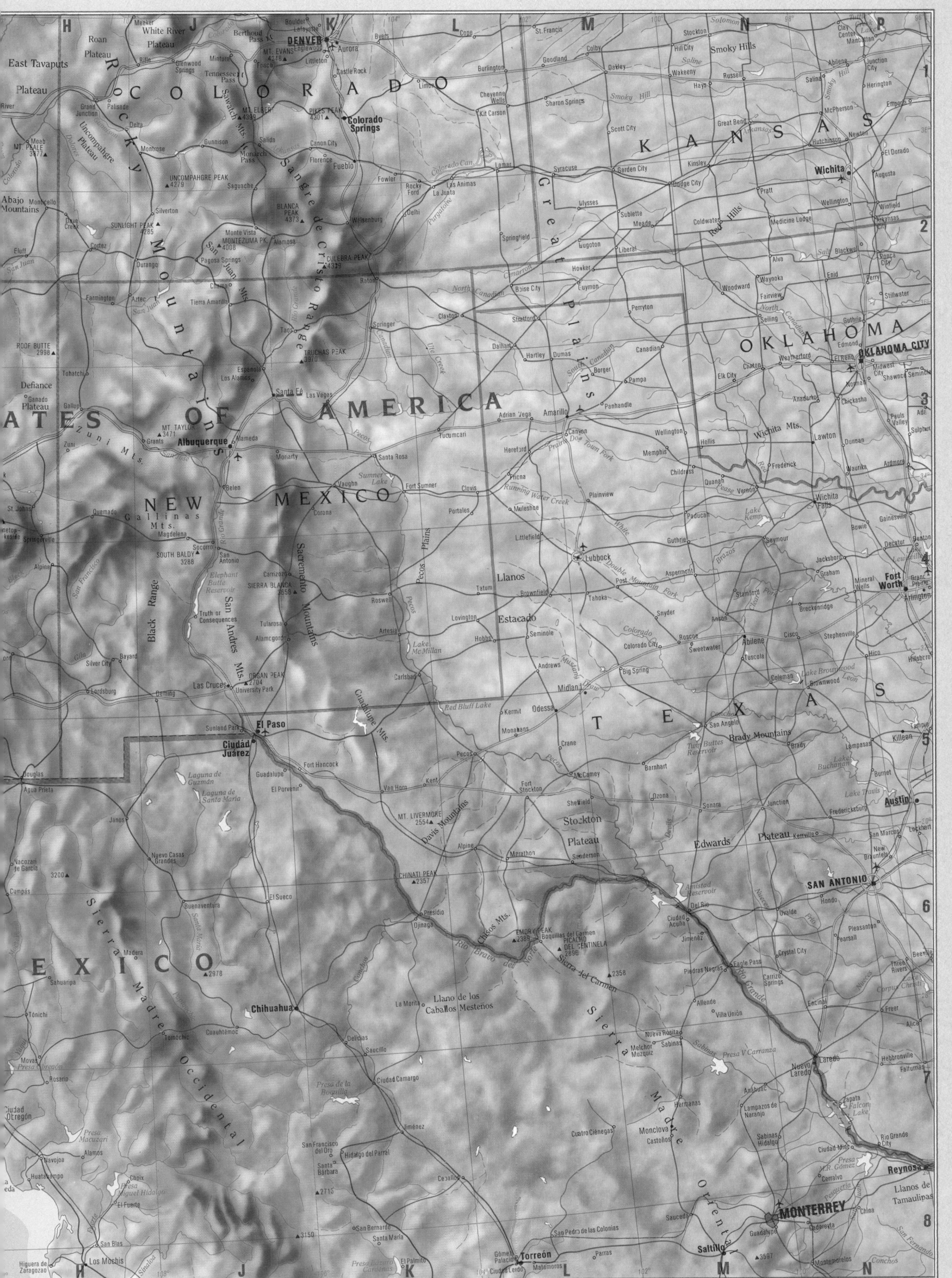

Bipolar Oblique Conic Conformal Projection

West of Greenwich

Designed and produced by E.S.R.

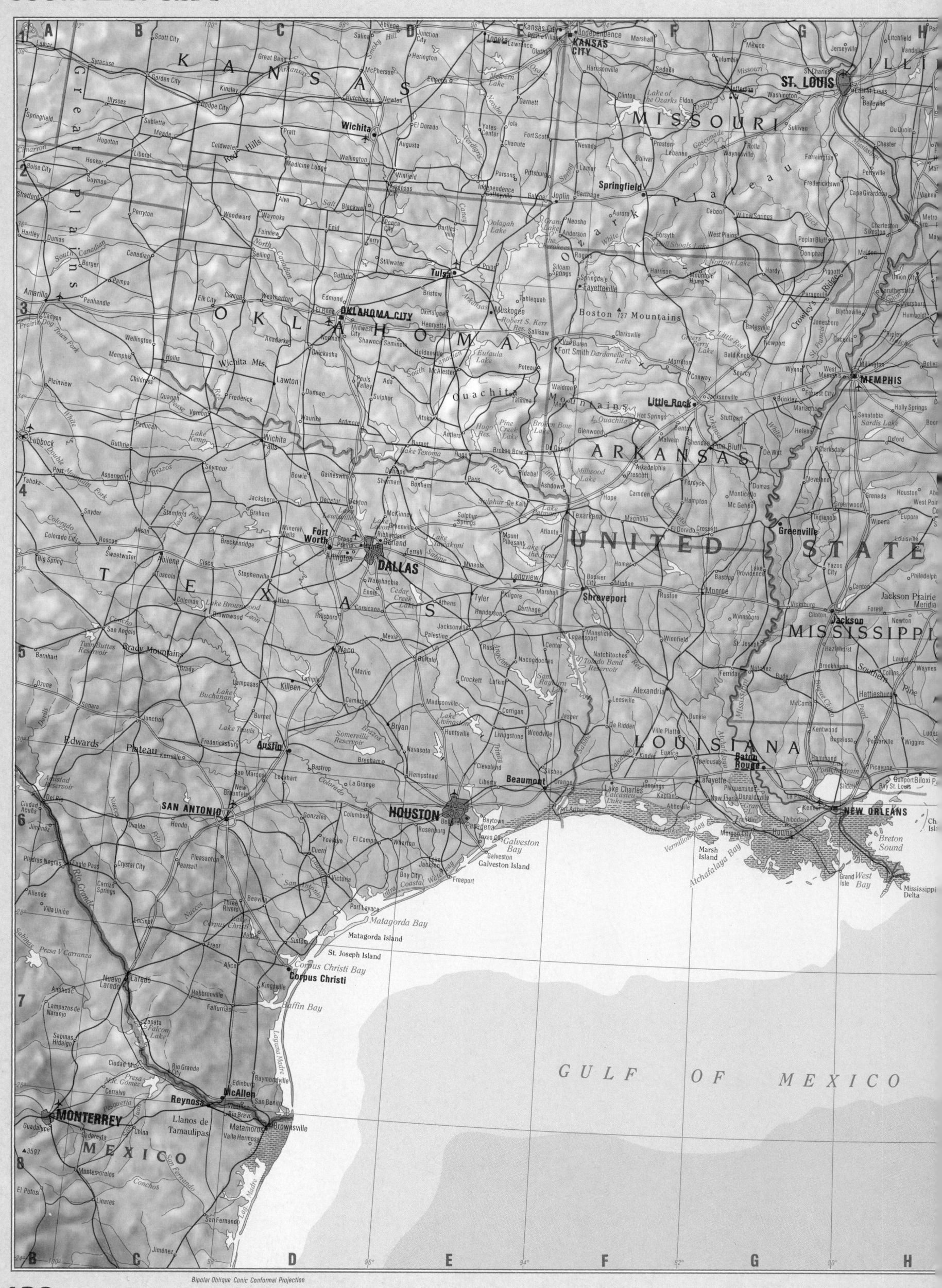

Bipolar Oblique Conic Conformal Projection

1:5,000,000

© COLOUR LIBRARY BOOKS

Designed and produced by E.S.R.

MEXICO

Bipolar Oblique Conic Conformal Projection

1:6,500,000

© COLOUR LIBRARY BOOKS

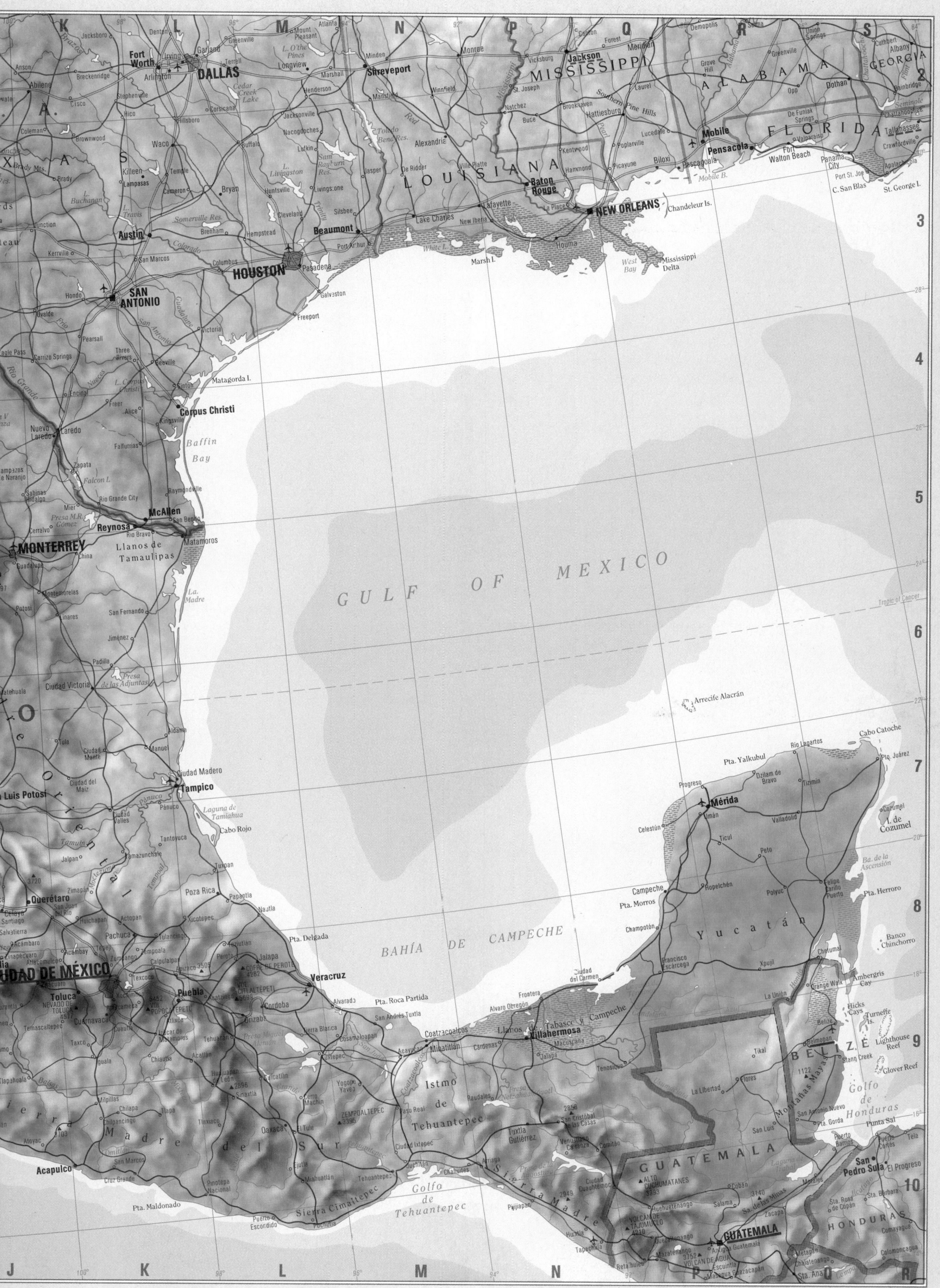

GULF OF MEXICO

BAHÍA DE CAMPECHE

Bipolar Oblique Conic Conformal Projection

1:7,000,000

| 0 | 50 | 100 | 150 | 200 | 250 | 300 | 350 | 400 KILOMETRES |

| 0 | 50 | 100 | 150 | 200 | 250 STATUTE MILES |

© COLOUR LIBRARY BOOKS

ATLANTIC

OCEAN

Tropic of Cancer

BAHAMAS

San Salvador
(Watling I.)

Rum Cay

Long I.
Clarence
Town

Samana Cray

Crooked I. Passage

Crooked I.

Snug
Corner

Mayaguana I.

Acklins I.

Mayaguana
Bay

Hogsty Reef

Caicos Is. (U.K.)

Little
Inagua I.

Turks I. Passage

Turks I. (U.K.)

Salt Cay

Lucrecia

Great
Inagua

Moa

Matthew
Town

Baracoa

Cabo Maisí

Puerto Rico Trench

Guantánamo

Île de la Tortue

Monte
Cristi

C. Isabela

Cap Haïtien

Puerto Plata

Ba. de
Escocesa

Santiago

San Francisco
de Macorís

C. Samaná

Ba. de Samaná

Windward Passage

Golfe de la
Gonâve

Hinche

Cordillera

La Vega

Yuna

Sabana de la Mar

Virgin
Islands

Anegada (U.K.)

Île de la Gonâve

PICO DUARTE

C. Engaño

Aguadilla

Arecibo

SAN JUAN

St Thomas
(U.S.A.)

Road
Town

Virgin Gorda (U.K.)

Leeward Islands

HAITI

St Marc

San Juan

SANTO
DOMINGO

Higüey

Bayamón

Caguas

Charlotte
Amalie

St John
(U.S.A.)

Tortola (U.K.)

Anguilla
(U.K.)

Saint Martin (Fr.)

PORT-AU-PRINCE

Lago
Enriquillo

LA SELLE

Barahona

San Pedro
de Macorís

La Romana

Mayagüez

CERRO DE
PUNTA 1338

Ponce

Vieques

Sint Maarten
(Neth.)

Saba
(Neth.)

Barbuda

C. Dame
Marie

Massif de la Hotte
2347

Jérémie

Jacmel

Île-à-Vache

Pedernales

DOMINICAN
REPUBLIC

I. Saona

C. Rojo

I. Mona

Puerto Rico
(U.S.A.)

Fredericksted

St Eustatius
(Neth.)

St Croix (U.S.A.)

Antigua
St John's

ANTIGUA
AND
BARBUDA

Dame
Marie
(U.S.A.)

Les Cayes

Pte.-à-
Gravois

Isla Beata

Cabo Beata

Mona Passage

Basseterre

ST. KITTS-
NEVIS

Montserrat
(U.K.)

Plymouth

Guadeloupe (France)

La Désirade

A n t i l l e s

Pointe-à-Pitre

Basse Terre

Marie-Galante (France)

Iles des Saintes

BEAN SEA

I. de Aves
(Bird I.)
(Ven.)

DOMINICA

Marigot

Roseau

Lesser Antilles

Martinique Passage

Martinique
(France)

Fort-de-France

St Lucia Channel

Castries

Windward Islands

ST. LUCIA

St. Vincent Passage

Kingstown

Bridgetown

ST. VINCENT

BARBADOS

The

L e s s e r   A n t i l l e s

Grenadines

Carriacou

Punta Gallinas

Oranjestad

Aruba
(Neth.)

Curaçao
(Neth.)

Bonaire
(Neth.)

Is. Las Aves
(Ven.)

I. Orchila
(Ven.)

I. Blanquilla
(Ven.)

GRENADA

St. George's

Península
de Guajira

Pto. Estrella

Carrizal

Castilletes

Amuay

Penín.
de
Paraguaná

Pueblo Nuevo

Punto Fijo

Pto. Cumarebo

Is. Los Roques
(Ven.)

Los Testigos
(Ven.)

Tobago

Scarborough

Riohacha

Golfo de
Venezuela

Maicao

Caro

Bonaire Trench

Isla de
Margarita
(Ven.)

La Asunción

Porlamar

TRINIDAD
AND
TOBAGO

Santa
Marta

Cabo de
la Aguja

Ciénaga

PICO CRISTÓBAL
COLÓN 5775

San Rafael

Capatárida

Miramar

Churuguara

CARACAS

Maiquetía

Guatire

Guarenas

Cabo Codera

Barcelona

Cumaná

Carúpano

Río Caribe

Penín. de Paria

Port of
Spain

Dragon's
Mouth

Trinidad

anquilla

Sabanalarga

Valledupar

Robles La Paz

Maracaibo

Cabimas

Sta. Rita

San Felipe

Valencia

Los Teques

Pto. Cabello

Maracay

Villa de Cura

Golfo de
Paria

Pto. La Cruz

San Mateo

Maturín

Pt. Fortin

San
Fernando

Serpent's
Mouth

Galeota Pt.

artagena

Calamar

Ciudad
Ojeda

Lagunillas

Barquisimeto

El Tocuyo

Yaritagua

Tinaco

Carora

Aragua de
Barcelona

Caripito

Pedernales

Santa Rosa de El Amparo

Lago de
Maracaibo

Machiques

La Ceiba

Trujillo

Acarigua

San
Carlos

Calabozo

Valle de
la Pascua

Zaraza

El Tigre

Mata Negra

Boca
Grande

OMBIA

El Banco

Barranca

La Fría

Valera

Guanare

Nueva
Florida

Las Mercedes

Tucupita

Ocaña

Cordillera
de
Mérida

PICO BOLÍVAR
5007

Barinas

Ciudad Guayana

San José de
Amacuro

Majagual

Simití

ALTO DE
TAMAR
2350

El VIEJO
4100

Mérida

El Vigía

San Silvestre

Bruzual

San Fernando
de Apure

Maipure

Ciudad
Bolívar

Represa
Raúl Leoni

Port Kaituma

Caucasia

V E N E Z U E L A

Ciudad Piar

GUYANA

Cúcuta

San Cristóbal

La Urbana

Boca del
Pao

CERRO MATO
1863

Upata

802

Guasipati

El Callao

Tumeremo

Bucaramanga

San Antonio
de Caparo

Rubio

Guasdualito

La Paragua

San Pedro
de las Bocas

El Dorado

Barrancabermeja

Banadía

Arauca

Santa María

El Samán
de Apure

Mantecal

Guchipas

La Urbana

Karlani

West of Greenwich

133

Bipolar Oblique Conic Conformal Projection

1:16,000,000

| 0 | 100 | 200 | 300 | 400 | 500 | 600 | 700 | 800 KILOMETRES |

| 0 | 100 | 200 | 300 | 400 | 500 STATUTE MILES |

© COLOUR LIBRARY BOOKS

PACIFIC

OCEAN

SOUTH

ATLANTIC

OCEAN

Tropic of Capricorn

BELO
HORIZONTE
Vitória
Valadares
Linhares

Sete Lagoas
Araxá

Campos
Petrópolis
São Gonçalo
Niterói
RIO DE JANEIRO
Muiz de Fora
NOVI
IGUAÇU
São José
dos Campos
Taubaté
Santos

Ribeirão
Prêto
San
Carlos
Campinas
Jundiaí
SÃO
PAULO

Represa de
Furnas
Uberaba

Piracicaba
Sorocaba
CURITIBA

Joinville

Londrina
Marília
Maringá
Florianópolis

Campo
Grande
Dourados
Vilarrica
Santa Maria

PORTO ALEGRE
Canoas
Caxias
do Sul

Rio Grande

Pelotas

*Lagoa
dos Patos*

Serra do Mar

PARAGUAY

Asunción
Paraguari

Villarica

Corrientes
Posadas
Resistencia

Paraná

Pilcomayo

Bermejo

Tarija

San Salvador
de Jujuy
Salta

*Salinas
Grandes*

San Miguel
de Tucumán

Santiago
del Estero

Córdoba
Santa Fe

Paraná
Rosario
San Pedro

BUENOS AIRES
La Plata
MONTEVIDEO
URUGUAY
Salto
Paysandú
Mercedes

Río de la Plata

Mar del Plata

Dolores
Azul
Chivilcoy
Rufino
Trenque Lauquen
Tres
Arroyos

Río Cuarto

San Luis
Mendoza
San Juan

Salado

Santa Rosa

Bahía Blanca

Colorado

Negro

General
Roca

Cutral-Có
Neuquén

Limay

Valdivia

Puerto Montt

Castro
Isla de
Chiloé

*Archipiélago
de los Chonos*

*Península
de Taitao*

Isla
Wellington

*Archipiélago
de la Reina
Adelaida*

CERRO SAN
VALENTÍN

Trelew

*Golfo
San Matías*

*Península
Valdés*

*Golfo
de
San Jorge*

Puerto Deseado

Comodoro
Rivadavia

Chico

Deseado

Río Gallegos
*Bahía
Grande*

Punta
Arenas

*Tierra
del
Fuego*

I. de los Estados

Ushuaia
Cabo de Hornos

Falkland Islands
(U.K.)
Stanley
East Falkland
West Falkland

South Georgia
(U.K.)

Desierto de Atacama

Antofagasta

María Elena

Iquique

I. San Félix
(Chile)
I. San Ambrosio
(Chile)

Islas de Juan Fernández
(Chile)

La Serena
Copiapó

Viña del Mar
Valparaíso
SANTIAGO
Rancagua
Talca

Chillán
Talcahuano
Concepción

Temuco
Osorno

CHILE

Andes

ARGENTINA

Pampas

Patagonia

*Gran
Chaco*

F

E

D

C

B

A

5

6

7

West of Greenwich

Designed and produced by E.S.R.

Bipolar Oblique Conic Conformal Projection

1:11,000,000

© COLOUR LIBRARY BOOKS

| 0 | 100 | 200 | 300 | 400 | 500 | 600 | 700 | 800 KILOMETRES |
| 0 | 100 | 200 | 300 | 400 | 500 STATUTE MILES |

N O R T H   A T L A N T I C   O C E A N

SURINAME
Paramaribo Nieuw Amsterdam
Totness Groningen Moengo Albina
Affobakka Saint Iracoubo Sinamary
Laurent Kourou
Oranje Grand Santi Cayenne
Pontoetoe Gebretale Roura
Kapiting **FRENCH**
Serra **GUIANA**
Tumucumaque (Inini)
(France)

Cabo Orange
Cabo Caciporé
Punta Grande

AMAPÁ
Serra Lombarda
Regina
Amapá
Ilha de Maracá

Ponta Grossa
Serra do Navio

Macapá Pôrto Grande
Mouths of
the Amazon
Chaves Salinópolis
Soure Curuçá
Ilha Grande Tijoca Capanema
do Gurupá Viseu
Almeirim Ponta de Pedras
Gurupá Melgaço Curralinho **BELÉM**
Abaetetuba São José de Gurupi
Pombal Igarapé-Miri Mojú
Cametá Mocajuba
Baião

Ilhas de São João
Cururupu
Turiaçu
Marassuré
Alcântara

PARÁ

Altamira Serra dos Carajás Tucuruí Breu Branco

MARANHÃO

São Luís
Rosário
Itapecuru Mirim
Viana

Tutóia
Parnaíba
Araioses
Brejo
Luzilândia
Chapadinha
Coroatá Piracuruca
Codó Miguel Alves
Pedreiras Peritoró Pipiri
Caxias Maior

Camocim Acaraú
Massapê Sobral
Tianguá Itapipoca
Maranguape Caucaia
Baturité **FORTALEZA**
Cascavel

Jacundá **Teresina**
Bacabal Presidente Dutra
Imperatriz Barra do Colinas
Corda

PIAUÍ
São Miguel
do Tapuio Valença
do Piauí **CEARÁ**
Várzea Grande

Quixadá Morada Nova
Mombaça Quixeramobim
Senador Pompeu Iguatu Russas
Crateús Aracati
Campos Sales Piranhas
Juazeiro **RIO GRANDE**
do Norte **DO NORTE**
Iguatú Currais Novos **Natal**

Punta da Maceió
Mossoró Macau
Areia Branca
Cabo de São Roque
Nova Cruz

B R A Z I L

Serra do Cachimbo
Cachimbo

Conceição do Araguaia
Araguacema

Serra das
Carolina Araras
Pau d' Arco Araguaína
Couto Magalhães
Balsas

Loreto
Eliseu Martins
São João do Piauí Paulistana
Simplício Mendes Paulistana
Oeiras Ouricurí
Floriano Arneiroz
Picos Cajazeiras
Jaicós Juàzeiro
do Norte **PARAÍBA**
Flores Patos
Sta. Luzia **Campina
Grande** **João Pessoa**
Cabo Branco
Itabaiana
Sapé
Guarabira
Limoeiro Paulista
Olinda
RECIFE
Caruaru Carpina **Jaboatão**

Miracema do Norte Lizarda Serra do Piauí
São Raimundo Nonato
Redenção Remanso Bom Jesus
Nova Remanso

**TRANS-AMAZONIAN
HIGHWAY**
Ipuaçu
Vitória de
Sta. Rita Cabo
Pesqueira Garanhuns
Santana
do Ipanema
PERNAMBUCO
Palmares
União dos Palmares
ALAGOAS
Arapiraca **Maceió**
São Miguel dos Campos

Planalto do
Cachoeira
Von Martius

MATO GROSSO
Serra do Roncador

O GROSSO

Serra dos Xavantes
Ilha do Bananal

Pôrto Nacional
Cristalândia
Natividade
Peixe
Alvorada

Xique-Xique
Barra
Irecê
Capixaba Jacobina
Morpara Morro do Chapéu
Ipupiara Mundo Novo
Serrinha
Euclides da Cunha
Tucano
Ribeira do Pombal Penedo
Itabaiana Pontal do Manguinha
Estância **Aracaju**
SERGIPE
Jaguaripe

Senhor do Bonfim
Canudos
Uauá

Mato Grosso

DO GROSSO
Pedra

Nobres
São Bugres

Cuiabá
Alto Coité
Guiratinga Poxoréu
Rondonópolis
Anhumas
Alto Araguaia

Pôrto dos Gauchos

MATO GROSSO
Pantanal do
Rio Negro
DO SUL
esperança

BAHIA

Angical
Taguatinga
Barreiras
Santana
São Domingos
Bom Jesus da Lapa
Riacho de Santana
Carinhanha
Sítio da Abadia
Manga
167B

Morpara
Macaúbas
Andaraí
Ipirá
Seabra
Itaberaba Castro
Alves **Feira de Santana**
Santo Amaro
Nazaré Cachoeira
Valença I. de Tinharé
Teporão I. Boipeba
Ubaíra Ponta do Mutá

Jequié
Brumado
Vitória da
Conquista
Itabuna
Ilhéus
Una

Cabo Tromba Grande

**DISTRITO
FEDERAL** **BRASÍLIA**
Jaraguá Itaberaí
Luziânia
Anápolis
Goiânia Leopoldo Bulhões
Hidrolândia
Silvânia
Cristalina
Paracatu

GOIÁS
Ceres
Aruanã
San Miguel do Araguaia
Cavalcante
Uruaçu
Niquelândia
Formosa
Brasília
São Romão

Formosa do Rio Prêto

Serra Geral de Goiás

Serra da
Tabatinga

Arraias

Janaúba
Monte Azul
Condeúba

Vitória da
Conquista

Itapetinga
Itambé

Ponta Santo Antônio
Pôrto Seguro
Escondido
Ponta da Baleia

Jataí
Rio Verde
Morrinhos
Caiapônia
Piracanjuba
Itumbiara
Goiatuba

Paraúna
Pires do Rio
Ipameri

Montes Claros
Bocaiúva
Pirapora
Coromandel
Patrocínio

**MINAS
GERAIS**

Curvelo
Diamantina
PICO DE ITAMBÉ
2040
Guanhães
Teófilo Otoni
Governador
Valadares

Caravelas Ponta da Baleia
Helvécia

ESPÍRITO SANTO
São Mateus

Uberlândia
Araguari
Patos de Minas
Abaeté

Canoeiras
Capelinha
Almenara

West of Greenwich

137

Designed and produced by E.S.R.

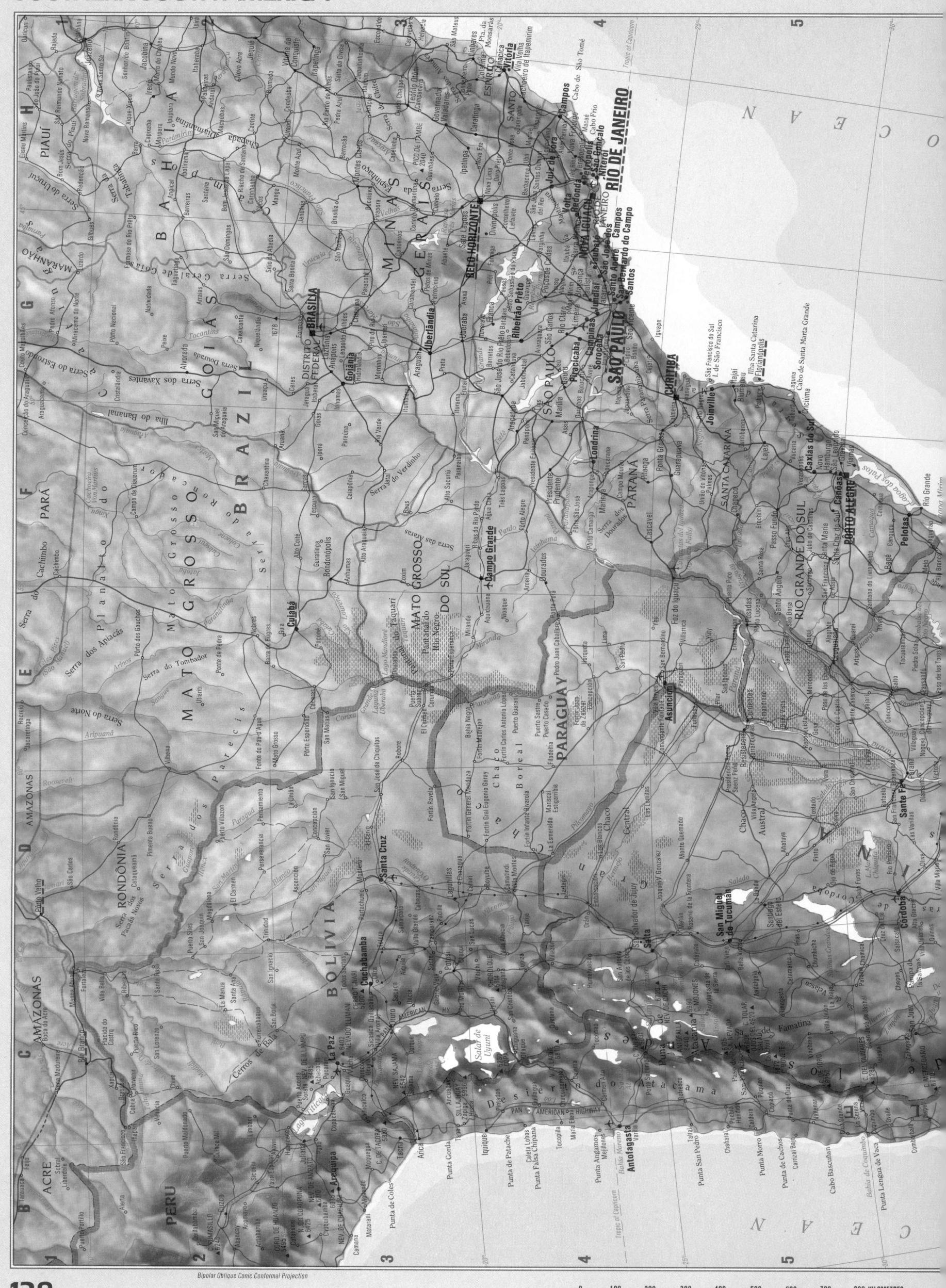

Bipolar Oblique Conic Conformal Projection

1:11,000,000

| 0 | 100 | 200 | 300 | 400 | 500 | 600 | 700 | 800 KILOMETRES |

| 0 | 100 | 200 | 300 | 400 | 500 STATUTE MILES |

© COLOUR LIBRARY BOOKS

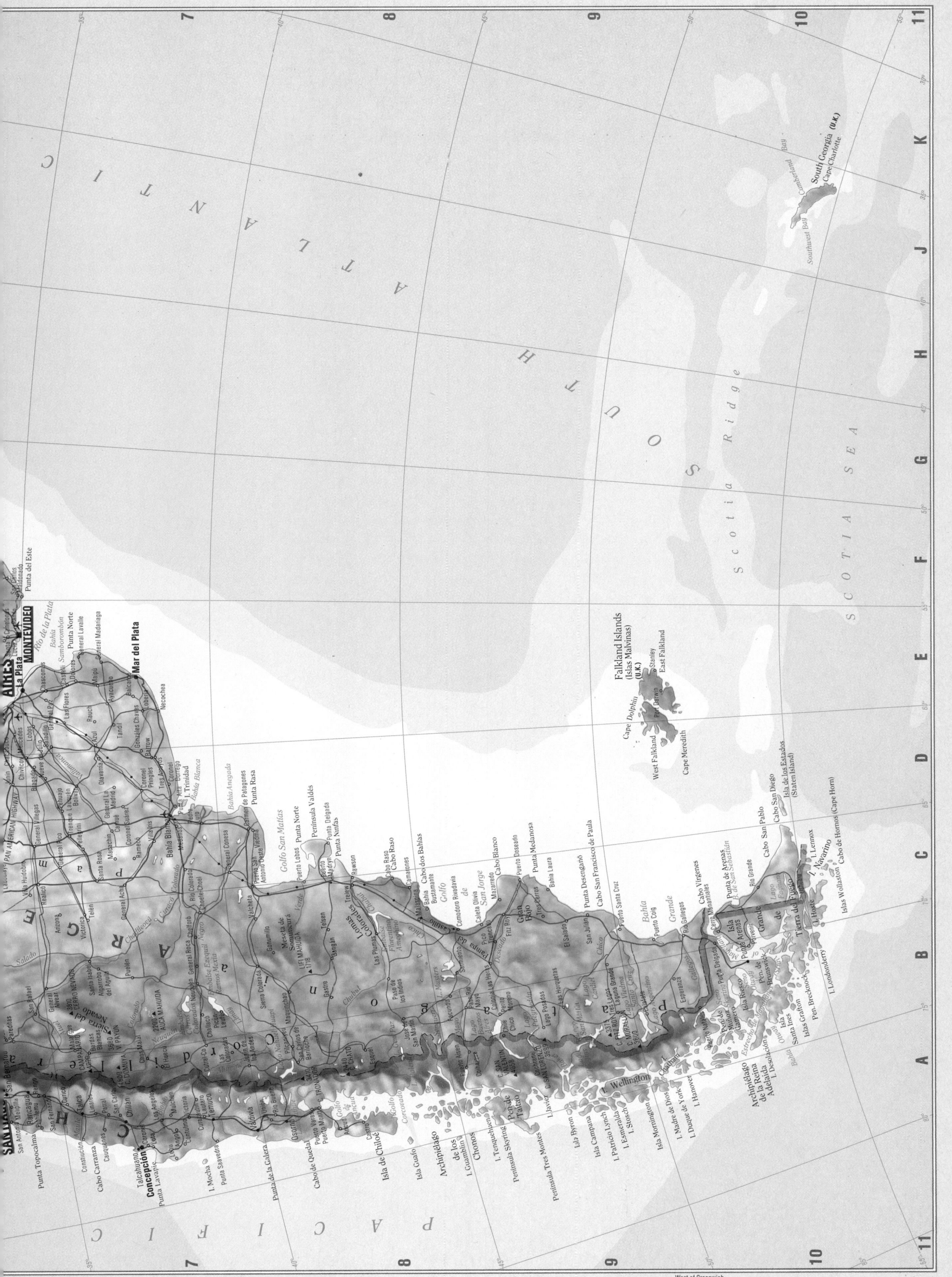

West of Greenwich

Designed and produced by E.S.R.

THE ARCTIC

Polar Stereographic Projection

Scale 1:30,000,000 (Approx.)

© COLOUR LIBRARY BOOKS

| | 250 | 500 | 750 | 1000 | 1250 | 1500 KILOMETRES |
| 0 | 250 | 500 | 750 | | 1000 STATUTE MILES |

PACIFIC OCEAN

Aleutian Is.

BERING SEA

Andreanof Islands

West of Greenwich / East of Greenwich

Near Is. (U.S.A.)

JAPAN

SAPPORO

Asahi Kaw

Hokkaido

Os. Iturup

Kuril'skiye Ostrova

Komandorskiye Ostrova (U.S.S.R.)

KLYUCHEVSKAYA SOPKA 4750

Sredinnyy Khrebet

Okhotskoye More

Sakhalin

Khabarovsk

Nikolayevsk-na-Amure

Komsomol'sk-na-Amure

Magadan

Koryakskiy Khrebet

Anadyr

Khrebet Kolymskiy

Khrebet Dzhugdzhur

Kodiak I.

Aleutian Range

Nuniyak I.

St. Lawrence I.

Nome

Seward Peninsula

Chukotskiy Poluostrov

Arctic Circle

U.S.S.R.

Gulf of Alaska

Anchorage

Alaska Range

MT. McKINLEY 6194

ALASKA (U.S.A.)

Fairbanks

MT. FAIRWEATHER 4670

Vancouver Island

Queen Charlotte Is.

Alexander Archipelago

Prince Rupert

Coast Mountains

C. Lisburne

Pevek

Ambarchik

Kolyma

Os. Vrangelya

Chukchi Sea

Yakutsk

MT. ROBSON 3954

Rocky Mountains

Dawson

Barrow

Prudhoe Bay

Point Barrow

Brooks Range

Indigirka

Vostochno Sibirskoye More

Verkhoyanskiy Khrebet

Olenek

Tiksi

Mackenzie Mts.

Inuvik

McKenzie

BEAUFORT SEA

Novosibirskiye Ostrova

More Laptevykh

Great Slave Lake

Great Bear Lake

C. Bathurst

Yellowknife

Banks Island

Amundsen Gulf

Lake Athabasca

McClure Strait

Victoria Island

NORTH WEST TERRITORIES

Reindeer Lake

Lomonosov Ridge

M. Chelyuskin

Khatanga

Poluostrov Taymyr

Sredne Sibirskoye Ploskogor ye

CANADA

Back

Prince of Wales I.

North Magnetic Pole (1987)

Queen Elizabeth Islands

ARCTIC OCEAN

North Pole

Severnaya Zemlya

Churchill

Boothia Peninsula

Ellesmere Island

Dikson

Southampton I.

Melville Peninsula

Hudson Bay

Foxe Basin

Smith Sound

Lincoln Sea

North Geomagnetic Pole (1985)

Thule

Melville Bugt

K. Morris Jesup

Wandel Sea

Zemlya Frantsa-Iosifa (U.S.S.R.)

Pol. Yamal

Obskaya Guba

Zapadno Sibirskaya Ravnina

Peninsule d' Ungave

2591

Oikiqtaluk (Baffin Island)

Baffin Bay

Upernavik

Nordaustlandet

Svalbard (Norway)

Novaya Zemlya

Karskoye More

Vorkuta

GORA NARODNAYA 1894

Uralskiy Khrebet

Hudson Strait

Cumberland Sound

Scheffervville

Labrador

C. Chidley

Davis Strait

Godthåb (Nuuk)

GREENLAND (Denmark)

MT. FOREL 3360

Ammassalik

Barentsevo More

Ostrov Kolguyev

Pechora

Ukhta

CHELYABINSK

Goose Bay

C. Bauld

Newfoundland

Denmark Strait

K. Farvel

Maximum extent of pack ice

Greenland Sea

Storesbysund

Nordkapp

MURMANSK

Kol'skiy Poluostrov

Beloye More

Arkhangel'sk

Kirov

KIRYBYSM

NORWEGIAN SEA

Arctic Circle

Reykjavik

ICELAND

Onezhskoye Ozero

Ladozhskoye Ozero

Kuybyshevsk Volkhr.

Føroyar (Denmark)

Helsingfors

LENINGRAD

MOSKVA

ATLANTIC OCEAN

Shetland Is.

Orkney Is.

North Sea

FINLAND

SWEDEN

NORWAY

OSLO

STOCKHOLM

Baltic Sea

MINSK

KHAR'KOV

Edinburgh

KØBENHAVN DENMARK

UNITED KINGDOM

WARSZAWA

POLAND

U.S.S.R.

IRELAND

Dublin

AMSTERDAM

NETH.

EAST GER.

BERLIN

PRAHA

CZECH.

KIEV

ODESSA

LONDON

BELG.

Bonn

WEST GERMANY

MÜNCHEN

BRUXELLES

LUX.

Rhein

WIEN

AUSTRIA

HUNG.

BUDAPEST

ROMANIA

BUCURESTI

Black Sea

PARIS

FRANCE

Bern

SWITZ.

Donau

ANKARA

LYON

Alps

BEOGRAD

YUGOSLAVIA

SOFIYA

BULG.

ISTANBUL

TURKE

MARSEILLE

Loire

AND.

ITALY

ROMA

Tiranë

ALB.

GREECE

ATHINAI

CYP

SPAIN

Bilbao

BARCELONA

ATHINAI

Mediterranean Sea

LEB.

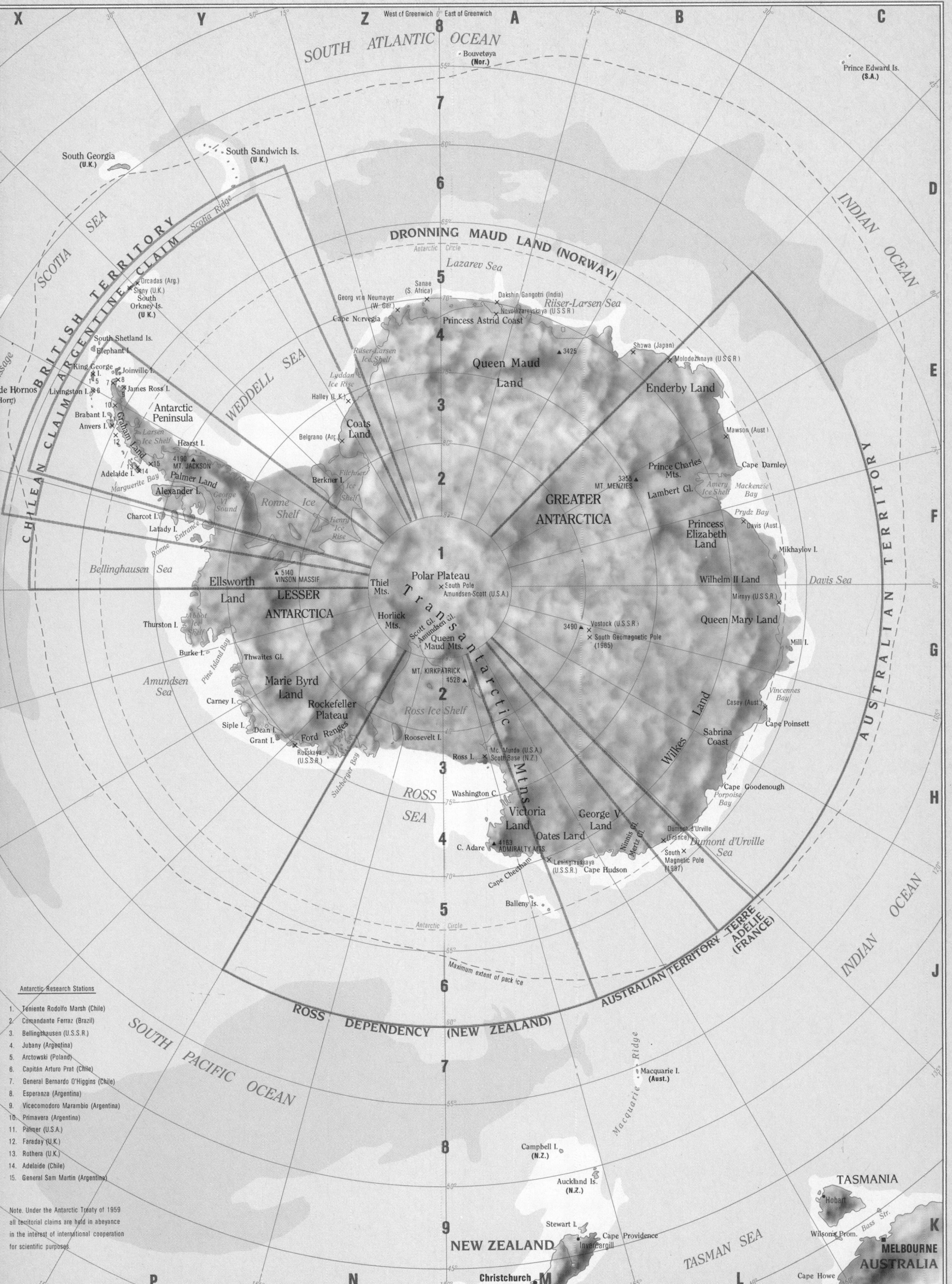

THE ANTARCTIC

SOUTH ATLANTIC OCEAN

Bouvetøya (Nor.)

Prince Edward Is. (S.A.)

SCOTIA SEA

South Georgia (U.K.)

South Sandwich Is. (U.K.)

INDIAN OCEAN

DRONNING MAUD LAND (NORWAY)

Antarctic Circle

Lazarev Sea

Riiser-Larsen Sea

Sanae (S. Africa)
Georg von Neumayer (W. Ger.)
Dakshin Gangotri (India)
Novolazarevskaya (U.S.S.R.)

Cape Norvegia
Princess Astrid Coast

Queen Maud Land

Showa (Japan)
Molodezhnaya (U.S.S.R.)

Riiser-Larsen Ice Shelf

Lyddan Ice Rise

Enderby Land

BRITISH TERRITORY
ARGENTINE CLAIM
Scotia Ridge

Orcadas (Arg.)
Signy (U.K.)
South Orkney Is. (U.K.)

Halley (U.K.)

Coats Land

Mawson (Aust)

Cape Darnley

South Shetland Is.
Elephant I.
King George I.
Joinville I.
James Ross I.

Belgrano (Arg.)

Prince Charles Mts.

Mackenzie Bay

de Hornos (Horn)
Livingston I.
Brabant I.
Anvers I.
Graham Land

Antarctic Peninsula

Hearst I.

Berkner I.

MT. MENZIES 3355

Lambert Gl.

Amery Ice Shelf

Prydz Bay

Davis (Aust)

Larsen Ice Shelf

MT. JACKSON 4190

Filchner Ice Shelf

GREATER ANTARCTICA

Princess Elizabeth Land

Mikhaylov I.

Adelaide I.
Palmer Land
Alexander I.

Marguerite Bay

George VI Sound

Ronne Ice Shelf

Henry Ice Rise

Wilhelm II Land

Davis Sea

CHILEAN CLAIM

Charcot I.
Latady I.

Bonne Entrance

Bellinghausen Sea

Ellsworth Land

VINSON MASSIF 5140

LESSER ANTARCTICA

Polar Plateau
South Pole
Amundsen-Scott (U.S.A.)

Mirnyy (U.S.S.R.)

Queen Mary Land

Thiel Mts.

Horlick Mts.

Scott Gl.
Amundsen Gl.
Queen Maud Mts.

3490
Vostock (U.S.S.R.)
South Geomagnetic Pole (1985)

Mill I.

Thurston I.

Abbot Ice Shelf

Transantarctic

MT. KIRKPATRICK 4528

Vincennes Bay

Amundsen Sea

Burke I.

Thwaites Gl.

Marie Byrd Land

Ross Ice Shelf

Casey (Aust)
Cape Poinsett

Pine Island Bay

Rockefeller Plateau

Roosevelt I.

Mc. Murdo (U.S.A.)
Scott Base (N.Z.)

Wilkes Land

Sabrina Coast

Carney I.
Siple I.
Dean I.
Grant I.
Ford Ranges

Ross I.

Cape Goodenough

Russkaya (U.S.S.R.)

Mtns.

Porpoise Bay

ROSS SEA

Washington C.

Victoria Land

George V Land

Ninnis Gl.
Mertz Gl.

Dumont d'Urville (France)

South Magnetic Pole (1987)

Dumont d'Urville Sea

Oates Land

C. Adare
ADMIRALTY MTS. 4163

Leningradskaya (U.S.S.R.)
Cape Hudson

AUSTRALIAN TERRITORY

Cape Cheetham

TERRE ADÉLIE (FRANCE)

Balleny Is.

Antarctic Circle

INDIAN OCEAN

Maximum extent of pack ice

ROSS DEPENDENCY (NEW ZEALAND)

AUSTRALIAN TERRITORY

SOUTH PACIFIC OCEAN

Macquarie Ridge

Macquarie I. (Aust.)

Campbell I. (N.Z.)

Auckland Is. (N.Z.)

TASMANIA

Hobart

Bass Str.

Stewart I.
Cape Providence
Invercargill

Wilsons Prom.

NEW ZEALAND

Christchurch

TASMAN SEA

Cape Howe

MELBOURNE
AUSTRALIA

Antarctic Research Stations

1. Teniente Rodolfo Marsh (Chile)
2. Comandante Ferraz (Brazil)
3. Bellingshausen (U.S.S.R.)
4. Jubany (Argentina)
5. Arctowski (Poland)
6. Capitán Arturo Prat (Chile)
7. General Bernardo O'Higgins (Chile)
8. Esperanza (Argentina)
9. Vicecomodoro Marambio (Argentina)
10. Primavera (Argentina)
11. Palmer (U.S.A.)
12. Faraday (U.K.)
13. Rothera (U.K.)
14. Adelaide (Chile)
15. General Sam Martin (Argentina)

Note. Under the Antarctic Treaty of 1959 all territorial claims are held in abeyance in the interest of international cooperation for scientific purposes.

Polar Stereographic Projection

Designed and produced by E.S.R.

141

Mercator Projection

1:85,000,000 (Scale at the Equator)

G   East of Greenwich   West of Greenwich   H   J   K   L   M

TIC OCEAN

1

Ellesmere
Island

Queen

Kane
Basin

Elizabeth

GREENLAND
(Denmark)

Islands

*otochno
irskoye
tore*

Banks
Island

Viscount Melville
Sound

Baffin Bay

Beaufort Sea

Ostrov Vrangelya

Pt. Barrow

Amundsen
Gulf

Victoria Island

Oikiqtaluk

Davis Str.

Denmark Strait

*Chucki
Sea*

2

Arctic Circle

Kolymsky

Brooks Range

Mackenzie Mts.

Great Bear Lake

Back

Foxe
Basin

Reykjavik
ICELAND

ALASKA
(U.S.A.)

Anadyrskiy
Zaliv

McKinley
6194

Bering Str.

Yukon

Great Slave Lake

Hudson Str.

Hudson Bay

Labrador Sea

Kap Farvel

60°

*Bering
Sea*

Alaska Range

Gulf of Alaska

Rocky Mountains

L. Athabasca

Reindeer Lake

CANADA

Labrador

Kodiak I.

Aleutian Islands

Vancouver I.

L. Winnipeg

Great
Lakes

Newfoundland

Aleutian Trench

*NORTH
PACIFIC
OCEAN*

Columbia

*Great
Plains*

Missouri

St. Lawrence

Ottawa

*NORTH
ATLANTIC
OCEAN*

3

CHICAGO

NEW YORK

UNITED STATES

Gt. Salt Lake

SAN FRANCISCO

OF

AMERICA

PHILADELPHIA
Washington

Appalachian Mts.

Açores
(Port.)

Colorado

Mississippi

LOS ANGELES

Rio Grande

Bermuda
(U.K.)

Hawaiian

Isla de
Guadalupe
(Mex.)

30°

Islands

Gulf of Mexico

BAHAMAS
Nassau

Tropic of Cancer

MEXICO
CIUDAD DE
MÉXICO

La Habana

CUBA

West Indies

DOMINICAN REP.

**CAPE
VERDE**

HAWAII
(U.S.A.)

Islas de Revillagigedo
(Mex.)

Port au Prince
HAITI

Puerto Rico (U.S.A.)
Santo Domingo

4

Belmopan
BELIZE

Kingston
JAMAICA

Leeward Is.

Praia

Territory of
ic Islands

GUATEMALA
Guatemala
San Salvador
SALVADOR
Managua

HONDURAS
Tegucigalpa

Caribbean Sea

Windward Is.

BARBADOS

Marshall Is.

NICARAGUA
San José
COSTA RICA

Caracas
Panamá
VENEZUELA

**TRINIDAD
AND TOBAGO**

NAURU

Tarawa
Gilbert
Is.

PANAMA

Orinoco

Georgetown
Paramaribo
Cayenne
FRENCH GUIANA

Equator

Christmas I.

Bogotá
COLOMBIA

GU **SUR**

0°

Phoenix Is.

Quito

Islas Galápagos
(Ecuador)

ECUADOR

Negro

Isla Fernando
de Noronha
(Brazil)

MON ISLANDS

TUVALU

KIRIBATI

Santa
Cruz
Is.

Fanafuti

Iles Marquises
(Fr.)

PERU

Amazonas

BRAZIL

5

iara

W.
SAMOA

Cook Islands
(N.Z.)

LIMA

Planalto do

NUATU

Iles
Wallice
(Fr.)

Apia
Samoa
(U.S.A.)

French Polynesia
(Fr.)

Iles Tuamotu

*SOUTH
PACIFIC
OCEAN*

Mato Grosso

Brasília

Vila

FIJI
Suva

TONGA
Nuku'alofa

Iles de la
Société

La Paz
BOLIVIA
Sucre

Madeira

São Paulo

Ilha da Trindade
(Brazil)

*Tonga
Trench*

Pitcairn I.
(U.K.)
Ducie I.
(U.K.)

Iles Gambier

PARAGUAY

SÃO PAULO

RÍO DE JANEIRO

Tropic of Capricorn

Isla de Pascua
(Easter I.)
(Chile)

Asunción

30°

Islas Juan
Fernández
(Chile)

ACONCAGUA
6960

URUGUAY

nan Sea

Santiago

ARGENTINA

BUENOS AIRES
Montevideo

*SOUTH
ATLANTIC
OCEAN*

EW ZEALAND
Wellington

Chatham Is.
(N.Z.)

Patagonia

6

Auckland Is.
(N.Z.)

Falkland Is.
(U.K.)

acquarie Is.
(Aus.)

Cabo de Hornos

South Georgia
(U.K.)

Scotia Sea

South
Sandwich
Is. (U.K.)

G   H   J   K   L   M

GLOSSARY AND ABBREVIATIONS

Language abbreviations in glossary

Afr	Afrikaans	*Dut*	Dutch	*I-C*	Indo-Chinese	*Mal*	Malay
Alb	Albanian	*Fin*	Finnish	*Ice*	Icelandic	*Mlg*	Malagasy
Ar	Arabic	*Fr*	French	*Ind*	Indonesian	*Mon*	Mongolian
Ber	Berber	*Gae*	Gaelic	*It*	Italian	*Nor*	Norwegian
Bul	Bulgarian	*Ger*	German	*Jap*	Japanese	*Per*	Persian
Bur	Burmese	*Gr*	Greek	*Khm*	Khmer	*Pol*	Polish
Ch	Chinese	*Heb*	Hebrew	*Kor*	Korean	*Por*	Portuguese
Cz	Czechoslovakian	*Hin*	Hindi	*Lao*	Laotian	*Rom*	Romanian
Dan	Danish	*Hun*	Hungarian	*Lat*	Latvian	*Rus*	Russian

S-C	Serbo-Croat				
Som	Somali				
Sp	Spanish				
Swe	Swedish				
Th	Thai				
Tib	Tibetan				
Tu	Turkish				
Vt	Vietnamese				
Wel	Welsh				

Glossary

A

Ābār *(Ar)* – wells
Abyār *(Ar)* – wells
Adasi *(Tu)* – island
Adrar *(Ber)* – mountains
Aïn *(Ar)* – spring, well
'Ain *(Ar)* – spring, well
'Aïn *(Ar)* – spring, well
Ákra *(Gr)* – cape, point
Alb *(Ger)* – mountains
Alpen *(Ger)* – mountains
Alpes *(Fr)* – mountains
Alpi *(It)* – mountains
Alto *(Por)* – high
-älv *(Swe)* – river
-älven *(Swe)* – river
Appennino *(It)* – mountain range
'Aqabat *(Ar)* – pass
Archipiélago *(Sp)* – archipelago
Arquipiélago *(Por)* – archipelago
Arrecife *(Sp)* – reef
Ayia *(Gr)* – saint
Áyios *(Gr)* – saint
'Ayn *(Ar)* – spring, well

B

Bāb *(Ar)* – strait
Bad *(Ger)* – spa
Bādiyah *(Ar)* – desert
Bælt *(Dan)* – strait
Baharu *(Mal)* – new
Bahía *(Sp)* – bay
Bahr *(Ar)* – bay, canal, lake, stream
Bahr *(Ar)* – bay, canal, lake, stream
Bahrat *(Ar)* – lake
Baia *(Por)* – bay
Baie *(Fr)* – bay
Baja *(Sp)* – lower
Ban *(Khm, Lao, Th)* – village
-bana *(Jap)* – cape, point
Banco *(Sp)* – bank
-bandao *(Ch)* – peninsula
Bandar *(Per)* – bay
Baraji *(Tu)* – reservoir
Barqā *(Ar)* – hill
Barragem *(Por)* – reservoir
Bassin *(Fr)* – basin, bay
Batin *(Ar)* – depression
Beinn *(Gae)* – mountain
Beloyy *(Rus)* – white
Ben *(Gae)* – mountain
Bereg *(Rus)* – bank, shore
Berg *(Ger)* – mountain
Berge *(Afr)* – mountains
Bheinn *(Gae)* – mountain
Bi'ār *(Ar)* – wells
Bir *(Ar)* – well
Bi'r *(Ar)* – well
Birkat *(Ar)* – well
Birket *(Ar)* – well
Boca *(Sp)* – river mouth
Bocche *(It)* – mouths, estuary
Bodden *(Ger)* – bay
Boğazi *(Tu)* – strait
Boka *(S-C)* – gulf, inlet
Bol'shoy *(Rus)* – big
Bol'shoye *(Rus)* – big
Bory *(Pol)* – forest
Bratul *(Rom)* – river channel
Bucht *(Ger)* – bay
Bugt *(Dan)* – bay
Buhayrat *(Ar)* – lagoon, lake
Bukit *(Mal)* – hill, mountain
Bukt *(Nor)* – bay
Bulak *(Rus)* – spring
Burnu *(Tu)* – cape, point
Burun *(Tu)* – cape, point
Busen *(Ger)* – bay
Büyük *(Tu)* – big

C

Cabo *(Por, Sp)* – cape, point
Cachoeira *(Sp)* – waterfall
Cap *(Fr)* – cape, point
Campos *(Sp)* – upland
Cao Nguyen *(Th)* – plateau, tableland
Cataratas *(Sp)* – waterfall
Çayi *(Tu)* – stream
Cayo *(Sp)* – islet, rock
Cerro *(Sp)* – hill
Chaco *(Sp)* – jungle
Chaîne *(Fr)* – mountain chain
Chapada *(Por)* – hills
Ch'eng *(Ch)* – town
Chiang *(Ch)* – river
Chiang *(Th)* – town
Chott *(Ar)* – marsh, salt lake
Chute *(Fr)* – waterfall
Ciénaga *(Sp)* – marshy lake
Ciudad *(Sp)* – city, town
Co *(Tib)* – lake
Col *(Fr)* – pass
Colinas *(Sp)* – hills
Cordillera *(Sp)* – mountain range
Costa *(Sp)* – coast, shore
Côte *(Fr)* – coast, slope
Coteau *(Fr)* – hill, slope
Coxilha *(Por)* – mountain pasture
Cuchillas *(Sp)* – hills

D

Dağ *(Tu)* – mountain
Dağı *(Tu)* – mountain
Dağları *(Tu)* – mountains
-dake *(Jap)* – peak
-dal *(Nor)* – valley
Dao *(Ch)* – island
Darreh *(Per)* – valley
Daryâcheh *(Per)* – lake
Dasht *(Per)* – desert
Denizi *(Tu)* – sea
Desierto *(Sp)* – desert
Djebel *(Ar)* – mountain
-djik *(Dut)* – dyke
Do *(Kor, Jap, Vt)* – island
Dolina *(Rus)* – valley
Dolok *(Ind)* – mountain
Dolna *(Bul)* – lower
Dolní *(Cz)* – lower
Dūr *(Ar)* – mountains

E

Eiland *(Dut)* – island
Eilanden *(Dut)* – islands
-elva *(Nor)* – river
Embalse *(Sp)* – reservoir
Erg *(Ar)* – sandy desert
Estero *(Sp)* – bay, estuary, inlet
Estrecho *(Sp)* – strait
Étang *(Fr)* – lagoon, pond
Ezers *(Lat)* – lake

F

Feng *(Ch)* – mountain, peak
Fels *(Ger)* – rock
Firth *(Gae)* – estuary
-fjäll *(Swe)* – mountains
Fjeld *(Dan)* – mountain
-fjell *(Nor)* – mountain
-flói *(Ice)* – bay
-fjörður *(Ice)* – fjord
Förde *(Ger)* – inlet
Forêt *(Fr)* – forest
-foss *(Ice)* – waterfall

G

-gan *(Jap)* – rock
Gang *(Ch)* – harbour
Ganga *(Hin)* – river
Gata *(Jap)* – inlet, lagoon
Gave *(Fr)* – torrent
Gebel *(Ar)* – mountain
Gebirge *(Ger)* – mountains
Ghat *(Hin)* – range of hills
Ghubbat *(Ar)* – bay
Glen *(Gae)* – valley
Gletscher *(Ger)* – glacier
Gobi *(Mon)* – desert
Golfe *(Fr)* – bay, gulf
Golfo *(It, Sp)* – bay, gulf
Gölü *(Tu)* – lake
Gora *(Bul)* – forest
Gora *(Rus)* – mountain
Gorá *(Pol)* – mountain
-gorod *(Rus)* – small town
Gory *(Rus)* – mountains
Góry *(Pol)* – mountains
Grada *(Rus)* – mountain range
Grad *(Bul, Rus, S-C)* – city, town
Gross *(Ger)* – big
Gryada *(Rus)* – ridge
Guba *(Rus)* – bay
-guntō *(Jap)* – island group
Gunung *(Ind, Mal)* – mountain

H

Hādh *(Ar)* – sand dunes
Hafen *(Ger)* – harbour, port
Haff *(Ger)* – bay, lagoon
Hai *(Ch)* – sea
Haixia *(Ch)* – strait
-holm *(Dan)* – island
Halvø *(Dan)* – peninsula
-hama *(Jap)* – beach
Hamada *(Ar)* – plateau
-hamar *(Ice)* – mountain
Hammādah *(Ar)* – plain, stony desert
Hāmūn *(Per)* – marsh
-hantō *(Jap)* – peninsula
Harrat *(Ar)* – lava field
Hav *(Swe)* – gulf
Havet *(Nor)* – sea
-havn *(Dan, Nor)* – harbour
Hawr *(Ar)* – lake
He *(Ch)* – river
Heide *(Ger)* – heath, moor
-hisar *(Tu)* – castle
Ho *(Ch)* – river
Höhe *(Ger)* – hills
Horn *(Ger)* – peak, summit
Hu *(Ch)* – lake
-huk *(Swe)* – cape, point

I

Idd *(Ar)* – well
Idhan *(Ar)* – sand dunes
Île *(Fr)* – island
Îles *(Fr)* – islands
Ilha *(Por)* – island
Ilhas *(Por)* – islands
Insel *(Ger)* – island
Inseln *(Ger)* – islands
'Irq *(Ar)* – sand dunes
Irmak *(Tu)* – large river
Isfjord *(Dan)* – glacier
Iskappe *(Dan)* – icecap
Isla *(Sp)* – island
Islas *(Sp)* – islands
Isola *(It)* – island
Isole *(It)* – islands
Istmo *(Sp)* – isthmus

J

Jabal *(Ar)* – mountain
-järvi *(Fin)* – lake
Jazā 'ir *(Ar)* – islands
Jazīrat *(Ar)* – island
Jazovir *(Bul)* – reservoir
Jbel *(Ar)* – mountain
Jebel *(Ar)* – mountain
Jezero *(Alb, S-C)* – lake
Jezioro *(Pol)* – lagoon, lake
Jezïrat *(Ar)* – island
-jiang *(Ch)* – river
Jibāl *(Ar)* – mountain
Jiddat *(Ar)* – gravel plain
-jima *(Jap)* – island
-joki *(Fin)* – river
-jökull *(Ice)* – glacier

K

Kaap *(Afr)* – cape, point
-kai *(Jap)* – bay, sea
-kaikyō *(Jap)* – strait
Kanaal *(Dut)* – canal
Kap *(Ger)* – cape, point
-kapp *(Nor)* – cape, point
Kas *(Khm)* – island
Kavir *(Per)* – desert
-kawa *(Jap)* – river
Kēnet *(Alb)* – inlet
Kep *(Alb)* – cape, point
Kepulauan *(Ind)* – archipelago, islands
Kereb *(Ar)* – hill, ridge
Khalij *(Ar)* – bay, gulf
Khawr *(Ar)* – wadi
Khrebet *(Ru)* – mountain range
Kiang *(Ch)* – river
Klein *(Afr, Ger)* – small
Ko *(Th)* – island
-ko *(Jap)* – inlet, lake
Koh *(Khm)* – island
Kólpos *(Gr)* – gulf
Kolymskoye *(Rus)* – mountain range
Körfezi *(Tu)* – bay, gulf
Kosa *(Rus)* – spit
Kotlina *(Cz, Pol)* – basin, depression
Kraj *(Cz, Pol, S-C)* – region
Krasnyy *(Rus)* – red
Kray *(Rus)* – region
Kreis *(Ger)* – district
Kryazh *(Rus)* – mountains
Küçük *(Tu)* – small
Kūh *(Per)* – mountain
Kūhhā *(Per)* – mountains
Kum *(Rus)* – sandy desert
Kyst *(Dan)* – coast
Kyun *(Bur)* – island
Kyunzu *(Bur)* – islands

L

La *(Tib)* – pass
Lac *(Fr)* – lake
Lacul *(Rom)* – lake
Laem *(Th)* – point
Lago *(It, Por, Sp)* – lake
Lagoa *(Por)* – lagoon
Laguna *(Sp)* – lagoon, lake
Lam *(Th)* – stream
Lande *(Fr)* – heath, sandy moor
Laut *(Ind)* – sea
Ling *(Ch)* – mountain range
Liman *(Rus)* – bay, gulf
Límni *(Gr)* – lagoon, lake
Llano *(Sp)* – plain, prairie
Llanos *(Sp)* – plains, prairies
Llyn *(Wel)* – lake
Loch *(Gae)* – lake
Lough *(Gae)* – lake

M

Mae Nam *(Th)* – river
Mala *(S-C)* – small
Malaya *(Rus)* – small
Malé *(Cz)* – small
Maloye *(Rus)* – small
Malyy *(Rus)* – small
Mar *(Por, Sp)* – sea
Mare *(It)* – sea
Maşirah *(Ar)* – channel
Massif *(Fr)* – mountains
Mato *(Por)* – forest
Meer *(Afr, Dut, Ger)* – lake, sea
Menor *(Por, Sp)* – lesser, smaller
Mer *(Fr)* – sea
Mesa *(Sp)* – tableland
Minami *(Jap)* – south
-misaki *(Jap)* – cape, point
Mont *(Fr)* – mountain
Montagna *(It)* – mountain
Montagne *(Fr)* – mountain
Montagnes *(Fr)* – mountains
Montaña *(Sp)* – mountain
Montañas *(Sp)* – mountains
Monte *(It, Por, Sp)* – mountain
Monti *(It)* – mountains
More *(Rus)* – sea
Mull *(Gae)* – cape, point, promontory
Munkhafad *(Ar)* – depression
Muntii *(Rom)* – mountains
Mynydd *(Wel)* – mountain
Mys *(Rus)* – cape, point

N

-nada *(Jap)* – gulf, sea
Nádrž *(Cz)* – reservoir
Nafūd *(Ar)* – desert, dune
Nagor'ye *(Rus)* – highland, uplands
Nagy- *(Hun)* – great
Nahr *(Ar)* – river
Namakzār *(Per)* – desert, salt flat
Nei *(Ch)* – inner
Ness *(Gae)* – cape, promontory
Neu *(Ger)* – new
Nevada *(Sp)* – snow capped mountains
Nevado *(Sp)* – mountain
Ngoc *(Vt)* – mountain, peak
-nísi *(Gr)* – island
Nísoi *(Gr)* – islands
Nísos *(Gr)* – island
Nizhnyaya *(Rus)* – lower
Nizina *(Pol)* – depression, lowland
Nizmennost' *(Rus)* – lowland
Noord *(Dut)* – north
Nord *(Dan, Fr, Ger)* – north
Norte *(Por, Sp)* – north
Nos *(Bul, Rus)* – point, spit
Nosy *(Mlg)* – island
Nova *(Bul)* – new
Nová *(Cz)* – new
Novaya *(Rus)* – new
Nové *(Cz)* – new
Novi *(Bul)* – new
Nudo *(Sp)* – mountain
Nuruu *(Mon)* – mountain range
Nuur *(Mon)* – lake

O

Ø *(Dan)* – island
Oblast' *(Rus)* – province
Occidental *(Fr, Rom, Sp)* – western
Oki *(Jap)* – bay
-oog *(Ger)* – island
Ojo *(Sp)* – spring
Oraşul *(Rom)* – city
Óri *(Gr)* – mountains
Oriental *(Fr, Rom, Sp)* – eastern
Órmos *(Gr)* – bay
Óros *(Gr)* – island

144

Ort *(Ger)* – cape, point
Ostrov *(Rus)* – island
Ostrova *(Rus)* – islands
Otok *(S-C)* – island
Otoki *(S-C)* – islands
Ouadi *(Ar)* – wadi, dry watercourse
Oued *(Ar)* – dry river bed, wadi
Ovasi *(Tu)* – plain
Ozero *(Rus)* – lake

P

Pampa *(Sp)* – plain
Paniai *(Ind)* – lake
Paso *(Sp)* – pass
Passage *(Fr)* – pass
Passo *(It)* – pass
Pasul *(Rom)* – pass
Pélagos *(Gr)* – sea
Pendi *(Ch)* – basin
Pengunungan *(Ind)* – mountain range
Peninsola *(It)* – peninsula
Peninsule *(Fr)* – peninsula
Pereval *(Rus)* – pass
Peski *(Rus)* – desert, sands
Phnom *(Khm)* – hill, mountain
Phu *(Vt)* – mountain
Pic *(Fr)* – peak
Picacho *(Sp)* – peak
Pico *(Sp)* – peak
Pik *(Rus)* – peak
Pingyuan *(Ch)* – plain
Pizzo *(It)* – peak
Planalto *(Por)* – plateau
Plana *(S-C, Sp)* – plain
Planina *(Bul, S-C)* – mountains
Plato *(Afr, Bul, Rus)* – plateau
Ploskogor'ye *(Rus)* – plateau
Ploskogorje *(Rus)* – plateau
Poco *(Ind)* – peak
Pohorie *(Cz)* – mountain range
Pointe *(Fr)* – cape, point
Pojezierze *(Pol)* – plateau
Poluostrov *(Rus)* – peninsula
Pólwysep *(Pol)* – peninsula
Ponta *(Por)* – cape, point
Presa *(Sp)* – reservoir
Proliv *(Sp)* – strait
Pueblo *(Sp)* – village

Puerto *(Sp)* – harbour, pass
Pulau *(Ind, Mal)* – island
Puna *(Sp)* – desert plateau
Puncak *(Ind)* – peak
Punta *(It, Sp)* – cape, point
Puy *(Fr)* – peak

Q

Qalamat *(Ar)* – well
Qalib *(Ar)* – well
Qararat *(Ar)* – depression
Qolleh *(Per)* – mountain
Qornet *(Ar)* – peak
Qundao *(Ch)* – archipelago

R

Ramlat *(Ar)* – dunes
Ra's *(Ar, Per)* – cape, point
Râs *(Ar)* – cape, point
Rass *(Som)* – cape, point
Ravnina *(Rus)* – plain
Recife *(Por)* – reef
Represa *(Por)* – dam
Reshteh *(Per)* – mountain range
-rettō *(Jap)* – island chain
Rijeka *(S-C)* – river
Rio *(Por)* – river
Rio *(Sp)* – river
Rivière *(Fr)* – river
Rt *(S-C)* – cape, point
Rubha *(Gae)* – cape, point
Ruck *(Ger)* – mountain
Rücken *(Ger)* – ridge
Rūd *(Per)* – river
Rudohorie *(Cz)* – mountains
Rzeka *(Pol)* – river

S

Sabkhat *(Ar)* – salt flat
Sāgar *(Hin)* – lake
Saharā *(Ar)* – desert
Sahl *(Ar)* – plain
Sahrā *(Ar)* – desert
Sa'īd *(Ar)* – highland
-saki *(Jap)* – cape, point
Salar *(Sp)* – salt pan
Salina *(Sp)* – salt pan

San *(Sp)* – saint
-san *(Jap)* – mountain
-sanchi *(Jap)* – mountainous area
Sankt *(Ger, Swe)* – saint
Santa *(Sp)* – saint
São *(Por)* – saint
Sar *(Kur)* – mountain
Satu *(Rom)* – village
Şawqirah *(Ar)* – bay
Se *(I-C)* – river
See *(Ger)* – lake
Selat *(Ind)* – channel, strait
-selka *(Fin)* – bay
Selva *(Sp)* – forest
Serra *(Por)* – mountain range
Serrania *(Sp)* – mountains
Severnaya *(Rus)* – southern
Sfintu *(Rom)* – saint
Shamo *(Ch)* – desert
Shan *(Ch)* – mountains
Shandi *(Ch)* – mountainous area
Shatt *(Ar)* – river mouth, river
-shima *(Jap)* – islands
Shiqqat *(Ar)* – interdune trough
-shotō *(Jap)* – group of islands
Sierra *(Sp)* – mountain range
Sint *(Afr, Dut)* – saint
Slieve *(Gae)* – range of hills
Sø *(Dan, Nor)* – lake
Söder- *(Swe)* – southern
Søndre *(Dan, Nor)* – southern
Song *(Vt)* – river
Spitze *(Ger)* – peak
Sredne *(Rus)* – middle
Stadt *(Ger)* – town
Stará *(Cz)* – old
Staraya *(Rus)* – old
Stenón *(Gr)* – strait, pass
Step' *(Rus)* – plain, steppe
Strelka *(Rus)* – spit
Stretto *(It)* – strait
-suidō *(Jap)* – channel, strait
Sund *(Swe)* – sound, strait
Szent- *(Hun)* – saint

T

-take *(Jap)* – peak
Tall *(Ar)* – hill
Tallât *(Ar)* – hills
Tanggula *(Tib)* – pass
Tanjong *(Ind, Mal)* – cape, point
Tanjon'i *(Mlg)* – cape, point
Tanjung *(Ind, Mal)* – cape, point
Tao *(Ch)* – island
Taraq *(Ar)* – hills
Tassili *(Ber)* – rocky plateau
Tau *(Rus)* – mountains
Taung *(Bur)* – mountain, south
Tekojärvi *(Fin)* – reservoir
Tell *(Ar)* – hill
Teluk *(Ind)* – bay
Ténéré *(Fr)* – desert
Terre *(Fr)* – land
Thale *(Tha)* – lake
Thamad *(Ar)* – well
Tir'at *(Ar)* – canal
Tjärn *(Swe)* – lake
Tso *(Tib)* – lake
Tonle *(Khm)* – lake
Tutūl *(Ar)* – hills

J

Ujung *(Ind)* – cape, point
-ura *(Jap)* – inlet
'Urayq *(Ar)* – sand ridge
'Urūq *(Ar)* – dunes
Ust *(Rus)* – river mouth
Uul *(Mon)* – mountain

V

Valea *(Rom)* – valley
-város *(Hun)* – town
-varre *(Nor)* – mountain
-vatten *(Swe)* – lake
Vaux *(Fr)* – valleys
Velika *(S-C)* – big
Velikaya *(Rus)* – big
Verkhne *(Rus)* – upper
-vesi *(Fin)* – lake, water
Ville *(Fr)* – town
Vinh *(Vt)* – bay

Virful *(Rom)* – peak
Vodokhranilishche *(Rus)* – reservoir
Volcán *(Sp)* – volcano
Vorota *(Rus)* – strait
Vostochnyy *(Rus)* – eastern
Vozvyshennost' *(Rus)* – hills, upland
Vpadina *(Rus)* – depression

W

Wadi *(Ar)* – river, stream
Wāḥat *(Ar)* – oasis
Wai *(Ch)* – outer
Wald *(Ger)* – forest
Wan *(Ch)* – bay
Wasser *(Ger)* – lake, water
Wenz *(Ar)* – river
Wielka *(Pol)* – big

X

Xan *(Ch)* – strait
Xi *(Ch)* – stream, west
Xia *(Ch)* – gorge, lower
Xian *(Ch)* – county
Xiao *(Ch)* – small
Xu *(Ch)* – island

Y

Yam *(Heb)* – lake
-yama *(Jap)* – mountain
Yarimadasi *(Tu)* – peninsula
Yazovir *(Bul)* – reservoir
Ye *(Bur)* – island
Yoma *(Bur)* – mountain range
Yugo- *(Rus)* – southern
Yuzhnyy *(Rus)* – southern

Z

Zaki *(Jap)* – cape, point
Zalew *(Pol)* – bay, inlet
Zaliv *(Rus)* – bay
-zan *(Jap)* – mountain
Zapadno *(Rus)* – western
Zatoka *(Pol)* – bay
Zee *(Dut)* – sea
Zemlya *(Rus)* – island, land
-zhen *(Ch)* – town

Abbreviations

A

A. – Alp, Alpen, Alpi
Ákr. – Ákra
And. – Andorra
Arch. – Archipelago
Arr. – Arrecife
A.S.S.R. – Autonomous Soviet Socialist Republic
Aust. – Australia
Áy. – Áyios

B

B. – Bahía, Baia, Baie, Bay, Bucht, Bukt
Ba. – Bahía
Bang. – Bangladesh
Bah. – Bahrain
Bel. – Belgium
Ben. – Benin
Bg. – Berg
Bhu. – Bhutan
Bk. – Bukit
Bol. – Bol'shoy, Bol'shoye
Br. – Burnu, Burun
Bru. – Brunei
Bt. – Bukit
Bu. – Burundi
Bü. – Büyük
Bulg. – Bulgaria
Bur. Faso – Burkina Faso

C

C. – Cabo, Cap, Cape; Cerro
Can. – Canal, Canale
Cga. – Ciénaga
Chan. – Channel
Co. – Cerro
Col. – Colombia
Cord. – Cordillera
Cr. – Creek
Czech. – Czechoslovakia

D

D. – Dağ, Dağı, Dağları; Daryācheh
D.C. – District of Colombia

Den. – Denmark
Djib. – Djibouti

E

E. – East
Eq. – Equatorial
Est. – Estrecho

F

Fd. – Fjord
Fk. – Fork
Fr. – France
Ft. – Fort

G

G. – Golfe, Golfo, Guba, Gulf; Gora, Gunung
Gd. – Grand
Gde. – Grande
Geb. – Gebirge
Gen. – General
Geog. – Geographical
Ger. – Germany
Gh. – Ghana
Gl. – Glacier
Gr. – Grande, Gross
Gt. – Great
Guy. – Guyana

H

Har. – Harbour
Hd. – Head
Hung. – Hungary

I

I. – Île, Ilha, Insel, Isla, Island, Isle, Iscla, Isole
Is. – Ilhas, Îles, Islands, Islas, Isles
Isth. – Isthmus

J

J. – Jabal, Jbel, Jebel; Jezioro, Jezero, Jazā'ir
Jor. – Jordan

K

K. – Kap; Kūh, Kūhhā; Koh; Kólpos
Kam. – Kampuchea
Kan. – Kanal, Kanaal
Kep. – Kepulauan
Khr. – Khrebet
Kör. – Körfezi
Kuw. – Kuwait

L

L. – Lac, Lacul, Lago, Lake, Limni, Llyn, Loch, Lough
Lag. – Lagoon, Laguna
Leb. – Lebanon
Liech. – Liechtenstein
Lit. – Little
Lux. – Luxembourg

M

M. – Mys
Mal. – Malawi
Mex. – Mexico
Mgne. – Montagne
Mt. – Mont, Mount, Mountain
Mti. – Monti
Mţii. – Munţii
Mts. – Monts, Mounts, Mountains

N

N. – Nord, North; Nos
Neb. – Nebraska
Neth. – Netherlands
Nev. – Nevado
N.H. – New Hampshire
Nizh. – Nizhnyaya
Nizm. – Nizmennost'
Nor. – Norway
N.Z. – New Zealand

O

O. – Ost; Ostrov
Os. – Ostrova
Oz. – Ozero

P

P. – Point
Pass. – Passage
Penn. – Pennsylvania
Peg. – Pegunungan
Pen. – Peninsola, Peninsula, Peninsule
Pk. – Peak, Puncak
Pl. – Planina
Pol. – Poluostrov
Port. – Portugal
Prom. – Promontory
Pt. – Point
Pta. – Ponta, Punta
Pte. – Pointe
Pto. – Puerto; Punto

Q

Qat. – Qatar

R

R. – Reshteh
Ra. – Range
Rep. – Republic
Res. – Reservoir
Rés. – Réservoir
Rom. – Romania
R.S.F.S.R. – Russian Soviet Federal Socialist Republic
Rw. – Rwanda

S

S. – Shatt; South
Sa. – Serra, Sierra
S.A. – South Africa
Sd. – Sound, Sund
Sp. – Spain
Sprs. – Springs
S.S.R. – Soviet Socialist Republic
St. – Saint, Sint
Sta. – Santa
Ste. – Sainte
Str. – Strait
Sur. – Suriname
Switz. – Switzerland

T

Tg. – Tanjong, Tanjung
Tk. – Teluk

U

U.A.E. – United Arab Emirates
U.K. – United Kingdom
U.S.A. – United States of America
U.S.S.R. – Union of Soviet Socialist Republics

V

V. – Volcano
Vdkhr. – Vodokhranilishche
Ven. – Venezuela
Verkh. – Verkhne
Vn. – Volcán
Vol. – Volcán, Volcano

W

W. – Wadi; Wald; West

Y

Y. – Yarimadasi
Yug. – Yugoslavia

Z

Zal. – Zaliv

INDEX

The index includes an alphabetical list of all names appearing in the map section of the Atlas. Names on the maps and in the index are generally in the local language. For names in languages not written in the Roman alphabet, the officially accepted transliteration system has been used.

The order of names in the index is strictly alphabetical, diacritical marks are disregarded.

Most features are indexed to the largest scale map on which they appear. Extensive features are usually indexed to maps that show the features completely or show them in their relationship to surrounding areas. For extensive regional features, locations are given for the approximate centre of the feature, those for linear features are given at the position of the name.

Each entry in the index is located by a page number and an alphanumeric grid reference on that particular page. The grid is defined by letters, positioned at the top and at the bottom of the map spread, and numbers, shown at the sides of the spread. For example, Bandung in Indonesia has the reference 90 D7. It can thus be found on page 90 in the grid square D7.

Where two identical names are referenced to the same page and grid square, it should be noted that they relate to different adjacent features. For example, the name Avon appears twice in the index and in both cases it is referenced to 52E3. These two entries locate firstly the county of Avon and secondly the River Avon.

Abū Kamāl	94 E4
Abū Latt	96 E7
Abū Madd, Ra's	96 C4
Abū Mūsā	95 M9
Abū Qa'ṭūr	77 G5
Abu Shagara, Râs	96 C6
Abut Head	115 C5
Abu Tig	102 F2
Abu Zabad	102 E5
Abū Ẓabī	97 M4
Abwong	103 F6
Åby	63 G7
Abyaḍ, Ar Ra's al	96 D5
Åbyälven	62 J4
Åbybro	63 C8
Abyek	95 K3
Acalayong	105 G5
Acámbaro	131 J7
Acambay	131 K8
Acandí	132 J10
Acaponeta	130 G6
Acapulco	131 K9
Acaraí, Serra	136 F3
Acaraú Brazil	137 J4
Acaraú Brazil	137 J4
Acarigua	136 D2
Acatlán Mexico	130 H7
Acatlán Mexico	131 K8
Acatzingo	131 L8
Acayucan	131 M9
Acceglio	68 A3
Accra	104 E4
Accrington	55 G3
Achacachi	138 C3
Achavanich	56 E2
Acheng	88 A3
Achikouya, Plateau des	106 B3
Achill	58 C5
Achill Head	58 B5
Achill Island	58 B5
Achim	70 C2
Achinsk	84 E5
Achmore	56 B2
Achnacroish	57 C4
Achosnich	57 B4
Acigöl	76 F3
Acipayam	76 C4
Acireale	69 E7
Acklins Island	133 K3
Acle	53 J2
Acomayo	136 C6
Aconcagua, Cerro	139 C6
Aconchi	127 G6
Açores	48 F3
Acoyapa	132 E9
Acqui Terme	68 B3
Acre Brazil	136 C5
Acre Brazil	136 D5
Acre Israel	94 B5
Actopan	131 K7
Açú	137 K5
Ada Ghana	104 F4
Ada Oklahoma, U.S.A.	128 D3
Adair, Bahia de	126 F5
Adaja	66 D2
Adak Island	118 Ac9
Adalia	76 D4
Adam	97 N5
Adaminaby	113 K6
'Adan	96 G10
Adana	76 F4
Adapazari	76 D2
Adare	59 E7
Adda	68 B2
Adda	68 B3
Ad Dakhla	100 B4
Ad Dammām	97 K3
Ad Darb	96 F8
Ad Dawādimī	96 G4
Ad Dawḥah	97 K4
Ad Dila	97 K7
Ad Dilam	96 H5
Ad Dir'īyah	96 H4
Ad Dūwānīyah	94 G6
Ad Duwayd	96 F1
Adel	124 C6
Adelaide Antarctic	141 V5
Adelaide Australia	113 H5
Adelaide Bahamas	129 P8
Adelaide Island	141 V5
Adelaide Peninsula	120 G4
Aden	96 G10
Aden, Gulf of	103 J5
Adh Dhayd	97 M4
Adi	114 A2
Ādī Ārk'ay	96 C10
Ādī Da'iro	96 D9
Adige	68 C3
Adīgrat	96 D9
Adigüzel Baraji	76 C3
Ādī K'eyah	96 D9
Adilabad	92 E5
Adilcevaz	77 K3
Adin	122 D7
Adirondack Mountains	125 N4
Ādīs Ābeba	103 G6
Ādī Ugrī	96 D9
Adiyaman	77 H4
Adjud	73 J2
Adjuntas, Presa de las	131 K6
Adka	118 Ac9
Adlington	55 G3
Admello	68 C2
Admiralty Gulf	112 F1
Admiralty Inlet	120 J3
Admiralty Island Canada	119 Q2
Admiralty Island U.S.A.	118 J4
Admiralty Islands	114 D2
Admund Ringnes Island	120 G2
Ado-Ekiti	105 G4
Adonara	91 G7
Adoni	92 E5
Adorf	70 E3
Adoumaoua, Massif de l'	105 H4
Adour	65 C7
Adra	66 E4
Adráno	69 E7
Adrar	100 E3
Adré	102 D5
Adria	68 D3
Adrian Michigan, U.S.A.	124 J6
Adrian Texas, U.S.A.	127 L3
Adriatic Sea	68 E4
Ādwa	96 D9
Adwick le Street	55 H3
Adycha	85 P3
Adzhar A.S.S.R.	79 G7
Adzhima	88 G1
Adz'vavom	78 K2
Aegean Sea	75 H3
Afafura, Laut	91 K7
Afanasevo	78 J4
Affopakka	137 F3
Affric	56 C3
Afghanistan	92 B2
Afgooye	107 J2
'Afif	96 F5
Afikpo	105 G4
Afmadow	107 H2
Afognak Island	118 E4
Afon Efyrnwy	52 D2
'Afrīn	77 G4
Afşin	77 G3
Afyon	76 D3
Agadez	101 G5
Agadir	100 D2
Agadyr'	86 C2
Agaie	105 G4
Agalta, Sierra de	132 E7
Agano	89 G7
Agapa U.S.S.R.	84 D2
Agapa U.S.S.R.	84 D2
Agapitovo	84 D3
Agartala	93 H4
Agaruut	87 K3
Agats	114 B3
Agatti	92 D6
Agattu Island	118 Aa9
Agbaja	105 G4
Agboville	104 E4
Agdam	94 H2
Agde	65 E7
Agematsu	89 F8
Agen	65 D6
Aghada	59 F9
Agha Jārī	95 J6
Agiabampo, Estero de	130 E4
Ağin	77 H3
Agira	69 E7
Ağlasun	76 D4
Ágnanda	75 F4
Agno	68 C3
Agnone	69 E5
Agout	65 D7
Agra	92 E3
Agram	72 C3
Agreda	67 F2
Agri	69 F5
Ağri	77 K3
Agrigento	69 D7
Agrínion	75 F3
Agropoli	69 E5
Água Clara	138 F4
Aguadas	136 B2
Aguadilla	133 P5
Aguanaval	130 H5
Agua Prieta	127 H5
Aguascalientes	130 H7
Agua, Volcán de	132 B7
Aguelhok	100 F5
Aguemour	101 F3
Aguilar de Campóo	66 D1
Aguilas	67 F4
Aguja, Cabo de la	133 K9
Aguja, Punta	136 A5
Agulhas, Kaap	108 D6
Agusan	91 H4
Ahar	94 H2
Åheim	62 A5
A'himahasoa	109 J4
Ahipara Bay	115 D1
Ahititi	115 E3
Ahlat	77 K3
Ahmadabad	92 D4
Ahmadī	95 N8
Ahmadnagar	92 D5
Ahmadpur	92 D3
Ahmar Mountains	103 H6
Ahoskie	129 P2
Ahram	95 K7
Ähtäri	62 L5
Ähtärinjärvi	62 L5
Ahuachapán	132 C8
Ahvāz	94 J6
Ahvenanmaa	63 H6
Aḥwar	96 H10
Aiddejavrre	62 K2
Aidhipsós	75 G3
Aigen	68 D1
Aigues	65 F6
Aiken	129 M4
Ailao Shan	93 K4
Ailsa Craig	57 C5
Aim	85 N5
Aimorés, Serra dos	138 H3
Ain	65 F5
Aïn Beïda	101 G1
Aïn Bessem	67 H4
Ain Defla	67 G4
Aïn El Hadjel	67 H5
Aïn Oulmène	67 J5
Aïn Sefra	100 E2
Ainsworth	123 Q6
Aioun el Atrouss	100 D5
Aiquile	138 C3
Aïr	101 G5
Airbangis	90 B5
Airdrie	57 E5
Aire France	64 F4
Aire U.K.	55 J3
Airedale	55 H3
Aire-sur-l'Adour	65 C7
Air Force Island	120 M4
Airgin Sum	87 L3
Airi-selkä	62 L3
Aisne	64 E4
Aitape	114 C2
Aith	56 F1
Aix-en-Provence	65 F7
Aix-les-Bains	65 F6
Aíyina	75 G4
Aiyínion	75 G2
Aíyion	75 G3
Aizawl	93 H4
Aizpute	63 J8
Aizu-Wakamatsu	89 G7
Ajaccio	69 B5
Ajana	112 C4
Ajanta Range	92 E4
Ajdābiyā	101 K2
Ajlun	94 B5
'Ajmān	97 M4
Ajmer	92 D3
Akaishi-sanchi	89 G8
Akalkot	92 E5
Akamkpa	105 G4
Akaroa Head	115 D5
Akbou	67 J4

Akbulak	79	K5
Akçaabat	77	H2
Akçaakale	77	H4
Akçadağ	77	G3
Akçakoca	76	D2
Akçaova	76	C4
Akçay	76	C4
Akchatau	86	C2
Ak Dağlari	76	C4
Akdağmadeni	77	F3
Ak Dovurak	84	E6
Akershus	63	D6
Akeşhir Gölü	76	D3
Aketi	106	D2
Akgevir	77	J4
Akhalkalaki	77	K2
Akhaltsikhe	77	K2
Akhdar, Al Jabal al	101	K2
Akhdar, Jabal	97	N5
Akhḍar, Wadi	96	C3
Akhelóös	75	F3
Akhiok	118	E4
Akhisar	76	B3
Akhmîm	103	F2
Akhtubinsk	79	H6
Akhtyrka	79	E5
Aki	89	D9
Akimiski Island	121	K7
Akincilar	77	H2
Akinkeen	59	D9
Akinli	77	J4
Akita	88	H6
Akjoujt	100	C5
Akkavare	62	J3
Akkeshi	88	K4
'Akko	94	B5
Akköy	76	B4
Akkuş	77	G2
Aklavik	118	H2
Akniste	63	L8
Akola	92	E4
Akonolinga	105	H5
Ak'ordat	96	C9
Akören	76	E4
Akosombo Dam	104	E4
Akot	92	E4
Akpatok Island	121	N5
Akpinar	76	E3
Akqi	86	D3
Akranes	62	T12
Akron	125	K6
Akşar	77	K2
Aksaray	76	E3
Aksay *China*	86	G4
Aksay *U.S.S.R.*	79	J5
Akşehir	76	D3
Akseki	76	D4
Aksenovo-Zilovskoye	85	K6
Aks-e Rostam	95	M7
Aksha	85	J6
Akshimrau	79	J7
Aksu *China*	86	E3
Aksu *Turkey*	76	D4
Aksu *U.S.S.R.*	79	J5
Aksu-Ayuly	86	C2
Aksu Çayi	76	D4
Āksum	96	D9
Aksumbe	86	B3
Aktau	84	A6
Aktí	75	H2

Aktogay	86	D2
Akulivik	120	L5
Akune	89	C9
Akun Island	118	Ae9
Akure	105	G4
Akureyri	62	V12
Akuse	104	F4
Akutan Island	118	Ae9
Akwanga	105	G4
Akyab	93	H4
Akyatan Gölü	76	F4
Akyazi	76	D2
Akyurt	76	E2
Akzhar	86	C3
Al Aaiún	100	C3
Alabama *U.S.A.*	129	J4
Alabama *U.S.A.*	129	J4
Alaca	76	F2
Alacahan	77	G3
Alaçam	77	F2
Alaçam Dağlari	76	C3
Alacrán, Arrecife	131	Q6
Alagoas	137	K5
Alagoinhas	137	K6
Alagón *Spain*	66	C2
Alagón *Spain*	67	F2
Al 'Aḥmadī	97	J2
Al 'Ajā'iz	97	N7
Alajärvi	62	K5
Alajuela	132	E9
Alakanuk	118	C3
Alakol', Ozero	86	E2
Alakylä	62	L3
Al 'Amārah	94	H6
Alameda *California, U.S.A.*	126	A2
Alameda *New Mexico, U.S.A.*	127	J3
Alamicamba	132	E8
Alamo	126	E2
Alamogordo	127	K4
Alà, Monti di	69	B5
Alamos	127	H7
Alamosa	127	K2
Åland	63	H6
Ålands hav	63	M6
Alanya	76	E4
Alaotra, Lake	109	J3
Alapayevsk	84	Ad5
Al 'Āqūlah	97	J5
Alarcón, Embalse de	66	E3
Al Arṭāwīyah	96	G3
Alaşehir	76	C3
Al Ashkhirah	97	P6
Alaska	118	E3
Alaska, Gulf of	118	F4
Alaska Peninsula	118	Af8
Alaska Range	118	E3
Alassio	68	B4
Alatna	118	E2
Alatyr	78	H5
Alausi	136	B4
Alaverdi	77	L2
Alavus	62	K5
Al 'Ayn	97	M4
Alayor	67	J3
Alayskiy Khrebet	86	C4
Al Azamīyah	77	L6
Alazeya	85	S2
Alba	68	B3
Al Bâb	77	G4
Albacete	67	F3

Alba de Tormes	66	D2
Al Badī	96	H5
Al Badi	77	J5
Alba Iulia	73	G2
Albæk	63	D8
Alba, Mount	115	B6
Albanel, Lake	121	M7
Albania	74	E2
Albano	137	F4
Albany *Australia*	112	D5
Albany *Canada*	121	K7
Albany *Georgia, U.S.A.*	129	K5
Albany *Kentucky, U.S.A.*	124	H8
Albany *New York, U.S.A.*	125	P5
Albany *Oregon, U.S.A.*	122	C5
Albarracín	67	F2
Al Basrah	94	H6
Albatross Bay	113	J1
Albatross Point	115	E3
Al Bayḍā	96	G10
Albayrak	77	L3
Albemarle	129	M3
Albemarle Island	136	A7
Albemarle Sound	129	P2
Albenga	68	B3
Albentosa	67	F2
Alberche	66	D2
Alberga	113	G4
Albergaria-a-Velha	66	B2
Alberique	67	F3
Albert	64	E3
Alberta	119	M5
Albert Edward, Mount	114	D3
Albert Kanaal	64	F3
Albert, Lake	107	F2
Albert Lea	124	D5
Albert Nile	107	F2
Albertville *France*	65	G6
Albertville *Zaire*	107	E4
Albi	65	E7
Albina	137	G2
Al Bi'r	96	C2
Al Birk	96	E7
Albocácer	67	G2
Albo, Monti	69	B5
Alborán, Isla de	66	E5
Ålborg	63	D8
Ålborg Bugt	63	D8
Alborz, Reshteh-ye Kühtä ye	95	K3
Albro	113	K3
Albufeira	66	B4
Ālbū Gharz, Sabkhat	77	J5
Albuquerque	127	J3
Al Buraymī	97	M4
Albury	113	K6
Al Buşayyah	94	H6
Al Buzūn	97	K9
Alcácer do Sal	66	B3
Alcalá de Henares	66	E2
Alcamo	69	D7
Alcañices	66	C2
Alcañiz	67	F2
Alcántara	66	C3
Alcântara	137	J4
Alcántara, Embalse de	66	C3
Alcaraz	66	E3
Alcaraz, Sierra de	66	E3
Alcaudete	66	D4
Alcázar de San Juan	66	E3
Alcester	53	F2

Alcolea del Pinar	66	E2
Alcoutim	66	C4
Alcoy	67	F3
Alcubierre, Sierra de	67	F2
Alcublas	67	F3
Alcudia	67	H3
Aldabra Islands	82	C7
Aldama	131	K6
Aldan *U.S.S.R.*	85	M5
Aldan *U.S.S.R.*	85	N4
Aldanskoye Nagor'ye	85	M5
Alde	53	J2
Aldeburgh	53	J2
Aldeia Nova	66	C4
Alderley Edge	55	G3
Alderney	53	M6
Aldershot	53	G3
Aldridge	53	F2
Aleg	100	C5
Alegrete	138	E5
Aleksandra, Mys	85	P6
Aleksandriya	79	E6
Aleksandrov	78	F4
Aleksandrovac	73	F4
Aleksandrov Gay	79	H5
Aleksandrovsk	78	K4
Aleksandrovskoye	79	G7
Aleksandrovsk-Sakhalinskiy	85	Q6
Aleksandry, Ostrov	80	F1
Alekseyevka *Kazakhstan S.S.R., U.S.S.R.*	84	A6
Alekseyevka *Rossiyskaya S.F.S.R., U.S.S.R.*	79	F5
Aleksin	78	F5
Além Paraíba	138	H4
Alençon	64	D4
Alenquer	137	G4
Alentejo	66	C3
Alenuihaha Channel	126	S10
Aleppo	77	G4
Aléria	69	B4
Alerta	136	C6
Alès	65	F6
Alëshki	78	H2
Alessandria	68	B3
Alessio	74	E2
Ålesund	62	B5
Aleutian Islands	118	Ab9
Aleutian Range	118	D4
Aleutian Trench	143	H3
Alevina, Mys	85	S5
Alexander Archipelago	118	J4
Alexander Bay	108	C5
Alexander, Cape	119	P2
Alexander City	129	K4
Alexander Island	141	V4
Alexander, Kap	120	M2
Alexandra *Australia*	113	K6
Alexandra *New Zealand*	115	B6
Alexandretta	77	G4
Alexandria *Egypt*	102	E1
Alexandria *Romania*	73	H4
Alexandria *South Africa*	108	E6
Alexandria *U.K.*	57	D5
Alexandria *Louisiana, U.S.A.*	128	F5
Alexandria *Minnesota, U.S.A.*	124	C4
Alexandria *Virginia, U.S.A.*	125	M7
Alexandroúpolis	75	H2
Aleysk	84	C6
Al Fallūjah	77	K6

Alfambra *Spain*	67	F2	Alingsås	63	E8	Almáciles	66	E4	Al Qāmishlī	94	E3
Alfambra *Spain*	67	F2	Alinskoye	84	D4	Almada	66	B3	Al Qaryatayn	77	G5
Alfaro	136	B4	Alipka	84	D5	Al Maḍḍah	96	F7	Al Qaṭīf	97	J3
Alfatar	73	J4	'Al 'Īsawiyah	94	C6	Almadén	66	D3	Al Qaṭn	97	J9
Al Faw	94	J7	Alisos	126	G5	Al Madīnah	96	D4	Al Qayşumah	96	H2
Alfeld	70	C3	Alistáti	75	G2	Almagro	66	E3	Al Qubbah	101	K2
Alfiós	75	F4	Aliwal North	108	E6	Al Maḥmūdīyah	94	G5	Alqueva, Barragem de	66	C3
Alford *Grampian, U.K.*	56	F3	Al Jaghbūb	101	K2	Al Majma'ah	96	G4	Alquippa	125	K6
Alford *Lincolnshire, U.K.*	55	K3	Al Jahrah	97	H2	Almalyk	86	B3	Al Qunfudhah	96	E7
Alfreton	55	H3	Al Jawārah	97	N7	Al Manāmah	97	K3	Al Quraynī	97	L6
Al Fuḥayḥīl	97	J2	Al Jawf *Libya*	101	K4	Almanor, Lake	122	D7	Al Qurayyāt	97	P5
Al Fujayrah	97	N4	Al Jawf *Saudi Arabia*	96	D2	Almansa	67	F3	Al Qurnah	94	H6
Al Fuqah'ā	101	J3	Al Jazīrah	77	J4	Al Mansūrīyah	96	F9	Al Quţayfah	94	C5
Al Furāt	77	J5	Al Jubayl	97	J3	Almanzor, Pic de	66	D2	Al Quwayīyah	96	G4
Algård	63	A7	Aljustrel	66	B4	Al Māriyah	97	L5	Al Quzah	97	J9
Algarrobo del Aguila	139	C7	Al Kalban	97	P6	Al Marj	101	K2	Al Ramādī	77	K6
Algarve	66	B4	Al Kāmil	97	P5	Al Maşna'ah	97	N5	Als	70	C1
Algatart	86	C3	Al Khābūrah	97	N5	Al Mawşil	77	K4	Alsace	64	G4
Algeciras	66	D4	Al Khālis	94	G5	Al Mayādīn	77	J5	Alsask	123	K2
Algena	96	D8	Al Khalūf	97	P6	Al Mayyah	96	F3	Alsasua	67	E1
Alger, Baie 'd	67	H4	Al Khaşab	97	N3	Almazán	66	E2	Alsek	118	H4
Algeria	101	F3	Al Khatt	97	N4	Almeirim	137	G4	Alsfeld	70	C3
Al Ghaydah	97	L8	Al Khawr	97	K4	Almelo	64	G2	Alsh, Loch	56	C3
Alghero	69	B5	Al Khubar	97	K3	Almendra, Embalse de	66	C2	Alsten	62	E4
Algiers	101	F1	Al Khufrah	101	K4	Almería	66	E4	Alstermo	63	F8
Algoa Bay	108	E6	Al Khums	101	H2	Almeria, Golfo de	66	E4	Alston	55	G2
Algodões	137	K5	Al Khuraybah	97	J9	Al'met'yevsk	78	J5	Alta	62	P2
Algodonales	66	D4	Al Khuwayr	97	K3	Älmhult	63	F8	Altaelv	62	K2
Algona	124	C5	Alkmaar	64	F2	Al Midhnab	96	G4	Altafjord	62	K1
Algonquin Park	125	L4	Al Kūfah	94	G5	Almina, Punta	66	D5	Alta Gracia	138	D6
Algueirão	109	F4	Al Kūt	94	G5	Al Miqdādīyah	94	G5	Altagracia	133	M9
Al Ḥadd	97	P5	Al Kuwayt	97	H2	Almiropótamos	75	H3	Altai	86	G2
Al Hadīthah	94	F4	Allada	105	F4	Almirós	75	G3	Altamaha	129	M5
Al Ḥaḍr	77	K5	Al Lādhiqīyah	77	F5	Almiroú, Kólpos	75	H5	Altamira	137	G4
Al Ḥalfāyah	94	H6	Allahabad	92	F3	Al Mish'āb	96	J3	Altamura	69	F5
Al Ḥallānīyah	97	N8	Allahüekber Dağlari	77	K2	Almodôvar	66	B4	Altamura, Isla de	130	E5
Al Ḥamar	96	H5	Allakh-Yu'n	85	P4	Almond	57	E4	Alta, Sierra	67	C2
Alhambra	66	E3	Allanmyo	93	J5	Almonte	66	D3	Altay *U.S.S.R.*	84	Ae4
Al Ḥanākīyah	96	E4	Allanridge	108	E5	Almora	92	E3	Altay *U.S.S.R.*	86	F2
Al Ḥarīq	96	H5	Allaqi, Wadi	103	F3	Al Mubarraz	97	J4	Altay *U.S.S.R.*	86	H2
Al Has'ā	97	J3	Allariz	66	C1	Al Mudawwara	94	B7	Altdorf	68	B2
Al Hasakah	77	J4	Alldays	108	E4	Al Muḍaybī	97	P5	Altenburg	70	E3
Al Hāshimīyah	94	G5	Allegheny	125	L6	Al Muḍayrib	97	P5	Altinekin	76	E3
Al Ḥawṭah	96	H9	Allegheny Mountains	124	J8	Al Muḥarraq	97	K3	Altinhisar	76	F3
Al Ḥayy	94	H5	Allegheny Plateau	125	K7	Al Mukallā	97	J9	Altinkaya	76	D4
Al Ḥillah *Iraq*	94	G5	Allen *Philippines*	91	G3	Al Mukhā	96	F10	Altin Köprü	77	L5
Al Ḥillah *Saudi Arabia*	96	H5	Allen *U.K.*	52	C4	Almuradiel	66	E3	Altinova	76	B3
Al Ḥilwah	96	H5	Allen, Bog of	59	H6	Al Musaymīr	96	G10	Altinözü	77	G4
Al Ḥudaydah	96	F9	Allendale	129	M4	Al Musayyib	94	G5	Altintaş	76	D3
Al Hufūf	96	J4	Allende	127	M6	Almus Baraji	77	G2	Altkirche	65	G5
Al Ḥuraydah	97	J9	Allen, Lough	58	F4	Al Mūwayh	96	E5	Altmark	70	D2
Alīābād	94	H4	Allenstein	71	J2	Al Muwaylih	96	B3	Altmühl	70	D4
Alīabad	95	M7	Allentown	125	N6	Aln	57	G5	Altnaharra	56	D2
Aliağa	76	B3	Alleppey	92	E7	Alness	56	D3	Alto Araguaia	138	F3
Aliaga	67	F2	Aller	70	D2	Alnwick	55	H1	Alto Coité	138	F3
Aliákmon	75	G2	Allerston	55	J2	Alofi	111	T4	Alto Molocue	109	G3
'Alī al Gharbī	94	H5	Allevard	65	G6	Alor	91	G7	Alton *Hampshire, U.K.*	53	G3
Alibag	92	D5	Allgäuer Alpen	68	C2	Alora	66	D4	Alton *Staffordshire, U.K.*	53	F2
Alibey, Ozero	73	L3	Alliance *Nebraska, U.S.A.*	123	N6	Alor, Kepulauan	91	G7	Altoona	125	L6
Alibunar	73	F3	Alliance *Ohio, U.S.A.*	125	K6	Alotau	114	E4	Alto Sucuriú	138	F3
Alicante	67	F3	Allier	65	E5	Alpe-d'Huez	65	G6	Altrincham	55	G3
Alice	128	C7	Allik	121	Q6	Alpena	124	J4	Altun Shan	92	F1
Alice, Punta	69	F6	Al Līth	96	E6	Alpercatas, Serra das	137	J5	Alturas	122	D7
Alice Springs	113	G3	Alloa	57	E4	Alpine *Arizona, U.S.A.*	127	H4	Al 'Ubaylah	97	K6
Aligarh	92	E3	Al Luhayyah	96	F9	Alpine *Texas, U.S.A.*	127	L5	Alucra	77	H2
Alīgūdarz	95	J5	Allur	92	F6	Alps	50	J6	Alūksne	63	M8
Alijūq, Kūh-e	95	K6	Alma *Canada*	125	Q2	Alpu	76	D3	Al 'Ulā	96	C3
Al Ikhwān	97	N10	Alma *Michigan, U.S.A.*	124	H5	Al Qaffāy	97	K4	Aluminé	139	B7
Alima	106	C3	Alma *Nebraska, U.S.A.*	123	Q7	Al Qā'im	77	J5	Al 'Uqayr	97	K4
Alindao	102	D6	Alma-Ata	86	D3	Al Qalibah	96	C2	Alur Setar	90	C4

Al' Uwayja	96	G5	Amboise	65	D5	Amsterdam *U.S.A.*	125	N5	'Andām, Wadi	97	P6
Alva	128	C2	Ambon *Indonesia*	91	H6	Am Timan	102	D5	Andanga	78	H4
Alvarado	131	M8	Ambon *Indonesia*	91	H6	Amuay	133	M9	Andapa	109	J2
Alvaro Obregón	131	N8	Ambositra	109	J4	Amundsen Glacier	141	P1	Andaraí	137	J6
Alvdal	63	H5	Ambovombe	109	J5	Amundsen-Scott	141	A1	Ãndeba Ye Midir Zerf Ch'af	96	E9
Älvdalen	63	F6	Ambriz	106	B4	Amundsen Sea	141	S5	Andeg	78	J2
Alvito	66	C3	Ambrym	114	U12	Amuntai	90	F6	Andenes	62	G2
Alvorada	137	H6	Amchitka Island	118	Ab9	Amur *China*	87	N1	Andermatt	68	B2
Älvsborg	63	E8	Amchitka Pass	118	Ab9	Amur *U.S.S.R.*	85	Q6	Anderson *Canada*	118	K2
Alvsbyn	62	J4	Amdassa	91	J7	Amuri Pass	115	D5	Anderson *Indiana, U.S.A.*	124	H6
Al Wajh	96	C3	Amderma	84	Ad3	Amursk	85	P6	Anderson *Missouri, U.S.A.*	124	C8
Al Wakrah	97	K4	Amdo	93	H2	Amurskaya Oblast'	85	M6	Anderson *S.Carolina, U.S.A.*	129	L3
Alwar	92	E3	Ameca	130	G7	Amur, Wadi	103	F4	Anderson Bay	113	K7
Alwen Reservoir	55	F3	Amecameca	131	K8	Amvrakikós Kólpos	75	F3	Andes	136	B2
Alwinton	57	F5	Amendolara	69	F6	Amvrosiyevka	79	F6	Andevoranto	109	J3
Al Wusayl	97	K4	Ameralik	120	R5	Anabar	84	J2	Andfjorden	62	G2
Alyaskitovyy	85	Q4	American	122	D8	Anaco	133	Q10	Andhra Pradesh	92	E5
Alyat	94	J2	American Falls Reservoir	122	H6	Anaconda	122	H4	Andikíthira	75	G5
Alyth, Forest of	57	E4	American Samoa	111	U4	Anadarko	128	C3	Andīmeshk	94	J5
Alytus	71	L1	Americus	129	K4	Anadyr' *U.S.S.R.*	85	W4	Andímilos	75	H4
Alzamay	84	F5	Amersham	53	G3	Anadyr' *U.S.S.R.*	85	X4	Andíparos	75	H4
Amadeus, Lake	112	G3	Amery Ice Shelf	141	E5	Anadyrskiy Khrebet	85	W3	Andípaxoi	75	F3
Amādīyah	77	K4	Ames	124	D5	Anáfi *Greece*	75	H4	Andirin	77	G4
Amadjuak Lake	120	M5	Amesbury	53	F3	Anáfi *Greece*	75	H4	Andizhan	86	C3
Amagasaki	89	E8	Amfíklia	75	G3	Anåfjället	62	E5	Andkhovy	95	S3
Amager	63	E9	Amfilokhía	75	F3	'Ānah	77	J5	Andoas	136	B4
Amahai	91	H6	Amfípolis	75	G2	Anaheim	126	D4	Andong	89	B7
Amakusa-Shimo-shima	89	C9	Ámfissa	75	G3	Anáhuac	128	B7	Andongwei	87	M4
Åmål	63	E7	Amga *U.S.S.R.*	85	N4	Anakapalle	92	F5	Andorra	66	G1
Amalfi	69	E5	Amga *U.S.S.R.*	85	N4	Anaktuvuk	118	E2	Andorra la Vella	67	G1
Amaliás	75	F4	Amgu	88	F3	Analalava	109	J2	Andover	53	F3
Amalner	92	E4	Amguema	85	Y3	Anambas, Kepulauan	90	D5	Andøya	62	F2
Amami-Ō-shima	89	B11	Amgun'	85	P6	Anamur	76	E4	Andraitx	67	H3
Amami-shotō	89	J10	Amherst *Canada*	121	P8	Anamur Burun	76	E4	Andrascoggin	125	Q4
Amandola	69	D4	Amherst *U.S.A.*	125	L8	Anan	89	E9	Andravídha	75	F4
Amantea	69	F6	Amiata, Monte	69	C4	Anánes	75	H4	Andreafsky	118	C3
Amanzimtoti	108	F6	Amiens	64	E4	Anantapur	92	E6	Andreanof Islands	118	Ac9
Amapa	137	G3	Amikino	85	L6	Anantnag	92	E2	Andrews	127	L4
Amapá	137	G3	Amilḥayt, Wadi al	97	L7	Anan'yev	73	K2	Andreyevka	79	J5
Amarante	66	B2	Amindivi Islands	92	D6	Anan'yevo	86	D3	Andreyevo Ivanovka	73	L2
Amarapura	93	J4	Amirante Islands	82	D7	Anápolis	138	J3	Andreyevsk	85	J5
Amargosa	126	D3	Amistad Reservoir	127	M6	Anapu	137	G4	Andria	69	F5
Amarillo	127	M3	Amitioke Peninsula	120	K4	Anār	95	M6	Andrijevica	72	E4
Amaro	69	E4	Amka	85	Q5	Anārak	95	L5	Andringitra	109	J4
Amasiya	77	K2	Amland	64	F2	Anār Darreh	95	Q5	Andropov	78	F4
Amasra	76	E2	Amlia Island	118	Ad9	Añatuya	138	D5	Andros	132	H2
Amasya	77	F2	Amlwch	55	E3	Anauá	136	E3	Ándros *Greece*	75	H4
Amatignak Island	118	Ac9	Amman	94	B6	Anavilhanas, Arquipiélago das	136	E4	Ándros *Greece*	75	H4
Amatrice	69	D4	Ammanford	52	C3	A Nazrēt	103	G6	Androth	92	D6
Amazon	137	G4	Ammer	70	D4	Anbei	86	H3	Andújar	66	D3
Amazonas	137	G4	Ammersee	70	D5	Ancenis	65	C5	Andulo	106	C5
Amazon, Mouths of the	137	G4	Amol	95	L3	Ancha	85	P4	Andyngda	85	K3
Ambala	92	E2	Amorgós *Greece*	75	H4	Anchi	105	G4	Anegada	133	Q5
Ambalavao	109	J4	Amorgós *Greece*	75	J4	Anchorage	118	F3	Anegada, Bahía	139	D8
Ambanja	109	J2	Amos	125	L2	Anchor Island	115	A6	Aného	105	F4
Ambar	84	E3	Åmot *Buskerud, Norway*	63	C7	Ancohuma, Nevado	138	C3	Aneityum	114	U13
Ambarchik	85	U3	Åmot *Telemark, Norway*	63	C7	Ancona	68	D4	Anelghowhat	114	U14
Ambarnyy	78	E2	Åmotfors	63	E7	Ancrum	57	F4	Aneto, Pic D'	67	G1
Ambato	136	B4	Ampana	91	G6	Ancuabe	109	G2	Anfield Plain	55	H2
Ambato-Boeny	109	J3	Ampanihy	109	H4	Ancuaque	138	C3	Angamos, Punta	138	B4
Ambatolampy	109	J3	Ampato, Nevado de	138	B3	Ancud	139	B8	Angar	114	A2
Amberg	70	D4	Amposta	67	G2	Ancud, Golfo de	139	B8	Angara	84	E5
Ambergris Cay	132	D5	Ampthill	53	G2	Anda	87	P2	Angara Basin	140	A1
Ambérieu-en-Bugey	65	F6	Amqui	125	S2	Andalgalá	138	C5	Angarsk	84	G6
Ambert	65	E6	Amrān	96	F9	Åndalsnes	62	B5	Ånge	62	F5
Ambikapur	92	F4	Amravati	92	E4	Andalucia	66	D4	Angel de la Guarda, Isla	126	F6
Ambilobe	109	J2	Amritsar	92	D2	Andalusia	129	J5	Angeles	91	G2
Amble-by-the-Sea	55	H1	Amroha	92	E3	Andaman Islands	93	H6	Angel Falls	136	E2
Ambleside	55	G2	Amrum	70	C1	Andaman Sea	93	J6	Ängelholm	63	E8
Ambodifototra	109	J3	Amsterdam *Netherlands*	64	F2	Andamarca	136	C6	Angelino	128	E5

Archidona	66	D4	Argolikós Kólpos	75	G4	Armeniya S.S.R.	79	G7	Art	114	V15
Arcis-sur-Aube	64	F4	Argonne, Forêt d'	64	F4	Armidale	113	L5	Árta	75	F3
Arco	122	H6	Argopuro, Gunung	90	E7	Armori	92	E4	Artá	67	H3
Arcos de la Frontera	66	D4	Argo Reefs	114	S9	Armoy	58	K2	Artashat	94	G2
Arctic Bay	120	J3	Árgos	75	G4	Armstrong	124	F1	Arteaga	130	H8
Arctic Ocean	140	A1	Argostólion	75	F3	Armthorpe	55	H3	Artem	88	D4
Arctic Red	118	J2	Arguello, Point	126	B3	Armu	88	F2	Artemisa	132	F3
Arctic Red River	118	J2	Argun	85	K6	Armutlu	76	C2	Artem-Ostrov	79	J7
Arctowski	141	W6	Argungu	105	F3	Armutova	76	B3	Artemovsk	79	F6
Arda	73	H5	Argunsk	85	L6	Armyansk	79	E6	Artemovskiy	84	Ad5
Ardabīl	94	J2	Arguvan	77	H3	Arnaía	75	G2	Artenay	65	D4
Ardahan	77	K2	Argyle, Lake	112	F2	Arnarfjörður	62	S12	Artesia	127	K4
Årdalstangen	63	B6	Argyll	57	C4	Arnaud	121	M5	Arthur's Pass	115	C5
Ardanuç	77	K2	Arhavi	77	J2	Arnauti, Akra	76	E5	Arthur's Town	133	K2
Ardara	58	F3	Ar Horqin Qi	87	M3	Arnedo	67	E1	Arti	78	K4
Ardarroch	56	C3	Århus	63	D8	Arneiroz	137	J5	Artigas	138	E6
Ardee	58	J5	Ariano Irpino	69	E5	Arnhem	64	F2	Artillery Lake	119	P3
Ardennes	64	F3	Arica	138	B3	Arnhem, Cape	113	H1	Artois	64	E3
Ardentinny	57	D4	Ariège	65	D7	Arnhem Land	113	G1	Artova	77	G2
Ardeşen	77	J2	Arīḥa	77	G5	Arno	68	C4	Artrutx, Cabo d'	67	H3
Ardestān	95	L5	Arilje	72	F4	Arnold	53	F2	Artsiz	79	D6
Ardfert	59	C8	Arima	136	E1	Arnon	65	E5	Artux	86	D4
Ardglass	58	L4	Arinagour	57	B4	Arnøy	62	J1	Artvin	77	J2
Ardgour	57	C4	Arinos	137	F6	Arnprior	125	M4	Artyk	85	R4
Ardh es Suwwān	94	C6	Aripuanã	136	E5	Ærø	70	D1	Arua	107	F2
Ardila	66	C3	Arisaig, Sound of	57	C4	Aroab	108	C5	Aruanã	137	G6
Ardino	73	H5	Aristazabal Island	118	K5	Aroeira	138	F4	Aruba	133	N8
Ardivacher Point	56	A3	Arivonimamo	109	J3	Arona	68	B3	Aru, Kepulauan	114	A3
Ardlussa	57	C4	Arivruaich	56	B2	Aroostook	125	R3	Arumã	136	E4
Ardminish	57	C5	Ariza	67	E2	Arorae	111	S2	Arun	53	G4
Ardmore	128	D3	Arizaro, Salar de	138	C4	Aroroy	91	G3	Arunachal Pradesh	93	H3
Ardnacross Bay	57	C5	Arizona Argentina	139	C7	Arosa	68	B2	Arundel	53	G4
Ardnamurchan	57	B4	Arizona U.S.A.	126	F3	Arpa	77	K2	Arun Qi	87	N2
Ardnamurchan Point	57	B4	Årjäng	63	E7	Arpaçay	77	K2	Aruppukkottai	92	E7
Ardnave Point	57	B5	Arjeplog	62	H3	Arpavla	84	Ad4	Arusha	107	G3
Ardrossan	57	D5	Arjona	136	B1	Arraias	137	H6	Arus, Tanjung	91	G5
Ards Peninsula	58	L3	Arkadak	79	G5	Ar Ramādī	94	F5	Aru, Tanjung	90	F6
Ardtalla	57	B5	Arkadelphia	128	F3	Arran	57	C5	Aruwimi	106	E2
Ardvasar	57	C3	Arkaig, Loch	57	B4	Ar Raqqah	77	H5	Arvayheer	87	J2
Ardvule, Rubha	56	A3	Arkalyk	84	Ae6	Arras	64	E3	Arvidsjaur	62	M4
Areão	137	H4	Arkansas U.S.A.	128	E3	Ar Rass	96	F4	Arvika	63	E7
Arecibo	133	P5	Arkansas U.S.A.	128	F3	Ar Rawdah	96	F6	Årviksand	62	J1
Areia Branca	137	K4	Arkansas City	128	D2	Ar Rāwuk	97	J9	Arxang	86	F3
Arena de las Ventas, Punta	130	E5	Arkhángelos	75	K4	Arrecife	100	C3	Arys'	86	B3
Arena, Point	122	B8	Arkhangel'sk	78	G3	Arrée, Monts d'	64	B4	Arzamas	78	G4
Arena, Punta	130	E6	Arkhipovka	88	D4	Arriaga	131	N9	Arzanah	97	L4
Arenas de San Pedro	66	D2	Arklow	59	K7	Ar Rifāʿī	94	H6	Arzew	100	E1
Arenas, Punta de	139	C10	Árkoi	75	J4	Arrino	112	D4	Arzew, Golfe d'	67	F5
Arendal	63	C7	Arkona, Kap	70	E1	Ar Riyād	96	H4	Arzúa	66	B1
Areópolis	75	G4	Arkticheskogo Instituta, Ostrova	84	C1	Arromanches	64	C4	Ås	63	D7
Arequipa	138	A3	Arlagnuk Point	120	K4	Arroux	65	F5	Asadābād	94	J4
Arévalo	66	D2	Arlanza	66	E1	Arrow	52	E2	Asad, Buḥayrat al	77	H5
Arezzo	68	C4	Arlberg Pass	68	C2	Arrow, Lough	58	F4	Aşağipinar	76	E3
Arfersiorfik	120	R4	Arles France	65	E7	Arrowtown	115	B6	Asahi-Dake	88	J4
Arga	67	F1	Arles France	65	F7	Arroyo Verde	139	C8	Asahi Kawa	88	J4
Argan	86	F3	Arlington Oregon, U.S.A.	122	D5	Ar Ru'ays	97	L4	Asālem	94	J3
Arganil	66	B2	Arlington S.Dakota, U.S.A.	123	R5	Ar Rub al Khālī	97	L6	Asamankese	104	E4
Argelès-Gazost	65	C7	Arlington Virginia, U.S.A.	125	M7	Ar Rumaytha	97	K4	Asansk	84	F5
Argens	65	G7	Arlon	64	F4	Ar Rumaythah	94	G6	Asansol	92	G4
Argent	65	E5	Armadale	57	E5	Ar Ruşāfah	77	H5	Asap	77	H2
Argenta	68	C3	Armagh U.K.	58	J4	Ar Rustāq	97	N5	Åsarna	62	F5
Argentan	64	C4	Armagh U.K.	58	J4	Ar Ruţbah	94	E5	Asbestos Mountains	108	D5
Argentat	65	D6	Armagnac	65	D7	Års	63	C8	Asbury Park	125	P6
Argentera	68	A3	Armah, Wadi	97	K8	Ars	94	H3	Ascención	138	D3
Argenteuil	64	E4	Arman	85	S4	Arsaynshand	87	L3	Ascension	99	B7
Argentina	139	C7	Armançon	65	E5	Arsenajan	95	L7	Ascensión, Bahía de la	131	R8
Argentino, Lago	139	B10	Armathia	75	J5	Arsen'yev	88	D3	Aschaffenburg	70	C4
Argenton-sur-Creuse	65	D5	Armavir	79	G6	Arsin	77	H2	Aschersleben	70	D3
Argeş	73	H3	Armenia	136	B3	Arsk	78	H4	Asco	69	B4
Argo	102	F4	Armeniş	73	G3	Arslanköy	76	F4	Ascoli Piceno	69	D4

Name	Map	Grid	Name	Map	Grid	Name	Map	Grid	Name	Map	Grid
Austin, Lake	112	D4	Axel-Heiberg Island	120	H2	Azoum	102	D5	Badby	53	F2
Australia	110	F6	Axim	104	E5	Azov, Sea of	79	F6	Bad Doberan	70	D1
Australian Capital Territory	113	K6	Axiós	75	G2	Azovskoye More	79	F6	Bad Ems	70	B3
Austria	68	D2	Ax-les-Thermes	65	D7	Azpeitia	66	E1	Baden	68	B2
Austurhorn	62	X12	Axminster	52	D4	Azraq, Bahr el	103	F5	Baden-Baden	70	C4
Autazes	136	F4	Ayabe	89	E8	Azrou	100	D2	Badenoch	57	D4
Authie	64	D3	Ayacucho *Argentina*	139	E7	Aztec	127	H2	Badgastein	68	D2
Autlán	130	G8	Ayacucho *Peru*	136	C6	Azuaga	66	D3	Bad Homburg	70	C3
Autun	65	F5	Ayaguz	86	F2	Azuari	137	G3	Badiet esh Shām	94	D5
Auvergne *Australia*	112	G2	Ayamonte	66	C4	Azuero, Península de	132	G11	Bad Ischl	68	D2
Auvergne *France*	65	E6	Ayan *U.S.S.R.*	84	H5	Azul *Argentina*	139	E7	Bad Kissingen	70	D3
Auxerre	65	E5	Ayan *U.S.S.R.*	85	P5	Azul *Mexico*	131	Q9	Bad Kreuznach	70	B4
Avallon	65	E5	Ayancik	76	F2	Azul, Cordillera	136	B5	Bad Lands	123	N4
Avanos	76	F3	Ayaş	76	E3	Azur, Côte d'	65	G7	Bad Mergentheim	70	C4
Avaré	138	G4	Ayaviri	136	C6	Azvaday	76	E2	Badminton	52	E3
Ávas	75	H2	Ayayei	96	C10	Az Zabadānī	77	G6	Bad Neustadt	70	D3
Avcilar	76	C2	Aya-Yenahin	104	E4	Aẓ Ẓafīr	96	E7	Bad Oldesloe	70	D2
Avebury	53	F3	Aybasti	77	G2	Aẓ Ẓahrān	97	K3	Ba Don	93	L5
Aveiro *Portugal*	66	B2	Aydarkul', Ozero	86	B3	Az Zarqā	97	L4	Badong	93	M2
Aveiro *Portugal*	66	B2	Aydere	95	N2	Az Zawiyah	101	H2	Badrah	94	G5
Avellino	69	E5	Aydin	76	B4	Az Zaydīyah	96	F9	Badr Ḥunayn	96	D5
Avelon Peninsula	121	R8	Aydinça	77	G2	Az Zilfī	96	G3	Bad Segeberg	70	D2
Aversa	69	E5	Aydincik	76	E4	Az Zubaydiyah	94	G5	Bad Tölz	70	D5
Aves, Isla de	133	R7	Aydin Dağlari	76	C3	Az Zubayr	94	H6	Badulla	92	F7
Avesnes	64	E3	Ayerbe	67	F1	Az Zuhrah	96	F9	Bad Wildungen	70	C3
Avesta	63	G6	Ayers Rock	112	G4	Az Zuqur	96	F9	Badzhal	85	N6
Aveyron	65	E6	Ayeshka	84	E6				Badzhal'skiy Khrebet	85	N6
Avezzano	69	D4	Ayía Ánna	75	G3				Bae Can	93	L4
Avgó	75	H5	Ayía Marína	75	J5	Baaba	114	W16	Baena	66	D4
Aviemore	57	E3	Áyios	75	G4	Baalbek	77	G5	Baeza	136	B4
Aviemore, Lake	115	C6	Áyios Andreas	75	G4	Baamonde	66	C1	Bafa Gölü	76	B4
Avigliano	69	E5	Áyios Evstrátios	75	H3	Baardheere	107	H2	Bafang	105	H4
Avignon	65	F7	Áyios Kírikos	75	J4	Babadag	73	K3	Bafatá	104	C3
Ávila	66	D2	Áyios Nikólaos *Greece*	75	F3	Babaeski	76	B2	Baffin	120	H3
Ávila, Sierra de	66	D2	Áyios Nikólaos *Greece*	75	H5	Babahoyo	136	B4	Baffin Bay *Canada*	120	N3
Avilés	66	D1	Áyios Pétros	75	F3	Babai Gaxun	87	J3	Baffin Bay *U.S.A.*	128	D7
Avisio	68	C2	Aykathonísi	75	J4	Bāba, Koh-i-	92	C2	Baffin Island	120	L3
Aviz	66	C3	Aykhal	84	J3	Babar	91	H7	Bafia	105	H5
Avlum	63	C8	Aylesbury	53	G3	Babar, Kepulauan	91	H7	Bafing Makàna	100	C6
Avoca *Australia*	113	J6	Ayllón	66	E2	Babayevo	78	F4	Bafoulabé	100	C6
Avoca *Iowa, U.S.A.*	124	C6	Aylmer, Lake	119	P3	Babbacombe Bay	52	D4	Bafoussam	105	H4
Avola	69	E7	Aylsham	53	J2	Babelthuap	91	J4	Bāfq	95	M6
Avon *Devon, U.K.*	52	D4	Ayn al Bayd'ā	77	G5	Babine Lake	118	K5	Bafra	77	F2
Avon *Hampshire, U.K.*	53	F4	Ayni	86	B4	Babo	114	A2	Bafra Burun	77	F2
Avon *U.K.*	52	E3	'Ayn Ţarfāwī	77	K5	Bābol	95	L3	Bāft	95	N7
Avon *U.K.*	52	E3	Ayn, Wadi al	97	M5	Bābol Sar	95	L3	Bafwasende	106	E2
Avonmouth	52	E3	Ayod	102	F6	Baboua	102	B6	Bagamoya	107	G4
Avon Park	129	M7	Ayon	85	V3	Babstovo	88	D1	Bagan Datuk	90	C5
Avon Water	57	D5	Ayon, Ostrov	85	V3	Babushkin	84	H6	Bagansiapiapi	90	C5
Avranches	64	C4	Ayora	67	F3	Babuyan *Philippines*	91	F4	Baganyuvam	78	K2
Avrig	73	H3	Ayr *U.K.*	57	D5	Babuyan *Philippines*	91	G2	Bagaryak	84	Ad5
Avuavu	114	K6	Ayr *U.K.*	57	D5	Babuyan Channel	91	G2	Bagdad	126	F3
Awaji-shima	89	E8	Ayranci	76	E4	Babuyan Islands	91	G2	Bağdere	77	J3
Awālī	97	K3	Ayre, Point of	54	E2	Bacabal	137	J4	Bagé	138	F6
Awanui	115	D1	Aysgarth	55	H2	Bacan	91	H6	Bagenalstown	59	J7
Awārik, 'Uruq al	96	H7	Ayshirak	86	C2	Bacău	73	J2	Baggs	123	L7
Awarua Point	115	A6	Aytos	73	J4	B'acceg'alhaldde	62	J2	Baghdād	77	L6
Awa-shima	89	G6	Ayun	97	L8	Back	119	R2	Bagherhat	93	G4
Āwash Wenz	103	H5	Ayutthaya	93	K6	Backa	63	E6	Bagheria	69	D6
Awaso	104	E4	Ayvacik	76	B3	Backaland	56	F1	Baghlān	92	C1
Awatere	115	D4	Ayvali	76	D4	Bačka Topola	72	E3	Bagh nam Faoileann	56	A3
Awbārī	101	H3	Azambuja	66	B3	Backe	62	G5	Bağisli	77	L4
Aweil	102	E6	Azamgarh	92	F3	Bac Ninh	93	L4	Bagnères-de-Bigorre	65	D7
Awe, Loch	57	C4	Āzarān	94	H3	Bacolod	91	G3	Bagnères-de-Luchon	65	D7
Awful, Mount	115	B6	A'zāz	77	G4	Bacup	55	G3	Bagnoles-de-l'Orne	64	C4
Awgu	105	G4	Azazga	67	J4	Badagara	92	E6	Bagnolo Mella	68	C3
Awjilah	101	K2	Azbine	101	G5	Badajoz	66	C3	Bagoé	104	D3
Axbridge	52	E3	Azerbaydzhan S.S.R.	79	H7	Badalona	67	H2	Bagrationovsk	71	J1
Axe *Dorset, U.K.*	52	E4	Azezo	96	C10	Badanah	94	E6	Bagshot	53	G3
Axe *Somerset, U.K.*	52	E3	Azogues	136	B4	Bad Aussee	68	D2	Baguio	91	G2

Name	Pg	Grid	Name	Pg	Grid	Name	Pg	Grid	Name	Pg	Grid
Banda, Punta la	126	D5	Ban Khemmarat	93	L5	Baran	92	E3	Barmby Moor	55	J3
Bandar Abbās	95	N8	Ban Khok Kloi	93	J7	Barang, Dasht-i-	95	Q5	Barmer	92	D3
Bandarbeyla	103	K6	Banks Island *Australia*	114	C4	Barankul'	84	Ae6	Barmouth	52	D2
Bandar-e Anzalī	94	J3	Banks Island *British Columbia, Canada*	118	J5	Baranof Island	118	H4	Barnard Castle	55	H2
Bandar-e Deylam	95	K6				Baranovichi	71	L2	Barnaul	84	C6
Bandar-e Lengeh	95	M8	Banks Island *NW.Territories, Canada*	119	L1	Baraoltului, Munţii	73	H2	Barnes Ice Cap	120	M3
Bandar e Ma'shur	94	J6				Barapasai	114	B2	Barnet	53	G3
Bandar-e Moghūyeh	95	M8	Banks Islands	111	Q4	Barat Daya, Kepulauan	91	H7	Barnhart	127	M5
Bandar-e Rīg	95	K7	Banks Peninsula	115	D5	Barbacena	138	H4	Barnoldswick	55	G3
Bandar-e Torkeman	95	M3	Banks, Point	118	E4	Barbados	133	T6	Barnsley	55	H3
Bandar Khomeynī	94	J6	Banks Strait	113	K7	Barbas, Cap	100	B4	Barnstaple	52	C3
Bandar Seri Begawan	90	E5	Ban Kui Nua	93	J6	Barbastro	67	G1	Barnstaple Bay	52	C3
Bande	66	C1	Bankura	93	G4	Barberton *South Africa*	108	F5	Baro	105	G4
Band-e-pay	95	L3	Bankya	73	G4	Barberton *U.S.A.*	125	K6	Baroda	92	D4
Bandiagara	100	E6	Ban Mae Sariang	93	J5	Barbezieux	65	C6	Barony, The	56	E1
Bandirma	76	B2	Banmauk	93	J4	Barbuda	133	S6	Barquilla	66	D3
Bandol	65	F7	Ban Me Thuot	93	L6	Barcaldine	113	K3	Barquinha	66	B3
Bandon *Ireland*	59	E9	Bann	58	K3	Barcelona *Spain*	67	H2	Barquisimeto	136	D1
Bandon *Ireland*	59	E9	Ban Nabo	93	L5	Barcelona *Venezuela*	136	E2	Barra *Brazil*	137	J6
Bandundu	106	C3	Ban Na San	93	J7	Barcelonnette	65	G6	Barra *U.K.*	57	A4
Bandung	90	D7	Bannockburn	108	E4	Barcelos *Brazil*	136	E4	Barra do Bugres	138	E3
Bāneh	94	G4	Bannu	92	D2	Barcelos *Portugal*	66	B2	Barra do Corda	137	H5
Banes	133	K4	Bañolas	67	H1	Barcin	71	G2	Barra Head	57	A4
Banff *Canada*	122	G2	Bánovce	71	H4	Barcoo	113	J3	Barra Mansa	138	H4
Banff *U.K.*	56	F3	Ban Pak Chan	93	J6	Barcs	72	D3	Barranca *Peru*	136	B4
Banfora	104	E3	Ban Sao	93	K5	Barda	79	H7	Barranca *Venezuela*	133	L10
Bangalore	92	E6	Banská Bystrica	71	H4	Bardai	102	C3	Barrancabermeja	136	C2
Bangangté	105	H4	Banská Stiavnica	71	H4	Bardas Blancas	139	C7	Barrancas	133	R10
Bangassou	102	D7	Bansko	73	G5	Barddhamān	93	G4	Barrancos	66	C3
Bangeta, Mount	114	D3	Banstead	53	G3	Bardejov	71	J4	Barránqueras	138	E5
Banggai	91	G6	Banswara	92	D4	Barðneshorn	62	Y12	Barranquilla	136	C1
Banggai, Kepulauan	91	G6	Bantaeng	91	F7	Bardney	55	J3	Barra, Sound of	57	A3
Banggi	91	F4	Ban Takua Pa	93	J7	Bardsey Island	52	C2	Barre	125	P4
Banghāzī	101	K2	Ban Tan	93	K6	Bareilly	92	E3	Barreiras	137	H6
Bangka	90	D6	Banteer	59	E8	Barentsevo More	78	F2	Barreiro	66	B3
Bangkalan	90	E7	Ban Tha Sala	93	J7	Barentsøya	80	D2	Barren Island, Cape	110	L10
Bangkaru	90	B5	Bantry	59	D9	Barents Sea	78	F2	Barren Islands	118	E4
Bangka, Selat	90	D6	Bantry Bay	59	C9	Barentu	103	G4	Barren River Lake	124	H8
Bangko	90	D6	Banya	73	H4	Bareo	90	F5	Barretos	138	G4
Bangkok	93	K6	Banyak, Kepulauan	90	B5	Barfleur, Point de	64	C4	Barrhead *Canada*	119	N5
Bangkok, Bight of	93	K6	Banyo	105	H4	Barford	53	F2	Barrhead *U.K.*	57	F4
Bangladesh	93	G4	Banyuls	65	E7	Bargrennan	57	D5	Barrhill	57	D5
Bangor *Down, U.K.*	58	L3	Banyuwangi	90	E7	Barguzinskiy Khrebet	84	H6	Barrie	125	L4
Bangor *Gwynedd, U.K.*	54	E3	Banzyville	106	D2	Barh	92	G3	Barrier, Cape	115	E2
Bangor *U.S.A.*	125	R4	Baoding	87	M4	Barhaj	92	F3	Barriere	122	D2
Bangor Erris	58	C4	Baofeng	93	M2	Barham	53	J3	Barrington Tops	113	L5
Bang Saphan Yai	93	J6	Baoji	93	L2	Bar Harbor	125	R4	Barrocão	138	H3
Bangui *Central African Rep.*	102	C7	Baoqing	88	D2	Bári	69	F5	Barrow *Argentina*	139	D7
Bangui *Philippines*	91	G2	Baoshan	93	J4	Barīdī, Ra's	96	C4	Barrow *Ireland*	59	H8
Bangweulu, Lake	107	E5	Baoting	93	L5	Barika	67	J5	Barrow *U.S.A.*	118	D1
Bangweulu Swamps	107	E5	Baotou	87	L3	Barinas	136	C2	Barrowford	55	G3
Ban Hat Yai	93	K7	Baoxing	88	C1	Baring, Cape	119	M1	Barrow-in-Furness	55	F2
Ban Houei Sai	93	K4	Bapatla	92	F5	Baripada	92	G4	Barrow Islands	112	D3
Bani	100	D6	Bapaume	64	E3	Bari Sadri	92	D4	Barrow, Point	118	D1
Baní	133	M5	Ba'qūbah	77	L6	Barisal	93	H4	Barrow Range	112	F4
Baniara	114	D3	Bar *U.S.S.R.*	73	J1	Barisan, Pegunungan	90	C6	Barrow Strait	120	G3
Banika	114	J6	Bar *Yugoslavia*	77	E1	Barito	90	E6	Barry	52	D3
Banī Khaṭmah	96	G7	Bara	102	F5	Barkā	97	N5	Barry's Bay	125	M4
Banī Ma'āriḍ	96	H7	Baraawe	107	H2	Barkan, Ra's-e	95	J7	Barsalpur	92	D3
Bani Walid	101	H2	Barabai	90	F6	Barking	53	H3	Barsi	92	E5
Bāniyās	94	B5	Bara Banki	92	F3	Barkley Sound	122	B3	Barstow	126	D3
Bāniyas	94	B4	Barabinsk	84	B5	Barkly East	108	E6	Bar-sur-Aube	64	F4
Bani Zaynān, Ḥādh	97	J6	Barabinskaya Step'	84	B6	Barkly Tableland	113	H2	Bar-sur-Seine	64	F4
Banja Luka	72	D3	Baracoa	133	K4	Barkol	86	F3	Barth	70	E1
Banjarmasin	90	E6	Bărăganul	73	J3	Barkston	53	G2	Bartica	136	F2
Banjul	104	B3	Barahona	133	M5	Barle	52	D3	Bartin	76	E2
Banka Banka	113	G2	Barail Range	93	H3	Bar-le-Duc	64	F4	Bartle Frere, Mount	113	K2
Ban Kantang	93	J7	Baraka	96	C8	Barlee, Lake	112	D4	Bartlesville	128	D2
Ban Keng Phao	93	L6	Barakkul'	84	Ae6	Barlestone	53	F2	Barton *Philippines*	91	F3
Bankfoot	57	E4	Baram	90	E5	Barletta	69	F5	Barton *U.S.A.*	125	P4

Behshahr	95	L3	Belgium	64	E3	Belorusskaya Gryada	71	L2	Ben Lomond	57	D4
Bei'an	87	P2	Belgorod	79	F5	Belot, Lac	118	K2	Ben Loyal	56	D2
Beibu Wan	93	L4	Belgorod-Dnestrovskiy	79	E6	Belo-Tsiribihina	109	H3	Ben Lui	57	D4
Beihai	93	L4	Belgrade	72	F3	Belousovka	84	C6	Ben Macdui	57	E3
Beila	100	B5	Belgrano	141	X3	Belovo	84	D6	Ben MórCoigach	56	C3
Beinn a' Ghlo	57	E4	Belica	71	L2	Beloye More	78	F2	Ben More *Central, U.K.*	57	D4
Beinn Bheigier	57	B5	Beli Lom	73	J4	Beloye Ozero	78	F3	Ben More *Strathclyde, U.K.*	56	B4
Beinn Dearg *Highland, U.K.*	56	D3	Beli Manastir	72	E3	Belozersk	78	F4	Ben More Assynt	56	D2
Beinn Dearg *Tayside, U.K.*	57	E4	Belimbing	90	C7	Belozerskoye	84	Ae5	Benmore, Lake	115	C6
Beinn Dorain	57	D4	Belin	65	C6	Belper	55	H3	Bennachie	56	F3
Beinn Eighe	56	C3	Belinskiy	79	G5	Belsay	57	G5	Benn Cleuch	57	E4
Beinn Fhada	56	C3	Belinyu	90	D6	Belterra	137	F4	Bennetta, Ostrov	85	R1
Beinn Ime	57	D4	Belitsa	73	G5	Belton	55	J3	Ben Nevis	57	C4
Beinn Mhor	56	A3	Belitung	90	D6	Bel'tsy	73	J2	Bennington	125	P5
Beinn na Caillich	57	C3	Belize	132	C6	Belturbet	58	H4	Benoni	108	E5
Beinn Resipol	57	C4	Belkina, Mys	88	F3	Belukha, Gora	86	F2	Be, Nosy	109	J2
Beinn Sgritheall	57	C3	Belknap, Mount	122	H8	Belvedere Marittimo	69	E6	Ben Rinnes	56	E3
Beipiao	87	N3	Bel'kovskiy, Ostrov	85	P1	Belvidere	124	F5	Bensheim	70	C4
Beira	109	F3	Bella Bella	118	K5	Belvoir, Vale of	53	G2	Benson *U.K.*	53	F3
Beirut	76	F6	Bellac	65	D5	Belyando, River	113	K3	Benson *U.K.*	126	G5
Bei Shan	86	H3	Bella Coola	118	K5	Belyayevka	73	L2	Ben Starav	57	C4
Beit Lahm	94	B6	Bellaire	128	E6	Belyy, Ostrov	85	A2	Bent	95	P8
Beiuş	73	G2	Bellary	92	E5	Belyy Yar	84	D5	Bentinck Island	93	J6
Beja	66	C3	Bella Vista *Argentina*	138	C5	Bełżyce	71	K3	Bent Jbail	94	B5
Béja	101	G1	Bella Vista *Argentina*	138	E5	Bemaraha, Plateau du	109	J3	Bentley	55	H3
Bejaïa	101	G1	Belleek	58	F4	Bembridge	53	F4	Benton	128	F3
Bejaïa, Golfe de	67	J4	Bellefontaine	124	J6	Bemidji	124	C3	Benton Harbor	124	G5
Béjar	66	D2	Belle Fourche *South Dakota, U.S.A.*	123	N5	Benabarre	67	G1	Bentung	90	C5
Bejestän	95	P4	Belle Fourche *Wyoming, U.S.A.*	123	M5	Ben Alder	57	D4	Benue	105	G4
Beji	92	C3	Belle Glade	129	M7	Benalla	113	K6	Ben Venue	57	D4
Bekdast	79	J7	Belle Île	65	B5	Benares	92	F3	Ben Vorlich	57	D4
Békéscsaba	73	F2	Belle Isle	121	Q7	Benavente	66	D2	Benwee	58	C5
Bekily	109	J4	Bellême	64	D4	Ben Avon	57	E3	Benwee Head	58	C4
Bekopaka	109	H3	Belleville *Canada*	125	M4	Benbaun	59	C5	Ben Wyvis	56	D3
Bekwai	104	E4	Belleville *Illinois, U.S.A.*	124	F7	Ben Chonzie	57	E4	Benxi	87	N3
Bela *India*	92	F3	Belleville *Kansas, U.S.A.*	123	R8	Bencorr	59	C5	Beo	91	H5
Bela *Pakistan*	92	C3	Bellevue *Idaho, U.S.A.*	122	G6	Ben Cruachan	57	C4	Beograd	72	F3
Bélabo	105	H5	Bellevue *Washington, U.S.A.*	122	C4	Bend	122	D5	Beppu	89	C9
Belaga	90	E5	Belley	65	F6	Bende	105	G4	Beqa	114	R9
Belang	91	G5	Bellingham *U.K.*	57	F5	Bender Qaasim	103	J5	Berat	74	E2
Bela Palanka	73	G4	Bellingham *U.S.A.*	122	C3	Bendery	79	D6	Berau, Teluk	114	A2
Bela Vista	109	F5	Bellinghaussen Sea	141	U5	Bendigo	113	J6	Berber	103	F4
Belawan	90	B5	Bellingshausen	141	W6	Benešov	70	F4	Berbera	103	J5
Belaya *U.S.S.R.*	78	K4	Bellinzona	68	B2	Benevento	69	E5	Berbérati	102	C7
Belaya *U.S.S.R.*	85	W3	Bello	136	B2	Bengbu	87	M5	Berck	64	D3
Belaya-Kalitva	79	G6	Bellona Island	114	J7	Benghazi	101	K2	Berdichev	79	D6
Belaya Kholunitsa	78	J4	Bellona Reefs	111	N6	Bengkalis	90	C5	Berdigestyakh	85	M4
Belayan	90	F5	Bellpuig	67	G2	Bengkulu	90	C6	Berdyansk	79	F6
Belaya Tserkov'	79	E6	Bellshill	57	D5	Bengo, Baia do	106	B4	Berea	124	H8
Belcher Channel	120	G2	Belluno	68	D2	Bengoi	91	J6	Bereeda	103	K5
Belcher Islands	121	L6	Bell Ville	138	D6	Bengtsfors	63	E7	Beregovo	79	C6
Belchiragh	94	S4	Belly	122	H3	Benguela	106	B5	Berens	119	R5
Belchite	67	F2	Belmont	56	A1	Benguérua, Ilha	109	G4	Berens River	119	R5
Belcoo	58	G4	Belmonte *Portugal*	66	C2	Benha	102	F1	Bere Regis	52	E4
Belderg	58	C4	Belmonte *Spain*	66	E3	Ben Hope	56	D2	Berettyo	73	F2
Belebey	78	J5	Belmopan	132	C6	Beni *Bolivia*	136	D6	Berettyoujfalu	73	F2
Beledweyne	103	J7	Belmullet	58	B4	Beni *Zaïre*	107	E2	Bereza	71	L2
Belém	137	H4	Belogorsk	79	E6	Beni Abbes	100	E2	Berezhany	71	L4
Belen *Turkey*	76	E4	Belogorye	71	M4	Benicarló	67	G2	Berezhnykh, Mys	85	Q1
Belen *U.S.A.*	127	J3	Belogradchik	73	G4	Benidorm	67	F3	Berezina	78	D5
Bélep, Îles	114	V15	Belo Horizonte	138	K4	Benî Mazâr	102	F2	Berezino	78	D5
Belesar, Embalse de	66	C1	Beloit	124	F5	Beni Mellal	100	D2	Berezna	79	E5
Belev	79	F5	Belokorovichi	79	D5	Benin	105	F4	Berezniki	78	K4
Belfast *New Zealand*	115	D5	Belomorsk	78	E3	Benin, Bight of	105	F4	Berezno	71	M3
Belfast *U.K.*	58	L3	Belorado	66	E1	Benin City	105	G4	Berezovka *Rossiyskaya S.F.S.R., U.S.S.R.*	78	K3
Belfast Lough	58	L3	Belorechensk	79	F7	Beni Saf	100	E1			
Belfield	123	N4	Belören	76	E4	Beni Suef	102	F2	Berezovka *Rossiyskaya S.F.S.R., U.S.S.R.*	85	K5
Belford	57	G5	Belorussiya S.S.R.	71	L2	Ben Klibreck	56	D2			
Belfort	65	G5	Belorusskaya Gryada			Ben Lawers	57	D4	Berezovka *Rossiyskaya S.F.S.R., U.S.S.R.*	85	T3
Belgaum	92	D5	Belören	76	E4	Ben Ledi	57	D4			

Berezovka *Ukraine S.S.R., U.S.S.R.*	**79** E6	Beru	**111** S2
Berezovo *U.S.S.R.*	**84** Ae4	Beruri	**136** E4
Berezovo *U.S.S.R.*	**85** W4	Berwick	**125** M6
Berezovskaya	**85** K5	Berwick-upon-Tweed	**57** F5
Berg	**108** C6	Berwyn Mountains	**52** D2
Berga	**67** G1	Berzence	**72** D2
Bergama	**76** B3	Besalampy	**109** H3
Bergamo	**68** B3	Besançon	**65** G5
Bergeforsen	**62** G5	Besar, Kai	**91** J7
Bergen *E. Germany*	**70** E1	Besbre	**65** E5
Bergen *Norway*	**63** J6	Beshneh	**95** M7
Bergen op Zoom	**64** F3	Beşiri	**77** J4
Bergerac	**65** D6	Beskidy Zachodnie	**71** H4
Bergfors	**62** H2	Beslan	**79** G7
Bergisch-Gladbach	**70** B3	Besni	**77** G4
Bergsviken	**62** J4	Bessarabia	**73** K2
Berhala, Selat	**90** C6	Bessarabka	**73** K2
Beringa, Ostrov	**81** T4	Bessbrook	**58** K4
Bering Glacier	**118** G3	Bessemer *Alabama, U.S.A.*	**129** J4
Beringovskiy	**85** X4	Bessemer *Winconsin, U.S.A.*	**124** F3
Bering Sea	**143** H3	Bestamak *U.S.S.R.*	**86** D2
Bering Strait	**118** B2	Bestamak *U.S.S.R.*	**79** K6
Berislav	**79** E6	Bestobe	**84** A6
Beris, Ra's	**95** Q9	Bestuzhevo	**78** G3
Berja	**66** E4	Betafo	**109** J3
Berkåk	**62** C5	Betanzos	**66** B1
Berkakit	**85** L5	Bétaré Oya	**105** H4
Berkeley *U.K.*	**52** E3	Bethal	**108** E5
Berkeley *U.S.A.*	**126** A2	Bethanie	**108** C5
Berkhamsted	**53** G3	Bethany	**124** C6
Berkner Island	**141** W3	Bethel	**118** C3
Berkovitsa	**73** G4	Bethel Park	**125** L6
Berkshire	**53** F3	Bethesda *U.K.*	**54** E3
Berkshire Downs	**53** F3	Bethesda *U.S.A.*	**125** M7
Berkshire Mountains	**125** P5	Bethlehem *Israel*	**94** B6
Berlevåg	**62** N2	Bethlehem *South Africa*	**108** E5
Berlin *E. Germany*	**70** E2	Bethulie	**108** E6
Berlin *U.S.A.*	**125** Q4	Béthune *France*	**64** D4
Bermeja, Sierra	**66** D4	Béthune *France*	**64** E3
Bermejo *Argentina*	**138** C6	Betioky	**109** H4
Bermejo *Argentina*	**138** D4	Betpak-Dala	**86** B2
Bermeo	**66** E1	Bet-Pak-Data	**86** B2
Bermillo de Sayago	**66** C2	Betroka	**109** J4
Bermuda	**117** N5	Betsiamites	**125** R2
Bern	**68** A2	Betsiboka	**109** J3
Bernau	**70** E2	Bettiah	**92** F3
Bernay	**64** D4	Bettyhill	**56** D2
Bernburg	**70** D3	Betul	**92** E4
Berne	**68** A2	Betwa	**92** E4
Berner Alpen	**68** A2	Betws-y-coed	**54** F3
Berneray *U.K.*	**57** A4	Beuvron	**65** D5
Berneray *U.K.*	**56** A3	Beverley *Australia*	**112** D5
Bernina, Piz	**68** B2	Beverley *U.K.*	**55** J3
Béroroha	**109** J4	Beverly Hills	**126** C3
Berounka	**70** E4	Bexhill	**53** H4
Berre, Étang de	**65** F7	Beykoz	**76** C2
Berriedale	**56** E2	Beyla	**104** D4
Berriedale Water	**56** E2	Beylul	**96** F10
Berrigan	**113** K6	Beyneu	**79** K6
Berringarra	**112** D4	Beypazari	**76** D2
Berrouaghia	**67** H4	Beypinar	**77** G3
Berry *Australia*	**113** L5	Beyşehir	**76** D4
Berry *France*	**65** E5	Beyşehir Gölü	**76** D4
Berryessa, Lake	**122** C8	Beyton	**53** H2
Berry Head	**52** D4	Beytüşşebap	**77** K4
Berry Islands	**132** J1	Bezhetsk	**78** F4
Bershad'	**73** K1	Béziers	**65** E7
Berthoud Pass	**123** L8	Bezmein	**95** P2
Bertoua	**105** H5	Bhadgaon	**92** G3
		Bhadrachalam	**92** F5

Bhadrakh	**92** G4	Bigadiç	**76** C3
Bhadravati	**92** E6	Big Bay	**114** T11
Bhagalpur	**92** G3	Big Belt Mountains	**122** J4
Bhakkar	**92** D2	Big Blue	**123** R7
Bhamo	**93** J4	Bigbury Bay	**52** D4
Bhandara	**92** E4	Biggar *Canada*	**123** K1
Bhanrer Range	**92** F4	Biggar *U.K.*	**57** E5
Bharatpur *Pradesh, India*	**92** F4	Biggleswade	**53** G2
Bharatpur *Rajasthan, India*	**92** E3	Big Horn	**123** K5
Bharuch	**92** D4	Big Horn Mountains	**123** L5
Bhatinda	**92** D2	Big Island	**120** M5
Bhatpara	**93** G4	Big Pine	**126** C2
Bhavnagar	**92** D4	Big Piney	**123** J6
Bhawanipatna	**92** F5	Big Sheep Mountains	**123** L4
Bhilwara	**92** D3	Big Sioux	**123** R5
Bhima	**92** E5	Big Snowy Mount	**122** K4
Bhiwani	**92** E3	Big Spring	**127** M4
Bhopal	**92** E4	Big Stone Gap	**124** J8
Bhopalpatnam	**92** F5	Big Timber	**123** J5
Bhor	**92** D5	Big Trout Lake	**119** T4
Bhubaneshwar	**92** G4	Bihac	**72** C3
Bhuj	**92** C4	Bihar	**92** G4
Bhumiphol Dam	**93** J5	Bihār	**92** G3
Bhusawal	**92** E4	Biharamulo	**107** F3
Bhutan	**93** G3	Bihoro	**88** K4
Bía	**136** D4	Bihu	**87** M6
Biābān	**95** N8	Bijagos, Arquipelago dos	**104** B3
Biabānak	**95** S5	Bijapur	**92** E5
Biak	**114** B2	Bijār	**94** H4
Biała Podlaska	**71** K2	Bijeljina	**72** E3
Białobrzegi	**71** J3	Bijelo Polje	**72** E4
Białowieża	**71** K2	Bijie	**93** L3
Bialystok	**71** K2	Bijnor	**92** E3
Bianco	**69** F6	Bikaner	**92** D3
Biankouma	**104** D4	Bikin *U.S.S.R.*	**88** E2
Biaro	**91** H5	Bikin *U.S.S.R.*	**88** F2
Biarritz	**65** C7	Bikoro	**106** C3
Biasca	**68** B2	Bilād Banī Bū 'Alī	**97** P5
Biba	**102** F2	Bilād Ghāmid	**96** E6
Bibai	**88** H4	Bilād Zahran	**96** E6
Bibala	**106** B5	Bilaspur	**92** F4
Bibby Island	**119** S3	Bilauktaung Range	**93** J6
Biberach	**70** C4	Bilbao	**66** E1
Bibury	**53** F3	Bil'chir	**85** J6
Bicester	**53** F3	Bilecik	**76** C2
Bicheno	**113** K7	Biled	**73** F3
Bickle Knob	**125** L7	Bilé Karpaty	**71** G4
Bida	**105** G4	Bilesha Plain	**107** H2
Bidar	**92** E5	Bilgoraj	**71** K3
Biddeford	**125** Q5	Bili	**106** E2
Biddulph	**55** G3	Bilin	**93** J5
Bidean Nam Bian	**57** C4	Billabalong	**112** D4
Bideford	**52** C3	Billericay	**53** H3
Bideford Bay	**52** C3	Billingham	**55** H2
Bidford-on-Avon	**53** F2	Billings	**123** K5
Bidokht	**95** P4	Billingshurst	**53** G3
Bidzhan *U.S.S.R.*	**88** C1	Bilma	**101** H5
Bidzhan *U.S.S.R.*	**88** C2	Bilma, Grand Erg de	**101** H5
Biebrza	**71** K2	Biloela	**113** L3
Biel	**68** A2	Bilo Gora	**72** D3
Bielefeld	**70** C2	Biloxi	**128** H5
Biella	**68** B3	Biltine	**102** D5
Bielsko-Biala	**71** H4	Bilugyun	**93** J5
Bielsk Podlaski	**71** K2	Binālūd, Kūh-e	**95** P3
Bien Hoa	**93** L6	Binatang	**90** E5
Bienne	**68** A2	Binder	**87** L2
Bienveneu	**137** G3	Bindloe Island	**136** A7
Bienville, Lac	**121** M6	Bindura	**108** F3
Biferno	**69** E5	Binéfar	**67** G2
Biga	**76** B2	Binga	**108** E3

Borzhomi	77	K2
Borzya	85	K7
Bosa	69	B5
Bosanski Brod	72	E3
Bosanski Novi	72	D3
Bosanski Petrovac	72	D3
Boscastle	52	C4
Bose	93	L4
Bos Gradiška	72	D3
Boshruyeh	95	N5
Bosilegrad	73	G4
Boskovice	71	G4
Bosna	72	E3
Bosnik	114	B2
Bosobolo	106	C2
Bōsō-hantō	89	H8
Bosphorus	76	C2
Bossambélé	102	C6
Bossangoa	102	C6
Bossier City	128	F4
Bostan *Iran*	94	H6
Bostan *Pakistan*	92	C2
Bostānābād	94	H3
Bosten Bagrax Hu	86	F3
Boston *U.S.A.*	53	G2
Boston *U.S.A.*	125	Q5
Boston Mountains	128	E3
Botesdale	53	J2
Botev	73	H4
Botevgrad	73	G4
Bothel	55	F2
Bothnia, Gulf of	62	J5
Botna	73	K2
Botoşani	73	J2
Botsmark	62	J4
Botswana	108	D4
Botte Donato	69	F6
Bottenhavet	63	H6
Bottenviken	62	K4
Bottesford	53	G2
Bottineau	123	P3
Bottisham	53	H2
Bottrop	70	B3
Botucatu	138	G4
Bouaflé	104	D4
Bouaké	104	D4
Bouar	102	C6
Bouàrfa	100	E2
Boucant Bay	113	G1
Bouchegouf	69	A7
Bougainville	114	E3
Bougainville, Cape	112	F1
Bougainville Reef	113	K2
Bougainville Strait	114	J5
Bougaroun, Cap	101	G1
Bougie	67	J4
Bougouni	100	D6
Bougzdul	67	H5
Bouhalloufa	67	G4
Bouillon	64	F4
Bouira	67	H4
Bou Ismaïl	67	H4
Boujdour	100	C3
Bou Kadir	67	G4
Boulay	64	G4
Boulder	123	M8
Boulder City	126	E3
Boulogne-sur-Mer	64	D3
Boumbé I	102	C7
Boumbé II	102	C7

Boumo	102	C6
Bouna	104	E4
Boundiali	104	D4
Boung Long	93	L6
Boun Tai	93	K4
Bountiful	122	J7
Bounty Islands	111	S11
Bourail	114	W16
Bourbon-l'Archambault	65	E5
Bourbonnais *France*	65	E5
Bourbonnais *U.S.A.*	124	G6
Bourbonne-les-Bains	65	F5
Bourem	100	E5
Bourganeuf	65	D6
Bourg-en-Bresse	65	F5
Bourges	65	E5
Bourgogne	65	F5
Bourgogne, Canal de	65	E5
Bourg-Saint-Andéol	65	F6
Bourke	113	K5
Bourne	53	G2
Bournemouth	53	F4
Bou Saâda	101	F1
Boussac	65	E5
Bousso	102	C5
Boutilimit	100	C5
Boves	68	A3
Bovey	52	D4
Bovey Tracy	52	D4
Bovingdon	53	G3
Bovino	69	E5
Bow	122	H2
Bowbells	123	N3
Bowen	113	K3
Bowers Bank	118	Ab9
Bowes	55	G2
Bowfell	55	F2
Bowie	128	D4
Bow Island	122	J3
Bowkan	94	H3
Bowland, Forest of	55	G2
Bowling Green *Kentucky, U.S.A.*	124	G8
Bowling Green *Ohio, U.S.A.*	124	J6
Bowman	123	N4
Bowman Bay	120	M4
Bowness	55	G2
Bowness-on-Solway	55	F2
Bowraville	113	L5
Boxford	53	H2
Bo Xian	93	N2
Boxing	87	M4
Box Tank	113	J5
Boyabat	76	F2
Boyang	87	M6
Boyarka	84	F2
Boyd Lake	119	Q3
Boyer	124	C6
Boyle	58	F5
Boyne	58	K5
Boynton Beach	129	M7
Boyuibe	138	D4
Bozburun	76	C4
Bozcaada	75	H3
Boz Dağlari	76	B3
Bozdoğan	76	C4
Bozeman	122	J5
Bozen	68	C2
Boże Pole	71	G1
Bozkir	76	E4

Bozkurt	76	E2
Bozoum	102	C6
Bozova	77	H4
Bozqūsh, Kūh-e	94	H3
Bozüyük	76	D3
Bra	68	A3
Brabant Island	141	V6
Brabourne	53	H3
Brač	72	D4
Bracadale	56	B3
Bracadale, Loch	56	B3
Bracciano	69	D4
Bräcke	62	F5
Brackley	53	F2
Bracknell	53	G3
Brad	73	G2
Bradano	69	F5
Bradda Head	54	E2
Bradenton	129	L7
Bradford *U.K.*	55	H3
Bradford *U.S.A.*	125	L6
Bradford-on-Avon	52	E3
Bradwell Waterside	53	H3
Brady	127	N5
Brady Mountains	127	N5
Brae	56	A1
Braemar	57	E3
Braemore	56	E2
Braeswick	56	F1
Braga	66	B2
Bragado	139	D7
Bragança	66	C2
Bragança Paulista	138	G4
Bragar	56	B2
Brahman Baria	93	H4
Brāhmani	92	G4
Brahmapur	92	F5
Brahmaputra	93	H3
Braidwood	113	K6
Brăila	73	J3
Brailsford	53	F2
Brainerd	124	C3
Braintree	53	H3
Braishfield	53	F3
Brake	70	C2
Brakel	70	C3
Brállos	75	G3
Bramdean	53	F3
Bramham	55	H3
Bramming	63	C9
Brampton *Canada*	125	L5
Brampton *U.K.*	55	G2
Bramsche	70	B2
Brancaster	53	H2
Brancaster Bay	53	H2
Branco	136	E3
Branco, Cabo	137	L5
Brandberg	108	B4
Brandbu	63	D6
Brande	63	C9
Brandenburg	70	E2
Brandesburton	55	J3
Brandon *Canada*	123	Q3
Brandon *U.S.A.*	125	P5
Brandon Bay	59	B8
Brandon Mount	59	B8
Brandon Point	59	B8
Brandval	63	E6
Brăneşti	73	J3
Braniewo	71	H1

Bran, Pasul	73	H3
Brantford	125	K5
Brantley	129	J5
Brantôme	65	D6
Brasileia	136	D6
Brasília *Distrito Federal, Brazil*	138	F3
Brasília *Minas Gerais, Brazil*	138	H3
Braslav	63	M9
Braşov	73	H3
Brassey Range	91	F5
Brates, Lacul	73	K3
Bratislava	71	G4
Bratsk	84	G5
Bratslav	73	K1
Braunau	68	D1
Braunsberg	71	H1
Braunschweig	70	D2
Braunton	52	C3
Brava	104	L7
Brava, Costa	67	H2
Bravo del Norte, Río	127	L6
Brawley	126	E4
Bray	59	K6
Bray Head	59	B9
Bray Island	120	L4
Brazil	137	G5
Brazos	128	D5
Brazzaville	106	C3
Brčko	72	E3
Brda	71	G2
Breadalbane	57	D4
Breaksea Sound	115	A6
Brean	52	D3
Brebes	90	D7
Brechfa	52	C3
Brechin	57	F4
Breckenridge *Minnesota, U.S.A.*	124	B3
Breckenridge *Texas, U.S.A.*	128	C4
Breckland	53	H2
Brecknock, Península	139	B10
Břeclav	71	G4
Brecon	52	D3
Brecon Beacons	52	D3
Breda	64	F3
Bredon Hill	53	F3
Bredstedt	70	C1
Breezewood	125	L7
Bregenz	68	B2
Bregovo	73	G3
Breiðafjörður	62	T12
Brejo	137	J4
Brekken	62	D5
Brekstad	62	C5
Bremen *U.S.A.*	129	K4
Bremen *W. Germany*	70	C2
Bremerhaven	70	C2
Bremer Range	112	E5
Bremerton	122	C4
Bremervörde	70	C2
Brendon Hills	52	D3
Brenham	128	D5
Brenig, Llyn	55	F3
Brenish	56	A2
Brenner Pass	68	C2
Breno	68	C3
Brenta	68	C3
Brentford	53	G2
Brentwood *U.K.*	53	H3

Buffalo *Texas, U.S.A.*	128	D5	Bunkie	128	F5	Burnie	113	K7	Buurhakaba	107	H2

Place	Page	Ref
Buffalo *Texas, U.S.A.*	128	D5
Buffalo *Wyoming, U.S.A.*	123	L5
Buffalo Lake	119	M3
Buffalo Narrows	119	P4
Buftea	73	H3
Bug	71	K2
Buga	136	B3
Bugdayli	95	M2
Bugel, Tanjung	90	E7
Bugøynes	62	N2
Bugrino	78	H2
Bugsuk	91	F4
Bugul'ma	78	J5
Buguruslan	78	J5
Buhl	122	G6
Buhuşi	73	J2
Buie, Loch	57	B4
Builth Wells	52	D2
Buin	114	G5
Buinsk	78	H5
B'uin Zahrā	95	K4
Buitrago del Lozoye	66	E2
Bujaraloz	67	F2
Buje	72	B3
Bujumbura	107	E3
Bük	72	D2
Buka	114	E3
Bukama	106	E4
Bukavu	107	E3
Bukhara	80	H6
Bukittinggi	90	D6
Bükk	72	F1
Bukoba	107	F3
Bukoloto	107	F2
Bula	114	A2
Bulanash	84	Ad5
Bulancak	77	H2
Bulandshahr	92	E3
Bulanik	77	K3
Bulanovo	79	K5
Bulawayo	108	E4
Buldan	76	C3
Buldana	92	E4
Buldir Island	118	Ab9
Buldurty	79	J6
Bulgan *Mongolia*	86	G2
Bulgan *Mongolia*	87	J2
Bulgaria	73	G4
Buliluyan, Cape	91	F4
Bulkeley	55	G3
Bulle	68	A2
Buller	115	C4
Bullhead City	126	E3
Bull Shoals Lake	128	F2
Bulolo	114	D3
Bulum	85	M2
Buma	114	K6
Bumba	106	D2
Buna	74	E2
Bunbeg	58	F2
Bunbury	112	D5
Bunclody	59	J7
Buncrana	58	H2
Bundaberg	113	L3
Bundoran	58	F4
Bungalaut, Selat	90	B6
Bungay	53	J2
Bungo-suidō	89	D9
Bunguran Utara, Kepulauan	90	D5
Bunia	107	F2

Place	Page	Ref
Bunkie	128	F5
Bunratty	59	E7
Buntingford	53	G3
Buntok	90	E6
Bünyan	77	F3
Buolkalakh	85	K2
Buol Kheyr	95	K7
Buorkhaya, Guba	85	N2
Buorkhaya, Mys	85	N2
Buqayq	97	J4
Buqūm, Ḥarrat al	96	F6
Buram	102	E5
Buran	86	F2
Buraydah	96	F3
Burbage	53	F3
Burbank	126	C3
Burco	103	J6
Burdalyk	95	S2
Burdekin	113	K3
Burdur	76	D4
Burdur Gölü	76	D4
Bure	53	J2
Bureå	62	J4
Burentsogt	87	L2
Bureya *U.S.S.R.*	85	M7
Bureya *U.S.S.R.*	85	N6
Burg	70	D2
Burgas	73	J4
Burgdorf	68	A2
Burgeo	121	Q8
Burgersdorp	108	E6
Burgess Hill	53	G4
Burghead	56	E3
Burghead Bay	56	E3
Burgh-le-Marsh	55	K3
Burgos	66	E1
Burgsteinfurt	70	B2
Burgsvik	63	H8
Burguete	67	F1
Burhan Budai Shan	93	J1
Burhaniye	76	B3
Burhanpur	92	E4
Burias	91	G3
Burica, Punta	132	F10
Burin Peninsula	121	Q8
Buri Peninsula	96	D9
Buriram	93	K5
Burj Sāfītā	77	G5
Burke Island	141	S4
Burketown	113	H2
Burkhala	85	R4
Burkina Faso	104	E3
Burley	122	H6
Burli	79	J5
Burlington *Canada*	125	L5
Burlington *Colorado, U.S.A.*	123	N8
Burlington *Iowa, U.S.A.*	124	E6
Burlington *N. Carolina, U.S.A.*	129	N2
Burlington *Vermont, U.S.A.*	125	P4
Burlington *Washington, U.S.A.*	122	C3
Burlton	52	E2
Burlyu-Tobe	86	D2
Burma	93	J4
Burmantovo	78	L3
Burnaby	122	C3
Burneston	55	H2
Burnet	128	C5
Burnham-on-Crouch	53	H3
Burnham-on-Sea	52	E3

Place	Page	Ref
Burnie	113	K7
Burnley	55	G3
Burns	122	E6
Burntwood	119	R4
Burqān	97	H2
Burqin	86	F2
Burra	113	H5
Burravoe	56	A1
Burray	56	F2
Burren, The	59	D6
Burriana	67	F3
Burrow Head	54	E2
Burrs Junction	122	F6
Burrundie	112	G1
Burry Port	52	C3
Bursa	76	C2
Bur Safâga	103	F2
Bûr Sa'îd	103	F1
Bur Sudan	96	C7
Burt, Mount	112	F4
Burton Joyce	53	F2
Burton Lake	121	L7
Burton Latimer	53	G2
Burton upon Stather	55	J3
Burton-upon-Trent	53	F2
Burträsk	62	J4
Buru	91	H6
Burūm	97	J9
Burundi	107	E3
Burunnoye	79	J5
Bururi	107	E3
Burwick	56	F2
Bury	55	G3
Buryatskaya A.S.S.R.	85	H6
Burylbaytal	86	C2
Burynshik	79	J6
Bury Saint Edmunds	53	H2
Busayṭa, Al	96	D1
Bushat	74	E2
Büshehr	95	K7
Bushimaie	106	D4
Bushmills	58	J2
Businga	106	D2
Busira	106	C3
Busk	71	L4
Buskerud	63	C6
Busko	71	J3
Busselton	112	D5
Bussol', Proliv	85	S7
Bustakh, Ozero	85	Q2
Busto Arsizio	68	B3
Busuanga	91	G3
Buta	106	D2
Butang Group	93	J7
Butare	107	E3
Bute	57	C5
Bute, Sound of	57	C5
Butiaba	107	F2
Butler	125	L6
Butmah	77	K4
Butte	122	H5
Buttermere	55	F2
Butterworth *Malaysia*	90	C4
Butterworth *South Africa*	108	E6
Buttevant	59	E8
Button Islands	121	P5
Butuan	91	H4
Butung	91	G7
Buturlinovka	79	G5
Buulobarde	103	J7

Place	Page	Ref
Buurhakaba	107	H2
Buwātah	96	D4
Buxton	55	H3
Buy	78	G4
Buyba	84	E6
Buynaksk	79	H7
Buyr Nuur	87	M2
Büyük Ağri Daği	77	L3
Büyüklaçin	76	F2
Büyük Menderes	76	C4
Buzançais	65	D5
Buzău *Romania*	73	J3
Buzău *Romania*	73	J3
Buzi	109	F3
Buzovyazy	78	K5
Buzuluk	84	Ae6
Buzuluk	79	J5
Byam Martin, Cape	120	L3
Byam Martin Island	120	F2
Byczyna	71	H3
Bydgoszcz	71	G2
Byers	123	M8
Byfleet	53	G3
Byglandsfjord	63	B7
Bykhov	79	E5
Bykovo *U.S.S.R.*	79	H6
Bykovo *U.S.S.R.*	78	H3
Byla Slatina	73	G4
Bylot Island	120	L3
Byrock	113	K5
Byron, Cape	113	L4
Byron, Isla	139	A9
Byrranga, Gory	84	E2
Byrum	63	D8
Byserovo	78	J4
Byske	62	J4
Byskeälven	62	J4
Bystra	71	H4
Bystraya	85	T6
Bystrzyca Kłodzka	71	G3
Bytantay	85	N3
Bytča	71	H4
Byten'	71	L2
Bytom	71	H3
Bytów	71	G1
Byxelkrok	63	G8
Caála	106	C5
Caatingas	137	H5
Caballeria, Cabo	67	J2
Caballos Mesteños, Llano de los	127	K6
Cabanatuan	91	G2
Cabano	125	R3
Cabeza de Buey	66	D3
Cabeza Lagarto, Punta	136	B6
Cabezas	138	D3
Cabimas	136	C1
Cabinda *Angola*	106	B4
Cabinda *Angola*	106	B4
Cabo	137	L5
Cabo Colnet	126	D5
Cabo Gracias á Dios, Punta	132	F7
Cabonga, Réservoir	125	M3
Cabool	124	D8
Caboolture	113	L4
Cabora Bassa Dam	109	F3
Cabo Raso	139	C8
Caborca	126	F5

Canal Cockburn	**139** B10	Canutama	**136** E5	Carentan	**64** C4	Carpina	**137** K5
Cananea	**126** G5	Canvey Island	**53** H3	Carey, Lake	**112** E4	Carra, Lough	**58** D5
Canarias, Islas	**100** B3	Canyon	**127** M3	Carhaix-Plouguer	**64** B4	Carranza, Cabo	**139** B7
Canarreos, Archipiélago de los	**132** G4	Cao Bang	**93** L4	Carhué	**139** D7	Carranza, Presa V.	**127** M7
Canary Islands	**100** B3	Caombo	**106** C4	Cariacica	**138** H4	Carrara	**68** C3
Canastota	**125** N5	Capanaparo	**136** D2	Cariboa Lake	**124** F1	Carrauntoohil	**59** C9
Canaveral, Cape	**129** M6	Capanema	**137** H4	Cariboo Mountains	**119** L5	Carriacou	**133** S8
Cañaveras	**66** E2	Capão Bonito	**138** G4	Caribou *Canada*	**119** R4	Carrick	**57** D5
Canberra	**113** K6	Capatárida	**136** C1	Caribou *U.S.A.*	**125** S3	Carrickfergus	**58** L3
Çancarli	**76** B3	Cap de la Madeléine	**125** P3	Caribou Mountains	**119** M4	Carrickmacross	**58** J5
Candarli Körfezi	**75** J3	Cape Breton Island	**121** P8	Cariñena	**67** F2	Carrick-on-Shannon	**58** F5
Candé	**65** C5	Cape Coast	**104** E4	Carinhanha	**137** J6	Carrick-on-Suir	**59** H8
Candelaria	**131** P8	Cape Coral	**129** M7	Carinish	**56** A3	Carrigallen	**58** G5
Candia	**75** H5	Cape Dorset	**120** L5	Caripito	**133** R9	Carrigtwohill	**59** F9
Çandir	**76** E2	Cape Dyer	**120** P4	Carleton, Mount	**125** S3	Carrington	**123** Q4
Cando	**123** Q3	Cape Egmont	**115** D3	Carlingford	**58** K4	Carrión	**66** D1
Canea	**75** H5	Cape Girardeau	**124** F8	Carlingford Lough	**58** K4	Carrizal	**136** C1
Canelones	**139** E6	Capel	**53** G3	Carlisle *U.K.*	**55** G2	Carrizal Bajo	**138** B5
Cañete	**67** F2	Capelinha	**138** H3	Carlisle *U.S.A.*	**125** M6	Carrizo Springs	**127** N6
Caney	**128** E2	Capella	**114** C2	Carlos Chagas	**138** H3	Carrizozo	**127** K4
Cangallo	**136** C6	Cape Town	**108** C6	Carlow *Ireland*	**59** J7	Carroll	**124** C5
Cangamba	**106** C5	Cape Verde	**104** L7	Carlow *Ireland*	**59** J7	Carrollton *Georgia, U.S.A.*	**129** K4
Cangas de Narcea	**66** C1	Cape York Peninsula	**113** J1	Carloway	**56** C2	Carrollton *Kentucky, U.S.A.*	**124** H7
Cangas de Onís	**66** D1	Cap-Haïtien	**133** L5	Carlsbad *Czechoslovakia*	**70** E3	Carron	**56** D3
Canguaretama	**137** K5	Capim	**137** H4	Carlsbad *California, U.S.A.*	**126** D4	Carron, Loch	**56** C3
Canguçu	**138** F6	Capitán Arturo Prat	**141** V6	Carlsbad *New Mexico, U.S.A.*	**127** K4	Carrot	**119** Q5
Cangzhou	**87** M4	Capixaba	**138** J6	Carlton *Nottinghamshire, U.K.*	**53** F2	Carrowkeel	**58** H2
Caniapiscau *Canada*	**121** N7	Cappoquin	**59** G8	Carlton *N. Yorkshire, U.K.*	**55** H2	Carrowmore Lough	**58** C4
Caniapiscau *Canada*	**121** N6	Capraia, Isola di	**68** B4	Carlyle	**123** N3	Carryduff	**58** L3
Caniapiscau, Lac	**121** N7	Caprera, Isola	**69** B5	Carmacks	**118** H3	Carşamba	**76** E4
Canicattì	**69** D7	Capricorn Channel	**113** L3	Carmagnola	**68** A3	Carşamba	**77** G2
Canik Dağlari	**77** G2	Capri, Isola di	**69** E5	Carmarthen	**52** C3	Carşibaşi	**77** H2
Canisp	**56** C2	Caprivi Strip	**108** D3	Carmarthen Bay	**52** C3	Carson City	**126** C1
Canjáyar	**66** E4	Captieux	**65** C6	Carmaux	**65** E6	Carson Sink	**122** E8
Çankaya	**76** E3	Capua	**69** E5	Carmel Head	**54** E3	Carsphairn	**57** D5
Çankiri	**76** E2	Caquetá	**136** C4	Carmelo	**139** E6	Cartagena *Colombia*	**136** B1
Canna	**57** B3	Carabinani	**136** E4	Carmen	**136** B2	Cartagena *Spain*	**67** F4
Cannanore	**92** E6	Caracal	**73** H3	Carmen Alto	**138** C4	Cartago *Colombia*	**136** B3
Canna, Sound of	**57** B3	Caracarai	**136** E3	Carmen de Patagones	**139** D8	Cartago *Costa Rica*	**132** F10
Cannes	**65** G7	Caracas	**136** D1	Carmen, Isla	**126** G8	Cartaret	**53** N7
Cannich *U.K.*	**56** D3	Carajari	**137** G4	Carmen, Sierra del	**127** L6	Cartaxo	**66** B3
Cannich *U.K.*	**56** D3	Carajás, Serra dos	**137** G5	Carmi	**124** F7	Cartaya	**66** C4
Canning	**118** F2	Carangola	**138** H4	Carmona	**66** D4	Carteret	**64** C4
Canning Basin	**112** E2	Caratasca	**132** F7	Carnarvon *Australia*	**112** C3	Carterton	**115** E4
Cannington	**52** D3	Caratasca, Laguna	**132** F7	Carnarvon *South Africa*	**108** D6	Carthage *Missouri, U.S.A.*	**124** C8
Cannock	**53** E2	Caratinga	**138** H3	Carn Ban	**57** D3	Carthage *Texas, U.S.A.*	**128** E4
Cann River	**113** K6	Carauari	**136** D4	Carnedd Llewelyn	**54** F3	Cartier Island	**110** F4
Canõas	**138** F5	Caravaca de la Cruz	**67** F3	Carnegie, Lake	**112** E4	Cartwright	**121** Q7
Canoas	**138** F5	Caravelas	**137** K7	Carnew	**59** K7	Caruara	**137** K5
Canoeiros	**138** G3	Carballo	**66** B1	Carney Island	**141** R4	Carumbo	**106** C4
Canoe Lake	**119** P4	Carbonara, Capo	**69** B6	Carnforth	**55** G2	Carúpano	**136** E1
Canon City	**127** K1	Carbondale	**125** N6	Carn Glas-choire	**56** E3	Caruthersville	**128** H2
Canosa di Puglia	**69** F5	Carbonear	**121** R8	Carniche, Alpi	**68** D2	Carvoeiro, Cabo	**66** B3
Canta	**136** B6	Carboneras de Guadazaóri	**67** F3	Car Nicobar	**93** H7	Cary	**52** E3
Cantábrica, Cordillera	**66** D1	Carbonia	**69** B6	Carnlough	**58** L3	Casablanca	**100** D2
Cantábrico, Mar	**66** D1	Carcans, Étang de	**65** C6	Carnlough Bay	**58** L3	Casa Grande	**126** G4
Cantanhede	**66** B2	Carcans-Plage	**65** C6	Carnot	**102** C7	Casale Monferrato	**68** B3
Canterbury	**53** J3	Carcaraña	**138** D6	Carnsore Point	**59** K8	Casalmaggiore	**68** C3
Canterbury Bight	**115** D6	Carcassonne	**65** E7	Carnwath	**118** K2	Casamance	**104** B3
Canterbury Plains	**115** C6	Carcross	**118** J3	Carolina	**137** H5	Casanare	**136** C2
Can Tho	**93** L6	Çardak	**76** C4	Caroline Islands	**91** K4	Casas Ibañez	**67** F3
Canton *China*	**93** M4	Cardamon Hills	**92** E7	Carondelet Reef	**111** U3	Cascade	**122** F5
Canton *Illinois, U.S.A.*	**124** E6	Cárdenas	**131** N9	Caroni	**136** E2	Cascade Mountains	**122** D3
Canton *Mississippi, U.S.A.*	**128** H4	Cardiel, Lago	**139** B9	Carora	**133** M9	Cascade Point	**115** B5
Canton *New York, U.S.A.*	**125** N4	Cardiff	**52** D3	Carpathians	**73** F1	Cascade Range	**122** C6
Canton *Ohio, U.S.A.*	**125** K6	Cardigan	**52** C2	Carpatii Meridionali	**73** G3	Cascais	**66** B3
Canton *S. Dakota, U.S.A.*	**123** R6	Cardigan Bay	**52** C2	Carpentaria, Gulf of	**113** H1	Cascapédia	**125** S2
Canudos *Amazonas, Brazil*	**136** F5	Cardona	**67** G2	Carpentras	**65** F6	Cascavel *Ceará, Brazil*	**137** K4
Canudos *Bahia, Brazil*	**137** K5	Cardston	**122** H3	Carpi	**68** C3	Cascavel *Paraná, Brazil*	**138** F4
Canumã	**136** F4	Carei	**73** G2			Caschuil	**138** C5

Name	Page	Grid
Chad *U.S.S.R.*	78	K4
Chadan	84	E6
Chadderton	55	G3
Chaddesley Corbett	53	E2
Chadileovú	139	C7
Chad, Lake	102	B5
Chadobets	84	F5
Chadron	123	N6
Chāgai Hills	92	B3
Chagda	85	N5
Chaghcharan	95	S4
Chagny	65	F5
Chagoda	78	F4
Chagos Archipelago	82	F7
Chahah Burjah	95	R6
Chāh Bahār	95	Q9
Chahbounia	67	H5
Ch'aho	88	B5
Chahuites	131	M9
Chāïbāsa	92	G4
Chai Buri	93	K5
Chaiya	93	J7
Chaiyaphum	93	K5
Chajari	138	E6
Chala	136	C7
Chalais	65	D6
Chalap Dalan	92	B2
Chala, Punta	136	B7
Chalatenango	132	C7
Chaldonka	85	K6
Chale	53	F4
Chaleur, Baie de	121	N8
Chaleur Bay	125	T3
Chalhuanca	136	C6
Chalisgaon	92	E4
Challacó	139	C7
Challacombe	52	D3
Challans	65	C5
Challis	122	G5
Chal'mny Varre	78	F2
Chalna	93	G4
Châlon-sur-Marne	64	F4
Chalon-sur-Saône	65	F5
Châlus	65	D6
Chālūs	95	K3
Cham	70	E4
Chama	127	J2
Chaman	92	C2
Chamba *India*	92	E2
Chamba *U.S.S.R.*	84	G4
Chambal	92	E3
Chamberlain *Australia*	112	F2
Chamberlain *U.S.A.*	123	Q6
Chambersburg	125	M7
Chambéry	65	F6
Chamela	130	G8
Chamical	138	C6
Chamonix	65	G6
Chamouchouane	125	P2
Champagne	64	F4
Champagnole	65	F5
Champaign	124	F6
Champflower	52	D3
Champlaine, Lake	125	P4
Champlitte	65	F5
Champotón	131	P8
Chamrajnagar	92	E6
Chamusca	66	B3
Chañaral	138	B5
Chanārān	95	P3
Chança	66	C4
Chandalar	118	F2
Chandausi	92	E3
Chandeleur Islands	128	H6
Chandigarh	92	E2
Chandler	121	P8
Chandmanĭ *Mongolia*	86	G2
Chandmanĭ *Mongolia*	86	H2
Chandpur	93	H4
Chandrapur	92	E5
Chandvad	92	D4
Chānf	95	Q8
Chang'an	93	L2
Changane	109	F4
Changbai	88	B5
Changbai Shan	88	B4
Changchun	87	P3
Changde	93	M3
Chang-hua	87	N7
Chang Jiang	87	M5
Chang, Ko	93	K6
Changle	87	M4
Changling	87	N3
Changma	86	H4
Changnyön	87	P4
Changsan-got	87	N4
Changsha	93	M3
Changshan	87	M6
Changtai	87	M7
Changting	87	M6
Changwu	93	L1
Changxing	87	M5
Changyi	87	M4
Changzhi	87	L4
Changzhou	87	M5
Channel Islands	53	M7
Channel-Port-aux-Basques	121	Q8
Chantada	66	C1
Chanthaburi	93	K6
Chantilly	64	E4
Chantonnay	65	C5
Chantrey Inlet	120	G4
Chanute	128	E2
Chany, Ozero	84	B6
Chao	136	B5
Chao Hu	87	M5
Chao Phraya	93	K5
Chaor He	87	N2
Chaouên	100	D1
Chaoyang *China*	87	N3
Chaoyang *China*	87	N3
Chaozhou	87	M7
Chapadinha	137	J4
Chapala, Laguna de	130	H7
Chapanda	85	N5
Chapayevo	79	J5
Chapayevsk	79	H5
Chapayev-Zheday	85	K4
Chapchachi	79	H6
Chapeco	138	F5
Chapel-en-le-Frith	55	H3
Chapel Hill	129	N3
Chapeltown *Grampian, U.K.*	56	E3
Chapeltown *S. Yorkshire, U.K.*	55	H3
Chapleau	124	J3
Chaplygin	79	F5
Chapman	112	F2
Chapman, Cape	120	J4
Chapman Islands	119	P2
Chaqui	138	C3
Chara *U.S.S.R.*	85	K5
Chara *U.S.S.R.*	85	K5
Charagua	138	D3
Chārak	95	M8
Charambirá, Punta	136	B3
Charcot Island	141	U5
Chard	52	E4
Chardzhou	80	H6
Charente	65	C6
Chari	102	C5
Chārikār	92	C1
Chariton *U.S.A.*	124	D6
Chariton *U.S.A.*	124	D6
Charkhari	92	E3
Charlemount	58	J4
Charleroi	64	F3
Charlesbourg	125	Q3
Charles, Cape	125	N8
Charles City	124	D5
Charles Island *Canada*	120	M5
Charles Island *Ecuador*	136	A7
Charleston *Illinois, U.S.A.*	124	F7
Charleston *Missouri, U.S.A.*	124	F8
Charleston *S. Carolina, U.S.A.*	129	N4
Charleston *W. Virginia, U.S.A.*	125	K7
Charlestown	58	E5
Charlestown of Aberlour	56	E3
Charleville	113	K4
Charleville-Mézières	64	F4
Charlotte	129	M3
Charlotte Amalie	133	Q5
Charlotte, Cape	139	J10
Charlotte Harbour	129	L7
Charlottesville	125	L7
Charlottetown	121	P8
Charlton	113	J6
Charlton Island	121	L7
Charmes	64	G4
Charnley	112	F2
Charolles	65	F5
Charters Towers	113	K3
Chartres	64	D4
Charwelton	53	F2
Charybdis Reef	114	Q8
Charyn	86	D3
Chascomús	139	E7
Chasel'ka	84	C3
Chaslands Mistake	115	B7
Chasong	87	P3
Chasovo	78	J3
Chasseeneuil	65	D6
Chāt	95	M3
Châteaubriant	65	C5
Château Chinon	65	E5
Châteaudun	65	D4
Château-Gontier	65	C5
Château-la-Vallière	65	D5
Châteaulin	64	A4
Châteauneuf-en-Thimerais	64	D4
Châteauneuf-sur-Loire	65	E5
Châteaurenault	65	D5
Châteauroux	65	D5
Château-Salins	64	G4
Château-Thierry	64	E4
Châtellerault	65	D5
Chatham *New Brunswick, Canada*	125	T3
Chatham *Ontario, Canada*	124	J5
Chatham *U.K.*	53	H3
Chatham, Isla	139	B10
Chatham Island *Ecuador*	136	A7
Chatham Island *New Zealand*	115	F7
Chatham Islands	115	G7
Châtillon	68	A3
Châtillon-sur-Indre	65	D5
Châtillon-sur-Seine	65	F5
Chato, Cerro	139	B8
Chattahoochee	129	K5
Chattanooga	129	K3
Chatteris	53	H2
Chatyrtash	86	D3
Chaudiere	125	Q3
Chaumont	64	F4
Chaunskaya Guba	85	V3
Chauny	64	E4
Chautauqua Lake	125	L5
Chavantina	138	G6
Chaves *Brazil*	137	H4
Chaves *Portugal*	66	C2
Chaviva	136	C3
Chāy Khanah	77	L5
Chaykovskiy	78	J4
Chazhegovo	78	J3
Cheadle	55	G3
Cheb	70	E3
Cheboksary	78	H4
Cheboygan	124	H4
Checheningush A.S.S.R.	79	H7
Chechen', Ostrov	79	H7
Chech, Erg	100	E3
Chechuysk	84	H5
Chęciny	71	J3
Chedabucto Bay	121	P8
Cheddar	52	E3
Cheduba	93	H5
Cheetham, Cape	141	L4
Chef-Boutonne	65	C5
Chehalis	122	C4
Chehel Dokhtarān	95	R4
Cheju	87	P5
Cheju do	87	P5
Chekhov	88	H2
Chekunda	85	N6
Chekurovka	85	M2
Chekuyevo	78	F3
Chelan	122	D4
Chelan, Lake	122	D3
Chela, Serra da	106	B6
Cheleken	95	L2
Chelforó	139	C7
Cheliff, Oued	100	F1
Chelkar	51	U6
Chełm	71	K3
Chelmsford	53	H3
Chelmuzhi	78	F3
Chelosh	84	D6
Cheltenham	53	E3
Chelva	67	F3
Chelyabinsk	84	Ad5
Chelyuskin	84	G1
Chelyuskin, Mys	81	M2
Chemba	109	F3
Chemillé	65	C5
Chemnitz	70	E3
Chenab	92	D2
Cheney	122	F4
Chengde	87	M3
Chengdu	93	K2
Chenghai	87	M7
Chengjiang	93	K4

Chon Thanh	**93**	L6
Chop	**79**	C6
Chorley	**55**	G3
Chorolque	**138**	C4
Chortkov	**79**	D6
Chorzele	**71**	J2
Chōshi	**89**	H8
Chosica	**136**	B6
Chos-Malal	**139**	B7
Choson-Man	**87**	P4
Choszczno	**70**	F2
Chota	**136**	B5
Choteau	**122**	H4
Choybalsan	**87**	L2
Christchurch *New Zealand*	**115**	D5
Christchurch *U.K.*	**53**	F4
Christiansfeld	**63**	C9
Christianshåb	**120**	R4
Christie Bay	**119**	N3
Christmas Creek	**112**	F2
Christmas Island *Australia*	**83**	J8
Christmas Island *Kiribati*	**143**	H4
Chrzanów	**71**	H3
Chu	**86**	C3
Chubartau	**86**	D2
Chubut	**139**	C8
Chudleigh	**52**	D4
Chudovo	**78**	E4
Chudskoye Ozero	**63**	M7
Chugach Mountains	**118**	G3
Chūgoku-sanchi	**89**	D8
Chugunash	**84**	D6
Chuguyevka	**88**	D3
Chukchi Sea	**118**	B2
Chuken	**88**	F2
Chukhloma	**78**	G4
Chukotat	**121**	L5
Chukotskiy Khrebet	**85**	W3
Chukotskiy Poluostrov	**81**	V3
Chulak-Kurgan	**86**	B3
Chula Vista	**126**	D4
Chulman	**85**	L5
Chulmleigh	**52**	D4
Chulym *U.S.S.R.*	**84**	C5
Chulym *U.S.S.R.*	**84**	C5
Chum	**78**	L2
Chumbicha	**138**	C5
Chumek	**86**	F2
Chumikan	**85**	P6
Chumphon	**93**	J6
Chuna	**84**	F5
Ch'unch'ŏn	**87**	P4
Ch'ungju	**87**	P4
Chunhua	**88**	C4
Chunoyar	**84**	F5
Chunya	**107**	F4
Chunyang	**88**	B4
Ch'unyang	**89**	B7
Chuquibamba	**138**	B3
Chuquicamata	**138**	B4
Chur	**68**	B2
Churan	**85**	L4
Chûrapcha	**85**	N4
Churchill *Canada*	**119**	S4
Churchill *Canada*	**119**	S4
Churchill *Newfoundland, Canada*	**121**	P7
Churchill, Cape	**119**	S4
Churchill Falls	**121**	P7
Churchill Peak	**118**	L4

Church Stretton	**52**	E2
Churia Ghati Hills	**92**	G3
Churín	**136**	B6
Churu	**92**	D3
Churuguara	**136**	D1
Chushevitsy	**78**	G3
Chushul	**92**	E2
Chusovaya	**78**	K4
Chusovov	**78**	K4
Chust	**86**	C3
Chute des Passes	**125**	Q2
Chuŭronjang	**88**	B5
Chuvash A.S.S.R.	**78**	H4
Chuxiong	**93**	K4
Chu Yang Sin	**93**	L6
Chwārtā	**94**	G4
Chyulu Range	**107**	G3
Cianjur	**90**	D7
Çiçekdaği	**76**	F3
Cicia	**114**	S8
Cide	**76**	E2
Cidones	**66**	E2
Ciéchanow	**71**	J2
Ciego de Avila	**132**	H4
Ciénaga	**136**	C1
Cienfuegos	**132**	G3
Cieszyn	**71**	H4
Cieza	**67**	F3
Çiftehan	**76**	F4
Çifteler	**76**	D3
Cifuentes	**66**	E2
Cihanbeyli	**76**	E3
Cijara, Embalse de	**66**	D3
Cilacap	**90**	D7
Çildir	**77**	K2
Çildir Gölü	**77**	K2
Cilo Daği	**77**	L4
Cimarron	**128**	A2
Cimone, Monte	**68**	C3
Cîmpeni	**73**	G2
Cîmpina	**73**	H3
Cîmpulung	**73**	H3
Cîmpuri	**73**	J2
Çinar	**77**	J4
Cinaruco	**136**	D2
Cina, Tanjung	**90**	C7
Cinca	**67**	G2
Cinčer	**72**	D4
Cincinnati	**124**	H7
Cinderford	**52**	E3
Çine	**76**	C4
Çinguş	**77**	H3
Cinto, Monte	**69**	B4
Circeo, Capo	**69**	D5
Circle *Alaska, U.S.A.*	**118**	G2
Circle *Montana, U.S.A.*	**123**	M4
Circular Reef	**114**	D2
Cirebon	**90**	D7
Cirencester	**53**	F3
Ciri	**136**	E5
Ciria	**67**	E2
Ciro	**69**	F6
Cisco	**128**	C4
Cislău	**73**	J3
Cisna	**71**	K4
Cisneros	**136**	B2
Cistierna	**66**	D1
Citac, Nevado	**136**	C6
Citlaltépetl, Volcán	**131**	L8
Citt à di Castello	**68**	D4

Cittanova	**69**	F6
Ciucului, Munţii	**73**	H2
Ciudad Acuña	**127**	M6
Ciudad Bolivar	**136**	E2
Ciudad Camargo	**127**	K7
Ciudad Cuauhtémoc	**131**	P10
Ciudad del Carmen	**131**	P8
Ciudad del Maíz	**131**	K6
Ciudad de México	**131**	K8
Ciudadela	**67**	H3
Ciudad Guayana	**136**	E2
Ciudad Guzmán	**130**	H8
Ciudad Ixtepec	**131**	M9
Ciudad Juárez	**127**	J5
Ciudad Lerdo	**127**	L8
Ciudad Madero	**131**	L6
Ciudad Mante	**131**	K6
Ciudad Mier	**128**	C7
Ciudad Obregón	**127**	H7
Ciudad Ojeda	**133**	M9
Ciudad Piar	**133**	R11
Ciudad Real	**66**	E3
Ciudad Rodrigo	**66**	C2
Ciudad Valles	**131**	K7
Ciudad Victoria	**131**	K6
Civa Burun	**77**	G2
Cividale del Friuli	**68**	D2
Cívita Castellana	**69**	D4
Civitanova Marche	**68**	D4
Civitavecchia	**69**	C4
Civray	**65**	D5
Çivril	**76**	C3
Cizre	**77**	K4
Clach Leathad	**57**	D4
Clacton-on-Sea	**53**	J3
Cladich	**57**	C4
Claerwen Reservoir	**52**	D2
Clain	**65**	D5
Claire, Lac à l'Eau	**121**	M6
Claire, Lake	**119**	N4
Clamecy	**65**	E5
Clane	**59**	J6
Clanton	**129**	J4
Clanwilliam	**108**	C6
Claonaig	**57**	C5
Clare *Australia*	**113**	H5
Clare *Ireland*	**59**	D7
Clare Island	**58**	B5
Claremont	**125**	P5
Claremorris	**58**	D5
Clarence *New Zealand*	**115**	D5
Clarence *New Zealand*	**115**	D5
Clarence, Cape	**120**	H3
Clarence Head	**120**	L2
Clarence Strait *Australia*	**112**	G1
Clarence Strait *U.S.A.*	**118**	J4
Clarence Town	**133**	K3
Clarinda	**124**	C6
Clarion	**125**	L6
Clark	**123**	K5
Clarke River	**113**	K2
Clark Fork *Montana, U.S.A*	**122**	H4
Clark Fork *Washington, U.S.A.*	**122**	F3
Clark, Lake	**118**	E3
Clarksburg	**125**	K7
Clarksdale	**128**	G3
Clarks Hill Lake	**129**	L4
Clarkston	**122**	F4
Clarksville *Arkansas, U.S.A.*	**128**	F3

Clarksville *Tennessee, U.S.A.*	**129**	J2
Clàr, Loch nan	**56**	D2
Clatteringshaws Loch	**57**	D5
Claughton	**55**	G2
Clavering Ø	**120**	X3
Claxton	**129**	M4
Clay Center	**123**	R8
Clay Cross	**55**	H3
Claydon	**53**	J2
Clayton *Georgia, U.S.A.*	**129**	L3
Clayton *New Mexico, U.S.A.*	**127**	L2
Clear, Cape	**59**	C10
Clearfield *Pennsylvania, U.S.A.*	**125**	L6
Clearfield *Utah, U.S.A.*	**122**	J7
Clear Fork	**127**	N4
Clear Hills	**119**	M4
Clear Island	**59**	D10
Clear Lake *California, U.S.A.*	**122**	C8
Clear Lake *Iowa, U.S.A.*	**124**	D5
Clear Lake Reservoir	**122**	D7
Clearwater *Canada*	**122**	G1
Clearwater *Canada*	**119**	P4
Clearwater *Florida, U.S.A.*	**129**	L7
Clearwater *Idaho, U.S.A.*	**122**	F4
Clearwater Mountains	**122**	G4
Cleethorpes	**55**	J3
Clerke Reef	**112**	D2
Clermont *Australia*	**113**	K3
Clermont *France*	**64**	E4
Clermont-Ferrand	**65**	E6
Clermont-l'Hérault	**65**	E7
Clervaux	**64**	G3
Cleve	**113**	H5
Clevedon	**52**	E3
Cleveland *U.K.*	**55**	H2
Cleveland *Mississippi, U.S.A.*	**128**	G4
Cleveland *Ohio, U.S.A.*	**125**	K6
Cleveland *Tennessee, U.S.A.*	**129**	K3
Cleveland *Texas, U.S.A.*	**128**	E5
Cleveland, Cape	**113**	K2
Cleveland Hills	**55**	H2
Cleveland, Mount	**122**	H3
Cleveleys	**55**	F3
Clew Bay	**58**	C5
Clifden *Ireland*	**59**	B6
Clifden *New Zealand*	**115**	A7
Cliffe	**53**	H3
Cliffs of Moher	**59**	D7
Clifton	**55**	G2
Clincha Alta	**136**	B6
Clinch Mountains	**129**	L2
Clingmans Dome	**129**	L3
Clinton *Canada*	**122**	D2
Clinton *Illinois, U.S.A.*	**124**	F6
Clinton *Iowa, U.S.A.*	**124**	E6
Clinton *Mississippi, U.S.A.*	**128**	G4
Clinton *Missouri, U.S.A.*	**124**	D7
Clinton *N. Carolina, U.S.A.*	**129**	N3
Clinton *Oklahoma, U.S.A.*	**128**	C3
Clinton-Colden Lake	**119**	P3
Clipperton Island	**117**	J7
Clisham	**56**	B3
Clisson	**65**	C5
Clitheroe	**55**	G3
Cliza	**138**	C3
Cloates, Point	**112**	C3
Clogheen	**59**	G8
Clogherhead	**58**	K5
Clogher Head	**58**	K5

Constância dos Baetas	**136** E5	Corbières	**65** E7	Corrientes, Cabo *Cuba*	**132** E4	Cowbridge	**52** D3
Constanţa	**73** K3	Corbigny	**65** E5	Corrientes, Cabo *Mexico*	**130** G7	Cowdenbeath	**57** E4
Constantina	**66** D4	Corbin	**124** H8	Corrigan	**128** E5	Cowes	**53** F4
Constantine	**101** G1	Corbones	**66** D4	Corrigin	**112** D5	Cowfold	**53** G4
Constantine Bay	**52** B4	Corbridge	**55** G2	Corry	**125** L6	Cowlitz	**122** C4
Constantine, Cape	**118** D4	Corby	**53** G2	Corryvreckan, Gulf of	**57** C4	Cowra	**113** K5
Constantinople	**76** C2	Corby Glen	**53** G2	Corse	**69** B4	Coxim	**138** F3
Constitución	**139** B7	Corcaigh	**59** E9	Corse, Cap	**68** B4	Cox's Bazar	**93** H4
Contamana	**136** C5	Corcovado, Golfo	**139** B8	Corsewall Point	**57** C5	Coxwold	**55** H2
Contas	**137** J6	Corcubión	**66** B1	Corsica	**69** B4	Cozumel	**131** R7
Contratacion	**136** C2	Cordele	**129** L5	Corsicana	**128** D4	Cozumel, Isla de	**131** R7
Contrexéville	**64** F4	Cordoba	**131** L8	Corte	**69** B4	Cracow	**71** H3
Contulmo	**139** B7	Córdoba *Argentina*	**138** D6	Cortegana	**66** C4	Cradock	**108** E6
Contwoyto Lake	**119** N2	Córdoba *Spain*	**66** D4	Cortez	**127** H2	Craig	**123** L7
Conway *Arkansas, U.S.A.*	**128** F3	Cordoba, Sierras de	**138** D6	Cortina d'Ampezzo	**68** D2	Craigavon	**58** K4
Conway *New Hampshire, U.S.A.*	**125** Q5	Córdova	**136** B6	Cortland	**125** M5	Craignure	**57** C4
Conway *S. Carolina, U.S.A.*	**129** N4	Cordova	**118** F3	Cortona	**68** C4	Craignure	
		Corfe	**52** D4	Corubal	**104** C3	Crail	**57** F4
Conway Bay	**54** F3	Corfu *Greece*	**74** E3	Coruche	**66** B3	Crailsheim	**70** D4
Conwy	**54** F3	Corfu *Greece*	**74** E3	Çoruh	**77** J2	Craiova	**73** G3
Coober Pedy	**113** G4	Coria	**66** C2	Çorum	**76** F2	Cramlington	**55** H1
Cook	**112** G5	Corigliano Calabro	**69** F6	Corumbá	**138** E3	Cranborne	**53** F4
Cook, Cape	**122** A2	Corinda	**113** H2	Corumba	**138** G3	Cranbrook	**122** G3
Cookeville	**129** K2	Corinth *Greece*	**75** G4	Corunna	**66** B1	Crane	**127** L5
Cook Inlet	**118** E3	Corinth *U.S.A.*	**128** H3	Corvallis	**122** C5	Cranleigh	**53** G3
Cook Islands	**143** H5	Corinth, Gulf of	**75** G3	Corve	**52** E2	Cranstown, Kap	**120** Q3
Cook, Mount	**115** C5	Corinto *Brazil*	**138** H3	Corwen	**52** D2	Craponne-sur-Arzon	**65** E6
Cook, Récif de	**114** W15	Corinto *Nicaragua*	**132** D8	Cos	**75** J4	Crasna *Romania*	**73** G2
Cookstown	**58** J3	Corixa Grande	**138** E3	Cosamaloapan	**131** M8	Crasna *Romania*	**73** J2
Cook Strait	**115** E4	Cork *Ireland*	**59** E9	Cosamozza	**69** B4	Crater Lake	**122** C6
Cooktown	**113** K2	Cork *Ireland*	**59** E9	Cosenza	**69** F6	Crateús	**137** J5
Coolibah	**112** G2	Corlay	**64** B4	Cosigüina, Volcán	**132** D8	Crati	**69** F6
Coolidge	**126** G4	Corleone	**69** D7	Cosmoledo Islands	**82** C7	Crato	**137** K5
Cooma	**113** K6	Corlu	**76** B2	Cosne	**65** E5	Cravo Norte	**136** C2
Coomnadiha	**59** C9	Cornafulla	**59** F6	Costa, Cordillera de la	**133** N9	Crawford	**123** N6
Coomscarrea	**59** B9	Corner Brook	**121** Q8	Costa Rica	**132** E9	Crawford Point	**91** F3
Coonamble	**113** K5	Cornhill-on-Tweed	**57** F4	Costeşti	**73** H3	Crawfordville	**129** K5
Coondapoor	**92** D6	Corning	**125** M5	Cotabato	**91** G4	Crawley	**53** G3
Coongan	**112** D3	Corn Islands	**132** F8	Cotacachi	**136** B3	Crazy Mountains	**123** J4
Coopers Creek	**113** H4	Cornudilla	**66** E1	Cotagaita	**138** C4	Creach Bheinn	**57** C4
Cooroy	**113** L4	Cornwall *U.K.*	**52** C4	Cotahuasi	**138** B3	Creag Meagaidh	**57** D3
Coosa	**129** J4	Cornwall *U.K.*	**125** N4	Cotentin	**64** C4	Creagorry	**56** A3
Coos Bay *U.S.A.*	**122** B6	Cornwallis Island	**120** H2	Cotiella	**67** G1	Crediton	**52** D4
Coos Bay *U.S.A.*	**122** B6	Cornwall Island	**120** H2	Cotonou	**105** F4	Cree *Canada*	**119** P4
Cootamundra	**113** K5	Coro	**136** D1	Cotopaxi	**136** B4	Cree *U.K.*	**57** D5
Cootehill	**58** H4	Coroatá	**137** J4	Cottage Grove	**122** C6	Cree Lake	**119** P4
Copacabana	**138** C3	Corocoro	**138** C3	Cottbus	**70** F3	Creeslough	**58** G2
Copa, Cerro	**138** C4	Coromandel *Brazil*	**138** G3	Cottingham	**55** J3	Creetown	**54** E2
Cope	**123** N8	Coromandel *New Zealand*	**115** E2	Cottonwood	**126** F3	Creggan	**58** H3
Copenhagen	**63** E9	Coromandel Coast	**92** F6	Coubre, Pointe de la	**65** C6	Creggs	**58** F5
Copiapó	**138** B5	Coromandel Peninsula	**115** E2	Coulommiers	**64** E4	Crema	**68** B3
Copinsay	**56** F2	Corona	**127** K3	Coulonge	**125** M3	Cremona	**68** B3
Cöpköy	**76** B2	Coronado, Bahía de	**132** E10	Council Bluffs	**124** C6	Crepaja	**72** F3
Copper	**118** G3	Coronation Gulf	**119** N2	Coupar Angus	**57** E4	Creran, Loch	**57** C4
Copper Center	**118** F3	Coronel	**139** B7	Courantyne	**136** F3	Cres *Yugoslavia*	**72** C3
Coppermine *Canada*	**119** M2	Coronel Dorrego	**139** D7	Courchevel	**65** G6	Cres *Yugoslavia*	**72** C3
Coppermine *Canada*	**119** N2	Coronel Pringles	**139** D7	Couronne, Cap	**65** F7	Crescent	**122** D6
Copper Mount	**122** F2	Coronel Suárez	**139** D7	Courtenay	**122** B3	Crescent City	**122** B7
Copplestone	**52** D4	Corovodë	**75** F2	Courtmacsherry Bay	**59** E9	Crest	**65** F6
Copşa Mică	**73** H2	Corps	**65** F6	Coutances	**64** C4	Creston	**124** C6
Coquet	**57** G5	Corpus Christi	**128** D7	Couto Magalhães	**137** H5	Crestview	**129** J5
Coquimbo	**138** B5	Corpus Christi Bay	**128** D7	Coutras	**65** C6	Crete	**75** H5
Coquimbo, Bahia de	**138** B5	Corpus Christi, Lake	**128** D6	Cove	**56** C3	Cretin, Cape	**114** D3
Corabia	**73** H4	Corque	**138** C3	Coventry	**53** F2	Creus, Cap	**67** H1
Coracora	**136** C7	Corran	**57** C4	Covilhã	**66** C2	Creuse	**65** D5
Coral Harbour	**120** K5	Corraun Peninsula	**58** C5	Covington *Kentucky, U.S.A.*	**124** H7	Crevillente	**67** F3
Coral Sea Plateau	**113** K2	Corrib, Lough	**59** D6	Covington *Virginia, U.S.A.*	**125** L8	Crewe	**55** G3
Corantijn	**136** F3	Corrientes *Argentina*	**138** E5	Cowall	**57** C4	Crewkerne	**52** E4
Corbeil-Essonnes	**64** E4	Corrientes *Peru*	**136** B4	Cowan, Lake	**112** E5	Crianlarich	**57** D4
Corbière	**53** M7	Corrientes, Cabo *Colombia*	**136** B2	Cowbit	**53** G2	Criccieth	**52** C2
						Criciúma	**138** G5

Name	Page	Ref
Decatur *Illinois, U.S.A.*	124	F7
Decatur *Indiana, U.S.A.*	124	H6
Decatur *Texas, U.S.A.*	128	D4
Decazeville	65	E6
Deccan	92	E5
Deception	108	D4
Déception	120	M5
Dechang	93	K3
Decize	65	E5
Decorah	124	E5
Deda	73	H2
Deddington	53	F3
Dedéagach	75	H2
Dedegöl Dağlari	76	D4
Dedeköy	76	E2
Dédougou	104	E3
Dedu	87	P2
Dee *Cheshire, U.K.*	55	G3
Dee *Dumfries and Galloway, U.K.*	54	F2
Dee *Grampian, U.K.*	57	F3
Dee, Linn of	57	E4
Deep River	125	M3
Deeps, The	56	A2
Deering, Mount	112	F4
Deer Lake	121	Q8
Deer Lodge	122	H4
Defiance	124	H6
Defiance Plateau	127	H3
Deflotte, Cape	114	X16
De Funiak Springs	129	J5
Degeberga	63	F9
Degeh Bur	103	H6
Dégelis	125	R3
Degerhamn	63	G8
Deggendorf	70	E4
De Grey	112	E3
Dehaj	95	M6
Dehak	95	R8
Dehalak Desēt	103	H4
Deh Bīd	95	L6
Deh-Dasht	95	K6
Deheq	95	K5
Dehiwala	92	E7
Dehkhvāreqan	94	G3
Dehlorān	94	H5
Dehra Dun	92	E2
Deh Salm	95	P6
Dehui	87	P3
Deim Zubeir	102	E6
Dej	73	G2
De Kalb *Illinois, U.S.A.*	124	F6
De Kalb *Texas, U.S.A.*	128	E4
Dek'emhāre	96	D9
Dekese	106	D3
Delami	102	F5
Delano	126	C3
Delārām	95	R5
Delaware *Ohio, U.S.A.*	124	J6
Delaware *Pennsylvania, U.S.A.*	125	N6
Delaware *U.S.A.*	125	N7
Delaware Bay	125	N7
Delčevo	73	G5
Delémont	68	A2
Delft	64	F2
Delfzijl	64	G2
Delgada, Punta	131	L8
Delgado, Cabo	109	H2
Delgerhaan	87	J2
Delgo	102	F3
Delhi *India*	92	E3
Delhi *India*	92	E3
Delhi *Colorado, U.S.A.*	127	L2
Delhi *New York, U.S.A.*	125	N5
Delice *Turkey*	76	E3
Delice *Turkey*	76	F2
Delicias	127	K6
Delījān	95	K4
Delingha	93	J1
Delitzsch	70	E3
Delle	65	G5
Dellys	101	F1
Delmenhorst	70	C2
Delnice	72	C3
De Long Mountains	118	C2
Deloraine	113	K7
Delray Beach	129	M7
Del Rio	127	M6
Delsbo	63	G6
Delta *Colorado, U.S.A.*	127	H1
Delta *Utah, U.S.A.*	126	F1
Delta Junction	118	F3
Delvin	58	H5
Dema	78	J5
Demanda, Sierra de la	66	E1
Demba	106	D4
Dembī Dolo	103	F6
Demer	64	F3
Demerara	136	F2
Deming	127	J4
Demini	136	E3
Demirci	76	C3
Demir Kazik	76	F4
Demirköy	76	B2
Demmin	70	E2
Demnate	100	D2
Demopolis	129	J4
Dempo, Gunung	90	C6
Demyanskoye	84	Ae5
Denakil	103	H5
Denan	103	H6
Denau	86	B4
Denbigh	55	F3
Denbigh, Cape	118	C3
Denby Dale	55	H3
Dendang	90	D6
Dendermonde	64	F3
Dendi	103	G6
Denezhkino	84	D3
Dengkou	87	K3
Dêngqen	93	J2
Den Haag	64	F2
Den Helder	64	F2
Denia	67	G3
Deniliquin	113	K6
Denio	122	E7
Denison *Iowa, U.S.A.*	124	C6
Denison *Texas, U.S.A.*	128	D4
Denison, Mount	118	E4
Denizli	76	C4
Denmark	63	B9
Denmark Strait	116	S2
Denner Pass	122	D8
Dennis Head	56	F1
Denny	57	E4
Denpasar	90	F7
Densongi	91	G6
Denta	73	F3
Denton	128	D4
D'Entrecasteaux Islands	114	E3
D'Entrecasteaux, Point	112	D5
Denver	123	M8
Deogarh	92	F4
Deoghar	92	G4
Declali	92	D5
Decsai, Plains of	92	E2
Dep	85	M6
Dêcên	93	J3
Deqing	93	M4
De Queen	128	E3
Dera Bugti	92	C3
Dera Ghazikhan	92	D2
Dera Ismail Khan	92	D2
Derajat	92	D2
Derazhno	71	M3
Derazhnya	73	J1
Derbent	79	H7
Derby *Australia*	112	E2
Derby *U.K.*	53	F2
Derbyshire	55	H3
Dereköy	76	B2
Dereli	77	H2
Derg	58	G3
Derg, Lough *Donegal, Ireland*	58	G3
Derg, Lough *Tipperary, Ireland*	59	F7
De Ridder	128	F5
Derik	77	J4
Derinkuyu	76	F3
Derna	101	K2
Dêrong	93	J3
Derravaragh, Lough	58	H5
Derry	58	H2
Derrynasaggart Mountains	59	D9
Derryveagh Mountains	58	F2
Derudeb	103	G4
Dervéni	75	G3
Derventa	72	D3
Derwent *Australia*	113	K7
Derwent *Derbyshire, U.K.*	55	H3
Derwent *N. Yorkshire, U.K.*	55	J2
Derwent Reservoir	55	H2
Derwent Water	54	E2
Derzhavinsk	84	Ae6
Desaguadero *Argentina*	138	C6
Desaguadero *Bolivia*	138	C3
Descanso	126	D4
Deschambault Lake	119	Q5
Deschutes	122	D5
Desē	103	G5
Deseado	139	C9
Desemboque	126	F5
Desengaño, Punta	139	C9
Desert Center	126	E4
Desert Peak	122	H7
Des Moines *U.S.A.*	124	D6
Des Moines *U.S.A.*	124	D6
Desna	79	E5
Desolación, Isla	139	B10
Des Plaines	124	G5
Dessau	70	E3
Deštná	71	G3
Dete	108	E3
Detmold	70	C3
Detour, Point	124	G4
Detroit	124	J5
Detroit Lakes	124	C3
Deutschlandsberg	68	E2
Deva	73	G3
Devakottai	92	E7
Devdevdyak	84	H4
Devecikonaği	76	C3
Devecser	72	D2
Devegedçidi Baraji	77	H3
Develi	76	F3
Deventer	64	G2
Deveron	56	F3
Devils	127	M5
Devil's Bridge	52	D2
Devils Lake	123	Q3
Devils Paw	118	J4
Devils Tower	123	M5
Devin	73	H5
Devizes	53	F3
Devli	92	E3
Devnya	73	J4
Devoll	75	F2
Devon	52	D4
Devon Island	120	J2
Devonport	115	E2
Devrek	76	D2
Devrekani	76	E2
Devrez	76	E2
Devyatkova	84	Ae5
Dewangiri	93	H3
Dewas	92	E4
De Witt	128	G3
Dewsbury	55	H3
Dey-Dey, Lake	112	G4
Deyhuk	95	N5
Deylaman	95	J3
Deyong, Tanjung	114	B3
Deyyer	95	K8
Dez	94	J5
Dezfūl	94	J5
Dezhneva, Mys	118	B2
Dezhou	87	M4
Dhaka	93	G4
Dhamār	96	G9
Dhampur	92	E3
Dhamtari	92	F4
Dhanbad	92	G4
Dhandhuka	92	D4
Dhang Range	92	F3
Dhankuta	93	G3
Dhar	92	E4
Dharmapuri	92	E6
Dharmavaram	92	E6
Dharmjaygarh	92	F4
Dhārwād	92	D5
Dhaulāgiri	92	F3
Dhaulpur	92	E3
Dhenkanal	92	G4
Dhenoúsa	75	H4
Dhermatás, Ákra	75	G3
Dhërmi	74	E2
Dheskáti	75	F3
Dhespotikó	75	H4
Dhíalvos Zákinthou	75	F4
Dhidhimótikhon	75	J2
Dhíkti Óri	75	H5
Dhírfis	75	G3
Dhodhekánisos	75	J4
Dhomokós	75	G3
Dhoraji	92	D4
Dhoxáton	75	H2
Dhrangadhra	92	D4
Dhrépanon, Ákra	75	G3
Dhuburi	93	G3

Dhule	92	D4	Dinard	64	B4	Djolu	106	D2	Dolgellau	52	D2
Día	75	H5	Dinas Head	52	C2	Djougou	105	F4	Dolginovo	71	M1
Diamante	138	D6	Dinbych	55	F3	Djourab	102	C4	Dolgiy, Ostrov	84	Ac3
Diamantina Australia	113	H4	Dinbych-y-pysgod	52	C3	Djúpivogur	62	X12	Dolgoye	71	K4
Diamantina Brazil	138	H3	Dinder	96	B10	Djurdjura	67	J4	Dolina	79	C6
Diamantina, Chapada	137	J6	Dindigul	92	E6	Djursland	63	D8	Dolinsk	88	J2
Diamond Lake Junction	122	D6	Dinek	76	E4	Dmitriya Lapteva, Proliv	85	Q2	Dolinskaya	79	E6
Diaoling	88	B3	Dinggyê	93	G3	Dmitrov	78	F4	Dollar	57	E4
Diavata	75	G2	Dingle	59	B8	Dnepr	79	E6	Dollar Law	57	E5
Dibā al Ḥiṣn	97	N4	Dingle Bay	59	B8	Dneprodzerzhinsk	79	E6	Dolni Královice	70	F4
Dibaya	106	D4	Dingle Peninsula	59	B8	Dnepropetrovsk	79	F6	Dolok, Tanjung	114	A3
Dibdibah, Ad	96	H2	Dinguiraye	104	C3	Dneprovskaya Nizmennost'	79	D5	Dolomitiche, Alpi	68	C2
Dibrugarh	93	H3	Dingwall	56	D3	Dneprovsko-Bugskiy Kanal	71	L2	Dolo Odo	103	H7
Dickinson	123	N4	Dingxi	93	K1	Dnestr	73	K2	Dolores Argentina	139	E7
Dickson	129	J2	Dingxin	86	H3	Dnestrovskiy Liman	73	L2	Dolores Uruguay	139	E6
Dicle	77	J4	Dingxing	87	M4	Dno	78	E4	Dolores U.S.A.	122	K8
Didcot	53	F3	Dinh Lap	93	L4	Doaktown	125	T3	Dolphin and Union Strait	119	N1
Didinga Hills	103	F7	Dinnington	55	H3	Doba	102	C6	Dolphin, Cape	139	E10
Didnovarre	62	K1	Dinosaur	123	K7	Dobbiáco	68	D2	Dolsk	71	G3
Didwana	92	D3	Dionard	56	D2	Döbeln	70	E3	Domaniç	76	C3
Die	65	F6	Diorbivol	104	C2	Dobiegniew	70	F2	Dombås	63	C5
Diébougou	104	E3	Diouloulou	104	B3	Dobo	114	A3	Dombe	109	F3
Diefenbaker, Lake	123	L2	Diourbel	104	B3	Doboj	72	E3	Dombe Grande	106	B5
Diégo-Suarez	109	J2	Dipolog	91	G4	Dobra	71	H3	Dombóvár	72	E2
Diélette	53	N6	Dir	92	D1	Dobre Miasto	71	J2	Dombrád	73	F1
Dien Bien Phu	93	K4	Direction, Cape	113	J1	Dobrič	73	J4	Dôme, Puy de	65	E6
Diepholz	70	C2	Dirē Dawa	103	H6	Dobrodzień	71	H3	Domett	115	D5
Dieppe	64	D4	Direkli	77	G3	Dobrogea	73	K3	Domfront	64	C4
Dietfurt	70	D4	Dirk Hartogs Island	112	C4	Dobrovol'sk	71	K1	Dominica	133	S7
Diffa	101	H6	Dirra	102	E5	Dobrush	79	E5	Dominical	132	F10
Digby	121	N9	Dirranbandi	113	K4	Dobryanka	78	K4	Dominican Republic	133	M5
Digges Island	120	L5	Disappointment, Cape	122	B4	Dobšina	71	J4	Dominion, Cape	120	M4
Digne	65	G6	Disappointment, Lake	112	E3	Dobson	115	C5	Domo	103	J6
Digoin	65	F5	Discovery Bay	113	J6	Dochart	57	D4	Domodossola	68	B2
Digor	77	K2	Dishna Egypt	103	F2	Docking	53	H2	Domuya, Cerro	139	B7
Digul	114	C3	Dishna U.S.A.	118	D3	Dodecanese	75	J4	Don Grampian, U.K.	56	F3
Diinsoor	107	H2	Disko	120	R4	Dodge City	127	M2	Don S. Yorkshire, U.K.	55	H3
Dijlah, Nahr	77	K5	Disko Bay	120	R4	Dodman Point	52	C4	Don U.S.S.R.	79	G6
Dijon	65	F5	Disna U.S.S.R.	63	M9	Dodoma	107	G4	Donaghadee	58	L3
Dikākah, Ad	97	K7	Disna U.S.S.R.	63	N9	Doetinchem	64	G3	Donaldsville	128	G5
Dikanäs	62	G4	Dispur	93	H3	Dofa	91	H6	Donau	68	E1
Dikbiyik	77	G2	Diss	53	J2	Dogai Coring	93	G2	Donauwörth	70	D4
Dikili	76	B3	Dissen	96	E8	Doğanbey	76	D4	Don Benito	66	D3
Dikson	84	C2	Distrito Federal	138	G3	Doğanhisar	76	D3	Doncaster	55	H3
Dikwa	105	H3	Ditchling Beacon	53	G4	Doğankent	76	F4	Dondo	106	B4
Dili	91	H7	Ditinn	104	C3	Doğanşehir	77	G3	Dondra Head	92	F7
Di Linh	93	L6	Dittaino	69	E7	Doğanyol	77	H3	Donegal Ireland	58	F3
Dilizhan	77	L2	Ditton Priors	52	E2	Doğanyurt	76	E2	Donegal Ireland	58	G3
Dilliá	101	H5	Diu	92	D4	Dog Creek	122	C2	Donegal Bay	58	F3
Dilling	102	E5	Dīvāndarreh	94	H4	Dogên Co	93	H2	Donegal Point	59	C7
Dillingen	70	D4	Divinópolis	138	G4	Dog Lake	124	F2	Donenbay	86	D2
Dillingham	118	D4	Divi Point	92	F5	Dōgo	89	D7	Doneraile	59	E8
Dillon	122	H5	Divisor, Serra do	136	C5	Dogondoutchi	101	F6	Donetsk	79	F6
Dilolo	106	D5	Divnoye	79	G6	Doğubeyazit	77	L3	Dong'an Heilongjiang, China	88	E2
Dimapur	93	H3	Divriği	77	H3	Doğukardeniz Dağlari	77	J2	Dong'an Hunan, China	93	M3
Dimashq	77	G6	Dixcove	104	E5	Doha	97	K4	Dongara	112	C4
Dimbelenge	106	D4	Dixon Entrance	118	J5	Doi Luang	93	K5	Dongbolhai Shan	93	G2
Dimbokro	104	E4	Diyadin	77	K3	Dojran	73	G5	Dongchuan	93	K3
Dîmbo vita	73	H3	Diyālá	94	G4	Dojransko Jezero	73	G5	Dongfang	93	L5
Dimitrovgrad Bulgaria	73	H4	Diyarbakir	77	J4	Doka Indonesia	114	A3	Dongfanghong	88	D2
Dimitrovgrad U.S.S.R.	78	H5	Diza	77	L3	Doka Sudan	96	B10	Donggala	91	F6
Dîmona	94	B6	Dja	105	H5	Dokkum	64	G2	Dong Hoi	93	L5
Dimovo	73	G4	Djado	101	H4	Dokshitsy	63	M9	Dongjingcheng	88	B3
Dinagat	91	H3	Djambala	106	B3	Dokurcun	76	D2	Dongliu	87	M5
Dinajpur	93	G3	Djanet	101	G4	Dolak	114	B3	Donglük	86	F4
Dinan	64	B4	Djelfa	101	F2	Dolak, Tanjung	91	K7	Dongning	88	C3
Dinanagar	92	E2	Djéma	102	E6	Dolanog	52	D2	Dongola	102	F4
Dinant	64	F3	Djenne	100	E6	Dolbeau	125	P2	Dongping	87	M4
Dinar	76	D3	Djibouti	103	H5	Dol-de-Bretagne	64	C4	Dongshan	87	N5
Dinara Planina	72	D3	Djibouti	103	H5	Dôle	65	F5	Dongsheng	87	K4

Name	Page	Grid
Dongtai	87	N5
Donguena	106	B6
Dong Ujimqin Qi	87	M2
Dongxi Lian Dao	87	M5
Donington	53	G2
Doniphan	124	E8
Donji Vakuf	72	D3
Dønna	62	E3
Donnington	52	E2
Dooagh	58	B5
Doon	57	D5
Doonbeg	59	C7
Doonerak, Mount	118	E2
Doon, Loch	57	D5
Doorin Point	58	F3
Dor	95	R6
Dorada, Costa	67	G2
Dora, Lake	112	E3
Dora Riparia	68	A3
Dorbiljin	86	E2
Dorchester	52	E4
Dorchester, Cape	120	L4
Dordogne	65	C6
Dordrecht	64	F3
Dore	65	E6
Doré Lake	119	P5
Dore, Mont	65	E6
Dorgali	69	B5
Dori	104	E3
Dorking	53	G3
Dormo, Ras	96	F10
Dornbirn	68	B2
Dornie	56	C3
Dornoch	56	D3
Dornoch Firth	56	D3
Dorofeyevskaya	84	C2
Dorohoi	73	J2
Dorotea	62	G4
Dorovitsa	78	H4
Dorset	52	E4
Dörtdivan	76	E2
Dortmund	70	B3
Dörtyol	77	G4
Doruokha	84	J2
Dorutay	77	L3
Dosatuy	85	K7
Dosso	101	F6
Dossor	79	J6
Dothan	129	K5
Douai	64	E3
Douala	105	G5
Douarnenez	64	A4
Double Mountain Fork	127	M4
Doubs	65	F5
Doubtful Sound	115	A6
Doubtless Bay	115	D1
Doué-la-Fontaine	65	C5
Douentza	100	E5
Douglas South Africa	108	D5
Douglas Isle of Man, U.K.	54	D2
Douglas Strathclyde, U.K.	57	E5
Douglas Arizona, U.S.A.	127	H5
Douglas Georgia, U.S.A.	129	L5
Douglas Wyoming, U.S.A.	123	M6
Doullens	64	E3
Doulus Head	59	B9
Doumé	105	H5
Doune	57	D4
Dourada, Serra	137	H6
Dourados Brazil	138	E3
Dourados Brazil	138	F4
Dourados, Serra dos	138	F4
Douro	66	B2
Dove	55	H3
Dove Dale	55	H3
Dover U.K.	53	J3
Dover Delaware, U.S.A.	125	N7
Dover New Hampshire, U.S.A.	125	Q5
Dover Ohio, U.S.A.	125	K6
Dover-Foxcroft	125	R4
Dover, Strait of	53	J4
Dovrefjell	62	C5
Dowa	107	F5
Dowlatābād Afghanistan	95	R5
Dowlatābād Afghanistan	95	S3
Dowlatābād Iran	95	N7
Dowlat Yār	92	C2
Down	58	L4
Downham Market	53	H2
Downpatrick	58	L4
Downpatrick Head	58	D4
Downs, The	53	J3
Downton	53	F4
Dow Rūd	94	J5
Dowshī	92	C1
Dōzen	89	D7
Drâa, Oued	100	D3
Drac	65	F6
Dračevo	73	F5
Drachten	64	G2
Dragalina	73	J3
Drăgăşani	73	H3
Dragoman	73	G4
Dragonera, Isla	67	H3
Dragon's Mouth	133	S9
Dragsfjärd	63	K6
Draguignan	65	G7
Dra, Hamada du	100	D3
Drake	123	P4
Drakensberg	108	E6
Drake Passage	141	V7
Dráma	75	H2
Drammen	63	H7
Drangedal	63	C7
Draperstown	58	J3
Dras	92	E2
Drau	68	E2
Drava	72	E3
Dravograd	72	C2
Drawa	70	F2
Drawsko, Jezioro	71	G2
Drayton Valley	119	N5
Dren	73	G4
Drenewydd	52	D2
Dresden	70	E3
Dresvyanka	78	K2
Dreux	64	D4
Drin	75	F2
Drina	72	E3
Drin i zi	74	E1
Drøbak	63	H7
Drobin	71	H2
Drogheda	58	K5
Drogichin	71	L2
Drogobych	79	C6
Drohiczyn	71	K2
Droichead Atha	58	K5
Droichead Nua	59	J6
Droitwich	53	E2
Drokiya	73	J1
Drôme	65	F6
Dromedary, Cape	113	L6
Dromore	58	K4
Dronfield	55	H3
Dronne	65	D6
Dronning Maud Land	141	Z5
Dropt	65	D6
Drovyanaya	84	A2
Drumcollogher	59	E8
Drumheller	122	H2
Drummond	122	H4
Drummond Islands	124	J3
Drummond Range	113	K3
Drummondville	125	P4
Drummore	54	E2
Drumochter, Pass of	57	D4
Drumshanbo	58	F4
Druridge Bay	55	H1
Druskininkai	71	K1
Druzhba Kazakstan S.S.R., U.S.S.R.	86	E2
Druzhba Rossiyskaya, S.F.S.R., U.S.S.R.	71	J1
Druzhina	85	R3
Drvar	72	D3
Drwęca	71	H2
Dry	112	G2
Dry Bay Canada	121	N6
Dry Bay U.S.A.	118	H4
Dryden	124	D2
Drysdale, River	112	F2
Dschang	105	H4
Dūāb	94	J4
Dualo	91	G6
Duarte, Pico	133	M5
Quba	96	B3
Dubai	97	M4
Dubawnt Lake	119	Q3
Dubayy	97	M4
Dubbagh, Jambal Ad	96	B3
Dubbo	113	K5
Dubenskiy	79	K5
Dublin Ireland	59	K6
Dublin Ireland	59	K6
Dublin U.S.A.	129	L4
Dublin Bay	59	K6
Dubna	78	F4
Dubno	79	D5
Du Bois	125	L6
Dubois Idaho, U.S.A.	122	H5
Dubois Wyoming, U.S.A.	123	K6
Dubossary	79	D6
Dubreka	104	C4
Dubrovitsa	71	M3
Dubrovka U.S.S.R.	79	E5
Dubrovka U.S.S.R.	79	G6
Dubrovnik	72	E4
Dubrovskoye	84	J5
Dubuque	124	E5
Duchang	87	M6
Duchesne U.S.A.	123	J7
Duchesne U.S.A.	123	J7
Duchess	113	H3
Ducie Island	143	J5
Duck	129	J3
Ducklington	53	F3
Duck Mountain	119	Q5
Duddington	53	G2
Dudinka	84	D3
Dudley	53	E2
Dueñas	66	D2
Duero	66	D2
Duffield	53	F2
Duff Islands	114	N6
Dufftown	56	E3
Dufton	55	G2
Duga Zapadnaya, Mys	85	R5
Dughaill, Loch	56	C3
Dugi Otok	72	C3
Duisburg	70	B3
Dukambīya	96	C9
Dukat	73	G4
Duk Fadiat	102	F6
Duk Faiwil	102	F6
Dukhān	97	K4
Duki Bolen	85	P6
Dukla	71	J4
Dukou	93	K3
Dulan	93	J1
Dul'durga	85	J6
Duleek	58	K5
Dulga-Kyuyel'	84	J4
Dulgalakh	85	N3
Dullingham	53	H2
Dull Lake	118	C3
Dulnain	56	E3
Dulovo	73	J4
Duluth	124	D3
Dūmā	77	G6
Dumaguete	91	G4
Dumai	90	C5
Dumaran	91	F3
Dumas Arkansas, U.S.A.	128	G4
Dumas Texas, U.S.A.	127	M3
Dumbarton	57	D5
Dumbéa	114	X17
Ďumbier	71	H4
Dumfries	55	F1
Dumfries and Galloway	57	E5
Dumitreşti	73	J3
Dumka	93	G4
Dumlu	77	J2
Dumlupinar	76	C3
Dumoine	125	M3
Dumont d'Urville	141	K5
Dumont d'Urville Sea	141	J6
Dumyât	103	F1
Duna	72	E2
Dunaj	71	H5
Dunajec	71	J3
Dunany Point	58	K5
Dunărea	73	J3
Dunaújvaros	72	E2
Dunav	73	H4
Dunay Moldavia S.S.R., U.S.S.R.	73	K3
Dunay Rossiyskaya S.F.S.R., U.S.S.R.	88	D4
Dunayevtsy	73	J1
Dunay, Ostrov	85	L2
Dunbar Australia	113	J2
Dunbar U.K.	57	F4
Dunblane	57	E4
Dunboyne	59	K6
Duncan Canada	122	C3
Duncan U.S.A.	128	D3
Duncan Passage	93	H6
Duncansby Head	56	E2
Dunchurch	53	F2
Dundaga	63	K8

Name	Page	Grid
Dundalk *Ireland*	58	K4
Dundalk *U.S.A.*	125	M7
Dundalk Bay	58	K5
Dundas	120	M2
Dundas, Lake	112	E5
Dundas Peninsula	120	D3
Dundas Strait	112	G1
Dun Dealgan	58	K4
Dundee *South Africa*	108	F5
Dundee *U.K.*	57	F4
Dundonald	57	D5
Dundonnell	56	C3
Dundrennan	54	F2
Dundrod	58	K3
Dundrum	58	L4
Dundrum Bay	58	L4
Dundwa Range	92	F3
Dunecht	57	F3
Dunedin *New Zealand*	115	C6
Dunedin *U.S.A.*	129	L6
Dunfanaghy	58	G2
Dunfermline	57	E4
Dungannon	58	J3
Dungarpur	92	D4
Dungarvan	59	G8
Dungarvan Harbour	59	G8
Dungeness	53	H4
Dungiven	58	J3
Dungloe	58	F3
Dungu	107	E2
Dungun	90	C5
Dunholme	55	J3
Dunhua	88	B4
Dunhuang	86	F3
Dunkeld	113	J6
Dunkerque	64	E3
Dunkirk	125	L5
Dunkur	103	G5
Dunkwa	104	E4
Dun Laoghaire	59	K6
Dunlavin	59	J6
Dunleer	58	K5
Dunmanus Bay	59	C9
Dunmanway	59	D9
Dunmore Town	132	J2
Dunmurry	58	K3
Dunnet Bay	56	E2
Dunnet Head	56	E2
Dunoon	57	D5
Dunragit	54	E2
Duns	57	F4
Dunseith	123	P3
Dunsford	52	D4
Dunstable	53	G3
Dunstan Mountains	115	B6
Dunster	52	D3
Duntelchaig, Loch	56	D3
Duntroon	115	C6
Dunvegan	56	B3
Dunvegan Head	56	B3
Dupang Ling	93	M3
Dupree	123	P5
Duque de York, Isla	139	A10
Du Quoin	124	F7
Durağan	76	F2
Durance	65	F7
Durand, Récif	114	Y17
Durango *Mexico*	130	G5
Durango *U.S.A.*	127	J2
Durankulak	73	K4
Durant	128	D3
Durazno	138	E6
Durazzo	74	E2
Durban	108	F6
Dúrcal	66	E4
Durdevac	72	D2
Durelj	87	J4
Düren	70	B3
Durg	92	F4
Durgapur *Bangladesh*	93	H3
Durgapur *India*	93	G4
Durham *U.K.*	55	H2
Durham *U.K.*	55	H2
Durham *U.S.A.*	129	N2
Durisdeer	57	E5
Durmä	96	H4
Durmitor	72	E4
Durness	56	D2
Durness, Kyle of	56	D2
Durrës	74	E2
Dursey Head	59	B9
Dursey Island	59	B9
Dursley	52	E3
Dursunbey	76	C3
D'Urville Island	115	D4
Dury Voe	56	B1
Dushak	95	Q3
Dushan	93	L3
Dushanbe	86	B4
Dushanzi	86	G4
Düskotna	73	J4
Düsseldorf	70	B3
Dutch Harbor	118	Ae9
Dutovo	78	K3
Duvan	78	K4
Duyun	93	L3
Düzce	76	D2
Düzköy	77	H2
Dvinskaya Guba	78	F3
Dvorets	84	F5
Dwarka	92	C4
Dyadino	84	H5
Dyat'kovo	79	E5
Dyatlovo	71	L2
Dybvad	63	D8
Dyce	56	F3
Dyer, Cape	120	P4
Dyersburg	128	H2
Dyfed	52	C3
Dyfi	52	D2
Dyje	71	G4
Dykh Tau	79	G7
Dynów	71	K4
Dyrnesvågen	62	B5
Dyulino	73	J4
Dzamïn Üüd	87	L3
Dzaoudzi	109	J2
Dzavhan Gol	86	G2
Dzaygil Hid	86	H2
Dzerzhinsk *Belorussiya S.S.R., U.S.S.R.*	78	D5
Dzerzhinsk *Rossiyskaya S.F.S.R., U.S.S.R.*	78	G4
Dzhalal-Abad	86	C3
Dzhalinda	85	L6
Dzhambeyty	79	J5
Dzhambul *U.S.S.R.*	86	C2
Dzhambul *U.S.S.R.*	86	C3
Dzhambul *U.S.S.R.*	79	J6
Dzhamm	85	N2
Dzhankoy	79	E6
Dzhebel *Bulgaria*	73	H5
Dzhebel *U.S.S.R.*	95	M2
Dzhelinde	84	J2
Dzhezkazgan	80	H5
Dzhirgatal'	86	C4
Dzhizak	86	B3
Dzhugdzhur, Khrebet	85	P5
Dzhul'fa	94	G2
Dzhungarskiy Alatau, Khrebet	86	E2
Dzhurin	79	D6
Dzhusaly	86	A2
Działdowo	71	J2
Działoszyn	71	H3
Dzilam de Bravo	131	Q7
Dzungarian Basin	86	F2
Dzüünbayan	87	L3
Dzuunbulag	87	M2
Eagle *Newfoundland, Canada*	121	Q7
Eagle *Yukon, Canada*	118	H2
Eagle *U.S.A.*	118	G3
Eagle Lake *Canada*	124	D2
Eagle Lake *U.S.A.*	122	D7
Eagle, Mount	59	B8
Eagle Pass	127	M6
Eagle Point	114	D4
Eaglesham	57	D5
Eagles Hill	59	B9
Eaglestone Reef	111	S4
Ealing	53	G3
Earby	55	G3
Earlsferry	57	F4
Earl Shilton	53	F2
Earlston	57	F4
Earl Stonham	53	J2
Earn	57	E4
Earn, Loch	57	D4
Earp	126	E3
Easingwold	55	H2
East Anglian Heights	53	H2
Eastbourne	53	H4
East Brent	52	E3
East Bridgford	53	G2
East Cape	115	G2
East China Sea	87	P6
East Cleddau	52	C3
East Dean	53	H4
East Dereham	53	H2
Easter Island	143	K5
Eastern Ghats	92	E6
Eastern Ross	56	D3
East Falkland	139	E10
East Germany	70	E3
East Grinstead	53	G3
East Haddon	53	F2
East Hoathly	53	H4
East Ilsley	53	F3
East Kilbride	57	D5
East Lake Tarbert	56	B3
Eastleigh	53	F4
East Linton	57	F4
East Loch Roag	56	B2
East London	108	E6
Eastmain *Canada*	121	L7
Eastmain *Canada*	121	M7
Eastmain-Opinaca, Réservoir	121	L7
Eastman	129	L4
East Midlands Airport	53	F2
East Millnocket	125	R4
Eastoft	55	J3
Easton *U.K.*	52	E4
Easton *U.S.A.*	125	N6
East Point *Prince Edward Island, Canada*	121	P8
East Point *Québec, Canada*	121	P8
Eastport	125	S4
East Retford	55	J3
Eastry	53	J3
East Saint Louis	124	E7
East Siberian Sea	85	T2
East Sussex	53	H3
East Tavaputs Plateau	123	K8
Eastville	55	K3
East Wittering	53	G4
Eastwood	55	H3
Eatonton	129	L4
Eau Claire	124	E4
Ebbw Vale	52	D3
Ebe-Basa	85	M4
Ebebiyin	105	H5
Ebeltoft	63	D8
Eber Gölü	76	D3
Ebersberg	70	D4
Eberswalde	70	E2
Ebinur Hu	86	E3
Eboli	69	E5
Ebolowa	105	H5
Ebrach	70	D4
Ebro	66	G2
Ecclefechan	57	E5
Eccles	55	G3
Eccleshall	52	E2
Eccleston	55	G3
Eceabat	76	B2
Ech Cheliff	100	F1
Echeng	93	M2
Echigo-sammyaku	89	G7
Echo Bay *NW. Territories, Canada*	119	M2
Echo Bay *Ontario, Canada*	124	H3
Echternach	64	G4
Echuca	113	J6
Écija	66	D4
Eckernförde	70	C1
Eclipse Sound	120	L3
Ečmiadzin	77	L2
Ecuador	136	B4
Ēd	103	H5
Ed	63	H7
Edah Wagga	112	D4
Edam	64	F2
Eday	56	F1
Ed Damazin	103	F5
Ed Damer	96	A8
Ed Debba	102	F4
Ed-Déffa	102	E1
Edderton	56	D3
Eddrachillis Bay	56	C2
Ed Dueim	103	F5
Ede *Netherlands*	64	F2
Ede *Nigeria*	105	F4
Edéa	105	H5
Edehon Lake	119	R3
Edel Land	112	C4
Eden *Australia*	113	K6
Eden *Cumbria, U.K.*	55	G2

Name	Page	Grid	Name	Page	Grid	Name	Page	Grid	Name	Page	Grid
Eden *Kent, U.K.*	53	H3	Eilsleben	70	D2	El Dorado *Kansas, U.S.A.*	128	D2	Ellesmere	52	E2
Eden *U.S.A.*	123	K6	Einbeck	70	C3	El Dorado *Venezuela*	133	S11	Ellesmere Island	120	K2
Edenderry	59	H6	Eindhoven	64	F3	Eldoret	107	G2	Ellesmere, Lake	115	D5
Edgecumbe	115	F2	Eiriksjökull	62	U12	Elektrostal'	78	F4	Ellesmere Port	55	G3
Edgeley	123	Q4	Eirunepé	136	D5	Elephant Butte Reservoir	127	J4	Ellice	119	Q2
Edgell Island	121	P5	Eisenach	70	D3	Elephant Island	141	W6	Ellington	114	R8
Edgemont	123	N6	Eisenhüttenstadt	70	F2	Eleşkirt	77	K3	Elliot	108	E6
Edgeøya	80	D2	Eisenkappel	68	E2	El Eulma	101	G1	Elliot Lake	124	J3
Edgeworthstown	58	G5	Eishort, Lake	57	C3	Eleuthera	132	J2	Elliot, Mount	113	K2
Édhessa	75	G2	Eisleben	70	D3	Elevsís	75	G3	Elliston	113	H5
Edievale	115	B6	Eitorf	70	B3	El Faiyûm	102	F2	El Llano	132	H10
Edinburg	128	D7	Ejea de los Caballeros	67	F1	El Fasher	102	E5	Ellon	56	F3
Edinburgh	57	E5	Ejido Insurgentes	130	D5	El Fashn	102	F2	Ellsworth	125	R4
Edirne	76	B2	Ejin Horo Qi	87	K4	El Ferrol	66	B1	Ellsworth Land	141	U4
Edisto	129	M4	Ejin Qi	86	J3	El Fuerte	127	H7	Ellwangen	70	D4
Edith River	112	G1	Ejutla	131	L9	Elgepiggen	63	D5	Elmadağ	76	E3
Edjeleh	101	G3	Ekenäs	63	K6	El Geteina	103	F5	Elma Daği	76	E3
Edland	63	B7	Eket	105	G5	Elgin *U.K.*	56	E3	El Mahalla El Kubra	102	F1
Edmond	128	D3	Eketahuna	115	E4	Elgin *Illinois, U.S.A.*	124	F5	Elmali	76	C4
Edmonds	122	C4	Ekhinádhes	75	F3	Elgin *N. Dakota, U.S.A.*	123	P4	El Manaqil	103	F5
Edmonton	119	N5	Ekhínos	75	H2	El Gîza	102	F1	El Mansûra	102	F1
Edmunston	125	R3	Ekibastuz	84	B6	Elgol	57	B3	El Mesellemiya	103	F5
Édolo	68	C2	Ekimchan	85	N6	El Golea	101	F2	El Milk	102	E4
Edremit	76	B3	Ekonda	84	G3	El Golfo de Santa Clara	126	E5	El Minya	102	F2
Edremit Körfezi	76	B3	Eksjö	63	F8	Elgon, Mont	107	F2	Elmira	125	M5
Edson	119	M5	Ekwan	121	K7	El Hawata	96	B10	Elmore	113	J6
Edward, Lake	107	E3	El Affroun	67	H4	El Hodna, Chott	67	J5	Elmshorn	70	C2
Edwardson, Cape	115	B7	Elafónisos	75	G4	El Homra	102	F5	El Muglad	102	E5
Edwards Plateau	127	M5	El Araïche	100	D1	El Hosh	103	F5	El Nido	91	F3
Edzhen	85	P4	El Arco	126	F7	El Huecú	139	B7	El Obeid	102	F5
Eeklo	64	E3	El' Arîsh	103	F1	Elikón	75	G3	El Odaiya	102	E5
Eel	122	B7	Elassón	75	G3	Elisabethville	107	E5	Elorza	136	D2
Efate	114	U12	Elat	94	B7	Elíseu Martins	137	J5	El Oued	101	G2
Eferding	68	E1	Elâziğ	77	H3	Elista	79	G6	Eloy	126	G4
Eflâni	76	E2	El Azraq	94	C6	Elizabeth *Australia*	113	H5	El Palmito	127	K8
Efyrnwy, Llyn	52	D2	El Bahri, Borg	67	H4	Elizabeth *U.S.A.*	125	N6	El Pardo	66	E2
Egå	63	D8	Elba, Isole d'	69	C4	Elizabeth City	129	P2	El Paso *Illinois, U.S.A.*	124	F6
Egadi, Isole	69	D7	El Balyana	103	F2	Elizabeth Reef	113	M4	El Paso *Texas, U.S.A.*	127	J5
Egersund	63	B7	El'ban	85	P6	Elizabethton	129	L2	Elphin	56	C2
Egerton, Mount	112	D3	El Banco	136	C2	Elizabethtown	124	H8	El Porvenir	127	K5
Eggan	105	G4	El Barco de Avila	66	D2	Elizondo	67	F1	El Potosí	128	B8
Egg Lagoon	113	J6	El Barco de Valdeorras	66	C1	El Jadida	100	D2	El Progreso	132	D7
Egglescliffe	55	H2	Elbasan	74	F2	El Jafr	94	C6	El Puente del Arzobispo	66	D3
Eggum	62	E2	El Bayadh	100	F2	El Jebelein	103	F5	El Qâ'hira	102	F1
Egham	53	G3	Elbe	70	C2	El Jerid, Chott	101	G2	El Qasr	102	E2
Eghol	114	H6	Elbert, Mount	123	L8	Elk	122	G3	El Qunayţirah	94	B5
Egilsstaðir	62	X12	Elberton	129	L3	Ełk	71	K2	El Real	132	J10
Egiyn Gol	86	J1	Elbeuf	64	D4	El Kala	69	B7	El Reno	128	D3
Eglinton	58	H2	Elbeyli	77	G4	El Kamlin	103	F5	El Ronquillo	66	C4
Eglinton Island	120	C2	Elbing	71	H1	Elk City	128	C3	El Rosario	126	E5
Egmount, Mount	115	E3	Elbistan	77	G3	El Khalil	94	B6	El Sahuaro	126	F5
Egremont	55	F2	Elbląg	71	H1	El Khârga	102	F2	El Salado	139	C9
Eğridir	76	D4	Elbrus	79	G7	Elkhart	124	H6	El Salto	130	G6
Eğridir Gölü	76	D3	El Burgo de Osma	66	E2	El Khartum	103	F4	El Salvador	132	C8
Egvekinot	85	Y3	El Cajon	126	D4	Elkhorn	123	Q6	El Sam'án de Apure	133	N11
Egypt	102	E2	El Callao	136	E2	Elkhotovo	79	G7	El Sauzal	126	D5
Ehingen	70	C4	El Campo	128	D6	Elkhovo	73	J4	Elsham	55	J3
Eibar	66	E1	El Carmen *Bolivia*	138	E3	Elkin	129	M2	El Socorro	126	F5
Eidem	62	D4	El Carmen *Bolivia*	136	E6	Elkins	125	L7	Elster	70	E3
Eidfjord	63	B6	El Centro	126	E4	Elko	122	G7	Elsterwerda	70	E3
Eiði	62	Z14	El Cerro	138	D3	El K'oran	103	H6	El Sueco	127	J6
Eidsvold	113	L4	El Chaparro	136	D2	El Korima, Oued	100	E2	El Suweis	103	F2
Eidsvoll	63	D6	Elche	67	F3	El Lagowa	102	E5	El Tambo	136	B4
Eifel	70	B3	Elche de la Sierra	67	F3	Elland	55	H3	Eltham	115	E3
Eigg	57	C4	El'dikan	85	P4	Ellef Ringnes Island	120	F2	El Thamad	96	B2
Eigg, Sound of	57	B4	Eldivan	76	E2	Ellen	55	F2	El Tigre	133	Q10
Eight Degree Channel	92	D7	El Djazaïr	101	F1	Ellendale *Australia*	112	E2	El Tîh	96	A2
Eighty Mile Beach	112	E2	El Djouf	100	D4	Ellendale *U.S.A.*	123	Q5	Eltisley	53	G2
Eilerts de Haan Geb	137	F3	Eldon	124	D7	Ellen, Mount	122	J8	El Tocuyo	133	N10
Eil, Loch	57	C4	El Dorado *Arkansas, U.S.A.*	128	F4	Ellensburg	122	D4	Elton *U.K.*	53	G2

Elton *U.S.S.R*	79	H6	Enfield *U.K.*	53	G3	Ereenstav	87	M2	Escondido *U.S.A.*	126	D4
El Tule	131	L9	Engaño, Cabo	133	N5	Ereğli *Turkey*	76	D2	Escrick	55	H3
El Tûr	96	A2	Engaño, Cape	91	G2	Ereğli *Turkey*	76	F4	Escuintla	132	B7
Eluru	92	F5	Engaru	88	J3	Erek Daği	77	K3	Ese-Khayya	85	N3
Elvanfoot	57	E5	Engel's	79	H5	Erenhot	87	L3	Esemer	77	K3
Elvas	66	C3	Enggano	90	C7	Erentepe	77	K3	Eşen	76	C4
Elveden	53	H2	Engger Us	87	J3	Eresma	66	D2	Esendere	77	L4
Elverum	63	D6	Engineer Group	114	E4	Eressós	75	H3	Eşfahān	95	K5
El Viejo	133	L11	Englehart	125	L3	Erfelek	76	F2	Esfarayen, Reshteh ye	95	N3
El Vigia	136	C2	Englewood	123	M8	Erfurt	70	D3	Eshan	93	K4
Elwy	55	F3	English Channel	50	G5	Ergani	77	H3	Esha Ness	56	A1
Ely *Cambridgeshire, U.K.*	53	H2	Énguera	67	F3	Ergene	76	B2	Esh Sheikh, Jbel	77	G6
Ely *Mid Glamorgan, U.K.*	52	D3	Enguera, Sierra de	67	F3	Ērgli	63	L8	Esino	68	D4
Ely *Minnesota, U.S.A.*	124	E3	Enid	128	D2	Ergun He	85	K6	Esk	57	E5
Ely *Nevada, U.S.A.*	126	E1	Enkhuizen	64	F2	Ergun Zuoqi	87	N1	Eskdale	57	E5
Elze	70	C2	Enköping	63	G7	Eriboll, Loch	56	D2	Eske, Lough	58	F3
Ema	63	M7	Enna	69	E7	Ericht, Loch	57	D4	Eskifjörður	62	Y12
Emaé	114	U12	Ennadai Lake	119	Q3	Ericiyas Daği	76	F3	Eskilstuna	63	G7
Emāmrud	95	M3	En Nahud	102	E5	Erie	125	K5	Eskimalatya	77	H3
Emām Taqī	95	P4	Ennedi	102	D4	Erie, Lake	125	K5	Eskimo Lakes	118	J2
Emån	63	G8	Ennell, Lough	59	H6	Erikoúsa	74	E3	Eskimo Point	119	S3
Emao	114	U12	Ennerdale Water	55	F2	Erímanthos	75	F4	Eskipazar	76	E2
Emba	79	K6	Enning	123	N5	Erimo-misaki	88	J5	Eskishir	76	D3
Embarcación	138	D4	Ennis *Ireland*	59	E7	Eriskay	57	A3	Esla	66	D1
Embleton	55	H1	Ennis *U.S.A.*	128	D4	Erkelenz	70	B3	Eslamābād-e Gharb	94	H4
Embona	75	J4	Enniscorthy	59	J7	Erkilet	76	F3	Eslām Qal'eh	95	Q4
Embrun	65	G6	Enniskillen	58	G4	Erkowit	96	C7	Eşme	76	C3
Embu	107	G3	Ennistymon	59	D7	Erlandson Lake	121	N6	Esmeralda, Isla	139	A9
Emden	70	B2	Enns	68	E1	Erlangen	70	D4	Esmeraldas	136	B3
Emerald	113	K3	Enonkoski	62	N5	Erldunda	113	G4	Espalion	65	E6
Emerald Island	120	D2	Enontekiö	62	K2	Erme	52	D4	Espanola *Canada*	125	K3
Emerson	123	R3	Enrekang	91	F6	Ermelo	108	F5	Espanola *U.S.A.*	127	J3
Emet	76	C3	Enschede	64	G2	Ermenak	76	E4	Española, Isla	136	A7
Emeti	114	C3	Ensenada	126	D5	Ernakulam	92	E7	Espenberg, Cape	118	C2
Emi	84	F6	Enshi	93	L2	Erne	58	H5	Esperance	112	E5
Emigrant Pass	122	F7	Enstone	53	F3	Erne, Lower Lough	58	G4	Esperance Bay	112	E5
Emin	86	E2	Entebbe	107	F2	Erne, Upper Lough	58	G4	Esperanza *Antarctic*	141	W6
Emine, Nos	73	J4	Enterprise	129	K5	Erode	92	E6	Esperanza *Argentina*	139	B10
Emirdağ	76	D3	Entinas, Punta de las	66	E4	Eromanga	113	J4	Esperanza *Argentina*	138	D6
Emir Daği	76	D3	Entraygues	65	E6	Er Rachidia	100	E2	Espiel	66	D3
Emita	113	K7	Entrecasteaux, Recifs d'	111	N5	Er Rahad	102	F5	Espinhaço, Serra da	138	H3
Emmaboda	63	F8	Enugu	105	G4	Errego	109	G3	Espinho	66	B2
Emmaste	63	K7	Enurmino	118	A2	Errigal	58	F2	Espinosa de los Monteros	66	E1
Emmen	64	G2	Enz	70	C4	Erris Head	58	B4	Espírito Santo	138	H3
Emory Peak	127	L6	Eo	66	C1	Errochty, Loch	57	D4	Espíritu Santo	114	T11
Empalme	126	G7	Eolie	69	E6	Errogie	56	D3	Espíritu Santo, Cape	91	H3
Empangeni	109	F5	Epano Fellos	75	H4	Erromango	114	U13	Espíritu Santo, Isla	130	D5
Empedrado	138	E5	Epanomi	75	G2	Ersekë	75	F2	Espiye	77	H2
Empingham	53	G2	Épernay	64	E4	Erskine	124	C3	Espoo	63	N6
Empoli	68	C4	Ephrata	122	E4	Ertai	86	G2	Esposende	66	B2
Emporia *Kansas, U.S.A.*	128	D1	Épi	114	U12	Eruh	77	K4	Espot	67	G1
Emporia *Virginia, U.S.A.*	125	M8	Epinal	64	G4	Erwigol	86	F3	Espungabera	109	F4
Ems	70	B2	Epping	53	H3	Eryuan	93	J3	Esquel	139	B8
Emu	88	B4	Eppynt, Mynydd	52	D2	Erzen	74	E2	Es Sahrâ en Nûbîya	96	B6
Enard Bay	56	C2	Epşi	77	J4	Erzgebirge	70	E3	Essaouira	100	D2
Encantada, Cerro Del La	126	E5	Epsom	53	G3	Erzin	84	F6	Es Semara	100	C3
Encarnacion	138	E5	Eqlïd	95	L6	Erzincan	77	H3	Essen	70	B3
Enchi	104	E4	Equatorial Guinea	105	G5	Erzurum	77	J3	Essex	53	H3
Encinal	128	C6	Equeipa	136	E2	Esa-Ala	114	E3	Essex, Punta	136	A7
Encontrados	136	C2	Erap	114	D3	Esan-misaki	88	H5	Esslingen	70	C4
Encounter Bay	113	H6	Erbaa	77	G2	Esashi *Japan*	88	H5	Esso	85	T5
Endau	90	C5	Erba, Jebel	96	C6	Esashi *Japan*	88	J3	Estacado, Llanos	127	L4
Ende	91	G7	Erçek	77	K3	Esbjerg	63	C9	Estados, Isla de los	139	D10
Endeavour Strait	113	J1	Erciş	77	K3	Esbo	63	N6	Eştahbānāt	95	M7
Enderbury Island	111	U2	Ercsi	72	E2	Escalona	66	D2	Estância	138	K6
Enderby Land	141	D5	Erdek	76	B2	Escambia	129	J5	Estcourt	108	E5
Endicott Mountains	118	C2	Erdemli	76	F4	Escanaba	124	G4	Este	68	C3
Ene	136	C6	Erdenet	87	J2	Escarpé, Cape	114	X16	Estelí	132	D8
Enez	76	B2	Erdre	65	C5	Escocesa, Bahía de	133	N5	Estella	67	E1
Enfield *Ireland*	59	J6	Erechim	138	F5	Escondido *Brazil*	138	J3	Estepona	66	D4

Forez, Monts du	65	E6
Forfar	57	F4
Forgandenny	57	E4
Fork	123	K5
Forks	122	B4
Forlì	68	D3
Formartin	56	F3
Formby	55	F3
Formby Point	55	F3
Formentera	67	G3
Formentor, Cabo de	67	H3
Formia	69	D5
Formiga	138	G4
Formosa	87	N7
Formosa *Argentina*	138	E5
Formosa *Brazil*	138	G3
Formosa do Rio Prêto	137	H6
Føroyar	62	Z14
Forres	56	E3
Forrest	112	F5
Forrest City	128	G3
Forsayth	113	J2
Forsnäs	62	H3
Forsnes	62	C5
Forssa	63	K6
Forsyth *Missouri, U.S.A.*	124	D8
Forsyth *Montana, U.S.A.*	123	L4
Fort Albany	121	K7
Fortaleza *Bolivia*	136	D5
Fortaleza *Brazil*	137	K4
Fort Archambault	102	C6
Fort Beaufort	108	E6
Fort Benton	123	J4
Fort Bragg	122	C8
Fort Charlet	101	G4
Fort Chipewyan	119	N4
Fort Collins	123	M7
Fort Coulonge	125	M4
Fort-Dauphin	109	J5
Fort-de-France	133	S7
Fort de Polignac	101	G3
Fort Dodge	124	C5
Fortescue	112	D3
Fort Flatters	101	G3
Fort Foureau	105	J3
Fort Frances	124	D2
Fort Franklin	118	L2
Fort Good Hope	118	K2
Forth	57	D4
Fort Hall	107	G3
Fort Hancock	127	K5
Forth, Firth of	57	F4
Fortín Carlos Antonio López	138	E4
Fortín General Mendoza	138	D4
Fortín Gral Eugenio Garay	138	D4
Fortín Infante Rivarola	138	D4
Fortín Juan de Zalazar	138	E4
Fortín Madrejon	138	E4
Fortin Ravelo	138	D3
Fort Jameson	107	F3
Fort Kent	125	R3
Fort Lamy	102	C5
Fort Lauderdale	129	M7
Fort Liard	118	L3
Fort Macleod	122	H3
Fort McMurray	119	N4
Fort McPherson	118	J2
Fort Madison	124	E6
Fort Manning	107	F5
Fort Morgan	123	N7

Fort Myers	129	M7
Fort Nelson	119	L4
Fort Norman	118	K3
Fortore	69	E5
Fort Payne	129	K3
Fort Peck	123	L3
Fort Peck Dam	123	L4
Fort Peck Reservoir	123	L4
Fort Pierce	129	M7
Fort Portal	107	F2
Fort Providence	119	M3
Fort Qu'Appelle	123	N2
Fort Randall	118	Af8
Fort Resolution	119	N3
Fortrose	56	D3
Fort Rosebery	107	E5
Fort Saint James	118	L5
Fort Saint John	119	L4
Fort Scott	124	C8
Fort Severn	120	J6
Fort Shevchenko	79	J7
Fort Simpson	119	L3
Fort Smith *Canada*	119	N3
Fort Smith *U.S.A.*	128	E4
Fort Soufflay	106	B2
Fort Stockton	127	L5
Fort Sumner	127	K3
Fort Trinquet	100	D1
Fortuna	122	B7
Fortune Bay	121	Q8
Fort Valley	129	L4
Fort Vermilion	119	M4
Fort Victoria	108	F4
Fort Walton Beach	129	J5
Fort Wayne	124	H6
Fort William	57	C4
Fort Worth	128	D4
Fort Yukon	118	F2
Forür	95	M8
Foshan	93	M4
Fosheim Peninsula	120	K2
Fosna	62	D5
Fossombrone	68	D4
Fossvellir	62	X12
Foster	113	K6
Fougères	64	C4
Foula	56	A2
Foula Morie	104	C3
Foulden	57	F4
Foulness Island	53	H3
Foulness Point	53	H3
Foulwind, Cape	115	C4
Foumban	105	H4
Foundiougne	104	B3
Fountainhall	57	F5
Four Mountains, Islands of the	118	Ad9
Foúrnoi	75	J4
Foveaux Strait	115	B7
Fowey *U.K.*	52	C4
Fowey *U.K.*	52	C4
Fowler	127	K1
Fowler, Point	112	G5
Fowlers Bay	112	G5
Fowman	94	J3
Fox *Canada*	118	K4
Fox *U.S.A.*	124	F6
Foxe Basin	120	L4
Foxe Peninsula	120	L5
Foxford	58	D5
Fox Islands	118	Ae9

Foxton	115	E4
Foyers, Falls of	56	D3
Foyle	58	H3
Foyle, Lough	58	H2
Foynes	59	D7
Foz do Iguaçu	138	F5
Fraga	67	G2
Framington	125	Q5
Framlingham	53	J2
Frampol	71	K3
Franca	138	G4
Français, Récif des	114	V15
France	65	C5
France, Île de	64	E4
Frances *Australia*	113	J6
Frances *Canada*	118	K3
Franceville	106	B3
Franche Comte	65	G5
Francis Case, Lake	123	Q6
Francisco Escárcega	131	P8
Francistown	108	E4
Francois Lake	118	K5
Frangista	75	F3
Frankfort *Indiana, U.S.A.*	124	G6
Frankfort *Kentucky, U.S.A.*	124	H7
Frankfurt	70	F2
Frankfurt am Main	70	C3
Fränkischer Alb	70	D4
Franklin *Indiana, U.S.A.*	124	H7
Franklin *Louisiana, U.S.A.*	128	G6
Franklin *N. Carolina, U.S.A.*	129	L3
Franklin *Pennsylvania, U.S.A.*	125	L6
Franklin *Tennessee, U.S.A.*	129	J3
Franklin Bay	118	K2
Franklin D Roosevelt Lake	122	E3
Franklin, Lake	119	R2
Franklin Mountains	118	K3
Franklin, Point	118	D1
Franklin Strait	120	G3
Frank's Peak	123	K6
Fränsta	62	G5
Frantsa-Iosifa, Zemlya	80	G2
Frascati	69	D5
Fraserburg	108	D6
Fraserburgh	56	F3
Fraserdale	125	K2
Fraser Island	113	L4
Fraser, Mount	112	D4
Frasertown	115	F3
Frauenfeld	68	B2
Fray Bentos	138	E6
Frazer	122	D2
Freckleton	55	G3
Fredericia	63	C9
Frederick *Maryland, U.S.A.*	125	M7
Frederick *Oklahoma, U.S.A.*	128	C3
Frederick Reef	110	M6
Fredericksburg	125	M7
Frederick Sound	118	J4
Fredericktown	124	E8
Fredericton	125	S4
Frederikshåb	120	S5
Frederikshåbs Isblink	120	S5
Frederikshavn	63	D8
Frederiksted	133	Q6
Fredonia	125	L5
Fredrika	62	M4
Fredrikshamn	63	M6
Fredrikstad	63	D7
Freeling, Mount	113	G3

Freeport *Illinois, U.S.A.*	124	F5
Freeport *Texas, U.S.A.*	128	E6
Freeport City	132	H1
Freer	128	C7
Freetown	104	C4
Fregenal de la Sierra	66	C3
Fréhel, Cap	64	B4
Freiberg	70	E3
Freiburg	70	B4
Freising	70	D4
Freistadt	68	E1
Fréjus	65	G7
Fremantle	112	D5
Fremont *California, U.S.A.*	126	A2
Fremont *Nebraska, U.S.A.*	123	R7
Fremont *Utah, U.S.A.*	122	J8
French	125	K1
French Broad	129	L2
French Guiana	136	G3
Frenchman	123	L3
Frenchpark	58	F5
French Polynesia	143	J5
Frenda	100	F1
Frensham	53	G3
Fresco	137	G5
Freshfield, Mount	122	F2
Freshwater	53	F4
Fresnillo	130	H6
Fresno	126	C2
Freu, Cabo del	67	H3
Frias	138	C5
Fribourg	68	A2
Fridaythorpe	55	J2
Friedrichshafen	70	C5
Friesach	68	E2
Frio	127	N6
Frio, Cabo	138	H4
Friona	127	L3
Frisco	123	L8
Friza, Proliv	85	R7
Frobisher Bay	120	N5
Frobisher Lake	119	P4
Frodsham	55	G3
Frohavet	62	C5
Frolovo	79	G6
Frome *Dorset, U.K.*	52	E4
Frome *Somerset, U.K.*	52	E3
Frome, Lake	113	H5
Fronteira	66	C3
Frontera	131	N8
Front Royal	125	L7
Frosinone	69	D5
Frøya	62	C5
Frunze	86	C3
Frutal	138	G3
Frýdek Mistek	71	H4
Ftéri	75	F3
Fu'an	87	M6
Fudai	88	H5
Fuding	87	N6
Fudzin	88	E3
Fuengirola	66	D4
Fuente el Fresno	66	E3
Fuente Obejuna	66	D3
Fuentesaúco	66	D2
Fuentes de Oñoro	66	C2
Fuerte	127	H7
Fuerteventura	100	C3
Fufeng	93	L2
Fuga	91	G2

Name	Page	Ref	Name	Page	Ref	Name	Page	Ref	Name	Page	Ref
Gascogne	65	D7	Gediz *Turkey*	76	B3	George *South Africa*	108	D6	Ghardimaou	69	B7
Gascogne, Golfe de	65	C7	Gediz *Turkey*	76	C3	Georgeham	52	C3	Gharrat, Shatt al	94	H6
Gasconade	124	D8	Gedney Hill	53	G2	George Island	139	E10	Gharyān	101	H2
Gascoyne	112	C3	Gedser	70	D1	George, Lake	129	M6	Ghāt	101	H3
Gascuña, Golfo de	67	F1	Gee	64	F3	George Sound	115	A6	Ghatampur	92	F3
Gasht	95	Q8	Geelong	113	J6	Georgetown *Australia*	113	H5	Ghatere	114	J5
Gashua	105	H3	Geelvink Channel	112	C4	George Town *Australia*	113	K7	Ghayl Bā Wazīr	97	J9
Gask	95	P5	Geeveston	113	K7	Georgetown *Gambia*	104	C3	Ghayl Bin Yumayn	97	J9
Gasmata	114	E3	Gê'gyai	92	F2	Georgetown *Grand Cayman, U.K.*	132	G5	Ghazaouet	100	E1
Gaspar, Selat	90	D6	Geikie	119	Q4	Georgetown *Guyana*	136	F2	Ghaziabad	92	E3
Gaspé	121	P8	Geilo	63	C6	George Town *Malaysia*	90	C4	Ghazipur	92	E3
Gaspé, Cape	121	P8	Geita	107	F3	Georgetown *U.S.A.*	129	N4	Ghaznī	92	C2
Gaspé Peninsula	121	N8	Geitlandsjökull	62	U12	George V Land	141	K4	Gheorgheni	73	H2
Gastonia	129	M3	Gejiu	93	K4	George VI Sound	141	V4	Ghimeş-Făget	73	J2
Gaston, Lake	129	N2	Geka, Mys	85	X4	Georgia	129	K4	Ghisonaccia	69	B4
Gastoúni	75	F4	Gela	69	E7	Georgian Bay	125	K4	Ghisoni	69	B4
Gastre	139	C8	Geladī	103	J6	Georgia S.S.R.	77	K1	Ghubbah	97	P10
Gata, Cabo de	66	E4	Gelendost	76	D3	Georgia, Strait of	122	C3	Ghubeish	102	E5
Gátas, Akra	76	E5	Gelendzhik	79	F7	Georgina	113	H3	Ghudāf, Wadi al	94	E5
Gata, Sierra de	66	C2	Gelibolu	76	B2	Georgina Bay	121	K8	Ghūrīān	95	Q4
Gatchina	63	P7	Gelibolu Yarimadasi	75	J2	Georgiu-Dezh	79	F5	Giant's Causeway Head	58	J2
Gatehouse of Fleet	54	E2	Gelligaer	52	D3	Georgiyevka	86	E2	Giarre	69	E7
Gateshead	55	H2	Gelnhausen	70	C3	Georgiyevsk	79	G7	Gibostad	62	H2
Gateshead Island	119	Q1	Gelsenkirchen	70	B3	Georg von Neumayer	141	Z4	Gibraltar	66	D4
Gatineau	125	N3	Gemena	106	C2	Gera	70	E3	Gibraltar Point	55	K3
Gatooma	108	E3	Gemerek	77	G3	Geral de Goiás, Serra	137	H6	Gibraltar, Strait of	66	D5
Gaţrūyeh	95	M7	Gemlik	76	C2	Geraldine	115	C6	Gibson Desert	112	E3
Gatún Lake	132	H10	Gemlik Körfezi	75	K2	Geraldton *Australia*	112	C4	Gichgeniyn Nuruu	86	H2
Gatvand	94	J5	Gemona del Friuli	68	D2	Geraldton *U.S.A.*	124	G2	Gīdolē	103	G6
Gatwick	53	G3	Gemünd	70	B3	Gérardmer	64	G4	Gien	65	E5
Gaud-i-Zureh	95	R7	Genalē Wenz	103	H6	Gerasimovka	84	A5	Gieseckes Isfjord	120	Q3
Gauer Lake	119	R4	Genç	77	J3	Gercüs	77	J4	Giessen	70	C3
Gauhati	93	H3	Geneina	102	D5	Gerede *Turkey*	76	E2	Gifatîn	96	A3
Gauja	63	L8	General Acha	139	D7	Gerede *Turkey*	76	E2	Gifford Creek	112	D3
Gauldalen	62	D5	General Alvear	139	C7	Gereshk	92	B2	Gifhorn	70	D2
Gausta	63	C7	General Bernardo O'Higgins	141	W6	Gérgal	66	E4	Gifu	89	F8
Gaväter	95	Q9	General Conesa	139	D8	Gerger	77	H4	Giganta, Sierra de la	130	D5
Gāvbūs, Kūh-e	95	L8	General La Madrid	139	D7	Gerik	90	C4	Gigha Island	57	C5
Gavdhopoúla	75	G5	General Lavalle	139	E7	Geriş	76	D4	Gigha, Sound of	57	C5
Gávdhos	75	H5	General Madariaga	139	E7	Gerlachovsky	71	J4	Giglio, Isola di	69	C4
Gavião	66	C3	General Paz	139	E7	German Democratic Republic	70	E2	Gijón	66	D1
Gāv Koshī	95	N7	General Paz, Lago	139	B8	Germany, Federal Republic of	70	C2	Gijunabena Islands	114	J5
Gävle	63	G6	General Pico	139	D7	Germencik	76	B4	Gila	126	F4
Gävleborg	63	G6	General Roca	139	C7	Germi	94	J2	Gila Bend	126	F4
Gavrilov-Yam	78	F4	General Sam Martin	141	V5	Germiston	108	E5	Gilan Garb	94	G4
Gawler	113	H5	General Santos	91	H4	Gérona	67	H2	Gilbert	113	J2
Gawler Ranges	113	H5	General Villegas	139	D7	Gerrards Cross	53	G3	Gilbert Islands	111	R2
Gaxun Nur	86	J3	Geneseo	125	M5	Gerze	76	F2	Gilbert, Mount	122	B2
Gaya	92	G4	Genessee	125	L5	Geseke	70	C3	Gilbues	137	H5
Gaya La	92	F3	Geneva *Switzerland*	68	A2	Geta	63	G6	Gilé	109	G3
Gaydon	53	F2	Geneva *U.S.A.*	125	M5	Getafe	66	E2	Gilford	58	K4
Gayndah	113	L4	Geneva, Lake of	68	A2	Gettysburg *Pennsylvania, U.S.A.*	125	M7	Gilgandra	113	K5
Gaysin	73	K1	Genève	68	A2	Gettysburg *S. Dakota, U.S.A.*	123	Q5	Gilgit	92	D1
Gayvoron	79	D6	Gen He	87	N1	Geumapang	90	B5	Gillam	119	S4
Gâza	94	B6	Genichesk	79	E6	Gevān	95	N8	Gillen, Mount	113	G3
Gazelle Peninsula	114	E2	Genil	66	D4	Gevas	77	K3	Gillesnuole	62	G4
Gazelle, Récif de la	114	W16	Gennargentu, Monti del	69	B6	Geyik Daği	76	E4	Gillespie Point	115	B5
Gaziantep	77	G4	Genoa *Australia*	113	K6	Geyik Dağlari	76	E4	Gillette	123	M5
Gazimur	85	K6	Genoa *Italy*	68	B3	Geyve	76	D2	Gillian Lake	120	L4
Gazimurskiy Zavod	85	K6	Genova	68	B3	Gezi	77	F3	Gillingham	53	H3
Gazipaşa	76	E4	Genova, Golfo di	68	B3	Ghadāmis	101	G2	Gill, Lough	58	F4
Gbarnga	104	D4	Genovesa, Isla	136	B7	Ghaghara	92	F3	Gilroy	126	B2
Gboko	105	G4	Genriyetty, Ostrov	81	S2	Ghana	104	E4	Giluwe, Mount	114	C3
Gdańsk	71	H1	Gent	64	E3	Ghanzi	108	D4	Gimli	123	R2
Gdov	63	M7	Genteng	90	D7	Ghārah, Wadi	97	L8	Gimo	63	H6
Geary	56	B3	Genyem	91	L6	Gharbī, Al Hajār al	97	N4	Gimone	65	D7
Gebeit	96	C7	Geographe Bay	112	D5	Gharbîya, Es Sahrâ' el	103	E2	Gīnda	96	D9
Gebze	76	C2	Geographe Channel	112	C3	Ghardaia	101	F2	Gingin	112	D5
Geçitli	77	K4	Geokchay	79	H7				Gīnīr	103	H6
Gedaref	103	G5	George *Canada*	121	N6				Gioia del Colle	69	F5

Great Zab	**94**	F3	Grey Island	**121**	Q7	Guadalcanal *Solomon Is.*	**114**	J6	Guarico	**136**	D2
Gredos, Sierra de	**66**	D2	Grey Mare's Tail	**57**	E5	Guadalcanal *Spain*	**66**	D3	Guasave	**130**	E5
Greece	**75**	F3	Greymouth	**115**	C5	Guadalete	**66**	D4	Guasdualito	**136**	C2
Greeley	**123**	M7	Grey Range	**113**	J4	Guadalimar	**66**	E3	Guasipati	**136**	E2
Greely Fjord	**120**	K1	Greysteel	**58**	H2	Guadalmez	**66**	D3	Guastalla	**68**	C3
Green *Kentucky, U.S.A.*	**124**	G8	Greystones	**59**	K6	Guadalope	**67**	F2	Guatemala	**132**	B7
Green *Wyoming, U.S.A.*	**123**	J6	Greytown	**115**	E4	Guadalquivir	**66**	D4	Guatemala	**132**	B7
Green Bay *U.S.A.*	**124**	G4	Griefswald Bodden	**70**	E1	Guadalupe *Mexico*	**128**	B8	Guaviare	**136**	D3
Green Bay *U.S.A.*	**124**	G4	Griffin	**129**	K4	Guadalupe *Mexico*	**127**	J5	Guaxupe	**138**	G4
Green Bell, Ostrov	**80**	H1	Griffith	**113**	K5	Guadalupe *Spain*	**66**	D3	Guayaquil	**136**	B4
Greenbrier	**125**	K8	Griffith Island	**120**	G3	Guadalupe *Texas, U.S.A.*	**128**	D6	Guayaquil, Golfo de	**136**	A4
Greencastle	**58**	K4	Grigoriopol'	**73**	K2	Guadalupe Mountains	**127**	K5	Guaymas	**126**	G7
Greeneville	**129**	L2	Grimailov	**71**	M4	Guadalupe, Sierra de	**66**	D3	Guazacapán	**132**	B7
Greenfield	**125**	P5	Grim, Cape	**113**	J7	Guadalupe Victoria	**130**	G5	Guba	**103**	G5
Green Hammerton	**55**	H2	Grimsby	**55**	J3	Guadarrama *Spain*	**66**	D2	Guba Dolgaya	**84**	Ac2
Greenhead	**55**	G2	Grímsey	**62**	W11	Guadarrama *Spain*	**66**	D2	Gubakha	**78**	K4
Green Island	**115**	C6	Grimshaw	**119**	M4	Guadarrama, Sierra de	**66**	E2	Gubbio	**68**	D4
Greenisland	**58**	L3	Grimstad	**63**	C7	Guadeloupe	**133**	S6	Gubdor	**78**	K3
Green Islands	**114**	E2	Grindavík	**62**	T13	Guadeloupe Passage	**133**	S6	Guben	**70**	F3
Greenland	**116**	Q1	Grindsted	**63**	C9	Guadelupe	**126**	D4	Gücük	**77**	G3
Greenlaw	**57**	F4	Gringley on the Hill	**55**	J3	Guadiana	**66**	C4	Gúdar, Sierra de	**67**	F2
Greenlough	**112**	D4	Grinnell	**124**	D6	Guadiana, Bahía de	**132**	E3	Gudbrandsdalen	**63**	D6
Greenlowther	**57**	D5	Grinnell Peninsula	**120**	G2	Guadiana Menor	**66**	E4	Gudenå	**63**	C8
Green Mountains	**125**	P5	Grintavec	**68**	E2	Guadix	**66**	E4	Gudur	**92**	E6
Greenock	**57**	D5	Gris-Nez, Cap	**64**	D3	Guafo, Isla	**139**	B8	Gudvangen	**62**	B6
Green River *Papua New Guinea*	**114**	C2	Griva	**78**	J3	Guainia	**136**	D3	Guékedou	**104**	C4
Green River *Utah, U.S.A.*	**127**	G1	Grmeč Planina	**72**	D3	Guaiquinima, Cerro	**136**	E2	Guelma	**101**	G1
Green River *Wyoming, U.S.A.*	**123**	K7	Gröbming	**68**	D2	Guajira, Península de	**136**	C1	Guelph	**125**	K5
Greensboro	**129**	N2	Grodekovo	**88**	C3	Gualachulian	**57**	C4	Guéréda	**102**	D5
Greensburg	**125**	L6	Grodno	**71**	K2	Gualaquiza	**136**	B4	Guéret	**65**	D5
Greenstone Point	**56**	C3	Groix, Île de	**65**	B5	Gualeguay *Argentina*	**138**	E6	Guernsey *U.K.*	**53**	M7
Green Valley	**126**	G5	Grombalia	**69**	C7	Gualeguay *Argentina*	**138**	E6	Guernsey *U.S.A.*	**123**	M6
Greenville *Liberia*	**104**	D4	Grong	**62**	E4	Gualeguaychu	**138**	E6	Guerrero Negro	**126**	E6
Greenville *Alabama, U.S.A.*	**129**	J5	Groningen *Netherlands*	**64**	G2	Guam	**83**	N5	Gugu	**73**	G3
Greenville *Mississippi, U.S.A.*	**128**	G4	Groningen *Suriname*	**137**	F2	Guamá	**137**	H4	Guhakolak, Tanjung	**90**	D7
Greenville *N. Carolina, U.S.A.*	**129**	P3	Groot	**108**	D6	Guamblin, Isla	**139**	A8	Guia	**138**	E3
Greenville *S. Carolina, U.S.A.*	**129**	L3	Groote Eylandt	**113**	H1	Guampi, Sierra de	**136**	D2	Guide	**93**	K1
Greenville *Texas, U.S.A.*	**128**	D4	Grootfontein	**108**	C3	Guamúchil	**130**	E5	Guider	**105**	H4
Greenwood *Mississippi, U.S.A.*	**128**	G4	Grossa, Ponta	**137**	H3	Gua Musang	**90**	C5	Guidong	**93**	M3
Greenwood *S. Carolina, U.S.A.*	**129**	L3	Grosseto	**69**	C4	Guanare *Venezuela*	**136**	D2	Guiglo	**104**	D4
Greers Ferry Lake	**128**	F3	Grossevichi	**88**	G1	Guanare *Venezuela*	**136**	D2	Gui Jiang	**93**	M4
Gregório	**136**	C5	Gros Ventre Mountains	**123**	J6	Guanay, Sierra	**136**	D2	Guildford	**53**	G3
Gregory, Lake	**113**	H4	Grottaglie	**69**	F5	Guandi	**88**	B4	Guildtown	**57**	E4
Gregory Range	**113**	J2	Groundhog	**124**	J2	Guang'an	**93**	L2	Guilin	**93**	M3
Greian Head	**57**	A3	Grove	**53**	J3	Guangdong	**93**	M4	Guillestre	**65**	G6
Greifswald	**70**	E1	Grove City	**125**	K6	Guanghua	**93**	M2	Guimarães	**66**	B2
Grein	**68**	E1	Grove Hill	**129**	J5	Guangnan	**93**	L4	Guinea	**104**	C3
Greipstad	**62**	H2	Grover City	**126**	B3	Guangning	**93**	M4	Guinea Bissau	**104**	C3
Greiz	**70**	E3	Groznyy	**79**	H7	Guangping	**87**	M4	Guinea, Gulf of	**105**	F5
Gremikha	**78**	F2	Grudovo	**73**	J4	Guangxi	**93**	L4	Güines	**132**	F3
Gremyachinsk	**78**	K4	Grudziądz	**71**	H2	Guangyuan	**93**	L2	Guingamp	**64**	B4
Grenå	**63**	D8	Gruinard Bay	**56**	C3	Guangze	**87**	M6	Guiratinga	**138**	F3
Grenada	**133**	S8	Gruinart, Loch	**57**	B5	Guangzhou	**93**	M4	Güiria	**136**	E1
Grenada *U.S.A.*	**128**	H4	Grums	**63**	E7	Guanhães	**138**	H3	Guisanbourg	**137**	G3
Grenadines, The	**133**	S8	Grünaw	**108**	C5	Guanipa	**133**	R10	Guisborough	**55**	H2
Grenen	**63**	D8	Grünberg	**70**	F3	Guanoca	**136**	E1	Guise	**64**	E4
Grenfell	**123**	N2	Grund	**62**	U12	Guantánamo	**133**	K4	Guiseley	**55**	H3
Grenivík	**62**	V12	Grundarfjörður	**62**	T12	Guan Xian	**93**	K2	Guiting Power	**53**	F3
Grenoble	**65**	F6	Grundy	**124**	J8	Guapí	**136**	B3	Guiuan	**91**	H3
Grenville, Cape	**113**	J1	Gruziya S.S.R.	**77**	K1	Guápiles	**132**	F9	Guixi	**87**	M6
Gresford	**55**	G3	Gruznovka	**84**	H5	Guaporé	**136**	E6	Gui Xian	**93**	L4
Gresham	**122**	C5	Gryazi	**79**	F5	Guaqui	**138**	C3	Guiyang	**93**	L3
Gresik	**90**	E7	Gryazovets	**78**	G4	Guarabira	**137**	K5	Guizhou	**93**	L3
Greta	**55**	H1	Gryfice	**70**	F2	Guarapuava	**138**	F5	Gujarat	**92**	D4
Gretna	**55**	F2	Gryfino	**70**	F2	Guara, Sierra de	**67**	F1	Gujranwala	**92**	D2
Grevená	**75**	F2	Guabito	**136**	A2	Guarda *Portugal*	**66**	C2	Gujrat	**92**	D2
Greybull	**123**	K5	Guacanayabo, Golfo de	**132**	J4	Guarda *Portugal*	**66**	C2	Gulbarga	**92**	E5
			Guadajoz	**66**	D4	Guardo	**66**	D1	Gulbene	**63**	M8
			Guadalajara *Mexico*	**130**	H7	Guarenas	**136**	D1	Gülçayir	**76**	D3
			Guadalajara *Spain*	**66**	E2	Guaribas, Cachoeira	**137**	G4	Gul'cha	**86**	C3

Name	Page	Ref
Gulfport	128	H5
Gulian	87	N1
Gullane	57	F4
Gullfoss	62	V12
Gull Lake	123	K2
Gullspång	63	F7
Güllük	76	B4
Gülnar	76	E4
Gülpinar	76	B3
Gülşehir	76	F3
Gulyantsi	73	H4
Gumbaz	95	R6
Gummi	105	G3
Gümüşhaciköy	76	F2
Gümüşhane	77	H2
Guna	92	E4
Gundagi	113	K6
Gündoğmuş	76	E4
Gunedidalem	91	H6
Güney	76	C3
Güneydoğutoroslar	77	H3
Gungu	106	C4
Gunnedah	113	L5
Gunning	113	K5
Gunnison Colorado, U.S.A.	127	J1
Gunnison Colorado, U.S.A.	123	K8
Gunnison Utah, U.S.A	126	G1
Guntakal	92	E5
Guntersville	129	J3
Guntersville Lake	129	J3
Guntur	92	F5
Gunungsitoli	90	B5
Gunungsugih	90	D6
Gunzenhausen	70	D4
Gurban Obo	87	L3
Gürbulak	77	L3
Gurdim	95	Q9
Gurdzhaani	79	H7
Güre	76	C3
Gurgaon	92	E3
Gurgei, Jebel	102	D5
Gurghiului, Munţii	73	H2
Gurguéia	137	J5
Gur I Topit	75	F2
Gürpinar	77	K3
Gurué	109	G3
Gürün	77	G3
Gurupá	137	G4
Gurupa, Ilha Grande do	137	G4
Gurupí	137	H4
Gurupi, Serra do	137	H4
Guruzala	92	E5
Gur'yev	79	J6
Gusau	105	G3
Gusev	71	K1
Gusinoozersk	84	H6
Gu's-Khrustal'nyy	78	G4
Güstrow	70	E2
Gusyatin	73	J1
Gutcher	56	A1
Guthrie Oklahoma, U.S.A.	128	D3
Guthrie Texas, U.S.A.	127	M4
Gutian	87	M6
Guttenberg	124	E5
Güvem	76	E2
Guyana	136	F2
Guyenne	65	D6
Guymon	127	M2
Guyuan	93	L1
Güzelbağ	76	D4
Guzeloluk	76	F4
Güzelsu	77	K3
Güzelyurt	76	F3
Guzmán, Laguna de	127	J5
Gvardeysk	71	J1
Gvardeyskoye	73	J1
Gwa	93	H5
Gwabegar	113	K5
Gwadar	92	B3
Gwalior	92	E3
Gwanda	108	E4
Gweebarra Bay	58	F3
Gwelo	108	E3
Gwent	52	E3
Gweru	108	E3
Gwoza	105	H3
Gwydir,	113	K4
Gwynedd	52	D2
Gyangzê	93	G3
Gyaring Hu	93	J2
Gydanskaya Guba	84	B2
Gydanskiy Polucstrov	84	B2
Gydnia	71	H1
Gympie	113	L4
Gynymskaya	85	N5
Gyöngyös	72	E2
Gyönk	72	E2
Gyór	72	D2
Gypsumville	123	Q2
Gyueshevo	73	G4
Gyula	73	F2
Háabunga	62	W12
Ha'apai Group	111	U5
Haapajärvi	62	L5
Haapamäki	63	L5
Haapsalu	63	K7
Haardt	70	B4
Haarlem	64	F2
Haast New Zealand	115	B5
Haast New Zealand	115	B5
Haast Passage	115	B6
Hab	92	C3
Ḩabawnāh, Wadi	96	G8
Habbān	96	H9
Ḩabbānīyah	94	F5
Ḩabbānīyah, Hawr al	94	F5
Haberli	77	J4
Habirag	87	M3
Haboro	88	H3
Hachenburg	70	B3
Hachijō-jima	89	G9
Hachiman	89	F8
Hachinohe	88	H5
Hachiōji	89	G8
Hacibektaş	76	F3
Hacihalil Daği	77	K2
Haciömer	77	J3
Hackås	62	F5
Ḩaḍan, Ḩarrāt	96	E6
Ḩaḍārah	96	E7
Hadarba, Râs	96	C5
Haddenham	53	H2
Haddington	57	F5
Ḩadd, Ra's al	97	P5
Hadejia	105	G3
Hadera	94	B5
Haderslev	63	E9
Hadhālīl, Al	96	G2
Hadhramawt	97	J9
Hadīboh	97	P10
Hadim	76	E4
Hadleigh	53	H2
Hadley Bay	119	P1
Hadong	93	L4
Hadrian's Wall	57	F5
Hadsund	63	D8
Haeju	87	P4
Hafar al Baţin	96	H2
Hafik	77	G3
Ḩafit	97	M5
Hafnarfjörður	62	U12
Hafratindur	62	U12
Haft Gel	94	J6
Haftqala	95	R4
Hag 'Abdullah	103	F5
Hagemeister Island	118	A3
Hagen	70	B3
Hagen, Mount	114	C3
Hagerstown	125	M7
Hagfors	63	E6
Häggenås	62	F5
Hagi	89	C8
Ha Giang	93	K4
Hăgimaş	73	H2
Hagley	53	E2
Hagondange	64	G4
Hags Head	59	D7
Hague, Cap de la	64	C4
Haguenau	64	G4
Hai'an	93	M4
Haibei	88	A2
Haicheng	87	N3
Hai Duong	93	L4
Haifa	94	B5
Haifeng	87	M7
Haikang	93	M4
Haikou	93	M5
Hā'il	96	E3
Hailar	87	M2
Hailar He	87	M2
Hailsham	53	H4
Hailun	88	A2
Hailuoto Finland	62	L4
Hailuoto Finland	63	L2
Hainan Dao	93	M5
Haines	118	H4
Haines City	129	M6
Haiphong	93	L4
Haiti	133	L5
Haivare	114	C3
Haiya	96	C7
Ḩajarah, Al	96	F2
Hajdúböszörmeny	73	F2
Hajdúnánás	73	F2
Hajiki-saki	89	G6
Hajipur	92	G3
Ḩajjah	96	F9
Hajjīābād	95	M7
Hajmah	97	N7
Hajr, Wadi	97	J9
Hakataramea	115	C6
Hakkâri	77	K4
Hakkas	62	J3
Hakkibey	76	F4
Hakodate	88	H5
Haku-san	89	F7
Hala	92	C3
Halab	94	C3
Ḩalabān	96	G5
Halabja	94	G4
Halaib	103	G3
Ḩālat 'Ammār	96	C2
Hålaveden	63	F7
Halawa Hawaii, U.S.A.	126	S10
Halawa Hawaii, U.S.A.	126	T10
Halba	77	G5
Halberstadt	70	D3
Halcon, Mount	91	G3
Halden	63	D7
Haldensleben	70	D2
Halesowen	53	E2
Halesworth	53	J2
Halfeti	77	G4
Halfin, Wadi	97	N6
Halfmoon Bay	115	B7
Halfway	119	L4
Ḩalī	96	E7
Haliburton Highlands	125	L4
Halifax Canada	121	P9
Halifax U.K.	55	H3
Halifax Bay	113	K2
Halikarnassos	76	B4
Halīleh, Ra's-e	95	K7
Halin	88	B3
Halīsah	77	G4
Halitpaşa	76	B3
Halkapinar	76	F4
Halkett, Cape	118	E1
Hälla	62	G5
Halladale	56	E2
Hallanca	136	B5
Halland	63	E8
Hallandsås	63	E8
Halle	70	C3
Hällefors	63	F7
Hallen	62	F5
Halley	141	Y3
Hallingdal	63	C6
Hallingskarvet	63	B6
Hall Peninsula	120	N5
Halls Creek	112	F2
Hallstavik	63	H6
Hallum	64	F2
Halmahera	91	H5
Halmahera, Laut	91	H6
Halmstad	63	E8
Hals	63	D8
Halsinge-skogen	63	F6
Hälsingland	63	G6
Halstead	53	H3
Halton Lea Gate	55	G2
Ḩālūl	97	L4
Ham France	64	E4
Ham U.K.	56	A2
Hamada	89	D8
Hamad, Al	94	D6
Hamadān	94	J4
Hamāh	94	C4
Hamam	77	G4
Hamamatsu	89	F8
Hamar	63	D6
Hamâta, Gebel	96	B4
Hama-Tombetsu	88	J3
Hambantota	92	F7
Hambleton	55	G3
Hamburg U.S.A.	124	C6
Hamburg W. Germany	70	D2
Hamdaman, Dasht-i	95	Q4

Name	Page	Grid
Ḥamḍ, Wadi al	96	C4
Häme	63	L6
Hameln	70	C2
Hamhŭng	87	P4
Hami	86	F3
Hamilton	113	H3
Hamilton *Bermuda*	117	N5
Hamilton *Canada*	125	L5
Hamilton *New Zealand*	115	E2
Hamilton *U.K.*	57	D5
Hamilton *Alabama, U.S.A.*	129	J3
Hamilton *Montana, U.S.A.*	122	G4
Hamilton *Ohio, U.S.A.*	124	H7
Hamilton Inlet	121	Q7
Ḥamīm, Wadi al	101	K2
Hamina	63	M6
Hamitabat	76	D4
Hamm	70	B2
Hammar, Hawr al	94	H6
Hammarstrand	62	G5
Hämeenlinna	63	L6
Hammerdal	62	F5
Hammerfest	62	K1
Hammersley Range	112	D3
Hammond *Indiana, U.S.A.*	124	G6
Hammond *Louisiana, U.S.A.*	128	G5
Hammond *Montana, U.S.A.*	123	M5
Hamnavoe	56	A1
Hampden	115	C6
Hampshire	53	F3
Hampshire Downs	53	F3
Hampton *Arkansas, U.S.A.*	128	F4
Hampton *S. Carolina, U.S.A.*	129	M4
Hampton *Virginia, U.S.A.*	125	M8
Hamrā', Al Hammādah al	101	H3
Hamrånge	63	G6
Hamrin, Jebel	77	L5
Hamun-i Māshkel	92	B3
Hamur	77	K3
Hanahan	114	E3
Hanak	77	K2
Hanalei	126	R9
Hanamaki	88	H6
Hancheng	93	M1
Hancock	125	L7
Handa	89	F8
Handan	87	L4
Handeni	107	G4
Handlová	71	H4
Hanford	126	C2
Hangang	87	P4
Hangayn Nuruu	86	H2
Hanggin Houqi	87	K3
Hanggin Qi	87	K4
Hangö	63	K7
Hangzhou	87	N5
Hangzhou Wan	87	N5
Hanhongor	87	J3
Hani	77	J3
Ḥanīfah, Wadi	96	H4
Hanīsh al Kabīr	96	F10
Haniyah, Al	94	H7
Han Jiang	87	M7
Hanko	63	K7
Hanksville	126	G1
Hanna	122	H2
Hannah Bay	121	L7
Hannibal	124	E7
Hann, Mount	112	F2
Hannover	70	C2
Hanö-bukten	63	F9
Hanoi	93	L4
Hanover *Canada*	125	K4
Hanover *South Africa*	108	D6
Hanover *U.S.A.*	125	P5
Hanover, Isla	139	B10
Hanpan, Cape	114	E2
Han Pijesak	72	E3
Han Shui	93	M2
Hanson Bay	115	F6
Hanstholm	63	C8
Hantay	86	J2
Hanyuan	93	K3
Hanzhong	93	L2
Haparanda	62	L4
Happisburgh	53	J2
Hapsu	88	B5
Hapur	92	E3
Ḥaql	96	B2
Hara	87	K2
Ḥaraḍ *Saudi Arabia*	97	J4
Ḥaraḍ *Yemen*	96	F8
Harads	62	J3
Haramachi	89	H7
Harare	108	F3
Ḥarāsīs, Jiddat al	97	N7
Harbin	87	P2
Harbiye	77	G4
Harbour Breton	121	Q8
Harby	53	G2
Hardangerfjord	63	B6
Hardanger-Jøkulen	63	B6
Hardangervidda	63	B6
Hardin	123	L5
Hardoi	92	F3
Hardy	128	G2
Hare Bay	121	Q7
Härer	103	H6
Harewood	55	H3
Hargeysa	103	H6
Hargīgo	96	D9
Har Hu	93	J1
Ḥarīb	96	G9
Haridwar	92	E3
Harihari	115	C5
Harima-nada	89	E8
Harim, Jabal Al	97	N4
Hari-Rud	95	S4
Härjedalen	62	E5
Harlan	124	C6
Harlem	123	K3
Harleston	53	J2
Harlingen	64	F2
Harlow	53	H3
Harlowton	123	K4
Harmancik	76	C3
Harmil	96	E8
Harney Basin	122	D6
Harney Lake	122	E6
Härnösand	62	G5
Haro	66	E1
Haro, Cabo	126	G7
Haroldswick	56	A1
Harpanahalli	92	E6
Harpenden	53	G3
Harper	104	D5
Harper Passage	115	C5
Harpstedt	70	C2
Harrah, Ad	94	D6
Harran	77	H4
Harray, Loch of	56	E1
Harricanaw	125	M2
Harrietsham	53	H3
Harrington	55	F2
Harris	56	B3
Harrisburg *Illinois, U.S.A.*	124	F8
Harrisburg *Pennsylvania, U.S.A.*	125	M6
Harrismith	108	E5
Harrison	128	F2
Harrison Bay	118	E1
Harrisonburg	125	L7
Harrison, Cape	121	Q7
Harrison Lake	122	D3
Harrisonville	124	C7
Harris Ridge	140	A1
Harris, Sound of	56	A3
Harrogate	55	H3
Harrow	53	G3
Harṣit	77	H2
Harstad	62	G2
Harsvik	62	D4
Hart	118	H2
Hartbees	108	D5
Hartberg	68	E2
Hårteigen	63	B6
Hartford	125	P6
Harthill	57	E5
Hartkjølen	62	E4
Hartland	52	C4
Hartland Point	52	C3
Hartlepool	55	H2
Hartley	127	L3
Hartola	63	M6
Hartsville	129	M3
Hartwell Reservoir	129	L3
Hartz	108	E5
Harūt	97	L8
Harvey *Australia*	112	D5
Harvey *U.S.A.*	124	G6
Harwich	53	J3
Haryana	92	E3
Harz	70	D3
Hasan Daği	76	F3
Ḥashīsh, Ghubbat	97	P6
Hasköy	77	K2
Haslemere	53	G3
Haslingden	55	G3
Hassa	77	G4
Hassan	92	E6
Hassankeyf	77	J4
Hassela	63	L5
Hassi Habadra	101	F3
Hässleholm	63	E8
Hastings *Australia*	113	K7
Hastings *New Zealand*	115	F3
Hastings *U.K.*	53	H4
Hastings *Michigan, U.S.A.*	124	H5
Hastings *Nebraska, U.S.A.*	123	Q7
Hästveda	63	E8
Hasvik	62	K1
Haswell	55	H2
Hatanbulag	87	K3
Hatchie	128	H3
Hatfield *Hertfordshire, U.K.*	53	G3
Hatfield *S. Yorkshire, U.K.*	55	H3
Hatfield Peverel	53	H3
Hatgal	86	J1
Hathras	92	E3
Ḥāṭibah, Ra's	96	D6
Ha Tien	93	K6
Ha Tinh	93	L5
Hatip	76	E4
Hat Island	120	G4
Hato	136	A2
Hatohudo	91	H7
Hatskiy	84	D5
Hatteras, Cape	129	Q3
Hattiesburg	128	H5
Hatton	56	G3
Hattras Passage	93	J6
Hatunsaray	76	E4
Hatuoto	91	H6
Haugesund	63	A7
Haughton	53	E2
Hauhui	114	K6
Haukivesi	62	N5
Haukivuori	63	M5
Hauraha	114	K7
Hauraki Gulf	115	E2
Haut Atlas	100	D2
Hauts Plateaux	100	E2
Havana	124	E6
Havant	53	F4
Havasu	126	F3
Havasu, Lake	126	E3
Havel	70	E2
Havelock North	115	F3
Haverfordwest	52	C2
Haverhill *U.K.*	53	H2
Haverhill *U.S.A.*	125	Q5
Havøysund	62	L1
Havran	76	B3
Havre	123	K3
Havre-Saint-Pierre	121	P7
Havsa	76	B2
Havza	77	F2
Hawaii *U.S.A.*	126	R10
Hawaii *U.S.A.*	126	T11
Ḥawāyā, Al	97	J6
Hawea, Lake	115	B6
Hawera	115	E3
Hawes	55	G2
Haweswater Reservoir	55	G2
Hawick	57	F5
Hawke	121	Q7
Hawke Bay	115	F3
Hawke, Cape	113	L5
Hawkesbury	125	N4
Hawkhurst	53	H3
Hawkinge	53	J3
Hawknest Point	133	K2
Hawnby	55	H2
Hawng Luk	93	J4
Ḥawrā	97	J9
Ḥāwrān, Wadi	94	E5
Hawsker	55	J2
Hawthorne	126	C1
Haxby	55	H2
Hay *New South Wales, Australia*	113	J5
Hay *Northern Territory, Australia*	113	H3
Hay *Canada*	119	M3
Hayden	123	L7
Hayes	119	R4
Hayes Halvo	120	N2
Hayes, Mount	118	F3
Hayján	96	G8
Ḥayl	97	N4

Name	Page	Grid
Hirakud Reservoir	92	F4
Hirara	89	G11
Hiratsuka	89	G8
Hirfanli Baraji	76	E3
Hîrlău	73	J2
Hiroo	88	J4
Hirosaki	88	H5
Hiroshima	89	D8
Hirschberg	70	F3
Hîrşova	73	J3
Hirtshals	63	C8
Hirwaun	52	D3
Hisar	92	E3
Hisma	96	C2
Hissjön	62	J5
Hīt	94	F5
Hitachi	89	H7
Hitchin	53	G3
Hitoyoshi	89	C9
Hitra	62	C5
Hiu	114	T10
Hiuchi-nada	89	D8
Hiz	53	G2
Hizan	77	K3
Hjälmaren	63	G7
Hjalmer Lake	119	P3
Hjelmeland	63	B7
Hjørring	63	C8
Ho	104	F4
Hoa Binh	93	L4
Hobara	89	H7
Hobart	113	K7
Hobbs	127	L4
Hoboksar	86	F2
Hobro	63	C8
Hobyo	103	J6
Hocalar	76	C3
Hochalm Spitze	68	D2
Ho Chi Minh	93	L6
Höchstadt	70	D4
Hockley	53	H3
Hockley Heath	53	F2
Hodal	92	E3
Hodder	55	G3
Hoddesdon	53	G3
Hodge Beck	55	H2
Hódmezóvásárhely	72	F2
Hodna, Monts du	67	J5
Hodnet	52	E2
Hodonín	71	G4
Hoea	126	T10
Hoeryong	88	B4
Hof	70	D3
Höfðakaupstaður	62	U12
Hofmeyr	108	E6
Höfn *Iceland*	62	T11
Höfn *Iceland*	62	X12
Hofors	63	G6
Hofsjökull	62	V12
Hōfu	89	C8
Höganäs	63	E8
Hoggar	101	G4
Högsby	63	G8
Hogsty Reef	133	L4
Hohe Rhön	70	C3
Hohe Tauern	68	D2
Hohhot	87	L3
Hoh Xil Shan	92	G1
Hoi An	93	L5
Hoima	107	F2

Name	Page	Grid
Hökensås	63	F7
Hokianga Harbour	115	D1
Hokitika	115	C5
Hokkaidō	88	H3
Hokksund	63	C7
Hokota	89	H7
Hok'ou	93	K4
Hokunō	89	F8
Holárfjall	62	V12
Holbeach	53	H2
Holborn Head	56	E2
Holbrook	127	G3
Holdenville	128	D3
Holderness	55	J3
Holdrege	123	Q7
Holguín	132	J4
Holič	71	G4
Holitna	118	D3
Höljes	63	E6
Hollabrunn	68	F1
Holland	124	G5
Hollandstoun	56	F1
Hollis	128	C3
Hollywood	129	M7
Holm	62	E4
Holman Island	119	M1
Hólmavík	62	U12
Holme-on-Spalding-Moor	55	J3
Holmes Chapel	55	G3
Holmes Reef	113	K2
Holmfirth	55	H3
Holms Ø	120	Q3
Holmsund	62	J5
Holoin Gun	86	J3
Holstebro	63	C8
Holsteinsborg	120	R4
Holsworthy	52	C4
Holt	53	J2
Holton *Canada*	121	Q7
Holton *U.S.A.*	124	C7
Holy Cross	118	D3
Holyhead	54	E3
Holyhead Bay	55	E3
Holy Island *Gwynedd, U.K.*	54	E3
Holy Island *Northumberland, U.K.*	55	H1
Holy Island *Strathclyde, U.K.*	57	C5
Holyoke *Colorado, U.S.A.*	123	N7
Holyoke *Massachusetts, U.S.A.*	125	P5
Holywell	55	F3
Holywood *Down, U.K.*	58	L3
Holywood *Dumfries and Galloway, U.K.*	57	E5
Homalin	93	H4
Hombre Muerto, Salar de	138	C5
Home Bay	120	N4
Home Hill	113	K2
Home Point	115	E1
Homer	128	F4
Homer Tunnel	115	A6
Hommelvik	62	D5
Hommersåk	63	D6
Homoine	109	G4
Homs	77	G5
Honavar	92	D6
Honaz Daği	76	C4
Hon Chong	93	K6
Hondo *Mexico*	131	Q8
Hondo *U.S.A.*	128	C6

Name	Page	Grid
Honduras	132	C7
Honduras, Golfo de	132	C6
Hønefoss	63	D6
Honesdale	125	N6
Honey Lake	122	D7
Hong Kong	87	L7
Hongliuyuan	86	H3
Hongo	86	G2
Hongor *Mongolia*	87	L2
Hongor *Mongolia*	87	L2
Hongshui He	93	L4
Hong, Song	93	K4
Hongsong	87	P4
Honguedo Strait	121	P8
Hongxing Sichang	86	F3
Hongze	87	M5
Hongze Hu	87	M5
Honiara	114	J6
Honingham	53	J2
Honiton	52	D4
Honjō	88	G6
Hon Khoai	93	K7
Honningsvåg	62	L1
Honohina	126	T11
Honokaa	126	T10
Honolulu	126	S10
Honshū	89	E7
Hood	119	N2
Hood Canal	122	C4
Hood Island	136	A7
Hood, Mount	122	D5
Hood Point	114	D4
Hood River	122	D5
Hoogeveen	64	G2
Hooghly	93	G4
Hook	53	G3
Hooker	127	M2
Hook Head	59	J8
Hook Norton	53	F3
Hooper, Cape	120	N4
Höör	63	E9
Hoorn	64	F2
Hoover Dam	126	E2
Hopa	77	J2
Hope *Canada*	122	D3
Hope *U.K.*	55	H3
Hope *U.S.A.*	128	F4
Hopedale	121	P6
Hopelchén	131	Q8
Hope, Loch	56	D2
Hopen	80	D2
Hope Pass	115	C5
Hope, Point	118	B2
Hopes Advance, Cape	121	N5
Hopetown	108	D5
Hopewell	125	M8
Hopkins Lake	112	F3
Hopkinsville	124	G8
Hoquiam	122	C4
Horasan	77	K2
Hörby	63	E9
Hordaland	63	B6
Horezu	73	G3
Horley	53	G3
Horlick Mountains	141	R1
Hormoz	95	N8
Hormuz, Strait of	97	N3
Horn *Austria*	68	E1
Horn *Iceland*	62	T11
Hornavan	62	G3

Name	Page	Grid
Horn, Cape	139	C10
Horncastle	55	J3
Horndal	63	G6
Horndean	53	F4
Hörnefors	62	H5
Hornepayne	124	H2
Horn Head	58	G2
Horn, Îles de	111	T4
Horningsham	52	E3
Horn Mountains	119	L3
Hornos, Cabo de	139	C11
Hornsea	55	J3
Hořovice	70	E4
Horqin Youyi Qianqi	87	N2
Horqin Zuoyi Houqi	87	N3
Horqueta	138	E4
Horsehoe Bend	122	F6
Horsens	63	C9
Horsey	53	J2
Horsforth	55	H3
Horsham *Australia*	113	J6
Horsham *U.K.*	53	G3
Horsham Saint Faith	53	J2
Horsley	53	G3
Horšovský Týn	70	E4
Horten	63	D7
Horton	118	L2
Horwich	55	G3
Hosa'ina	103	G6
Hosap	77	K3
Hose Mountains	90	E5
Hoseynābād	94	H4
Hoshangabad	92	E4
Hoshiarpur	92	E2
Hospet	92	E5
Hospitalet	67	H2
Hossegor	65	C7
Hoste, Isla	139	C11
Hotamiş	76	E4
Hotan	92	F1
Hotazel	108	D5
Hoti	91	J6
Hoting	62	G4
Hot Springs *Arkansas, U.S.A.*	128	F3
Hot Springs *S. Dakota, U.S.A.*	123	N6
Hottah Lake	119	M2
Hotte, Massif de la	133	K5
Houaïlou	114	W16
Houdan	64	D4
Houghton	124	F3
Houghton-le-Spring	55	H2
Houlton	125	S3
Houma *China*	93	M1
Houma *U.S.A.*	128	G6
Houmt Souk	101	H2
Houndé	104	E3
Hounslow	53	G3
Houston *Mississippi, U.S.A.*	128	H4
Houston *Texas, U.S.A.*	128	E6
Houtman Rocks	112	C4
Hova	63	F7
Hovd	86	G2
Hovd Gol	86	G2
Hove	53	G4
Hoveyzeh	94	J6
Hovingham	55	J2
Hovlya	79	G6
Hövsgöl	87	K3
Hövsgöl Nuur	86	J1
Howa	102	E4

Howakil	96	E9
Howard City	124	H5
Howard Lake	119	P3
Howden Moor	55	H3
Howden Reservoir	55	H3
Howe, Cape	113	K6
Howe of the Mearns	57	F4
Howitt, Mount	113	K6
Howland Island	111	T1
Howrah	93	G4
Hoxtolgay	86	F2
Hoxud	86	F3
Hoy	56	E2
Høyanger	63	B6
Hoyerswerda	70	F3
Hoylake	55	F3
Hoyos	66	C2
Hoy Sound	56	E2
Hradeckrálové	70	F3
Hron	71	H4
Hrubieszów	71	K3
Hsin-ch'eng	87	N7
Hsin-chu	87	N7
Hsipaw	93	J4
Huab	108	B4
Huacho	136	B6
Huachuan	88	C2
Huacrachuco	136	B5
Huade	87	L3
Huadian	87	P3
Huaibei	93	N2
Huaide	87	N3
Huai He	93	M2
Huaihua	93	M3
Huaiji	93	M4
Huainan	87	M5
Huairou	87	M3
Huaiyin	87	M5
Huajuapan de León	131	L9
Huallaga	136	B5
Huallanca	136	B5
Huama	88	C2
Huamachuco	136	B5
Huambo	106	C5
Huampusirpi	132	E7
Huanan	88	C2
Huancane	138	C3
Huancavelica	136	B6
Huancayo	136	B6
Huangehuan	93	N2
Huang Hai	87	N4
Huang He	87	L4
Huanghua	87	M4
Huangling	93	L1
Huangpi	93	M2
Huangshi	93	M2
Huang Xian	87	N4
Huangyan	87	N6
Huangyuan	93	K1
Huanren	87	P3
Huanta	136	C6
Huánuco	136	B5
Huan Xian	93	L1
Huanzo, Cordillera	136	C6
Huara	138	C3
Huaral	136	B6
Huaraz	136	B5
Huarmey	136	B6
Huascarán, Nevado	136	B5
Huatabampo	127	H7

Huayin	93	M2
Huayuan	93	L3
Hubei	93	M2
Hubli	92	E5
Hucknall	55	H3
Huddersfield	55	H3
Hudiksvall	63	G6
Hudson *Florida, U.S.A.*	129	L6
Hudson *New York, U.S.A.*	125	P5
Hudson *New York, U.S.A.*	125	P5
Hudson Bay	116	L3
Hudson, Cape	141	L5
Hudson Land	120	X3
Hudson Strait	120	M5
Hue	93	L5
Huebra	66	C2
Huedin	73	G2
Huehuento, Cerro	130	G5
Huehuetenango	132	B7
Huelgoat	64	B4
Huelva *Spain*	66	C4
Huelva *Spain*	66	C4
Huércal Overa	67	F4
Huesca	67	F1
Huéscar	66	E4
Huetamo	131	J8
Huete	66	E2
Hufrah, Al	96	D2
Hughenden	113	J3
Hugh Town	52	K5
Hugo	128	E4
Hugo Reservoir	128	E3
Hugoton	127	M2
Huhehot	87	L3
Huiarau Range	115	F3
Huichapan	131	K7
Huicholes, Sierra de los	130	G6
Hŭich'ŏn	87	P3
Huila, Nevado del	136	B3
Huimin	87	M4
Huisne	65	D4
Huitong	93	L3
Huittinen	63	K6
Huixtla	131	N10
Huize	93	K3
Huizhou	87	L7
Hūj, Al	96	D2
Huka Falls	115	E3
Hukou	87	M6
Hula	114	D4
Hulan He	88	A2
Hulayfah	96	E4
Huld	87	K3
Hulin	88	D3
Hull *Canada*	125	N4
Hull *U.K.*	55	J3
Hultsfred	63	F8
Hulun	87	M2
Hulun Nur	87	M2
Huma	87	P1
Humahuaca	138	B4
Humaitá	136	E5
Humarkló	62	X12
Humaya	130	F5
Humber	55	J3
Humber, Mouth of the	55	K3
Humberside	55	J3
Humboldt *Canada*	123	M1
Humboldt *Nevada, U.S.A.*	122	E7
Humboldt *Tennessee, U.S.A.*	128	H3

Humboldt, Mount	114	X16
Humbolt Gletscher	120	P2
Hŭmedān	95	P9
Humphreys Peak	126	G3
Humpolec	70	F4
Húnaflói	62	U12
Hunan	93	M3
Hunchun	88	C4
Hünfeld	70	C3
Hungary	72	D2
Hungerford	53	F3
Hŭnghae	89	B7
Hŭngnam	87	P4
Hungry Hill	59	C9
Hunjiang	87	P3
Huns Mountains	108	C5
Hunsrück	70	B4
Hunstanton	53	H2
Hunsur	92	E6
Hunte	70	C2
Hunter	113	L5
Hunter, Cape	120	M3
Hunter Islands	113	J7
Huntingdon *U.K.*	53	G2
Huntingdon *U.S.A.*	125	M6
Huntington *Indiana, U.S.A.*	124	H6
Huntington *W. Virginia, U.S.A.*	124	J7
Huntington Beach	126	C4
Huntley	52	E3
Huntly *New Zealand*	115	E2
Huntly *U.K.*	56	F3
Huntsville *Canada*	125	L4
Huntsville *Alabama, U.S.A.*	129	J3
Huntsville *Texas, U.S.A.*	128	E5
Huolongmen	87	P2
Huon Gulf	114	D3
Huon Peninsula	114	D3
Hurd, Cape	125	K4
Hurdiyo	103	K5
Hure Qi	87	N3
Hurghada	103	F2
Hurimta	87	K2
Hurliness	56	E2
Hurn	53	F4
Huron	123	Q5
Huron, Lake	124	J4
Hurricane	126	F2
Hurrungane	63	B6
Hurunui	115	D5
Húsavík *Denmark*	62	Z14
Húsavík *Iceland*	62	W11
Husbands Bosworth	53	F2
Husbondliden	62	H4
Hushan	88	C3
Hushinish	56	A3
Huşi	73	K2
Huskvarna	63	F8
Ḩuşn Āl 'Abr	96	H8
Husum *Sweden*	62	H5
Husum *W. Germany*	70	C1
Hutag	86	J2
Hutaym, Ḩarrat	96	E3
Hutchinson *Kansas, U.S.A.*	128	D1
Hutchinson *Minnesota, U.S.A.*	124	C4
Hutou	88	D2
Hüttenberg	68	E2
Huttoft	55	K3
Hutton, Mount	113	K4
Hutubi	86	F3
Huwar	97	K4

Huxley, Mount	115	B6
Hüyük	76	D4
Huzhou	87	N5
Hvallátur	62	S12
Hvammstangi	62	U12
Hvar	72	D4
Hveragerði	62	U13
Hvítá	62	U12
Hwange	108	E3
Hwlffordd	52	C2
Hyannis *Massachusetts, U.S.A.*	125	Q6
Hyannis *Nebraska, U.S.A.*	123	P7
Hyargas Nuur	86	G2
Hyde *New Zealand*	115	C6
Hyde *U.K.*	55	G3
Hyderabad *India*	92	E5
Hyderabad *Pakistan*	92	C3
Hyères	65	G7
Hyères, Îles d'	65	G7
Hyesan	88	B5
Hyltebruk	63	E8
Hyndman Peak	122	G6
Hynish Bay	57	B4
Hyrynsalmi	62	N4
Hythe *Hampshire, U.K.*	53	F4
Hythe *Kent, U.K.*	53	J3
Hyūga	89	C9
Hyvinkää	63	L6
Iaco	136	D5
Iacobeni	73	H2
Ialomiţa	73	J3
Iapala	109	G2
Iar Connaught	59	D6
Iaşi	73	J2
Ib	78	J3
Iba	91	F2
Ibadan	105	F4
Ibague	136	B3
Ibarra	136	B3
Ibb	96	G10
Ibi	105	G4
Ibiapaba, Serra da	137	J4
Ibiza *Spain*	67	G3
Ibiza *Spain*	67	G3
Ibn Su'aydan, Ramlat	97	M6
Ibo	109	H2
Ibonma	91	J6
Ibotirama	138	J6
Ibrā	97	P5
Ibra, Wadi	102	D5
Ibrī	97	N5
İbriktepe	76	B2
Ibsley	53	F4
Ibusuki	89	C10
Ica	136	B6
Iça	136	D4
Icabarú	136	E3
Içana *Brazil*	136	D3
Içana *Brazil*	136	D3
İçel	76	F4
Iceland	62	V12
Ichalkaranji	92	D5
Ichchapuram	92	F5
Ichera	84	H5
Ichilo	138	D3
Ichinomiya	89	F8
Ichinoseki	88	H6

Ichnya	**79** E5
Ichoa	**138** C3
Icy Bay	**118** G4
Icy Cape	**118** C1
Icy Strait	**118** H4
Idabel	**128** E4
Idah	**105** G4
Idaho	**122** G5
Idaho Falls	**122** H6
Idanha-a-Nova	**66** C3
Idar-Oberstein	**70** B4
Ider	**86** H2
Idfu	**103** F3
Ídhi Óros	**75** H5
Ídhra	**75** G4
İdil	**77** J4
Idiofa	**106** C3
Idiouia	**67** G5
Idlib	**94** C4
Idre	**63** E6
Idrigill Point	**56** B3
Ieper	**64** E3
Ierápetra	**75** H5
Ierissós	**75** G2
Iesi	**68** D4
Ifanadiana	**109** J4
Ife	**105** F4
Iforas, Adrar des	**100** F5
Igara Paraná	**136** C4
Igarapé Miri	**137** H4
Igarka	**84** D3
İğdir	**76** E2
Iğdir	**77** L3
Iğdir Daği	**77** H2
Iggesund	**63** G6
Iglesia	**139** C6
Iglesias	**69** B6
Igloolik	**120** K4
Igluligarjuk	**119** S3
Ignace	**124** E2
İğneada	**76** B2
İğneada Burun	**76** C2
Igoumenítsa	**75** F3
Igra	**78** J4
Iguala	**131** K8
Igualada	**67** G2
Iguape	**138** G4
Iguatu	**137** K5
Iguazú, Cataratas del	**138** F5
Iguazú Falls	**138** F5
Iguidi, Erg	**100** D3
Iheya-rettō	**89** H10
Ih-Hayrhaan	**87** K2
Ihlara	**76** F3
Ihosy	**109** J4
İhsaniye	**76** D3
Iida	**89** F8
Iide-san	**89** G7
Iisalmi	**62** M5
Ijebu Ode	**105** F4
IJmuiden	**64** F2
IJssel	**64** F2
IJsselmeer	**64** F2
Ijzer	**64** E3
Ik	**78** J4
Ika	**84** H5
Ikaalinen	**63** K6
Ikariá	**75** J4
Ikast	**63** C8
Iked	**89** D8

Ikeda	**88** J4
Ikela	**106** D3
Iki-shima	**89** B9
Ikizce	**76** E3
İkizdere	**77** J2
Ikom	**105** G4
Ikomba	**107** F4
Ikongo	**109** J4
Ikpikpuk	**118** E1
Ikuno	**89** E8
Ila	**105** F4
Ilagan	**91** G2
Ilam	**94** H5
Ilanskiy	**84** F5
Ilaro	**105** F4
Iława	**71** H2
Ilbenge	**85** L4
Ileanda	**73** G2
Ilebo	**106** D3
Ilek	**79** J5
Ilesha	**105** F4
Ilfracombe	**52** C3
Ilgaz	**76** E2
Ilgaz Dağlari	**76** F2
Ilgin	**76** D3
Ilhéus	**137** K6
Ili	**86** D3
Ilia	**73** G3
Iliamna Lake	**118** D4
İliç	**77** H3
Iligan	**91** G4
Ilikurangi	**115** G2
Il'inskiy	**88** J1
Il'intsy	**73** K1
Iliodhrómia	**75** G3
Iliômar	**91** H7
Ilja	**71** M1
Ilkeston	**53** F2
Ilkley	**55** H3
Ilkley Moor	**55** H3
Illampu, Nevado de	**138** C3
Illapel	**138** B6
Illbille, Mount	**112** G4
Iller	**70** D4
Illescas	**66** E2
Illimani, Nevado	**138** C3
Illinois *U.S.A.*	**124** E6
Illinois *U.S.A.*	**124** E6
Illizi	**101** G3
Illo	**105** F3
Illote, Punta	**136** A4
Ilm	**70** D3
Il'men', Ozero	**78** E4
Ilminster	**52** E4
Iloilo	**91** G3
Ilorin	**105** F4
Il'pyrskiy	**85** U5
Ilsin-dong	**88** B5
Ilwaki	**91** H7
Ilych	**78** K3
Iłża	**71** J3
Iłżanka	**71** J3
Ima	**85** K5
Imabari	**89** D8
Imamoğlu	**77** F4
Iman	**88** E3
Imandra, Ozero	**62** Q3
Imari	**89** B9
Imataca, Serranía de	**136** E2
Imatra	**63** N6

Imese	**106** C2
Imishli	**94** J2
Immenstadt	**70** D5
Immingham	**55** J3
Imola	**68** C3
Imotski	**72** D4
Imperatriz	**137** H5
Imperia	**68** A4
Imperial	**123** P7
Imperieuse Reef	**112** D2
Impfondo	**106** C2
Imphal	**93** H4
Imrali	**76** C2
Imst	**68** C2
Imundsen Gulf	**118** L1
Imuris	**126** G5
Ina	**89** F8
Inagh	**59** D7
Inakona	**114** K6
In Aménas	**101** G3
Inangahua Junction	**115** C4
Inanwatan	**91** J6
Iñapari	**136** D6
Inari	**62** M2
Inarijärvi	**62** M2
Inawashiro-ko	**89** H7
Inca	**67** H3
Incebel Dağlari	**77** G3
İnce Burun	**76** F1
İnçekum Burun	**76** E4
İncesu	**76** F3
Inchard, Loch	**56** C2
Inch'on	**87** P4
Inchôpe	**109** F3
Indalsälven	**62** G5
Inda Silasē	**96** D9
Indefatigable Island	**136** A7
Independence *California, U.S.A.*	**126** C2
Independence *Kansas, U.S.A.*	**128** E2
Independence *Missouri, U.S.A.*	**124** C7
Independence Mountains	**122** F7
Inderborskiy	**79** J6
India	**92** E4
Indiana *Pennsylvania, U.S.A.*	**125** L6
Indiana *U.S.A.*	**124** G6
Indianapolis	**124** G7
Indian Ocean	**142** D5
Indianola	**128** G4
Indian Springs	**126** E2
Indiga	**78** H2
Indigirka	**85** R2
Indispensable Reefs	**111** P4
Indispensable Strait	**114** K6
Indonesia	**90** D6
Indore	**92** E4
Indragiri	**90** C6
Indramayu	**90** D7
Indrapura	**90** D6
Indravati	**92** F5
Indre	**65** D5
Indre Arna	**63** A6
Indura	**71** K2
Indus	**92** C4
Indus, Mouths of the	**92** C4
İnebolu	**76** E2
İnece	**76** B2
İnecik	**76** B2
İnegöl	**76** C2

In Ekker	**101** G4
Ineu	**73** F2
Infiernillo, Presa del	**130** J8
Ingatestone	**53** H3
Ingersoll	**125** K5
Inggen	**87** J3
Ingham *Australia*	**113** K2
Ingham *U.K.*	**53** H2
Ingida	**84** Aa3
Ingleborough	**55** G2
Inglefield Land	**120** M2
Ingleton	**55** G2
Inglewood	**115** E3
Ingoda	**85** J6
Ingoldmells	**55** K3
Ingólfshöfði	**62** W13
Ingolstadt	**70** D4
Ingrãj Bazar	**93** G3
Ingul	**79** E6
Ingulets	**79** E6
Inguri	**77** J1
Inhambane	**109** G4
Inhambupe	**137** K6
Inharrime	**109** G4
Inhassôro	**109** G4
Inhumas	**138** G3
Inini	**137** G3
Inírida	**136** D3
Inishark	**58** B5
Inishbofin *Donegal, Ireland*	**58** F2
Inishbofin *Galway, Ireland*	**58** B5
Inishcrone	**58** D4
Inisheer	**59** C6
Inishkea North	**58** B4
Inishkea South	**58** B4
Inishmaan	**59** C6
Inishmore	**59** C6
Inishmurry	**58** E4
Inishnabro	**59** A8
Inishowen Head	**58** J2
Inishowen Peninsula	**58** H2
Inishtooskert	**59** A8
Inishtrahull	**58** H2
Inishturk	**58** B5
Inishvickillane	**59** A8
Inkberrow	**53** F2
Inkisi	**106** C4
Inle, Lake	**93** J4
Inndyr	**62** F3
Inner Hebrides	**57** B4
Innerleithen	**57** E5
Inner Mongolian Autonomous Region	**87** L3
Inner Sound	**56** C3
Innisfail	**113** K2
Innokent'evskiy	**88** H1
Innoko	**118** D3
Innsbruck	**68** C2
Inongo	**106** C3
Inowrocław	**71** H2
In Salah	**101** F3
Insein	**93** J5
Inskip	**55** G3
Insko	**70** F2
Insterburg	**63** J9
Instow	**52** C3
Insty	**78** G2
Inta	**78** L2
İntepe	**76** B2
Interlaken	**68** A2

Kaf

Kaffrine	104 B3	Kakogawa	89 E8	Kall	62 E5	Kamloops	122 D2
Kafírévs, Ákra	75 H3	Kaktovik	118 G1	Kallavesi	62 M5	Kamloops Lake	122 D2
Kafue *Zambia*	106 E6	Kalabagh	92 D2	Kalloni	75 J3	Kammenoye, Ozero	62 P4
Kafue *Zambia*	107 E6	Kalabahi	91 G7	Kallsjön	62 E5	Kamnik	72 C2
Kafue Dam	108 E3	Kalabáka	75 F3	Kalmar *Sweden*	63 G8	Kamo *Japan*	88 G6
Kaga Bandoro	102 C6	Kalabakan	91 F5	Kalmar *Sweden*	63 G8	Kamo *U.S.S.R.*	77 L2
Kağizman	77 K2	Kalabo	106 D6	Kalmarsund	63 G8	Kamp	68 E1
Kagmar	102 F5	Kalach	79 G5	Kalmykovo	79 J6	Kampala	107 F2
Kagoshima	89 C10	Kalachinsk	84 A5	Kalmytskaya A.S.S.R.	79 H6	Kampar	90 C5
Kagoshima-wan	89 C10	Kalach-Na-Donu	79 G6	Kalni	93 H4	Kampen	64 F2
Kagul	79 D6	Kaladar	125 M4	Kalomo	106 E6	Kamphaeng Phet	93 J5
Kahama	107 F3	Ka Lae	126 T11	Kalón	75 G2	Kampot	93 K6
Kahan	92 C3	Kalahari	108 D4	Kalpeni	92 D6	Kampuchea	93 K6
Kahayan	90 E6	Kalai-Khumb	86 C4	Kalpi	92 E3	Kamsack	123 P2
Kahnūj	95 N8	Kalajoki *Finland*	62 K4	Kalpin	86 D3	Kamskiy	78 J3
Kahoku	89 H6	Kalajoki *Finland*	62 L5	Kal-Shūr, Rūd-e	95 P3	Kamskoye Vodokhranilishche	78 K4
Kahoolawe	126 S10	Kalakan	85 K5	Kaluga	78 F5	Kāmyārān	94 H4
Kahramanmaraş	77 G4	Kalámai	75 G4	Kaluku	91 F6	Kamyshin	79 H5
Kâhta	77 H4	Kalamáta	75 G4	Kalush	79 C6	Kamzar	97 N3
Kahuku	126 R10	Kalamazoo *U.S.A.*	124 H5	Kalutara	92 E7	Kan	84 E5
Kahurak	95 P7	Kalamazoo *U.S.A.*	124 H5	Kalvarija	71 K1	Kana	84 H4
Kahurangi Point	115 D4	Kalao	91 G7	Kal'ya	78 K3	Kanab	126 F2
Kaiama	105 F4	Kalaotoa	91 G7	Kalyan	92 D5	Kanab Creek	126 F2
Kaiapoi	115 D5	Kalapana	126 T11	Kalyazin	78 F4	Kanab Plateau	126 F2
Kaibab Plateau	126 F2	Kalar	85 K5	Kama	84 Ad4	Kanaga Island	118 Ac9
Kai Besar	114 A3	Kalarash	73 K2	Kamaishi	88 H6	Kanairiktok	121 P7
Kaifeng	93 M2	Kälarne	62 G5	Kamalia	92 D2	Kananda	84 G4
Kaihu	115 D1	Kalat	92 C3	Kaman	76 E3	Kananga	106 D4
Kai Kecil	114 A3	Kalaupapa	126 S10	Kamarān	96 F9	Kanash	78 H4
Kai, Kepulauan	91 J7	Kalavardha	75 J4	Kamaria Falls	136 F2	Kanastraíon, Ákra	75 G3
Kaikohe	115 D1	Kalávrita	75 G3	Kamativi	108 E3	Kanawha	124 K7
Kaikoura	115 D5	Kalb, Ra's	97 J9	Kambalda	112 E5	Kanazawa	89 F7
Kaikoura Range	115 D5	Kalce	72 C3	Kambarka	78 J4	Kanchanaburi	93 J6
Kailahun	104 C4	Kaldakvísl	62 V12	Kambia	104 C4	Kanchenjunga	93 G3
Kailu	87 N3	Kaldungborg	63 D9	Kamchatka *U.S.S.R.*	85 T5	Kanchipuram	92 E6
Kailua *U.S.A.*	126 S10	Kale *Turkey*	76 C4	Kamchatka *U.S.S.R.*	85 S5	Kandahār	92 C2
Kailua *U.S.A.*	126 S11	Kale *Turkey*	76 C4	Kamchatka Oblast'	85 U5	Kandalaksha	62 Q3
Kaimana	91 J6	Kale *Turkey*	77 H2	Kamchiya	73 J4	Kandalakshskaya Guba	78 E2
Kaimanawa Mountains	115 F3	Kalecik	76 E2	Kamen'	63 N9	Kandang	90 B5
Kaimur Range	92 F4	Kalémié	107 E4	Kamenets Podol'skiy	73 J1	Kandangan	90 F6
Kainantu	114 D3	Kal-e-Shūr	95 P4	Kamen, Gora	84 F3	Kándanos	75 G5
Kainji Reservoir	105 F3	Kalety	71 H3	Kamenjak, Rt	72 B3	Kandat	84 D5
Kaipara Harbour	115 E2	Kalevala	62 P4	Kamenka *Kazakhstan S.S.R.,*		Kandi	105 F3
Kaiping	93 M4	Kalewa	93 H4	*U.S.S.R.*	79 J5	Kandira	76 D2
Kairouan	101 H1	Kaleybar	94 H2	Kamenka *Moldavia S.S.R.,*		Kandrian	114 D3
Kairuku	114 D3	Kálfafell	62 W13	*U.S.S.R.*	73 K1	Kandukur	92 E5
Kaiserslautern	70 B4	Kalgoorlie	112 E5	Kamenka *U.S.S.R.*	84 F5	Kandy	92 F7
Kaisiadorys	71 L1	Kaliakra, Nos	73 K4	Kamenka *U.S.S.R.*	79 G5	Kane	125 L6
Kaitaia	115 D1	Kalianda	90 D7	Kamenka *U.S.S.R.*	78 G2	Kane Basin	120 M2
Kaitangata	115 B7	Kalima	106 E3	Kamen Kashirskiy	79 D5	Kaneohe	126 S10
Kaiteur Falls	136 F3	Kalimantan	90 E5	Kamen'-na-Obi	84 C6	Kanevskaya	79 F6
Kaitumälven	62 J3	Kálimnos *Greece*	75 J4	Kamennyy, Mys	85 S1	Kangal	77 G3
Kaiwaka	115 E2	Kálimnos *Greece*	75 J4	Kamen Rybolov	88 C3	Kangalassy	85 M4
Kaiwi Channel	126 S10	Kalinin	78 F4	Kamensk-Shakhtinskiy	79 G6	Kangan	95 L8
Kaiyuan *Liaoning, China*	87 N3	Kalininabad	86 B4	Kamensk-Ural'skiy	84 Ad5	Kangar	90 C4
Kaiyuan *Yunnan, China*	93 K4	Kaliningrad	71 J1	Kamenyuki	71 K2	Kangaroo Island	113 H6
Kaiyuh Mountains	118 D3	Kalinino	78 K4	Kamenz	70 F3	Kangāvar	94 H4
Kajaani	62 M4	Kalininsk	79 G5	Kames	57 C5	Kangaz	73 K2
Kajo Kaji	102 F7	Kalinkovichi	79 D5	Kameshkovo	78 G4	Kangding	93 K2
Kaka	103 F5	Kalinovka	79 D6	Kamienna Góra	70 F3	Kangean	90 F7
Kakabeka Falls	124 F2	Kalis	103 J6	Kamién Pombrski	70 F2	Kangerdtuk	120 R3
Kakamari	107 F2	Kali Sindh	92 E4	Kamieńsk	71 H3	Kanggye	87 P3
Kakamas	108 D5	Kalispell	122 G3	Kamilukuak Lake	119 Q3	Kangiqsualujjuaq	121 N6
Kakamega	107 F2	Kalisz *Poland*	70 F2	Kamina	106 E4	Kangiqsujuaq	121 M5
Kakapotahi	115 C5	Kalisz *Poland*	71 H3	Kaminak Lake	119 R3	Kangirsuk	121 N5
Kake	89 D8	Kaliua	107 F4	Kaminuriak Lake	119 R3	Kangnŭng	89 B7
Kakhovskoye Vodokhranilishche	79 E6	Kalix	62 K4	Kamishak Bay	118 E4	Kangping	87 N3
Kākī	95 K7	Kalixälven	62 K3	Kamişli	76 F4	Kangri Karpo Pass	93 J3
Kākināda	92 F5	Kalkan	76 C4	Kamkaly	86 C3	Kani	93 H4
Kakisa Lake	119 M3	Kalkandere	77 J2	Kamla	93 G3	Kaniama	106 D4

Kanibadam	86	B3
Kaniet Islands	114	D2
Kanigigsualujak	121	L7
Kanin Nos	78	G2
Kanin Nos, Mys	78	G2
Kanin, Poluostrov	78	G2
Kanjiža	72	F2
Kankaanpää	63	K6
Kankakee	124	G6
Kankan	104	D3
Kanker	92	F4
Kanmaw Kyun	93	J6
Kannapolis	129	M3
Kannonkoski	62	L5
Kannoura	89	E9
Kannus	62	N4
Kano	105	G3
Kanoya	89	C10
Kanpur	92	F3
Kansas	123	P8
Kansas City *Kansas, U.S.A.*	124	C7
Kansas City *Missouri, U.S.A.*	124	C7
Kansk	84	F5
Kansŏng	88	B6
Kant	86	D3
Kantemirovka	79	F6
Kānthi	93	G4
Kanton Island	111	U2
Kanturk	59	E8
Kanuku Mountains	136	F3
Kanye	108	E5
Kao	111	T5
Kao-hsiung	87	N7
Kaokoveld	108	B3
Kaolack	104	B3
Kaoma	106	D5
Kapanga	106	D4
Kapchagayskoye Vodokhranilishche	86	D3
Kapellskär	63	H7
Kapidaği Yarimadasi	76	B2
Kapiri Mposhi	107	E5
Kapit	90	E5
Kapiti Island	115	E4
Kapiting	137	F3
Kaplan	128	F5
Kaplice	70	F4
Kapoeta	103	F7
Kaposvár	72	D2
Kapsan	88	B5
Kapsukas	71	K1
Kaptanpaşa	77	J2
Kapuae	90	E6
Kapuas	90	D6
Kapuas Hulu, Pegunungan	90	E5
Kapudzhukh	94	H2
Kapuskasing *Canada*	124	J2
Kapuskasing *Canada*	124	J2
Kapustin Yar	79	H6
Kara *Togo*	104	F4
Kara *Turkey*	77	J3
Kara *U.S.S.R.*	84	Ae3
Kara Balta	86	C3
Karabas *U.S.S.R.*	86	C2
Karabas *U.S.S.R.*	86	D2
Karabekaul	95	S2
Karabiga	76	B2
Kara-Bogaz-Gol	79	J7
Kara-Bogaz-Gol, Proliv	79	J2
Kara-Bogaz-Gol, Zaliv	79	J2

Karabük	76	E2
Karabulak *China*	86	D3
Karabulak *U.S.S.R.*	86	E2
Karaburun	76	B3
Karacabey	76	C2
Karacadağ	77	H4
Karacaköy	76	C2
Karacali Daği	77	H4
Karacasu	76	C4
Karaçay	77	G4
Karachev	79	E5
Karacheyevsk	79	G7
Karachi	92	C4
Karad	92	D5
Karadeniz Boğazi	76	C2
Karadilli	76	D3
Karagach	84	A5
Karaganda	86	C2
Karagayly	86	D2
Karagel	95	L2
Karaginskiy, Ostrov	85	U5
Karagiye, Vpadina	79	J7
Karahalli	76	C3
Karaidel'	78	K4
Kāraikāl	92	E6
Karaikkudi	92	E6
Karaisali	76	F4
Karaj	95	K4
Karak	94	B6
Kara Kala	95	N2
Karakax He	92	E1
Karakeçili	76	E3
Karakelong	91	H5
Karakoçan	77	J3
Karakoram	92	E1
Karakuduk	84	B6
Karakul'	86	C4
Kara Kul'	86	C3
Kara-Kul', Ozero	86	C4
Karakumskiy Kanal	95	R3
Karakurt	77	K2
Karaman	76	E4
Karamay	86	E2
Karamea	115	D4
Karamea Bight	115	C4
Karamürsel	76	C2
Karand	94	H4
Karanja	92	E4
Karanlik	76	F3
Karanlik Burun	76	B3
Karapelit	73	J4
Karapinar	76	E4
Karasburg	108	C5
Kara Sea	84	A2
Karashoky	84	A6
Karasjok	62	L2
Karasu *Turkey*	76	D2
Karasu *U.S.S.R.*	84	A6
Karasu *U.S.S.R.*	86	E2
Karasuk	84	B6
Karatal	86	D2
Karataş	76	F4
Kara Tau	86	C3
Karatau, Khrebet *U.S.S.R.*	86	B3
Karatau, Khrebet *U.S.S.R.*	79	J7
Karatobe	79	J6
Karaton	79	J6
Karatsu	89	B9
Karaudanawa	136	F3
Karauli	92	E3

Karaulkel'dy	79	K6
Karavas	75	G4
Karawang	90	D7
Karayazi	77	K3
Karbalā'	94	G5
Kårböle	63	F6
Karcag	73	F2
Kardhámila	75	J3
Kardhitsa	75	F3
Kärdla	63	K7
Karesuando	62	K2
Kargasok	84	C5
Kargat	84	C5
Kargi *Turkey*	76	D4
Kargi *Turkey*	76	F2
Kargopol'	78	F3
Kariba	108	E3
Kariba, Lake	108	E3
Karibib	108	C4
Kaributo	88	H4
Karigasniemi	62	L2
Karikari, Cape	115	D1
Karima	103	F4
Karimata, Kepulauan	90	D6
Karimata, Selat	90	D6
Karimganj	93	H4
Karimnagar	92	E5
Karimunjawa, Kepulauan	90	E7
Karin	103	J5
Káristos	75	H3
Kārīz	95	Q4
Karkaralinsk	86	D2
Karkaralong, Kepulauan	91	H5
Karkar Island	114	D2
Karkas, Kūh-e	95	L5
Karkkila	63	L6
Karlino	70	F1
Karliova	77	J3
Karl-Marx-Stadt	70	E3
Karlobag	72	C3
Karlovac	72	C3
Karlovo	73	H4
Karlovy Vary	70	E3
Karlsborg	63	F7
Karlskoga	63	F7
Karlskrona	63	F8
Karlsruhe	70	C4
Karlstad *Sweden*	63	E7
Karlstad *U.S.A.*	124	B2
Karlstadt	70	C4
Karmanovka	79	J6
Karmøy	63	A7
Karnafuli Reservoir	93	H4
Karnal	92	E3
Karnali	92	F3
Karnataka	92	E6
Karnobat	73	J4
Karonie	112	E5
Karora	103	G4
Karossa, Tanjung	91	F7
Karousàdhes	74	E3
Karoy	86	D2
Kárpathos *Greece*	75	J5
Kárpathos *Greece*	75	J5
Kárpathos Straits	75	J5
Kárpathou, Stenón	75	J5
Karpenision	75	F3
Karpinsk	84	Ad5
Karpogory	78	G3
Karratha	112	D3

Karrats Fjord	120	R3
Karree Berge	108	D6
Kars *Turkey*	77	K2
Kars *Turkey*	77	K2
Karsakpay	86	B2
Kärsämäki	62	L5
Karsanti	76	F4
Karshi *Kazakhstan S.S.R., U.S.S.R.*	79	J7
Karshi *Uzbekistan S.S.R., U.S.S.R.*	80	H6
Karşiyaka	76	B3
Karskoye More	84	A2
Karsun	78	H5
Kartal	76	C2
Kartayel'	78	J3
Kartuni	133	T11
Kartuzy	71	H1
Karufa	91	J6
Kārūn	94	J6
Karviná	71	H4
Karwar	92	D6
Karym	84	Ae4
Karymskoye	85	J6
Kaş	76	C4
Kasai	106	C3
Kasaji	106	D5
Kasama	107	F5
Kasane	108	E3
Kasanga	107	F4
Kasangulu	106	C3
Kasaragod	92	D6
Kasar, Râs	96	D7
Kasba Lake	119	Q3
Kasba Tadla	100	D2
Kasempa	106	E5
Kasese	107	F2
Kashaf	95	Q3
Kāshān	95	K5
Kashary	79	G6
Kashgar	86	D4
Kashi	86	D4
Kashima	89	C9
Kashin	78	F4
Kashipur	92	E3
Kashira	78	F5
Kashiwazaki	89	G7
Kashkanteniz	86	C2
Kashkarantsy	78	F2
Kāshmar	95	P4
Kasimov	78	G5
Kasin	92	D2
Kasiruta	91	H6
Kaskinen	62	J5
Kaskö	62	J5
Kas Kong	93	K6
Kasli	84	Ad5
Kasmere Lake	119	Q4
Kasongo	106	E3
Kasongo-Lunda	106	C4
Kásos	75	J5
Kásos, Stenón	75	J5
Kaspiyskiy	79	H6
Kassala	103	G4
Kassándra	75	G2
Kassel	70	C3
Kasserine	101	G1
Kastamonu	76	E2
Kastanéai	75	J2
Kastélli	75	G5

Name	Page	Grid	Name	Page	Grid	Name	Page	Grid	Name	Page	Grid
Kitchener	125	K5	Kłodzko *Poland*	71	G3	Kodiak	118	E4	Koloubara	72	F3
Kitee	62	P5	Klos	75	F2	Kodiak Island	118	E4	Kolozsvar	73	G2
Kitgum	107	F2	Klosterneuberg	68	F1	Kodima	78	G3	Kolpashevo	84	C5
Kithira *Greece*	75	G4	Klosters	68	B2	Kodinar	92	D4	Kolpino	78	E4
Kithira *Greece*	75	G4	Klrovskiy	79	H6	Kodok	103	F6	Kol'skiy Poluostrov	78	F2
Kithnos *Greece*	75	H4	Kluane	118	H3	Kodomari	88	H5	Koltubanovskiy	79	J5
Kithnos *Greece*	75	H4	Kluane Lake	118	H3	Kodyma	73	L2	Koluszki	71	H3
Kitikmeot	119	N1	Kluczbork	71	H3	Kofçaz	76	B2	Kolva *U.S.S.R.*	78	K3
Kitimat	118	K5	Klyevka	84	A6	Koffiefontein	108	D5	Kolva *U.S.S.R.*	78	K2
Kitinen	62	M3	Klyuchevskaya Sopka	85	U5	Köflach	68	E2	Kolwezi	106	E5
Kitkiöjoki	62	K3	Klyuchi	85	U5	Koforidua	104	E4	Kolyma	85	U3
Kitsuki	89	C9	Klyukvinka	84	D5	Kōfu	89	G8	Kolymskaya Nizmennost'	85	T3
Kittanning	125	L6	Kmagta	114	J6	Køge	63	E9	Kolymskiy, Khrebet	85	T4
Kittilä	62	L3	Kmanjab	108	B3	Kogilnik	73	K2	Komadugu Gana	105	H3
Kitui	107	G3	K2, Mount	92	E1	Ko, Gora	88	F2	Komandorskiye Ostrova	81	T4
Kitunda	107	F4	Knapdale	57	C5	Kohat	92	D2	Komárno	71	H5
Kitwe	107	E5	Knaresborough	55	H2	Kohima	93	H3	Komárom	72	E2
Kitzbühel	68	D2	Knife	123	N4	Koh-i Qaisar	95	S5	Komatsu	89	F7
Kitzbüheler Alpen	68	D2	Knight Island	118	F3	Kohtla-Järve	63	M7	Komering	90	C6
Kitzingen	70	D4	Knighton	52	D2	Koide	89	G7	Komi A.S.S.R.	78	J3
Kivalo	62	L3	Knin	72	D3	Koi Sanjaq	94	G3	Kommunarsk	79	F6
Kivijärvi	62	L5	Knjaževac	73	G4	Koitere	62	P5	Komodo	91	F7
Kivu, Lake	107	E3	Knockadoon Head	59	G9	Koivu	62	L3	Komoé	104	E4
Kiyev	79	E5	Knockalla Mount	58	G2	Kōje	89	B8	Kom Ombo	103	F3
Kiyevka	88	D4	Knockanaffrin	59	G8	Kojonup	112	D5	Komoran	91	K7
Kiyevskoye Vodokhranilishche	79	E5	Knockaunapeebra	59	G8	Kokand	86	B3	Komosomolets, Ostrov	81	L1
Kiyiköy	76	C2	Knocklayd	58	K2	Kokas	91	J6	Komotiní	75	H2
Kizel	78	K4	Knockmealdown Mountains	59	G8	Kokchetav	84	Ae6	Komovi	74	E1
Kizema	78	H3	Knocknaskagh	59	F8	Kokemäenjoki	63	K6	Kompong Cham	93	L6
Kizilağac	77	J3	Knottingley	55	H3	Kokenau	91	K6	Kompong Chhnang	93	K6
Kizilcabölük	76	C4	Knox, Cape	118	J5	Kokkola	62	K5	Kompong Som	93	K6
Kizilcadağ	76	C4	Knoxville *Iowa, U.S.A.*	124	D6	Koko	105	G4	Kompong Speu	93	K6
Kizilhisar	76	C4	Knoxville *Tennessee, U.S.A.*	129	L3	Kokoda	114	D3	Kompong Sralao	93	L6
Kizilirmak	76	E2	Knoydart	57	C3	Kokomo	124	G6	Kompong Thom	93	K6
Kizil Irmak	77	F2	Knud Rasmussen Land	120	P2	Kokpekty	86	E2	Komrat	79	D6
Kizilkaya	76	D4	Knutholstind	63	C6	Koksoak	121	N6	Komsomolets, Zaliv	79	J6
Kizilören	76	E4	Knutsford	55	G3	Kokstad	108	E6	Komsomol'sk	79	E6
Kiziltepe	77	J4	Knyazhaya Guba	62	Q3	Koktas	86	C2	Komsomol'skiy	79	J6
Kizlyar	79	H7	Knyazhevo	78	G4	Kokubu	89	C10	Komsomol'sk-na-Amure	85	P6
Kizyl-Arvat	95	N2	Knysna	108	D6	Kokuora	85	R2	Konakovo	78	F4
Kizyl-Atrek	95	M3	Knyszyn	71	K2	Kokura	89	C9	Končanica	72	D3
Kizyl Ayak	95	S3	Koba	90	D6	Kokuy	85	K6	Konch	92	E3
Kizyl-Su	95	L2	Kobarid	72	B2	Kok-Yangak	86	C3	Konda *Indonesia*	91	J6
Kjøllefjord	62	M1	Kobayashi	89	C10	Kola	62	Q2	Konda *U.S.S.R.*	84	Ae4
Kjøpsvick	62	L2	Kobberminebugt	120	R5	Kolaka	91	G6	Kondagaon	92	F5
Kladanj	72	E3	Kobelyaki	79	E6	Kolar	92	E6	Kondinin	112	D5
Kladno	70	F3	København	63	E9	Kolari	62	K3	Kondinskoye	84	Ae5
Kladovo	73	G3	Koblenz	70	B3	Kolarovgrad	73	J4	Kondoa	107	G3
Klagenfurt	68	E2	Kobowre, Pegunungan	91	K6	Kolašin	72	E4	Kondon	85	P6
Klaipėda	63	L9	Kobrin	71	L2	Kolay	77	F2	Kondoponga	78	E3
Klamath *U.S.A.*	122	B7	Kobroor	91	J7	Kolberg	70	F1	Kondūz	92	C1
Klamath *U.S.A.*	122	C7	Kobuk	118	D2	Kolbuszowa	71	J3	Koné	114	W16
Klamath Falls	122	D6	Kobuleti	77	J2	Kol'chugino	78	F4	Konevo	78	F3
Klamath Mountains	122	C6	Kobya	85	M4	Kolda	104	C3	Kong	104	E4
Klamono	91	J6	Koca *Turkey*	76	B3	Kolding	63	C9	Kongan	89	J10
Klarälven	63	J6	Koca *Turkey*	76	C3	Kole	106	D3	Kong Christian den X Land	120	W3
Klatovy	70	E4	Koca *Turkey*	76	E2	Kolguyev, Ostrov	78	H2	Kong Karls Land	80	D2
Klekovača	72	D3	Kocapinar	77	K3	Kolhapur	92	D5	Kongolo	106	E4
Klenak	72	E3	Koçarli	76	B4	Kolín	70	F3	Kongsberg	63	C7
Klerksdorp	108	E5	Koceljevo	72	E3	Kolki	71	L3	Kongsvinger	63	E6
Klichka	85	K7	Koch Bihār	93	G3	Kolkuskull	62	V12	Kong Wilhelms Land	120	X2
Klimovichi	79	E5	Kochechum	84	G3	Kóllabuður	62	T12	Koniecpol	71	H3
Klin	78	F4	Kochegarovo	85	K5	Köln	70	B3	Königsberg	71	J4
Klínovec	70	E3	Kocher	70	C4	Kolno	71	J2	Königs Wusterhausen	70	E2
Klintsovka	79	H5	Kōchi	89	D9	Koloa	126	R10	Konin	71	H2
Klintsy	79	E5	Koch Island	120	L4	Kołobrzeg	70	F1	Kónitsa	75	F2
Klisura	73	H4	Kochkorka	86	D3	Kologriv	78	G4	Koniya	89	B11
Ključ	72	D3	Koch Peak	122	J5	Kolombangara	114	H5	Könkämäälv	62	J2
Kłobuck	71	H3	Kochumdek	84	E4	Kolomna	78	F4	Konkouré	104	C3
Kłodzka *Poland*	71	G3	Kodeń	71	K3	Kolono	91	G6	Könnern	70	D3

Kon

Konnevesi	62	M5
Konosha	78	G3
Konotop	79	E5
Konqi He	86	F3
Konskie	71	J3
Konstantinovka	79	F6
Konstantinovsk	79	G6
Konstanz	68	B2
Kontagora	105	G3
Kontcha	105	H4
Kontiomäki	62	N4
Kontum	93	L6
Kontum, Plateau du	93	L6
Konya	76	E4
Konya Ovasi	76	E3
Konzhakovskiy Kamen', Gora	78	K4
Kootenai	122	G3
Kootenay	122	F3
Kootenay Lake	122	F3
Kopaonik	73	F4
Kópasker	62	W11
Kópavogur	62	U12
Koper	72	B3
Kopervik	63	A7
Kopet Dag, Khrebet	95	N2
Kopeysk	84	Ad5
Köping	63	F7
Kopka	124	F1
Köpmanholmen	62	H5
Koppang	63	D6
Kopparberg *Sweden*	63	F7
Kopparberg *Sweden*	63	F6
Koppi *U.S.S.R.*	88	G1
Koppi *U.S.S.R.*	88	H1
Köprü	76	D4
Köprübaşi	76	C3
Köprülü	76	E4
Köprüören	76	C3
Kopychintsy	73	H1
Kor	95	L6
Kora	77	K2
Korab	72	F5
K'orahē	103	H6
Koraluk	121	P6
Korana	72	C3
Korba	69	C7
Korbach	70	C3
Korbu, Gunung	90	C5
Korcë	75	F2
Korčula	72	D4
Korda	84	F4
Kord Küv	95	M3
Korea Bay	87	N4
Korea, North	87	P4
Korea, South	87	P4
Korea Strait	89	B8
Korennoye	84	H2
Korenovsk	79	F6
Korf	85	V4
Korforskiy	88	E1
Korgan	77	G2
Korgen	62	E3
Korhogo	104	D4
Korido	91	K6
Korim	91	K6
Korinthiakós Kólpos	75	G3
Kórinthos	75	G4
Kōriyama	89	H7
Korkinitskiy Zaliv	79	E6
Korkodon	85	T4
Korkuteli	76	D4
Korla	86	F3
Kormakíti, Akra	76	E5
Kornat	72	C4
Koro	114	R8
Korocha	79	F5
Köroğlu Dağlari	76	E2
Korónia, Límni	75	G2
Koronowo	71	G2
Körös	72	F2
Korosten'	79	D5
Korostyshev	79	D5
Korotaikha	78	L2
Korovin Volcano	118	Ad9
Korpilombolo	62	K3
Korsakov	88	J2
Korsnäs	62	J5
Korsør	63	D9
Korti	103	F4
Kortrijk	64	E3
Korucu	76	B3
Koryakskaya Sopka	85	U6
Koryanskiy Khrebet	85	Z5
Koryazhma	78	H3
Korzybie	71	G1
Kos *Greece*	75	J4
Kos *Greece*	75	J4
Koschagyl	79	J6
Kościan	71	G2
Koscierzyna	71	G1
Kosciusco, Mount	113	K6
Kosciusko	128	H4
Köse	77	H2
Kos Gölü	76	B2
Koshiki-rettō	89	B10
Košice	71	J4
Koski	63	K6
Koslan	78	H3
Köslin	71	G1
Kosma	78	H2
Kosŏng	88	B6
Kosŏng-ni	88	B5
Kossou, Lac de	104	D4
Kossovo	71	L2
Kostajnica	72	D3
Kosti	103	F5
Kostino	84	D3
Kostomuksha	62	P4
Kostopol	71	M3
Kostroma *U.S.S.R.*	78	G4
Kostroma *U.S.S.R.*	78	G4
Kostrzyn	70	F2
Kosu-dong	89	B8
Kos'va	78	K4
Kos'yu	78	K2
Kos'yuvom	78	K2
Koszalin	71	G1
Kota	92	E3
Kotaagung	90	C7
Kota Baharu	90	C4
Kotabaru *Indonesia*	90	E6
Kotabaru *Indonesia*	90	F6
Kota Belud	90	F4
Kotabumi	90	C5
Kota Kinabalu	90	F4
Kotala	62	N3
Kotamubagu	91	G5
Kota Tinggi	90	C5
Kotel	73	J4
Kotel'nich	78	H4
Kotel'nikovo	79	G6
Kotel'nyy, Ostrov	85	P1
Kotikovo	88	E2
Kotka	63	M6
Kot Kapura	92	D2
Kotlas	78	H3
Kotli	92	D2
Kotlik	118	C3
Koto	85	P7
Kotor	72	E4
Kotovo	79	G5
Kotovsk *Rossiyskaya S.F.S.R., U.S.S.R.*	79	G5
Kotovsk *Ukraine S.S.R., U.S.S.R.*	79	D6
Kotri	92	C3
Kottagudem	92	F5
Kottayam	92	E7
Kotto	102	D6
Kotuy	84	G2
Kotyuzhany	73	K2
Kotzebue	118	C2
Kotzebue Sound	118	C2
Kouango	102	C6
Koudougou	104	E3
Koufonísi	75	J5
Koukajuak, Great Plain of the	120	M4
Kouki	102	C6
Koumac	114	W16
Koumenzi	86	F3
Koumra	102	C6
Koundara	104	C3
Koungou Mountains	106	B3
Kounradskiy	86	D2
Kourou	137	G2
Kouroussa	104	D3
Kousséri	105	J3
Koutiala	100	D6
Kouvola	63	M6
Kova	84	G5
Kovachevo	73	J4
Kovanlik	77	H2
Kovdor	62	P3
Kovdozero, Ozero	62	Q3
Kovel'	71	L3
Kovernino	78	G4
Kovero	62	P5
Kovik Bay	121	L5
Kovno	71	K1
Kovrov	78	G4
Kovylkino	78	G5
Kowalewo	71	H2
Kowloon	87	L7
Köyceğiz	76	C4
Koyda	78	G2
Koyuk	118	C3
Koyukuk	118	D3
Koyulhisar	77	G2
Koza	89	E9
Kozakli	76	F3
Kozan	77	F4
Kozáni	75	F2
Kozekovo	71	M1
Kozel'sk	78	F5
Kozhevnikovo	84	B5
Kozhikode	92	E6
Kozhim	78	K2
Kozhposelok	78	F3
Kozhva	78	K2
Kozlu	76	D2
Kozludere	77	G4
Kozluk	77	J3
Koz'modem'yansk	78	H4
Kōzu-shima	89	G8
Kpalimé	104	F4
Krabi	93	J7
Kragerø	63	C7
Kragujevac	73	F3
Kraków	71	H3
Krakowska, Jura	71	H3
Král Chlmec	71	K4
Kralendijk	133	N8
Kraljevo	72	F4
Kral'ovvany	71	H4
Kralupy	70	F3
Kramatorsk	79	F6
Kramfors	62	G5
Kraniá	75	F3
Kranídhion	75	G4
Kranj	72	C2
Kranskop	108	F5
Krasavino	78	H3
Krasino	84	Ab2
Kraskino	88	C4
Krasneno	85	X4
Krasnoarmeysk	84	Ae6
Krasnoarmeyskiy	85	W3
Krasnoborsk	78	H3
Krasnodar	79	F6
Krasnogorsk	88	J1
Krasnograd	79	F6
Krasnokamsk	78	K4
Krasnokutskoye	84	B6
Krasnolesnyy	79	F5
Krasnorechenskiy	88	E3
Krasnosel'kup	84	C3
Krasnoslobodsk	78	G5
Krasnotur'insk	84	Ad5
Krasnoufimsk	78	K4
Krasnousol'skiy	78	K5
Krasnovishersk	78	K3
Krasnovodsk	95	L2
Krasnovodskiy Poluostrov	79	J7
Krasnoyarsk	84	E5
Krasnoyarskiy Kray	84	E3
Krasnoye	78	G4
Krasnstaw	71	K3
Krasnyy Chikoy	84	H6
Krasnyye Okny	73	K2
Krasnyy Kholm	79	J5
Krasnyy Kut	79	H5
Krasnyy Luch	79	F6
Krasnyy Yar *U.S.S.R.*	79	G5
Krasnyy Yar *U.S.S.R.*	79	H6
Kratie	93	L6
Kraulshavn	120	Q3
Kravânh, Chuŏr Phnum	93	K6
Krefeld	70	B3
Kremenchug	79	E6
Kremenchugskoye Vodokhranilishche	79	E6
Kremnets	79	D5
Krems	68	E1
Krenitzin Islands	118	Ae9
Kreševo	72	E4
Kresttsy	78	E4
Kresty	84	D2
Krestyakh	85	K4
Krest'yanka	84	C2
Kretinga	63	J9

Kuybyshevskoye		
Vodokhranilishche	78	H4
Kuyeda	78	K4
Kuygan	86	C2
Kuytun	86	F3
Kuyucak	76	C4
Kuyumba	84	F4
Kuyus	84	D6
Kuzino	78	K4
Kuzitrin	118	C2
Kuz'movka	84	E4
Kuznetsk	79	H5
Kuznetsovo	88	G2
Kuzomen	78	F2
Kuzucubelen	76	F4
Kvaløy	62	H2
Kvaløya	62	K1
Kvalsund	62	L1
Kvarner	72	C3
Kvarnerić	72	C3
Kvichak Bay	118	D4
Kvidinge	63	E8
Kvigtind	62	E4
Kvikkjokk	62	G3
Kvina	63	B7
Kvorning	63	C8
Kwa	106	C3
Kwale	105	G4
Kwamouth	106	C3
Kwangju	87	P4
Kwango	106	C3
Kwansŏ-ri	88	B5
Kwatisore	91	J6
Kwekwe	108	E3
Kwidzyn	71	H2
Kwilu	106	C3
Kwoka	91	J6
Kyabé	102	C6
Kyaikto	93	J5
Kyakhta	84	H6
Kyaukpyu	93	H5
Kyaukse	93	J4
Kybartai	71	K1
Kychema	78	G2
Kyeburn	115	C6
Kyelang	92	E2
Kyle	57	D5
Kyleakin	56	C3
Kyle of Lochalsh	56	C3
Kylestrome	56	C2
Kymi	63	M6
Kymijoki	63	M6
Kynuna	113	J3
Kyoga, Lake	107	F2
Kyŏngju	89	B8
Kyōto	89	E8
Kyrdanyy	85	M3
Kyritz	70	E2
Kyrkheden	63	E6
Kyronjoki	62	K5
Kyrösjärvi	63	K6
Kyrta	78	K3
Kyssa	78	H3
Kystyk, Plato	85	L2
Kyuekh-Bulung	84	J3
Kyurdamir	79	H7
Kyūshū	89	C9
Kyūshū-sanchi	89	C9
Kyustendil	73	G4
Kyyjärvi	62	L5

Kyyvesi	63	M6
Kyzyk	79	J7
Kyzyl	84	E6
Kyzyldyykan	86	B2
Kyzylkoga	79	J6
Kyzyl-Kommuna	86	B2
Kyzylkum	80	H5
Kzyl-Dzhar	86	B2
Kzyl-Orda	86	B3
Kzyltu	84	A6
La Almunia de Doña Godina	67	F2
Laascaanood	103	J6
Laas Dhuure	103	J5
La Asunción	136	E1
Laâyoune	100	C3
La Baie	125	Q2
La Banda	138	D5
La Bañeza	66	D1
La Barca	130	H7
Labasa	114	R8
La Baule	65	B5
Labaz, Ozero	84	F2
Labbah, Al	96	E2
Labé	104	C3
Labe	70	F3
Labelle	125	N3
Laberge, Lake	118	H3
Labi	90	E5
Labin	72	C3
Labinsk	79	G7
Labis	90	C5
La Bisbal	67	H2
Labouheyre	65	C6
Laboulaye	139	D6
La Bourboule	65	E6
Labrador	121	P7
Labrador City	121	N7
Labrador Sea	121	Q6
Lábrea	136	E5
Labrit	65	C6
Labuha	91	H6
Labuhan	90	D7
Labuhanbajo	91	F7
Labuhanbilik	90	C5
Labytnangi	84	Ae3
Laç	74	E2
La Calzada de Calatrava	66	E3
Lacanau	65	C6
La Carlota	139	D6
La Carolina	66	E3
La Cava	67	G2
Laccadive Islands	92	D6
Laccadive Sea	92	E7
La Ceiba	132	D7
Lacepede Bay	113	H6
La Chaise-Dieu	65	E6
Lacha, Ozero	78	F3
La Charité	65	E5
La Chartre-sur-le-Loir	65	D5
La Châtre	65	D5
La Chaux-de-Fonds	68	A2
Lachin	94	H2
Lachlan	113	K5
La Chorrera	132	H10
Lachute	125	N4
La Cieneguita	126	G6
La Ciotat	65	F7
Lac la Biche	119	N5

Lac Mégantic	125	Q4
La Colorada	126	G6
Laconi	69	B6
Laconia	125	Q5
La Coruña	66	B1
La Croix, Lac	124	D2
La Crosse	124	E5
La Cruz *Costa Rica*	132	E9
La Cruz *Mexico*	130	F6
Lacul Razelm	73	K3
Ladakh Range	92	E2
Ladder Hills	56	E3
La Désirade	133	S6
Ladik	77	F2
Ladismith	108	D6
Lādīz	95	Q7
Ladozhskoye Ozero	63	P6
Ladybank	57	E4
Ladybower Reservoir	55	H3
Ladybrand	108	E5
Ladysmith *Canada*	122	C3
Ladysmith *South Africa*	108	E5
Ladysmith *U.S.A.*	124	E4
Ladyzhenka	84	Ae6
Ladyzhinka	79	D6
Lae	93	K5
Laem Ngop	93	K6
La Esmeralda *Paraguay*	138	D4
La Esmeralda *Venezuela*	136	D3
La Fayette	129	K3
Lafayette *Colorado, U.S.A.*	123	M8
Lafayette *Indiana, U.S.A.*	124	G6
Lafayette *Louisiana, U.S.A.*	128	F5
La Fé	132	E3
La Ferté-Bernard	64	D4
La-Ferté-Saint-Aubin	65	D5
Laffān, Ra's	97	K4
Lafia	105	G4
Lafiagi	105	G4
La Flèche	65	C5
La Follette	129	K2
La Fria	136	C2
Laft	95	M8
La Fuente de San Esteban	66	C2
La Galite	69	B7
Lagan	63	E8
Lagarfljót	62	X12
Lågen *Norway*	63	C6
Lågen *Norway*	63	D6
Laggan	57	D3
Laggan Bay	57	B5
Laggan, Loch	57	D4
Laghouat	101	F2
Lagny	64	E4
Lagonegro	69	E5
Lago Posadas	139	B9
Lagos *Nigeria*	105	F4
Lagos *Portugal*	66	B4
Lagos de Moreno	130	J7
La Grande *Canada*	121	M7
La Grande *U.S.A.*	122	E5
La Grande 2, Réservoir	121	L7
La Grande 3, Réservoir	121	L7
La Grande 4, Réservoir	121	M7
La Grange *Georgia, U.S.A.*	129	K4
La Grange *Kentucky, U.S.A.*	124	H7
La Grange *Texas, U.S.A.*	128	D6
La Granja	66	D2
La Gran Sabana	136	E2
La Guardia	66	B2

Laguardia	66	E1
La Gudiña	66	C1
La Guerche-de-Bretagne	65	C5
Laguna	138	G5
Laguna Grande	139	C9
Lagunillas *Bolivia*	138	D3
Lagunillas *Venezuela*	133	M9
Laha	87	N2
La Habana	132	F3
Lahad Datu	91	F4
Lahave	121	P9
Laḥij	96	G10
Lāhījān	95	J3
Lahn *W. Germany*	70	C3
Lahn *W. Germany*	70	C3
Lahore	92	D2
Lahr	70	B4
Lahti	63	L6
Laibach	72	C2
Laibin	93	L4
Lai Chau	93	K4
L'Aigle	64	D4
Laihia	62	J5
Laimbélé, Mount	114	T12
Lainá	75	J2
Laingsburg	108	D6
Lainioälven	62	K3
Lair	56	C3
Lairg	56	D2
Lais	90	C6
Laitila	63	J6
Laiwui	91	H6
Laixi	87	N4
Laiyang	87	N4
Laiyuan	87	L4
Laizhou Wan	87	M4
Lajes	138	F5
La Junta	127	L2
Lakaträsk	62	J3
Lake Andes	123	Q6
Lakeba	114	S9
Lakeba Passage	114	S9
Lake Cargelligo	113	K5
Lake Charles	128	F5
Lake City *Florida, U.S.A.*	129	L5
Lake City *S. Carolina, U.S.A.*	129	N4
Lake District	55	F2
Lake Grace	112	D5
Lake Harbour	120	N5
Lake Havasu City	126	E3
Lake Jackson	128	E6
Lake King	112	D5
Lake Kopiago	114	C3
Lakeland	129	M6
Lake Louise	122	F2
Lake Murray	114	C3
Lakeport	122	C8
Lake Providence	128	G4
Lakeview	122	D6
Lake Wales	129	M7
Lakewood	124	K6
Lakhdaria	67	H4
Lakhpat	92	C4
Lakki	92	D2
Lakonikós Kólpos	75	G4
Laksefjorden	62	M1
Lakselv	62	L1
Lakshadweep	92	D6
Lakuramau	114	E2
Lala Musa	92	D2

Place	Map	Ref
La Unión *Colombia*	136	B3
La Unión *El Salvador*	132	D8
La Unión *Mexico*	131	Q9
La Unión *Spain*	67	F4
Laupheim	70	C4
Laura	113	J2
La Urbana	133	P11
Laurel *Mississippi, U.S.A.*	128	H5
Laurel *Montana, U.S.A.*	123	K5
Laurencekirk	57	F4
Laurentian Scarp	125	M3
Laurentien, Plateau	121	M7
Laurenzana	69	E5
Lauria	69	E5
Laurinburg	129	N3
Lausanne	68	A2
Laut	90	F6
Lautaro	139	B7
Laut Kecil, Kepulauan	90	F6
Lautoka	114	Q8
Laval *Canada*	125	P4
Laval *France*	65	C4
Lāvān	95	L8
Lavapié, Punta	139	B7
La Vecilla	66	D1
La Vega	133	M5
La Venturosa	136	D2
Lavernock Point	52	D3
Laverton	112	E4
Lavina	123	K4
Lavon, Lake	128	D4
Lavras	138	H4
Lawas	90	F5
Lawdar	96	G10
Lawksawk	93	J4
Lawqah	96	F2
Lawra	104	E3
Lawrence *New Zealand*	115	B6
Lawrence *Kansas, U.S.A.*	124	C7
Lawrence *Massachusetts, U.S.A.*	125	Q5
Lawrenceburg	129	J3
Lawrenceville	124	G7
Lawton	128	C3
Lawu, Gunung	90	E7
Lawz, Jambal Al	96	B2
Laxay	56	B2
Laxford, Loch	56	C2
Laxo	56	A1
Lay	65	C5
Layar, Tanjung	90	F6
Laylá	96	H5
Laysār	94	J3
Lazarevac	72	F3
Lazarev Sea	141	A5
Lázaro Cárdenas	130	H8
Lázaro Cárdenas, Presa	127	K8
Lazdijai	71	K1
Lazo	88	D4
Lead	123	N5
Leadburn	57	E5
Leaden Roding	53	H3
Leader	123	K2
Leader Water	57	F5
Leaf	121	M6
Leaf Bay	121	N6
Leane, Lough	59	C8
Leatherhead	53	G3
Leavenworth *Kansas, U.S.A.*	124	C7
Leavenworth *Washington, U.S.A.*	122	D4
Łeba	71	G1
Lebak	91	G4
Lebane	73	F4
Lebanon	125	P5
Lebanon *Missouri, U.S.A.*	94	B4
Lebanon *Pennsylvania, U.S.A.*	129	J2
Lebanon *Tennessee, U.S.A.*	124	D8
Lebanon *Vermont, U.S.A.*	125	M6
Lebed'	84	D4
Lebedin	79	E5
Lebesby	62	M1
Le Blanc	65	D5
Lebombo Mountains	109	F4
Lębork	71	G1
Lebrija	66	C4
Łebsko, Jezioro	71	G1
Lebu	139	B7
Lebyazh'ye	84	B6
Le Cateau	64	E3
Lecce	69	G5
Lecco	68	B3
Lech *Austria*	68	C2
Lech *W. Germany*	70	D4
Lechang	93	M3
Lechlade	53	F3
Lechtaler Alpen	68	C2
Leconfield	55	J3
Le Conquet	64	A4
Le Creusot	65	F5
Le Croisic	65	B5
Lectoure	65	D7
Lecumberri	67	F1
Łęczna	71	K3
Łęczyca	71	H2
Ledbury	52	E2
Ledesma	66	D2
Lediba	106	C3
Ledmozero	62	Q4
Ledong	93	L5
Le Dorat	65	D5
Ledu	93	K1
Ledyanaya, Gora	85	W4
Lee	59	E9
Leech Lake	124	C3
Leeds	55	H3
Leedstown	52	B4
Leek	55	G3
Leemoore	126	C2
Leer	70	B2
Leesburg	129	M6
Leesville	128	F5
Leeuwarden	64	F2
Leeuwin, Cape	112	D5
Leeward Islands	133	R5
Le Faouët	65	B4
Lefroy, Lake	112	E5
Leganés	66	E2
Legaspi	91	G3
Legbourne	55	K3
Leghorn	68	C4
Legnago	68	C3
Legnica	71	G3
Leh	92	E2
Le Havre	64	D4
Leiah	92	D2
Leibnitz	68	E2
Leibo	93	K3
Leicester	53	F2
Leicestershire	53	F2
Leichhardt	113	H2
Leiden	64	F2
Leie	64	E3
Leigh *New Zealand*	115	E2
Leigh *U.K.*	55	G3
Leigh Creek	113	H5
Leighlinbridge	59	J7
Leighton Buzzard	53	G3
Leine	70	C3
Leinster	59	H6
Leinster, Mount	59	J7
Leipzig	70	E3
Leiria	66	B3
Leirvik	63	A7
Leisier, Mount	112	F3
Leiston	53	J2
Leitha	68	F2
Leitrim	58	F4
Leixlip	59	K6
Leiyang	93	M3
Lek	64	F3
Leksand	63	F6
Lekshmozero	78	F3
Leksozero, Ozero	62	P5
Leksvik	62	D5
Lelai, Tanjung	91	H5
Leland	62	E3
Le Lavandou	65	G7
Le Luc	65	G7
Leluova	114	M7
Lelysted	64	F2
Léman, Lac	68	A2
Le Mans	65	D4
Le Mars	124	B5
Lemberg	71	L4
Lemgo	70	C2
Lemmer	64	F2
Lemmon	123	N5
Lemnos	75	H3
Le Mont-Dore	65	E6
Lempa	132	C8
Lemreway	56	C2
Le Murge	69	F5
Lena	85	M2
Lénakel	114	U13
Lene, Lough	58	H5
Lengerich	70	B2
Lengshuijiang	93	M3
Lengua de Vaca, Punta	139	B6
Lenhovda	63	F8
Leninabad	86	B3
Leninakan	77	K2
Lenina, Pik	86	C4
Leningrad	63	N7
Leningradskaya	141	L5
Leninogorsk	78	J5
Leninskiy *Kazakhstan S.S.R., U.S.S.R.*	78	H4
Leninskiy *Rossiyskaya S.F.S.R., U.S.S.R.*	86	E2
Leninsk-Kuznetskiy	84	D6
Leninskoye *U.S.S.R.*	88	D2
Leninskoye *U.S.S.R.*	78	H4
Lenkoran'	94	J2
Lennox, Isla	139	C11
Lenoir	129	M3
Lens	64	E3
Lensk	85	J4
Lenti	72	D2
Lentini	69	E7
Lentura	62	N4
Leo	104	E3
Leoben	68	E2
Leominster	52	E2
León	130	J7
Leon	127	N5
León *Mexico*	132	D8
León *Nicaragua*	66	D1
Léon *Spain*	65	C7
Leonard Darwin, Gunung	91	K6
Leonforte	69	E7
Leonídhion	75	G4
Leon, Montanas de	66	C1
Leopoldina	138	H4
Leopoldo Bulhões	138	G3
Léopoldville	106	C3
Leovo	73	K2
Le Palais	65	B5
Lepaya	63	L8
Lepel'	63	N9
Lephepe	108	E4
Leping	87	M6
Lepini, Monti	69	D5
Lepontine, Alpi	68	B2
Lepsy	86	D2
Le Puy	65	E6
Lercara Friddi	69	D7
Léré	102	B6
L'Eree	53	M7
Lereh, Tanjung	91	F6
Lérida	67	G2
Lerma	66	E1
Lermontovka	88	E2
Léros	75	J4
Lerum	63	E8
Lerwick	56	A2
Leş	73	F2
Les Andelys	64	D4
Lesbos	75	J3
Les Cayes	133	L5
Les Ecrins	65	G6
Les Escoumins	125	R2
Leshan	93	K3
Leshukonskoye	78	H3
Lesjöfors	63	F7
Leskovac	73	F4
Lešnica	72	E3
Lesogorsk	85	Q7
Lesopil'noye	88	E2
Lesosibirsk	84	E5
Lesotho	108	E5
Lesozavodsk	88	D3
Lesparre-Médoc	65	C6
L'Esperance Rock	111	T8
Les Sables-d'Olonne	65	C5
Lesser Antarctica	141	T3
Lesser Antilles	133	Q6
Lesser Slave Lake	119	M4
Lesser Zab	94	F4
L'Estartit	67	H1
Lestijärvi	62	L5
Lésvos	75	J3
L'Etacq	53	M7
Letchworth	53	G3
Lethbridge	122	H3
Leticia	136	D4
Leti, Kepulauan	91	H7
Le Touquet-Paris-Plage	64	D3
Le Tréport	64	D3
Letsok-aw Kyun	93	J6

Name	Page	Grid
Letterfrack	59	C5
Letterkenny	58	G3
Lettermore	59	C6
Leuchars	57	F4
Leuser, Gunung	90	B5
Leuven	64	F3
Levádhia	75	G3
Levan	74	E2
Levanger	62	D5
Levdym	84	Ae4
Leven	57	E4
Leven, Loch *Highland, U.K.*	57	C4
Leven, Loch *Tayside, U.K.*	57	E4
Lévêque, Cape	112	E2
Leverburgh	56	A3
Le Verdon-sur-Mer	65	C6
Leverkusen	70	B3
Levice	71	H4
Le Vigan	65	E7
Levin	115	E4
Levis	125	Q3
Levittown	125	N6
Lévka Óri	75	G5
Levkás *Greece*	75	F3
Levkás *Greece*	75	F3
Levkímmi	74	F3
Levkosía	76	E5
Levoča	71	J4
Levozero	78	F2
Lev Tolstoy	79	F5
Levuka	114	R8
Lewannick	52	C4
Lewes	53	H4
Lewis	56	B2
Lewis, Butt of	56	B2
Lewisporte	121	Q8
Lewis Range	122	H3
Lewis Smith Lake	129	J3
Lewiston *U.K.*	56	D3
Lewiston *Maine, U.S.A.*	125	Q4
Lewiston *Montana, U.S.A.*	122	F4
Lewistown	123	K4
Lewisville, Lake	128	D4
Lexington *Kentucky, U.S.A.*	124	H7
Lexington *N. Carolina, U.S.A.*	129	M3
Lexington *Nebraska, U.S.A.*	123	Q7
Lexington *Virginia, U.S.A.*	125	L8
Lexington Park	125	M7
Leyburn	55	H2
Leye	93	L4
Leyland	55	G3
Leysdown-on-Sea	53	H3
Leyson Point	120	K5
Leyte	91	G3
Leyte Gulf	91	H3
Lezha	78	G4
Lezhë	74	E2
Lezno	71	G3
L'gov	79	F5
Lhasa	93	H3
Lhazê	93	G3
Lhokseumawe	90	B4
Liancheng	87	M6
Liangbingtai	88	B4
Liangdang	93	L2
Liangpran, Bukit	90	E5
Liangzhen	87	K4
Lianjiang	93	M4
Lianjiangkou	88	C2
Lian Xian	93	M3
Lianyungang	87	M5
Lianzhushan	88	C3
Liaodun	86	F3
Liao He	87	N3
Liaoning	87	N3
Liaoyang	87	N3
Liaoyuan	87	P3
Liapádhes	74	E3
Liard	119	L3
Liban, Jazâ'ir	94	B4
Liban, Jebel	77	F6
Líbano	136	B3
Libby	122	G3
Libenge	106	C2
Liberal	127	M2
Líberdale	136	C5
Liberec	70	F3
Liberia	104	D4
Liberia *Costa Rica*	132	E9
Liberty *New York, U.S.A.*	125	N6
Liberty *Texas, U.S.A.*	128	E5
Libobo, Tanjung	91	H6
Libourne	65	C6
Librazhd	75	F2
Libreville	106	A2
Librilla	67	F4
Libya	101	J3
Libyan Desert	102	E3
Libyan Plateau	102	E1
Licata	69	D7
Lice	77	J3
Lichfield	53	F2
Lichinga	109	G2
Lichtenburg	108	E5
Lichtenfels	70	D3
Lichuan	87	M6
Licking	124	J7
Licosa, Punta	69	E5
Lida	71	L2
Lidao	87	N4
Liddel Water	57	F5
Liddesdale	57	F5
Liden	62	G5
Lidingö	63	H7
Lidköping	63	E7
Lidzbark Warmiński	71	J1
Liebling	73	F3
Liechtenstein	70	C5
Liège	64	F3
Liegnitz	71	G3
Lielope	63	L8
Lienz	68	D2
Liepāja	63	L8
Lier	64	F3
Liestal	68	A2
Liezen	68	E2
Liffey	59	J6
Lifford	58	H3
Lifi Mahuida	139	C8
Lifou	114	X16
Ligger Bay	52	B4
Lighthouse Reef	132	D6
Ligonha	109	G3
Ligui	126	G8
Ligure, Appennino	68	B3
Ligurian Sea	68	B4
Lihir Group	114	E2
Lihou Reefs	113	L2
Lihue	126	R10
Lihula	63	K7
Lijiang	93	K3
Likasi	106	E5
Likhoslavl'	78	F4
Liku	90	D5
Likupang	91	H5
L'Ile-Rousse	69	B4
Lille	64	E3
Lille Bælt	63	C8
Lillebonne	64	D4
Lillehammer	63	D6
Lillesand	63	C7
Lillestrøm	63	H7
Lillhamra	63	F6
Lillhärdal	63	F6
Lillholmsjön	62	F5
Lillo	66	E3
Lillviken	62	G3
Lilongwe	107	F5
Liloy	91	G4
Lima *Paraguay*	138	E4
Lima *Peru*	136	B6
Lima *Portugal*	66	B2
Lima *Montana, U.S.A.*	122	H5
Lima *Ohio, U.S.A.*	124	H6
Līmah	97	N4
Limanköy	76	C2
Limavady	58	J2
Limay	139	C7
Limbang	90	E5
Limbani	136	D6
Limbe *Cameroon*	105	G5
Limbe *Malawi*	107	G6
Limburg	70	C3
Limeira	138	G4
Limenária	75	H2
Limén Vathéos	75	J4
Limerick *Ireland*	59	E8
Limerick *Ireland*	59	E7
Limfjorden	63	C8
Limín	75	H2
Limmen Bight	113	H1
Límni	75	G3
Límnos	75	H3
Limoeiro *Ceará, Brazil*	137	K5
Limoeiro *Pernambuco, Brazil*	137	K5
Limoges	65	D6
Limón	132	F9
Limon	123	N8
Limousin	65	D6
Limoux	65	E7
Limpopo	109	F4
Linaälv	62	J3
Līnah	96	F2
Linapacan Strait	91	F3
Linares *Chile*	139	B7
Linares *Mexico*	128	C8
Linares *Spain*	66	E3
Lincang	93	K4
Lincoln *New Zealand*	115	D5
Lincoln *U.K.*	55	J3
Lincoln *Illinois, U.S.A.*	124	F6
Lincoln *Maine, U.S.A.*	125	R4
Lincoln *Nebraska, U.S.A.*	123	R7
Lincoln City	122	B5
Lincoln Sea	140	R2
Lincolnshire	55	J3
Lincolnton	129	M3
Lindau	70	C5
Linde	85	L3
Linden *Guyana*	136	F2
Linden *U.S.A.*	129	J3
Linderödsåsen	63	E9
Lindesberg	63	F7
Lindi	107	G4
Lindley	108	E5
Líndos	75	K4
Lindsay *Canada*	125	L4
Lindsay *California, U.S.A.*	126	C2
Lindsay *Montana, U.S.A.*	123	M4
Lindu Point	114	S8
Linfen	93	M1
Lingao	93	L5
Lingayen	91	G2
Lingen	70	B2
Lingfield	53	G3
Lingga	90	C6
Lingga, Kepulauan	90	C6
Lingle	123	M6
Lingling	93	M3
Lingshi	87	L4
Lingshui	93	M5
Lingsugur	92	E5
Linguère	104	B2
Ling Xian	93	M3
Lingyuan	87	M3
Linhai	87	N6
Linhares	138	H3
Linhe	87	K3
Linh, Ngoc	93	L5
Linköping	63	F7
Linkou	88	C3
Linlithgow	57	E5
Linnhe, Loch	57	C4
Linosa	74	B5
Linru	93	M2
Lins	138	G4
Linsell	63	E5
Linslade	53	G3
Lintao	93	K1
Linton *U.K.*	53	H2
Linton *U.S.A.*	123	P4
Linwu	93	M3
Linxi	87	M3
Linxia	93	K1
Linyi *China*	87	M4
Linyi *China*	87	M4
Linz *Austria*	68	E1
Linz *W. Germany*	70	B3
Linze	86	J4
Lion, Golfe du	65	F7
Liouesso	106	C2
Lipa *Philippines*	91	G3
Lipa *Yugoslavia*	72	D3
Lipari, Isola	69	E6
Lipari, Isole	69	E6
Lipenská nádrž	70	F4
Lipetsk	79	F5
Lipiany	70	F2
Lipin Bor	78	F3
Liping	93	L3
Lipkany	79	D6
Lipljan	73	F4
Lipnishki	71	L2
Lipno	71	H2
Lippe	70	C3
Lipsói	75	J4
Lipsón	75	F3
Lipu	93	M4
Lipusz	71	G1

Lir

Name	Page	Ref
Lira	107	F2
Lircay	136	C6
Liri	69	D5
Lisabata	91	H6
Lisala	106	D2
Lisboa	66	B3
Lisbon *Portugal*	66	B3
Lisbon *U.S.A.*	123	R4
Lisburn	58	K3
Lisburne, Cape	118	B2
Liscannor Bay	59	D7
Lisdoonvarna	59	D6
Lishi	87	L4
Lishui	87	M6
Lisichansk	79	F6
Lisieux	64	D4
Liskeard	52	C4
L'Isle-Jourdain	65	D7
Lismore *Australia*	113	L4
Lismore *Ireland*	59	G8
Lismore *U.K.*	57	C4
Liss	53	G3
Listowel	59	D8
Lit	62	F5
Litang	93	K3
Litani	137	G3
Litchfield	124	F7
Litherland	55	G3
Lithgow	113	L5
Líthinon, Ákra	75	H5
Litos	66	C2
Litovko	85	P7
Little	128	E4
Little Abaco	132	J1
Little Aden	96	G10
Little Andaman	93	H6
Little Bahama Bank	132	H1
Little Barrier Island	115	E2
Little Belt Mountains	122	J4
Littleborough	55	G3
Little Bow	122	H2
Little Cayman	132	G5
Little Colorado	126	G3
Little Falls *Minnesota, U.S.A.*	124	C3
Little Falls *New York, U.S.A.*	125	N5
Littlefield	127	L4
Littlehampton	53	G4
Little Inagua Island	133	L4
Little Karoo	108	D6
Little Minch, The	56	B3
Little Missouri	123	M5
Little Nicobar	93	H7
Little Ouse	53	H2
Little Pamir	92	D1
Littleport	53	H2
Little Red	128	G3
Little Rock	128	F3
Little Rocky Mountains	123	K3
Little Scarcies	104	C4
Little Sitkin Island	118	Ab9
Little Smoky	119	M5
Little Snake	123	K7
Little South-west Miramichi	125	S3
Little Strickland	55	G2
Littleton *Colorado, U.S.A.*	123	M8
Littleton *New Hampshire, U.S.A.*	125	Q4
Little Wabash	124	F7
Little Waltham	53	H3
Litva S.S.R.	62	K9
Liulin	87	L4
Liupan Shan	93	L1
Liuyang	93	M3
Liuzhou	93	L4
Līvāni	63	M8
Live Oak	129	L5
Livermore	126	B2
Livermore, Mount	127	K5
Liverpool *Australia*	113	L5
Liverpool *U.K.*	55	G3
Liverpool Bay *Canada*	118	K1
Liverpool Bay *U.K.*	55	F3
Livingston *Canada*	121	N7
Livingston *U.K.*	57	E5
Livingston *Montana, U.S.A.*	123	J5
Livingston *Texas, U.S.A.*	128	E5
Livingstone	106	E6
Livingstone, Chutes de	106	B4
Livingstone Falls	106	B4
Livingstone Mountains	107	F4
Livingston Island	141	V6
Livingston, Lake	128	E5
Livno	72	D4
Livny	79	F5
Livojoki	62	M4
Livonia	124	J5
Livorno	68	C4
Liwiec	71	J2
Liwonde	107	G6
Li Xian	93	M3
Liyang	87	M5
Lizard	52	B4
Lizardo	137	H5
Lizard Point	52	B4
Ljósavatn	62	W12
Ljubinje	72	E4
Ljubišnja	72	E4
Ljubljana	72	C2
Ljungan	62	G5
Ljungby	63	E8
Ljusdal	63	G6
Ljusnan	63	F5
Llanarmon Dyffryn Ceiriog	52	D2
Llanbadarn Fynydd	52	D2
Llanbedr	52	C2
Llanberis	54	E3
Llanbrynmair	52	D2
Llandeilo	52	D3
Llandovery	52	D3
Llandrindod Wells	52	D2
Llandudno	54	F3
Llanelli	52	C3
Llanerchymedd	54	E3
Llanes	66	D1
Llanfaethlu	54	E3
Llanfair Caereinion	52	D2
Llanfairfechan	54	F3
Llanfair Talhaiarn	55	F3
Llanfyllin	52	D2
Llangefni	55	E3
Llanglydwen	52	C3
Llangollen	52	D2
Llangranog	52	C2
Llangurig	52	D2
Llanidloes	52	D2
Llanilar	52	C2
Llanos	136	D2
Llanquihue, Lago	139	B8
Llanrhystud	52	C2
Llanrwst	54	F3
Llantrisant	52	D3
Llanwenog	52	C2
Llanwrtyd Wells	52	D2
Llawhaden	52	C3
Llerena	66	C3
Lleyn Peninsula	52	C2
Lliria	67	F3
Llivia	67	G1
Llobregat	67	G2
Lloydminster	119	P5
Lluchmayor	67	H3
Llyswen	52	D2
Loa	138	C4
Loanhead	57	E5
Lobatse	108	E5
Löbau	70	F3
Lobería	139	E7
Łobez	70	F2
Lobito	106	B5
Lobos	139	E7
Lobos, Island	126	G7
Locarno	68	B2
Lochaber	57	D4
Lochailort	57	C4
Lochan Fada	56	C3
Loch Ard Forest	57	D4
Lochboisdale	57	A3
Lochearnhead	57	D4
Loches	65	D5
Lochgelly	57	E4
Lochgilphead	57	C4
Lochinver	56	C2
Lochmaben	57	E5
Lochmaddy	56	A3
Lochnagar	57	E4
Lochranza	57	C5
Loch Shin	56	D2
Lochy, Loch	57	D4
Lock	113	H5
Lockerbie	57	E5
Lockhart	128	D6
Lock Haven	125	M6
Lockport	125	L5
Lócri	69	F6
Löddeköpinge	63	E9
Loddon *Australia*	113	J6
Loddon *U.K.*	53	J2
Lodève	65	E7
Lodeynoye Pole	78	E3
Lodge Grass	123	L5
Lodgepole	123	M7
Lodi *Italy*	68	B3
Lodi *U.S.A.*	126	B1
Lødingen	62	F2
Lodja	106	D3
Lodwar	107	G2
Łódź	71	H3
Loeriesfontein	108	C6
Lofoten	62	E2
Loftus	55	J2
Logan	122	J7
Logan, Mount	118	G3
Logansport *Indiana, U.S.A.*	124	G6
Logansport *Louisiana, U.S.A.*	128	F5
Loge	106	B4
Logishin	71	M2
Logone	102	C5
Logroño	66	E1
Logrosan	66	D3
Loh	114	T10
Lohardaga	92	F4
Loharu	92	E3
Lohit	93	J3
Lohja	63	L6
Lohtaja	62	K4
Loikaw	93	J5
Loimaa	63	K6
Loimijoki	63	K6
Loing	65	E5
Loi, Phu	93	K4
Loir	65	C5
Loire	65	B5
Loja *Ecuador*	136	B4
Loja *Spain*	66	D4
Lokantekojärvi	62	M3
Lokhpodgort	78	M2
Lokhvitsa	79	E5
Lokichokio	107	F2
Lokilalaki, Gunung	91	G6
Lokka	62	M3
Loknya	78	E4
Lokoja	105	G4
Lokshak	85	N6
Lokuru	114	H6
Lol	102	E6
Lola	104	D4
Lolland	63	D9
Lolo	122	G4
Loloda	91	H5
Lolo Pass	122	G4
Lolvavana, Passage	114	U11
Lom *Bulgaria*	73	G4
Lom *Norway*	63	C6
Lomami	106	D3
Lomas Coloradas	139	C8
Łomazy	71	K3
Lombarda, Serra	137	G3
Lombe	107	G4
Lombez	65	D7
Lomblen	91	G7
Lombok	90	F7
Lomé	104	F4
Lomela	106	D3
Lomir	94	J2
Lomond Hills	57	E4
Lomond, Loch	57	D4
Lomonosov Ridge	140	A1
Lompobattang, Gunung	91	F7
Lompoc	126	B3
Łomża	71	K2
London *Canada*	125	K5
London *U.K.*	53	G3
Londonderry *U.K.*	58	H2
Londonderry *U.K.*	58	J3
Londonderry, Cape	112	F1
Londonderry, Isla	139	B11
Londoni	114	R8
Londrina	138	F4
Lone Pine	126	C2
Longa *Angola*	106	C5
Longa *Angola*	106	C6
Longa Island	56	C3
Long Akah	90	E5
Longa, Ostrova de	81	S2
Long Bay	129	N4
Long Beach *California, U.S.A.*	126	C4
Long Beach *New York, U.S.A.*	125	P6
Long Branch	125	P6
Longchang	93	L3
Longchuan	87	M7

Longde	93	L1	Lordegan	95	K6	Louvain	64	F3
Long Eaton	53	F2	Lord Howe Island	113	M5	Louviers	64	D4
Longford *Ireland*	58	G5	Lordsburg	127	H4	Lövånger	62	J4
Longford *Ireland*	58	G5	Loré	91	H7	Lovat'	78	E4
Longformacus	57	F5	Lorengau	114	D2	Lövberga	62	F5
Longframlington	57	G5	Lorentz	91	K7	Lovech	73	H4
Longhoughton	55	H1	Lorenzo	136	B3	Loveland	123	M7
Longhua	87	M3	Loreto *Brazil*	137	H5	Lovell	123	K5
Longhui	93	M3	Loreto *Colombia*	136	C4	Lóvere	68	C3
Long Island *Bahamas*	133	K3	Loreto *Mexico*	126	G7	Loviisa	63	M6
Long Island *Canada*	121	L7	Lorica	133	K10	Lovington	127	L4
Long Island *New Zealand*	115	A7	Lorient	65	B5	Lovisa	63	M6
Long Island *Papua New Guinea*	114	D3	Lorillard	119	S3	Lövnäs	62	F4
Long Island *U.S.A.*	125	P6	Lórinci	72	E2	Lovosice	70	F3
Long Island Sound	125	P6	Lorn	57	C4	Lóvua	106	D5
Longjiang	87	N2	Lorne	113	J6	Low, Cape	120	J5
Longjing	88	B4	Lorn, Firth of	57	C4	Lower Arrow Lake	122	E3
Longlac	124	G2	Lörrach	70	B5	Lower Hut	115	E4
Long Lake	124	G2	Lorraine	64	F4	Lowestoft	53	J2
Longli	93	L3	Los	63	F6	Łowicz	71	H2
Long, Loch	57	D4	Los Alamos	127	J3	Lowther Hills	57	E5
Long Melford	53	H2	Los Andes	139	B6	Lowther Island	120	G3
Longmen	87	L7	Los Angeles *Chile*	139	B7	Loyal, Loch	56	D2
Long Mynd, The	52	E2	Los Angeles *U.S.A.*	126	C4	Loyauté, Îles	114	X16
Longnan	87	L7	Los Angeles Aqueduct	126	C3	Loyma	78	H3
Longnawan	90	E5	Los Banos	126	B2	Loyne, Loch	57	C3
Longney	52	E3	Los Blancos	138	D4	Lozarevo	73	J4
Long Point *Canada*	125	K5	Los Filabres, Sierra de	66	E4	Lozère, Mont	65	E6
Long Point *New Zealand*	115	B7	Lošinj	72	C3	Loznica	72	E3
Long Preston	55	G2	Los Mochis	127	H8	Lozovaya	79	F6
Long Range	121	Q8	Los Pedraches	66	D3	Lualaba	106	E3
Long Range Mountains	121	Q7	Los Roques	136	D1	Lu'an	93	N2
Longreach	113	J3	Lossie	56	E3	Luanda	106	B4
Long Reef	114	E4	Lossiemouth	56	E3	Luang Prabang	93	K5
Longridge	55	G3	Los Teques	136	D1	Luangwa	107	F5
Longshan	93	L3	Los Testigos	133	R9	Luan He	87	M4
Longsheng	93	M3	Lost Trail Pass	122	H5	Luanjing	87	K4
Longs Peak	123	M7	Lostwithiel	52	C4	Luanping	87	M3
Long Stratton	53	J2	Lot	65	D6	Luanshya	107	E5
Longton	55	G3	Lota	139	B7	Luapula	107	E5
Longtown	57	F5	Lotfähäd	95	P3	Luarca	66	C1
Longuyon	64	F4	Lothian	57	E5	Luashi	106	D5
Longview *Texas, U.S.A.*	128	E4	Lotta	62	N2	Luau	106	D5
Longview *Washington, U.S.A.*	122	C4	Löttorp	63	G8	Lubalo	106	C4
Longwy	64	F4	Lo-tung	87	N7	Lubānas Ezers	62	M8
Longxi	93	K2	Lotzen	71	J1	Lubang Islands	91	G3
Long Xuyen	93	L6	Loudéac	64	B4	Lubango	106	B5
Longyan	87	M6	Loudun	65	D5	Lubartów	71	K3
Longyao	87	L4	Louga	104	B2	Lubawa	71	H2
Lons-le-Saunier	65	F5	Loughborough	53	F2	Lübben	70	E3
Looe	52	C4	Loughbrickland	58	K4	Lubbock	127	M4
Lookout, Cape	129	P3	Lougheed Island	120	E2	Lübeck	70	D2
Loongana	112	F5	Loughor	52	C3	Lubefu	106	D3
Loop Head	59	C7	Loughrea	59	E6	Lubenka	79	J5
Lopatin	79	H7	Loughsalt Mount	58	G2	Lubero	107	E3
Lopatino	79	H5	Lough Swilly	58	G2	Lubie, Jezioro	70	F2
Lopatka	85	T6	Louhans	65	F5	Lubién	71	H2
Lopatka, Mys	85	T6	Louisa	124	J7	Lublin	71	K3
Lop Buri	93	K6	Louisiade Archipelago	114	T10	Lubny	79	E5
Lopévi	114	U12	Louisiana	128	F5	Lubosalma	62	P5
Lopez, Cap	106	A3	Lou Island	114	D2	Lubsko	70	F3
Lop Nur	86	G3	Louis Trichardt	108	E4	Lübtheen	70	D2
Lopphavet	62	J1	Louisville *Kentucky, U.S.A.*	124	H7	Lubudi	106	E4
Lopra	62	Z14	Louisville *Mississippi, U.S.A.*	128	H4	Lubuklinggau	90	C6
Lopydino	78	J3	Loukhi	62	Q3	Lubumbashi	107	E5
Lora del Río	66	D4	Loulé	66	B4	Lubutu	106	E3
Lorain	124	J6	Loup	123	Q7	Lucan	59	K6
Loralai	92	C2	Lourdes	65	C7	Lucano, Appennino	69	E5
Lorca	67	F4	Louth *Ireland*	58	K5	Lucaya	129	N7
			Louth *U.K.*	55	K1	Lucca	68	C4

Lucea	132	H5
Luce Bay	54	E2
Lucedale	128	H5
Lucena *Philippines*	91	G3
Lucena *Spain*	66	D4
Lucena del Cid	67	F2
Lučenec	71	H4
Lucera	69	E5
Lucerne	68	B2
Lüchow	70	D2
Luckau	70	E3
Luckenwalde	70	E2
Lucknow	92	F3
Luçon	65	C5
Lucrecia, Cabo	133	K4
Lucusse	106	D5
Lüda	87	N4
Lüdensheid	70	B3
Lüderitz	108	C5
Ludford	55	J3
Ludgvan	52	B4
Ludhiana	92	E2
Ludington	124	G5
Ludlow *U.K.*	52	E2
Ludlow *U.S.A.*	126	D3
Ludogorie	73	J4
Luduş	73	H2
Ludvika	63	F6
Ludwigsburg	70	C4
Ludwigshafen	70	B4
Ludwigslust	70	D2
Ludza	63	M8
Luebo	106	D4
Luena	106	C5
Luepa	136	E2
Lüeyang	93	L2
Lufeng	87	M7
Lufkin	128	E5
Luga	63	N7
Lugano	68	B2
Lugano, Lago di	68	B3
Luganville	114	T11
Lugela	109	G3
Lugenda	109	G2
Lugg	52	E2
Lugnaquilla	59	K7
Lugo *Italy*	68	C3
Lugo *Spain*	66	C1
Lugoj	73	F3
Lugovoy	86	C3
Lugton	57	D5
Luiana	106	D6
Luichart, Loch	56	D3
Luik	64	F3
Luimneach	59	E7
Luing	57	D4
Luinne Bheinn	57	C3
Luiro	62	M3
Luiza	106	D4
Luján	139	C6
Lujiang	87	M5
Lukashkin Yar	84	B4
Lukeville	126	F5
Lukovit	73	H4
Lukovo	72	F5
Łuków	71	K3
Lukoyanov	78	G4
Lukulu	106	D5
Luleå	62	K4
Luleälven	62	J3

212

Madison *Nebraska, U.S.A.*	**123**	R7
Madison *S. Dakota, U.S.A.*	**123**	R5
Madison *Winconsin, U.S.A.*	**124**	F5
Madisonville *Kentucky, U.S.A.*	**124**	G8
Madisonville *Texas, U.S.A.*	**128**	E5
Madiun	**90**	E7
Mado Gashi	**107**	G2
Madoi	**93**	J2
Madona	**63**	M8
Madrakah, Ra's	**97**	N7
Madras *India*	**92**	F6
Madras *U.S.A.*	**122**	D5
Madre de Dios	**136**	D6
Madre de Dios, Isla	**139**	A10
Madre, Laguna *Mexico*	**128**	D8
Madre, Laguna *U.S.A.*	**128**	D7
Madre Occidental, Sierra	**127**	H6
Madre Oriental, Sierra	**127**	L7
Madre, Sierra	**91**	G2
Madrid	**66**	E2
Madridejos	**66**	E3
Madrigalejo	**66**	D3
Madrona, Sierra	**66**	D3
Madura *Australia*	**112**	F5
Madura *Indonesia*	**90**	E7
Madurai	**92**	E7
Madura, Selat	**90**	E7
Madzharovo	**73**	H5
Maebashi	**89**	G7
Mǎeruş	**73**	H3
Maesteg	**52**	D3
Maestra, Sierra	**132**	J4
Maevatanana	**109**	J3
Maéwo	**114**	U11
Mafa	**91**	H5
Mafeteng	**108**	E5
Mafia Island	**107**	G4
Mafikeng	**108**	E5
Mafra	**66**	B3
Mafraq	**94**	C5
Maga	**114**	S8
Magadan	**85**	S5
Magadan Oblast'	**85**	V3
Magadi	**107**	G3
Magallanes, Estrecho de	**139**	B10
Magangué	**136**	C2
Mağara	**76**	E4
Magarida	**114**	D4
Magburaka	**104**	C4
Magdagachi	**85**	M6
Magdalena *Bolivia*	**136**	E6
Magdalena *Colombia*	**136**	C2
Magdalena *Mexico*	**126**	F7
Magdalena *Mexico*	**126**	G5
Magdalena *Mexico*	**130**	H7
Magdalena, Isla	**130**	C5
Magdalena, Llano de la	**130**	D5
Magdalen Islands	**121**	P8
Magda Plateau	**120**	K3
Magdeburg	**70**	D2
Magdelena	**127**	J3
Magee, Island	**58**	L3
Magelang	**90**	E7
Magellan, Strait of	**139**	B10
Magenta, Lake	**112**	D5
Magerøya	**62**	L1
Maggiore, Lago	**68**	B3
Maghâgha	**102**	F2
Magharee Islands	**59**	B8
Maghera	**58**	J3

Magherafelt	**58**	J3
Magheramorne	**58**	L3
Magilligan Point	**58**	J2
Mágina	**66**	E4
Maglić	**72**	E4
Maglie	**69**	G5
Magnolia	**128**	F4
Magoe	**109**	F3
Magog	**125**	P4
Magpie	**121**	P7
Magro	**67**	F3
Magude	**109**	F5
Maguse Lake	**119**	R3
Maguse Point	**119**	S3
Magwe	**93**	H4
Mahābād	**94**	G3
Mahabe	**109**	J3
Mahabharat Range	**92**	G3
Mahabo	**109**	H4
Mahaddayweyne	**107**	J2
Mahadeo Hills	**92**	E4
Mahagi	**107**	F2
Mahajanga	**109**	J3
Mahakam	**90**	F5
Mahalapye	**108**	E4
Mahallāt	**95**	K5
Mahānadi	**92**	F4
Mahanoy City	**125**	M6
Mahao	**88**	A4
Maharashtra	**92**	E5
Mahārlū, Daryācheh-ye	**95**	L7
Maha Sarakham	**93**	K5
Mahavavy	**109**	J3
Mahbubnagar	**92**	E5
Mahdah	**97**	M4
Mahdia *Guyana*	**136**	F2
Mahdia *Tunisia*	**101**	H1
Mahé	**92**	E6
Mahébourg	**109**	L7
Mahenge	**107**	G4
Mahesana	**92**	D4
Mahi	**92**	D4
Mahia Peninsula	**115**	G3
Mahmudabad *India*	**92**	F3
Mahmudabad *Iran*	**95**	L3
Mahmudia	**73**	K3
Mahmudiye	**76**	D3
Mahnomen	**124**	B3
Mahón	**67**	J3
Mahrah, Al	**97**	K8
Mahukona	**126**	T10
Mahuva	**92**	D4
Maicao	**136**	C1
Maîche	**65**	G5
Maicuru	**137**	G4
Maidenhead	**53**	G3
Maidi	**91**	H5
Maidstone	**53**	H3
Maiduguri	**105**	H3
Maihar	**92**	F4
Maijdi	**93**	H4
Maikala Range	**92**	F4
Main *U.K.*	**58**	K3
Main *W. Germany*	**70**	C4
Main Barrier Range	**113**	J5
Main Channel	**125**	K4
Mai-Ndombe, Lac	**106**	C3
Maine *France*	**64**	C4
Maine *U.S.A.*	**125**	R4
Mainé Soroa	**101**	H6

Maingkwan	**93**	J3
Mainland *Orkney Is., U.K.*	**56**	E2
Mainland *Shetland Is., U.K.*	**56**	A1
Maintirano	**109**	H3
Mainua	**62**	M4
Mainz	**70**	C4
Maio	**104**	L7
Maipú	**139**	E7
Maiquetía	**133**	P9
Maira	**68**	A3
Maisí, Cabo	**133**	K4
Maiskhal	**93**	H4
Maitland *New South Wales, Australia*	**113**	L5
Maitland *S. Australia, Australia*	**113**	H5
Maíz, Islas del	**132**	F8
Maizuru	**89**	E8
Majagual	**136**	C2
Majene	**91**	F6
Maji	**103**	G6
Majiang	**93**	L3
Majin	**87**	M6
Majorca	**67**	H3
Maka *Senegal*	**104**	C3
Maka *Solomon Is.*	**114**	K6
Makale	**91**	F6
Makambako	**107**	F4
Makanza	**106**	C2
Makarikha	**78**	K2
Makarova	**84**	D2
Makarska	**72**	D4
Makaryev	**78**	G4
Makassar	**91**	F7
Makassar, Selat	**91**	F6
Makat	**79**	J6
Makatini Flats	**109**	F5
Makay, Massif du	**109**	J4
Makeni	**104**	C4
Makenu	**126**	S10
Makeyevka	**79**	F6
Makhachkala	**79**	H7
Makharadze	**77**	K2
Makhmûr	**94**	F4
Makhyah, Wadi	**97**	J8
Maki	**91**	J6
Makinsk	**84**	A6
Makkah	**96**	D6
Makkovik	**121**	Q6
Makkovik, Cape	**121**	Q6
Makogai	**114**	R8
Makokou	**106**	B2
Makondi Plateau	**107**	G5
Makov	**71**	H4
Makrá	**75**	H4
Makrai	**92**	E4
Makran	**92**	B3
Mákri	**75**	H2
Makronísi	**75**	H4
Maksatikha	**78**	F4
Maksim	**78**	K3
Maksimovka	**88**	F2
Makteir	**100**	C4
Mākū	**94**	G2
Makurazaki	**89**	C10
Makurdi	**105**	G4
Makushin Volcano	**118**	Ae9
Malå	**62**	M4
Malabang	**91**	G4
Malabar Coast	**92**	D6

Malabo	**105**	G5
Malacca, Strait of	**90**	C5
Malacky	**71**	G4
Mala Fatra	**71**	H4
Málaga *Colombia*	**136**	C2
Málaga *Spain*	**66**	D4
Malagarasi	**107**	F3
Malahide	**59**	K6
Malaita	**114**	K6
Malakal	**103**	F6
Malakanagiri	**92**	F5
Malakand	**92**	D2
Malakula	**114**	T12
Malang	**90**	E7
Malanje	**106**	C4
Malao	**114**	T11
Mala, Punta	**136**	B2
Mälaren	**63**	G7
Malargue	**139**	C7
Malartic	**125**	L2
Malaspina	**139**	C8
Malaspina Glacier	**118**	G4
Malatya	**77**	H3
Malatya Dağlari	**77**	H3
Malavate	**137**	G3
Mālavi	**94**	H5
Malaŵi	**107**	F5
Malawi, Lake	**107**	F5
Malaybalay	**91**	H4
Malāyer	**94**	J4
Malay Peninsula	**90**	C5
Malaysia	**90**	D5
Malazgirt	**77**	K3
Malbork	**71**	H1
Malchin *E. Germany*	**70**	E2
Malchin *Mongolia*	**86**	G2
Malcolm's Point	**57**	B4
Malden	**124**	F8
Maldives	**82**	F6
Maldon	**53**	H3
Maldonado	**139**	F6
Maldonado, Punta	**131**	K9
Malé	**82**	F6
Maléa, Ákra	**75**	G4
Malegaon	**92**	D4
Malé Karpaty	**71**	G4
Malema	**109**	G2
Malemba-Nkulu	**106**	E4
Máleme	**75**	G5
Maler Kotla	**92**	E2
Malesherbes	**64**	E4
Maleta	**84**	H6
Malevangga	**114**	H5
Malgobek	**79**	G7
Malgomaj	**62**	G4
Malhāt	**77**	K5
Malheur	**122**	F6
Malheur, Lake	**122**	E6
Mali	**100**	E5
Mali Hka	**93**	J3
Mali Kanal	**72**	E3
Mali Kyun	**93**	J6
Malimba, Mont	**107**	E4
Malin *Ireland*	**58**	H2
Malin *U.S.S.R.*	**79**	D5
Malin Beg	**58**	E3
Malindi	**107**	H3
Malin Head	**58**	H2
Malin More	**58**	E3
Malka	**85**	T6

Maradi	101	G6	Mariánské Lázně	70	E4	Marmelos	136	E5
Marāgheh	94	H3	Marias	122	J3	Marne	64	E4
Marajó, Baia de	137	H4	Marías, Islas	130	F7	Maro	102	C3
Marajó, Ilha de	137	H4	Mariato, Punta	132	G11	Marcantsetra	109	J3
Maralal	107	G2	Maria van Diemen, Cape	115	D1	Marclambo	109	J4
Maramasike	114	K6	Mariazell	68	E2	Marondera	109	F3
Maramba	106	E6	Ma'rib	96	G9	Maroni	137	G3
Maran	90	C5	Maribor	72	C2	Maros	91	F6
Marand	94	G2	Maridi	102	E7	Marotiri Islands	115	E1
Maranguape	137	K4	Marie Byrd Land	141	S3	Maroua	105	H3
Maranhão	137	H5	Marie Galante	133	S7	Marovoay	109	J3
Maranhão Grande, Cachoeira	137	F4	Mariehamn	63	H6	Marowÿne	137	G3
Mārān, Koh-i-	92	C3	Marienbad	70	E4	Marple	55	G3
Marañón	136	C4	Marienburg	71	H1	Marquette	124	G3
Marans	65	C5	Mariental	108	C4	Marquise	64	D3
Marari	136	D5	Marienwerder	71	H2	Marquises, Îles	143	J5
Mărăşeşti	73	J3	Mariestad	63	E7	Marra, Jebel	102	D5
Marassumé	137	H4	Marietta *Georgia, U.S.A.*	129	K4	Marrakech	100	D2
Marateca	66	B3	Marietta *Ohio, U.S.A.*	125	K7	Marrakesh	100	D2
Marathókambos	75	J4	Marigot	133	S7	Marrak Point	120	R5
Marathon *Canada*	124	G2	Mariinsk	84	D5	Marrawah	113	J7
Marathon *Florida, U.S.A.*	129	M8	Marina di Carrara	68	C3	Marree	113	H4
Marathon *Texas, U.S.A.*	127	L5	Marina di Léuca	69	G6	Marresale	84	Ae3
Marau	90	E6	Marina di Monasterace	69	F6	Marrupa	109	G2
Marau Point	115	G3	Marinette	124	G4	Marsa Alam	96	B4
Maravovo	114	J6	Maringa	106	D2	Marsabit	107	G2
Marbella	66	D4	Maringá	138	F4	Marsala	69	D7
Marble Bar	112	D3	Marion *Illinois, U.S.A.*	124	F8	Marsden *Australia*	113	K5
Marble Canyon	126	G2	Marion *Indiana, U.S.A.*	124	H6	Marsden *U.K.*	55	H3
Marburg	70	C3	Marion *Ohio, U.S.A.*	124	J6	Marseille	65	F7
Marcelino	136	D4	Marion *S. Carolina, U.S.A.*	129	N3	Mar, Serra do	138	G5
March	53	H2	Marion *Virginia, U.S.A.*	125	K8	Marsfjället	62	G3
Marche *Belgium*	64	F3	Marion, Lake	129	M4	Marshall *Minnesota, U.S.A.*	124	C4
Marche *France*	65	D5	Marion Reefs	113	L2	Marshall *Missouri, U.S.A.*	124	D7
Marchena	66	D4	Maripa	136	D2	Marshall *Texas, U.S.A.*	128	E4
Marchena, Isla	136	A7	Marisa	91	G5	Marshall Bennett Islands	114	E3
Mar Chiquita, Lago	138	D6	Mariscal Estigarribia	138	D4	Marshall Islands	143	G4
Marcigny	65	F5	Maritimes, Alpes	65	G6	Marshalltown	124	D5
Marcus Baker, Mount	118	F3	Maritsa	73	H4	Marshchapel	55	K3
Marcus Island	83	P4	Marīvān	94	H4	Marshfield	124	E4
Mardan	92	D2	Mariy A.S.S.R.	78	H4	Marsh Island	128	G6
Mar del Plata	139	E7	Märjamaa	63	L7	Marske-by-the-Sea	55	H2
Mardin	77	J4	Marjayoûn	94	B5	Märsta	63	G7
Maré	114	Y16	Markā	96	E7	Martaban	93	J5
Mareeba	113	K2	Marka	107	H2	Martaban, Gulf of	93	J5
Maree, Loch	56	C3	Markam	93	J3	Martapura	90	E6
Mareeq	103	J7	Market Deeping	53	G2	Martés, Sierra	67	F3
Mareuil	65	D6	Market Drayton	52	E2	Marthaguy	113	K5
Margai Caka	92	G1	Market Harborough	53	G2	Martha's Vineyard	125	Q6
Marganets	79	E6	Markethill	58	J4	Martigny	68	A2
Margaret, Cape	120	H3	Market Rasen	55	J3	Martigues	65	F7
Margaret River	112	F2	Market Weighton	55	J3	Martin *Poland*	71	H4
Margarita, Isla de	136	E1	Markha	85	K4	Martin *Spain*	67	F2
Margaritovo	88	E4	Markham	114	D3	Martin *S. Dakota, U.S.A.*	123	P6
Margate	53	J3	Marlborough *Australia*	113	K3	Martin *Tennessee, U.S.A.*	128	H2
Margeride, Monts de la	65	E6	Marlborough *Guyana*	136	F2	Martinavas	53	N6
Margita	73	F3	Marlborough *U.K.*	53	F3	Martinborough	115	E4
Margo, Dasht-i	95	R6	Marlin	128	D5	Martinique	133	S7
Marguerite	121	N7	Marlinton	125	K7	Martinique Passage	133	S7
Marguerite Bay	141	V5	Marlow	53	G3	Martin Lake	129	K4
Mari	114	C3	Marmagao	92	D5	Martin Point	118	G1
Maria Elena	138	C4	Marmande	65	D6	Martinsberg	68	E1
Maria, Golfo de Ana	132	H4	Marmara *Turkey*	76	B2	Martinsville	125	L8
María Madre, Isla	130	F7	Marmara *Turkey*	76	B2	Martock	52	E4
María Magdalena, Isla	130	F7	Marmara Denizi	76	C2	Marton *New Zealand*	115	E4
Marianas Islands	83	N5	Marmaraereğlisi	76	B2	Marton *U.K.*	55	J3
Marianas Trench	142	F4	Marmara Gölü	76	C3	Martorell	67	G2
Marian Lake	119	M3	Marmara, Sea of	76	C2	Martos	66	E4
Marianna *Arkansas, U.S.A.*	128	G3	Marmaris	76	C4	Martre, Lac La	119	M3
Marianna *Florida, U.S.A.*	129	K5	Marmblada	68	C2	Martuk	79	K5
						Martuni	79	H7
						Martyn	78	K2
						Martzé	136	D4
						Marudi	90	E5
						Marugame	89	D8
						Marum, Mount	114	U12
						Marunga	114	E2
						Marungu	107	E4
						Marv Dasht	95	L7
						Marvéjols	65	E6
						Marvine, Mount	122	J8
						Marwar	92	D3
						Mary	95	Q3
						Maryborough	113	L4
						Mar'yevka	84	Ae6
						Maryland	125	M7
						Maryport	55	F2
						Mary, Puy	65	E6
						Marystown	121	Q8
						Marysville *California, U.S.A.*	126	B1
						Marysville *Kansas, U.S.A.*	123	R8
						Maryvale	113	L4
						Maryville *Missouri, U.S.A.*	124	C6
						Maryville *Tennessee, U.S.A.*	129	L3
						Marzo, Cabo	132	J11
						Masagua	132	B7
						Masai Steppe	107	G3
						Masaka	107	F3
						Masally	94	J2
						Masan	89	B8
						Masasi	107	G5
						Masaya	132	D8
						Masbate *Philippines*	91	G3
						Masbate *Philippines*	91	G3
						Mascara	100	F1
						Mascarene Islands	109	L7
						Masela	91	H7
						Maseru	108	E5
						Mashābih	96	C4
						Masham	55	H2
						Mashan *Guangxi, China*	93	L4
						Mashan *Heilongjiang, China*	88	C3
						Mashhad	95	P3
						Mashike	88	H4
						Mashīz	95	N7
						Māshkīd	95	R8
						Masi	62	K2
						Masīlah, Wadi al	97	J9
						Masi-Manimba	106	C3
						Masindi	107	F2
						Maşīrah	97	P6
						Maşīrah, Khalīj	97	N7
						Maşīrah, Khawr al	97	P6
						Masiri	95	K6
						Masisi	107	E3
						Masjed Soleymān	94	J6
						Mask, Lough	58	D5
						Maskūtān	95	P8
						Maslen Nos	73	J4
						Masoala, Cap	109	K3
						Mason Bay	115	A7
						Mason City	124	D5
						Ma, Song	93	K4
						Masqaţ	97	P5
						Massa	68	C3
						Massachusetts	125	P5
						Massachusetts Bay	125	Q5
						Massakori	102	C5
						Massa Maríttima	68	C4
						Massangena	109	F4

Massapê	137	J4	Mátra	72	E2	Mayas, Montañas	132	C6	Mbuji-Mayi	106	D4

Massapê	137	J4
Massava	84	Ad4
Massénya	102	C5
Massigui	100	D6
Massillon	124	K6
Massinga	109	G4
Massingir	109	F4
Masteksay	79	H6
Masterton	115	E4
Mástikho, Ákra	75	J3
Mastuj	92	D1
Mãstūrah	96	D5
Masuda	89	C8
Masulch	94	J3
Masurai, Bukit	90	C6
Masvingo	108	F4
Maşyāf	94	C4
Mat	74	F2
Mataboor	91	K6
Mataca	109	G2
Matachel	66	C3
Matad	87	M2
Matadi	106	B4
Matafome	66	B3
Matagalpa	132	E8
Matagami Ontario, Canada	125	M2
Matagami Québec, Canada	125	M2
Matagami, Lac	125	M1
Matagorda Bay	128	D6
Matagorda Island	128	D6
Matakana Island	115	F2
Matakaoa Point	115	G2
Matala	106	C5
Matale	92	F7
Matam	104	C2
Matamata	115	E2
Matamoros Mexico	128	D8
Matamoros Mexico	127	L8
Matane	125	S2
Mata Negra	136	E2
Matanzas	132	G3
Matapán, Cape	75	G4
Matapédia	125	S2
Matara	92	F7
Mataram	90	F7
Matarani	138	B3
Mataranka	112	G1
Mataró	67	H2
Matata	115	F2
Matatiele	108	E6
Mataura New Zealand	115	B6
Mataura New Zealand	115	B7
Matawai	115	F3
Matay	86	D2
Matcha	86	B4
Matehuala	131	J6
Matera	69	F5
Mátészálka	73	G2
Mateur	101	G1
Matfors	62	G5
Matheson	125	K2
Mathis	128	D6
Mathry	52	B3
Mathura	92	E3
Mati	91	H4
Matlock	55	H3
Mato, Cerro	133	Q11
Mato Grosso	136	F6
Mato Grosso do Sul	138	E3
Mato Grosso, Planalto do	138	E3

Mátra	72	E2
Maţraḩ	97	P5
Matrosovo	71	J1
Matrûh	102	E1
Matsubara	89	J10
Matsue	89	D8
Ma-tsu Lieh-tao	87	M6
Matsumae	88	H5
Matsumoto	89	F7
Matsusaka	89	F8
Matsuyama	89	D9
Mattagami	121	K8
Mattancheri	92	E7
Mattawa	125	L3
Matterhorn Switzerland	68	A3
Matterhorn U.S.A.	122	G7
Matthews Peak	107	G2
Matthew Town	133	L4
Maţţi, Sabkhat	97	K10
Mattoon	124	F7
Matty Island	120	G3
Matua, Ostrov	85	S7
Matuku	114	R9
Maturín	136	E2
Matyushkinskaya	84	B5
Mau	92	F3
Maua	109	G2
Maubara	91	H7
Maubeuge	64	E3
Maubin	93	J5
Maubourguet	65	D7
Mauchline	57	D5
Maud	56	F3
Maués	136	F4
Mauganj	92	F4
Maui	126	S10
Maula	62	L4
Maule	139	B7
Mauléon-Licharre	65	C7
Maumere	91	G7
Maumtrasna	58	C5
Maumturk Mountains	59	C5
Maun	108	D4
Mauna Kea	126	T11
Mauna Loa	126	T11
Maungmagan Islands	93	J6
Maunoir, Lac	118	L2
Maures	65	G7
Mauriac	65	E6
Maurice, Lake	112	G4
Mauritania	100	C5
Mauritius	109	L7
Mauron	64	B4
Mauston	124	E5
Mautern	68	E2
Mavinga	106	D6
Mawbray	55	F2
Mawhai Point	115	G3
Mawlaik	93	H4
Mawson	141	E5
Maxaila	109	F4
Maxmo	62	K5
Maya	85	N5
Mayaguana Island	133	L3
Mayaguana Passage	133	L3
Mayagüez	133	P5
Mayak China	86	F2
Mayak U.S.S.R.	71	H1
Mayak U.S.S.R.	79	K5
Mayamey	95	M3

Mayas, Montañas	132	C6
Maybole	57	D5
May, Cape	125	N7
Maych'ew	96	D10
Maydh	103	J5
Mayenne France	64	C4
Mayenne France	65	C5
Mayero	84	G3
Mayfa'ah	97	H9
Mayfield U.K.	53	H3
Mayfield U.S.A.	124	F8
May, Isle of	57	F4
Maykop	79	G7
Maykor	78	K4
Maymakan U.S.S.R.	85	N5
Maymakan U.S.S.R.	85	P5
Maymyo	93	J4
Mayn	85	W4
Maynooth	59	J6
Mayo Argentina	139	B9
Mayo Canada	118	H3
Mayo Ireland	58	D5
Mayo Mexico	130	E4
Mayor Island	115	F2
Mayor, Pic	67	H3
Mayotte	109	J2
May Pen	132	J6
Mayraira Point	91	G2
Mayráta	75	F3
Maysville	124	J7
Mayumba	106	A3
Mayuram	92	E6
Mayville	123	R4
Mayyūn Island	96	F10
Mazalat	73	H4
Mazamari	136	C6
Mazamet	65	E7
Mazar	92	E1
Mazār-e Sharīf	92	C1
Mazarete	67	E2
Mazarredo	139	C9
Mazarrón	67	F4
Mazarsu	86	C3
Mazaruni	136	F2
Mazatenango	132	B7
Mazatlán	130	F6
Mazdaj	95	K5
Mazeikiai	63	K8
Mazgirt	77	H3
Maẕĥūr, Irq al	96	G3
Mazidaği	77	J4
Mazinan	95	N3
Mazirbe	63	K8
Mazury	71	J2
Mbabane	108	F5
Mbaiki	102	C7
Mbala	107	F4
Mbalavu	114	S8
Mbale	107	F2
Mbalmayo	105	H5
Mbalo	114	K6
Mbandaka	106	C2
M'Banza Congo	106	B4
Mbanza-Ngungu	106	B4
Mbarara	107	F3
Mbengwi	105	G4
Mbeya	107	F4
Mbouda	105	H4
Mbour	104	B3
Mbout	100	C5

Mbuji-Mayi	106	D4
Mchinji	107	F5
M'Clintock	119	S4
Meade Alaska, U.S.A.	118	D1
Meade Kansas, U.S.A.	127	M2
Meadie, Loch	56	D2
Mead, Lake	126	E2
Meadow Lake	119	P5
Meadville	125	K6
Mealhada	66	B2
Meana	95	Q3
Meath	58	J5
Meaux	64	E4
Mebula	91	G7
Mecca	96	D6
Mechelen	64	F3
Mecheria	100	E2
Mechigmen	118	A2
Mechigmen Zaliv	118	A2
Mecidie	76	B2
Meçitözü	76	F2
Mecklenburger Bucht	70	D1
Mecsek	72	E2
Mecufi	109	H2
Mecula	109	G2
Medak	92	E5
Medan	90	B5
Médanos	139	D7
Medanosa, Punta	139	C9
Medéa	101	F1
Medellín	136	B2
Medelpad	62	G5
Medenine	101	H2
Mederdra	100	B5
Medford	122	C6
Medgidia	73	K3
Medicine Bow Mountains	123	L7
Medicine Bow Peak	123	L7
Medicine Hat	123	J3
Medicine Lodge	127	N2
Medina Saudi Arabia	96	D4
Medina N. Dakota, U.S.A.	123	Q4
Medina New York, U.S.A.	125	L5
Medinaceli	66	E2
Medina del Campo	66	D2
Medina de Ríoseco	66	D2
Medina Sidonia	66	D4
Medina Terminal Canal	125	L5
Medinïpur	93	G4
Mediterranean Sea	98	D3
Medjerda, Monts de la	69	B7
Medkovets	73	G4
Mednyy, Ostrov	81	T4
Médoc	65	C6
Médole	68	C3
Medvezh'l, Ostrova	85	U2
Medvezh'yegorsk	78	E3
Medvyeditsa	78	F4
Medway	53	H3
Medyn'	78	F5
Medynskiy Zavorot, Poluostrov	78	K2
Meeberrie	112	D4
Meechkyn, Kosa	85	Y3
Meekatharra	112	D4
Meeker	123	L7
Meerut	92	E3
Meeteetse	123	K5
Mega	91	J6
Megálo Khorió	75	J4
Megalópolis	75	G4

Mégara	75	G3	Melville Hills	118	L2	Mercedes *Argentina*	138	E5	Mesudiye	77	G2

Mégara	75 G3	Melville Hills	118 L2	Mercedes *Argentina*	138 E5	Mesudiye	77 G2
Megève	65 G6	Melville Island *Australia*	112 G1	Mercedes *Uruguay*	138 E6	Meta	136 D2
Megget Reservoir	57 E5	Melville Island *Canada*	120 D2	Mercimek	77 F4	Metán	138 D5
Meghalaya	93 H3	Melville, Kap	120 P2	Mercimekkale	77 J3	Metapan	132 C7
Megion	84 B4	Melville, Lake	121 Q7	Mercurea	73 G3	Metaponto	69 F5
Megísti	76 C4	Melville Peninsula	120 K4	Mercury Bay	115 E2	Metema	103 G5
Megra *U.S.S.R.*	78 F3	Melvin, Lough	58 F4	Mercy, Cape	120 P5	Meteran	114 E2
Megra *U.S.S.R.*	78 G2	Mélykút	72 E2	Mere	52 E3	Methven *New Zealand*	115 C5
Mehamn	62 M1	Melyuveyem	85 W4	Meredith, Cape	139 D10	Methven *U.K.*	57 E4
Mehndawal	92 F3	Memba	109 H2	Meredoua	100 F3	Methwin, Mount	112 E4
Mehrān	94 H5	Memberamo	91 K6	Mére Lava	114 U11	Metković	72 D4
Meig	56 D3	Memboro	91 F7	Mereworth	53 H3	Metlika	72 C3
Meighen Island	120 G2	Memel	63 L9	Mergenovo	79 J6	Metropolis	124 F8
Meiktila	93 J4	Memmingen	70 D4	Mergui	93 J6	Métsovon	75 F3
Meiningen	70 D3	Mempawah	90 D5	Mergui Archipelago	93 J6	Metu	103 G6
Meira	66 C1	Memphis *Tennessee, U.S.A.*	128 H3	Meribah	113 J5	Metz	64 G4
Meissen	70 E3	Memphis *Texas, U.S.A.*	127 M3	Meriç	76 B2	Meulaboh	90 B5
Mei Xian	87 M7	Mena	128 E3	Mérida *Mexico*	131 Q7	Meureudu	90 B4
Mejez El Bab	69 B7	Menai Bridge	55 E3	Mérida *Spain*	66 C3	Meurthe	64 G4
Mejillones	138 B4	Ménaka	101 F5	Mérida *Venezuela*	136 C2	Meuse	64 F3
Mekambo	106 B2	Mendawai	90 E6	Mérida, Cordillera de	136 C2	Mexborough	55 H3
Mek'elē	103 G5	Mende	65 E6	Meriden	125 P6	Mexia	128 D5
Meknès	100 D2	Mendi	114 C3	Meridian	128 H4	Mexicali	126 E7
Mekong	93 L6	Mendip Hills	52 E3	Merig	114 T11	Mexico	130 H6
Mekong, Mouths of the	93 L7	Mendocino, Cape	122 B7	Merir	91 J5	Mexico *U.S.A.*	124 E7
Mela	62 U12	Mendoza	138 C6	Merirumā	137 G3	Mexico City	131 K8
Melaka	90 C5	Menemen	76 B3	Merkys	63 L9	Mexico, Gulf of	117 K6
Mélambes	75 H5	Menen	64 E3	Mermaid Reef	112 D2	Meydancik	77 K2
Melanesia	142 F4	Menfi	69 D7	Merowe	103 F4	Meydān e Gel	95 M7
Melawi	90 E6	Mengcheng	93 N2	Merredin	112 D5	Meydanī, Ra's e	95 P9
Melbourne *Australia*	113 J6	Mengcun	87 M4	Merrick	57 D5	Meymaneh	94 S4
Melbourne *U.S.A.*	129 M6	Mengen	76 E2	Merrill	124 F4	Meymeh	95 K5
Melbourne Island	119 Q2	Mengene Daği	77 L3	Merrillville	124 G6	Meynypil'gyno	85 X4
Melbu	62 F2	Menggala	90 D6	Merrimack	125 Q5	Meyrueis	65 E6
Melchor Muzquiz	127 M7	Menghai	93 K4	Merritt	122 D2	Mezdra	73 G4
Melenki	78 G4	Mengjiagang	88 C2	Merritt Island	129 M6	Mezen' *U.S.S.R.*	78 G2
Meleuz	78 K5	Mengjiawan	87 K4	Merriwa	113 L5	Mezen' *U.S.S.R.*	78 H2
Melfi *Chad*	102 C5	Mengla	93 K4	Mersa Fatma	96 E9	Mézenc, Mont	65 F6
Melfi *Italy*	69 E5	Mengshan	93 M4	Mersea Island	53 H3	Mezenskaya Guba	78 G2
Melfort	119 Q5	Mengyin	87 M4	Merseburg	70 D3	Mezenskiy	84 F2
Melgaço	137 G4	Meniet	101 F3	Merse, The	57 F5	Mezhdurechensk	84 D6
Melhus	62 D4	Menihek, Lac	121 N7	Mersey	55 G3	Mezhdusharskiy, Ostrov	80 G2
Melilla	100 E1	Meningie	113 H6	Merseyside	55 G3	Mezhgor'ye	71 K4
Melipilla	139 B6	Menk'ya	78 L3	Mersin	76 F4	Mezőtúr	72 F2
Melita	123 P3	Menominee *U.S.A.*	124 G4	Mersing	90 C5	Mezquital	130 G6
Melito di Porto Salvo	69 E7	Menominee *U.S.A.*	124 G4	Mērsrags	63 K8	Mezzana	68 C2
Melitopol'	79 F6	Menomonee Falls	124 F5	Merthyr Tydfil	52 D3	Mhangura	108 F3
Melk	68 E1	Menongue	106 C5	Mértola	66 C4	Mhow	92 E4
Melksham	53 E3	Menorca	67 J3	Mërtvyy Kultuk, Sor	79 J6	Miahuatlán	131 L9
Mellègue, Oued	101 G1	Mentawai, Kepulauan	90 B6	Mertz Glacier	141 K5	Miajadas	66 D3
Mellerud	63 E7	Mentawai, Selat	90 B6	Merzifon	76 F2	Miami *Arizona, U.S.A.*	126 G4
Melle-sur-Bretonne	65 C5	Mentok	90 D6	Merzig	70 B4	Miami *Florida, U.S.A.*	129 M8
Melling	55 G2	Menton	68 A4	Mesa	126 G4	Miami *Ohio, U.S.A.*	124 H7
Mellish Reef	113 M2	Mentor	125 K6	Mesaras, Kólpos	75 H5	Miami Beach	129 M8
Mellte	52 D3	Menyamya	114 D3	Meschede	70 C3	Miānābād	95 N3
Mělník	70 F3	Menzel Bourguiba	69 B7	Meselefors	62 G4	Miandowāb	94 H3
Melo	138 F6	Meon	53 F4	Meshik	118 D4	Mīāneh	94 H3
Melolo	91 G7	Meppel	64 G2	Meshra'er Req	102 E6	Miang, Pou	93 K5
Melozitna	118 E2	Meppen	70 B2	Mesolóngion	75 F3	Mianwali	92 D2
Melrhir, Chott	101 G2	Mequinenza	67 G2	Messina *Italy*	69 E6	Mianyang	93 K2
Melrose	124 C4	Merabéllou, Kólpos	75 H5	Messina *South Africa*	108 F4	Miarinarivo *Madagascar*	109 J3
Melsungen	70 C3	Merak	90 D7	Messina, Stretto di	69 E6	Miarinarivo *Madagascar*	109 J3
Meltaus	62 L3	Merano	68 C2	Messingham	55 J3	Miass	84 Ad5
Melton Mowbray	53 G2	Merauke	91 L7	Messíni	75 F4	Miastko	71 G1
Melun	64 E4	Mercan Daği	77 H3	Messiniakós Kólpos	75 F4	Micang Shan	93 L2
Melut	103 F5	Mercato Saraceno	68 D4	Messo	84 B3	Michalovce	71 J4
Melvern Lake	124 C7	Merced	126 B2	Messoyakha	84 B3	Michelson, Mount	118 G2
Melville	123 N2	Mercedario, Cerro	138 B6	Mesta	75 H2	Michigan	124 H5
Melville Bugt	120 P2	Mercedes *Argentina*	139 C6	Mestiya	77 K1	Michigan City	124 G6
Melville, Cape	113 J1	Mercedes *Argentina*	139 E6	Mestre	68 D3	Michigan, Lake	124 G5

Mittelmark	70	E2
Mitumba, Chaine des	107	E4
Mitwaba	107	E4
Mitzic	106	B2
Mixteco	131	K8
Miyāh, Wadi al	77	H5
Miyake-jima	89	G8
Miyake-shotō	89	G11
Miyako	88	H6
Miyako-jima	89	G11
Miyakonojō	89	C10
Miyaly	79	J6
Miyazaki	89	C10
Miyazu	89	E8
Miyoshi	89	D8
Mizdah	101	H2
Mizen Head *Cork, Ireland*	59	C10
Mizen Head *Wicklow, Ireland*	59	K7
Mizhi	87	L4
Mizil	73	J3
Mizoram	93	H4
Mizpe Ramon	94	B6
Mjölby	63	F7
Mjøsa	63	D6
Mladá Boleslav	70	F3
Mladenovac	72	F3
Mľawa	71	J2
Mljet	72	D4
Moa *Cuba*	133	K4
Moa *Indonesia*	91	H7
Moab	127	H1
Moa Island	114	C4
Moala	114	R9
Moate	59	G6
Moatize	109	F3
Moba	107	E4
Mobaye	102	D7
Mobayi-Mbongo	106	D2
Moberly	124	D7
Mobile	129	H5
Mobile Bay	129	H5
Mobridge	123	P5
Mobutu Sese Seko, Lake	107	F2
Moca	114	S9
Mocajuba	137	G4
Moçambique	109	H3
Moçâmedes	106	B6
Mocha, Isla	139	B7
Mochudi	108	E4
Mocímboa da Praia	109	H2
Moctexuma	127	H6
Moctezuma	131	K7
Mocuba	109	G3
Modder	108	E5
Modena *Italy*	68	C3
Modena *U.S.A.*	126	F2
Modesto	126	B2
Modica	69	E7
Modigliana	68	C3
Mödling	68	F1
Modowi	91	J6
Moe	113	K6
Moelv	63	D6
Moengo	137	G2
Moffat	57	E5
Moffat Peak	115	B6
Mogadishu	107	J2
Mogadouro	66	C2
Mogdy	85	N6
Mogilev	78	E5

Mogilev-Podol'skiy	79	D6
Mogi-Mirim	138	G4
Mogincual	109	H3
Moglicë	75	F2
Mogocha	85	L6
Mogoi	91	J6
Mogok	93	J4
Mogollon Plateau	126	G3
Mogotoyevo, Ozero	85	R2
Mogoyn	86	H2
Mogoytuy	85	J6
Moguer	66	C4
Mohács	72	E2
Mohaka	115	F3
Mohall	123	P3
Mohāmmadābād	95	Q6
Mohammadia	100	F1
Mohawk	125	N5
Moheli	109	H2
Mohill	58	G5
Mohoro	107	G4
Moi	63	B7
Moidart	57	C4
Moimenta da Beira	66	C2
Moindou	114	W16
Mointy	86	C2
Mo i Rana	62	F3
Moisie	121	N7
Moissac	65	D6
Moïssala	102	C6
Mojave	126	C3
Mojave Desert	126	D3
Moji	89	C9
Mojones, Cerro	138	C5
Mojú	137	H4
Mokai	115	E3
Mokelumne	122	D8
Moknine	101	H1
Mokohinau Island	115	E1
Mokokchung	93	H3
Mokolo	105	H3
Mokp'o	87	P5
Mokra Gora	72	F4
Moláoi	75	G4
Molat	72	C3
Mold	55	F3
Moldavia	73	J2
Moldaviya S.S.R.	79	D6
Molde	62	B5
Moldovà	73	J2
Moldova Nouă	73	F3
Moldoveanu	73	H3
Moldoviţa	73	H2
Mole *Devon, U.K.*	52	D4
Mole *Surrey, U.K.*	53	G3
Molepolole	108	E4
Molfetta	69	F5
Molina de Aragón	67	F2
Molina de Segura	67	F3
Moline	124	E6
Molkom	63	E7
Mollakendi	77	H3
Mollaosman	77	K3
Mollendo	138	B3
Mölln	70	D2
Mölnlycke	63	E8
Molodechno	71	M1
Molodezhnaya	141	D5
Molodo *U.S.S.R.*	85	L3
Molodo *U.S.S.R.*	85	L3

Mologa	78	F4
Molokai	126	S10
Moloma	78	H4
Molotov	78	K4
Moloundou	105	J5
Molsheim	64	G4
Molson Lake	119	R5
Moluccas	91	H6
Moma *Mozambique*	109	R3
Moma *U.S.S.R.*	85	Q3
Mombasa	107	G3
Mombetsu	88	J3
Momboyo	106	C3
Momi, Ra's	97	P9
Momol	71	L2
Mompós	136	C2
Møn	63	E9
Monach Islands	56	A3
Monach, Sound of	56	A3
Monaco	65	G7
Monadhliath Mountains	57	D3
Monaghan	58	J4
Monahans	127	L5
Mona, Isla	133	P5
Mona Passage	133	N5
Monarch Mount	118	K5
Monarch Pass	123	L8
Monar, Loch	56	C3
Monashe Mountains	122	E2
Monasterevin	59	H6
Monastir *Albania*	73	F5
Monastir *Italy*	69	B6
Monastir *Tunisia*	101	H1
Monastyriska	73	H1
Monatélé	105	H5
Moncalieri	68	A3
Monção	66	B1
Mönchdorf	68	E1
Monchegorsk	62	Q3
Monchique	66	B4
Monclova	127	M7
Moncontour	64	B4
Moncton	121	P8
Mondego	66	C2
Mondoñedo	66	C1
Mondovi	68	A3
Mondragone	69	D5
Mondsee	68	D2
Monemvasía	75	G4
Moneron, Ostrov	88	H2
Monesterio	66	C3
Moneymore	58	J3
Monfalcone	68	D3
Monforte	66	C3
Monforte de Lemos	66	C1
Monga	106	D2
Mongala	106	D2
Mongalla	103	F6
Mong Cai	93	L4
Mongga	114	H5
Mongge	91	J6
Mong Hang	93	J4
Monghyr	92	G3
Mong Lin	93	K4
Mongo	102	C5
Mongolia	86	G2
Mongororo	102	D5
Mongu	106	D6
Mönhhaan	87	L2
Moniaive	57	E5

Monifieth	57	F4
Moniquira	136	C2
Monitor Range	122	F8
Monkira	113	J3
Monkland	52	E2
Monkoto	106	D3
Monmouth *U.K.*	52	E3
Monmouth *U.S.A.*	124	E6
Monnow	52	E3
Mono	105	F4
Mono Lake	126	C2
Monólithos	75	J4
Monopoli	69	F5
Monóvar	67	F3
Monreal del Campo	67	F2
Monreale	69	D6
Monroe *Georgia, U.S.A.*	129	L4
Monroe *Louisiana, U.S.A.*	128	F4
Monroe *Michigan, U.S.A.*	124	J6
Monroe *N. Carolina, U.S.A.*	129	M3
Monroe *Wisconsin, U.S.A.*	124	F5
Monrovia	104	C4
Mons	64	E3
Monsarás, Ponta da	138	J3
Monselice	68	C3
Monserrat	67	F3
Montaigu	65	C5
Montalbán	67	F2
Montalbo	66	E3
Montalcino	68	C4
Montalto	69	E6
Montalvo	136	B4
Montamarta	66	D2
Montana	122	K4
Montánchez	66	C3
Montañita	136	B3
Montargis	65	E5
Montauban	65	D6
Montauk Point	125	Q6
Montbard	65	F5
Montbéliard	65	G5
Montblanch	67	G2
Montbrison	65	F6
Montceau-les-Mines	65	F5
Montcornet	64	F4
Mont-de-Marsan	65	C7
Montdidier	64	E4
Monte Alegre	137	G4
Monte Azul	138	H3
Monte Bello	136	B5
Montebello	125	N4
Monte Carlo	68	A4
Monte Caseros	139	E6
Montecatini Terme	68	C4
Monte Cristi	133	M5
Montecristo, Isola di	69	C4
Montego Bay	132	J5
Montélimar	65	F6
Montemaggiore Belsito	69	D7
Montemorelos	128	C8
Montemor-o-Novo	66	B3
Montepuez	109	G2
Montepulciano	68	C4
Monte Quemado	138	D5
Montereau-faut-Yonne	64	E4
Monterey	126	B2
Monterey Bay	126	B2
Montería	136	B2
Montero	138	D3
Monterotondo	69	D4

Monterrey	**128**	B8	Moradal, Sierra do	**66**	C3	Moronade, Cerro des	**130**	G7	Mostaganem	**100**	F1
Monte Santu, Capo di	**69**	B5	Mora de Rubielos	**67**	F2	Morondava	**109**	H4	Mostar	**72**	D4
Montes Claros	**138**	E3	Morafenobe	**109**	H3	Morón de la Frontera	**66**	D4	Mostiska	**71**	K4
Montevideo *Uruguay*	**139**	E6	Moråg	**71**	H2	Moroni	**109**	H2	Mosty	**71**	L2
Montevideo *U.S.A.*	**124**	C4	Morales	**132**	C7	Moron Us He	**93**	H2	Mostyn	**55**	F3
Monte Vista	**127**	J2	Moramanga	**109**	J3	Morotai	**91**	H5	Mosul	**77**	K4
Montezuma Peak	**127**	J2	Moran	**123**	J6	Moroto	**107**	F2	Mosŭlpo	**87**	P5
Montfort-sur-Meu	**64**	B4	Morant Cays	**132**	K6	Morozovsk	**79**	G6	Mot'a	**103**	G5
Montgomery *U.K.*	**52**	D2	Morant Point	**132**	J6	Morpara	**137**	J6	Mota	**114**	T10
Montgomery *U.S.A.*	**129**	J4	Moratuwa	**92**	E7	Morpeth	**55**	H1	Mota del Cuervo	**66**	E3
Montguyon	**65**	C6	Morava *Czechoslovakia*	**71**	G4	Morrilton	**128**	F3	Motala	**63**	F7
Monti	**69**	B5	Morava *Yugoslavia*	**73**	F3	Morrinhos	**138**	G3	Mota Lava	**114**	T10
Monticello *Arkansas, U.S.A.*	**128**	G4	Moraveh Tappeh	**95**	M3	Morrinsville	**115**	E2	Motegi	**89**	H7
Monticello *Florida, U.S.A.*	**129**	L5	Morawa	**112**	D4	Morris *Canada*	**123**	R3	Motherwell	**57**	E5
Monticello *New York, U.S.A.*	**125**	N6	Moray Firth	**56**	E3	Morris *U.S.A.*	**124**	C4	Motihari	**92**	F3
Monticello *Utah, U.S.A.*	**127**	H2	Morbi	**92**	D4	Morris Jesup, Kap	**140**	Q2	Motilla del Palancar	**67**	F3
Montiel, Campo de	**66**	E3	Mor Budějovice	**70**	F4	Morris, Mount	**112**	G4	Motovskiy Zaliv	**62**	G2
Montignac	**65**	D6	Mörbylånga	**63**	G8	Morristown	**129**	L2	Motril	**66**	E4
Montilla	**66**	D4	Morden	**123**	Q3	Morro Bay	**126**	B3	Motueka *New Zealand*	**115**	D4
Mont-Joli	**125**	R2	Mordoğan	**76**	B3	Morro do Chapéu	**137**	J6	Motueka *New Zealand*	**115**	D4
Mont Laurier	**125**	N3	Mordov A.S.S.R.	**78**	G5	Morro, Punta	**139**	B5	Motupiko Blenheim	**115**	D4
Montluçon	**65**	E5	Mordovo	**79**	G5	Morros, Punta	**131**	P8	Motykleyka	**85**	R5
Montmagny	**125**	Q3	Moreau	**122**	N5	Morrosquillo, Golfo de	**133**	K10	Moúdhros	**75**	H3
Montmédy	**64**	F4	Morebattle	**57**	F5	Mors	**63**	C8	Moudjéria	**100**	C5
Montmirail	**64**	E4	Morecambe	**55**	G2	Morshansk	**79**	G5	Mouka	**102**	D6
Montmorillon	**65**	D5	Morecambe Bay	**55**	E2	Mortagne	**64**	D4	Mould Bay	**120**	C2
Monto	**113**	L3	Moreda	**66**	E4	Mortain	**64**	C4	Moulins	**65**	E5
Montoro	**66**	D4	Moree	**113**	K4	Mortara	**68**	B3	Moulmein	**93**	J5
Montpelier	**122**	J6	Morehead *Papua New*			Morteau	**65**	G5	Moulouya, Oued	**100**	E2
Montpellier *France*	**65**	E7	*Guinea*	**114**	C3	Morte Bay	**52**	C3	Moulton	**55**	H2
Montpellier *U.S.A.*	**125**	P4	Morehead *U.S.A.*	**124**	J7	Mortes	**137**	G6	Moultrie	**129**	L5
Montraux	**68**	A2	Morehead City	**129**	P3	Morton *U.K.*	**53**	G2	Moultrie, Lake	**129**	M4
Montreal	**124**	H3	Morelia	**131**	J8	Morton *U.S.A.*	**122**	C4	Moúnda, Ákra	**75**	F3
Montréal	**125**	P4	Morella	**67**	F2	Morundah	**113**	K5	Mound City	**124**	C6
Montreal Lake	**119**	P5	More, Loch *U.K.*	**56**	D2	Morven *Australia*	**113**	K4	Moundou	**102**	C6
Montreal River Harbour	**124**	H3	More, Loch *U.K.*	**56**	E2	Morven *U.K.*	**57**	E3	Moung	**93**	K6
Montrose *U.K.*	**57**	F4	Morena, Sierra	**66**	D3	Morvern	**57**	C4	Mountain	**118**	K2
Montrose *U.S.A.*	**127**	J1	Moreno	**126**	G6	Morwell	**113**	K6	Mountain Ash	**52**	D3
Mont Saint-Michel	**64**	C4	Moreno, Bahía	**138**	B4	Mōsakula	**63**	L7	Mountain Home *Arkansas,*		
Montseny	**67**	H2	Møre og Romsdal	**62**	C5	Mosby	**63**	B7	*U.S.A.*	**128**	F2
Montserrat	**133**	R6	Moresby Island	**118**	J5	Moscow *U.S.A.*	**122**	F4	Mountain Home *Idaho, U.S.A.*	**122**	G6
Mont Wright	**121**	N7	Mores Island	**132**	J1	Moscow *U.S.S.R.*	**78**	F4	Mountain Village	**118**	C3
Monywa	**93**	J4	Moreton Bay	**113**	L4	Mosedale	**55**	F2	Mount Airy	**129**	M2
Monza	**68**	B3	Moreton-in-Marsh	**53**	F3	Mosel	**70**	B4	Mount Ararat	**77**	L3
Monzón	**67**	G2	Moreton Island	**113**	L4	Moselle	**64**	G4	Mount Bellew	**59**	E6
Moonie	**113**	K4	Morez	**65**	G5	Moses Lake	**122**	E4	Mount Desert Island	**125**	R4
Moopna	**112**	F5	Morgan City	**128**	G6	Moseyevo	**78**	H2	Mount Doreen	**112**	G3
Moora	**112**	D5	Morganton	**129**	M3	Mosgiel	**115**	C6	Mount Douglas	**113**	K3
Mooraberree	**113**	J4	Morgantown	**125**	L7	Mosha	**78**	G3	Mount Elba	**113**	H5
Moorcroft	**123**	M5	Morgongåva	**63**	G7	Moshchnyy, Ostrov	**63**	M6	Mount Gambier	**113**	J6
Moore, Lake	**112**	D4	Mori *China*	**86**	F3	Moshi	**107**	G3	Mount Hagen	**114**	C3
Moorfoot Hills	**57**	E5	Mori *Japan*	**88**	H4	Mosjøen	**62**	E4	Mount Isa	**113**	H3
Moorhead	**124**	B3	Moriarty	**127**	K3	Moskenesøya	**62**	E3	Mount Magnet	**112**	D4
Moorlands	**113**	H6	Morioka	**88**	H6	Moskosel	**62**	H4	Mountmellick	**59**	H6
Moorlinch	**52**	E3	Morlaix	**64**	B4	Moskva	**78**	F4	Mount Pleasant *Iowa, U.S.A.*	**124**	E6
Moose	**121**	K7	Morley	**55**	H3	Mosonmagyaróvár	**72**	D2	Mount Pleasant *Michigan,*		
Moosehead Lake	**125**	R4	Mörlunda	**63**	F8	Mosquera	**136**	B3	*U.S.A.*	**124**	H5
Moose Jaw	**123**	M2	Mormanno	**69**	F6	Mosquitia	**132**	E7	Mount Pleasant *Texas, U.S.A.*	**128**	E4
Moose Lake *Canada*	**119**	Q5	Mornington, Isla	**139**	A9	Mosquito Lake	**119**	Q3	Mount Pleasant *Utah, U.S.A.*	**126**	G1
Moose Lake *U.S.A.*	**124**	D3	Mornington Island	**113**	H2	Mosquitos, Costa de	**132**	F8	Mountrath	**59**	H6
Moose Mountain Creek	**123**	N2	Morobe	**114**	D3	Mosquitos, Golfo de los	**132**	G10	Mount's Bay	**52**	B4
Moosonee	**121**	K7	Morocco	**100**	D2	Moss	**63**	D7	Mount Shasta	**122**	C7
Mopêia Velha	**109**	G3	Morogoro	**107**	G4	Mossaka	**106**	C3	Mount Thule	**120**	L3
Mopti	**100**	E6	Moro Gulf	**91**	G4	Mossburn	**115**	B6	Mount Vernon *Alabama,*		
Moqor	**92**	C2	Morokovo	**85**	W3	Mosselbaai	**108**	D6	*U.S.A.*	**129**	H5
Moquequa	**138**	B3	Moroleón	**131**	J7	Mossley	**58**	L3	Mount Vernon *Illinois, U.S.A.*	**124**	F7
Mora *Cameroon*	**105**	H3	Morombe	**109**	H4	Mossman	**113**	K2	Mount Vernon *Indiana, U.S.A.*	**124**	G8
Mora *Portugal*	**66**	B3	Morón	**132**	H3	Mossoró	**137**	K5	Mount Vernon *Ohio, U.S.A.*	**124**	J6
Mora *Sweden*	**63**	F6	Mörön *Mongolia*	**86**	J2	Most	**70**	E3	Mount Vernon *Washington,*		
Moradabad	**92**	E3	Mörön *Mongolia*	**87**	L2	Mosta	**74**	C5	*U.S.A.*	**122**	C3

Moura *Brazil*	136	E4	Muconda	106	D5	Mull Head *U.K.*	56	F2	Mureş	73	F2
Moura *Portugal*	66	C3	Mucuim	136	E5	Mull Head *U.K.*	56	F1	Muret	65	D7
Mourdi, Depression du	102	D4	Múcur	76	F3	Mullinavat	59	H8	Murfreesboro *N. Carolina,*
Mourne Mountains	58	K4	Mudanjiang	88	B3	Mullingar	59	H5	*U.S.A.*	129	P2
Moussoro	102	C5	Mudan Jiang	88	B3	Mullsjö	63	E8	Murfreesboro *Tennessee,*
Moutong	91	G5	Mudanya	76	C2	Mull, Sound of	57	C4	*U.S.A.*	129	J3
Movas	127	H6	Mudayy	97	L8	Mulobezi	106	E6	Murgab *Tadzhikistan S.S.R.,*
Moville	58	H2	Muddy Gap Pass	123	L6	Mulrany	58	C5	*U.S.S.R.*	86	C4
Moy	58	D4	Mudgee	113	K5	Multan	92	D2	Murgab *Turkmeniya S.S.R.,*
Moyale	107	G2	Mudurnu	76	D2	Multanovy	84	A4	*U.S.S.R.*	95	R3
Moyamba	104	C4	Mueda	109	G2	Multia	62	L5	Mūrī	95	N3
Moyen Atlas	100	E2	Muelas	66	D2	Mulym'ya	84	Ad4	Muriaé	138	H4
Moygashel	58	J4	Muéo	114	W16	Mumbles, The	52	C3	Muriege	106	D4
Moyo *Indonesia*	91	F7	Mufulira	107	E5	Mumbwa	106	E6	Müritz See	70	E2
Moyo *Uganda*	106	F2	Mufu Shan	93	M3	Mumra	79	H6	Murmansk	78	E2
Moyobamba	136	B5	Muganskaya Step'	94	J2	Muna *Indonesia*	91	G7	Murmanskaya Oblast'	62	P2
Moyu	92	E1	Müghar	95	L5	Muna *U.S.S.R.*	85	L3	Murmansk Bereg	78	F2
Mozambique	109	G3	Mughshin	97	M7	Munayly	79	J6	Murmashi	62	Q2
Mozambique Channel	109	H3	Mugi	89	E9	Münchberg	70	D3	Murnau	70	D5
Mozhaysk	78	F4	Mugía	66	B1	München	70	D4	Murom	78	G4
Mozhga	78	J4	Mugila, Monts	107	E4	Münchengladbach	70	B3	Muromtsevo	84	B5
Mozyr'	79	D5	Muğla	76	C4	Muncie	124	H6	Muroran	88	H4
Mpanda	107	F4	Muhammad Qol	103	G3	Munda	114	H6	Muros	66	B1
Mpé	106	B3	Muḥammad, Ras	103	F2	Mundesley	53	J2	Muroto-zaki	89	E9
Mpika	107	F5	Muḥaywir	77	J6	Mundford	53	H2	Murphy	129	L3
Mporokoso	107	F4	Mühldorf	70	E4	Mundo	67	F3	Murra Murra	113	K4
Mpraeso	104	E4	Mühlhausen	70	D3	Mundo Novo	138	J6	Murray *Australia*	113	H5
Mrakovo	79	K5	Muhu	63	K7	Mungbere	107	E2	Murray *Kentucky, U.S.A.*	124	F8
M.R. Gómez, Presa	127	N7	Mui Bai Bung	93	K7	Munich	70	D4	Murray *Utah, U.S.A.*	122	J7
Mrkonjič Grad	72	D3	Muick	57	E3	Muniesa	67	F2	Murray Bridge	110	J9
Msaken	101	H1	Muirkirk	57	D5	Munkfors	63	E7	Murray Harbour	121	P8
M'Sila	67	J5	Muite	109	G2	Mun, Mae Nam	93	K5	Murray, Lake *Papua New*
Msta	78	E4	Mukachevo	79	C6	Muñoz Gamero, Península de	139	B10	*Guinea*	114	C3
Mstislav'	78	E5	Mukah	90	E5	Münster	70	B3	Murray, Lake *U.S.A.*	129	M3
Mtsensk	79	F5	Mukawa	88	H4	Munster	59	D8	Murraysburg	108	D6
Mtwara	107	G5	Mukawwar	96	C6	Münsterland	70	B3	Murree	92	D2
Mualo	109	G2	Mukdahan	93	K5	Muntenia	73	J3	Murrumbidgee	113	K5
Muang Chiang Rai	93	J5	Mukden	87	N3	Muntinlupa	91	G3	Mursal	77	H3
Muang Khon Kaen	93	K5	Mukhen	88	F1	Munzur Dağlari	77	H3	Mursala	90	B5
Muang Lampang	93	J5	Mukhor-Konduy	85	J6	Muong Khoua	93	K4	Murud	90	F5
Muang Lamphun	93	J5	Mukomuko	90	D6	Muong Ou Tay	93	K4	Murukta	84	G3
Muang Loei	93	K5	Mukur	79	J6	Muong Sing	93	K4	Murupara	115	F3
Muang Nan	93	K5	Mula	67	F3	Muonio	62	K3	Murwara	92	F4
Muang Phayao	93	J5	Mulaly	86	D2	Muoniojoki	62	K3	Murwillumbah	113	L4
Muang Phetchabun	93	K5	Mulan	88	B3	Muqdisho	107	J2	Murz	68	E2
Muang Phichit	93	K5	Mulanay	91	G3	Muqshin, Wadi	97	M7	Murzuq	101	H3
Muang Phitsanulok	93	K5	Mulayit Taung	93	J5	Mur	68	E2	Murzuq, Idhān	101	H4
Muang Phrae	93	K5	Mulchatna	118	D3	Mura	72	D2	Mürzzuschlag	68	E2
Muanza	109	F3	Mulchen	139	B7	Muradiye *Turkey*	76	B3	Muş	77	J3
Muar	90	C5	Mulde	70	E3	Muradiye *Turkey*	77	K3	Musala	73	G4
Muara	90	E4	Muleshoe	127	L3	Murallón, Cerro	139	B9	Muṣallam, Wadi	97	N5
Muarabungo	90	D6	Mulga Downs	112	D3	Murang'a	107	G3	Musan	88	B4
Muaraenim	90	D6	Mulgrave	121	P8	Murashi	78	H4	Musandam Peninsula	97	N3
Muaralesan	91	F5	Mulgrave Island	114	C4	Murat *France*	65	E6	Musay'īd	97	K4
Muarasiberut	90	B6	Mulhacén	66	E4	Murat *Turkey*	77	J3	Muscat	97	P5
Muarasigep	90	B6	Mülheim	70	B3	Muratbasi	77	K3	Musgrave Ranges	112	G4
Muarasipongi	90	B5	Mulhouse	65	G5	Murat Daği	76	C3	Mushāsh al Hādī	97	J3
Muaratebo	90	D6	Muligort	84	Ad4	Muratli	76	B2	Musheramore	59	D8
Muarateweh	90	E6	Muling *China*	88	C3	Muraysah, Ras al	101	K2	Mushie	106	C3
Mubende	107	F2	Muling *China*	88	C3	Murban	97	L5	Musi	90	C6
Mubi	105	H3	Muling He	88	D3	Murcheh Khvort	95	K5	Musian	94	H5
Mubrani	91	J6	Mull	57	C4	Murchison *Australia*	112	C4	Muskegon *U.S.A.*	124	G5
Mucajaí	136	E3	Mullaghanattin	59	C9	Murchison *Canada*	120	H4	Muskegon *U.S.A.*	124	H5
Muchinga Escarpment	107	F5	Mullaghanish	59	D9	Murchison *New Zealand*	115	D4	Muskingum	124	K7
Much Wenlock	52	E2	Mullaghareirk Mountains	59	D8	Murchison Sund	120	M2	Muskogee	128	E3
Muck	57	B4	Mullaghcleevaun	59	K6	Murcia *Spain*	67	F4	Musmar	103	G4
Muckanagh Lough	59	E7	Mullaghmore	58	J3	Murcia *Spain*	67	F3	Musoma	107	F3
Muckish Mount	58	G2	Muller, Pegunungan	90	E5	Murdo	123	P6	Mussau	114	D2
Muckle Roe	56	A1	Mullet, The	58	B4	Murdochville	125	T2	Musselburgh	57	E5
Muckross Head	58	E3	Mullewa	112	D4	Mürefte	76	B2	Musselshell	123	K4

Mussende	106	C5
Musserra	106	B4
Mussidan	65	D6
Mussuma	106	D5
Mussy	65	F5
Mustafakemalpaşa	76	C2
Mustang	92	F3
Mustang Draw	127	L4
Musters, Lago	139	C9
Mustvee	63	M7
Musu-dan	88	B5
Muswellbrook	113	L5
Mut *Egypt*	102	E2
Mut *Turkey*	76	E4
Mutá Ponta do	137	K6
Mutarara	109	G3
Mutare	109	F3
Mutki	77	J3
Mutnyy Materik	78	K2
Mutoko	109	F3
Mutoray	84	G4
Mutsu-wan	88	H5
Muurame	63	L5
Muurola	62	L3
Muwaffaq	97	M7
Muxima	106	B4
Muya	85	J5
Muyunkum, Peski	86	C3
Muzaffarabad	92	D2
Muzaffargarh	92	D2
Muzaffarnagar	92	E3
Muzaffarpur	92	G3
Muzon, Cape	118	J5
Muz Tagh Ata Range	92	E1
Mvuma	108	F3
Mwaniwowo	114	L7
Mwanza	107	F3
Mwaya	107	F4
Mweelrea	58	C5
Mwene Ditu	106	D4
Mwenezi *Zimbabwe*	108	F4
Mwenezi *Zimbabwe*	108	F4
Mwenga	107	E3
Mweru, Lake	107	E4
Mweru Wantipa, Lake	107	E4
Mwinilunga	106	D5
Myakit	85	S4
Myanaung	93	J5
Myaundzha	85	R4
Myaungmya	93	H5
Myeik Kyunzu	93	J6
Myingyan	93	J4
Myinmu	93	J4
Myitkyina	93	J3
Myitnge	93	J4
Myittha	93	J4
Myla	78	J2
Mymensingh	93	H4
Myre	62	F2
Mýri	62	W12
Myrtle Beach	129	N4
Myrviken	62	F5
Mysen	63	H7
Myśliborz	70	F2
Mysore	92	E6
Mys Shmidta	85	Y3
My Tho	93	L6
Mytishchi	78	F4
M'zab	101	F2
Mže	70	E4

Mzuzu	107	F5
Naalehu	126	T11
Naantali	63	K6
Naas	59	J6
Nabaõ	66	B3
Nabavatu	114	R8
Naberezhnyye	78	J4
Nabeul	101	H1
Nabire	91	K6
Nablus	94	B5
Nabouwalu	114	R8
Naburn	55	H3
Nacala-a-Velha	109	H2
Nacaome	132	D8
Nachiki	85	T6
Nachvak Fjord	121	P6
Nacogdoches	128	E5
Nacozari de García	127	H5
Nadachi	89	G7
Nadezhdinskoye	88	D1
Nadezhnyy, Mys	85	S2
Nadi	114	Q8
Nadiad	92	D4
Nădlac	72	F2
Nador	100	E1
Naduri	114	R8
Nadvornaya	71	L4
Nadym	84	A3
Naft-e Safid	94	J6
Nafūd, An	96	E2
Nafy	96	F4
Naga	91	G3
Nagagami	124	H2
Nagahama	89	D9
Naga Hills	93	H3
Nagai	89	G6
Nagaland	93	H3
Nagano	89	G7
Nagaoka	89	G7
Nagappattinam	92	E6
Nāgārjuna Sāgar	92	E5
Nagasaki	89	B9
Nagashima	89	F8
Nagato	89	C8
Nagaur	92	D3
Nagercoil	92	E7
Nagishot	103	F7
Nagles Mountains	59	F8
Nagornyy	85	L5
Nagorsk	78	J4
Nagoya	89	F8
Nagpur	92	E4
Nagqu	93	H2
Nags Head	129	Q3
Nagykanizsa	72	D2
Nagykáta	72	E2
Nagykőrös	72	E2
Naha	89	H10
Nahariya	94	B5
Nahāvand	94	J4
Nahe	70	B4
Nahoi, Cap	114	T11
Nahuel Huapi, Lago	139	B8
Naikliu	91	G7
Nailsea	52	E3
Nailsworth	52	E3
Naiman Qi	87	N3
Nā'īn	95	L5

Nain	121	P6
Naini Tal	92	E3
Nairai	114	R8
Nairn	56	E3
Nairobi	107	G3
Najafābād	95	K5
Najd	96	E4
Najibabad	92	E3
Najin	88	C4
N'Ajjer, Tassili	101	G3
Najrān	96	G8
Najrān, Wadi	96	G8
Nakadōri-shima	89	B9
Nakajo	89	G6
Nakamura	89	D9
Nakano	89	G7
Nakano-shima	89	B11
Nakatay	84	Ad5
Nakatsu	89	C9
Nakatsugawa	89	F8
Nak'fa	103	G4
Nakhichevan	77	L3
Nakhichevan A.S.S.R.	79	H8
Nakhl *Eygpt*	96	A2
Nakhl *Oman*	97	N5
Nakhodka *U.S.S.R.*	84	B3
Nakhodka *U.S.S.R.*	88	D4
Nakhon Pathom	93	J6
Nakhon Phanom	93	K5
Nakhon Ratchasima	93	K6
Nakhon Sawan	93	K5
Nakhon Si Thammarat	93	J7
Nakina	121	J7
Nakiri	89	F8
Naknek Lake	118	D4
Nakskov	63	F9
Naktong	87	P4
Nakuru	107	G3
Nakusp	122	F2
Nal'chik	79	G7
Nalgonda	92	E5
Nallamala Hills	92	E5
Nallihan	76	D2
Nālūt	101	H2
Namaa, Tanjung	91	H6
Namacunde	106	C6
Namacurra	109	G3
Namak, Daryācheh-ye	95	K4
Namakī	95	M6
Namakzar	95	Q5
Namakzar, Daryacheh-ye	95	Q5
Namangan	86	C3
Namapa	109	G2
Namaponda	109	G3
Namarroi	109	G3
Namasagali	107	F2
Namatanai	114	E2
Nambour	113	L4
Nam Can	93	K7
Nam Co	93	H2
Nam Dinh	93	L4
Nametil	109	G3
Namib Desert	108	B4
Namibe	106	B6
Namibia	108	C4
Namlea	91	H6
Namoi	113	L5
Namosi Peak	114	R8
Nampa	122	F6
Nampula	109	G3

Namsê La	92	F3
Namsen	62	E4
Namsos	62	D4
Namti	93	J3
Namtok	93	J5
Namuka-i-Lau	114	S9
Namuli	109	G3
Namur	64	F3
Namutoni	108	C3
Namwala	106	E6
Nana Barya	102	C6
Nanaimo	122	C3
Nanam	88	B5
Nanao	89	F7
Nancha	88	B2
Nanchang	87	M6
Nanchong	93	L2
Nancowry	93	H7
Nancy	64	G4
Nanda Devi	92	E2
Nandan	93	L3
Nānded	92	E5
Nandurbar	92	D4
Nandyal	92	E5
Nanfeng	87	M6
Nanga Eboko	105	H5
Nangahpinoh	90	E6
Nanga Parbat	92	D1
Nangatayap	90	E6
Nangong	87	M4
Nan Hai	83	K5
Nanjing	87	M5
Nanking	87	M5
Nan, Mae Nam	93	K5
Nanning	93	L4
Nanortalik	116	Q2
Nanpan Jiang	93	K4
Nanpara	92	F3
Nanpi	87	M4
Nanping	87	M6
Nansei-shotō	89	H10
Nansen Sound	120	H1
Nanshan Islands	90	E4
Nansha Qundao	90	E4
Nantais, Lac	121	M5
Nantes	65	C5
Nantong	87	N5
Nantua	65	F5
Nantucket Island	125	Q6
Nantucket Sound	125	Q6
Nantwich	55	G3
Nant-y-môch Reservoir	52	D2
Nanuku Passage	114	S8
Nanuku Reef	114	S8
Nanumanga	111	S3
Nanumea	111	S3
Nanusa, Kepulauan	91	H5
Nanyang	93	M2
Nanyuki	107	G2
Nao, Cabo de la	67	G3
Naococane, Lake	121	M7
Náousa	75	G2
Napa	126	A1
Napabalana	91	G6
Napalkovo	84	A2
Napas	84	C5
Nape	93	L5
Napier	115	F3
Naples *Italy*	69	E5
Naples *U.S.A.*	129	M7

Nikol'sk *U.S.S.R.*	79	H5
Nikol'sk *U.S.S.R.*	78	H4
Nikol'skiy	86	B2
Nikopol'	79	E6
Niksar	77	G2
Nĭkshahr	95	Q8
Nikšić	72	E4
Nikulino	84	D4
Nikumarora	111	U2
Nîl	103	F2
Nila	91	H7
Nilgiri Hills	92	E6
Nîl, Nahren	103	F2
Nilsiä	62	N5
Nimach	92	D4
Nimba Mountains	104	D4
Nîmes	65	F7
Nimmitabel	113	K6
Nimule	103	F6
Nina Bang Lake	120	L3
Nine Degree Channel	92	D7
Ninety Mile Beach	115	D1
Ninfas, Punta	139	D8
Ninfield	53	H4
Ning'an	88	B3
Ningbo	87	N6
Ningde	87	M6
Ningdu	87	M6
Ningguo	87	M5
Ninghe	87	M4
Ninghua	87	M6
Ningjing Shan	93	J2
Ningqiang	93	L2
Ningshan	93	L2
Ningwu	87	L4
Ningxia	93	L1
Ningyang	87	M4
Ninh Hoa	93	L6
Ninigo Group	114	C2
Ninnis Glacier	141	K5
Ninyako Vogumma	84	B2
Nioaque	138	E4
Niobrara	123	P6
Niono	100	D6
Nioro du Sahel	100	D5
Niort	65	C5
Nios	75	H4
Nipigon	124	F2
Nipigon, Lake	124	F2
Nipisiguit	125	S3
Nipissing, Lac	125	L3
Niquelândia	137	H6
Nīr	94	H2
Nirmal	92	E5
Nirmal Range	92	E5
Niš	73	F4
Nisa	66	C3
Nişāb	96	H9
Nišava	73	G4
Nishinoyama	89	E8
Nishi-suidō	89	B8
Nísiros	75	J4
Nisling	118	H3
Nisporeny	73	K2
Nissan	63	E8
Nisum Bredning	63	C8
Nitchequon	121	M7
Niterói	138	H4
Nith	57	E5
Nithsdale	57	E5

Nitra	71	H4
Niuafo'ou	111	T5
Niuatoputapu	111	U5
Niue	111	V5
Niulakita	111	S4
Niulan Jiang	93	K3
Niutao	111	S3
Nivelles	64	F3
Nivernais	65	E5
Nivshera	78	J3
Niwbwrch	54	E3
Nizamabad	92	E5
Nizhneangarsk	84	H5
Nizhneimbatskoye	84	D4
Nizhnekamsk	78	J4
Nizhnekamsko Vodokhranilishche	78	J4
Nizhneudinsk	84	F6
Nizhnevartovsk	84	B4
Nizhneye Bugayevo	84	Ab3
Nizhniy Lomov	79	G5
Nizhniy Yenangsk	78	H4
Nizhnyaya Bugayevo	78	J2
Nizhnyaya Chulym	84	B6
Nizhnyaya Omka	84	A5
Nizhnyaya Salda	84	Ad5
Nizhnyaya Shakhtama	85	K6
Nizhnyaya Tunguska	84	H5
Nizhnyaya Tura	78	K4
Nizhnyaya Voch	78	J3
Nizip	77	G4
Nízké Tatry	71	H4
Nizmennyy, Mys	88	E4
Njombe	107	F4
Njoroveto	114	H5
Njurundabommen	63	L5
Nkambe	105	H4
Nkayi	108	E3
Nkhotakota	107	F5
Nkongsamba	105	G5
Nmai Hka	93	J3
Noasca	68	A3
Noatak	118	C2
Nobeoka	89	C9
Nobres	137	F6
Nocera	69	E5
Nogales *Mexico*	126	G5
Nogales *U.S.A.*	126	G5
Nogata	89	C9
Nogent-le-Rotrou	64	D4
Nogent-sur-Seine	64	E4
Noginsk	78	F4
Noginskiy	84	E4
Nogoa	113	K3
Nogoyá	138	E6
Noheji	88	H5
Noire	93	K4
Noire, Montagnes	64	B4
Noirmoutier	65	B5
Noirmoutier, Île de	65	B5
Nok Kundi	92	B3
Nola *Central African Republic*	102	C7
Nola *Italy*	69	E5
Nolinsk	78	H4
Nomad	114	C3
Noma-misaki	89	C10
Nome	118	B3
Nomuka	111	U6
Nonburg	78	J2

Nonca	113	J3
Noncugl	114	C3
Nongan	87	P3
Nong Khai	93	K5
Nongoma	109	F5
Nonouti	111	R2
Nonthaburi	93	K6
Nontron	65	D6
Nookta Island	122	A3
Nootka Sound	122	A3
Nora	103	H4
Noranda	125	L2
Nordaustlandet	140	L2
Nordborg	63	E9
Nord Cap	62	T11
Norðdepil	62	Z14
Norden	70	B2
Nordenham	70	C2
Nordenshel'da, Arkhipelag	84	F1
Norderney	70	B2
Nordfjord	62	A6
Nordfjordeid	62	A6
Nordfold	62	F3
Nord-Friesische Inseln	63	C9
Nordhausen	70	D3
Nordhorn	70	B2
Nordkapp	62	L1
Nordkinn-halvøya	62	M1
Nord Kvaløy	62	H1
Nordland	63	E4
Nordmaling	62	H5
Nordostsee Kanal	70	C2
Norðoyar	62	Z14
Nordre Isortoq	120	R4
Nordre Strømfjord	120	R4
Nordstrand	70	C1
Norðurfjörður	62	U11
Nordvik	84	J2
Nordvik, Mys	84	J2
Nore	59	H8
Norfolk *U.K.*	53	H2
Norfolk *Nebraska, U.S.A.*	123	R6
Norfolk *Virginia, U.S.A.*	125	M8
Norfolk Island	111	Q7
Norfolk Lake	128	F2
Norheimsund	63	B6
Nori	84	A3
Noril'sk	84	D3
Norlat	78	J5
Norman *Australia*	113	J2
Norman *U.S.A.*	128	D3
Normanby	113	J1
Normanby Island	114	E3
Normandes, Îles	64	B4
Normandie	64	D4
Normandie, Collines de	64	C4
Normanton *Australia*	113	J2
Normanton *U.K.*	55	H3
Norman Wells	118	K2
Nornalup	112	D5
Norra Storfjället	62	F4
Norrbotten	62	M3
Nørresundby	63	C8
Norrfjärden	62	J4
Norristown	125	N6
Norrköping	63	L7
Norrland	62	F5
Norrtälje	63	H7
Norseman	112	E5
Norsjö	62	M4

Norsk	85	N6
Norsup	114	T12
Norte, Punta *Argentina*	139	D8
Norte, Punta *Argentina*	139	E7
Norte, Serra do	136	F6
Northallerton	55	H2
Northam	112	D5
Northampton *U.K.*	53	G2
Northampton *U.S.A.*	125	P5
Northamptonshire	53	G2
North Andaman	93	H6
North Arm	119	N3
North Astrolabe Reef	114	R9
North Battleford	119	P5
North Bay *Canada*	125	L3
North Bay *Ireland*	59	K8
North Bend	122	B6
North Berwick	57	F4
North Canadian	128	C3
North, Cape	121	P8
North Cape *New Zealand*	115	D1
North Cape *Norway*	62	L1
North Cape *U.S.A.*	118	A3
North Carolina	129	M3
North Cave	55	J3
North Channel *Canada*	124	J3
North Channel *U.K.*	58	L2
Northchapel	53	G3
North Charlton	55	H1
Northcliffe	112	D5
North Dakota	123	P4
North Dorset Downs	52	E4
North Downs	53	H3
Northeast Cape	118	B3
Northeast Providence Channel	132	J2
North Elmham	53	H2
Northern Ireland	58	H3
Northern Sporades	75	H3
Northern Territory	112	G3
North Esk	57	F4
Northfield	124	D4
North Flinders Range	113	H5
North Foreland	53	J3
North Geomagnetic Pole	140	S3
North Henik Lake	119	R3
North Korea	87	P4
North Kyme	55	J3
North Lakhimpur	93	H3
Northleach	53	F3
North Magnetic Pole	140	U3
North Miami Beach	129	M8
North Platte *U.S.A.*	123	N7
North Platte *U.S.A.*	123	P7
North Point *Canada*	121	P8
North Point *U.S.A.*	124	J4
North Pole	140	A1
North River	119	S4
North Roe	56	A1
North Ronaldsay	56	F1
North Ronaldsay Firth	56	F1
North Saskatchewan	119	P5
North Sea	50	H4
North Sentinel	93	H6
North Shields	55	H1
North Shoshone Peak	122	F8
North Sound	59	C6
North Sound, The	56	F1
North Stradbroke Island	113	L4
North Taranaki Bight	115	E3
North Tawton	52	D4

Nyong	105	H5
Nyons	65	F6
Nýrany	70	E4
Nyrud	62	N2
Nysa	71	G3
Nysh	85	Q6
Nyshott	63	N6
Nystad	63	J6
Nytva	78	K4
Nyuk, Ozero	62	P4
Nyuksenitsa	78	G3
Nyunzu	107	E4
Nyurba	85	K4
Nyurol'skiy	84	B5
Nyuya	85	J4
Nyvrovo	85	Q6
Nzambi	106	B3
Nzega	107	F3
Nzérékoré	104	D4
N'zeto	106	B4
Nzo	104	D4
Oadby	53	F2
Oahe Dam	123	P5
Oahe, Lake	123	P5
Oahu	126	S10
Oakdale	126	B2
Oakengates	52	E2
Oakes	123	Q4
Oakford	52	D4
Oakham	53	G2
Oak Hill	125	K8
Oakington	53	H2
Oakland California, U.S.A.	126	A2
Oakland Nebraska, U.S.A.	123	R7
Oak Lawn	124	G6
Oakley	123	P8
Oakover	112	E3
Oakridge	122	C6
Oak Ridge	129	K2
Oak Valley	125	N7
Oamaru	115	C6
Oa, Mull of	57	B5
Oates Land	141	L4
Oa, The	57	B5
Oatlands	113	K7
Oaxaca	131	L9
Ob'	84	Ae3
Oban	57	D4
Oberammergau	70	D5
Oberhausen	70	B3
Oberlin	123	P8
Obidos Brazil	137	F4
Obidos Portugal	66	B3
Obihiro	88	J4
Obi, Kepulauan	91	H6
Obil'noye	79	G6
Obion	128	H2
Obninsk	78	F4
Obo	102	E6
Obock	103	H5
Obŏk-tong	88	B5
Oborniki	71	G2
Oboyan'	79	F5
Obozerskiy	78	G3
Obregón, Presa	127	H6
Obruk	76	E3
Obryvistoye	85	Q7
Observatoire, Caye de l'	111	N6

Obskaya Guba	84	A3
Obuasi	104	E4
Ocala	129	L6
Ocaña Colombia	136	C2
Ocaña Spain	66	E3
Occidental, Cordillera Colombia	136	B3
Occidental, Cordillera Peru	136	B6
Occidental, Grand Erg	100	F2
Oceanside	126	D4
Ocejón, Pic	66	E2
Ochamchire	77	J1
Ochil Hills	57	E4
Ochiltree	57	D5
Ock	53	F3
Ockelbo	63	G6
Ocmulgee	129	L5
Ocna Mureş	73	G2
Oconee	129	L4
Ocotlán	130	H7
Ocracoke Island	129	Q3
Ocreza	66	C3
Ócsa	72	E2
Ŏda	89	D8
Oda	104	E4
Óðáðhraun	62	W12
Ŏdaejin	88	B5
Oda, Jebel	103	G3
Ŏdate	88	H5
Odawara	89	G8
Odda	63	B6
Odemira	66	B4
Ödemis	76	B3
Odendaalsrus	108	E5
Odense	63	D9
Oder	70	F2
Oderhaff	70	F2
Oderzo	68	D3
Ödeshög	63	F7
Odessa U.S.A.	127	L5
Odessa U.S.S.R.	79	E6
Odesskoye	84	A6
Odienné	104	D4
Ödmården	63	L6
Odorheiu Secuiesc	73	H2
Odra	70	F2
Odžaci	72	E3
Oeiras	137	J5
Oekussi	91	G7
Oelrichs	123	N6
Oena, Wadi	103	F2
Oenpelli Mission	113	G1
Of	77	J2
Ofanto	69	E5
Offaly	59	G6
Offenbach	70	C3
Offenburg	70	B4
Offord D'Arcy	53	G2
Ofidhoúsa	75	J4
Ofotfjord	62	G2
Ŏfunato	88	H6
Oga	88	G6
Ogadēn	103	H6
Ogaki	89	F8
Ogasawara-shoto	83	N4
Ogbomosho	105	F4
Ogden	122	J7
Ogdensburg	125	N4
Ogea	114	S9
Ogeechee	129	M4

Ogho	114	H5
Ogi	89	G7
Ogilvie Mountains	118	H3
Oginskiy, Kanal	71	L2
Ogle Point	120	G4
Oglethorpe, Mount	129	K3
Oglio	68	C3
Ognon	65	F5
Ogoamas, Gunung	91	G5
Ogoja	105	G4
Ogoki	121	J7
Ogooué	106	B3
Ogoron	85	M6
Ogosta	73	G4
Ogražden	73	G5
Ogre	63	L8
Ogurchinskiy, Ostrov	79	J8
Oğuz	77	H3
Oğuzeli	77	G4
Ogwashi-Uku	105	G4
Ohai	115	A6
Ohakune	115	E3
Ōhata	88	H5
Ohau, Lake	115	B6
O'Higgins, Lago	139	B9
Ohingaiti	115	E3
Ohio Kentucky, U.S.A.	124	F8
Ohio U.S.A.	124	J6
Ohre	70	D2
Ohře	70	E3
Ohrid	73	F5
Ohridska Jezero	72	F5
Ohura	115	E3
Oiapoque Brazil	137	G3
Oiapoque Brazil	137	G3
Oikiqtaluk	120	L3
Oil City	125	L6
Oise	64	E4
Oita	89	C9
Oituz, Pasul	73	J2
Oiwake	88	H4
Ojinaga	127	K6
Ojo de Agua	138	D5
Ojos del Salado	138	C5
Oka U.S.S.R.	78	G4
Oka U.S.S.R.	84	G6
Okaba	114	B3
Okahandja	108	C4
Okahukura	115	E3
Okaihau	115	D1
Okanagan Lake	122	E3
Okanogan U.S.A.	122	E3
Okanogan U.S.A.	122	E3
Okara	92	D2
Okarem	95	M2
Okaukuejo	108	C3
Okavango	108	D3
Okavango Delta	108	D3
Okaya	89	G7
Okayama	89	D8
Okazaki	89	F8
Okeechobee, Lake	129	M7
Okehampton	52	C4
Okene	105	G4
Oketo	88	J4
Okha	85	Q6
Okhota	85	Q5
Okhotsk	85	Q5
Okhotskoye More	85	R5
Okhotsk, Sea of	85	R5

Okinawa	89	H10
Okinawa-shotō	89	H10
Okinoerabu-shima	89	J10
Oki-shotō	89	D7
Okitipupa	105	F4
Oklahoma	127	N3
Oklahoma City	128	D3
Oklya	71	L3
Okmulgee	128	D3
Okondja	106	B3
Okoppe	88	J3
Oko, Wadi	103	G3
Øksfjord	62	K1
Oksino	78	J2
Okstindan	62	F3
Oktyabr'skiy U.S.S.R.	78	G3
Oktyabr'skiy U.S.S.R.	78	J5
Oktyabr'skiy U.S.S.R.	85	T6
Oktyabr'skoye	79	K5
Oktyabr'skoy Revolyutsii, Ostrov	81	L2
Oku	89	J10
Okulovka	78	E4
Okurchan	85	S5
Okushiri-tō	88	G4
Okwa	108	D4
Ólafsfjörður	62	V11
Ólafsvík	62	T12
Öland	63	G8
Olanga	62	P3
Olathe	124	C7
Olavarría	139	D7
Olbia	69	B5
Old Bedford River	53	H2
Oldcastle	58	H5
Old Crow	118	H2
Old Deer	56	F3
Oldenburg W. Germany	70	C2
Oldenburg W. Germany	70	D1
Oldham	55	G3
Old Head of Kinsale	59	E9
Old Hickory Lake	129	J2
Oldman	122	H3
Old Man of Coniston	55	F2
Old Man of Hoy	56	E2
Oldmeldrum	56	F3
Old Nene	53	H2
Old Post Point	121	P8
Olds	122	G2
Old Tongy	113	K4
Old Town	125	R4
Old Wives Lake	123	L2
Olean	125	L5
Olekma	85	L5
Olekminsk	85	L4
Olekmo-charskoye Nagor'ye	85	L5
Olema	78	H3
Ølen	63	A7
Olenegorsk	62	Q2
Olenëk	85	L2
Olenëkskiy Zaliv	85	N2
Oleniy, Ostrov	84	B2
Oléron, Île d'	65	C6
Olesko	71	L4
Olésnica	71	G3
Olevsk	79	D5
Olevugha	114	K6
Ølfjellet	62	F3
Ol'ga	88	E4
Olgiy	86	G2
Olgopol	73	K1

Orona	111	U2	Oskarshamn	63	G8	Oţelu Roşu	73	G3	Oulainen	62	L4
Oronsay	57	B5	Oskarström	63	E8	Otematata	115	C6	Oulmès	100	D2
Oronsay, Passage of	57	B5	Oskoba	84	G4	Othe, Forêt d'	65	E4	Oulu *Finland*	62	L4
Orontes	77	G5	Oskol	79	F5	Othonoí	74	E3	Oulu *Finland*	62	M4
Oropesa	66	D3	Oslo *Norway*	63	D7	Óthris	75	G3	Oulujärvi	62	M4
Oroqe.. Zizhiqi	87	N1	Oslo *Norway*	63	D7	Oti	104	F4	Oulujoki	62	M4
Oroquieta	91	G4	Oslob	91	G4	Otira	115	C5	Oulx	68	A3
Orosei, Golfo di	69	B5	Oslofjorden	63	H7	Otis	123	N7	Oum Chalouba	102	D4
Orosháza	72	F2	Osmānābād	92	E5	Otish, Monts	121	M7	Oum El Bouaghi	101	G1
Orotukan	85	S4	Osmancik	76	F2	Otjiwarongo	108	C4	Oum er Rbia, Oued	100	D2
Oroville *California, U.S.A.*	122	D8	Osmaneli	76	C2	Otley	55	H3	Ou, Nam	93	K4
Oroville *Washington, U.S.A.*	122	E3	Osmaniye	77	G4	Otlukbeli Dağlari	77	J2	Ounasjoki	62	L3
Oroville, Lake	122	D8	Osmington	52	E4	Otnes	63	D6	Oundle	53	G2
Orrin Reservoir	56	D3	Os'mino	63	N7	Otočac	72	C3	Ounianga Kebir	102	D4
Orsa	63	F6	Ösmo	63	G7	Otorohanga	115	E3	Oupu	87	P1
Orsa *Finnmark*	63	F6	Osnabrück	70	C2	Otoskwin	121	H7	Ouricurí	137	J5
Orsaro, Monte	68	C3	Osogovska Planina	73	G4	Otra	63	B7	Ourinhos	138	G4
Orsha	78	E5	Osorno *Chile*	139	B8	Otranto	69	G5	Ouro Prêto	138	H4
Ørsta	62	B5	Osorno *Spain*	66	D1	Otranto, Capo d'	69	G5	Ourthe	64	F3
Orta	76	E2	Osøyro	63	A6	Otranto, Strait of	74	E2	Ouse *Australia*	113	K7
Ortabağ	77	K4	Osprey Reef	113	K1	Ōtsu	89	E8	Ouse *U.K.*	55	H3
Ortaca	76	C4	Oss	64	F3	Otsu	89	H7	Oust	65	B5
Ortaköy *Turkey*	76	F2	Ossa	75	G3	Otta *Norway*	63	C6	Outardes, Réservoir	121	N7
Ortaköy *Turkey*	76	F3	Ossa, Mount	110	L10	Otta *Norway*	63	C6	Outer Hebrides	56	A3
Ortatoroslar	76	F4	Ossett	55	H3	Ottawa *Canada*	125	L3	Outokumpu	62	N5
Ortega	136	B3	Ossian, Loch	57	D4	Ottawa *Canada*	125	N4	Out Skerries	56	B1
Ortegal, Cabo	66	C1	Ossokmanuan Lake	121	P7	Ottawa Islands	121	K6	Outwell	53	H2
Ortelsburg	71	J2	Ostashkov	78	E4	Otter	52	D4	Ouvéa	114	X16
Orthez	65	C7	Östavall	62	F5	Otterburn	57	F5	Ouyen	113	J6
Ortigueira	66	C1	Østby	63	E6	Otter Rapids	125	K1	Ovacik *Turkey*	77	H4
Ortiz	133	P10	Oste	70	C2	Otterup	63	D9	Ovacik *Turkey*	77	J2
Ortles	68	C2	Osterburken	70	C4	Ottery	52	C4	Ovada	68	B3
Ortona	69	E4	Österdalälven	63	E6	Ottery Saint Mary	52	D4	Ovalau Batiki	114	R8
Orto-Tokoy	86	D3	Østerdalen	63	D5	Ottumwa	124	D6	Ovalle	138	B6
Orūmīyeh	77	L4	Ostergotland	63	F7	Oturkpo	105	G4	Ovau	114	H5
Orūmīyeh, Daryācheh-ye	94	G3	Osterode	71	H2	Otway, Bahía	139	B10	Ovejo	66	D3
Oruro	138	C3	Östersund	62	F5	Otway, Cape	113	J6	Oven	115	X17
Orvieto	69	D4	Østfold	63	D7	Otway, Seno	139	B10	Overbister	56	F1
Orwell	53	J3	Ost Friesische Inseln	70	B2	Otwock	71	J2	Øverbygd	62	H2
Oryakhovo	73	G4	Ostfriesland	70	B2	Otynya	71	L4	Överkalix	62	K3
Os	62	D5	Osthammar	63	H6	Ötztaler Alpen	68	C2	Övernäs	62	G3
Osa	78	K4	Ostíglia	68	C3	Ouachita	128	F4	Övertorneå	62	K3
Osage	124	D7	Ostra	68	D4	Ouachita, Lake	128	F3	Oviedo	66	D1
Ōsaka *Japan*	89	E8	Ostrava	71	H4	Ouachita Mountains	128	E3	Ovinishche	78	F4
Ōsaka *Japan*	89	F8	Ostróda	71	H2	Ouadda	102	D6	Øvre Årdal	63	B6
Ōsaka-wan	89	E8	Ostrog	79	D5	Ouagadougou	104	E3	Ovruch	79	D5
Osa, Península de	132	F10	Ostrogozhsk	79	F5	Ouahigouya	104	E3	Owahanga	115	F4
Osceola *Arkansas, U.S.A.*	128	H3	Ostrołeka	71	J2	Oualata	100	D5	Owaka	115	B7
Osceola *Iowa, U.S.A.*	124	D6	Ostrov	63	N8	Oua-n Ahagar, Tassili	101	G4	Owando	106	C3
Osh	86	B3	Ostrovnoy, Mys	88	D4	Ouanda Djailé	102	D6	Owase	89	F8
Oshamambe	88	H4	Ostrów	71	G3	Ouarâne	100	D4	Owatonna	124	D4
Oshawa	125	L5	Ostrowiec	71	J3	Ouargla	101	G2	Owbeh	95	R4
Ō-shima	89	G8	Ostrów Mazowiecki	71	J2	Ouarra	102	E6	Owel, Lough	58	H5
Oshkosh	124	F4	Ostuni	69	F6	Ouarsenis, Massif de l'	67	G5	Owenbeg	58	E4
Oshkur'ya	84	Ac3	Osum	75	F2	Ouarzazate	100	D2	Owenkillew	58	H3
Oshmarino	84	C2	Osŭm	73	H4	Ouatoais	125	M4	Owenmore	58	C4
Oshmyanskaya Vozvyshennost'	71	M1	Ōsumi-kaikyō	89	C10	Oubangui	106	C3	Owens	126	C2
Oshmyany	71	L1	Ōsumi-shotō	89	C10	Oudenaarde	64	E3	Owensboro	124	G8
Oshnovīyeh	94	G3	Osuna	66	D4	Oude Rijn	64	F2	Owens Lake	126	D2
Oshogbo	105	F4	Os'Van'	78	K2	Oudtshoorn	108	D6	Owen Sound	125	K4
Oshtorān Kūh	94	J5	Oswaldtwistle	55	G3	Oued Zem	100	D2	Owen Stanley Range	114	D3
Oshtorīnān	94	J4	Oswego	125	M5	Ouémé	105	F4	Owerri	105	G4
Oshwe	106	C3	Oswestry	52	D2	Ouen	114	X17	Owo	105	G4
Osijek	72	E3	Otaki	115	E4	Ouesso	106	C2	Owosso	124	H5
Osimo	68	D4	Otaru	88	H4	Ouezzane	100	D2	Owyhee *Nevada, U.S.A.*	122	F7
Osinniki	84	D6	Otava	70	E4	Oughterard	59	D6	Owyhee *Oregon, U.S.A.*	122	F6
Osipovichi	79	D5	Otavi	108	C3	Oughter, Lough	58	H4	Oxbow	123	N3
Oskaloosa	124	D6	Ōtawara	89	G7	Ouidah	105	F4	Oxelösund	63	G7
Oskamull	57	B4	Otchinjau	106	B6	Oujda	100	E2	Oxenholme	55	G2
Oskara, Mys	84	F1	Otelec	73	F3	Oujda	100	E2	Oxenhope	55	H3

Oxford *New Zealand*	115	D5	Padua	68	C3	Paldiski	63	L7	Pamplona *Spain*	67	F1
Oxford *U.K.*	53	F3	Paducah *Kentucky, U.S.A.*	124	F8	Palembang	90	C6	Pana	124	F7
Oxford *U.S.A.*	128	H3	Paducah *Texas, U.S.A.*	127	M4	Palena, Lago	139	B8	Panaca	126	E2
Oxfordshire	53	F3	Padunskoye More	62	P2	Palencia	66	D1	Panagyurishte	73	H4
Ox Mountains	58	E4	Paekariki	115	E4	Palermo	69	D6	Panaji	92	D5
Oxnard	126	C3	Paengnyŏng-do	87	N4	Palestine	128	E5	Panamá	132	G10
Oxton	55	H3	Paeroa	115	E2	Paletwa	93	H4	Panamá	132	H10
Oyaca	76	E3	Pag *Yugoslavia*	72	C3	Palghat	92	E6	Panamá, Bahía de	132	H10
Oyali	77	J4	Pag *Yugoslavia*	72	C3	Palgrave Point	108	B4	Panama Canal	136	B2
Oyapock	137	G3	Pagadian	91	G4	Palhoca	138	G5	Panama City	129	K5
Oyem	106	B2	Pagasitikós Kólpos	75	G3	Pali	92	D3	Panamá, Golfo de	136	B2
Oykel	56	D3	Pagatan	90	F6	Palisade	127	H1	Panandak	95	K4
Oykel Bridge	56	D3	Page	126	G2	Palit, Kep i	74	E2	Panaro	68	C3
Oymyakon	85	Q4	Pagosa Springs	127	J2	Pälkane	63	L6	Panay	91	G3
Oyo	105	F4	Pagwa River	124	H2	Palk Strait	92	E7	Pančevo	72	F3
Özalp	77	L3	Pagwi	114	C2	Pallaresa	67	G1	Panda	109	F4
Ozamiz	91	G4	Pahala	126	T11	Pallas Green	59	F7	Pandan *Philippines*	91	G3
Ozark Plateau	124	D8	Pahang	90	C5	Pallasovka	79	H5	Pandan *Philippines*	91	G3
Ozarks, Lake of the	124	D7	Pahia Point	115	A7	Pallastunturi	62	K2	Pandany	78	E3
Ozd	72	F1	Pahiatua	115	E4	Palliser Bay	115	E4	Pandharpur	92	E5
Ozernovskiy	85	T6	Pahlavī Dezh	95	M3	Palliser, Cape	115	E4	Pando	139	E6
Ozernoye	84	A5	Pahoa	126	T11	Palma *Mozambique*	109	H2	Pandunskoye More	78	E2
Ozersk	71	K1	Pahokee	129	M7	Palma *Spain*	67	H3	Panevėžys	63	N9
Ozhogina	85	R3	Pahra Kariz	95	Q4	Palma, Baia de	67	H3	Panfilov	86	E3
Ozieri	69	B5	Paia	126	S10	Palma del Río	66	D4	Pangalanes, Canal des	109	J4
Ozinki	79	H5	Paide	63	L7	Pal Malmal	114	E3	Pangani	107	G4
Ozona	127	M5	Paignton	52	D4	Palmanova	68	D3	Panggoé	114	H5
Ozora	72	E2	Päijänne	63	L6	Palmares	137	K5	Pangi	106	E3
Özyurt	76	F3	Pailolo Chan	126	S10	Palmar, Punta del	139	F6	Pangkalanbuun	90	E6
			Paimpol	64	B4	Palmas	138	G5	Pangkalpinang	90	D6
			Painswick	53	E3	Palmas, Cape	104	D5	Pangnirtung	120	N4
Paama	114	U12	Painted Desert	126	G2	Palmas, Golfo di	69	B6	Pangong Tso	92	E2
Paarl	108	C6	Paisley	57	D5	Palma Soriano	132	J4	Pangrango, Gunung	90	D7
Pabbay *U.K.*	56	A3	Paita	136	A5	Pal'matkina	85	V4	Pangtara	93	J4
Pabbay *U.K.*	57	A4	Païta	114	X17	Palmeira	138	F5	Pangururar	90	B5
Pabellón de Arteaga	130	H6	Paittasjärvi	62	K2	Palmeiras	137	J6	Pangutaran Group	91	G4
Pabjanice	71	H3	Pajala	62	K3	Palmer *Antarctic*	141	V6	Panhandle	127	M3
Pabna	92	G4	Pakaraima Mountains	136	E2	Palmer *U.S.A.*	118	F3	Paniai, Danau	114	B2
Pabradė	63	L9	Pakistan	92	C3	Palmer Land	141	V4	Panié, Mount	114	W16
Pacaás Novos, Serra dos	136	E6	Pak Lay	93	K5	Palmerston	115	C6	Panipat	92	E3
Pacaraima, Sierra	136	E3	Pakokku	93	H4	Palmerston Island	111	W5	Panjim	92	D5
Pacasmayo	136	B5	Pakpattan	92	D2	Palmerston North	115	E4	Panna	92	F4
Pachino	69	E7	Pakrac	72	D3	Palm Harbor	129	L6	Panovo	84	G5
Pachora	92	E4	Paks	72	E2	Palmi	69	E6	Pant *Essex, U.K.*	53	H3
Pachuca	131	K7	Pakse	93	L5	Palmira	136	B3	Pant *Shropshire, U.K.*	52	D2
Pacifica	126	A2	Pala	102	B6	Palm Springs	126	D4	Pantar	91	G7
Pacific Ocean	87	P7	Palabuhanratu	90	D7	Palmyra	94	D4	Pantelleria, Isola di	69	D7
Pacific Ocean, North	143	H3	Palafrugell	67	H2	Palmyras Point	92	G4	Pantones	66	E3
Pacific Ocean, South	143	J5	Palagruža	72	D4	Palo de las Letras	136	B2	Pánuco *Mexico*	131	K6
Pacitan	90	E7	Palaiókastron	75	J5	Palomar, Mount	126	D4	Pánuco *Mexico*	131	K6
Packwood	122	D4	Palaiokhóra	75	G5	Palopo	91	G6	Pan Xian	93	K3
Padang *Indonesia*	90	C6	Pāla Laharha	92	G4	Palos, Cabo de	67	F4	Panyam	105	G4
Padang *Indonesia*	90	C5	Palamós	67	H2	Palpetu, Tanjung	91	H6	Pão-de-Acucar	137	K5
Padangpanjang	90	D6	Palana	85	T5	Palu *Indonesia*	91	F6	Paola	69	F6
Padangsidimpuan	90	B5	Palanan Point	91	G2	Palu *Indonesia*	91	F6	Paoua	102	C6
Padasjoki	63	L6	Palanga	63	J9	Palu *Turkey*	77	H3	Pápa	72	D2
Padauirí	136	E3	Palangān, Kūh-e-	95	Q6	Palyavaam	85	W3	Papakura	115	E2
Paderborn	70	C3	Palangkaraya	90	E6	Pama	104	F3	Papantla	131	L7
Padeş	73	G3	Palanpur	92	D4	Pamban	92	E7	Paparoa	115	E2
Padiham	55	G3	Palapye	108	E4	Pamekasan	90	E7	Paparoa Range	115	C5
Padilla *Bolivia*	138	D3	Palar	92	E6	Pameungpeuk	90	D7	Papa Stour	56	A1
Padilla *Mexico*	131	K5	Palata	69	E5	Pamiers	65	D7	Papatoetoe	115	E2
Padina	73	J3	Palatka *U.S.A.*	129	M6	Pámisos	75	F4	Papa Westray	56	F1
Padje-Ianta	62	G3	Palatka *U.S.S.R.*	85	S4	Pamlico Sound	129	P3	Papenburg	70	B2
Padloping Island	120	P4	Palau	69	B5	Pampa	127	M3	Papigochic	127	J6
Padova	68	C3	Palau Islands	91	J4	Pampachiri	136	C6	Papisoi, Tanjung	114	A2
Padrão, Pointa do	106	B4	Palawan	91	F4	Pampas *Argentina*	139	D7	Paps of Jura	57	B5
Padrón	66	B1	Palawan Passage	91	F4	Pampas *Peru*	136	C6	Paps, The	59	D8
Padstow	52	C4	Palayankottai	92	E7	Pampilhosa da Serra	66	C2	Papua, Gulf of	114	C3
Padstow Bay	52	C4	Palazzola Acreide	69	E7	Pamplona *Colombia*	136	C2	Papua New Guinea	114	C2

Papuk	72	D3
Papun	93	J5
Pará	137	G4
Paracas, Península	136	B6
Paracatú *Brazil*	138	G3
Paracatú *Brazil*	138	G3
Paraćin	73	F4
Paradubice	70	F3
Paragould	128	G2
Paraguá	136	E6
Paragua	136	E2
Paraguaçu	137	J6
Paraguai	136	F7
Paraguaná, Península de	133	M8
Paraguari	138	E5
Paraguay	138	E4
Paraguay	138	E4
Paraíba	138	H4
Paraiba	137	K5
Parajuru	137	K4
Parakou	105	F4
Paraläkhemundi	92	F5
Paralkot	92	F5
Paramaribo	137	F2
Paramillo	136	B2
Parámirim	137	J6
Paramonga	136	B6
Paramushir, Ostrov	85	T6
Paraná	138	D6
Paranã	137	H6
Paranaguá	138	G5
Paranaíba *Maranhão, Brazil*	137	J4
Paranaíba *Mato Grosso do Sul, Brazil*	138	F3
Paranaíba *Minas Gerais, Brazil*	138	G3
Paranaidji	137	H5
Paranapanema	138	F4
Paranapiacaba, Serra	138	G4
Paranatinga	137	F6
Parangipettai	92	E6
Paraparaum	115	E4
Parapóla	75	G4
Paraúna	138	F3
Pārbatī	92	E4
Parbhani	92	E5
Parcel Islands	93	M5
Parchim	70	D2
Pardo	138	F4
Parecis, Serra dos	136	F6
Pareditas	139	C6
Pare Mountains	107	G3
Parengarenga Harbour	115	D1
Parepare	91	F6
Paria, Golfo de	133	R9
Pariaguán	136	E2
Paria, Península de	133	R9
Paricutin, Volcán el	130	H8
Parigi	91	G6
Parikkala	63	N6
Parima, Serra	136	E3
Parintins	137	F4
Paris *France*	64	E4
Paris *Kentucky, U.S.A.*	124	H7
Paris *Tennessee, U.S.A.*	129	H2
Paris *Texas, U.S.A.*	128	E4
Parkano	63	K5
Parker	126	E3
Parkersburg	125	K7
Parkes	113	K5

Parkgate	57	E5
Park Range	123	L7
Parksville	122	B3
Parma *Italy*	68	C3
Parma *U.S.A.*	125	K6
Parnaíba	137	J4
Parnamirim	137	K5
Parnassós	75	G3
Parnassus	115	D5
Párnis	75	G3
Párnon Óros	75	G4
Pärnu *U.S.S.R.*	63	L7
Pärnu *U.S.S.R.*	63	L7
Paro	93	G3
Paropamisus	95	R4
Páros *Greece*	75	H4
Páros *Greece*	75	H4
Parowan	126	F2
Parral	139	B7
Parras	127	L8
Parrett	52	E3
Parrsboro	121	P8
Parry Bay	120	K4
Parry Islands	120	C2
Parry, Kap	120	M2
Parry Peninsula	118	L2
Parry Sound	125	L4
Parsęta	71	G2
Parshino	85	J5
Parsons	128	E2
Partabpur	92	F4
Parthenay	65	C5
Partizansk	88	D4
Parton	57	D5
Partry Mountains	58	C5
Paru	137	G4
Parys	108	E5
Pasa Barris	137	K6
Pasadena *California, U.S.A.*	126	C3
Pasadena *Texas, U.S.A.*	128	E6
Pasado, Cabo	136	A4
Pa Sak, Mae Nam	93	K5
Pasarwajo	91	G7
Pascagoula *U.S.A.*	128	H5
Pascagoula *U.S.A.*	128	H5
Paşcani	73	J2
Pasco	122	E4
Pascua, Isla de	143	K5
Pasewalk	70	F2
Pashiya	78	K4
Pashkovo	88	C1
Pasig	91	G3
Pasinler	77	J3
Pasirpangarayan	90	C5
Pasłęk	71	H1
Pasley, Cape	112	E5
Pasmajärvi	62	L3
Pasman	72	C4
Pasni	92	B3
Paso de los Indios	139	C8
Paso de los Libres	138	E5
Paso de los Toros	138	E6
Paso Real	131	M9
Paso Rio Mayo	139	B9
Paso Robles	126	B3
Pasquia Hills	119	Q5
Passage East	59	J8
Passage West	59	F9
Passamaquoddy Bay	125	S4
Passau	70	E4

Passero, Capo	69	E7
Passo Fundo	138	F5
Passos	138	G4
Pastaza	136	B4
Pas, The	119	Q5
Pasto	136	B3
Pastol Bay	118	C3
Pastos Bons	137	J5
Pastrana	66	E2
Pasuruan	90	E7
Patache, Punta de	138	B4
Patagonia	139	C9
Patan *India*	92	D4
Patan *Nepal*	92	G3
Patani	91	H5
Patea	115	E3
Pateley Bridge	55	H2
Paterno	69	E7
Paterson	125	N6
Pathankot	92	E2
Pathfinder Reservoir	123	L6
Pathhead	57	F4
Patiala	92	E2
Patkai Bum	93	J3
Patman, Lake	128	E4
Pátmos	75	J4
Patna	92	G3
Patnagarh	92	F4
Patnos	77	K3
Patomskoye Nagor'ye	85	J4
Patos	137	K5
Patos de Minas	138	G3
Patos, Lagoa dos	138	F6
Patquia	138	C6
Pátrai	75	F3
Patras	75	F3
Patrasuy	78	L3
Patricio Lynch, Isla	139	A9
Patrington	55	J3
Patrocínio	138	G3
Pattani	93	K7
Patterdale	55	G2
Patti	69	E6
Patú	137	K5
Patuca	132	E7
Patuca, Punta	132	E7
Pátzcuaro	130	J8
Pátzcuaro, Laguna	130	J8
Pau	65	C7
Pau d'Arco	137	H5
Pau dos Ferros	137	K5
Pau, Gave de	65	C7
Pauini *Brazil*	136	D5
Pauini *Brazil*	136	D5
Paulilatino	69	B5
Paulista	137	K5
Paulistana	137	J5
Pauls Valley	128	D3
Paungde	93	J5
Pauni	92	E4
Pauri	92	E2
Pauto	136	C2
Pavarandocito	136	B2
Păveh	94	H4
Pavia	68	B3
Păvilosta	63	J8
Pavlikeni	73	H4
Pavlodar	84	B6
Pavlof Volcano	118	Af8
Pavlograd	79	F6

Pavlovo	78	G4
Pavlovsk	79	G5
Pavlovskaya	79	F6
Pavullo nel Frigano	68	C3
Pavuvu	114	J6
Pawan	90	E6
Paxoí	75	F3
Paxton	57	F4
Payakumbuh	90	D6
Payette *U.S.A.*	122	F5
Payette *U.S.A.*	122	F5
Payne, Lake	121	M6
Paynes Find	112	D4
Paysandú	138	E6
Payún, Volcán	139	C7
Păzanan	95	J6
Pazar	77	J2
Pazarbaşi Burun	76	D2
Pazarcik	77	G4
Pazardzhik	73	H4
Pazarören	77	G3
Pazaryeri	76	C2
Paz, Bahía de la	130	D5
Pazin	72	B3
Pcim	71	H4
Peabody Bugt	120	N2
Peace *Canada*	119	N4
Peace *U.S.A.*	129	M7
Peacehaven	53	M4
Peace River	119	M4
Peaima Falls	136	E2
Pea Island	129	Q3
Peak Hill	112	D4
Peale, Mount	123	K8
Pearl	128	H5
Pearl City	126	R10
Pearl Harbor	126	R10
Pearsall	128	C6
Peary Channel	120	F2
Pease	127	N3
Pebane	109	G3
Peć	72	F4
Pechenezhin	71	L4
Pechenga	62	P2
Pechora	78	J2
Pechorskaya Guba	78	J2
Pechorskoye More	78	J2
Pechory	63	M8
Pecos *U.S.A.*	127	L5
Pecos *U.S.A.*	127	L5
Pecos Plains	127	K4
Pécs	72	E2
Pedasí	132	G11
Pededze	63	M8
Pedernales	133	M5
Pedo La	92	F3
Pedorovka	79	J5
Pedra Azul	138	H3
Pedregal	132	F10
Pedreiras	137	J4
Pedro Afonso	137	H5
Pedro Cays	132	J6
Pedro Juan Caballero	138	E4
Pedro Luro	139	D7
Peebles	57	E5
Pee Dee	129	N3
Peel *Canada*	118	J2
Peel *U.K.*	54	E2
Peel Sound	120	G3
Peene	70	E2

Poggibonsi	68	C4
Pohang	89	B7
Pohjois-Karjala	62	N5
Pohorelá	71	J4
Pohorje	72	C2
Poiana Teiului	73	J2
Poinsett, Cape	141	H5
Pointe-à-Pitre	133	S6
Pointe-Noire	106	B3
Point Etienne	100	B4
Point Fortin	133	S9
Point Hope	118	B2
Point Lake	119	N2
Point Pleasant	124	J7
Poipet	93	K6
Poitiers	65	D5
Poitou	65	C5
Poix	64	D4
Pokataroo	113	K4
Pokhara	92	F3
Pokka	62	L2
Pokrovka *Kirgiziya S.S.R., U.S.S.R.*	86	D3
Pokrovka *Rossiyskaya S.F.S.R., U.S.S.R.*	88	C4
Pokrovsk	85	M4
Pokrovskoye	84	Ae5
Polacca Wash	126	G3
Pola de Laviana	66	D1
Polān	95	Q9
Połana	71	H4
Poland	71	G2
Polar Plateau	141	A1
Polati	76	E3
Pole Khatun	95	Q3
Pol-e Safid	95	L3
Polesie Lubelskie	71	K3
Polessk	71	J1
Poles'ye	79	D5
Polgár	73	F2
Políaigos	75	H4
Policastro, Golfo di	69	E6
Poligny	65	F5
Poligus	84	E4
Polikastron	75	G2
Políkhnitos	75	J3
Polillo Islands	91	G3
Polis	76	E5
Polisan, Tanjung	91	H5
Politovo	78	H3
Políyiros	75	G2
Pol'kyko	84	F2
Pollachi	92	E6
Pollino, Monte	69	F6
Polmak	62	N2
Polmont	57	E5
Polna	63	N7
Polnovat	84	Ae4
Polonnoye	79	D5
Polotsk	63	N9
Polperro	52	C4
Polski Trŭmbesh	73	H4
Poltava	79	E6
Poltavka	84	A6
Poltsamaa	63	L7
Polunochnoye	84	Ad4
Poluostrov Shirokostan	85	P2
Poluy	84	Ae3
Pol'yanovo	84	Ae4
Polyarnik	85	Y3

Polyarnyy	62	Q2
Polynesia	143	H4
Polyuc	131	Q8
Pombal *Pará, Brazil*	137	G4
Pombal *Paraiba, Brazil*	137	K5
Pombal *Portugal*	66	B3
Pomerania	70	E2
Pomona	126	D3
Pomorskie, Pojezierze	70	F2
Pomorskiy Proliv	78	H2
Pompano Beach	129	M7
Pompeyevka	88	C1
Pomyt	84	Ae4
Ponca City	128	D2
Ponce	133	P5
Ponce de Leon Bay	129	M8
Poncheville, Lac	125	M1
Pondicherry	92	E6
Pond Inlet	120	L3
Pondo	114	E2
Ponérihouen	114	W16
Ponferrada	66	C1
Pon'goma	78	E2
Ponnaiyar	92	E6
Ponnani	92	E6
Pono	114	A3
Ponomarevka	78	J5
Ponoy *U.S.S.R.*	78	F2
Ponoy *U.S.S.R.*	78	G2
Pons	65	C6
Pont	57	G5
Ponta de Pedras	137	G4
Ponta Grossa	138	F5
Pont-à-Mousson	64	G4
Ponta Porã	138	E4
Pontardulais	52	C3
Pontarlier	65	G5
Pontchartrain, Lake	128	G5
Ponte de Barca	66	B2
Ponte de Pedra	137	F6
Pontedera	68	C4
Ponte de Sor	66	B3
Pontefract	55	H3
Ponteland	55	H1
Ponte Nova	138	H4
Ponterwyd	52	D2
Pontevedra	66	B1
Ponthierville	106	E3
Pontiac	124	J5
Pontianak	90	D6
Pontivy	64	B4
Pont-l'Abbé	65	A5
Pontoetoe	137	F3
Pontois	64	E4
Pontremoli	68	B3
Pontrilas	52	E3
Ponts	67	G2
Pontypool	52	D3
Pontypridd	52	D3
Ponziane, Isole	69	D5
Poole	53	F4
Poole Bay	53	F4
Poolewe	56	C3
Pooley Bridge	55	G2
Poona	92	D5
Poopó, Lago	138	C3
Poor Knights Islands	115	E1
Popayán	136	B3
Popigay *U.S.S.R.*	84	H2
Popigay *U.S.S.R.*	84	J2

Poplar Bluff	124	E8
Poplarville	128	H5
Popocatépetl, Volcán	131	K8
Popokabaka	106	C4
Popoli	69	D4
Popomanaseu, Mount	114	K6
Popondetta	114	D3
Porbandar	92	C4
Porcher Island	118	J5
Porcuna	66	D4
Porcupine	118	G2
Pordenone	68	D3
Pordim	73	H4
Pore	136	C2
Poreč	72	B3
Pori	63	J6
Porirua	115	E4
Porjus	62	H3
Porkhov	63	N8
porlákshöfn	62	U13
Porlamar	136	E1
Porlock	52	D3
Porlock Bay	52	D3
Pornic	65	B5
Porog *U.S.S.R.*	78	F3
Porog *U.S.S.R.*	78	K3
Poronaysk	85	Q7
Póros *Greece*	75	G4
Póros *Greece*	75	G4
Porosozero	78	E3
Porozhsk	78	J3
Porozovo	71	L2
Porpoise Bay	141	J5
Porrentruy	68	A2
Porsangen	62	L1
Porsanger-halvøya	62	L1
Porsgrunn	63	C7
pórshöfn	62	X11
Porsuk	76	D3
Porsuk Baraji	76	D3
Pors'yakha	84	A3
Portachuelo	138	D3
Portadown	58	K4
Portaferry	58	L4
Portage	124	F5
Portage la Prairie	119	R5
Portal	123	N3
Port Alberni	122	B3
Port Albert	113	K6
Portalegre	66	C3
Port Alice	122	A2
Port Angeles	122	C3
Port Antonio	132	J5
Portarlington	59	H6
Port Arthur *Australia*	113	K7
Port Arthur *U.S.A.*	128	F6
Port Askaig	57	B5
Port Augusta	113	H5
Port-au-Prince	133	L5
Port Austin	124	J4
Portavogie	58	M4
Port-Bergé	109	J3
Port Blair	93	H6
Portboil	53	N7
Port Burwell	121	P5
Port Cartier	121	N7
Port Chalmers	115	C6
Port Charlotte	129	L7

Port Clarence	118	B2
Port Clinton	124	J6
Port Coquitlam	122	C3
Port Darwin	139	E10
Port-de-Paix	133	L5
Port Dickson	90	C5
Portel	66	C3
Port Elgin	125	K4
Port Elizabeth	108	E6
Port Ellen	57	C5
Port Erin	54	E2
Porterville	126	C2
Port-Eynon	52	C3
Port Francqui	106	D3
Port Gentil	106	A3
Port Glasgow	57	F4
Port Harcourt	105	G5
Port Hardy	118	K5
Porthcawl	52	D3
Port Heiden	118	D4
Port Herald	107	G6
Porthleven	52	B4
Porthmadog	52	C2
Porth Neigwl	52	C2
Port Huron	124	J5
Port Il'ich	94	J2
Portimão	66	B4
Port Isaac	52	C4
Port Isaac Bay	52	C4
Portishead	52	E3
Port Jackson	113	L5
Port Jervis	125	N6
Port Kaituma	136	F2
Port Kembla	113	L5
Port Kenney	113	G5
Portknockie	56	F3
Port Láirge	59	H8
Portland *Australia*	113	J6
Portland *New Zealand*	115	E1
Portland *Indiana, U.S.A.*	124	H6
Portland *Maine, U.S.A.*	125	Q5
Portland *Oregon, U.S.A.*	122	C5
Portland Bay	113	J6
Portland, Bill of	52	E4
Portland, Cape	113	K7
Portland, Isle of	52	E4
Portland Point	132	J6
Portland Promontory	121	L6
Port Laoise	59	H6
Port Lavaca	128	D6
Port-Leucate	65	E7
Port Lincoln	113	H5
Portlock Reefs	114	C3
Port Loko	104	C4
Port Louis	109	L7
Port McArthur	113	H2
Port Macquarie	113	L5
Port Menier	121	P8
Port Moresby	114	D3
Portnacroish	57	C4
Portnahaven	57	B5
Port Nelson	119	S4
Port Nolloth	108	C5
Portnyagino, Ozero	84	H2
Porto	66	B2
Pôrto Alegre	138	F4
Porto Alexandre	106	B6
Porto Amboim	106	B5
Pôrto Camargo	138	F4
Porto d'Ascoli	69	D4

Pôrto dos Gauchos	137	F6
Pôrto Esperança	138	E3
Pôrto Esperidião	138	E3
Portoferráio	69	C4
Port-of-Spain	136	E1
Pôrto Grande	137	G3
Portogruaro	68	D3
Pôrto Lucena	138	F5
Pörtom	62	J5
Portomaggiore	68	C3
Pôrto Nacional	138	H6
Porto Novo *Benin*	105	F4
Porto Novo *Cape Verde*	104	L7
Port Orford	122	B6
Porto San Stéfano	69	C4
Pôrto São José	138	F4
Pôrto Seguro	137	K7
Porto Socompa	138	C4
Porto Tolle	68	D3
Porto Torres	69	B5
Porto-Vecchio	69	B5
Pôrto Velho	136	E5
Portoviejo	136	A4
Portpatrick	54	D2
Port Pegasus	115	A7
Port Phillip Bay	113	J6
Port Pirie	113	H5
Portraine	59	K6
Portreath	52	B4
Portree	56	B3
Portrush	58	J2
Port Said	103	F1
Port Saint Joe	129	K6
Port Saint Johns	108	E6
Port-Saint-Louis	65	F7
Port Sandwich	114	T12
Port Saunders	121	Q7
Port Shepstone	108	F6
Portskerra	56	E2
Portsmouth *U.K.*	53	F4
Portsmouth *New Hampshire,*		
U.S.A.	125	Q5
Portsmouth *Ohio, U.S.A.*	124	J7
Portsmouth *Virginia, U.S.A.*	125	M8
Portsoy	56	F3
Port Stephens	113	L5
Portstewart	58	J2
Port Sudan	103	G4
Port Talbot	52	D3
Porttipahdan tekojärvi	62	M2
Port Townsend	122	C3
Portugal	66	B3
Portuguesa	136	D2
Portumna	59	F6
Port Washington	124	G5
Port William	54	E2
Porvenir *Bolivia*	136	D6
Porvenir *Chile*	139	B10
Porvoo	63	L6
Posadas	138	E5
Posen	71	G2
Poshekhon'ye Volodarsk	78	F4
Posht-e Badam	95	M5
Poso	91	G6
Posof	77	K2
Post	127	M4
Postavy	63	M9
Poste Weygand	100	F4
Postmasburg	108	D5
Postojna	72	C3

Posušje	72	D4
Pos'yet	88	C4
Potamiá	75	F4
Potamós	75	G4
Potapovo	84	D3
Potchefstroom	108	E5
Poteau	128	E3
Potenza	69	E5
Potes	66	D1
Potgietersrus	108	E4
Poti	77	J1
Potiskum	105	H3
Potlogi	73	H3
Potnarvin	114	U13
Potomac	125	M7
Potosi	138	C3
Potsdam *U.S.A.*	125	N4
Potsdam *W. Germany*	70	E2
Pott	114	V15
Potters Bar	53	G3
Pottstown	125	N6
Pottsville	125	M6
Pouébo	114	W16
Poughkeepsie	125	P6
Poulaphouca Reservoir	59	J6
Poulter	55	H3
Poulton-le-Fylde	55	G3
Poundstock	52	C4
Pouso Alegre	138	G4
Pouzauges	65	C5
Povenets	78	E3
Poverty Bay	115	G3
Povorino	79	G5
Povungnituk	121	L6
Povungnituk Bay	121	L6
Powder	123	M5
Powell	123	K5
Powell, Lake	126	F2
Powell River	122	B3
Power Head	59	F9
Powys	52	D2
Poya	114	W16
Poyang Hu	87	M6
Poyraz	77	H3
Poysdorf	68	F1
Pöytya	63	K6
Pozanti	76	F4
Požarevac	73	F3
Poza Rica	131	L7
Pozharskoye	88	E2
Poznań	71	G2
Pozoblanco	66	D3
Pozohondo	67	F3
Pozzuoli	69	E5
Prabumulih	90	D6
Prachin Buri	93	K6
Prachuap Khiri Khan	93	J6
Praděd	71	G3
Pradelles	65	E6
Prades	65	E7
Prague	70	F3
Praha	70	F3
Prahova	73	H3
Praia	104	L7
Prainha *Amazonas, Brazil*	136	E5
Prainha *Pará, Brazil*	137	G4
Prairie Dog Town Fork	127	L3
Prairie du Chien	124	E5
Prairies, Coteau des	124	C5
Prairie Village	124	C7

Prapat	90	B5
Prasonísí, Ákra	75	J5
Præstø	63	E9
Prata	138	G3
Prato	68	C4
Pratt	127	N2
Pravets	73	G4
Pravia	66	C1
Predazzo	68	C2
Predcal	73	H3
Predeal, Pasul	73	H3
Predivinsk	84	E5
Predlitz	68	D2
Premer	113	K5
Premuda	72	C3
Prenai	71	K1
Prentice	124	E4
Prenzlau	70	E2
Preobrazhenka	84	H5
Preparis	93	H6
Preparis North Channel	93	H5
Preparis South Channel	93	H6
Přerov	71	G4
Prescot	55	G3
Prescott *Arizona, U.S.A.*	126	F3
Prescott *Arkansas, U.S.A.*	128	F4
Prescott Island	120	G3
Preseli, Mynydd	52	C3
Preservation Inlet	115	A7
Preševo	73	F4
Presho	123	Q6
Presídencia Roque Saenz		
Peña	138	D5
Presidente Dutra	137	J4
Presidente Epitácio	138	F4
Presidente Prudente	138	E4
Presidio	127	K6
Preslav	73	J4
Presnovka	84	Ae6
Prešov	71	J4
Prespansko Jezero	75	F2
Presque Isle	125	S3
Pressburg	71	G4
Prestatyn	55	F3
Presteigne	52	D2
Preston *U.K.*	55	G3
Preston *Minnesota, U.S.A.*	124	D5
Preston *Missouri, U.S.A.*	124	D8
Prestonburg	124	J8
Prestonpans	57	F5
Prestwick	57	F4
Pretoria	108	E5
Préveza	75	F3
Prey Veng	93	L6
Pribilof Islands	118	Ad8
Pribinić	72	D3
Příbram	70	F4
Price	126	G1
Price, Cape	93	H6
Prichard	129	H5
Priego	66	E2
Priego de Córdoba	66	D4
Prieska	108	D5
Priest Lake	122	F3
Priest River	122	F3
Prievidza	71	H4
Prignitz	70	D2
Prijedor	72	D3
Prikaspiyskaya Nizmennost'	79	J6
Prilep	73	F5

Priluki *Rossiyskaya S.F.S.R.,*		
U.S.S.R.	78	G3
Priluki *Ukraine S.S.R., U.S.S.R.*	79	E5
Primavera	141	V6
Primorsk *Azerbaydzhan S.S.R.,*		
U.S.S.R.	79	H7
Primorsk *Ukraine, S.S.R.,*		
U.S.S.R.	79	F6
Primorsk *U.S.S.R.*	79	H6
Primorsk *U.S.S.R.*	63	N6
Primorskiy Kray	88	E3
Primorsko	73	J4
Primorsko-Akhtarsk	79	F6
Primrose Lake	119	P5
Prince Albert *Canada*	119	P5
Prince Albert *South Africa*	108	D6
Prince Albert Peninsula	119	N1
Prince Albert Road	108	D6
Prince Albert Sound	119	N1
Prince Alfred, Cape	120	B3
Prince Charles Island	120	L4
Prince Charles Mountains	141	E4
Prince Edward Island	121	P8
Prince Edward Islands	142	C6
Prince George	119	L5
Prince Gustav Adolph Sea	120	E2
Prince of Wales, Cape		
Canada	121	M5
Prince of Wales, Cape *U.S.A.*	118	B2
Prince of Wales Island		
Australia	114	C4
Prince of Wales Island		
Canada	120	G3
Prince of Wales Island *U.S.A.*	118	J4
Prince of Wales Strait	119	M1
Prince Patrick Island	120	B2
Prince Regent Inlet	120	H3
Prince Rupert	118	J5
Princes Risborough	53	G3
Princess Astrid Coast	141	A4
Princess Charlotte Bay	113	J1
Princess Elizabeth Land	141	F4
Princess Marie Bay	120	L2
Princethorpe	53	F2
Princeton *Canada*	122	D3
Princeton *Illinois, U.S.A.*	124	F6
Princeton *Kentucky, U.S.A.*	124	G8
Princeton *Missouri, U.S.A.*	124	D6
Princeton *W. Virginia, U.S.A.*	125	K8
Prince William Sound	118	F3
Príncipe	105	G5
Prineville	122	D5
Prins Karls Forland	80	C2
Prinzapolca	132	E8
Priozersk	63	P6
Pripet Marshes	79	D5
Pripyat'	71	M2
Priština	73	F4
Pritzwalk	70	E2
Privas	65	F6
Privolzhskaya Vozvyshennost'	79	H5
Prizzi	69	D7
Prnjavor	72	D3
Probolinggo	90	E7
Proddatur	92	E6
Progreso	131	Q7
Prokhladnyy	79	G7
Prokletije	74	E1
Prokop'yevsk	84	D6
Prokuplje	73	F4

Name	Page	Grid
Qaṭ'ah	77	J5
Qaṭanā	94	C5
Qatar	97	K4
Qatrāna	94	C6
Qattâra Depression	102	E2
Qattâra, Munkhafed el	102	E2
Qâyen	95	P5
Qazvīn	95	K3
Qeisûm	96	A3
Qena	103	F2
Qeshm *Iran*	95	N8
Qeshm *Iran*	95	N8
Qeydār	94	J3
Qeys	95	L8
Qezel Owzan	94	J3
Qez'iot	94	B6
Qian'an	87	N2
Qianjiang	93	L3
Qianwei	87	N3
Qianxi	93	L3
Qianxinan	93	K3
Qiaowan	86	H3
Qidong *Hunan, China*	93	M3
Qidong *Jiangsu, China*	87	N5
Qiemo	92	G1
Qihe	87	M4
Qihreg	87	L3
Qijiaojing	86	F3
Qikou	87	M4
Qila Ladgasht	92	B3
Qila Saifullah	92	C2
Qilian Shan	86	H4
Qināb, Wadi	97	J8
Qing'an	88	A2
Qingdao	87	N4
Qinggang	87	P2
Qinghai	93	J2
Qinghai Hu	93	K1
Qinghai Nanshan	93	J1
Qinghe	88	B2
Qing Xian	87	M4
Qingyang	93	L1
Qingyuan *Liaoning, China*	87	N3
Qingyuan *Zhejiang, China*	87	M6
Qinhuangdao	87	M4
Qin Ling	93	L2
Qinshui	93	M1
Qin Xian	87	L4
Qinyuan	87	L4
Qinzhou	93	L4
Qionglai	93	K2
Qionglai Shan	93	K2
Qiongzhong	93	L5
Qiongzhou Haixia	93	L4
Qiqihar	87	N2
Qīr	95	L7
Qīshn	97	K9
Qishrān	96	E6
Qitai	86	F3
Qitaihe	87	Q2
Qitbīt, Wadi	97	M7
Qixing He	88	D2
Qixingpao	88	C2
Qiyang	93	M3
Qizil Bulak	95	Q4
Qojūr	94	H3
Qolleh-ye Damāvand	95	L4
Qom	95	K4
Qomishēh	95	K5
Qomolangma Feng	92	G3
Qornetes Saouda	94	B4
Qorveh	94	H4
Qoṭbābād	95	N8
Qoṭūr *Iran*	77	L3
Qoṭūr *Iran*	77	L3
Quaidabad	92	D2
Quairading	112	D5
Quakenbrück	70	B2
Quanah	127	N3
Quang Ngai	93	L5
Quang Tri	93	L5
Quang Yen	93	L4
Quan Long	93	L7
Quannan	87	L7
Quan Phu Quoc	93	K6
Quantock Hills	52	D3
Quanzhou *Fujian, China*	87	M7
Quanzhou *Guangxi, China*	93	M3
Qu'Appelle	123	N2
Quaqtaq	121	N5
Quaraí *Brazil*	138	E6
Quaraí *Brazil*	138	E6
Quartu San Elena	69	B6
Quartzsite	126	E4
Quatsino Sound	122	A2
Quayṭī	97	J9
Quchan	95	P3
Qudaym	77	H5
Queanbeyan	113	K6
Québec *Canada*	121	L7
Québec *Canada*	125	Q3
Quedal, Cabo de	139	B8
Queen Bess, Mount	122	B2
Queen, Cape	120	L5
Queen Charlotte Islands	118	J5
Queen Charlotte Sound	118	K5
Queen Charlotte Strait	118	K5
Queen Elizabeth Islands	120	G2
Queen Mary Land	141	G4
Queen Maud Gulf	119	Q2
Queen Maud Land	141	A4
Queen Maud Mountains	141	N1
Queensbury	55	H3
Queens Channel	112	F1
Queensferry *Clwyd, U.K.*	55	F3
Queensferry *Lothian, U.K.*	57	E5
Queensland	113	J3
Queenstown *Australia*	113	K7
Queenstown *New Zealand*	115	B6
Queenstown *South Africa*	108	E6
Queija, Sierra de	66	C1
Queimadas	137	K6
Quela	106	C4
Quelimane	109	G3
Quelpart Island	87	P5
Quemado	127	H3
Quembo	106	C5
Quepos	132	E10
Que Que	108	E3
Querétaro	131	J7
Queshan	93	M2
Quesnel	119	L5
Quesnel Lake	119	L5
Quetena	138	C4
Quetta	92	C2
Quettehou	64	C4
Quevedo	136	B4
Quezaltenango	132	B7
Quezon City	91	G3
Quibala	106	B5
Quibaxi	106	B4
Quibdó	136	B2
Quiberon	65	B5
Quiberon, Baie de	65	B5
Quilengues	106	B5
Quillabamba	136	C6
Quillacollo	138	C3
Quillagua	138	C4
Quillan	65	E7
Quill Lakes	123	M2
Quillota	139	B6
Quilon	92	E7
Quilpie	113	J4
Quimbele	106	C4
Quimper	64	A4
Quimperlé	65	B5
Quinag	56	C2
Quince Mil	136	C6
Quincy *California, U.S.A.*	122	D8
Quincy *Illinois, U.S.A.*	124	E7
Quincy *Massachusetts, U.S.A.*	125	Q5
Quines	139	C6
Qui Nhon	93	L6
Quintanar de la Orden	66	E3
Quintero	139	B6
Quipungo	106	B5
Quiroga	66	C1
Quissanga	109	H2
Quita Sueño Bank	132	G7
Quito	136	B4
Quixadá	137	K4
Qu Jiang	93	L2
Qujing	93	K3
Qulbān Layyah	94	H7
Qumarlêb	93	J2
Qumbu	108	E6
Qunayfidhah, Naṭūd	96	G4
Qucin Point	108	C6
Qucrn	113	H5
Qucrndon	53	F2
Qūrū Gol Pass	94	G2
Qus	103	F2
Quseir	103	F2
Qūtīābād	94	J4
Quṭū	96	E7
Quzhou	87	M6
Raab *Austria*	68	E2
Raab *Hungary*	72	D2
Raahe	62	L4
Rääkkylä	62	N5
Raanes Peninsula	120	J2
Raanujärvi	62	L3
Raasay	56	B3
Raasay, Sound of	56	B3
Rab	72	C3
Rába	72	D2
Raba *Indonesia*	91	F7
Raba *Poland*	71	H4
Rabastens	65	D7
Rabat *Morocco*	100	D2
Rabat *Turkey*	77	J2
Rabaul	114	E2
Rabi	114	S8
Rābigh	96	D5
Rābor	95	N7
Rabyānah, Ramlat	101	K4
Race, Cape	121	R8
Rach Gia	93	L6
Racibórz	71	H3
Racine	124	G5
Rackwick	56	E2
Racoon	124	C5
Racoon Mountains	129	J3
Radā'	96	G9
Rădăuţi	73	H2
Radcliff	124	H8
Radde	88	C1
Radekhov	71	L3
Radford	125	K8
Radisson	121	L7
Radna	73	F2
Radnice	70	E4
Radnor Forest	52	D2
Radom	71	J3
Radomsko	71	H3
Radomyshl'	79	D5
Radoviš	73	G5
Radstadt	68	D2
Radstock	52	E3
Radstock, Cape	113	G5
Radzyń Podlaski	71	K3
Rae	119	M2
Rae Bareli	92	F3
Rae Isthmus	120	J4
Raetihi	115	E3
Rafaela	138	D6
Rafaī	102	D6
Rafalovka	71	L3
Rafḥā	96	F2
Rafsanjān	95	M6
Raga	102	E6
Ragged Cays	133	K3
Raghtin More	58	H2
Raglan Harbour	115	E2
Ragusa *Italy*	69	E7
Ragusa *Yugoslavia*	72	E4
Rahad	96	B10
Rahaṭ, Ḥarrat	96	E5
Rahimyar Khan	92	D3
Rahuri	92	D5
Raichur	92	E5
Raigarh *Madhya Pradesh, India*	92	F4
Raigarh *Orissa, India*	92	F5
Rainbow City	129	J4
Rainham	53	H3
Rainier, Mount	122	D4
Rainy	124	C2
Rainy Lake	124	D2
Raippaluoto	62	J5
Raipur	92	F4
Raisduoddarhaldde	62	J2
Raistakka	62	N3
Rajada	137	J5
Rajahmundry	92	F5
Rajang	90	E5
Rajanpur	92	D3
Rajapalaiyam	92	E7
Rajapur	92	D5
Rajasthan	92	D3
Rajasthan Canal	92	D3
Rajgarh	92	E4
Rajgród	71	K2
Rajkot	92	D4
Rajmahal Hills	93	G4
Raj Nandgaon	92	F4
Rajpipla	92	D4

Reggio di Calabria	69	E6	Retalhuleu	132	B7	Ribeiro do Pombal	137	K6	Ringmer	53	H4
Reggio nell 'Amelia	68	C3	Rethel	64	F4	Ribérac	65	D6	Ringselet	62	L3
Regina *Brazil*	137	G3	Réthimnon	75	H5	Riberalta	136	D6	Ringvassøy	62	H2
Regina *Canada*	123	M2	Retiche, Alpi	68	C2	Ribnica	72	C3	Ringwood	53	F4
Reguengos de Monsaraz	66	C3	Rétság	72	E2	Ribnitz-Damgarten	70	E1	Rinía	75	H4
Rehna	70	D2	Retuerta de Bullaque	66	D3	Riccall	55	H3	Rinjani, Gunung	90	F7
Rehoboth	108	C4	Réunion	109	L7	Rice Lake *Canada*	125	L4	Rinns Point	57	B5
Rehoboth Beach	125	N7	Reus	67	G2	Rice Lake *U.S.A.*	124	E4	Riobamba	136	B4
Rehovot	94	B6	Reuss	68	B2	Richard Collinson Inlet	119	N1	Río Branco *Brazil*	136	D5
Réidh, Rubha	56	C3	Reut	73	J2	Richards Island	118	H2	Río Branco *Uruguay*	138	F6
Reidsville	129	N2	Reutlingen	70	C4	Richardson	128	D4	Rio Bravo	128	D8
Reiff	56	C2	Revel	65	D7	Richardson Mountains	118	H2	Río Bueno	139	B8
Reigate	53	G3	Revelstoke	122	E2	Richelieu	125	P4	Río Caribe	136	E1
Reighton	55	J2	Reventador, Volcán	136	B4	Richfield	126	F1	Río Claro	136	E1
Ré, Île de	65	C5	Revillagigedo Island	118	J5	Richland	122	E4	Río Colorado	139	D7
Reims	64	F4	Revillagigedo, Islas	130	D8	Richlands	125	K8	Río Cuarto	138	D6
Reina Adelaida, Archipiélago			Rewa	92	F4	Richmond *Australia*	113	J3	Río de Janeiro *Brazil*	138	H4
de la	139	B10	Rewari	92	E3	Richmond *New Zealand*	115	D4	Río de Janeiro *Brazil*	138	H4
Reindeer Lake	119	Q4	Rexburg	122	J6	Richmond *South Africa*	108	D6	Rio de Oro, Baie de	100	B4
Reine	62	E3	Reyes, Point	122	C9	Richmond *Greater London,*			Río Gallegos	139	C10
Reinga, Cape	115	D1	Reyhanli	77	G4	*U.K.*	53	G3	Río Grande *Argentina*	139	C10
Reinheimen	62	B5	Rey, Isla del	132	H10	Richmond *North Yorkshire,*			Río Grande *Brazil*	138	F6
Reinosa	66	D1	Reykjaheiði	62	W12	*U.K.*	55	H2	Río Grande *U.S.A.*	130	H6
Reitz	108	E5	Reykjahhð	62	W12	Richmond *Indiana, U.S.A.*	124	H7	Rio Grande City	128	C7
Relizane	100	F1	Reykjanestá	62	T13	Richmond *Kentucky, U.S.A.*	124	H8	Río Grande de Santiago	130	G7
Remada	101	H2	Reykjavík	62	U12	Richmond *Virginia, U.S.A.*	125	M8	Rio Grande do Norte	137	K5
Rembang	90	E7	Reynivellir *Iceland*	62	U12	Richmond Range	115	D4	Rio Grande do Sul	138	F5
Remeshk	95	P8	Reynivellir *Iceland*	62	W12	Rickmansworth	53	G3	Ríohacha	136	C1
Remiremont	65	G4	Reynosa	128	C7	Ricla	67	F2	Río Hato	132	G10
Remontnoye	79	G6	Rēzekne	63	M8	Ricobayo, Embalse de	66	D2	Río Lagartos	131	Q7
Remoulins	65	F7	Rhätikon Pratigau	68	B2	Ridgecrest	126	D3	Riom	65	E6
Remscheid	70	B3	Rhayader	52	D2	Ridgeland	129	M4	Riom-és-Montagnes	65	E6
Rena *Norway*	63	D6	Rheda-Wiedenbrück	70	C3	Ridgway	125	L6	Río Mulatos	138	C3
Rena *Norway*	63	D6	Rhee	53	G2	Riding Mountain	123	P2	Rionegro	136	C2
Renaix	64	E3	Rhein	70	B3	Ridsdale	57	F5	Rio Negro *Brazil*	138	G5
Renard Islands	114	E4	Rheine	70	B2	Ried	68	D1	Rio Negro *Spain*	66	C1
Rendova Island	114	H6	Rhewl	55	F3	Rienza	68	C2	Río Negro, Embalse del	138	E6
Rendsburg	70	C1	Rhiconich	56	D2	Riesa	70	E3	Rio Negro, Pantanal do	138	E3
Renfrew *Canada*	125	M4	Rhine	64	G4	Riesco, Isla	139	B10	Rioni	77	J1
Renfrew *U.K.*	57	D5	Rhinelander	124	F4	Rietfontein	108	D4	Rio Pardo de Minas	138	H3
Rengat	90	D6	Rhino Camp	107	F2	Rieti	69	D4	Rio Primero	138	D6
Rengo	139	B6	Rhir, Cap	100	D2	Rifle	123	L8	Rio São Gonçalo	138	H4
Renish Point	56	B3	Rho	68	B3	Rifstangi	62	W11	Ríosucio *Colombia*	136	B2
Renk	103	F5	Rhode Island	125	Q6	Riga	63	L8	Ríosucio *Colombia*	136	B2
Renmark	113	J5	Rhodes	75	J4	Riga, Gulf of	63	K8	Rio Verde	138	F3
Renmin	87	P2	Rhodopi Planina	73	G4	Rīgān	95	P7	Ripley *Ohio, U.S.A.*	124	J7
Rennell Island	114	K7	Rhondda	52	D3	Rigistān	92	B2	Ripley *Tennessee, U.S.A.*	128	H3
Rennes	64	C4	Rhône	65	F7	Rigolet	121	Q7	Ripley *W. Virginia, U.S.A.*	125	K7
Reno *Italy*	68	C3	Rhoose	52	D3	Rihāb, Ar	94	G6	Ripoll	67	H1
Reno *U.S.A.*	122	E8	Rhosneigr	55	E3	Rihand	92	F4	Ripon	55	H2
Reo	91	G7	Rhuddlan	55	F3	Riiser-Larsen Sea	141	B5	Ripponden	55	H3
Repetek	95	R2	Rhum	57	B3	Rijeka	72	C3	Risca	52	D3
Repolovo	84	Ae4	Rhum, Sound of	57	B4	Rika	71	K4	Rishiri-tō	88	H3
Republican	123	R7	Rhydaman	52	C3	Rikā, Wadi al	96	G5	Rishon le Zion	94	B6
Repulse Bay *Australia*	113	K3	Rhyl	55	F3	Rīmah, Wadi al	96	E3	Risle	64	D4
Repulse Bay *Canada*	120	J4	Rhynie	56	F3	Rimāl, Ar	97	L6	Risør	63	C7
Requena *Peru*	136	C5	Riachão do Jacuípe	138	K6	Rimavská Sobota	71	J4	Risøyhamn	62	F2
Requena *Spain*	67	F3	Riacho de Santana	138	J6	Rimbo	63	H7	Ritchie's Archipelago	93	H6
Rere	114	K6	Riaño	66	D1	Rimini	68	D3	Ritter, Mount	122	E9
Reşadiye *Turkey*	76	B4	Riánsares	66	E3	Rimna	73	J3	Ritzville	122	E4
Reşadiye *Turkey*	77	G2	Riau, Kepulauan	90	C5	Rîmnicu Sărat	73	J3	Riva	68	C3
Resen	73	F5	Riaza	66	E2	Rîmnicu Vîlcea	73	H3	Rivas	132	E9
Resia, Passo de	68	C2	Ribadeo	66	C1	Rimouski	125	R2	Rivera	138	E6
Resistencia	138	E5	Ribadesella	66	D1	Rinca	91	F7	River Falls	124	D4
Reşiţa	73	F3	Ribas do Rio Pardo	138	F4	Rinchinlhumbe	86	H1	Riverina	113	K5
Resolution Island *Canada*	121	P5	Ribat	95	R5	Ringe	63	D9	Riversdale	108	D6
Resolution Island *New*			Ribatejo	66	B3	Ringebu	63	D6	Riverside	126	D4
Zealand	115	A6	Ribble	55	G2	Ringgold Isles	114	S8	Riverton *Australia*	113	H5
Resolution Lake	121	P6	Ribe	63	C9	Ringkøbing	63	C8	Riverton *Canada*	123	R2
Restigouche	125	S3	Ribeirão Prêto	138	G4	Ringkøping Fjord	63	C9	Riverton *New Zealand*	115	B7

Riverton *U.S.A.*	123	K6
Rivière-du-Loup	125	R3
Rivoli	68	A3
Riwaka	115	D4
Riwoqê	93	J2
Riyan	97	J9
Rize	77	J2
Rizhskiy Zaliv	63	K8
Rizokarpaso	76	F5
Rjukan	63	C7
Rjuven	63	B7
Roa	66	E2
Road Town	133	Q5
Roan Fell	57	F5
Roanne	65	F5
Roanoke *N. Carolina, U.S.A.*	129	P2
Roanoke *U.S.A.*	125	L8
Roanoke *U.S.A.*	125	L8
Roanoke Rapids	129	P2
Roan Plateau	123	K8
Robat	95	R6
Robāţ Karīm	95	K4
Robat Thand	95	Q7
Röbel	70	E2
Robert Brown, Cape	120	K4
Roberton	57	E5
Robertsbridge	53	H4
Robertsfors	62	J4
Robert S. Kerr Reservoir	128	E3
Robertson Range	112	E3
Robertsport	104	C4
Roberval	125	P2
Robinson	124	G7
Robinson Ranges	112	D4
Robleda	66	C2
Robledollano	66	D3
Robles La Paz	136	C1
Roblin	123	P2
Robore	138	E3
Rob Roy Island	114	H5
Robson, Mount	119	M5
Roca, Cabo da	66	B3
Roca Partida, Isla	130	C8
Roca Partida, Punta	131	M8
Roccella Ionica	69	F6
Rocha	139	F6
Rocha da Gale, Barragem	66	C4
Rochdale	55	G3
Rochechouart	65	D6
Rochefort	65	C6
Rochelle	124	F6
Rochester *Kent, U.K.*	53	H3
Rochester *Northumberland, U.K.*	57	F5
Rochester *New Hamshire, U.S.A.*	125	Q5
Rochester *New York, U.S.A.*	125	M5
Rochester *Winconsin, U.S.A.*	124	D4
Rochford	53	H3
Rochfortbridge	59	H6
Rock	124	F5
Rockefeller Plateau	141	R3
Rock Falls	124	F6
Rockford	124	F5
Rockglen	123	L3
Rockhampton	113	L3
Rockingham *Australia*	112	D5
Rockingham *U.S.A.*	129	N3
Rockingham Bay	113	K2
Rock Island	124	E6

Rockland *Maine, U.S.A.*	125	R4
Rockland *Michigan, U.S.A.*	124	F3
Rock Springs *Montana, U.S.A.*	123	L4
Rock Springs *Wyoming, U.S.A.*	123	K7
Rockwood	125	R4
Rocky Ford	127	L1
Rocky Mount	129	P3
Rocky Mountain House	119	N5
Rocky Mountains	116	G3
Rocroi	64	F4
Rødberg	63	C6
Rødby	63	D9
Rödeby	63	F8
Rodel	56	B3
Roden	52	E2
Rodez	65	E6
Ródhos *Greece*	75	J4
Ródhos *Greece*	75	K4
Rodi Gargánico	69	E5
Roding	53	H3
Rodinga	113	G3
Rodna	73	H2
Rodnei, Munţii	73	H2
Rodney, Cape *New Zealand*	115	E2
Rodney, Cape *U.S.A.*	118	B3
Rodonit, Kep i	74	E2
Rodosto	76	B2
Roebuck Bay	112	E2
Roermond	64	F3
Roeselare	64	E3
Roes Welcome Sound	120	J5
Rogachev	79	E5
Rogaland	63	B7
Rogatin	71	L4
Rogers	128	E2
Rogers, Mount	125	K8
Roggeveld Berge	108	D6
Rogliano	68	B4
Rognan	62	F3
Rogoźno	71	G2
Rohri	92	C3
Rohtak	92	E3
Rois Bheinn	57	C3
Rojas	139	D6
Rojo, Cabo *Mexico*	131	L7
Rojo, Cabo *U.S.A.*	133	P6
Rokan	90	C5
Rokel	104	C4
Rokiškis	63	L9
Rolla	124	E8
Rolleston	113	K3
Roma *Australia*	113	K4
Roma *Italy*	69	D5
Roma *Sweden*	63	H8
Romain, Cape	129	N4
Romaine	121	P7
Romaldkirk	55	G2
Roman	73	J2
Romang	91	H7
Romania	73	G3
Romano, Cape	129	M8
Romanovka	85	J6
Romans-sur-Isere	65	F6
Romanzof, Cape	118	B3
Romão	136	E4
Romblon	91	G3
Rome *Italy*	69	D5
Rome *U.S.A.*	129	K3
Romerike	63	D6

Romilly	64	E4
Romney	125	L7
Romny	79	E5
Rømø	63	C9
Romorantin	65	D5
Romsey	53	F4
Rona	56	C3
Ronay	56	A3
Roncador, Cayos	132	G8
Roncador, Serra do	137	G6
Ronco	68	D3
Ronda *India*	92	E1
Ronda *Spain*	66	D4
Rondane	63	C6
Ronda, Sierra de	66	D4
Rønde	63	D8
Rondeslottet	63	C6
Rondônia *Brazil*	136	E6
Rondônia *Brazil*	136	E6
Rondonópolis	138	F3
Ronge, Lac La	119	Q4
Rong Jiang	93	L4
Rong, Kas	93	K6
Rongshui	93	L3
Rong Xian	93	M4
Rønne	63	H9
Ronneby	63	F8
Ronne Entrance	141	U4
Ronne Ice Shelf	141	V3
Ronse	64	E3
Roodepoort	108	E5
Roof Butte	127	H2
Roosendaal	64	F3
Roosevelt	136	E5
Roosevelt Island	141	P3
Roosevelt, Mount	118	K4
Ropcha	78	J3
Roper	113	G1
Ropi	62	J2
Roquefort	65	C6
Rora Head	56	E2
Roraima	136	E3
Roraima, Mount	136	E2
Røros	62	D5
Rørvik	62	D4
Rosa, Cap	69	B7
Rosalía, Punta	126	E6
Rosa, Monte	68	A3
Rosário	137	J4
Rosario *Argentina*	138	D6
Rosario *Mexico*	130	G6
Rosario *Mexico*	127	H7
Rosario de la Frontera	138	D5
Rosarito	126	F6
Roscoe	127	M4
Roscommon *Ireland*	58	F5
Roscommon *Ireland*	58	F5
Roscrea	59	G7
Roseau	133	S7
Roseberth	113	H4
Rosebery	113	K7
Rosebud	122	H2
Roseburg	122	C6
Rosedale Abbey	55	J2
Rosehearty	56	F3
Rose Island	111	V4
Rosenburg	128	E6
Rosenheim	70	E5
Rose Point	118	J5
Roses	67	H1

Roses, Golfo de	67	H1
Roseto d'Abruzzi	69	D4
Rosetown	123	K2
Rosetta	102	F1
Roshkhvār	95	P4
Roşiori de Vede	73	H3
Rositsa	73	H4
Roskilde	63	E9
Roslavl'	78	E5
Ross *New Zealand*	115	C5
Ross *U.K.*	57	G5
Rossall Point	55	F3
Rossano	69	F6
Rossan Point	58	E3
Rosscarbery Bay	59	D9
Ross Dependency	141	P7
Rossel Island	114	E4
Rosses Bay	58	F2
Rosses Point	58	E4
Rosses, The	58	F3
Ross Ice Shelf	141	N2
Rossington	55	H3
Ross Island	141	M3
Rossiyskaya S.F.S.R.	78	E4
Rosslare Harbour	59	K8
Ross-on-Wye	52	E3
Rossosh'	79	F5
Ross River	118	J3
Ross Sea	141	N3
Røst	62	E3
Rostāq	95	L8
Rostock	70	E1
Rostonsölkä	62	J2
Rostov	78	F4
Rostov-na-Donu	79	F6
Rostrevor	58	K4
Roswell *Georgia, U.S.A.*	129	K3
Roswell *New Mexico, U.S.A.*	127	K4
Rotemo	63	B7
Rotenburg	70	C2
Rothaargebirge	70	C3
Rothbury	57	G5
Rothbury Forest	57	G5
Rother *Kent, U.K.*	53	H3
Rother *W. Sussex, U.K.*	53	G4
Rothera	141	V5
Rotherham	55	H3
Rothesay	57	C5
Rothiesholm	56	F1
Rothwell *Northamptonshire, U.K.*	53	G2
Rothwell *W. Yorkshire, U.K.*	55	H3
Roti	91	G8
Rotja, Punta	67	G3
Roto	113	K5
Rotondella	69	F5
Rotorua	115	F3
Rottenberg	70	C3
Rottenburg *W. Germany*	70	C4
Rottenburg *W. Germany*	70	E4
Rotterdam	64	F3
Rottweil	70	C4
Rotuma	111	S4
Rötz	70	E4
Roubaix	64	E3
Rouen	64	D4
Rouge	93	K4
Rouillac	65	C6
Round Hill Head	113	L3
Roundup	123	K4

Safid Kuh	**95**	R4
Safid Rūd	**95**	J3
Safonovo	**78**	E4
Safranbolu	**76**	E2
Şafwān	**94**	H6
Saga *China*	**92**	G3
Saga *Japan*	**89**	C9
Sagami-nada	**89**	G8
Sagamoso	**133**	L11
Saganthit Kyun	**93**	J6
Sagar *Karnataka, India*	**92**	D6
Sagar *Madhya Pradesh, India*	**92**	E4
Saggart	**59**	K6
Saginaw	**124**	J5
Saginaw Bay	**124**	J5
Sagiz *U.S.S.R.*	**79**	J6
Sagiz *U.S.S.R.*	**79**	J6
Sagiz *U.S.S.R.*	**79**	J6
Sağkaya	**77**	F4
Saglek Bay	**121**	P6
Sagone, Golfe de	**69**	B4
Sagres	**66**	B4
Saguache	**127**	J1
Sagua la Grande	**132**	G3
Saguenay	**121**	M8
Sagunto	**67**	F3
Sahagún	**66**	D1
Sahand, Kūh-e	**94**	H3
Sahara	**98**	C4
Saharanpur	**92**	E3
Şahin	**76**	B2
Sahiwal *Pakistan*	**92**	D2
Sahiwal *Pakistan*	**92**	D2
Şaḥm	**97**	N4
Sahra al Ḥijārah	**94**	G6
Sahuaripa	**127**	H6
Sahuayo	**130**	H7
Sa Huynh	**93**	L6
Šahy.	**71**	H4
Saibai Island	**114**	C3
Saïcla	**94**	B5
Saïda *Algeria*	**100**	F2
Saïda *Lebanon*	**76**	F6
Sa'īdābād	**95**	M7
Saidapet	**92**	F6
Saidor	**114**	D3
Saidpur	**93**	G3
Saigon	**93**	L6
Saijo	**89**	D9
Saimaa	**63**	M6
Saimbeyli	**77**	G3
Saindak	**95**	Q7
Sa'īndezh	**94**	H3
Saint Abb's Head	**57**	B5
Saint-Affrique	**65**	E7
Saint-Agathe-des-Monts	**125**	N3
Saint Agnes *U.K.*	**52**	B4
Saint Agnes *U.K.*	**52**	K5
Saint-Agrève	**65**	F6
Saint Albans *U.K.*	**53**	G3
Saint Albans *Vermont, U.S.A.*	**125**	P4
Saint Albans *W. Virginia, U.S.A.*	**124**	K7
Saint Alban's Head	**53**	E4
Saint Aldhelm's	**53**	E4
Saint-Amand-Montrond	**65**	E5
Saint-Ambroix	**65**	F6
Saint André, Cap	**109**	H3
Saint Andrew	**53**	M7
Saint Andrews *New Zealand*	**115**	C6

Saint Andrews *U.K.*	**57**	F4
Saint Andrews Bay	**57**	F4
Saint-Anne-des-Monts	**125**	S2
Saint Annes	**53**	M6
Saint Ann's Bay	**132**	J5
Saint Ann's Head	**52**	B3
Saint Anthony *Canada*	**121**	Q7
Saint Anthony *U.S.A.*	**122**	J6
Saint Arnaud	**115**	D4
Saint Asaph	**55**	F3
Saint Aubin	**53**	M7
Saint Augustin	**121**	Q7
Saint Augustine	**129**	M6
Saint Augustin Saguenay	**121**	Q7
Saint Austell	**52**	C4
Saint Austell Bay	**52**	C4
Saint Bees	**55**	F2
Saint Bees Head	**55**	F2
Saint Benoit	**109**	L7
Saint Blazey	**52**	C4
Saint Brides	**52**	B3
Saint Brides Bay	**52**	B3
Saint-Brieuc	**64**	B4
Saint-Calais	**65**	D5
Saint Catherines	**125**	L5
Saint Catherines Island	**129**	M5
Saint Catherine's Point	**53**	F4
Saint-Céré	**65**	D6
Saint-Chamond	**65**	F6
Saint Charles	**124**	E7
Saint Clair, Lake	**124**	J5
Saint-Claude	**65**	F5
Saint Clears	**52**	C3
Saint Cloud *Florida, U.S.A.*	**129**	M6
Saint Cloud *Minnesota, U.S.A.*	**124**	C4
Saint Columb Major	**52**	C4
Saint Croix *Canada*	**125**	S4
Saint Croix *Minnesota, U.S.A.*	**124**	D4
Saint Croix *U.S.A.*	**133**	Q6
Saint Croix Falls	**124**	D4
Saint David's	**52**	B3
Saint David's Head	**52**	B3
Saint-Denis	**64**	E4
Saint Denis	**109**	L7
Sainte-Foy-la-Grande	**65**	D6
Saint Elias, Mount	**118**	G3
Saint Elias Mountains	**118**	H3
Sainte-Marie	**109**	J3
Sainte-Marie-aux-Mines	**64**	G4
Sainte Marie, Cap	**109**	J5
Sainte-Maxime	**65**	G7
Sainte-Menehould	**64**	F4
Sainte Nazaire	**65**	B5
Saintes	**65**	C6
Saintes, Îles des	**133**	S7
Saintes-Maries-de-la-Mer	**65**	F7
Saint Étienne	**65**	F6
Saint Eustatius	**133**	R6
Saint-Fargeau	**65**	E5
Saintfield	**58**	L4
Saint Finan's Bay	**59**	B9
Saint-Florent, Golfe de	**69**	B4
Saint-Florentin	**65**	E4
Saint-Flour	**65**	E6
Saint Francis *Canada*	**125**	P4
Saint Francis *Arkansas, U.S.A.*	**128**	G3
Saint Francis *Kansas, U.S.A.*	**123**	P8
Saint Francis, Cape	**108**	D6

Saint Gallen	**68**	B2
Saint-Gaudens	**65**	D7
Saint George *Australia*	**113**	K4
Saint George *U.S.A.*	**126**	F2
Saint George, Cape *Canada*	**121**	Q8
Saint George, Cape *Papua New Guinea*	**114**	E2
Saint George Head	**113**	L6
Saint George Island *Alaska, U.S.A.*	**118**	Ae8
Saint George Island *Florida, U.S.A.*	**129**	K6
Saint Georges	**125**	Q3
Saint George's	**133**	S8
Saint Georges Bay	**121**	Q8
Saint George's Channel *Papua New Guinea*	**114**	E2
Saint George's Channel *U.K.*	**52**	B3
Saint-Germain	**64**	D4
Saint-Gildas-de-Rhuys	**65**	B5
Saint-Gilles-Croix-de-Vie	**65**	C5
Saint-Girons	**65**	D7
Saint Gotthard Pass	**68**	B2
Saint Govan's Head	**52**	C3
Saint Helena	**99**	C8
Saint Helena Bay	**108**	C6
Saint Helens *Australia*	**113**	K7
Saint Helens *U.K.*	**55**	G3
Saint Helens, Mount	**122**	C4
Saint Helens Point	**113**	K7
Saint Helier	**53**	M4
Saint Ignace	**124**	H4
Saint Ignatius	**122**	G4
Saint Ives *Cambridgeshire, U.K.*	**53**	G2
Saint Ives *Cornwall, U.K.*	**52**	B4
Saint Ives Bay	**52**	B4
Saint James, Cape	**118**	J5
Saint-Jean-d'Angély	**65**	C6
Saint-Jean-de-Luz	**65**	C7
Saint-Jean-de-Maurienne	**65**	G6
Saint-Jean-de-Monts	**65**	B5
Saint-Jean, Lac	**125**	P2
Saint-Jean-Pied-de-Port	**65**	C7
Saint-Jean-Sur-Richelieu	**125**	P4
Saint Jérôme	**125**	P4
Saint John *Canada*	**121**	N8
Saint John *Canada*	**121**	N8
Saint John *U.K.*	**53**	M7
Saint John *U.S.A.*	**133**	Q5
Saint John Bay	**121**	Q7
Saint John's *Antigua*	**133**	S6
Saint John's *Canada*	**121**	R8
Saint Johns *Arizona, U.S.A.*	**127**	H3
Saint Johns *Florida, U.S.A.*	**129**	M6
Saint Johns *Michigan, U.S.A.*	**124**	H5
Saint Johnsbury	**125**	Q4
Saint John's Point *Ireland*	**58**	F3
Saint John's Point *U.K.*	**58**	L4
Saint Joseph *Arkansas, U.S.A.*	**128**	G5
Saint Joseph *Missouri, U.S.A.*	**124**	C7
Saint Joseph Island	**128**	D7
Saint-Junien	**65**	D6
Saint Just	**52**	B4
Saint Keverne	**52**	B4
Saint Kitts-Nevis	**133**	R6
Saint Laurent	**137**	G2
Saint Lawrence *Australia*	**113**	K3
Saint Lawrence *Canada*	**121**	N8
Saint Lawrence *Canada*	**121**	Q8

Saint Lawrence, Gulf of	**121**	P8
Saint Lawrence Island	**118**	B3
Saint Lawrence Seaway	**125**	N4
Saint Leonard	**125**	S3
Saint-Léonard-de-Noblat	**65**	D6
Saint Lewis	**121**	Q7
Saint Lô	**64**	C4
Saint Louis *Minnesota, U.S.A.*	**124**	D3
Saint Louis *Missouri, U.S.A.*	**124**	E7
Saint Louis *Senegal*	**104**	B2
Saint Lucia	**133**	S6
Saint Lucia, Cape	**109**	F5
Saint Lucia Channel	**133**	S7
Saint Lucia, Lake	**109**	F5
Saint Magnus Bay	**56**	A1
Saint-Maixent-l'École	**65**	C5
Saint Malo	**64**	B4
Saint-Malo, Golfe de	**64**	C4
Saint Marc	**133**	L5
Saint-Marcellin	**65**	F6
Saint Margaret's-at-Cliffe	**53**	J3
Saint Maries	**122**	F4
Saint Martin *France*	**133**	R5
Saint Martin *U.K.*	**53**	M7
Saint Martin, Lake	**123**	Q2
Saint Martin's	**52**	L5
Saint-Martin-Vésubie	**65**	G6
Saint Mary Peak	**113**	H5
Saint Marys *Australia*	**113**	K7
Saint Mary's *Cornwall, U.K.*	**52**	L5
Saint Mary's *Orkney Islands, U.K.*	**56**	F2
Saint Marys *Florida, U.S.A.*	**129**	M5
Saint Marys *Pennsylvania, U.S.A.*	**125**	L6
Saint Mary's Loch	**57**	E5
Saint Matthias Group	**114**	D2
Saint-Maurice	**121**	M8
Saint Maurice	**125**	P3
Saint Mawes	**52**	B4
Saint-Maximin	**65**	F7
Saint Michael	**118**	C3
Saint-Mihiel	**64**	F4
Saint Monance	**57**	F4
Saint Moritz	**68**	B2
Saint Neots	**53**	G2
Saint Niklaas	**64**	F3
Saint Ninian's Island	**56**	A2
Saintogne	**65**	C6
Saint Omer	**64**	E3
Saint Pamphile	**125**	R3
Saint Pascal	**125**	R3
Saint Paul *Alberta, Canada*	**119**	N5
Saint Paul *Québec, Canada*	**121**	Q7
Saint Paul *Liberia*	**104**	C4
Saint Paul *Minnesota, U.S.A.*	**124**	D4
Saint Paul Island	**118**	Ad8
Saint Peter	**124**	D4
Saint Peter Port	**53**	M7
Saint Petersburg	**129**	L7
Saint Pierre *Canada*	**121**	Q8
Saint Pierre *France*	**109**	L7
Saint Pierre Bank	**121**	Q8
Saint Pol	**64**	E3
Saint-Pol-de-Léon	**64**	B4
Saint-Pölten	**68**	E1
Saint-Pons	**65**	E7
Saint-Pourçain	**65**	E5
Saint Queens Bay	**53**	M7
Saint-Quentin	**64**	E4

Shahr-e Kord	95	K5	Shashi	93	M2	Shepparton	113	K6	Shīndand	95	R5
Shahr Rey	95	K4	Shasta Lake	122	C7	Sheppey, Isle of	53	H3	Shin Falls	56	D3
Shah Rud	95	J3	Shasta, Mount	122	C7	Shepshed	53	F2	Shingū	89	E9
Shajapur	92	E4	Shatsk	78	G5	Shepton Mallet	52	E3	Shinjō	88	H6
Shakhauz	94	G2	Shatura	78	F4	Sheragul	84	G6	Shinness	56	D2
Shakhs, Ras	96	E9	Shaubak	94	B6	Sherard, Cape	120	K3	Shinshār	77	G5
Shakhty	79	G6	Shaunavon	123	K3	Sherborne	52	E4	Shinyanga	107	F3
Shakhun'ya	78	H4	Shaw	55	G3	Sherbro	104	C4	Shiogama	89	H6
Shaki	105	F4	Shawano	124	F4	Sherbro Island	104	C4	Shiono-misaki	89	E9
Shakotan-misaki	88	H4	Shawbury	52	E2	Sherbrooke	125	Q4	Shiosawa	89	G7
Shaktoolik	118	C3	Shawinigan	125	P3	Sherburne Reef	114	D2	Shiping	93	K4
Shālamzār	95	K5	Shawnce	128	D3	Sherburn in Elmet	55	H3	Shipley	55	H3
Shaler Mountains	119	N1	Sha Xi	87	M6	Shereik	96	A7	Shippensburg	125	M6
Shalfleet	53	F4	Sha Xian	87	M6	Sheridan Arkansas, U.S.A.	128	F3	Shippigan Island	121	P8
Shalkhar, Ozero	79	J5	Shaybārā	96	C4	Sheridan Wyoming, U.S.A.	123	L5	Shipston-on-Stour	53	F2
Shaluli Shan	93	J2	Shaytanovka	78	K3	Sheringham	53	J2	Shipton	55	H2
Shama, Ash	94	D6	Shchara	71	L2	Sherlovaya Gora	85	K6	Shipton-under-Wychwood	53	F3
Shamary	78	K4	Shchekino	78	F5	Sherman	128	D4	Shipunovo	84	C6
Shambe	102	F6	Shchel'yayur	78	J2	's-Hertogenbosch	64	F3	Shirakawa	89	H7
Shamīl	95	N8	Shcherbakovo	85	U3	Shetland	56	A1	Shirane-san Japan	89	G8
Shāmīyah	94	D4	Shchigry	79	F5	Shetland Islands	56	A1	Shirane-san Japan	89	G7
Sham, Jambal	97	N5	Shchirets	71	K4	Shetpe	79	J7	Shīrāz	95	L7
Shammar	96	E3	Shchors	79	E5	Shevchenko	79	J7	Shire	107	F6
Shand	95	R6	Shchuchin	71	L2	Shewa Gīmīra	103	G6	Shirebrook	55	H3
Shandan	86	J4	Shchuchinsk	84	A6	Sheya	85	K4	Shiretoko-misaki	88	K3
Shandong	87	M4	Shchuch'ye	84	Ad5	Sheyang	87	N5	Shiriya-saki	88	H5
Shangani	108	E3	Shebalino	84	D6	Sheyenne	123	Q4	Shīr Kūh	95	M6
Shanghang	87	M7	Shebekino	79	F5	Shiant Islands	56	B3	Shirten Holoy Gobi	86	H3
Shangqiu	93	N2	Sheberghān	92	C1	Shiant, Sound of	56	B3	Shīrvān	95	N3
Shangrao	87	M6	Sheboygan	124	G5	Shiashkotan, Ostrov	85	S7	Shishaldin Volcano	118	Af9
Shang Xian	93	L2	Shebshi Mountains	105	H4	Shibām	97	J9	Shivpuri	92	E3
Shangzhi	87	P2	Shebunino	88	H2	Shibata	89	G7	Shivwits Plateau	126	F2
Shanklin	53	F4	Sheelin, Lough	58	H5	Shibecha	88	K4	Shiwan Dashan	93	L4
Shannon Ireland	59	E7	Sheenjek	118	G2	Shibetsu Japan	88	J3	Shiyan	93	M2
Shannon New Zealand	115	E4	Sheep Haven	58	G2	Shibetsu Japan	88	K4	Shizhu	93	L3
Shannon, Mouth of the	59	C7	Sheep's Head	59	C9	Shibîn el Kôm	102	F1	Shizugawa	88	H6
Shantarskiye Ostrova	85	P5	Sheerness	53	H3	Shibotsu-jima	88	L4	Shizuishan	87	K4
Shantou	87	M7	Sheffield Alabama, U.S.A.	129	J3	Shibushi	89	C10	Shizuoka	89	G8
Shanxi	93	M1	Sheffield Texas, U.S.A.	127	M5	Shickshock Mountains	125	S2	Shkodër	74	E1
Shan Xian	93	N2	Sheffield U.K.	55	H3	Shiel Bridge	56	C3	Shkumbin	74	E2
Shanyin	87	L4	Shegmas	78	H3	Shieldaig	56	C3	Shmidta, Ostrov	81	L1
Shaoguan	93	M4	Shekhupura	92	D2	Shiel, Loch	57	C4	Shōbara	89	D8
Shaowu	87	M6	Sheki	79	H7	Shiḥan, Wadi	97	L8	Shokal'skogo, Ostrov	84	A2
Shaoxing	87	N6	Shelagskiy	85	W2	Shihezi	86	F3	Shorapur	92	E5
Shaoyang	93	M3	Shelagskiy, Mys	85	V2	Shiikh	103	J6	Shorawak	95	S6
Shap	55	G2	Shelburne	121	N9	Shijiazhuang	87	L4	Shoreham-by-Sea	53	G4
Shapinsay	56	F1	Shelburne Bay	113	J1	Shikarpur	92	C3	Shorkot	92	D2
Shapkina	78	J2	Shelby Montana, U.S.A.	122	J3	Shikoku	89	D9	Shoshone	122	G6
Shaqrā'	96	G4	Shelby N. Carolina, U.S.A.	129	M3	Shikoku-sanchi	89	D9	Shoshone Mountains	122	F8
Sharanga	78	H4	Shelbyville Indiana, U.S.A.	124	H7	Shikong	87	K4	Shoshoni	123	K6
Sharbithāt, Ra's	97	N8	Shelbyville Tennessee, U.S.A.	129	J3	Shikotan-tō	88	L4	Shostka	79	E5
Shari	88	K4	Shelikhova, Zaliv	85	T5	Shikotsu-ko	88	H4	Shouguang	87	M4
Shārī, Buḥayrat	77	L5	Shelikof Strait	118	E4	Shildon	55	H2	Shouning	87	M6
Shark Bay	112	C4	Shell Creek Range	122	G8	Shilega	78	G3	Showa	141	C5
Sharlauk	95	M2	Shelly	122	H6	Shiliguri	93	G3	Showak	96	B9
Sharlyk	79	J5	Shelton	122	C4	Shilka U.S.S.R.	85	K6	Shozhma	78	G3
Sharmah	96	B2	Sheltozero	78	F3	Shilka U.S.S.R.	85	L6	Shpikov	73	K1
Sharm el Sheikh	96	B3	Shemakha	79	H7	Shillingstone	52	E4	Shpola	79	E6
Sharon	125	K6	Shemonaikha	84	C6	Shillong	93	H3	Shrankogl	68	C2
Sharon Springs	127	M1	Shenandoah Iowa, U.S.A.	124	C6	Shilovo	78	G5	Shreveport	128	F4
Sharqī, Al Hajar ash	97	P5	Shenandoah Virginia, U.S.A.	125	L7	Shimabara	89	C9	Shrewsbury	52	E2
Sharqi, Jazā'ir esh	94	C5	Shendam	105	G4	Shimada	89	G8	Shrewton	53	F3
Sharqi, Jebel esh	77	G6	Shendi	103	F4	Shimanovsk	85	M6	Shrigonda	92	D5
Sharqīyah, Ash	97	P5	Shenge	104	C4	Shimian	93	K3	Shropshire	52	E2
Sharqîya, Sahrâ' Esh	103	F2	Shenkursk	78	G3	Shimizu	89	G8	Shrule	59	D5
Sharūrah	96	H8	Shenton, Mount	112	E4	Shimoda	89	G8	Shu'ab, Ra's	97	P9
Sharwayn, Ra's	97	K9	Shenyang	87	N3	Shimoga	92	E6	Shuanghezhen	87	P3
Sharya	78	H4	Shepetovka	79	D5	Shimonoseki	89	C9	Shuangliao	87	N3
Shashe	108	E4	Shepherd Bay	120	H4	Shinano	89	G7	Shuangyashan	87	Q2
Shashemenē	103	G6	Shepherd Islands	114	U12	Shinās	97	N4	Shubar-Kuduk	79	K6

Sir Sanford, Mount	122	F2	Skattkärr	63	E7	Slane	58	J5	Smiltene	63	M8
Sirsi	92	D6	Skaudvilė	63	K9	Slaney	59	J8	Smirnykh	85	Q7
Sirte	101	J2	Skaulo	62	J3	Slaný	70	F3	Smith Arm	118	L2
Sirte, Gulf of	101	J2	Skawina	71	H4	Slapin, Loch	57	B3	Smith Bay *Canada*	120	L2
Şirvan	77	K3	Skeena	118	K5	Slatina	73	H3	Smith Bay *U.S.A.*	118	E1
Sisak	72	D3	Skeena Mountains	118	K4	Slave	119	N4	Smithfield *N. Carolina,*		
Sisaket	93	K5	Skegness	55	K1	Slave Lake	119	N4	*U.S.A.*	129	N3
Sisophon	93	K6	Skeiðarársandur	62	W13	Slavgorod *Rossiyskaya S.F.S.R.,*			Smithfield *Utah, U.S.A.*	122	J7
Sisseton	123	R5	Skelda Ness	56	A2	*U.S.S.R.*	84	B6	Smith Island	121	L5
Sissonne	64	E4	Skellefteå	62	J4	Slavgorod *Ukraine S.S.R.,*			Smith Mount Lake	125	L8
Sīstan	95	P8	Skellefteälven	62	H4	*U.S.S.R.*	79	F6	Smiths Falls	125	N4
Sīstan, Daryācheh-ye-	95	Q6	Skelmersdale	55	G3	Slavo	85	Q6	Smith Sound	120	M2
Sisteron	65	F6	Skelton	55	J2	Slavyanka	88	C4	Smithton	113	K7
Sistig-Khem	84	F6	Skerpioenpunt	108	D5	Slavyansk	79	F6	Smjörfjöll	62	X12
Sistranda	62	C5	Skerries	58	K5	Slavyansk-na-Kubani	79	F6	Smoky	119	M4
Sitamau	92	E4	Skerries, The	54	E3	Sławno	71	G1	Smoky Cape	113	L5
Sitapur	92	F3	Skhíza	75	F4	Sławoborze	70	F2	Smoky Falls	121	K7
Sitges	67	G2	Ski	63	D7	Slea	55	J3	Smoky Hill	123	R8
Sithoniá	75	G2	Skíathos	75	G3	Sleaford	53	G2	Smoky Hills	123	Q8
Sitía	75	J5	Skibbereen	59	D9	Sleat, Sound of	57	C3	Smøla	62	C5
Sitian	86	F3	Skiddaw	55	F2	Sleetmute	118	D3	Smolenka	79	H5
Sitidgi Lake	118	J2	Skidegate	118	J5	Sleights	55	J2	Smolensk	78	E5
Sítio da Abadia	138	H6	Skidel'	71	L2	Slidell	128	H5	Smólikas	75	F2
Sitka	118	H4	Skien	63	C7	Slieve Anieren	58	G4	Smolyan	73	H5
Sittang	93	J5	Skierniewice	71	J3	Slieveanorra	58	K2	Smolyaninovo	88	D4
Sittingbourne	53	H3	Skiftet Kihti	63	J6	Slieveardagh Hills	59	G7	Smooth Rock Falls	125	K2
Sittwe	93	H4	Skikda	101	G1	Slieve Aughty Mountains	59	E6	Smorgon'	71	M1
Situbondo	90	E7	Skipton	55	G3	Slieve Beagh	58	H4	Smotrich	73	J1
Siuri	93	G4	Skiropoúla	75	H3	Slieve Bloom Mountains	59	G6	Smyrna	76	B3
Siuruanjoki	62	M4	Skíros *Greece*	75	H3	Slieve Callan	59	D7	Snaefell	54	E2
Sivas	77	G3	Skíros *Greece*	75	H3	Slieve Car	58	C4	Sn'afell	62	X12
Sivasli	76	C3	Skive	63	C8	Slieve Donard	58	L4	Sn'afellsjökull	62	T12
Siverek	77	H4	Skj'akerhatten	62	E4	Slieve Elva	59	D6	Snaith	55	H3
Siverskiy	63	P7	Skjalfandafljot	62	W12	Slieve Gamph	58	E4	Snake	122	E4
Sivrice	77	H3	Skjálfandi	62	W11	Slieve Kimalta	59	F7	Snake Range	122	G8
Sivrihisar	76	D3	Skjern	63	C9	Slieve League	58	E3	Snake River Plain	122	H6
Sivrihisar Dağlari	76	D3	Skjervøy	62	J1	Slieve Mish Mountains	59	C8	Snap Point	132	J3
Sivuk	85	Q6	Sklad	85	L2	Slieve Miskish	58	C9	Snap, The	56	B1
Siwa	102	E2	Skoghall	63	E7	Slieve Na Calliagh	58	H5	Snares Islands	111	Q11
Siwalik Range	92	F3	Skole	71	K4	Slieve Rushen	58	G4	Snåsa	62	E4
Siwan	92	F3	Skomer Island	53	B3	Slieve Snaght	58	H2	Snåsavatn	62	E4
Si Xian	87	M5	Skópelos *Greece*	75	G3	Sligo *Ireland*	58	E4	Sneek	64	F2
Sixmilebridge	59	E7	Skópelos *Greece*	75	G3	Sligo *Ireland*	58	F4	Sneem	59	C9
Sixpenny Handley	53	E4	Skópelos Kaloyeroi	75	H3	Sligo Bay	58	E4	Snettisham	53	H2
Siya	78	G3	Skopin	79	F5	Slioch	56	C3	Śnežka	70	F3
Siyâl Islands	96	C5	Skopje	73	F4	Slipper Island	115	E2	Snežnik	72	C3
Sizin	84	F6	Skopun	62	Z14	Sliven	73	J4	Sniardwy, Jezioro	71	J2
Sjælland	63	D9	Skorodum	84	A5	Slobodchikovo	78	H3	Snina	71	K4
Sjørup	63	C8	Skorovatn	62	E4	Slobodka	73	K2	Snizort, Loch	56	B3
Skadarsko Jezero	74	E1	Skoruvik	62	X11	Slobodskoy	78	J4	Snodland	53	H3
Skadovsk	79	E6	Skövde	63	E7	Slobodzeya	73	K2	Snøhetta	62	C5
Skaftá	62	V13	Skovorodino	85	L6	Slobozia *Romania*	73	H3	Snoqualmie Pass	122	D4
Skagafjörður	62	V12	Skowhegan	125	R4	Slobozia *Romania*	73	J3	Snoul	93	L6
Skagaflös	62	T12	Skreia	63	D6	Slonim	71	L2	Snowdon	54	E3
Skagen	63	D8	Skudenshavn	63	D6	Slot, The	114	J6	Snowtown	113	H5
Skagerrak	63	C8	Skulgam	62	H2	Slough	53	G3	Snowville	122	H7
Skagit	122	D3	Skull	59	C9	Sluch'	79	D5	Snowy, Mount	122	G3
Skagway	118	H4	Skulyany	73	J2	Slunj	72	C3	Snug Corner	133	L3
Skaill	56	F2	Skuodas	63	J8	Słupsk	71	G1	Snyatyn	73	H1
Skala-Podol'skaya	73	J1	Skuteč	70	F4	Slussfors	62	G4	Snyder	127	M4
Skanderborg	63	C8	Skutskär	63	G6	Slutsk	79	D5	Soalala	109	J3
Skanör	63	E9	Skvira	79	D6	Slyne Head	59	B6	Soalara	109	H4
Skansholm	62	G4	Skwierzyna	70	F2	Slyudyanka	84	G6	Soan Kundo	87	P5
Skantzoúra	75	H3	Skye	56	B3	Småland	63	F8	Soa Pan	108	E4
Skara	63	E7	Skyring, Península	139	B9	Smallwood Reservoir	121	P7	Soar	53	F2
Skaraborg	63	E7	Skyring, Seno	139	B10	Smcanli	76	D3	Soa-Siu	91	H5
Skærbæk	63	C9	Slagelse	63	D9	Smederevo	73	F3	Soavinandriana	109	J3
Skarð	62	V12	Slagnäs	62	H4	Smela	79	E6	Soay	57	B3
Skardu	92	E1	Slamannan	57	E5	Smethwick	53	E2	Soay Sound	57	B3
Skarnes	63	D6	Slamet, Gunung	90	D7	Smidovich	88	D1	Sobat	103	F6

Sobinka	78	F4	Solimões	136	E4
Sobopol	85	M3	Solingen	70	B3
Sobradinho, Barragem de	137	J5	Sollefteå	62	G5
Sobrado	137	G5	Sóller	67	H3
Sobral *Acre, Brazil*	136	C5	Solnechnogorsk	78	F4
Sobral *Ceará, Brazil*	137	J4	Solo	90	E7
Sobv'yevsk	85	K7	Solobkovtsy	73	J1
Soca	72	B2	Solok	90	D6
Socha	136	C2	Solomon	123	Q3
Sochi	79	F7	Solomon Islands	114	J5
Société, Îles de la	143	H5	Solon Springs	124	E3
Socorro *Colombia*	136	C2	Solontsovo	85	K6
Socorro *U.S.A.*	127	J4	Solor, Kepulauan	91	G7
Socorro, Isla	130	D8	Solothurn	68	A2
Socotra	97	P10	Solotobe	86	B3
Soda Lake	126	D3	Solov'yevsk	85	L6
Sodankylä	62	M3	Solta	72	D4
Soda Springs	122	J6	Soltānābād	95	P3
Söderala	63	G6	Solţānīyeh	94	J3
Söderhamn	63	G6	Soltau	70	C2
Söderköping	63	G7	Sol'tsy	78	E4
Södermanland	63	G7	Sölvesborg	63	F8
Södertälje	63	G7	Solway Firth	55	F2
Södra Rätansbyn	62	F5	Solwezi	106	E5
Soë	91	G7	Soma	76	B3
Soest	70	C3	Sōma	89	H7
Sofia *Bulgaria*	73	G4	Somalia	103	J6
Sofia *Madagascar*	109	J3	Sombor	72	E3
Sofiya	73	G4	Sombrerete	130	H6
Sofiysk	85	P6	Sombrero Channel	93	H7
Sogamoso *Colombia*	136	C2	Somerset *Kentucky, U.S.A.*	124	H8
Sogamoso *Colombia*	136	C2	Somerset *Pennsylvania,*		
Sogndalsfjøra	63	B6	*U.S.A.*	125	L6
Sognefjorden	63	A6	Somerset *U.K.*	52	D3
Sogn og Fjordan	63	B6	Somerset East	108	E6
Sogod	91	G3	Somerset Island	120	H3
Söğüt *Turkey*	76	C4	Somerton	52	E3
Söğüt *Turkey*	76	D2	Somerville Reservoir	128	D5
Söğütlü	76	D2	Someş	73	G2
Sog Xian	93	H2	Somes Point	115	F6
Sohâg	103	F2	Somme	64	D3
Sohano	114	E3	Sömmerda	70	D3
Sohela	92	F4	Somosomo	114	S8
Sohŭksan	87	P5	Sompolno	71	H2
Soissons	64	E4	Somport, Puerto de	67	F1
Sojat	92	D3	Somuncurá, Meseta de	139	C8
Sojotan Point	91	G4	Son	92	F4
Sokal	71	L3	Sonakh	85	P6
Söke	76	B4	Sonapur	92	F4
Soko Banja	73	F4	Sonara	127	M5
Sokodé	104	F4	Sønderborg	63	C9
Sokol	78	G4	Søndre Isortoq	120	R4
Sokolo	100	D6	Søndre Strømfjord	120	R4
Sokolovka	88	D4	Søndre Sund	120	Q3
Sokołów Podlaski	71	K2	Sondrio	68	B2
Sokoto *Nigeria*	105	F3	Songea	107	G5
Sokoto *Nigeria*	105	G3	Songhua	88	B2
Sola	71	H4	Songhua Jiang	87	P2
Solander Island	115	A7	Sŏngjin	88	B5
Solāpur	92	E5	Songkhla	93	K7
Sol, Costa del	66	D4	Songololo	106	B4
Soledad	133	K9	Sonhat	92	F4
Soledade	136	D5	Sonid-Youqi	87	L3
Sølen	63	D6	Sonid Zuoqi	87	L3
Solent, The	52	F4	Sonipat	92	E3
Solhan	77	J3	Sonkajärvi	62	M5
Soligorsk	79	D5	Sonkovo	78	F4
Solihull	53	F2	Son La	93	K4
Solikamsk	78	K4	Sonmiani	92	C3
Sol'lletsk	79	J5	Sonmiani Bay	92	C3

Sonoita	126	F5
Sonora	126	G6
Sonoran Desert	126	F4
Sonsonate	132	C8
Sonsorol Island	91	J4
Son Tay	93	L4
Sooghemeghat	118	B3
Sopi, Tanjung	91	H5
Sopot	71	H1
Sopron	72	D2
Sopur	92	D2
Sor	66	B3
Sora	69	D5
Sorada	92	F5
Söråker	62	G5
Sorata	138	C3
Sorbas	67	E4
Sore	65	C6
Sorel	125	P3
Sorgun	76	F3
Soria	66	E2
Sorisdale	57	B4
Sorka	78	F4
Sorkh, Kūh-e	95	M5
Sörmjöle	62	J5
Sorocaba	138	G4
Sorochinsk	79	J5
Soroki	79	D6
Sorong	91	J6
Sorot	63	N7
Soroti	107	F2
Sørøya	62	K1
Sørøysundet	62	K1
Sorraia	66	B3
Sorrento	69	E5
Sorsele	62	G4
Sorso	69	B5
Sorsogon	91	G3
Sortavala	63	P6
Sortland	62	F2
Sør-Trøndelag	62	D6
Sørvágsvatn	62	Z14
Sørvágur	62	Z14
Sorvær	62	K1
Sörvattnet	63	E5
Sos del Rey-Catóico	67	F1
Sosnogorsk	78	J3
Sosnovka	84	H6
Sosnovo	63	P6
Sosnovo-Ozerskoye	85	J6
Sosnowiec	71	H3
Sosunova, Mys	88	G2
Sos'va	84	Ad5
Sotik	107	G3
Sotra	63	A6
Sotuélamos	66	E3
Soubré	104	D4
Soudan	113	H3
Souflíon	75	J2
Souk Ahras	101	G1
Soumntam	67	J4
Soûr	94	B5
Sour al Ghozlane	67	H4
Soure	137	H4
Souris *Manitoba, Canada*	123	P3
Souris *Prince Edward Island,*		
Canada	121	P8
Sousse	101	H1
South Africa, Republic of	108	D6
Southampton *U.K.*	53	F4

Southampton *U.S.A.*	125	P6
Southampton Island	120	K5
Southampton Water	53	F4
South Andaman	93	H6
South Baldy	127	J4
South Baymouth	124	J4
South Bend *Indiana, U.S.A.*	124	G6
South Bend *Washington,*		
U.S.A.	122	C4
South Benfleet	53	H3
Southborough	53	H3
South Boston	125	L8
South Canadian	128	D3
South Cape *Fiji*	114	R8
South Cape *U.S.A.*	126	T11
South Carolina	129	M3
South China Sea	87	L7
South Creake	53	H2
South Dakota	123	N5
South Dorset Downs	52	E4
South Downs	53	G4
Southeast Cape	118	B3
South East Cape	113	K6
Southend	119	Q4
Southend-on-Sea	53	H3
Southern Alps	115	C5
Southern Cross	112	D5
Southern Indian Lake	119	R4
Southern Pine Hills	128	H5
Southern Pines	129	N3
Southern Uplands	57	E5
Southery	53	H2
South Esk	57	E4
South Foreland	53	J3
South Forty Foot Drain	53	G2
South Geomagnetic Pole	141	H3
South Georgia	139	J10
South Glamorgan	52	D3
South Harbour	56	A2
South Haven	124	G5
South Hayling	53	G4
South Henik Lake	119	R3
South Hill	125	L8
South Korea	87	P4
South Lake Tahoe	126	C1
South Magnetic Pole	141	K5
Southminster	53	H3
South Molton	52	D3
South Morar	57	C4
South Nahanni	118	K3
South Negril Point	132	H5
South Orkney Islands	141	W4
South Platte	123	N7
South Point	133	K3
South Pole	141	A1
Southport	55	F3
South River	125	L4
South Ronaldsay	56	F2
South Sandwich Islands	141	Y7
South Saskatchewan	123	L2
South Seal	119	R4
South Shields	55	H2
South Sister	122	D5
South Skirlaugh	55	J3
South Sound	59	C6
South Taranaki Bight	115	E3
South Twin Island	121	K7
South Tyne	55	G2
South Uist	56	A3
Southwell	55	J3

Thompson Sound	115	A6
Thomson *Australia*	113	J3
Thomson *U.S.A.*	129	L4
Thonon-les-Bains	65	G5
Thornaby	55	H2
Thornbury	52	E3
Thornby	53	F2
Thorndon	53	J2
Thorne	55	J3
Thorney	53	G2
Thornhill	57	E5
Thornley	55	H2
Thornton	55	F3
Thouars	65	C5
Thouet	65	C5
Thrakikón Pélagos	75	H2
Thrapston	53	G2
Three Forks	122	J5
Three Kings Islands	111	R8
Three Points, Cape	104	E5
Three Rivers *Michigan, U.S.A.*	124	H6
Three Rivers *Texas, U.S.A.*	128	C6
Three Sisters Islands	114	K7
Threshfield	55	G2
Throsell Range	112	E3
Thueyts	65	F6
Thuin	64	F3
Thule	120	N2
Thun	68	A2
Thunder Bay	124	F2
Thunder Mount	118	C2
Thung Song	93	J7
Thüringer Wald	70	D3
Thurles	59	G7
Thurloo Downs	113	J4
Thurnscoe	55	H3
Thursby	55	F2
Thurso *U.K.*	56	E2
Thurso *U.K.*	56	E2
Thurston Island	141	T4
Thusis	68	B2
Thwaites Glacier	141	S3
Tiancang	86	H3
Tianchang	87	M5
Tiandong	93	L4
Tian'e	93	L3
Tiangua	137	J4
Tianjin	87	M4
Tianjun	93	J1
Tianqiaoling	88	B4
Tianshui	93	L2
Tianyang	93	L4
Tianzhen	87	L3
Tianzhu	93	K1
Tiaret	100	F1
Tibati	105	H4
Tiber	69	D4
Tiberias	94	B5
Tibesti	102	C3
Tibet	92	F2
Tibet, Plateau of	92	F2
Tiboku Falls	136	F2
Tiburón, Isla	126	F6
Tichitt	100	D5
Ticino	68	B3
Ticul	131	Q7
Tidaholm	63	E7
Tidjikdja	100	C5
Tieli	88	B2
Tieling	87	N3

Tien Shan	86	D3
Tien Yen	93	L4
Tierp	63	G6
Tierra Amarilla	127	J2
Tierra Blanca	131	L8
Tierra del Fuego, Isla Grande de	139	C10
Tiétar	66	D2
Tietê	138	F4
Tifton	129	L5
Tifu	91	H6
Tiger	122	F3
Tigharry	56	A3
Tigil' *U.S.S.R.*	85	T5
Tigil' *U.S.S.R.*	85	T5
Tignish	121	P8
Tigre *Peru*	136	B4
Tigre *Venezuela*	136	E2
Tigres, Baia dos	106	B6
Tigris	94	H6
Tigzerte, Oued	100	D3
Tigzirt	67	J4
Tihāmat ash Shām	96	E7
Tihāmat 'Asir	96	F8
Tihsimir	77	J3
Tijoca	137	H4
Tijuana	126	D4
Tikal	132	C6
Tikamgarh	92	E4
Tikanlik	86	F3
Tikhoretsk	79	G6
Tikhvin	78	E4
Tikitiki	115	G2
Tikopica	111	Q4
Tikrīt	77	K5
Tiksi	85	M2
Tilburg	64	F3
Tilbury	53	H3
Tilemsi, Vallée du	100	F5
Till	57	F5
Tillabéri	100	F6
Tillanchang	93	H7
Tillicoultry	57	E4
Tilomar	91	H7
Tílos	75	J4
Tilsit	71	J1
Tilt	57	E4
Timanskiy Kryazh	78	H3
Timar	77	K3
Timaru	115	C6
Timashevsk	79	F6
Timbákion	75	H5
Timbédra	100	D5
Timbo *Guinea*	104	C3
Timbo *Liberia*	104	D4
Timbuktu	100	E5
Timfristós	75	F3
Timimoun	100	F3
Timiris, Cap	100	B5
Timiş	73	G3
Timişoara	73	F3
Timkapaul'	84	Ad4
Timmernabben	63	G8
Timmins	125	K2
Timok	73	G3
Timolin	59	J7
Timor	91	H7
Timor, Laut	91	H7
Timoshino	78	F3
Timsher	78	J3

Tinaca Point	91	H4
Tinaco	133	N10
Tinahely	59	K7
Tinakula	114	M7
Tindivanam	92	E6
Tindouf	100	D3
Tineo	66	C1
Tinglev	63	C9
Tingo María	136	B5
Tingsryd	63	F8
Tingvoll	62	C5
Tinharé, Ilha de	137	K6
Tinogasta	138	C5
Tinompo	91	G5
Tínos *Greece*	75	H4
Tínos *Greece*	75	H4
Tintinara	113	J6
Tinto *Spain*	66	C4
Tinto *U.K.*	57	E5
Tinto Hills	57	E5
Tinwald	115	C5
Tiomilaskogen	63	E6
Tipaza	67	H4
Tipitapa	132	D8
Tippecanoe	124	G6
Tipperary *Ireland*	59	F8
Tipperary *Ireland*	59	G7
Tipton	124	H6
Tiptree	53	H3
Tiquicheo	131	J8
Tiracambu, Serra do	137	H4
Ţirân	96	B3
Tirana	74	E2
Tiranë	74	E2
Tirano	68	C2
Tiraspol'	79	D6
Tire	76	B3
Tirebolu	77	H2
Tiree	57	C4
Tirga Mor	56	B3
Tîrgovişte	73	H3
Tîrgu Bujor	73	J3
Tîrgu Cărbuneşti	73	G3
Tîrgu Frumos	73	J2
Tîrgu Jiu	73	G3
Tîrgu Mureş	73	H2
Tîrgu Neamţ	73	J2
Tîrgu Ocna	73	J2
Tirich Mir	92	D1
Tîrnava Mare	73	H2
Tîrnava Mică	73	H2
Tírnavos	75	G3
Tirol	68	C2
Tirpul	95	Q4
Tirso	69	B6
Tirua Point	115	E3
Tiruchchirāppalli	92	E6
Tirumangalam	92	E7
Tirunelveli	92	E7
Tirupati	92	E6
Tiruppur	92	E6
Tiruvannamalai	92	E6
Tisa	72	F3
Tisisat Falls	103	G5
Tissa	71	K4
Tissington	55	H3
Tista	93	G3
Tisza	72	F2
Tit-Ary	85	M2
Titchfield	53	F4

Titicaca, Lago	138	C3
Titograd	72	E4
Titova Mitrovica	73	F4
Titovo Užice	72	E4
Titovo Velenje	72	C2
Titov Veles	73	F5
Titran	62	C5
Tittmoning	70	E4
Titu	73	H3
Titusville	129	M6
Tiumpan Head	56	B2
Tivaouane	104	B2
Tiveden	63	F7
Tiverton	52	D4
Tivoli	69	D5
Ţiwī	97	P5
Tiyās	77	G5
Tizimin	131	Q7
Tizi Ouzou	101	F1
Tiznit	100	D3
Tjåmotis	62	H3
Tjørnuvík	62	Z14
Tjøtta	62	E4
Tlaltenango	130	H7
Tlapa	131	K9
Tlapehuala	131	J8
Tlaxiaco	131	L9
Tlemcen	100	E2
Toad River	118	K4
Toamasina	109	J3
Tobago	133	S9
Toba Kākar Ranges	92	C2
Tobercurry	58	E4
Tobermory *Canada*	125	K4
Tobermory *U.K.*	57	B4
Toberonochy	57	C4
Tobi	91	J5
Tobin Lake	112	F3
Tobi-shima	88	G6
Toboali	90	D6
Tobol	84	Ae5
Tobol'sk	84	Ae5
Tobseda	78	J2
Tobysh	78	J3
Tocache Nuevo	136	B5
Tocantins	137	H4
Toccoa	129	L3
Toco	133	S9
Toconao	138	C4
Tocopilla	138	B4
Tocuyo	133	N9
Todeli	91	G6
Tödi	68	B2
Todi	69	D4
Todmorden	55	G3
Todog	86	E3
Todos os Santos, Baia de	137	K6
Todos Santos *Bolivia*	138	C3
Todos Santos *Mexico*	130	D6
Todos Santos, Bahia de	126	D5
Toe Head *Ireland*	59	D10
Toe Head *U.K.*	56	A3
Toetoes Bay	115	B7
Tofino	122	B3
Toft	56	A1
Tofte	63	D7
Tofua	111	T5
Toga	114	T10
Togi	89	F7
Togiak	118	C4

Tulare Lake	126	C3	Tuquan	87	N2	Tuttle Creek Lake	123	R8	Tyuli	84	Ae4
Tularosa	127	K4	Túquerres	136	B3	Tuttlingen	70	C5	Tyung	85	L4
Tulcán	136	B3	Tura *India*	93	H3	Tutuila	111	U4	Tywi	52	C3
Tulcea	73	K3	Tura *U.S.S.R.*	84	Ad5	Tuvalu	111	S3	Tywyn	52	C2
Tul'chin	73	K1	Tura *U.S.S.R.*	84	G4	Tuvinskaya A.S.S R.	84	E6	Tzaneen	108	F4
Tuléar	109	H4	Turabah	96	E6	Tuvuca	114	S8	Tzoumérka	75	F3
Tulik Volcano	118	Ae9	Turabah, Wadi	96	E6	Tuwayq, Jabal *Saudi Arabia*	96	G4			
Tulkarm	94	B5	Turama	84	F4	Tuwayq, Jabal *Saudi Arabia*	96	H5			
Tullahoma	129	J3	Turan	84	E6	Tuxford	55	J3	Uainambi	136	C3
Tullamore	59	H6	Turana, Khrebet	85	N6	Túxpan	130	G7	Uapao, Cape	114	X16
Tulle	65	D6	Turangi	115	E3	Tuxpan *Mexico*	130	H8	Uapés	136	D4
Tullow	59	J7	Turbaco	136	BI	Tuxpan *Mexico*	131	L7	Uatumã	136	F4
Tully	113	K2	Turbat	92	B3	Tuxtepec	131	L8	Uaupés	136	D3
Tullybrack	58	G4	Turbo	136	B2	Tuxtla Gutiérrez	131	N9	Uavá	137	K5
Tulovo	73	H4	Turda	73	G2	Túy	66	B1	Ubá	138	H4
Tulpan	78	K3	Turek	71	H2	Tuyao	86	F3	Ubaitaba	137	K6
Tulsa	128	E2	Turfan Depression	86	F3	Tuyen Quang	93	L4	Ube	89	C9
Tulsk	58	F5	Turgay	84	A6	Tuy Hoa	93	L6	Ubeda	66	E3
Tuluá	136	B3	Türgen Uul	86	G2	Tuymazy	78	J5	Ubekendt Ø	120	R3
Tulun	84	G6	Tŭrgovishte	73	J4	Tüysarkān	94	J4	Uberaba	138	J3
Tulungagung	90	E7	Turgutlu	76	B3	Tuzantla	131	J8	Uberaba, Laguna	138	E3
Tuma	78	G4	Turhal	77	G2	Tuz Gölü	76	E3	Uberlândia	138	G3
Tumaco	136	B3	Türi	63	L7	Tuz Khurmātū	77	L5	Ubinskoye	84	B5
Tumaco, Bada de	136	B3	Turia	67	F3	Tuzla	72	E3	Ubolratna Reservoir	93	K5
Tumanskiy	85	X4	Turiaçu	137	G4	Tuzluca	77	K2	Ubombo	109	F5
Tumany	85	T4	Turiaçú	137	G4	Tuzlukçu	76	D3	Ubon Ratchathani	93	K5
Tumbarumba	113	K6	Turin	68	A3	Tvedestrand	63	C7	Ubundu	106	E3
Tumbes	136	A4	Turinsk	84	Ad5	Tvøroyri	62	Z14	Ucayali	136	C4
Tumd Youqi	87	L3	Turiy Rog	88	C3	Tweed	57	F5	Üçdam	77	J3
Tumen *China*	88	B4	Turka	71	K4	Tweedsmuir	57	E5	Uch Adzhi	95	R2
Tumen *China*	88	B4	Turkana, Lake	107	G2	Tweedsmuir Hills	57	E5	Uchami	84	F4
Tumeremo	136	E2	Türkeli	76	F2	Twelve Pins, The	59	C5	Ucharal	86	F2
Tumereng	133	S11	Turkestan	86	B3	Twentynine Palms	126	E3	Uchiura-wan	88	H4
Tumkur	92	E6	Turkestan, Bandi-	95	S4	Twin Bridges	122	H5	Uchte	70	C2
Tummel Bridge	57	D4	Turkey	76	E3	Twin Buttes Reservoir	127	M5	Uchur	85	N5
Tummel, Loch	57	E4	Turkey Creek	112	F2	Twin Falls	122	G6	Ückermark	70	E2
Tump	92	B3	Turkmeniya S.S.R.	80	G6	Two Bridges	52	D4	Uckfield	53	H4
Tumpat	90	C4	Türkoğlu	77	G4	Two Rivers	124	G4	Ucluelet	122	B3
Tumu	104	E3	Turks Island	133	M4	Twrch	52	D2	Uda	85	N6
Tumucumaque, Serra	137	G3	Turks Island Passage	133	M4	Twycross	53	F2	Udachnyy	84	J3
Tunari, Cerro	138	D3	Turku	63	M6	Twyford *Berkshire, U.K.*	53	G3	Udaipur	92	D4
Tunbal Kubrá	95	M8	Turku-Pori	63	K6	Twyford *Hampshire, U.K.*	53	F3	'Udayd, Ra's al	97	K4
Tunbridge Wells	53	H3	Turnagain	118	K4	Twyford *Leicestershire, U.K.*	53	G2	Udbina	72	C3
Tunceli	77	H3	Turnagain, Cape	115	F4	Tyachev	71	K4	Uddevalla	63	D7
Tunduru	107	G5	Turneffe Island	132	D6	Tyana Shan'	86	D3	Uddjaur	62	G4
Tundzha	73	J4	Turnhout	64	F3	Tyanya	85	K5	Udine	68	D2
Tungabhadra	92	E5	Türnitz	68	E2	Tychany	84	F4	Udmurt A.S.S.R.	78	J4
Tungozero	62	P4	Turnov	70	F3	Tychy	71	H3	Udon Thani	93	K5
Tungurahua, Volcán	136	B4	Turnu Măgurele	73	H4	Tygda	85	M6	Udskoye	85	N6
Tunguska	84	E4	Turnu Roşu, Pasul	73	H3	Tyler	128	E4	Udupi	92	D6
Tunguskoye Plato	84	E4	Turpan	86	F3	Tylöskog	63	F7	Ueckermünde	70	F2
Tuni	92	F5	Turriff	56	F3	Tym	84	C5	Ueda	89	G7
Tunis	101	H1	Tursunzade	86	B4	Tymovskoye	85	Q6	Uele *U.S.S.R.*	84	J2
Tunis, Golfo di	69	C7	Turta	86	J1	Tynda	85	L5	Uele *Zaïre*	106	D2
Tunisia	101	G2	Turtas	84	Ae5	Tyndall, Mount	115	C5	Uelen	81	V3
Tunja	136	C2	Turtkul'	80	H5	Tyndrum	57	D4	Uel'kal	85	Y3
Tunka	84	G6	Turtle Mountain	123	P3	Tyne	55	H2	Uelzen	70	D2
Tunnsjøen	62	E4	Turukhansk	84	D3	Tyne and Wear	55	H2	Ufa *U.S.S.R.*	78	K4
Tunungayualok Island	121	P6	Tur'ya	71	L3	Tynemouth	55	H1	Ufa *U.S.S.R.*	78	K5
Tunxi	87	M6	Tuscaloosa	129	J4	Tynset	62	D5	Ugab	108	B4
Tuo Jiang	93	K3	Tuscania	69	C4	Tyr	85	P6	Uganda	107	F2
Tuomioja	62	L4	Tuscola	127	N4	Tyre	94	B5	Ugashik Bay	118	D4
Tuostakh	85	P3	Tustumena Lake	118	E3	Tyret'	84	G6	Ugashik Lakes	118	D4
Tupana	136	E4	Tutak	77	K3	Tyrma	85	N6	Ughelli	105	G4
Tupanaoca	136	E4	Tutayev	78	F4	Tyrone *U.K.*	58	H3	Ugíjar	66	E4
Tupelo	128	H3	Tuticorin	92	E7	Tyrone *U.S.A.*	125	L6	Uglich	78	F4
Tupinambaranas, Ilha	136	F4	Tutóia	137	J4	Tyrrhenian Sea	69	D5	Ugljane	72	D4
Tupiza	138	C4	Tutonchana	84	E3	Tysnesøy	63	A7	Ugra	78	E5
Tupos	62	L4	Tutonchany	84	E4	Tyukalinsk	84	A5	Ugun	85	M5
Tupungato, Cerro	139	C6	Tutrakan	73	J3	Tyul'gan	79	K5	Uğurlu	77	J2

Ugu

Uğurludağ	76	F2	Ulubey *Turkey*	77	G2	Universales, Montes	67	F2	Urubu	136	F4
Ugut	84	A4	Uluborlu	76	D3	University Park	127	J4	Uruçuí	137	J5
Uherské Hradiště	71	G4	Uluçinar	77	F4	Unnão	92	F3	Urucuia	138	G3
Úhlava	70	E4	Uludağ	76	C2	Unst	56	B1	Uruçuí, Serra do	137	J5
Uhrusk	71	K3	Ulu Daği	76	C2	Untaek	88	A5	Uruguaiana	138	E5
Uig	56	B3	Uludere	77	K4	Ünye	77	G2	Uruguay	138	E6
Uíge	106	C4	Uluguru Mountains	107	G4	Unzha	78	G4	Urumchi	86	F3
Uil *U.S.S.R.*	79	J6	Ulukişla	76	F4	Uodgan	96	D8	Ürümqi	86	F3
Uil *U.S.S.R.*	79	J6	Ulunkhan	85	J6	Uoyan	85	J5	Urupadi	137	F4
Uinskoye	78	K4	Ulus	76	E2	Upata	133	R10	Urup, Ostrov	85	S7
Uinta Mountains	122	J7	Ulva	57	B4	Upavon	53	F3	Uruti Point	115	F4
Uisŏng	89	B7	Ulverston	55	F2	Upemba, Lake	106	E4	Urville, Tanjung d'	114	B2
Uitenhage	108	E6	Ul'yanovsk	78	H5	Upernavik	120	Q3	Uryupinsk	79	G5
Ujiji	107	E3	Ulysses	127	M2	Upernavik Isfjord	120	R3	Urzhum	78	H4
Uji-shotō	89	B10	Ulzburg	70	C2	Upington	108	D5	Urziceni	73	J3
Ujjain	92	E4	Umala	138	C3	Upolu	111	U4	Usa	78	K2
Újpest	72	E2	Uman'	79	E6	Upolu Point	126	T10	Uşak	76	C3
Ujście	71	G2	Umán	131	Q7	Upper Arrow Lake	122	F2	Usambara Mountains	107	G3
Ujung Pandang	91	F7	Umanak Fjord	120	R3	Upper Broughton	53	G2	Usedom	70	F1
Uka	85	U5	Umari	114	B2	Upper Hutt	115	E4	Ushant	64	A4
Ukholovo	79	G5	Umarkot	92	C3	Upper Klamath Lake	122	D6	Ushitsa	73	J1
Ukhta	78	J3	Umba	78	E2	Upper Seal Lake	121	M6	Ushtobe	86	D2
Ukhunku	85	L3	Umbertide	68	D4	Uppingham	53	G2	Ushuaia	139	C10
Uki	114	K7	Umboi Island	114	D3	Uppsala *Sweden*	63	G6	Usk *Gwent, U.K.*	52	E3
Ukiah	122	C8	Umbro-Marchigiano, Appennino	68	D4	Uppsala *Sweden*	63	L7	Usk *Powys, U.K.*	52	D3
Ukmergė	63	L9	Umeå	62	J5	Upsala	124	E2	Usk Reservoir	52	D3
Ukraine S.S.R.	79	D6	Umeälven	62	H4	Upstart Bay	113	K2	Üsküdar	76	C2
Ukta	71	J2	Umm al Qaywayn	97	M4	Uqla Sąwāb	77	J6	Uslar	70	C3
Uku	106	B5	Umm as Samim	97	M6	Urad Qianqi	87	K3	Usman'	79	F5
Uku-jima	89	B9	Umm Bel	102	E5	Urad Zhongqi	87	K3	Usol'ye	78	K4
Ukuma	106	C5	Umm Keddada	102	E5	Urak	85	Q5	Usol'ye-Sibirskoye	84	G6
Ula	76	C4	Umm Lajj	96	C4	Urakan	84	H5	Uspenka	84	B6
Ulaangom	86	G2	Umm Ruwaba	102	F5	Urakawa	88	J4	Ussel	65	E6
Ulan Bator	87	K2	Umm Said	97	K4	Ural	79	J6	Ussuri	88	E2
Ulan-Erge	79	G6	Umm Urūmah	96	C4	Ural Mountains	78	K3	Ussuriysk	88	C4
Ulanhad	87	M3	Umnak Island	118	Ae9	Ural'sk	79	J5	Ust'-Barguzin	84	H6
Ulan-Khol	79	H6	Umred	92	E4	Ural'skiy Khrebet	78	K3	Ust'-Belaya	85	W3
Ulan Tohoi	86	J3	Umtali	109	F3	Urandangi	113	H3	Ust'-Chara	85	L4
Ulan-Ude	84	H6	Umtata	108	E6	Urandí	137	J6	Ust'Chizhapka	84	B5
Ulan Ula	93	H2	Umzingwani	108	E4	Uranium City	119	P4	Ustica, Isola di	69	D6
Ulaş	77	G3	Una *Brazil*	137	K7	Uraricoera	136	E3	Ust'Ilimsk	84	G5
Ulawa	114	K6	Una *Yugoslavia*	72	C3	Urawa	89	G8	Ust'-Ilimskiy Vodokhranilishche	84	J4
Ulchin	89	B7	Unalaska Island	118	Ae9	Uray'irah	97	J4	Ust'-Ilych	84	Ac4
Ulcinj	74	E2	Unare	133	Q10	'Urayq, Al	96	D2	Ústi nad Lebem	70	F3
Uled Saidan	101	J3	'Unayzah	96	F3	'Urayq, Nafūd al	96	F4	Ustinov	78	J4
Ulfborg	63	C8	Uncia	138	C3	Urbana	124	J6	Ustka	71	G1
Ulgumdzha	85	K4	Uncompahgre Peak	123	L8	Urbino	68	D4	Ust'Kamchatsk	85	U5
Ulhasnagar	92	D5	Uncompahgre Plateau	122	K8	Urda	79	H6	Ust'-Kamenogorsk	86	E2
Uliastay	86	H2	Underwood	123	P4	Urdzhar	86	E2	Ust'-Kamo	84	F4
Ulithi Atoll	91	K4	Unecha	79	E5	Uren	78	H4	Ust'-Kan	84	E5
Uljan	72	C3	Uneiuxi	136	D4	Urengoy	84	B3	Ust'-Kara	84	Ad3
Uljma	73	F3	Ungava Bay	121	N6	Uréparapara	114	T10	Ust'-Karenga	85	K6
Ulla	66	B1	Ungave, Peninsule d'	121	L5	Ures	126	G6	Ust'Katav	78	K5
Ullaanbaatar	87	K2	Unggi	88	C4	Urfa	77	H4	Ust'-Kulom	78	J3
Ullånger	62	H5	União dos Palmares	137	K5	Urgal	85	N6	Ust'-Kut	84	H5
Ullapool	56	C3	União do Vitória	138	E5	Urgel, Llanos de	67	G2	Ust'-Kuyga	85	P3
Ullock	55	F2	Unije	72	C3	Urgench	80	G5	Ust'-Labinsk	79	F6
Ullswater	55	G2	Unimak Island	118	Af9	Ürgüp	76	F3	Ust'Luga	63	N7
Ullŭng-do	89	C7	Unimak Pass	118	Ae9	Urho	86	F2	Ust'Maya	85	N4
Ulm	70	C4	Unini	136	E4	Uritskiy	84	Ae6	Ust'-Mayn	85	W3
Ulog	72	E4	Union	129	M3	Urkan	85	M6	Ust'-Mil'	85	N5
Ulongue	109	F2	Union City	128	H2	Urla	76	B3	Ust'-Muya	85	K5
Ulricehamn	63	E8	Uniondale	108	D6	Urlingford	59	G7	Ust'Nem	78	J3
Ulsan	89	B8	Union of Soviet Socialist			Urmi	88	D1	Ust'-Nera	85	Q4
Ulsta	56	A1	Republics	49	H3	Uroševac	73	F4	Ust'Niman	85	N6
Ulsteinvik	62	A5	Union Springs	129	K4	Urr Water	57	E5	Ust'Omchug	85	R4
Ulster	58	H3	Uniontown	125	L7	Ursat'yevskaya	86	B3	Ust'-Ordynskiy	84	G6
Ulster Canal	58	H4	United Arab Emirates	97	L5	Uruaçu	137	H6	Ustovo	73	H5
Ulubat Gölü	76	C2	United States of America	116	H4	Uruapan	130	H8	Ust'-Ozernoye	84	D5
Ulubey *Turkey*	76	C3	Unity	122	E5	Urubamba	136	C6	Ust'Penzhino	85	V4

Vat

Vatilau	114	J6
Vatnajökull	62	W12
Vatneyri	62	A2
Vatoa	111	T5
Vatomandry	109	J3
Vatra Dornei	73	H2
Vättern	63	F7
Vatu-i-Ra Channel	114	R8
Vatulele	114	Q9
Vaughn	127	K3
Vaupés	136	C3
Vavatenina	109	J3
Vava'u Group	111	U5
Vavuniya	92	F7
Vaxholm	63	H7
Växjö	63	F8
Vayalpad	92	E6
Vaygach	84	Ac2
Vaygach, Ostrov	84	Ac2
Veberöd	63	E9
Vebomark	62	J4
Vecht	64	G2
Vechta	70	C2
Vechte	70	B2
Veddige	63	E8
Vega *Norway*	62	D4
Vega *U.S.A.*	127	L3
Vegorritis, Límni	75	F2
Vegreville	119	N5
Veidholmen	62	B5
Veinge	63	E8
Vejen	63	C9
Vejer de la Frontera	66	D4
Vejle	63	C9
Velanidhia	75	G4
Vèlas, Cabo	132	E9
Velasco, Sierra de	138	C5
Velay, Monts du	65	E6
Velebit Planina	72	C3
Velestínon	75	G3
Vélez Málaga	66	D4
Vélez Rubio	67	E4
Velhas	138	H3
Velichayevskoye	79	H7
Velika Gorica	72	D3
Velika Kapela	72	C3
Velikaya *U.S.S.R.*	78	H2
Velikaya *U.S.S.R*	85	W4
Velikaya Kema	88	F3
Veliki Kanal	72	E3
Velikiy Bereznyy	71	K4
Velikiye Luki	78	E4
Velikonda Range	92	E6
Veliko Türnovo	73	H4
Veliky Ustyug	78	H3
Vélingara	104	C3
Velingrad	73	H4
Velizh	78	E4
Vella Gulf	114	H5
Vella Lavella	114	H5
Velletri	69	D5
Vellore	92	E6
Vel'sk	78	G3
Vel't	78	J2
Velvestad	62	E4
Venado Tuerto	139	D6
Venafro	69	E5
Venaria	68	A3
Venda Nova	66	C2
Vendas Novas	66	B3

Vendôme	65	D5
Vendsyssel	63	D8
Venecia	136	D6
Venezia	68	D3
Venezia, Golfo di	68	D3
Venezuela	136	D2
Venezuela Basin	134	C1
Venezuela, Golfo de	136	C1
Vengurla	92	D5
Veniaminof Volcano	118	Ag8
Venice *Italy*	68	D3
Venice *U.S.A.*	128	H6
Venkatapuram	92	F5
Venlo	64	G3
Vennesla	63	C7
Venta	63	J8
Ventimiglia	68	A4
Ventnor	53	F4
Ventry	59	B8
Ventspils	63	N8
Ventuari	136	D3
Ventura	126	C3
Venus Bay	113	K6
Venustiano Carranza *Mexico*	130	G5
Venustiano Carranza *Mexico*	131	N9
Vera *Argentina*	138	D5
Vera *Spain*	67	F4
Veracruz	131	L8
Veranópolis	138	F5
Veraval	92	D4
Verbania	68	B3
Vercelli	68	B3
Verdalsøra	62	D5
Verde *Mexico*	131	L9
Verde *U.S.A.*	126	G3
Verden	70	C2
Verdigris	124	C8
Verdinho, Serra do	138	F3
Verdon	65	G7
Verdun	64	F4
Vereeniging	108	E5
Vereshchagino	78	J4
Verga, Cap	104	C3
Verín	66	C2
Verin Talin	77	K2
Verkhne-Avzyar	78	K5
Verkhnedvinsk	63	M9
Verkhne-Imanskiy	88	E3
Verkhneimbatskoye	84	D4
Verkhne Matur	84	D6
Verkhne Nil'dino	84	Ad4
Verkhne Skoblino	84	D5
Verkhnetulomskiy	62	P2
Verkhne Tura	78	K4
Verkhnevilyuysk	85	L4
Verkhniy Baskunchak	79	H6
Verkhniy Shar	78	J2
Verkhnyaya Amga	85	M5
Verkhnyaya Inta	78	L2
Verkhnyaya Toyma	78	H3
Verkhotur'ye	84	Ad5
Verkhov'ye	79	F5
Verkhoyansk	85	N3
Verkhoyanskiy Khrebet	85	M3
Verkhyaya Nil'dino	78	L3
Vermilion	119	N5
Vermilion Bay	128	G6
Vermilion Lake	124	D3
Vermillion	123	R6
Vermillion Bay	124	D2

Vermont	125	P5
Vernal	123	K7
Verneuil	64	D4
Vernon *Canada*	122	E2
Vernon *France*	64	D4
Vernon *U.S.A.*	127	N3
Véroia	75	G2
Verona	68	C3
Versailles	64	E4
Vert, Cape	104	B3
Verviers	64	F3
Vervins	64	E4
Veryan Bay	52	C4
Veryuvom	78	L2
Veshenskaya	79	G6
Vesløs	63	C8
Veslyana	78	J3
Vesoul	65	G5
Vest-Agder	63	B7
Vesterålen	62	F2
Vestfjorden	62	F2
Vest-Fold	63	D7
Vestre Jakobselv	62	N1
Vestvågøy	62	E2
Vesuvio	69	E5
Ves'yegonsk	78	F4
Veszprém	72	D2
Vetekhtina	85	K5
Vetlanda	63	F8
Vetluga *U.S.S.R*	78	H4
Vetluga *U.S.S.R*	78	H4
Vetluzskiy	78	H4
Vettore, Monte	69	D4
Veun Kham	93	L6
Veurne	64	E3
Vevey	68	A2
Veyatie, Loch	56	C2
Vézelay	65	E5
Vézère	65	D6
Vezirköprü	76	F2
Viacha	138	C3
Viamao	138	F6
Viana	137	J4
Viana do Castelo	66	B2
Viangchan	93	K5
Viareggio	68	C4
Viaur	65	E6
Viborg	63	C8
Víbo Valéntia	69	F6
Vicecomodoro Marambio	141	W6
Vicente Guerrero	130	H6
Vicenza	68	C3
Vich	67	H2
Vichada	136	D3
Vichuga	78	G4
Vichy	65	E5
Vicksburg	128	G4
Vico	69	B4
Viçosa	137	K5
Victor Emanuel Range	114	C3
Victor Harbor	113	H6
Victoria *Argentina*	138	D6
Victoria *Northern Territory, Australia*	112	G2
Victoria *Victoria, Australia*	113	J6
Victoria *Cameroon*	105	G5
Victoria *Canada*	122	C3
Victoria *Chile*	139	B7
Victoria *Hong Kong*	90	E1
Victoria *Malaysia*	90	F4

Victoria *Seychelles*	82	D7
Victoria *U.S.A.*	128	D6
Victoria de las Tunas	132	J4
Victoria Falls	108	E3
Victoria Island	119	P1
Victoria, Lake	107	F3
Victoria Land	141	L4
Victoria, Mount *Burma*	93	H4
Victoria, Mount *Papua New Guinea*	114	D3
Victoria Nile	107	F2
Victoria Peak	118	K5
Victoria Strait	119	Q2
Victoriaville	125	Q3
Victoria West	108	D6
Victorica	139	C7
Victorville	126	D3
Vicuña	138	B6
Vidago	66	C2
Vidalia	129	L4
Viðareiði	62	Z14
Viðidalur	62	X12
Vidim	84	G5
Viðimyri	62	V12
Vidin	73	G4
Vidisha	92	E4
Viðivellir	62	X12
Vidomlya	71	K2
Vidsel	62	J4
Viedma	139	D8
Viedma, Lago	139	B9
Viella	67	G1
Vienna *Austria*	68	F1
Vienna *Illinois, U.S.A.*	124	F8
Vienna *Ohio, U.S.A.*	125	K7
Vienne *France*	65	D5
Vienne *France*	65	F6
Vientiane	93	K5
Vieques	133	Q5
Vierwaldstätter See	68	B2
Vierzon	65	E5
Vieste	69	F5
Vietnam	93	L5
Vif	65	F6
Vigan	91	G2
Vigevano	68	B3
Viggiano	69	E5
Vigia	137	G4
Viglio, Monte	69	D5
Vigo	66	B1
Vigrestad	63	A7
Viiala	63	K6
Vijayawada	92	F5
Vijosë	74	E2
Vik	62	E4
Vík	62	V13
Vikajärvi	62	M3
Vikersund	63	D7
Vikhorevka	84	G5
Vikna	62	D4
Viksøyri	63	B6
Vila	114	U12
Vilâdikars	77	K2
Vila Franca	66	B3
Vilaine	65	C5
Vilaller	67	G1
Vilanculos	109	G4
Vila Nova	137	F4
Vila Nova de Famalicão	66	B2
Vila Pouca de Aguiar	66	C2

Vozhe, Ozero	78	F3
Voznesensk	79	E6
Voznesen'ye	78	F3
Vozvyshennost' Karabil'	95	R3
Vrancei, Munţii	73	J3
Vrangelya, Mys	85	P6
Vrangelya, Ostrov	81	U2
Vranje	73	F4
Vranov	71	J4
Vratsa	73	G4
Vrbas	72	D3
Vrbovsko	72	C3
Vrede	108	E5
Vrhnika	72	C3
Vrindavan	92	E3
Vrlika	72	D4
Vrondádhes	75	J3
Vršac	73	F3
Vrsacki Kanal	73	F3
Vryburg	108	D5
Vryheid	108	F5
Vučitrn	73	F4
Vukovar	72	E3
Vulavu	114	J6
Vulcan	73	G3
Vulcano, Isola	69	E6
Vung Tau	93	L6
Vunisea	114	R9
Vuokatti	62	N4
Vuollerim	62	J3
Vyartsilya	62	P5
Vyatka	78	J4
Vyatskiye Polyany	78	J4
Vyazemskiy	88	E2
Vyaz'ma	78	E4
Vyazniki	78	G4
Vyborg	63	N6
Vychegda	78	H3
Vydrino	84	F5
Vygoda	73	L2
Vygozero, Ozero	78	F3
Vyhorlát	71	K4
Vyksa	78	G4
Vym'	78	J3
Vyrnwy	52	D2
Vyshniy-Volochek	78	E4
Vysokoye	71	K2
Vytegra	78	F3
Vyzhva	71	L3
Wa	104	E3
Waal	64	F3
Waat	103	F6
Wabana	121	R8
Wabasca	119	N4
Wabash	124	G7
Wabē Gestro Wenz	103	H6
Wabē Shabelē Wenz	103	H6
Wabigoon Lake	124	D2
Wabowden	119	R4
Wabush	121	N7
Waccasassa Bay	129	L6
Waco	128	D5
Wad Banda	102	E5
Waddān	101	J3
Waddeneilanden	64	F2
Waddenzee	64	F2
Waddesdon	53	G3
Waddington, Mount	118	K5

Wadebridge	52	C4
Wadena	124	C3
Wâdi Gimâl	96	B4
Wadi Halfa	102	F3
Wad Medani	103	F5
Wadomari	89	J10
Wad Rawa	103	F4
Wafra	97	H2
Wager Bay	120	J4
Wagga Wagga	113	K6
Wagin	112	D5
Wahai	91	H6
Waharoa	115	E2
Wahiawa	126	R10
Wahïbah, Ramlat ahl	97	P6
Waḥidï	96	H9
Wahoo	123	R7
Wahpeton	123	R4
Waialua	126	R10
Waianae	126	R10
Waiau *New Zealand*	115	A6
Waiau *New zealand*	115	D5
Waiau *New Zealand*	115	D5
Waibeem	91	J6
Waidhofen *Austria*	68	E2
Waidhofen *Austria*	68	E1
Waigeo	91	J6
Waiheke Island	115	E2
Waihi	115	E2
Waikabubak	91	F7
Waikato	115	E3
Waikerie	113	H5
Waikouaiti	115	C6
Wailuku	126	S10
Waimakariri	115	D5
Waimamaku	115	D1
Waimate	115	C6
Wainganga	92	E4
Waingapu	91	G7
Waini Point	136	F2
Wainwright	118	D1
Waiotapu	115	F3
Waiouru	115	E3
Waipa	115	E2
Waipahi	115	B7
Waipara	115	D5
Waipawa	115	F3
Waipiro	115	G3
Waipu	115	E1
Waipukurau	115	F3
Wairau	115	D4
Wairau Valley	115	D4
Wairio	115	B7
Wairoa	115	F3
Waitaki	115	C6
Waitangi	115	F6
Waitara	115	E3
Waitoa	115	E2
Waiuku	115	E2
Wajima	89	F7
Wajir	107	H2
Wakasa-wan	89	E8
Waka, Tanjung	91	H6
Wakatipu, Lake	115	B6
Wakaya	114	R8
Wakayama	89	E8
Wake	89	E8
Wakeeny	123	Q8
Wakefield	55	H3
Wakkanai	88	H3

Wakool *Australia*	113	J6
Wakool *Australia*	113	J6
Waku Kungo	106	C5
Walachia	73	H3
Walade	114	K6
Walagan	87	N1
Wałbrzych	71	G3
Walcha	113	L5
Walcheren	64	E3
Wałcz	71	G2
Waldenburg	71	G3
Waldon	52	C4
Waldron	128	E3
Waldshut	70	C5
Wales	118	A2
Wales Island	120	J4
Walgett	113	K4
Walikale	107	E3
Walinga	114	D3
Walker	122	E8
Walkeringham	55	J3
Walker Lake	122	E8
Wallace	129	P3
Wallaceburg	124	J5
Wallal Downs	112	E2
Wallasey	55	F3
Walla Walla	122	E4
Walldürn	70	C4
Wallhallow	113	H2
Wallingford	53	F3
Wallis, Îles	111	T4
Wallowa	122	F5
Walls	56	A1
Wallsend	55	H2
Walney, Island of	55	F2
Walpole	114	Y17
Walsall	53	F2
Walsenburg	127	K2
Walsingham, Cape	120	P4
Walsrode	70	C2
Walterboro	129	M4
Walter F. George Reservoir	129	K5
Waltham Abbey	53	H3
Walton	53	G3
Walvis Bay	108	B4
Wama	106	C5
Wamba *Nigeria*	105	G4
Wamba *Zaïre*	106	C4
Wami	114	A2
Wana	92	C2
Wanaaring	113	J4
Wanaka	115	B6
Wanaka, Lake	115	B6
Wanapiri	91	K6
Wanapitei	124	K3
Wanda Shan	88	C3
Wandel Sea	140	P2
Wandingzhen	93	J4
Wanganui *New Zealand*	115	E3
Wanganui *New Zealand*	115	E3
Wangaratta	113	K6
Wangary	113	H5
Wangerooge	70	B2
Wangiwangi	91	G7
Wangjiadian	88	C2
Wangkui	87	P2
Wang, Mae Nam	93	J5
Wangqing	88	B4
Wanie-Rukula	106	E2
Wankaner	92	D4

Wankie	108	E3
Wanlaweyn	107	H2
Wanquan	87	L3
Wantage	53	F3
Wanxian	93	L2
Wanyuan	93	L2
Wanzai	93	M3
Wapenamanda	114	C3
Wapsipinicon	124	E5
Warangal	92	E5
Waratah Bay	113	K6
Warboys	53	G2
Warbreccan	113	J3
Warburg	70	C3
Warburton	113	H4
Ward	115	E4
Wardha	92	E4
Ward Hunt, Cape	114	D3
Ward Hunt Strait	114	E3
Ware *Canada*	118	K4
Ware *U.K.*	53	G3
Ware *U.S.A.*	125	P5
Wareham	53	E4
Waren *E.Germany*	70	E2
Waren *Indonesia*	91	K6
Warka	71	J3
Wark Forest	57	F5
Warkworth	115	E2
Warlingham	53	G3
Warmbad	108	C5
Warminster	53	E3
Warm Springs	126	D1
Warner Robins	129	L4
Warnow	70	D2
Warora	92	E4
Warracknabeal	113	J6
Warrego	113	K5
Warren *Minnesota, U.S.A.*	124	B2
Warren *Ohio, U.S.A.*	125	K6
Warren *Pennsylvania, U.S.A.*	125	L6
Warrenpoint	58	K4
Warrenton *South Africa*	108	D5
Warrenton *U.S.A.*	125	M7
Warri	105	G4
Warrina	113	H4
Warrington *U.K.*	55	G3
Warrington *U.S.A.*	129	J5
Warrior Reefs	114	C3
Warrnambool	113	J6
Warroad	124	C2
Warsaw	71	J2
Warshiikh	107	J2
Warsop	55	H3
Warszawa	71	J2
Warta	71	G2
Waru	91	J6
Warwick *Australia*	113	L4
Warwick *U.K.*	53	F2
Warwick *U.S.A.*	125	Q6
Warwick Channel	113	H1
Warwickshire	53	F2
Wasbister	56	E1
Wasco	126	C3
Wasdale Head	55	F2
Washburn Lake	119	P1
Washim	92	E4
Washington *U.K.*	55	H2
Washington *District of Columbia, U.S.A.*	125	M7
Washington *Georgia, U.S.A.*	129	L4

Washington *Indiana, U.S.A.*	124	G7
Washington *Missouri, U.S.A.*	124	E7
Washington *N.Carolina, U.S.A.*	129	P3
Washington *Pennsylvania, U.S.A.*	125	K6
Washington *U.S.A.*	122	D4
Washington Cape	141	M4
Washington Land	120	N1
Washington, Mount	125	Q4
Wash, The	53	H2
Wasian	91	J6
Wasior	91	J6
Wasisi	91	H6
Waskaganish	121	L7
Waspán	132	E7
Wast Water	55	F2
Watam	114	C2
Watampone	91	G6
Watansoppeng	91	F6
Watchet	52	D3
Waterbeach	53	H2
Waterbury	125	P6
Wateree	129	M3
Waterford *Ireland*	59	G8
Waterford *Ireland*	59	H8
Watergrasshill	59	F8
Waterloo *Belgium*	64	F3
Waterloo *U.S.A.*	124	D5
Waterlooville	53	F4
Waternish	56	B3
Waternish Point	56	B3
Waterside	57	D5
Watertown *New York, U.S.A.*	125	N4
Watertown *S.Dakota, U.S.A.*	123	R5
Watertown *Wisconsin, U.S.A.*	124	F5
Waterville *Ireland*	59	B9
Waterville *U.S.A.*	125	R4
Watford	53	G3
Watford City	123	N4
Watheroo	112	D5
Watkaremoana, Lake	115	F3
Watling Island	133	K2
Watlington	53	F3
Watroa	115	F3
Watsa	107	E2
Watseka	124	G6
Watson	123	M1
Watson Lake	118	K3
Watsonville	126	B2
Watten	56	E2
Watten, Loch	56	E2
Watton	53	H2
Watubela, Kepulauan	91	J6
Wau *Papua New Guinea*	114	D3
Wau *Sudan*	102	E6
Wauchope	113	G3
Waukarlycarly, Lake	112	E3
Waukegan	124	G5
Waurika	128	D3
Wausau	124	F4
Wave Hill	112	G2
Waveney	53	J2
Waverly	125	M5
Wavre	64	F3
Wawa	124	H3
Waxahachie	128	D4
Waya	114	Q8
Wayabula	91	H5
Waycross	129	L5

Way, Lake	112	E4
Waynesboro *Georgia, U.S.A.*	129	L4
Waynesboro *Mississippi, U.S.A.*	128	H5
Waynesboro *Pennsylvania, U.S.A.*	125	M7
Waynesburg	125	K7
Waynesville *Missouri, U.S.A.*	124	D8
Waynesville *Tennessee, U.S.A.*	129	L3
Waynoka	128	C2
Wda	71	H2
We	90	B4
Wé	114	X16
Weald, The	53	H3
Wear	55	H2
Weardale	55	H2
Weasenham	53	H2
Weatherall Bay	120	E2
Weatherford	128	C3
Weaver	55	G3
Webi Shabeelle	103	J7
Webster	123	R5
Webster City	124	D5
Weda	91	H5
Weddell Sea	141	W4
Wedel	70	C2
Weduar, Tanjung	91	J7
Weeley	53	J3
Weemelah	113	K4
Węgorzewo	71	J1
Węgorzyno	70	F2
Weichang	87	M3
Weiden	70	E4
Weifang	87	M4
Weihai	87	N4
Weihe	88	B3
Wei He	93	L2
Weilu	87	L3
Weimar	70	D3
Weinan	93	L2
Weingarten	70	C5
Weiser	122	F5
Weissenburg	70	D4
Weissenfels	70	D3
Weiss Lake	129	K3
Weitra	68	E1
Weixin	93	K3
Wejherowo	71	H1
Welch	125	K8
Welcome Kop	108	C6
Welda	70	E3
Weldiya	103	G5
Welkom	108	E5
Welland	53	G2
Wellesley Islands	113	H2
Wellingborough	53	G2
Wellington *New Zealand*	115	E4
Wellington *South Africa*	108	C6
Wellington *Shropshire, U.K.*	52	E2
Wellington *Somerset, U.K.*	52	D4
Wellington *Kansas, U.S.A.*	128	D2
Wellington *Texas, U.S.A.*	127	M3
Wellington Channel	120	H2
Wellington, Isla	139	B9
Wells *U.K.*	52	E3
Wells *U.S.A.*	122	G7
Wellsford	115	E2
Wells-next-the-Sea	53	H2
Welney	53	H2

Wels	68	D1
Welshpool	52	D2
Welwyn Garden City	53	G3
Wemindji	121	L7
Wenasaga	123	T2
Wenatchee	122	D4
Wenchang	93	M5
Wenchuan	93	K2
Wendover	122	G7
Wengen	68	A2
Wenling	87	N6
Wenlock Edge	52	E2
Wenshan	93	K4
Wensleydale	55	H2
Wensu	86	E3
Wen Xian	93	K2
Wenzhou	87	N6
Wepener	108	E5
Weri	91	J6
Wernigerode	70	D3
Werra	70	D3
Werris Creek	113	L5
Wertach	70	D4
Weser	70	C2
Weslaco	128	D7
Wessel Islands	113	H1
West Auckland	55	H2
West Bay	128	H6
West Bengal	93	G4
West Branch Susquehanna	125	M6
West Bromwich	53	E2
Westbrook	125	Q5
West Burra	56	A2
Westbury	53	E3
Westbury-sub-Mendip	52	E3
Westby	124	E5
West Calder	57	E5
West End	129	N7
Westerdale	55	J2
Westerham	53	H3
Westerland	70	C1
Western Australia	112	E3
Western Desert	103	E2
Western Ghats	92	D5
Western Isles	56	A3
Westernport	125	L7
Western Ross	56	C3
Western Sahara	100	C4
Western Samoa	111	U4
Westerschelde	64	E3
Westerstede	70	B2
Westerwald	70	B3
West Falkland	139	E10
Westfield *U.K.*	56	E2
Westfield *Massachusetts, U.S.A.*	125	P5
Westfield *New York, U.S.A.*	125	L5
West Frankfort	124	F8
Westgate	55	G2
West Gerinish	56	A3
West Germany	70	B4
West Glamorgan	52	D3
West Glen	53	G2
West Harptree	52	E3
West Heslerton	55	J2
West Hoathly	53	G3
West Indies	48	D4
West Kilbride	57	D5
West Kirby	55	F3
West Linton	57	E5

Westlock	119	N5
Westmeath	59	G6
West Memphis	128	G3
West Meon	53	F3
West Mersea	53	H3
West Midlands	53	F2
West Moors	53	F4
Westmoreland	113	H2
Weston	125	K7
Weston-Super-Mare	52	E3
West Palm Beach	129	M7
West Plains	124	E8
West Point *Mississippi, U.S.A.*	128	H4
West Point *Nebraska, U.S.A.*	123	R7
Westport *Ireland*	58	C5
Westport *New Zealand*	115	C4
Westport Quay	58	C5
Westray	56	F1
Westray Firth	56	E1
West Road	118	L5
West Sussex	53	G4
West Tavaputs Plateau	122	J8
West Virginia	125	K7
West Wellow	53	F4
West Wyalong	113	K5
West Yellowstone	122	J5
West Yorkshire	55	H3
Wetar	91	H7
Wetar, Selat	91	H7
Wetaskiwin	119	N5
Wetherby	55	H3
Wewahitchka	129	K5
Wewak	114	C2
Wexford *Ireland*	59	J8
Wexford *Ireland*	59	K8
Wexford Bay	59	K8
Wey	53	G3
Weybridge	53	G3
Weyburn	123	N3
Weyhill	53	F3
Weymouth	52	E4
Weymouth Bay *Australia*	113	J1
Weymouth Bay *U.K.*	52	E4
Whakataki	115	F4
Whakatane	115	F2
Whalsay	56	A1
Whanganui Inlet	115	D4
Whangaparaoa	115	G2
Whangarei	115	E1
Whangaruru Harbour	115	D1
Whaplode	53	G2
Wharanui	115	E4
Wharfe	55	H2
Wharfedale	55	H3
Wharton	128	D6
Whataroa	115	C5
Wheatland	123	M6
Wheatley *Nottinghamshire, U.K.*	55	J3
Wheatley *Oxfordshire, U.K.*	53	F3
Wheeler Peak	122	G8
Wheeling	125	K6
Whernside	55	G2
Whidbey, Point	113	H5
Whitburn *Lothian, U.K.*	57	E5
Whitburn *Tyne and Wear, U.K.*	55	H2
Whitby	55	J2
Whitchurch *Avon, U.K.*	52	E3
Whitchurch *Hampshire, U.K.*	53	F3

Whitchurch *Shropshire, U.K.*	52	E2
White *Canada*	118	G3
White *Arkansas, U.S.A.*	128	G3
White *Indiana, U.S.A.*	124	G7
White *Missouri, U.S.A.*	124	D8
White *S.Dakota, U.S.A.*	123	P6
White *Texas, U.S.A.*	127	M4
Whiteadder Reservoir	57	F5
White Bay	121	Q7
Whitecourt	119	M5
Whitefish	122	G3
Whitefish Lake	119	P3
Whitefish Point	124	H3
White Gull Lake	121	P6
Whitehall	125	P5
White Handkerchief, Cape	121	P6
Whitehaven	55	F2
Whitehead	58	L3
Whitehorse	118	H3
Whitehorse Hill	53	F3
White Island	115	F2
White, Lake	112	F3
White Lake	128	F6
Whiteman Range	114	E3
White Mountains	118	F2
White Mount Peak	122	E9
Whitemouth	124	B2
Whiten Head	56	D2
Whiteparish	53	F3
White Pass	118	H4
White River	124	H2
White River Plateau	123	L8
White Salmon	122	D5
White Sea	78	F2
White Sulphur Springs	122	J4
White Volta	104	E4
Whitewater	124	F5
Whitewood	123	N2
Whitfield Moor	55	G2
Whithorn	54	E2
Whiting Bay	57	C5
Whitley Bay	55	H1
Whitmore	52	E2
Whitney, Mount	126	C2
Whitney-on-Wye	52	D2
Whitsand Bay	52	C4
Whitstable	53	J3
Whittlesey	53	G2
Whitton	55	J3
Whittonstall	55	H2
Whitworth	55	G3
Wholdaia Lake	119	Q3
Whyalla	113	H5
Wiarton	125	K4
Wiay	56	A3
Wichita	128	D2
Wichita Falls	127	N4
Wichita Mountains	128	C3
Wick *U.K.*	56	E2
Wick *U.K.*	56	E2
Wickenburg	126	F4
Wickford	53	H3
Wickham	55	H2
Wickhambrook	53	H2
Wickham, Cape	113	J6
Wicklow *Ireland*	59	K7
Wicklow *Ireland*	59	K7
Wicklow Head	59	L7
Wicklow Mountains	59	K6
Widawka	71	H3

Wide Firth	56	E1
Widnes	55	G3
Widyān, Al	94	E6
Wieleń	70	G2
Wieluń	71	H3
Wien	68	F1
Wiener Neustadt	68	F2
Wieprz	71	K3
Wieren	70	D2
Wiesbaden	70	C3
Wigan	55	G3
Wiggins	128	H5
Wighill	55	H3
Wight, Isle of	53	F4
Wigmore	52	E2
Wigry, Jezioro	71	K1
Wigston	53	F2
Wigton	55	F2
Wigtown	54	E2
Wigtown Bay	54	E2
Wil	68	B2
Wilbur	122	E4
Wilcannia	113	J5
Wild Spitze	68	C2
Wilhelm II Land	141	F4
Wilhelm, Mount	114	D3
Wilhelm-Pieck-Stadt	70	F3
Wilhelmshaven	70	C2
Wilkes-Barre	125	N6
Wilkes Land	141	J4
Wilkhaven	56	E3
Wilkins Sound	120	D2
Willamette	122	B5
Willard	126	G6
Willaumez Peninsula	114	D2
Willemstad	136	D1
Willeroo	112	G2
William, Mount	113	J6
Williams *Australia*	112	D5
Williams *U.S.A.*	122	C8
Williamsburg	125	M8
Williams Lake	119	L5
Williamson	124	J8
Williamsport	125	M6
Williamston	129	P3
Willingboro	125	N6
Willington *Derbyshire, U.K.*	53	F2
Willington *Durham, U.K.*	55	H2
Willipa Bay	122	B4
Willis Group	110	M5
Williston *South Africa*	108	D6
Williston *Florida, U.S.A.*	129	L6
Williston *N.Dakota, U.S.A.*	123	N3
Williston Lake	118	L4
Williton	52	D3
Willmar	124	C4
Willoughby-on-the-Wolds	53	F2
Willow Bunch	123	M3
Willowmore	108	D6
Willow Springs	124	E8
Wills, Lake	112	F3
Wilmington *Australia*	113	H5
Wilmington *N.Carolina, U.S.A.*	129	P3
Wilmington *New Jersey, U.S.A.*	125	N7
Wilmot Passage	115	A6
Wilmslow	55	G3
Wilson	129	P3
Wilson's Promontory	113	K6
Wilstedt	70	C2

Wilton	53	F3
Wiltshire	53	F3
Wiluna	112	E4
Wimbleball Lake	52	D3
Wimborne Minster	53	F4
Wincanton	52	E3
Winchcombe	53	F3
Winchelsea	53	H4
Winchester *U.K.*	53	F3
Winchester *Kentucky, U.S.A.*	124	H8
Winchester *Tennessee, U.S.A.*	129	J3
Winchester *Virginia, U.S.A.*	125	L7
Wind	118	H2
Winder	129	L4
Windermere *Canada*	122	G2
Windermere *U.K.*	55	G2
Windermere, Lake	55	G2
Windhoek	108	C4
Windischgarsten	68	E2
Windom	124	C5
Windorah	113	J4
Wind River Range	123	K6
Windrush	53	F3
Windsor *Australia*	113	L5
Windsor *Newfoundland, Canada*	121	Q8
Windsor *Ontario, Canada*	124	J5
Windsor *Québec, Canada*	125	Q4
Windsor *U.K.*	53	G3
Windsor *U.S.A.*	129	P3
Windsor, Lake	133	L4
Windward Islands	133	S7
Windward Passage	133	K5
Winfield *Alabama, U.S.A.*	129	J4
Winfield *Kansas, U.S.A.*	128	D2
Winisk *Canada*	121	J7
Winisk *Canada*	121	J6
Winkler	123	R3
Winneba	104	E4
Winnemucca	122	F7
Winnenvicca, Lake	122	E7
Winner	123	Q6
Winnfield	128	F5
Winnibigoshish Lake	124	C3
Winning Pool	112	C3
Winnipeg *Canada*	123	R3
Winnipeg *Canada*	123	S2
Winnipeg, Lake	123	R2
Winnipegosis, Lake	119	Q5
Winnipesaukee, Lake	125	Q5
Winnsboro	128	G4
Winona *Minnesota, U.S.A.*	124	E4
Winona *Mississippi, U.S.A.*	128	H4
Winschoten	64	G2
Winsford	55	G3
Winslow *U.K.*	53	G3
Winslow *U.S.A.*	126	G3
Winslow Reef	111	U2
Winston-Salem	129	M2
Winterbourne Abbas	52	E4
Winter Garden	129	M6
Winterthur	68	B2
Wintinna	113	G4
Winton *Australia*	113	J3
Winton *New Zealand*	115	B7
Wiqia	86	C4
Wirksworth	55	H3
Wirraminna	113	H5
Wisbech	53	H2

Wisconsin *U.S.A.*	124	E5
Wisconsin *U.S.A.*	124	E4
Wisconsin *U.S.A.*	124	F4
Wisconsin Rapids	124	F4
Wishaw	57	E5
Wiślany, Zalew	71	H1
Wisłok	71	K3
Wismar	70	D2
Wissembourg	64	G4
Wistanstow	52	E2
Witbank	108	E5
Witham *Essex, U.K.*	53	H3
Witham *Lincolnshire, U.K.*	55	J3
Witheridge	52	D4
Withernsea	55	J3
Withington *Gloucestershire, U.K.*	53	F3
Withington *Hereford and Worcester, U.K.*	52	E2
Witney	53	F3
Witten	70	B3
Wittenberg	70	E3
Wittenberge	70	D2
Wittingen	70	D2
Witti Range	90	F5
Wittstock	70	E2
Witu	107	H3
Witu Islands	114	D2
Wkra	71	J2
Władysławowo	71	H1
Włocławek	71	H2
Włodawa	71	K3
Włoszczowa	71	H3
Wodzisław	71	J3
Wodzisław Slaski	71	H3
Woitape	114	D3
Wokam	91	J7
Woken	88	C2
Woking	53	G3
Wokingham	53	G3
Wolds, The	55	J3
Wolf	124	F4
Wolf Point	123	M3
Wolfsberg	68	E2
Wolfsburg	70	D2
Wolf, Volcán	136	A7
Wolin	70	F2
Wollaston, Cape	119	M1
Wollaston, Islas	139	C11
Wollaston Lake	119	Q4
Wollaston Peninsula	119	M2
Wollongong	113	L5
Wologisi Mountains	104	C4
Wołomin	71	J2
Wolstenholme, Cape	120	L5
Wolsztyn	70	G2
Wolverhampton	53	E2
Wolverton	53	G2
Wolviston	55	H2
Wombourne	53	E2
Wombwell	55	H3
Wondoola	113	J2
Wŏnju	87	P4
Wonosobo	90	D7
Wŏnsan	87	P4
Wonthagg	110	L9
Wood	123	L3
Woodbourne	115	D4
Woodbridge	53	J2
Woodburn	113	L4
Woodhall Spa	55	J3

Yamunanagar	92	E2	Yartsevo *U.S.S.R.*	84	D4	Yelantsy	84	H6	Yeste	66	E3
Yamyshevo	84	B6	Yartsevo *U.S.S.R.*	78	E4	Yelets	79	F5	Yeu, Île d'	65	B5
Yamzho Yumco	93	H3	Yarty	52	D4	Yeletskiy	78	L2	Yevlakh	79	H7
Yana	85	P2	Yarumal	136	B2	Yelizarovo	84	Ae4	Yevpatoriya	79	E6
Yanam	92	F5	Yary	84	Ae3	Yelizavety, Mys	85	Q6	Yevreyskaya Ao	88	D1
Yan'an	93	L1	Yasawa	114	Q8	Yelkenli	77	K3	Ye Xian	87	M4
Yanaul	78	J4	Yasawa Group	114	Q8	Yell	56	A1	Yeysk	79	F6
Yanbu'al Baḥr	96	D4	Yaselda	71	L2	Yellandu	92	F5	Y-Fenni	52	D3
Yancheng	87	N5	Yashbum	96	H9	Yellel	67	G5	Yhú	138	E5
Yanchi	87	K4	Yashiro-jima	89	D9	Yellowhead Pass	119	M5	Yi'an	87	P2
Yanchuan	87	L4	Yashkul'	79	H6	Yellowknife *Canada*	119	N3	Yiannitsá	75	G2
Yandé	114	V16	Yasin	92	D1	Yellowknife *Canada*	119	N3	Yibin	93	K3
Yandrakinot	118	A3	Yasinya	71	L4	Yellow River	87	M4	Yichang	93	M2
Yandun	86	F3	Yasnaya Polyana	88	F3	Yellow Sea	87	N4	Yicheng	93	M2
Yangarey	78	L2	Yass	113	K5	Yellowstone	123	M4	Yichun	87	P2
Yangchun	93	M4	Yasuj	95	K6	Yellowstone Lake	123	J5	Yidu	93	M2
Yanghe	87	M5	Yasun Burun	77	G2	Yell Sound	56	A1	Yidun	93	J2
Yangjiang	93	M4	Yata	136	D6	Yel'nya	78	E5	Yiğilca	76	D2
Yangquan	87	L4	Yatağan	76	C4	Yemen Arab Republic	96	G8	Yilan	88	B2
Yangshan	93	M4	Yaté	114	X17	Yemen, People's Democratic			Yildizeli	77	G3
Yangshuo	93	M4	Yates Center	128	E2	Republic of	97	J8	Yimianpo	88	A3
Yangtze	93	L2	Yates Point	115	A6	Yemetsk	78	G3	Yimuhe	87	N1
Yangyang	88	B6	Yathkyed Lake	119	R3	Yemtsa	78	G3	Yinchuan	87	K4
Yangzhou	87	M5	Yatsushiro	89	C9	Yen Bai	93	K4	Yindarlgooda, Lake	112	E5
Yanina	75	F3	Yatta Plateau	107	G3	Yendi	104	E4	Yingde	93	M4
Yanis'yarvi, Ozero	62	P6	Yatton	52	E3	Yengisar *China*	86	D4	Ying He	93	M2
Yanji	88	B4	Yauri Espinar	136	C6	Yengisar *China*	86	E3	Yingkou	87	N3
Yankton	123	R6	Yavatmal	92	E4	Yengue	105	G5	Yining	86	E3
Yanqi	86	F3	Yavi, Cerro	136	D2	Yenice *Turkey*	76	B3	Yin Shan	87	K3
Yanshou	88	B3	Yavlenka	84	Ae6	Yenice *Turkey*	77	F3	Yinxian	87	N6
Yantai	87	N4	Yavorov	71	K4	Yenice *Turkey*	76	F4	Yioúra *Greece*	75	H4
Yantra	73	H4	Yavr	62	N2	Yeniceoba	76	E3	Yioúra *Greece*	75	H3
Yanxing	88	C2	Yavu	77	G3	Yenikem	76	E3	Yirga Álem	103	G6
Yanzhou	87	M4	Yavuzeli	77	G4	Yeniköy *Turkey*	77	G4	Yirol	102	F6
Yao	102	C5	Yawatahama	89	D9	Yeniköy *Turkey*	77	K2	Yishui	87	M4
Yaoquanzi	86	H4	Yawng-hwe	93	J4	Yenipazar	76	C4	Yithion	75	G4
Yaoundé	105	H5	Yawri Bay	104	C4	Yenişarbademli	76	D4	Yitong	87	P3
Yaoxiaolong	88	A1	Ya Xian	93	L5	Yenişehir	76	C2	Yi Xian	87	N3
Yapen	91	K6	Yaxley	53	G2	Yenisey	84	D3	Yixing	87	M5
Yapen, Selat	91	K6	Yaya	84	D5	Yeniseysk	84	E5	Yiyang	93	M3
Yap Islands	91	K4	Yaygin	77	J3	Yeniseyskiy Zaliv	84	C2	Ylihärmä	62	N4
Yaprakali	76	E2	Yayla	77	J3	Yenotayevka	79	H6	Yli-kitka	62	N3
Yaqui	127	H6	Yayladaği	77	G5	Yéoryios	75	G4	Yli-li	62	L4
Yar *U.K.*	53	F4	Yazd	95	M6	Yeovil	52	E4	Ylitornio	62	K3
Yar *U.S.S.R.*	78	J4	Yazd-e Khvāst	95	L6	Yeraliyev	79	J7	Ylivieska	62	L4
Yaraka	113	J3	Yazihan	77	H3	Yerbent	95	P2	Y Llethr	52	C2
Yaransk	78	H4	Yazoo City	128	G4	Yerbogachen	84	H4	Yntaly	86	C2
Yarashev	73	J1	Yazovir Dimitrov	73	H4	Yerema	84	H4	Yoakum	128	D6
Yardley Hastings	53	G2	Ybbs	68	E1	Yerevan	77	L2	Yogope Yaveo	131	M9
Yare	53	J2	Ydseram	105	H3	Yergeni	79	G6	Yogyakarta	90	E7
Yarenga	78	H3	Ye	93	J5	Yerköy	76	F3	Yójoa, Laguna de	132	D7
Yarensk	78	H3	Yealmpton	52	C4	Yermak	84	B6	Yokadouma	105	J5
Yariga-take	89	F7	Yecheng	92	E1	Yermaki	84	H5	Yokkaichi	89	F8
Yarim	96	G9	Yecla	67	F3	Yermakovo	84	D3	Yokohama *Japan*	89	G8
Yarimca	76	C2	Yedinka	88	G2	Yermitsa	78	J2	Yokohama *Japan*	88	H5
Yaritagua	136	D2	Yedinsty	79	D6	Yermolayevo	79	K5	Yokosuka	89	G8
Yarkant He	92	E1	Yedoma *U.S.S.R.*	78	G3	Yerofey-Pavlovich	85	L6	Yokote	88	H6
Yarkovo	84	Ae5	Yedoma *U.S.S.R.*	78	J2	Yerolimín	75	G4	Yola	105	H4
Yarlung Zangbo Jiang	93	H3	Yedondin	85	J6	Yershov	79	H5	Yolaina, Cordillera de	132	E9
Yarma	76	E4	Yeeda River	112	E2	Yerupaja, Cerro	136	B6	Yom, Mae Nam	93	J5
Yarmolintsy	73	J1	Yéfira	75	G3	Yerushalayim	94	B6	Yonabaru	89	H10
Yarmouth	121	N9	Yefremov	79	F5	Yeşil	77	G2	Yonago	89	D8
Yarongo	84	Ae3	Yegorova, Mys	88	F3	Yeşilçay	76	C2	Yŏnam-dong	88	B5
Yaroslavl	78	F4	Yegor'yevsk	78	F4	Yeşilgölcük	76	F3	Yŏn dŏk	89	B7
Yarraloola	112	D3	Yei	102	F7	Yeşilhisar	76	F3	Yonezawa	89	H7
Yarra Yarra Lakes	112	D4	Yeijo, Cerro	136	B4	Yeşilkent	77	G4	Yŏng-an	88	B5
Yarroto	84	A3	Yekaterininka	78	L3	Yesilova	76	C4	Yong'an	87	M6
Yarrow	57	E5	Yekaterinoslavka	85	M6	Yeşilova	76	E3	Yongchang	86	J4
Yar Sale	84	A3	Yekhegnadzor	77	L3	Yeşilyurt	77	G3	Yongchuan	93	L3
Yarsomovy	84	A4	Yelabuga	78	J4	Yessey	84	G3	Yongdeng	93	K1